THE HOLY SPIRIT AND
CHRISTIAN ORIGINS

James D. G. Dunn

THE HOLY SPIRIT AND CHRISTIAN ORIGINS

Essays in Honor of James D. G. Dunn

Edited by

Graham N. Stanton,
Bruce W. Longenecker,
&
Stephen C. Barton

WILLIAM B. EERDMANS PUBLISHING COMPANY
GRAND RAPIDS, MICHIGAN

Wm. B. Eerdmans Publishing Co.
4035 Park East Court SE, Grand Rapids, Michigan 49546
www.eerdmans.com

Hardcover edition 2004
Paperback edition 2020

ISBN 978-0-8028-7925-7

Contents

Contributors

Robert J. Banks is Research and Development Fellow in the Macquarie Christian Studies Institute and Adjunct Professor in Ancient History, Macquarie University, Sydney, Australia. His books include *Jesus and the Law in the Synoptic Tradition* (Cambridge: Cambridge University Press, 1975), *God, the Worker* (Sydney: Albatross, 1992/Valley Forge: Judson, 1994), and *Paul's Idea of Community* (rev. ed.; Peabody, Mass.: Hendrickson, 1994).

John M. G. Barclay is, since 2003, Lightfoot Professor of Divinity in the Department of Theology, University of Durham. His books include *Obeying the Truth* (Edinburgh: T&T Clark, 1988), *Jews in the Mediterranean Diaspora from Alexander to Trajan* (Edinburgh: T&T Clark, 1996), and *Colossians and Philemon* (Sheffield: Sheffield Academic Press, 1996).

Stephen C. Barton is Reader in New Testament in the Department of Theology, University of Durham, England, and an assistant curate at St. John's Church, Neville's Cross, Durham. His books include *Discipleship and Family Ties in Mark and Matthew* (Cambridge: Cambridge University Press, 1994), *Life Together: Family, Sexuality and Community in the New Testament and Today* (Edinburgh: T&T Clark, 2001), and, as editor, *Holiness Past and Present* (Edinburgh: T&T Clark, 2003).

Richard Bauckham, FBA, FRSE, is Professor of New Testament Studies and Bishop Wardlaw Professor in the University of St. Andrews, Scotland. His recent books include *James: Wisdom of James, Disciple of Jesus the Sage* (London /

New York: Routledge, 1999), *Gospel Women: Studies of the Named Women in the Gospels* (Grand Rapids: Eerdmans; Edinburgh: T&T Clark, 2002), *God and the Crisis of Freedom* (Louisville/ London: Westminster John Knox, 2002).

Peder Borgen is Professor Emeritus of New Testament, University of Trondheim, Trondheim, Norway. His books include *Philo, John and Paul: New Perspectives on Judaism and Early Christianity* (Atlanta: Scholars Press, 1987), *Early Christianity and Hellenistic Judaism* (Edinburgh: T&T Clark, 1996), *Philo of Alexandria — An Exegete for His Time* (Leiden: Brill, 1997), and *The Philo Index: A Complete Greek Word Index to the Writings of Philo of Alexandria* (with K. Fuglseth and R. Skarsten; Grand Rapids: Eerdmans, and Leiden: Brill, 2000).

David Catchpole is Scholar in Residence (New Testament) at Sarum College, Salisbury, and Professor Emeritus of Theological Studies at the University of Exeter. His most recent books are *The Quest for Q* (Edinburgh: T&T Clark, 1993) and *Resurrection People* (London: Darton, Longman & Todd, 2000).

Gordon D. Fee is Professor Emeritus of New Testament Studies at Regent College, Vancouver, British Columbia. His books include *The First Epistle to the Corinthians* (NICNT; Grand Rapids: Eerdmans, 1987), *New Testament Exegesis: A Handbook for Students and Pastors* (3rd ed.; Louisville: Westminster John Knox, 2002), *God's Empowering Presence: The Holy Spirit in the Letters of Paul* (Peabody, Mass.: Hendrickson, 1994), *Paul's Letter to the Philippians* (NICNT; Grand Rapids: Eerdmans, 1995), and *To What End Exegesis? Studies Textual, Exegetical, and Theological* (Grand Rapids: Eerdmans, 2001).

Victor Paul Furnish is University Distinguished Professor Emeritus of New Testament, Southern Methodist University, Dallas, Texas. His books include *The Moral Teaching of Paul: Selected Issues* (2nd ed.; Nashville: Abingdon, 1985), *Jesus according to Paul* (Cambridge and New York: Cambridge University Press, 1993), and *The Theology of the First Letter to the Corinthians* (Cambridge and New York: Cambridge University Press, 1999).

Beverly Roberts Gaventa is Helen H. P. Manson Professor of New Testament Literature and Exegesis, Princeton Theological Seminary, Princeton, New Jersey. Her publications include *From Darkness to Light: Aspects of Conversion in the New Testament* (Philadelphia: Fortress, 1986), *Mary: Glimpses of the Mother of Jesus* (Columbia, S.C.: University of South Carolina Press, 1995), *I and II Thessalonians* (Louisville: Westminster John Knox, 1998), and *The Acts of the Apostles* (Nashville: Abingdon, 2003).

Joel B. Green is Dean of Academic Affairs and Professor of New Testament Interpretation, Asbury Theological Seminary, Wilmore, Kentucky. His publications include *The Gospel of Luke* (NICNT; Grand Rapids: Eerdmans, 1997), *Introducing the New Testament: Its Literature and Theology* (with Paul J. Achtemeier and Marianne Meye Thompson; Grand Rapids: Eerdmans, 2001), *Narrative Reading, Narrative Preaching: Reuniting New Testament Interpretation and Proclamation* (with Michael Pasquarello III; Grand Rapids: Baker Academic, 2003), and *What about the Soul? Neuroscience and Christian Anthropology* (Nashville: Abingdon, 2004).

Morna Hooker is Lady Margaret's Professor Emerita in the University of Cambridge, and a Fellow of Robinson College. Her recent books include *From Adam to Christ: Essays on Paul* (Cambridge: Cambridge University Press, 1990), *A Commentary on the Gospel according to St Mark* (London: A. & C. Black/Peabody, Mass.: Hendrickson, 1991), *Not Ashamed of the Gospel* (Carlisle: Paternoster: 1994/Grand Rapids,: Eerdmans, 1995), *The Signs of a Prophet* (London: SCM/Harrisburg, Pa.: Trinity Press International, 1997), *Beginnings: Keys That Open the Gospels* (London: SCM/Harrisburg, Pa.: Trinity Press International, 1998), *Paul: A Short Introduction* (Oxford: Oneworld, 2003), and *Endings: Invitations to Discipleship* (London: SCM/Peabody, Mass.: Hendrickson, 2003). She is editor of the Black New Testament Commentaries (London: Continuum) and has been joint editor of the *Journal of Theological Studies* since 1985.

Robert Jewett is the Harry R. Kendall Professor Emeritus at Garrett-Evangelical Theological Seminary. Since 2000 he has served as Guest Professor of New Testament at the University of Heidelberg, where he is directing an archive project. His books on the New Testament include *A Chronology of Paul's Life* (Philadelphia: Fortress, 1979), *Letter to Pilgrims: A Commentary on the Epistle to the Hebrews* (New York: Pilgrim, 1981), and *Paul the Apostle to America: Cultural Trends and Pauline Scholarship* (Louisville: Westminster/John Knox, 1994). His hermeneutical studies include *Christian Tolerance: Paul's Message to the Modern Church* (Philadelphia: Westminster, 1982) and *Saint Paul Returns to the Movies: Triumph over Shame* (Grand Rapids: Eerdmans, 1999). Jewett's recent publications in cultural criticism are *The Myth of the American Superhero* (Grand Rapids: Eerdmans, 2002) and *Captain America and the Crusade against Evil: The Dilemma of Zealous Nationalism* (Grand Rapids: Eerdmans, 2003), both of which are co-authored with John Shelton Lawrence. He is currently finishing a commentary on Romans.

Hermann Lichtenberger is Professor for New Testament and Ancient Judaism at Tübingen University and Director of the Institut für antikes Judentum und hellenistische Religionsgeschichte. He serves as chief editor of the *Jüdische Schriften aus hellenistisch-römischer Zeit* and has contributed to the research on the Dead Sea Scrolls. His most recent book is *Das Ich Adams und das Ich der Menschheit* (Tübingen: Mohr [Siebeck], forthcoming).

Bruce W. Longenecker lectures in New Testament at the University of St. Andrews, Scotland. His recent publications include *The Triumph of Abraham's God* (Nashville: Abingdon, 1998), *Narrative Dynamics in Paul: A Critical Assessment* (ed.; Louisville: Westminster John Knox, 2002), and *The Lost Letters of Pergamum: A Story from the New Testament World* (Grand Rapids: Baker Academic, 2003). He is currently finishing a book provisionally entitled *Chain-Link Interlock in New Testament Texts: Structure, Theology, History.*

Ulrich Luz is Professor Emeritus for New Testament at the Theological Faculty of the University of Bern, Switzerland. Among his recent publications are *The Theology of Matthew* (Cambridge: Cambridge University Press, 1995), *Matthew 8–20* (Hermeneia; Minneapolis: Fortress, 2001), *Das Evangelium nach Matthäus (Mt 26–28)* (EKKNT I/4; Neukirchen/Düsseldorf: Neukirchener/Patmos, 2002), *Jesus oder Buddha* (together with Axel Michaels; Munich: C. H. Beck, 2002), *Albert Schweitzer: Vorträge, Vorlesungen und Aufsätze, Werke aus dem Nachlass* (ed. U. Luz et al.; Munich: C. H. Beck, 2003). Ulrich Luz is editor of *Evangelisch-Katholischer Kommentar zum Neuen Testament* and of *Albert Schweitzer: Werke aus dem Nachlass.*

I. Howard Marshall is Honorary Research Professor of New Testament at the University of Aberdeen. His recent publications include *A Critical and Exegetical Commentary on the Pastoral Epistles* (in collaboration with Philip H. Towner; The International Critical Commentary; Edinburgh: T&T Clark, 1999), W. F. Moulton and A. S. Geden, *Concordance to the Greek New Testament: Sixth Edition Fully Revised* (London: T&T Clark, 2002), and I. Howard Marshall, Stephen Travis, and Ian Paul: *Exploring the New Testament,* vol. 2: *The Letters and Revelation* (London: SPCK, 2002).

Scot McKnight is the Karl A. Olsson Professor in Religious Studies at North Park University, Chicago, Illinois. His publications include *A Light among the Gentiles* (Minneapolis: Fortress, 1992), *A New Vision for Israel* (Grand Rapids: Eerdmans, 1999), *Turning to Jesus* (Louisville: Westminster John Knox, 2002), and "2 Peter and Jude," in *The Eerdmans Commentary on the Bible* (Grand Rapids: Eerdmans, 2003). He is co-editor of *Currents in Biblical Research* and joint editor for *The Journal for the Study of the Historical Jesus.*

Walter Moberly is Reader in Theology at the University of Durham. He has written *The Old Testament of the Old Testament* (Minneapolis: Fortress, 1992; Eugene, Ore.: Wipf & Stock, 2001) and *The Bible, Theology, and Faith: A Study of Abraham and Jesus* (Cambridge: Cambridge University Press, 2000).

Robert Morgan is priest-in-charge of Sandford-on-Thames and Reader in New Testament Theology at the University of Oxford, and Vice-Principal of Linacre College. He edited *The Religion of the Incarnation: Anglican Essays in Commemoration of Lux Mundi* (Bristol: Bristol Classical Press, 1989), and wrote *Biblical Interpretation* (with John Barton; Oxford: Oxford University Press, 1988) and *Romans* (Sheffield: Sheffield Academic Press, 1995).

J. Lionel North was until retirement the Barmby Senior Lecturer in New Testament Studies at the University of Hull. His most recent publication is the article on Brooke Foss Westcott in *Theologische Realenzyklopädie* (Berlin/New York: de Gruyter, 2003), 35:675-79.

Graham Stanton is Lady Margaret's Professor of Divinity at the University of Cambridge and a Fellow of Fitzwilliam College. He is most recently the author of *A Gospel for a New People: Studies in Matthew* (Edinburgh: T&T Clark, 1992), *Gospel Truth?* (London: HarperCollins, 1995), *The Gospels and Jesus* (Oxford: Oxford University Press, 2nd ed. 2002), and *Jesus and Gospel* (Cambridge: Cambridge University Press, 2004). He is General Editor of the International Critical Commentaries.

Loren T. Stuckenbruck is B. F. Westcott Professor in Biblical Studies at the University of Durham. His books include *Angel Veneration and Christology* (Tübingen: Mohr [Siebeck], 1995) and *The Book of Giants from Qumran* (Tübingen: Mohr [Siebeck], 1997). He has published extensively in the areas of ancient Jewish apocalyptic thought and the Dead Sea Scrolls, and has edited (with Wendy North) *Exploring Early Jewish and Christian Monotheism* (London: T&T Clark International, 2004) and (with Christoph Auffarth) *The Fall of the Angels* (Leiden: Brill, 2004).

Peter Stuhlmacher is Professor Emeritus for New Testament in the University of Tübingen. His recent publications include *Paul's Letter to the Romans* (trans. Scott J. Hafemann; Louisville: Westminster/John Knox, 1994), *Biblische Theologie des Neuen Testaments* (2 vols.; Göttingen: Vandenhoeck & Ruprecht, 1992-99), *Revisiting Paul's Doctrine of Justification* (with an essay by Donald A.

Hagner) (Downers Grove, Ill.: InterVarsity, 2001), and *Biblische Theologie und Evangelium* (Tübingen, Mohr Siebeck, 2002).

Anthony C. Thiselton is Emeritus Professor of Christian Theology in Residence, University of Nottingham, and Visiting Research Professor in Christian Theology, Chester University College; also Canon Theologian of Leicester Cathedral and of Southwell Minster. His books include *The Two Horizons* (Carlisle: Paternoster; Grand Rapids: Eerdmans, 1980; Korean trans. 1990), *New Horizons in Hermeneutics* (London: HarperCollins; Carlisle: Paternoster; Grand Rapids: Zondervan, 1992), *Interpreting God and the Postmodern Self* (Edinburgh: T&T Clark; Grand Rapids: Eerdmans, 1995), *The First Epistle to the Corinthians: A Commentary on the Greek Text* (Grand Rapids: Eerdmans; Carlisle: Paternoster, 2000), and *A Concise Encyclopaedia of the Philosophy of Religion* (Oxford: Oneworld, 2002).

Marianne Meye Thompson is Professor of New Testament Interpretation, Fuller Theological Seminary, Pasadena, California. She is the author of *The Promise of the Father: Jesus and God in the New Testament* (Louisville: Westminster John Knox, 2000) and *The God of the Gospel of John* (Grand Rapids: Eerdmans, 2001).

Paul Trebilco is Professor of New Testament Studies and Head of the Department of Theology and Religious Studies at the University of Otago, Dunedin, New Zealand. He is the author of *Jewish Communities in Asia Minor* (Cambridge: Cambridge University Press, 1991) and *The Early Christians in Ephesus from Paul to Ignatius* (Tübingen: Mohr Siebeck, 2004).

Max Turner is Professor of New Testament Studies and Vice-Principal of London School of Theology, an Associated College of Brunel University. His published works include *Power from on High: The Spirit in Israel's Restoration and Witness in Luke-Acts* (Sheffield: Sheffield Academic Press; 1996), *The Holy Spirit and Spiritual Gifts: Then and Now* (Carlisle: Paternoster, 1996), and (ed. with Joel Green) *Between Two Horizons: Spanning New Testament Studies and Systematic Theology* (Grand Rapids: Eerdmans, 2000).

Alexander Wedderburn is Professor of New Testament, Ludwig-Maximilians-Universität, Munich. His recent publications include *Beyond Resurrection* (London: SCM/Peabody, Mass.: Hendrickson, 1999) and *A History of the First Christians* (London/New York: T&T Clark International, 2004)

Abbreviations

AB	Anchor Bible
AGJU	Arbeiten zur Geschichte des antiken Judentums und des Urchristentums
AnBib	Analecta Biblica
ANF	Ante-Nicene Fathers
AzTh	Arbeiten zur Theologie
BAR	*Biblical Archaeology Review*
BDAG	Bauer, W., F. W. Danker, W. F. Arndt, and F. W. Gingrich, *A Greek-English Lexicon of the New Testament and Other Early Christian Literature.* 3rd ed. Chicago, 2000
BETL	Bibliotheca ephemeridum theologicarum lovaniensium
BEvT	Beiträge zur evangelischen Theologie
BNTC	Black's New Testament Commentaries
BR	*Biblical Research*
BSac	*Bibliotheca Sacra*
BZ	*Biblische Zeitschrift*
BZNW	Beiheft zur Zeitschrift für die neutestamentliche Wissenschaft
CBQ	*Catholic Biblical Quarterly*
CC	Corpus Christianorum
CCSG	Corpus Christianorum, Series Graeca. Turnhout, 1977-
CCSL	Corpus Christianorum, Series Latina. Turnhout, 1953-
CGTSC	Cambridge Greek Testament for Schools and Colleges
CPG	*Clavis Patrum Graecorum.* Ed. M. Geerard. 5 vols. Turnhout, 1974-87

CSCO	Corpus scriptorum christianorum orientalium
CSEL	Corpus scriptorum ecclesiasticorum latinorum
EDNT	*Exegetical Dictionary of the New Testament*
EKKNT	Evangelisch-katholischer Kommentar zum Neuen Testament
EOMIA	*Ecclesiae Occidentalis Monumenta Iuris Antiquissima.* Ed. C. H. Turner. Oxford, 1899-1939
EQ	*Evangelical Quarterly*
ETS	Erfurter theologische Studien
ExpTim	*Expository Times*
FRLANT	Forschungen zur Religion und Literatur des Alten und Neuen Testaments
GCS	Die griechische christliche Schriftsteller der ersten [drei] Jahrhunderts
HERE	*Encyclopedia of Religion and Ethics.* Ed. J. Hastings. Edinburgh, 1908-26
HNT	Handbuch zum Neuen Testament
HNTC	Harper's New Testament Commentaries
HTKNT	Herders theologischer Kommentar zum Neuen Testament
HTR	*Harvard Theological Review*
HUT	Hermeneutische Untersuchungen zur Theologie
ICC	International Critical Commentary
IKZ	*Internationale kirchliche Zeitschrift*
JBL	*Journal of Biblical Literature*
JPT	*Journal of Pentecostal Theology*
JPTSup	Journal of Pentecostal Theology Supplements
JSJ	*Journal for the Study of Judaism in the Persian, Hellenistic, and Roman Periods*
JSNT	*Journal for the Study of the New Testament*
JSNTSup	Journal for the Study of the New Testament: Supplement Series
JSOT	*Journal for the Study of the Old Testament*
JTS	*Journal of Theological Studies*
LD	Lectio divina
NA^{27}	*Novum Testamentum Graecum.* Ed. B. and K. Aland et al. 27th ed. Stuttgart, 1993
N.F.	Neue Folge
n.s.	new series
NCB	New Century Bible
NEB	*New English Bible*
NICNT	New International Commentary on the New Testament

NIDNTT	*New International Dictionary of New Testament Theology.* Ed. C. Brown. 3 vols. Grand Rapids, 1975-85
NIGTC	New International Greek Testament Commentary
NovT	*Novum Testamentum*
NovTSup	Novum Testamentum Supplements
NTA	*New Testament Abstracts*
NTAbh	Neutestamentliche Abhandlungen
NTD	Das Neue Testament Deutsch
NTOA	Novum Testamentum et Orbis Antiquus
NTS	*New Testament Studies*
OBT	Overtures to Biblical Theology
PG	*Patrologia Graeca*
PL	*Patrologia Latina*
PO	*Patrologia Orientalis*
PS	*Patristica Sorbonensia*
QD	Quaestiones disputatae
REB	Revised English Bible
RNT	Regensburger Neues Testament
SBLDS	Society of Biblical Literature Dissertation Series
SBT	Studies in Biblical Theology
SC	Sources chrétiennes
SNTS	Studiorum Novi Testamenti Societas
SNTSMS	Society for New Testament Studies Monograph Series
SP	*Studia Patristica*
SR	*Studies in Religion*
STh	*Summa Theologiae* (Thomas Aquinas)
STS	Strassburger Theologische Studien
TANZ	Texte und Arbeiten zum neutestamentlichen Zeitalter
TDNT	*Theological Dictionary of the New Testament.* Ed. G. Kittel and G. Friedrich. Trans. G. W. Bromiley. 10 vols. Grand Rapids, 1964-76
TGl	*Theologie und Glaube*
THKNT	Theologischer Handkommentar zum Neuen Testament
ThZ	*Theologische Zeitschrift*
TR	Textus Receptus
TRE	*Theologische Realenzyklopädie.* Ed. G. Krause and G. Müller. Berlin, 1977-
TU	Texte und Untersuchungen zur Geschichte der altchristlicher Literatur
TynB	*Tyndale Bulletin*

UNT	Untersuchungen zum Neuen Testament
WBC	Word Biblical Commentary
WMANT	Wissenschaftliche Monographien zum Alten und Neuen Testament
WUNT	Wissenschaftliche Untersuchungen zum Neuen Testament
ZBK	Zürcher Bibelkommentare
ZNW	*Zeitschrift für die neutestamentliche Wissenschaft*
ZThK	*Zeitschrift für Theologie und Kirche*

Editors' Preface

Anyone who is interested in the rigorous study of early Christianity and who has not engaged with the works of Professor James D. G. Dunn is not interested in the rigorous study of early Christianity. No one would dispute that Professor Dunn (known to his friends as 'Jimmy') is one of the most prolific New Testament scholars of the late twentieth and early twenty-first centuries. And while a handful of scholars might have a list of publications to rival his own extensive publications list, none of them could claim to have set the agenda of scholarly study to the extent that Jimmy has done for a sustained period of time since the 1970s.

Jimmy's academic interests span virtually the whole spectrum of canonical New Testament writings, and his writings draw on a vast knowledge of Jewish and Graeco-Roman texts that help to reveal the context in which the early Christian movement emerged. Equally impressive is his awareness of the voluminous secondary literature pertaining to these primary sources, as well as his ability to tease out and engage with the most significant strands of contemporary scholarship. In any of his publications, the pertinent data will have been carefully appraised and clearly discussed in an argument that is well organised, accessible, and forceful.

Seven major monographs, a handful of commentaries, a variety of important shorter books, and a veritable plethora of significant articles[1] have so far appeared as a result of Jimmy's prodigious study of early Christianity in its

1. Many of his articles appear in the two-volume collection *Christ and the Spirit,* vol. 1: *Christology;* vol. 2: *Pneumatology* (Grand Rapids: Eerdmans; Edinburgh: T&T Clark, 1998).

historical context. But until Jimmy's pen dries up, any enumeration of his most significant works will almost inevitably be out of date almost as soon as it appears.

In retrospect, Jimmy's first four monographs can be seen to hang together in a progressive and related series. His 1968 PhD dissertation, written at Cambridge under the supervision of C. F. D. Moule, appeared in revised format in 1970 as *Baptism in the Holy Spirit.*[2] In that book he evaluates certain contemporary views concerning the Spirit and the Christian life in light of the New Testament evidence. The book caught a wave of interest when it was released and, most unusually for a published PhD thesis, continues to be influential some three decades later.

His continuing interest in issues pertaining to the Spirit, combined with his teaching a course at Nottingham University entitled 'The Beginning of Christianity', led to the appearance in 1975 of one of his most significant books: *Jesus and the Spirit: A Study of the Religious and Charismatic Experience of Jesus and the First Christians as Reflected in the New Testament.*[3] In that book, the New Testament data pertaining to early Christian religious experience are judiciously and engagingly analysed. The third section of that book deals with Paul and his churches, and as such prefigured the extensive work in Paul and Pauline Christianity that would become the primary focus of Jimmy's attention throughout the 1980s and 1990s.

The fourth section of *Jesus and the Spirit* deals with diverse varieties of Christian religious experience as reflected in the New Testament. This part laid the foundations for his third monograph, published just two years later in 1977 but crafted earlier in a Master's course of the same name: *Unity and Diversity in the New Testament: An Inquiry into the Character of Earliest Christianity.*[4] This book ranges widely but deftly over a series of complex issues, with Jimmy concluding that the unifying element within the New Testament writings is 'the unity between the historical Jesus and the exalted Christ'.[5] For some reviewers

2. London: SCM, 1970; Philadelphia: Westminster, 1977; trans. *El Bautismo del Espiritu Santo* (Buenos Aires: La Aurora, 1977).

3. London: SCM; Philadelphia: Westminster, 1975; trans. *Jesus y el Espiritu* (Salamanca: Secretariado Trinitario, 1981).

4. London: SCM, 1977; 2nd rev. ed.: London: SCM; Valley Forge, Pa.: Trinity Press International, 1990.

5. Dunn (p. 370) characterised this point of New Testament unity as 'the conviction that the wandering charismatic preacher from Nazareth has ministered, died and been raised from the dead to bring God and man finally together' and as 'the recognition that the divine power through which they now worshipped and were encouraged and accepted by God was one and the same person, Jesus, the man, the Christ, the Son of God, the Lord, the life-giving Spirit'.

this was a rather minimalist conclusion, but attempts to challenge it on the basis of the New Testament evidence have not overturned the potency of his case.

A mere three years later Jimmy published his fourth major book, *Christology in the Making: An Inquiry into the Origins of the Doctrine of the Incarnation.*[6] His *Unity and Diversity* had underlined the extent to which Christology is the major unifying factor in early Christian writings, so a fuller discussion of New Testament Christology was a natural next step. While Jimmy's work was carried out in relation to the theological debates of the late 1970s and early 1980s regarding what was then termed 'the myth of God incarnate', Jimmy's own contribution to that debate has withstood the test of time better than other contributions of the period. His chapters 'The Son of God', 'The Son of Man', 'The Last Adam', 'Spirit or Angel?', 'The Wisdom of God', and 'The Word of God' still contribute to scholarly consideration of those titles and concepts.

In the early 1980s, in the wake of E. P. Sanders' significant work *Paul and Palestinian Judaism* in 1977,[7] Jimmy began to turn his probing attention to a reevaluation of Paul in the light of Sanders' portrait of Early Judaism as a religion characterised by 'covenantal nomism'. In this enterprise Jimmy soon became the most outspoken advocate of what he termed 'the new perspective on Paul', in which Paul's engagement with 'Judaism' (as he calls it in Gal. 1:13) is understood in a fresh light apart from the traditional portrait of his religious heritage as one of hard-edged 'legalism'. A series of important articles emerged during this period that prepared the way for other notable accomplishments. Among them is Jimmy's significant two-volume commentary on Romans (1988),[8] the first commentary to offer a sustained reading of a single text informed by the 'new perspective on Paul'. This was followed in 1993 by a spirited commentary on Galatians[9] and a companion volume, *The Theology of Paul's Letter to the Galatians.*[10] His work on Paul culminated in his 1998 monograph of over 800 pages entitled *The Theology of Paul the Apostle.*[11] This monumental work has no rivals in English, assessing Paul's letters through analysis of their main theological convictions in relation to their situational context.

6. London: SCM; Philadelphia: Westminster, 1980; 2nd ed., with new Foreword: London: SCM, 1989; Grand Rapids: Eerdmans, 1996.

7. London: SCM, 1977.

8. WBC, vol. 38; Dallas: Word, 1988. See also his *Romans: The People's Bible Commentary* (Oxford: Bible Reading Fellowship, 2001).

9. *A Commentary on the Epistle to the Galatians* (BNTC; London: A&C Black, 1993).

10. Cambridge: Cambridge University Press, 1993; trans. into Japanese; Tokyo: Shinkyo Shuppansha, 1998.

11. Grand Rapids: Eerdmans; Edinburgh: T&T Clark, 1998; trans. as *La teologia dell'apostolo Paolo* (Introduzione allo studio della Bibbia, Supplementi 5; Brescia: Paideia, 1999).

Meanwhile, studies in Early Judaism and Early Christianity continued to emerge from Jimmy's work. His important book *The Partings of the Ways between Christianity and Judaism* appeared in 1991,[12] in which the central convictions of Early Judaism are sensitively exhibited, along with an ensuing analysis of the points at which first-century Christians parted company with 'Judaism', sometimes reluctantly, sometimes bitterly. And in 2003 Jimmy's monograph *Jesus Remembered* appeared.[13] In that book (consisting of over 1,000 pages), Jimmy's extensive discussion of methodological, historical, and theological matters offers an informed taxonomy of key issues in contemporary scholarly debate, and breaks new ground in a variety of ways. Not least, Jimmy seeks to 'alter the default setting' of Jesus studies[14] by doggedly pursuing the implications of the fact that the culture of Jesus and his followers was predominantly oral/aural and performatory in character. For Jimmy, both 'stability' and 'variability' can be shown to have characterized the traditioning processes of the early Christian communities as they remembered their Lord in stories about his life and teaching.[15] At the time of going to press, we await the two companion volumes of *Jesus Remembered.* Together they will comprise an ambitious three-volume study of the Christian movement from its inception until the middle of the second century, a project whose overarching title bears the obvious imprint of its author: Christianity in the Making.

These phenomenal academic accomplishments have spanned Jimmy's institutional involvement as Lecturer and Reader with the University of Nottingham (1970-82), as Professor of Divinity with the University of Durham (1982-2003), and as Lightfoot Professor of Divinity with the University of Durham (1990-2003). The productivity of those years is even more remarkable when some of Jimmy's other activities are kept in mind. Throughout his career he has carried a heavy teaching load, as well as being responsible for a variety of departmental and university administrative duties. He has successfully supervised more than thirty PhD candidates, many of whose theses have since been published. He attends national and international conferences more assiduously than most. He is a founding father of the British New Testament Society, with its annual conference promoting scholarship within Britain. He served as trea-

12. London: SCM; Philadelphia: Trinity Press International, 1991.

13. Grand Rapids: Eerdmans, 2003.

14. Cf. his article, 'Altering the Default Setting: Re-envisaging the Early Transmission of the Jesus Tradition', *NTS* 49 (2003): 139-75.

15. This emphasis on both stability and variability recalls his earlier interest in unity and diversity in the New Testament (cf. also his *The Evidence for Jesus* [London: SCM, 1985]), as well as his theological interests in the authority of Scripture for the Christian church (cf. his *The Living Word* [London: SCM, 1987]).

surer of Studiorum Novi Testamenti Societas (SNTS) from 1982 to 1992, later hosting its gathering in Durham in 2002 and serving as its president from 2002 to 2003. He has helped to set up extensive initiatives to promote New Testament scholarship in the developing world, has lectured widely in North America and Britain, preaches regularly, and even finds time to sing in a local choral society. Moreover, he is a devoted husband and father who ensures that the pressures of modern academic life do not upset his strong commitments to family and friends.

This Festschrift is offered with the greatest of respect and appreciation to honor Jimmy Dunn on his sixty-fifth birthday. It comprises a selection of original articles that engage a topic (i.e., the Spirit) that has held a prominent and distinctive place in the majority of his publications.[16] We hope that this collection of articles, written in sympathy with Jimmy's strong historical and theological interests, will help to stimulate further discussion and reflection in the theological academy and in the Christian church — two sectors that Jimmy has consistently and passionately sought to straddle, nurture, and refresh.

Since the number of potential contributors to this volume is nearly as lengthy as the number of entries in its honoree's list of publications, the editors have unfortunately had to exercise restraint in their invitations to contribute articles. And a few scholars who originally accepted their invitation were ultimately prevented from contributing for one reason or another. Nonetheless, the amount of goodwill expressed by the contributors, the publishers, and others in getting this project off the ground has been significant and sincere, and reflects the high regard in which Jimmy is held throughout the guild of New Testament studies. For the editors (one being a close friend from the heady days of PhD study, one being a long-standing colleague, and one being an admiring former PhD student), this project represents not simply a salute to an influential scholar but a token of affection for one whose friendship is as significant as his scholarship.

THE EDITORS

16. The word 'Spirit' appears in the title of over twenty-five of his publications.

1 Unity and Diversity in New Testament Talk of the Spirit

Robert Morgan

From his Cambridge cradle to his Durham presidency of Studiorum Novi Testamenti Societas, from Professor Moule's happy group ('school' is hardly the word) where even the geese felt like swans, to the Durham chair made awesome by the weight of his distinguished predecessor, Professor Barrett, our honorand has written and taught New Testament theology with an eye to the experiential dimension indicated by the subject of this Festschrift. His book which comes closest to being a New Testament theology is from his equally happy Nottingham period: *Unity and Diversity in the New Testament* (1977). It is dedicated to Charlie Moule and recalls the revered teacher's *Birth of the New Testament* (1962). Our shared love and appreciation of our aged teacher, and a shared fascination with a methodological essay of William Wrede and with the provocative contributions of Ernst Käsemann, pointed me back to that early Nottingham synthesis when reflecting on our all-too-sporadic thirty-odd year conversation about our shared aims and methods, and differing emphases. Our very different denominational backgrounds and personal experiences (not least with respect to the Spirit) will at least add to the diversity of this volume and confirm that the unity which the Spirit gives is still a sheer miracle.

Like most of Jimmy Dunn's work, this admirable book is historical and exegetical, but inspired by theological questioning and rich with theological consequences. That is enough to classify it as 'New Testament theology' even if it is not, and does not claim to be, *a* New Testament theology. The subtitle, 'An Inquiry into the Character of Earliest Christianity', implies historical and descriptive but also conceptual work. What is described is bound to have theological implications for any Protestant preacher guided, inspired, and in some sense 'normed' by Scripture, though what these might be is far from clear. As a biblical theologian Dr. Dunn includes 'a few remarks at the close of several chapters relating the conclusions to the present day' (p. xi). He has 'outlined some of the corollaries for our understanding of "the Authority of the New Testament" in the final section' (p. xi) entitled 'Has the Canon a Continuing Function?' But the New Testament scholar's primary task is to understand first-century historical reality, and in the 1970s it still seemed necessary almost to apologize ('I have taken the liberty') for these 'few' hermeneutical 'remarks'.

In fact the book owes its origin and much of its importance to the significance of its topic for Christian theological use of Scripture. The issues had been sharply profiled over the previous thirty years by Ernst Käsemann,[1] whose pervasive influence throughout this book is evident in its insistence on the theological diversity to be found in the New Testament, and in the phrase 'the canon within the canon', in the dubious use of the categories 'apocalyptic', 'enthusiasm', and 'early catholicism', and in the somewhat uncritical reception of Walter Bauer's stimulating work, *Orthodoxy and Heresy in Earliest Christianity* (1934, Eng. trans. 1971).

Like Käsemann, Dunn asked how 'the New Testament functions as a "canon", as a criterion for orthodoxy, as a norm for Christians of later generations' (p. 374), and while he admits that 'these are questions which require a much fuller discussion' (p. 374), he goes on to indicate some of the relevance of his own historical study to that theological question.

Also like Käsemann, Dunn finds a unifying christological centre to the New Testament and rightly insists that this implies limits to acceptable diversity. But unlike Käsemann and earlier discussions of the Bible as a norm and criterion, Dunn can celebrate the diversity: the New Testament '*canonizes the diversity* of Christianity' (p. 376), and 'to recognize the canon of the New Testament is to affirm the diversity of Christianity' (p. 377). What for a relatively orthodox Protestant and dialectical theologian like Käsemann was a problem has become for a relatively liberal Protestant a matter for rejoicing. The sceptical critic was a quite conservative theologian; the more conservative critic is a more liberal theologian.[2]

1. *Das Neue Testament als Kanon* (Göttingen: Vandenhoeck und Ruprecht, 1970) reprints and contains a lengthy critical discussion with fifteen important contributions, including his own essay, 'Begründet der neutestamentliche Kanon die Einheit der Kirche?' (1951; Eng. trans. 'The Canon of the New Testament and the Unity of the Church', in *Essays on New Testament Themes* (London: SCM, 1964). Several of Käsemann's other essays are cited in Dunn's footnotes and bibliography.

2. Käsemann wrote in 1964 of a similar change of fronts in comparing Jeremias and the Bultmann school: 'Blind Alleys in the "Jesus of History" Controversy', in *New Testament Questions of Today* (London: SCM, 1969), pp. 23-65.

Dunn's liberal delight in diversity is striking because that is not usually combined with the use of Scripture as a doctrinal norm, whereas Dunn recognizes and begins to define the importance of the New Testament for Christian doctrinal identity. The reason why its 'unity' is important to most Christians, and why Käsemann was worried by what historical research had uncovered, was that conflicting theologies seemed to prevent the New Testament from constituting a doctrinal norm.[3] His own solution of making his 'canon within the canon' the norm is picked up by Dunn and taken in a rather different direction.

Of course Dunn is right to identify (with Käsemann) and to celebrate (without him) the diversity of early Christianity. We are all theological pluralists now. Paths explored by liberal Protestants have been widely followed, and not even orthodox Anglicans claim that their true-to-Scripture theology is that of the whole Bible. We may further agree that some defences of 'orthodoxy' have been, and still are, unsustainable. Historical study is genuinely liberating and has broken up the older definitions of orthodoxy, however important it remains for Christians to distinguish between authentic and inauthentic forms of their faith and its institutions.

Dunn believes that the canon sets limits to legitimate diversity (p. 378). Christians must acknowledge Jesus to be human (no problem) and exalted (rather less straightforward). Whether that is sufficient definition to preserve Christian identity may be doubted, and Dunn echoes Schleiermacher's account of the essence of Christianity, where 'everything is related to the redemption accomplished by Jesus of Nazareth'.[4] His christological centre relates to other essential elements in early Christian belief and practice, including Spirit (p. 370). These wider ramifications of his 'unifying centre' qualify the 'minimal unity' (p. 374) implied by some of his formulations. The New Testament writers would not have accepted that their distinctive reference to Jesus crucified and risen would without elaboration suffice to define their unity of faith, and neither would any competent theologian before the eighteenth century, if then. Brief summaries (the creed or rule of faith or essence of Christianity) are helpful in guiding Christian interpretations of Scripture; they do not replace it as a norm of Christian faith and theology. That remains Scripture, however difficult it is to make appeals to Scripture persuasive when its interpretation is contested.[5] Those who insist on the New Testament canon, read in a correct rela-

3. This was one reason why F. C. Baur's Hegelian conflict account of the development of early Christian theology caused alarm.

4. *The Christian Faith* (1830/31^2; Eng. trans. Edinburgh: T&T Clark, 1928), §11, p. 52.

5. For my suggestion, see 'The New Testament Canon of Scripture and Christian Identity', in *Die Einheit der Schrift und die Vielfalt des Kanons* (hrsg. John Barton und Michael Wolter; Berlin: de Gruyter, 2003), pp. 151-93.

tionship to the Old, as a norm (as well as a source) of Christian faith and theology are claiming to share a common faith with all the New Testament writers, however variously that was and is articulated. Whether a common faith, still held by most Christians today, can be perceived behind or within the historical and theological diversity persuasively described by Dunn, is the conceptual question this essay seeks to address by reference to the different ways New Testament writers talk of the (Holy) Spirit. My conclusion will be that the blunt affirmation of the Nicene Creed, prior to the Constantinopolitan elaborations, is something that all the New Testament writers were agreed on: we believe in the Holy Spirit. The theological elaborations are (for reasons to be clarified) not the place to look.

Schleiermacher's 'essence of Christianity' was not an account of what united the New Testament writers, neither did he intend his formula to function as a norm identifying authentic Christianity. It was drawn from Christian history, especially the New Testament origins, and guided the historical and Christian reading of Scripture and tradition which he called 'historical theology'.[6] Describing the unity of Scripture in terms of a lowest common doctrinal denominator and using this as a norm would be to underestimate the unity of faith which Christians frequently acknowledge despite their institutional, liturgical, and even some of their doctrinal divisions.

Among the summaries of Christianity which describe the New Testament writers' and their successors' views of the essential subject matter of Christian Scripture and so guide its interpretation, Schillebeeckx's 'salvation from God in Jesus'[7] is better than most because God, the God of Israel identified by the Old Testament, is fundamental, and salvation is what God in Jesus is all about. Unlike Schleiermacher, Dunn stresses neither 'redemption' nor 'the Redeemer',[8] and his few references to 'salvation' and 'the Saviour' say less than a New Testament theology would, but the challenge of his book (which was 'intended to be provocative', p. 6) lies less in the doctrines deselected, and more in the way he characterizes the unity he recognizes in the New Testament. As a historian he is rightly conscious of the diversity of theological expression in early Christianity. As a Christian theologian he is rightly interested in the underlying unity. The

6. *Brief Outline on the Study of Theology* (1810, 1830[2]; Richmond: John Knox, 1966). Schleiermacher did not think that a 'properly historical perspective on Christianity' (p. 39) excluded 'a definite interest in Christianity' (p. 21) which was not purely academic and involved speaking of God.

7. *Jesus: An Experiment in Christology* (London: Collins, 1979), pp. 19-24. All three terms are also found in Denney's formulation quoted by Dunn on p. 419.

8. 'Reconciliation' and 'atonement' are also absent, in contrast to Ritschl's emphasis on the former and Peter Stuhlmacher's overemphasis on the latter.

danger of coupling these terms is that of suggesting that they are to be found on the same level. Looking for the unity on the theological plane where diversity has been emphasized encourages the minimalist approach to unity favoured by some ecumenical politicians.

Dr Dunn knows better than to succumb to that residue of an older biblical theology. He has learned from Bultmann and Käsemann to find the unity on another level, sometimes in Jesus, sometimes in the 'Christ event', rather than in particular christologies. What 'Christ event' means beyond identifying Jesus the risen Christ with Jesus of Nazareth and so referring to Christian proclamation needs clarifying. Bultmann's kerygmatic talk of revelation implied its reception in faith and life, but this is obscured when New Testament theology is seen as part of, and articulated on analogy with, the history of doctrine, as was common prior to Bultmann[9] and has remained common where Bultmann's historical criticism has been assimilated but his understanding of theology only partly understood. The unity of the New Testament is found in its *Sache*, or essential content, the gospel, not in a doctrinal minimum. The gospel cannot be 'objectified',[10] however necessary historical and theological language are to express, communicate, and define it doctrinally. Käsemann's canon within the canon, or norm effective in Scripture, like Luther's (and Bultmann's), consisted in the Christ proclaimed, Jesus crucified and risen, the gospel he thought best expressed by Paul's 'justification of the ungodly'. It did not consist in that or any other doctrinal topic as such.

The unity of the New Testament is a unity of faith which can be intuited by interpreting these texts critically and theologically. Only in the act of interpretation is the *Sache* of the New Testament understood sufficiently to permit judgments (provisional, in view of human fallibility) about the authenticity or otherwise of some Christian doctrinal, moral, or liturgical proposal. This is the business of a New Testament theology that aims to be Christian *theology*, done by interpreting Scripture. It was not the professional concern of William Wrede (n. 9), and Wrede's renunciation of theological interpretation of these texts has been legitimately followed by many biblical scholars. Legitimately,

9. Thus for all his criticisms of Holtzmann's presenting the theologies of the New Testament in terms of 'doctrinal topics' and his denial that the New Testament contains much 'doctrine', William Wrede still saw New Testament theology as 'the first period of the history of doctrine, separated only in a formal way from the rest.' See *The Task and Methods of 'New Testament Theology'*, Eng. trans. R. Morgan, *The Nature of New Testament Theology* (London: SCM, 1973), pp. 75, 183.

10. See Käsemann's essay 'Is the Gospel Objective?' (1953) in *Essays on New Testament Themes* (London: SCM, 1964), pp. 48-62. This Bultmannian essay ends with a reference to the Holy Spirit, through whom alone faith is possible in obedient response to the Word preached.

but not obligatorily, for there is more to biblical interpretation than historical scholarship. Historians of early Christian religion and theology can describe the diversity, but 'the unity in the New Testament' is as elusive as 'the unity that the Spirit gives' (Eph. 4.3, NEB). We may seek it by historical research and try to define it in doctrinal terms, but neither approach will grasp it. What can be said about it is inadequate, but some approaches are more fruitful than others. It is recognized in moments when the gospel subject-matter of Scripture is acknowledged, but it cannot be pinned down definitively. Doctrinal formulations such as the divinity of Christ are necessary and useful shorthand for teaching Christianity, but not substitutes for Scripture, and not themselves the norm defining authentic Christianity or constituting the unity of, or in, the New Testament.

Theological interpreters of Scripture make synthetic judgments about what is authentically Christian, and they do this in ongoing conversation with other competent readers of Scripture. Their interpretative acts are endlessly repeated, as in all reading of a classic text. These readers bring expectations and pre-understandings to the text. These may be challenged by the text, but they also affect how it is read. In the case of Christians' theological interpretations of their Scriptures, prior beliefs about the identity of God (which includes a self-understanding), about God's decisive saving revelation in Jesus' life and death and vindication (which again includes a self-understanding), and about the power and presence of God as Spirit, at work in the community and the world (likewise), all shape the readers' understanding of the subject matter or *Sache* of Scripture. We may sum this up by saying that they interpret the New Testament with an eye to the subsequent history of Christianity, in particular to how they as Christians (or reading from a Christian perspective) understand their Christianity today.[11] The scholarship required to understand the New Testament is largely linguistic and historical, but the perspective from which it is read theologically is religious and specifically Christian. Whether or not these modern readers share the writers' convictions about God, this is the perspective from which the New Testament is understood theologically: as expressions of a Christian faith shared by millions today, not merely as sources for historical reconstructions of early Christianity and its beliefs and aspirations, whether these are described (inadequately) in doctrinal concepts or with Wrede's historical sensitivity.

11. This formulation says nothing about the interpreters' faith or personal commitment (which is invisible) but assumes a perspective derived from standing in a tradition, being familiar with it, and to some degree identifying with it, at least for this purpose. Only so can one speak of God *with* the New Testament writers, in contrast to describing their *religion,* from a distance.

Wrede answered his own question, 'What are we really looking for?' (p. 84), as follows: *'What was believed, thought, taught, hoped, required and striven for in the earliest period of Christianity'* (p. 84). He contrasted that with 'what certain writings say about faith, doctrine, hope etc.' (p. 85). He was not contrasting history and theology, but what he thought was good and bad historical description. He objected to the doctrinal language found even in historically responsible New Testament theologies, that it 'makes doctrine out of what in itself is not doctrine' (p. 75).

The use of doctrinal language can be defended (as Wrede might have conceded) as an analytic tool. It can also be appreciated (but not by Wrede) for making links with the subsequent tradition, which theological interpretation must do. Wrede attacked this method in the interests of better historical description, the task of his biblical scholarship, but we cannot respond merely by referring to the different aims of a New Testament theology conceived as theological interpretation of Scripture. This is an inadequate response because behind Wrede's objections to modelling the biblical theological disciplines on the old dogmatics textbooks stood the liberal Protestant view that a biblical theology modelled on these would not be a plausible expression of contemporary Christianity and so would not satisfy a major requirement of theological interpretation. For such a biblical theology to replace dogmatics (as proposed in pietism's reaction against Protestant orthodoxy[12]), a precritical view of revelation (identifying it with the Bible) was necessary. That had long been indefensible, but at least the older biblical theologies were theology — attempting to express Christianity as it is or should be in their own day. Wrede was not performing that theological task. Like Dr Dunn he was describing first-century Christianity, and on his view New Testament theology (wrongly so-called) could only be the first chapters of a history of Christian religion and theology. He criticized his contemporaries for the way they performed that historical task but did not suggest that if done properly this would yield a norm or canon for deciding what is authentic Christianity today. Bultmann and Käsemann thought this task of theological discrimination to be part of their brief as New Testament theologians, and therefore moved 'beyond' Wrede's New Testament history.[13]

Christian theology owes much to historical critics. Their sharp eyes for mundane realities have enriched the understanding of Scripture and advanced

12. For example, A. F. Büsching, *Gedanken von der Beschaffenheit und dem Vorzug der biblische-dogmatischen Theologie vor der alten und neuen scholastischen* (Lemgo, 1758).

13. H. Räisänen's reversion to Wrede's programme in his excellent book *Beyond New Testament Theology* (London: SCM, 1990, 2000^{2}) could therefore be called *Instead of New Testament Theology,* avoiding the value judgments implicit in beyond, behind, or beneath.

the theological agenda. But their frame of reference is different from theology's, and there is no reason for biblical theology to give up speaking of God and to speak instead of early Christian religion, important as that also is for understanding the New Testament. Talking of God in a self-involving way is simply a different project from studying the New Testament as historical source material.

New Testament theology has since 1800 combined these tasks, more or less successfully. Most successfully when a reigning idealist metaphysics of history suggested that the historical reconstruction of the Christian religion would reveal the divine Spirit moving through that history. F. C. Baur's attempt to interpret the Spirit language of the New Testament in terms of modern philosophical theology *(Religionsphilosophie)* was rendered implausible by subsequent historical research,[14] and idealist speculation about the meaning of history was replaced by a more positivistic historiography. The piety of most biblical scholars preserved a sense of what the Christian church believes the subject matter of Scripture to be, but the articulation of this was treated as a matter for dogmatic and practical theology, not 'scientific' biblical scholarship.

Whatever the flaws of Bultmann's 1920s synthesis of theology and historical criticism, it repaired much of the damage done to Christian proclamation by this divorce between biblical studies and constructive theology. But that was then. Over the following eighty years historical research has made some progress and the cultural climate has again changed, consigning that synthesis also to the history of theology, and again leaving a theological vacuum in biblical studies. Many are content to perform historical and exegetical tasks without engaging with theological problems, and that is surely preferable to making historical criticism perform tasks for which it was never designed. But churches which read Scripture as a source and a norm of their faith and theology still need interpretations which relate the texts to their own contemporary self-construals. The heuristic use of doctrinal concepts can help, but the traditional dogmatic frame of reference is a procrustean bed which does not fit the biblical data and no longer seems to speak of God when Scripture is no longer read as divine revelation but as a collection of fallible human witnesses to revelation. The history-of-religion frame of reference adopted by Wrede is even less theologically helpful now that Baur's metaphysics is dead. New Testament theology must therefore give different accounts of the unity and subject matter of Scripture, returning to a theological interpretation of texts, but one enriched by the historical insights of Wrede and his successors.

14. H. Gunkel, *Die Wirkungen des heiligen Geistes nach der populären Anschauung der apostolischen Zeit und nach der Lehre des Apostels Paulus* (Göttingen: Vandenhoeck und Ruprecht, 1888).

Bultmann pointed New Testament theology away from both the older doctrinal type of biblical theology and Wrede's flight from *theology* to a preference for (scientific) *history* of early Christian religion and theology, with his remark that 'the writings of the New Testament can be interrogated as the "sources" which the historian interprets in order to reconstruct a picture of primitive Christianity as a phenomenon of the historical past, or the reconstruction stands in the service of the interpretation of the New Testament writings under the presupposition that they have something to say to the present'.[15] He placed his own book in the latter category, despite its largely historical frame of reference, and rightly so. His interpretations of Paul and John are more than historical reconstructions. They include the *Sachkritik*, or critical assessment of the text in the light of its theological subject matter, which Bultmann always insisted was essential in theological interpretation or *Sachexegese.*

There is some ambiguity in Bultmann's understanding of *Sachkritik.* His appeals to Luther's canon criticism suggest more than his own immanent criticism of the texts, or correcting 'what is said' by 'what is meant'. Luther appeals to his own understanding of the gospel heard in Scripture when he asks, 'What preaches Christ?' and is willing if necessary to 'urge Christ against Scripture'. This is more like the evaluations made in literary criticism than a historical judgment. A move towards a literary frame of reference is also implied by Bultmann's making the necessary historical research serve 'the interpretation of the New Testament *writings*' (n. 15).

Rather than following this track, Bultmann explored the alternative of expanding the historian's role to encompass all human consciousness. History writing is not merely criticizing and correlating sources to reconstruct the past. It is a medium of self-understanding in the present. That existentialist account of history seemed the best way forward in 1925,[16] following the publication of the letters of Dilthey and the Graf Paul Yorck (1922-23), and in a generation when the historical frame of reference looked like the only possibility for a properly critical theological interpretation. However, the blossoming of modern literary approaches to the Bible since the 1980s has opened up new possibilities. Their attention to the impact of texts on readers may provide better models of how Scripture is a *source* of faith and theology than historical research does. Most literary approaches are less helpful in enabling Scripture to function as a *norm* because this requires authorial or textual intention and determinacy, but some literary criticism insists on historically responsible exegesis (in some

15. *Theology of the New Testament*, vol. 2 (London: SCM, 1955), p. 251.

16. At the end of 'Das Problem einer theologischen Exegese des neuen Testaments' Bultmann thought he had made historical and theological exegesis 'coincide'.

contexts) and allows the interpreter to speak (with the text) of *God* without insisting on translating the text's God talk into historical descriptions of religion. Literary criticism is thus today more immediately open to the language of revelation than is historical research without metaphysics. Dr Dunn (like both his great predecessor and his revered teacher) is rightly suspicious of anything which might threaten the primacy of historical research in the training of biblical scholars. We try to imagine ourselves into the ancient world. But our questions are modern, and some of them are theological, including those about the identity of Christianity. If the doctrinal type of New Testament theology fails to answer these, and the critical historical type in its purity (Wrede) does not even try, and even Dr Dunn's grappling with the problem leads to a more 'minimal unity' than most Christians expect and experience, then we need a different account of the unity in the New Testament. This will help define and preserve authentic (or biblical) Christianity and so give a Protestant view of the unity of the Spirit in the bond of peace today.

Some would appeal to a distinctive religious experience shared by the New Testament writers and associated with Jesus and the Spirit. Certainly 'religious experience was a factor of fundamental importance in the beginnings of Christianity' (Dunn, *Unity*, p. 199 and throughout his *oeuvre*). But these writers' experience is not accessible to us. All we have is their writings, especially what they say about Jesus and salvation; and the Spirit, and what they all presuppose about God. It is therefore more fruitful to look for the shared religious vocabulary of these texts. Since language shapes experience, this may point to the more elusive unity of faith which, like Paul in the first generation (1 Cor. 15.11), all those who gradually assembled the canon assumed all the writers and they themselves shared. It includes more than a reference to the earthly and exalted Jesus, believed to be one and the same. It includes above all a shared conviction of and reference to the God of Israel, the Creator of heaven and earth. It includes the royal messianic claim made for Jesus, and the language of sonship and lordship, all of which speak of his saving relationship to his followers as well as his relation to God whom he revealed. It includes the community of his followers, united in having memories of Jesus and shared beliefs and life-styles, Scripture and rituals, in a community described in a wealth of metaphors. It included the hope of Jesus' return, again expressed in a variety of traditional language. And it included frequent references to the Spirit of God, who is associated with Jesus in the present, however variously that is understood and articulated.

These various ways of speaking of the Spirit have been sufficiently discussed in this volume and elsewhere. The diversity of expression and perhaps theology is not disputed here, though most of what is said about the Spirit in the New Testament is pre-reflective. Dr Dunn's 'wide-ranging diversity' (p. 374) of theological expression in early Christianity can be found even among the writings which were included in the canon on the assumption that they expressed a common 'apostolic' faith. The subsequent impact of Scripture has demonstrated that they can be read to support a common faith, and the differences noted by modern historians (and sometimes exaggerated, in understandable reaction against harmonization) have not changed that. What these have rendered inadmissible is appeal to a normative dogmatics found in Scripture (cf. n. 18). But (unlike Marcion) that was not what the fathers (or Luther) expected from the witness of Scripture. That expectation originated with a few eighteenth-century pietists (n. 12) who were trying (rightly) to let Scripture liberate them from the stranglehold of Protestant scholasticism, as it had liberated the Reformers from medieval scholasticism. Historical criticism has liberated modern theology from both a deadly dogmatics and the misguided counterproposal of pietism. Both these misreadings of Scripture are still alive in all denominations, wherever critical biblical study is disregarded. That disregard is sadly understandable on account of the critics' frequent failure (and sometimes unwillingness) to co-ordinate their historical work (as Baur and Bultmann did) with a theological interpretation of these texts.

Bultmann's existential theological interpretation of John's Gospel, like Käsemann's theological interpretation of Romans, showed how historical exegesis and hypothetical reconstructions can serve theological interpretations, even though these particular proposals have now been consigned to the history of theology. They remain healthy examples to a new generation whose emphasis on texts rather than history could easily mislead believers into reading the biblical texts as legislation, defining what is to be believed and done rather than as witness to the gospel. That appeal to the letter excludes the Spirit. In accord with Dr Dunn's intentions *(das Gemeinte),* but in tension with some of *das Gesagte,* the proposal implied by this respectful *Auseinandersetzung* with the most productive British scholar of our generation has opposed finding the 'unity in the New Testament' in a minimal christological statement which can serve as a doctrinal norm. To look for it instead in the dialectical relationship between Scripture and the Christ event or gospel means to write a historically responsible New Testament theology. These interpretations of the whole New Testament in the context of Old Testament belief in God contribute to the church's listening to the witness of Scripture in the ongoing correction of its faith, and doing so by joining in the ongoing conversation between competent readers of Scripture. Instead of using historical methods to extract doctrinal information from authoritative texts, or to reconstruct the history of doctrine, it gives historical work an essential role in listening to the witness of these ancient religious texts as they are being interpreted with a view to expressing Christian faith today. That literary and theological task of interpreting the New Testament writings in ways that do justice to its religious subject matter is normally done from within the religious tradition and community which reads them as Scripture. It respects their intentions and treasures the language they use without necessarily agreeing with every formulation found in them.

And what about what they say about the Holy Spirit?

Constructing a doctrine of the Holy Spirit today is a task for systematic, not biblical theology. Systematicians who read the Scriptures will hardly need telling how important the Spirit was in early Christian language and experience. They could be referred to the incredulity implied at Acts 19.2. But it is not only the reality of the Spirit that is implied here. The New Testament writers are agreed about more than that, and Christians who learn the grammar and vocabulary of their faith from Scripture will want to take note. They will learn that the Spirit is from God, and that God is Spirit. The fourth-century church was to argue about the divinity of the Holy Spirit and the shape of trinitarian theology, but such arguments are not found in the New Testament. Its writers inherited spirit-language from their mainly Jewish tradition and interpreted their own and their co-religionists' experience in the light of biblical prophecies. Paul and John had reflected deeply, and Luke perhaps less deeply, on the relationship between what they said about the Spirit and what they were saying about the risen Jesus, but not even Paul and John are helpfully described in terms of their respective 'doctrines of the Spirit'. The word 'doctrine' implies settled convictions which result from reflection at some distance from the immediacy of early Christian experience. The New Testament witnesses are a source of faith and provide resources for later doctrinal definition, but it is a category mistake to treat some of these occasional comments as already settled doctrine, and it is therefore inappropriate to use them as 'proof-texts' in doctrinal arguments. Church reports cite them as a kind of shorthand rather than as theological demonstration, but the so-called biblical theological movement was rightly criticized if it supposed its constructions could replace systematic theology.

These witnesses preserved the gospel story and generated or transmitted a vocabulary which could be used in proclamation, worship, and theological construction and argument. The imposition in the West of a tighter theological unity on this diverse collection arose from its use in doctrinal disputes between Protestants and Roman Catholics. When some Christians broke with the catholic magisterium a new authority and legitimation was needed, and it was found in 'Scripture alone'. The unity of faith which Paul had celebrated in 1 Cor. 15.1-11 was sometimes hardened into doctrines which could be thought biblical and therefore true and authentically Christian. These could be sharpened into biblical theological weapons strong enough to do battle with the papacy and give to a church deprived of its living authority an alternative basis and legitimacy. The Protestant belief that Scripture alone could provide a doctrinal norm encouraged its use as a doctrinal handbook as early as Melanchthon's *Loci Communes* of 1521, and later led to proof-texting support for dogmatics. Protestant self-understanding survived the demise of the latter, but when critical historical investigation found theological disagreements in Scripture, the foundations of Protestantism seemed to some to be threatened.

That misunderstanding of Luther's scriptural principle[17] was destroyed by historical criticism and corrected in the theological interpretation of Barth and Bultmann and their best pupils. 'There can be no normative Christian dogmatics'[18] drawn from the New Testament. Rather, Scripture is heard, read, marked, learned, and inwardly digested as a whole and (more usually) in bits, by believers (weak and strong) who hear its witness when they recognize in it the gospel they themselves acknowledge and confess (weakly or strongly). This requires learning its language, not only its vocabulary but its grammar, not only words like Spirit, but also how they all relate conceptually and in experience to the 'salvation from God in Jesus', the crucified and risen Lord in whom all the New Testament writers and all orthodox Christians *semper et ubique* see the revelation of God: we beheld his glory. . . . Nobody has ever seen God. . . . God is Spirit. . . . And Jesus gone to the Father sends another Paraclete, the Spirit of truth. Or as St Paul wrote in a verse very important to our honorand, the last Adam became a life-giving Spirit (1 Cor. 15.45). To conclude from these differences in what Paul and John say about the Spirit that their shared belief in the Spirit is not part of what unites them and all Christians who let their faith be normed as well as informed by Scripture would be absurd. In the light of later disputes about the *filioque* one might wish that the conciliar fathers at Constantinople (381) had stuck with the Creed of Nicaea, and not made the necessary theological elaborations a matter of faith. New Testament theology cannot resolve this dispute between East and West, only contribute to the ongoing conversation. This fruitful discussion continues within that generous and liberal orthodoxy which can be learned from a joyful Jimmy Dunn delighting in a legitimate diversity.

17. Corrected in several writings of G. Ebeling, notably in *The Word of God and Tradition* (London: Collins, 1968), pp. 102-47, reprinted and supported by Käsemann, *Kanon* (see n. 1).

18. So Bultmann, *Theology of the New Testament*, vol. 2 (London: SCM, 1955), p. 237.

11 Spirits and Demons in the Dead Sea Scrolls

Hermann Lichtenberger

I. Introduction

The conviction that the Spirit of God is at work in the lives of ordinary individuals is one that animates the literature of earliest Christianity and beyond. But it is a conviction that comes to life most fully only when seen against a contextual background in which spirits and demons were frequently thought to influence people toward certain ends. A broad stream of traditions in the ancient world testifies precisely to the frequency of this conviction in the ancient world.

The Qumran-Essene writings share with this broad stream of traditions the notion that no one is a master of his own person, nor free in his decisions; instead he is subject to suprahuman powers reigning over him. Though these powers are to be differentiated from him, they nonetheless are active in his inner being, rendering him to be in a powerless state. A systematic statement of this situation is found in the well-known treatise on the two spirits in 1QS 3.13–4.26,[1] from which some lines from the beginning are given here:

1. For the discussion of this passage until 1980, see Hermann Lichtenberger, *Studien zum Menschenbild in Texten der Qumrangemeinde* (Göttingen: Vandenhoeck & Ruprecht, 1980), pp. 123-42; the translation of the quoted passage is slightly revised from James H. Charlesworth, *The Dead Sea Scrolls: Rule of The Community. Photographic Multi-Language Edition* (Philadelphia: American Interfaith Institute/World Alliance, 1996), p. 58. For a long time this treatise was thought to be the very portrayal of Qumran-Essene demonology, but recent scholarship has come to the conclusion that the treatise goes back to pre-Essene tradition and was later incorporated into the Qumran-Essene text of the *Rule of the Community;* see Armin Lange, *Weisheit und Prädestination: Weisheitliche Urordnung und Prädestination in den Textfunden von Qumran*

> He (= God) created man for the dominion of the earth and designed for him two spirits in which to walk until the appointed time for his visitation; these are the spirits of truth and deceit. In the spring of light emanates the nature of truth and from a well of darkness emerges the nature of deceit. In the hand of the Prince of Lights (is) the dominion of all the Sons of Righteousness; in the ways of light they walk. But in the hand of the Angel of Darkness (is) the dominion of the Sons of Deceit; and in the ways of darkness they walk. (3.17-21)

Of course, the Qumran literature does not always resort to categories of angelology and demonology to depict the lack of freedom in human existence. Occasionally astronomical categories are used (as in the horoscopes),[2] and the concept of the heavenly tablets or books serves a similar deterministic function.[3] Nonetheless, in the Qumran literature the prevailing illustration of the "unfree" and dependent existence of humanity is demonology.

Since this demonology is part of a cosmological dualism comprising both *space* and *time*, it is a dualism that consequently operates within the parameters of Jewish monotheism. *Space* encompasses the whole world, humankind, and angels (including the princes of the angels) on the one hand and, on the other hand, demons, evil angels, and their princes (e.g., Belial). *Time* ranges from primeval times to the present and the eschaton: In the eschaton God will destroy all negative powers (bad spirits, evil angels, demons, Belial Mastema) definitively. The present period, however, is the time of the reign of Belial, to whom in his inscrutable mysteries God hands over *space* and *time* to be the context for his reign.[4]

In the paragraphs that follow, I shall highlight four significant passages illustrating the demonological convictions of the Qumran community in order to provide something of a backdrop for early Christian convictions about the influence of the Holy Spirit.

(Leiden, New York, Köln: E. J. Brill, 1995), pp. 121-70. For the background in terms of the history of religions, see the earlier studies by A. Dupont-Sommer, "L'instruction sur les deux Esprits dans le 'Manuel de Discipline,'" *Revue de l'Histoire des Religions* 142 (1952): 5-35, and K. G. Kuhn, "Die Sektenschrift und die iranische Religion," *ZThK* 49 (1952): 296-316 (discussed in Lichtenberger, *Menschenbild*, pp. 196-200), and especially Marc Philonenko, "La doctrine qoumrânienne des deux esprits: Ses origines iraniennes et ses prolongements dans le judaïsme essénien et le christianisme antique," in *Apocalyptique iranienne et dualisme qoumrânien* (ed. Geo Widengren, Anders Hultgård, and Marc Philonenko; Paris: Maisonneuve, 1995), pp. 163-211.

2. For example, 4Q186.

3. See Lange, *Weisheit und Prädestination*, pp. 69-79.

4. See 1QS 3.22-23.

II. Spirits and Demons in 11QPsAp^a (11Q11)[5]

11QPs^a 27.9-10[6] reports that among "David's Compositions" were four "songs for making music over the stricken."[7] James A. Sanders considers Psalm 91 to be one of the psalms which, according to rabbinic tradition, were to be sung over the stricken,[8] and J. P. M. van der Ploeg makes the same connection with regard to 11QPsAp^a: "Je me demande si les compositions 'apocryphes' de notre rouleau ne seraient pas les chants mentionnés dans le texte cité de 11QPs^a."[9]

The manuscript of 11QPsAp^a incorporates at least three songs against demons, with Psalm 91 following on directly as a fourth song of this sort. Spirits and demons *([hrw]ḥwt[ ]whšdim)* are closely connected in 2.3; demons occur also in 2.4: "These are [the de]mons." Incantation terminology is present in 1.7,

5. Final edition by Florentino García Martínez, Eibert J. C. Tigchelaar, and Adam S. van der Woude, *Qumran Cave 11, II, 11Q2-18, 11Q20-31* (Discoveries in the Judaean Desert 23; Oxford: Clarendon, 1998), pp. 181-205, Plates XXII-XXV.

6. James A. Sanders, *The Psalms Scroll of Qumrân Cave 11 (11QPs^a)* (Discoveries in the Judaean Desert 4; Oxford: Clarendon, 1965), pp. 91-93.

7. Trans. from Sanders, *Psalms Scroll,* p. 92.

8. Sanders, *Psalms Scroll,* p. 93; cf. also Marcus Jastrow, *A Dictionary of the Targumim, the Talmud Babli and Yerushalmi, and the Midrashic Literature* (New York: Pardes; repr., Philadelphia, 1903), p. 1135.

9. J. P. M. van der Ploeg, "Un petit rouleau de psaumes apocryphes (11QPsAp^a)," *Tradition und Glaube: Das frühe Christentum in seiner Umwelt* (ed. Gert Jeremias, Heinz-Wolfgang Kuhn, and Hartmut Stegemann; Göttingen: Vandenhoeck & Ruprecht, 1971), pp. 128-39, esp. p. 129. In opposition to van der Ploeg's identification, Maurice Baillet claims to find the collection for the stricken from 11QPs^a in the "Cantiques du Sage" (4Q510 and 511); *Qumran Cave 4, volume III, 4Q482-4Q520* (Discoveries in the Judaean Desert 7; Oxford: Clarendon, 1982), p. 215. In my opinion, the theory of van der Ploeg is more probable. See further Emile Puech, "11QPsAp^a: Un rituel d'exorcismes. Essai de reconstruction," *Revue de Qumran* 14 (1990): 377-408; idem, "Les deux derniers Psaumes davidiques du rituel d'exorcisme, 11QPsAp^a IV 4–V 14," *The Dead Sea Scrolls: Forty Years of Research* (ed. Devorah Dimant and Uriel Rappaport; Studies on the Texts of the Desert of Judah 10; Leiden, New York, Köln, Jerusalem: E. J. Brill, Yad Izhak Ben-Zvi, 1992), pp. 64-89; idem, "Les psaumes davidiques du rituel d'exorcisme (11Q11)", *Sapiential, Liturgical and Poetical Texts from Qumran* (ed. Daniel K. Falk, Florentino García Martínez, and Eileen M. Schuller; Leiden, Boston, Köln: Brill, 2000), pp. 160-81; James A. Sanders, *A Liturgy for Healing the Stricken (11QPsAp^a = 11Q11)* (Pseudepigraphic and Non-Masoretic Psalms and Prayers: The Princeton Theological Seminary Dead Sea Scrolls Project, Hebrew, Aramaic, and Greek Texts with English Translations; ed. James H. Charlesworth; vol. 4A (Tübingen and Louisville: Mohr [Siebeck] and Westminster John Knox, 1997), pp. 216-33; Hermann Lichtenberger, "Ps 91 und die Exorzismen in 11QPsAp^a," *Die Dämonen-Demons: Die Dämonologie der israelitisch-jüdischen und frühchristlichen Literatur im Kontext ihrer Umwelt — The Demonology of Israelite-Jewish and Early Christian Literature in Context of Their Environment* (ed. Armin Lange, Hermann Lichtenberger, and K. F. Diethard Römheld; Tübingen: Mohr [Siebeck], 2003), pp. 416-21.

3.4, and 5.1 *(mšbiʿ)*. Presumably Solomon is the one who "shall invoke" (2.2), and "YHWH will strike you with a [grea]t b[low] to destroy you" (4.4),[10] "and in his fury [he will send] against you a powerful angel" *(ml'k tqip)* (4.5). The demon is banished to the abyss (*thwm*, 2.5; 3.1) and to Sheol *(thwm rbh [wlš 'wl] htḥtih)* "who (scil. YHWH) [will bring] you [down] to the great abyss [and to] the deepest [Sheol]" (4.7-8).

Most important is the incantation of the demon in 5.4-11:

> (4) Of David. A[gainst . . . An incant]ation in the name of YHW[H. Invoke at an]y time
> (5) the heav[ens. When]he comes to you in the nig[ht,] you shall [s]ay to him:
> (6) 'Who are you, [O offspring of] man and seed of the ho[ly one]s? Your face is a face of
> (7) [delu]sion and your horns are horns of ill[us]ion, you are darkness and not light,
> (8) [injust]ice and not justice.[ ] the chief of the army, YHWH [will bring] you [down]
> (9) [to the] deepest [Sheo]l, [and he will shut the] two bronze [ga]tes th[rough which n]o
> (10) light [penetrates,] and [the] sun [will] not [shine for you] tha[t rises]
> (11) [upon the] just man to [

This third psalm (4.4–5.3) of the collection precedes the quotation of the biblical Psalm 91[11] with which it is closely connected. The following features illustrate the point:

1. The mention of danger in the night (5.4; see Ps. 91:5);
2. Asking for the name[12] of the demon *(mi 'th)* (5.6; see Ps. 91:2);
3. The description of the demon's futility and nothingness ("your face is a face of [delu]sion and your horns [i.e., your might] are horns of ill[us]ion, you are darkness and not light, [injust]ice and not justice," 5.6-8; see Ps. 91:3-8, 10, 13);

10. The translation here and in the following is that of García Martínez, Tigchelaar, and van der Woude, *Qumran Cave 11*.

11. For text-critical observations, see Otto Eißfeldt, "Eine Qumran-Textform des 91. Psalms," in *Bibel und Qumran: Beiträge zur Erforschung der Beziehungen zwischen Bibel- und Qumranwissenschaft* (ed. Siegfried Wagner; Berlin: Evangelische Haupt-Bibelgesellschaft, 1968), pp. 82-85, and Puech, Sanders, and Lichtenberger (n. 9).

12. A close parallel appears in Philonenko, "Doctrine," p. 173.

4. The description of YHWH's army and its chief *(sr)* (5.8 as in 4.5, the "powerful angel"; cf. Ps. 91:11-12, where the Lord's host and his angel come to deliver humanity).

Psalm 91 (in the manuscript, 5.3-14) is in its content clearly connected with the preceding three psalms. By means of its relationship with the preceding incantations, Psalm 91 itself serves the same purpose of deterring demonic influence. This becomes most evident from the fact that it is liturgically integrated by "Amen, Amen, Sela" (6.14; see 6.3 in the preceding psalm) into the collection and in the ascription to David (Ps. 91 was ascribed to David in LXX, as in 5.4, *ldwid*). But at the same time Ps. 91:2 appears to correct the preceding psalms and develop them further by insisting that the most effective protection from evil spirits is to turn to God himself:[13] ["He that lives]in the shelter[of the Most High, in the shadow of] the Almighty [he stays.] He who says [to YHWH: 'My refuge] and [my] fortress,[my God] is the safety in which [I trust']." In this way, Psalm 91 concludes the collection of incantations with the assurance of God's deliverance and acts as a keystone of faith in God against the power of demonic influence.

III. 11QPs^a 19.1-18 ("Plea for Deliverance")[14]

David Flusser[15] has drawn attention[16] to the "Plea for Deliverance" as an apotropaic prayer. Lines 13-16 confirm this interpretation:[17]

Forgive my sin, O Lord,
and purify me from my iniquity.
Vouchsafe to me a spirit of faith and knowledge,
And let me not be dishonoured in ruin.
Let not Satan rule over me,
Nor an unclean spirit;
Neither let pain nor the evil inclination
Take possession of my bones.

13. The text is 6.3-4.

14. The translation is that of Sanders, *Psalms Scroll,* pp. 76-79.

15. David Flusser, "Qumrân and Jewish 'Apotropaic' Prayers," *Israel Exploration Journal* 16 (1966): 194-205.

16. I owe the hint to Sanders, *Liturgy,* p. 217, n. 6.

17. The translation is that of Sanders, *Psalms Scroll,* p. 78.

Here we find the opposites "spirit of faith (i.e., truth)" (*rwḥ 'mwnh*, l. 14) and "Satan and a spirit of uncleanness" (*stn wrwḥ tm'h*, l. 15). A spirit of faithfulness is associated with (the spirit of) knowledge on the one hand, and on the other hand the dominion of Satan[18] is associated with an unclean spirit, pain, and the "evil inclination" (*yṣr r*ʿ[19]). As David Flusser notes:

> Unclean spirits were believed to emerge from Satan, and to cause pain and disease. Disease, in turn, was seen as a result of sin, which again is a product of man's evil inclination. In order to avert and banish these horrible dangers, the author of this Qumran prayer invoked the apotropaic protection of God: "Let Satan and an impure spirit not rule over me, neither let pain nor evil inclination claim power over my bones."[20]

IV. Spirit(s) in 1QGenesis Apocryphon

Crucial to our study is the passage in 20.16-32. After the praise of Sarai's beauty by Hirqanos (ll. 1-7), Pharaoh takes Sarai by force from Abraham (ll. 7-11). Abraham then prays to God (ll. 12-16), after which it is said in lines 16-17:

> That night, the God Most High sent him [i.e., Pharaoh] a chastising spirit *(rwḥ mkdš)*, to afflict him and all the members of his household, an evil spirit *(rwḥ b'yš)* that kept afflicting him and all the members of his household.

For two years the evil spirit is said to have tormented Pharaoh, preventing him from sexual intercourse with Sarai. Pharaoh then calls for the healers of Egypt, but they cannot heal him, "for the spirit *(rwḥ')* attacked all of them and they fled" (ll. 20-21). Hirqanos is told by Lot that these inflictions can cease only when Sarai is returned to Abraham, "and this plague and the spirit *(rwḥ)* of purulent evils will cease to afflict you" (l. 26). Abraham is asked by Pharaoh to pray for him and his household "so that this evil spirit *(rwḥ' d' b'yšt')* will be banished from us." Abraham states in lines 28-29: "I prayed that [he might be] cured and laid my hands upon his [hea]d. The plague was removed from him; the evil [spirit] ([*rwḥ'*] *b'yšt'*) was banished [from him] and he recovered."[21]

18. See also the *Testament of Levi* (Flusser, "'Apotropaic' Prayers," p. 194).

19. The meaning of *yṣr r*ʿ is not yet the technical one of rabbinic literature; on the *yṣr* see Lichtenberger, *Menschenbild*, pp. 77-81.

20. Flusser, "'Apotropaic' Prayers," p. 205.

21. The translation is that of Florentino García Martínez and Eibert J. C. Tigchelaar, *The*

The evil spirit here is clearly understood as a demon that inflicts plagues and punishment, rendering Pharaoh impotent for the time Sarai is in his control. Only by Abraham's prayer is the plague removed from him. A technical term for "demon" (e.g., *šd*) does not occur in this passage, but a demon ("evil spirit") has evidently taken possession of Pharaoh and his household. It is explicitly said that he is sent by God to hinder Pharaoh from approaching Sarai. Consequently God alone can — after Abraham's prayer — remove him.[22]

V. An Incantation Formula in 4Q560[23]

Douglas Penney and Michael Wise helpfully characterize this text in the following manner:

> 4Q560 preserves an Aramaic apotropaic magic formula that mentions concerns common to other similar texts: childbirth, demons and the diseases associated with them, sleep or dreams and perhaps safety of possessions. The preserved portions of the formula adjure the offending spirits, apparently by name.[24]

In the few preserved lines of this text, a whole panorama of ancient demonology is revealed before our eyes. So, in line 1 of column I "Beel]zebub" may be read, and there he is addressed directly ("you"); line 2 speaks of an "evil visitant," a *š[d]* ("demon"); line 3 seems to be an incantation: "I adjure you all who en]ter into the body, the male wasting-demon and the female wasting-demon";[25] line 4 obviously continues the incantation: "*Š[d]* I adjure you by the

Dead Sea Scrolls: Study Edition (Leiden, Boston, Köln, Brill; Grand Rapids, Cambridge: Eerdmans, 1997), vol. 1, pp. 42-43.

22. Prayer also plays a role in the "Prayer of Nabonid," but there is no notion of a "spirit" or demon; for this text and 1QGenApok, see Walter Kirchschläger, "Exorzismus in Qumran?" *Kairos* 18 (1976): 135-53. See Armin Lange, "The Essene Position on Magic and Divination," in *Legal Texts and Legal Issues: Proceedings of the Second Meeting of the International Organization for Qumran Studies Cambridge 1995: Published in Honour of Joseph M. Baumgarten* (ed. Moshe Bernstein, Florentino García Martínez, and John Kampen; Studies on the Texts of the Desert of Judah 23; Leiden, New York, Köln: E. J. Brill, 1997), pp. 377-435.

23. Most importantly, see Douglas L. Penney and Michael O. Wise, "By the Power of Beelzebub: An Aramaic Incantation Formula from Qumran (4Q560)," *JBL* 113 (1994): 627-50; see also Lange, "Magic," pp. 385-86.

24. Penney and Wise, "Beelzebub," p. 649.

25. The translation is that of Penney and Wise, "Beelzebub," p. 632.

name of YHWH, 'He who re]moves iniquity and transgression,'[26] O fever and chills and chest pain"; line 5 refers to "the male shrine-spirit and the female shrine-spirit,[27] breacher-demons (?) of . . ."; and in column II, line 5 reads: "And I adjure you, O spirit *(rwḥ)*, [that] you. . . ."

In this text, it is not prayer but incantation that serves to free man from spirits and demons who inflict suffering and pain upon him. It was not God who had sent the evil spirit(s) and demons, but nonetheless illness,[28] pain, and sleeplessness(?) will be driven out by calling the name of the God "[who re]moves iniquity and transgression."

VI. Summary

These four texts from the Dead Sea Scrolls show a great variety of aspects concerning the activities of (evil) spirits and demons in humanity. Those spirits and demons inflict suffering, lead to sin, and threaten life in every respect. In the special case of Pharaoh, their effect is for the benefit of the pious ones. We have encountered two ways to get rid of the evil spirits or demons: prayer to God and incantation in the name of God (YHWH). In the collection 11QPsAp[a] these two modes are combined: incantation in the first three psalms, the prayer of confidence in Ps. 91:2. In the years that lie ahead, may this verse from the Psalms be a companion to Jimmy Dunn, whom I ask to accept this small present as a token of friendship.

26. The quotation is either from Exod. 34:7 or from Num. 14:18; see Penney and Wise, "Beelzebub," p. 639.

27. For *prk* and *mḥtwri*, see Penney and Wise, "Beelzebub," pp. 642-46.

28. See in 11Q11 4.3 the name of Raphael.

III John's Baptism: A Prophetic Sign

Morna D. Hooker

It is self-evident that the unique feature that marked out John the Baptist from other prophets was the fact that he baptized: so unusual and distinctive was this that it gave him his name, 'the Baptist',[1] or 'the Baptizer'.[2] John's clothes marked him out as a prophet,[3] but his message was essentially contained in what he performed, which was primarily 'a baptism of repentance leading to the forgiveness of sins'.[4] Nowhere is it more plain than here that prophetic word and prophetic action belong closely together.[5] Although the baptism of Jews was without precedent, it was an appropriate symbol of cleansing. Not surprisingly, John's baptism has been described as an 'effective sign' or as a 'prophetic symbol'.[6] Our purpose in this chapter is to explore this idea of John's baptism as a prophetic sign more fully.

How would John's baptism have been understood? Attempts to trace the origin of his baptism to either proselyte baptism or the lustrations at Qumran have proved unconvincing to most scholars. The evidence for proselyte baptism, it is suggested, is too late; the rites at Qumran, unlike John's baptism, were

1. Matt. 3:1; 11:11-12; 14:2, 8; 16:14; 17:13; Mark 6:28; 8:25; Luke 7:20, 33; 9:19.

2. Mark 6:14, 24; also 1:4, according to B and some minuscules, including 33.

3. Cf. Mark 1:6 and parallels with Zech. 13:4 and 2 Kings 1:8.

4. Mark 1:4//Luke 3:3.

5. For a discussion of the connection between word and action, see W. D. Stacey, *Prophetic Drama in the Old Testament* (London: Epworth, 1990).

6. For example, J. D. G. Dunn, *Baptism in the Holy Spirit* (SBT, 2nd ser. 15; London: SCM, 1970), p. 17.

repeated regularly.[7] The relevance of both to our argument is more basic: both employ the symbolism of water. The proselyte entering Judaism needs to be cleansed of the sins and impurity of his or her past life; the initiate at Qumran seeks to maintain his purity. In each case, *water is an obvious symbol for interior cleansing.*

The image of washing as a metaphor for removing impurity or sin is common in the Old Testament.[8] The outward action symbolizes an inner reality. It is, then, no surprise that Mark and Luke describe John as proclaiming βάπτισμα μετανοίας εἰς ἄφεσιν ἁμαρτιῶν. But how should we understand that εἰς? Is forgiveness of sins something that takes place at the baptism in the Jordan? Or is it something that is *proclaimed* in this action but has not yet taken place? A comparison with Matthew is illuminating since he states only that John was preaching in the wilderness, calling on his hearers to repent — a theme echoed in John's declaration in Matt. 3:11: ἐγὼ μὲν ὑμᾶς βαπτίζω ἐν ὕδατι εἰς μετανοίαν. John summons men and women to repent (3:2), and those who are baptized confess their sins (3:6), but for Matthew forgiveness lies in the future, since it is brought by Jesus (9:6) and is made available to many through his death (26:28). Since Mark and Luke interpret John's proclamation of baptism as preparation for what was to come, they would surely have agreed with Matthew that John's baptism pointed forward to the forgiveness brought by Jesus.[9]

I. Prophetic Signs

Whatever the background to John's baptism, it would certainly have been *understood* as a 'prophetic sign' — a dramatic action which, like prophetic words, proclaimed the divine will.[10] Once performed, the prophetic sign — like the prophetic word — could not be undone. John's message and baptism both point forward to the one who follows him. His baptism is 'the beginning of the gospel'.[11] What, then, does it signify?

7. For brief accounts of the problem, see M. D. Hooker, *The Gospel according to St Mark* (BNTC; London: A. & C. Black, 1991), pp. 39-43; John P. Meier, *A Marginal Jew* (AB; New York: Doubleday, 1994), 2:49-52.

8. For example, Lev. 17:16; 2 Kings 5:10-14; Ps. 51:2, 7; Isa. 1:16: Jer. 4:14; Zech. 13:1-2. Cf. Josephus's interpretation of John's baptism in *Ant.* 18.5.2.

9. Cf. Meier, *Marginal Jew,* pp. 53-55; J. Marcus, *Mark 1–8* (AB; New York: Doubleday, 2000), pp. 155-56.

10. Stacey, *Prophetic Drama,* pp. 260-82.

11. Cf. E. Lohmeyer, *Das Evangelium des Markus*[17] (Göttingen: Vandenhoeck and Ruprecht, 1967), p. 19.

In the Old Testament, the prophetic action mimics what God is doing or is about to do. Isaiah goes 'naked and barefoot' as a symbol of Israel's coming shame (Isaiah 20); Jeremiah smashes a pot to symbolize the destruction of Jerusalem (Jer. 19:1-13); Ezekiel eats inferior bread, cooked with dung, and drinks a small measure of water each day to portray the terrible conditions that the people are going to endure (Ezek. 4:9-17). John announces the coming of the Lord — a coming that brings rejoicing but also demands repentance. His baptism could well symbolize the inner cleansing effected by forgiveness. Being submerged in water might also symbolize the death and destruction that will overwhelm the wicked,[12] just as emerging again could suggest salvation and new life.[13]

The link made in all the Gospels between John's baptism with water and the baptism with the Holy Spirit supports all these interpretations. Old Testament prophets warned of a coming Day of the Lord which would bring judgement and salvation: on the one hand, there would be purification and purging, on the other, renewal and recreation. Both ideas are linked with the expectation of God's רוּחַ as well as with the image of water. Like the Greek πνεῦμα, the Hebrew word רוּחַ can be translated into English by the word 'breath' as well as by 'wind' and 'spirit'. The wind that purifies and punishes comes from God himself. It is the Lord who will wash and cleanse Israel by means of 'a spirit of judgement' and 'a spirit of burning' in Isa. 4:4. It is the breath of the Lord which, like an overflowing stream, will 'sift the nations with the sieve of destruction' in Isa. 30:28.[14] The 'hot wind' that overwhelms Israel in judgement in Jer. 4:11 comes from the Lord; the prophet goes on to appeal to the people to 'wash [their] hearts clean of wickedness, so that [they] may be saved' (4:14). All these passages link future cleansing with purging or judgement; all of them combine the imagery of water or washing with the Spirit/wind/breath of God.[15]

Especially interesting for our investigation is Ezek. 36:25-28, where God promises on the one hand that he will remove his people's sins — a process that is symbolized by sprinkling them with water, an image taken from the cultic rite — and on the other that he will recreate them and put his own spirit within them, so that they obey his commands:

> I will sprinkle clean water upon you, and you shall be clean from all your uncleannesses, and from all your idols I will cleanse you. A new heart I will give you, and a new spirit I will put within you; and I will remove from your

12. Cf. Gen. 6:17, Jer. 47:2-4, and Ps. 106:11.

13. Cf. Jonah 2:5-6 and Ps. 18:16.

14. Cf. 2 Esdras 13:11.

15. For a similar link between the Spirit's cleansing from sin and the cleansing of flesh by water, see 1QS 3:6-9; 4:20-21. Cf. also *Jub.* 1:23, which associates a 'holy spirit' with cleansing.

> body the heart of stone and give you a heart of flesh. I will put my spirit within you, and make you follow my statutes and be careful to observe my ordinances. Then you shall live in the land that I gave to your ancestors: and you shall be my people, and I will be your God.

In Zech. 13:1, we are told that 'on that day, a fountain shall be opened for the house of David and the inhabitants of Jerusalem, to cleanse them from sin and impurity': idols, false prophets, and the unclean spirit will be removed. A few verses earlier, in Zech. 12:10, God had promised to 'pour out a spirit of compassion and supplication on the house of David and the inhabitants of Jerusalem'.

The Spirit of God is here a spirit of renewal. Water itself is, of course, greatly valued as the source of life,[16] and water in the wilderness, in particular, is seen as a symbol of regeneration.[17] The image of God 'pouring out' his Spirit, just as water is poured out, is used in Isa. 44:3-4, where we read: 'I will pour water on the thirsty land and streams on the dry ground. I will pour my spirit upon your descendants and my blessing on your offspring.'[18] Here renewal, the other side of what is expected, is emphasized. The Spirit of God, active at the creation (Gen. 1:2), will bring new life to the earth and to God's people.[19]

Although the 'spirit of judgement' and 'spirit of burning' expected by Isaiah (4:4) sound totally negative, closer examination shows that the *purpose* of this judgement was to purge: 'Whoever is left in Zion and remains in Jerusalem will be called holy' (v. 3). Moreover, this comes about 'once the Lord has washed away the filth of the daughters of Zion and cleansed the bloodstains of Jerusalem from its midst by a spirit of judgement and by a spirit of burning'. The image of God *purging* his people is common.[20] Washing and purging are likened to what takes place in the moral and spiritual sphere. Reward and punishment go together, as in Isa. 61:1-4, where the prophet, claiming that the Spirit of God rests upon him, declares that his task is to proclaim not only 'the year of the Lord's favour' but also 'the day of vengeance for our God'. The Baptist is portrayed in 'Q' as having threatened wrath and destruction by fire; he is also said to have expected the wheat to be gathered into the granary.

We suggest, then, that John's baptism with water was intended, not simply

16. Cf. Ezek. 17:5-6; 47:1-12.

17. Cf. Isa. 35:6-7; 41:18.

18. The targum of Isa. 44:3 specifically compares God's Spirit with water: 'As waters are poured upon a thirsty land, and flow down over the dry ground, so will I pour my holy spirit upon thy sons, and my blessing upon thy son's sons'.

19. Isa. 32:15; Ezek. 39:29; and Joel 2:28-29 also speak of God pouring out his Spirit on Israel.

20. For example, Job 23:10; Ps. 66:10; Isa. 1:25; 48:10; Jer. 6:29-30; 9:7; Zech. 13:9; Mal. 3:2-4.

as a symbol of cleansing, but as *a dramatic prophetic sign pointing to what God was about to do in a baptism with the Holy Spirit* — a pouring out of God's Spirit that would not only bring inner cleansing and punishment but would also renew his people. But how much of this is reflected in our Gospels?

II. Mark's Interpretation

Everything that the Evangelists tell us about John's baptism mark it out as preparatory. But each tells the story in a different way. Mark's brief account of John's activity begins with a quotation from Scripture which identifies him with Isaiah's voice, summoning men and women to 'prepare the way of the Lord'. His message, like his baptism, prepares those who respond for one who follows him. It consists of three points, all of which bear witness to his successor:

(1) Someone much stronger than John is coming after him.
(2) John is unworthy even to unfasten the thongs of this coming one's sandals.
(3) Whereas John has baptized with water, the coming one will baptize with the Holy Spirit.

Mark's next scene shows the baptism of Jesus, who is acknowledged by the heavenly voice as the beloved Son of God and as well pleasing to him. Jesus is clearly the one whose coming John has proclaimed. We understand now why John spoke of his unworthiness to serve him. As Mark's story unfolds, we see men and women recognizing this quality in Jesus, though rarely succeeding in expressing their awareness in words; indeed, it is only the centurion in charge of Jesus' execution who, echoing the words spoken in 1:11, confesses him to be 'Son of God' (15:39). Yet the belief that Jesus is the Son of God provides the explanation for the whole story. Unclean spirits acknowledge him to be 'the Holy One of God' (1:24), 'the Son of God' (3:11), and 'Son of the Most High God' (5:7). Men and women who see Jesus' mighty actions are overcome by fear (4:41; 5:15, 33) and terror (5:42), and ask wonderingly who he is (4:41). His opponents question him as to the source of his authority (1:27; 3:22; 11:28).

John's first promise was of someone 'stronger' than himself. Ἰσχυρότερος is hardly the word we would have expected, but it is clearly appropriate to Mark's story.[21] Following Jesus' baptism, we are told how he was tested by Satan in the wilderness, and though Mark does not tells us the outcome, the presence

21. God himself is characterised by strength in the Old Testament; see, e.g., Deut. 10:17; Ps. 24:8.

of wild beasts and angels suggests that he sees the confrontation as a cosmic battle. In 3:27, we realize from Jesus' parable that, since his exorcism of unclean spirits demonstrates that he has defeated Satan, he is clearly 'stronger' than Satan himself. Further proof of Jesus' strength is seen when he rebukes the wind and waves and subdues the storm (4:35-41). He then destroys a whole legion of unclean spirits and calms a man possessing supernatural strength, whom no one had previously been able to subdue (5:1-13).[22]

The promise concerning future baptism with the Holy Spirit appears at first sight to be the one that is most clearly picked up in Mark 1:9-13, for it is while Jesus is himself being baptized by John — with water — that the Spirit descends on him from heaven. This scene is linked by Mark to the next one with his favourite phrase — καὶ εὐθύς — suggesting that they belong together. The Spirit drives Jesus out into the wilderness to confront Satan. In the rest of his story, Mark leaves us in no doubt that what Jesus does is in the power of the Holy Spirit, for though the Spirit is rarely mentioned, the parable in which he compares Satan to a 'strong man' who has been bound concludes with the claim that what he is doing is in the power of the Holy Spirit (3:29-30).

But John's promise was that the coming one would baptize *you* — that is, those whom he himself has baptized with water — with the Holy Spirit. Mark's terse account of Jesus' baptism by John provides the explanation as to *how* the coming one is going to carry out this baptism, but there is no reference in the rest of Mark's Gospel to Jesus baptizing anyone, either with water or with the Spirit. Is this third element of John's message, then, unlike the other two, a promise whose fulfilment Mark fails to describe? This seems unlikely, since the three statements in Mark 1:7-8 clearly belong together: the first two refer to what Jesus is and does *during his ministry*, while the third saying points back to what we have been told about John's baptism: since his baptism prepared the way for the one who followed him, this suggests that it, too, pointed forward to something that Jesus would do *during his ministry.*

Is it possible that he thinks of Jesus as baptizing with the Holy Spirit *during his ministry?* This thesis was argued forty years ago by J. E. Yates,[23] though it has been generally ignored or rejected by other scholars. Yet there is much to be said for it, as we shall see.

In Mark, the recipients of John's baptism are described as 'the whole district of Judaea, together with everyone from Jerusalem'. Although this is clearly an exaggeration, the statement that all Jews throughout the nearby area have re-

22. Cf. Mark 9:18, where it is said that the disciples did not have the strength to cast out an unclean spirit.

23. *The Spirit and the Kingdom* (London: SPCK, 1963).

sponded to John's call is intended to indicate that the whole nation has been prepared for what is to come. In this prophetic action, the few represent the many. Those who, according to John, are to be baptized with the Holy Spirit are those whom he himself has baptized with water. If, then, it is *the whole nation* whom John has baptized and whom he addresses as ὑμᾶς, then it is *the whole nation* which is to be baptized with Holy Spirit,[24] and not Jesus' disciples alone.

We have seen that such a baptism with the Holy Spirit might well bring purification and destruction, as well as renewal and restoration. The Day of the Lord would bring both judgement and salvation, and God's people must expect the Lord to refine them as well as to bless them.[25] Mark has depicted Jesus as empowered during his ministry with the Holy Spirit (1:9-11). Everything he does will be in the power of the Holy Spirit — a fact confirmed in 3:20-30. Specifically, Mark shows how Jesus' authority over 'unclean spirits' — a phrase he uses eleven times — and over Satan himself is the work of the Holy Spirit (1:12-13; 3:29-30). Jesus is said to 'destroy' these unclean spirits (1:24), but those whom they possess are released, cleansed, and restored to health and to society (5:1-15). Jesus also forgives sins (2:1-12) and makes a leper clean (1:40-45). His healing miracles purge the sick not only from unclean spirits but also from impurity and sin (1:40–2:12; 5:21-34).

Jesus' message, too, is a call to purification. Because the rule or kingdom of God has drawn near, he calls on men and women to '*Repent* and believe the good news' (1:15). He calls sinners to follow him, and symbolizes God's forgiveness by eating with them (2:13-17). He demands *inner* purity and true love of God, not outward purification (7:1-30). At the end of his ministry he comes into the Temple and purges it of those who have substituted concern with the 'purity' of sacrifices for true worship (11:12-19; cf. Mal. 3:1-4). Jesus' prophetic action is a protest against the sham piety of the Temple and a demand for it to become a house of prayer, though Mark, writing after AD 70, inevitably saw it as pointing forward to its destruction.[26] Throughout his ministry, then, Jesus purifies Israel from sinfulness and uncleanness.

Side by side with Jesus' work of purification goes restoration. Some of his miracles appear to symbolize renewal and plenty — for example, the feedings (6:30-44; 8:1-10) or the restoration of nature (4:35-41). In his healing miracles,

24. Jesus, of course, begins his ministry in Galilee and does not reach Judaea until 10:1, but the crowds who come to hear him are said to come not only from Galilee, but 'from Judaea and from Jerusalem, from Idumea, from beyond Jordan, and from the region round Tyre and Sidon' (3:7).

25. Mal. 3:1-12.

26. See M. D. Hooker, *The Signs of a Prophet* (London: SCM and Harrisburg, Pa.: Trinity Press International, 1997), pp. 44-48.

he brings restoration of health, of limbs (2:1-12; 3:1-6), of sight (8:22-6; 10:46-52) and hearing (7:31-7), even of life itself (5:35-43). The verb σῴζω points us to the symbolic significance of these miracles, for salvation is what all long for (10:26; cf. 13:13, 20). Jesus' mission is to save life (3:4), and those who respond in faith are saved (5:34; 10:52). The sick are saved (5:23, 28; 6:56), since it is they who need a physician — but this physician has come to save sinners (2:17). He has come, too, to give his life as a ransom for many (10:45), and it is through his death that the many are saved: paradoxically, it is the one who refuses to save himself who is able to save others (15:30-31; cf. 8:35).

Apart from 1:1-13 and 3:29, Mark does not make the link between the Spirit and Jesus' ministry. Does this mean that it is unimportant? The emphasis on the Spirit in 1:1-13, which provides us with key information for understanding the Gospel, suggests the opposite. What we are told in the Prologue (Jesus as Messiah, Son of God, the fulfilment of Scripture, endowed with the Holy Spirit, confronting Satan) is worked out in the following narrative.

From time to time, however, there are reminders that the baptism of John points forward to that of Jesus. One significant example of this is in 11:27-33, where Jesus is questioned about his authority. To justify his actions, Jesus appeals to *the baptism* of John: the implication is clear — the baptism of John pointed forward to what Jesus has been doing in the Temple. As in 3:22-30, there are two possibilities regarding the source of John's authority and his own, but this time the choice is between God and men rather than between the Holy Spirit and Satan: to opt for 'men', however, is to deny Jesus' divine authority, and so in effect to opt for Satan.[27] Jesus invites his opponents to understand that what he is doing is the fulfilment of what John initiated in his baptism: just as John proclaimed the will of God, so now Jesus enacts it.

Other references to John suggest that Mark saw him as the forerunner of Jesus in his death. In 1:14, he is 'handed over' (παραδίδωμι); in 6:17-29, his death and burial foreshadow Jesus' own; in 9:12-13, the rejection of John, now identified as 'Elijah', seals Jesus' own fate. It is perhaps no accident that in 10:38-39, Jesus refers to his coming death as a 'baptism'. It will bring to others both condemnation (11:12-14, 20-21; 12:9) and salvation (10:45; 14:24).

In the light of Acts 2, commentators have tended to assume that the baptism with the Holy Spirit promised in Mark 1:8 must mean a pouring out of God's Spirit on believers, enabling them to prophesy, as foretold in Joel.[28] But

27. Cf. Mark 8:33, where Satan and 'men' are both opposed to what comes from God.

28. For example, C. K. Barrett, *The Holy Spirit and the Gospel Tradition* (London: SPCK, 1958), writes that Mark's form of this saying 'must doubtless have been understood by the Evangelist and his readers as a reference to the gift of the Spirit to the Church' (p. 125).

if the Holy Spirit is understood as the *agent* of the baptism that Jesus brings (as water is the agent of John's baptism), then we see that what Jesus does in his ministry is to baptize men and women with the Holy Spirit — to plunge them into God's purifying and creative power — bringing them cleansing and forgiveness, renewal and life. Those who respond to Jesus' message find salvation. For those who refuse to repent, however, this baptism inevitably brings judgement and punishment, since for those who resist the Holy Spirit there can be no forgiveness (3:29). It would seem, then, that Mark understands his Gospel to be the story of how Jesus 'baptized' men and women with the Holy Spirit.

We should not forget, moreover, that the enabling of the disciples depicted by Luke in Acts 2 is also one of Mark's themes. Jesus begins his ministry by calling disciples to share his work (1:16-20), and he appoints twelve to proclaim the gospel and to have authority over demons (3:14-15). When he sends them out, he gives them authority over unclean spirits (6:7). The disciples, then, are called to carry on his work of baptizing with the Holy Spirit. But they are also called to share the cup and baptism of suffering — to be baptized *with* him in death and resurrection (10:38-39).[29] They, however, are only partially successful: they cast out many demons (6:13) but then fail with the epileptic boy (9:14-29). The command to feed a crowd leaves them baffled (6:37), while they flee from danger and suffering (14:50, 66-72). But after the resurrection, the Holy Spirit will be working through them (13:11).

How, then, did Mark interpret the relationship between baptism with water and baptism with the Holy Spirit? If we have understood Mark correctly, it would seem that he presents John's baptism with water as a dramatic action by John, symbolizing *another* baptism. Like all such prophetic actions, it was *a way of proclaiming what God was doing or was about to do,* a prophetic sign of the baptism with the Holy Spirit carried out by Jesus.

III. Luke and Matthew

A comparison of Mark with Matthew and Luke raises problems regarding sources. For our purposes, the important question is whether their version of John's preaching might be earlier than Mark's.

In both Matthew and Luke, the saying comparing the two baptisms is split, and the other two sayings are sandwiched in between:

29. Cf. 8:34-38. See also Romans 6.

1a: I have baptized you with water;
2: The one who follows me is stronger than I;
3: I am not worthy to undo his sandals;
1b: He will baptize you with Holy Spirit and fire.

The other notable difference from the Markan version is the addition of the phrase 'and fire'. But *is* it an addition? Or is the 'Q' version[30] of the saying the more original?

The division and separation of the saying about baptism must surely be secondary. Instead of a comparison between the two baptisms we have a chiastic structure, with two short sayings about baptism surrounding the two other parallel sayings emphasizing Jesus' superiority. The effect is to relegate John to the past and focus our attention on Jesus.

What, however, are we to say about the reference to fire? Many commentators argue that this is original. Some of them argue that the earliest version of John's preaching contained no reference to the Spirit, referring only to a future baptism with fire: it should thus be understood as a threat of coming judgement.[31] This is supported by the context in Matthew and Luke, where John goes on to describe the way in which the coming one will winnow his wheat and burn the chaff with unquenchable fire.[32] Others suggest that πνεῦμα originally referred not to Spirit but to *wind,* and that the word ἁγίῳ was added later:[33] the wind is necessary to separate the chaff from the grain,[34] so that the simple πνεύματι καὶ πυρί would make excellent sense in the Matthaean and Lukan context. Both wind and fire would then be symbols of judgement and of destruction.[35]

30. The term 'Q' is used here simply to denote the material used in common by Matthew and Luke, and not to imply the use of a particular source or sources.

31. This suggestion has a venerable history. See, e.g., T. W. Manson, *The Sayings of Jesus* (London: SCM, 1949; original version, 1937), pp. 40-41; R. Bultmann, *The History of the Synoptic Tradition* (trans. John Marsh; Oxford: Blackwell, 1963), p. 111. Similarly, V. Taylor, *The Gospel according to St. Mark* (London: Macmillan, 1952), p. 157: 'Probably, then, the reference to the Holy Spirit has been introduced under the influence of the Christian practice of baptism'.

32. Matt. 3:12//Luke 3:17. Cf. also the threat of destruction by fire in Matt. 3:10//Luke 3:9.

33. For example, Barrett, *Holy Spirit,* p. 126. He points to the slight ms. evidence for the omission of the word in Luke 3:16. It is arguable, however, that the omission from Luke is not due to a recollection of a 'Q' version, but to the fact that 'wind' makes excellent sense in the immediate Lukan context. It will certainly not be what Luke himself wrote, however, since he understood the saying to point forward to the gift of the Holy Spirit at Pentecost. Among others who support 'wind and fire' as the original form, see E. Best, 'Spirit-Baptism', *NovT* 4 (1960): 236-43.

34. The image is used of destruction in Isa. 40:24 and 41:15-16.

35. Cf. Isa. 30:27-28; 66:15. The symbols are sometimes combined in images such as 'a hot wind' (Jer. 4:11-12), and 'breath of fire' (2 Esdr. 13:10).

Luke's inclusion of these 'harvest' sayings (3:17) is significant, since they are in apparent tension with his own understanding of John's promise that Jesus will baptize *with the Holy Spirit.* John's saying is echoed in Acts 1:5, where the risen Christ says, 'For John indeed baptized with water, but you shall be baptized in Holy Spirit, in a few days' time'.[36] This prophecy is fulfilled at Pentecost (2:1-4), and the phenomenon is associated with a noise 'like that of a rushing, violent wind' and the sight of 'divided tongues, as if of fire'.

Although Luke preserved the 'Q' sayings about judgement, therefore, he clearly understood John's words about the Holy Spirit as pointing forward to the gift of the Spirit to the disciples at Pentecost. Since he associated this experience with the image of fire, he apparently saw it as a purifying as well as an empowering experience.[37] The fire that destroys (Luke 3:9, 17) can also purge.[38] On the day of Pentecost, Peter urges the crowds to 'Repent, and be baptized . . . in the name of Jesus Christ, for the forgiveness of sins, and you will receive the gift of the Holy Spirit' (Acts 2:38). As in Luke 3:3, baptism points forward (εἰς) to the forgiveness of sins.[39] That this forgiveness is effected by the Holy Spirit is confirmed in Acts 10:43-44, where the Spirit is given *before* baptism and interpreted as proof that Cornelius and his household have already received forgiveness of sins. If we are puzzled by the fact that they are baptized *after* receiving the Spirit, that is because we do not appreciate the nature of the prophetic action, which does not necessarily precede what it signifies.[40]

In Luke 3:16, it seems likely that Luke understood the saying as primarily pointing forward to Pentecost and the experience of Christian believers. Yet this future baptism means also that they will be purged from sin. The Q context, which Luke has retained, stresses this negative aspect of what is expected, since it emphasizes the punishment and destruction of those who do *not* repent and respond. Luke has, however, tempered the negative element in John's teaching with positive advice to the repentant (3:10-14). Perhaps, then, Luke thought of two separate future baptisms — with the Spirit for some, and with the fire of judgement for others.[41] Yet 'Spirit' and 'fire' are linked together with καί, not presented as alternatives. Moreover, while the Spirit is poured out at Pentecost, condemnation and punishment still lie in the future, and will not occur until

36. Cf. also Acts 11:16 and Luke 24:49.

37. The wind in Acts 2:2 is referred to as πνοή and so can hardly be an echo of πνεῦμα in Luke 3:16.

38. God's Spirit is connected with the removal of sin in Jewish thought; cf. Isa. 4:4; 1QS 3:6; 4:20-21.

39. Cf. Acts 11:13-18; 15:8-9.

40. Stacey, *Prophetic Drama*, p. 277.

41. Cf. Origen, *Homiliae in Lucam* 24.

the coming of the Son of man and the restoration of Israel's kingdom (Luke 17:22-37; Acts 1:6).

Luke's references to the Spirit, like Mark's, are clustered at the beginning of the Gospel. In 4:14, Jesus comes into Galilee 'in the power of the Spirit'. Immediately following, he enters the synagogue in Nazareth, reads the passage from Isaiah 61 beginning 'The Spirit of God is upon me' (though the reference to 'the day of vengeance' is omitted), and declares, 'Today this scripture has been fulfilled in your hearing' (4:21). Like Mark, Luke thinks of Jesus as empowered by the Holy Spirit.

In the pages that follow, Luke shows Jesus fulfilling Isaiah 61's prophecy. He proclaims good news to the poor (4:43-44; 6:20-49), releases the captives and frees the oppressed — from unclean spirits (4:33-37), from sickness (4:38-41; 6:6-11), from leprosy (5:12-16), from sin (5:17-26), from death (7:11-17) — and announces the year of jubilee which changes everything (5:1-11, 27-28; 6:5). When John's disciples come to him in 7:18-20 to ask if he is 'the one who is to come', only the recovery of sight remains unfulfilled. In that very hour, says Luke, 'Jesus healed many from diseases, plagues, and evil spirits, and gave sight to many who were blind'. His message to John echoes Isa. 26:19 and 35:5-6, as well as Isa. 61:1. All that Jesus does he does because the Spirit of the Lord is on him; he is indeed the one proclaimed by John — 'the one who is to come' — the one who is to baptize with the Holy Spirit.

Jesus then asks the crowd about how they see John, and tells them that there is no one born of women who is greater than John; yet 'the least in the Kingdom of God is greater than he' (7:28). Luke comments that the people, having been baptized by John, acknowledged God to be righteous, but the Pharisees and scribes, who had refused baptism, rejected his will. For Luke, who recognizes that the entire population was *not* baptized by John,[42] the baptism which Jesus exercises is seen as positive, bringing forgiveness and renewal,[43] while those who rejected John — and so Jesus — will be punished. The final paragraph about John — the 'parable' about children at play (7:31-35) — reminds us that those who rejected John will also reject Jesus.

Luke ends this section with the story of the penitent woman who anoints Jesus' feet (7:36-50), a story which includes the parable of the two debtors (7:41-43). The theme is forgiveness and salvation, and it provides a fitting end to a section which began with the reading of Isaiah 61. The Pharisee's comment (v. 39) that if Jesus were a prophet he would have known that the woman was a sinner points us to the significance of the situation. Jesus does indeed

42. Contrast Luke 3:3 with Mark 1:5//Matt. 3:5.

43. Is this why he omits the reference to 'the day of vengeance' from Isaiah 61 in 4:19?

know that she is a sinner, and precisely because he is more than 'a prophet'[44] he brings her forgiveness and sets her free. In spite of Luke's Pentecost material, therefore, he presents Jesus throughout these chapters as the fulfilment of John's promise that his successor would baptize with the Holy Spirit. The 'power' that comes upon the disciples in Jerusalem (Acts 1:8) is *the power with which Jesus himself has worked.* They, too, now perform 'signs and wonders' (Acts 2:22, 43).

Matthew offers no parallel to the Pentecost story. Although his Gospel concludes with the dominical command to baptize 'into the name of the Father and of the Son and of the Holy Spirit' (Matt. 28:19), there is no hint that this baptism is to be ἐν πνεύματι ἁγίῳ. Like Mark, Matthew envisages the disciples as empowered with the Holy Spirit in the future when, following in Jesus' footsteps, they are 'handed over' and face false accusations.[45] Yet already during his ministry, Jesus gives his disciples authority over unclean spirits, a story found in all three Synoptics,[46] and in Matthew this authority over unclean spirits is clearly identified with the Holy Spirit (Matt. 12:28).[47] They are therefore clearly acting in the power and with the authority of the Holy Spirit.[48]

How, then, does Matthew understand John's promise that the coming one will baptize with the Holy Spirit and fire? Using the 'Q' tradition of John's teaching, he has emphasized the negative aspect of the Spirit's work. He points to a future judgement, when the wicked are destroyed in unquenchable fire (3:10, 12). Unlike Luke, he does not include teaching addressed to the repentant (Luke 3:10-14), so John's core teaching is immediately preceded by the denunciation of the Pharisees and Sadducees (Matt. 3:7-10), and followed by the reference to the winnowing fork, the threshing floor, and the burning of chaff. Moreover, in Matthew coming judgement is an important theme,[49] and fire is frequently referred to as the means of future punishment.[50] This corresponds

44. B* and Ξ read ὁ προφήτης, which is another way of making the same point.

45. Matt. 24:9//Mark 13:11. Cf. Matt. 10:19-20. These sayings all point to a specific occasion after the end of Jesus' ministry. Luke 11:13 suggests that his followers can ask for the Spirit at any time.

46. Matt. 10:1//Mark 6:7//Luke 9:1.

47. This saying is part of Jesus' response to those who accuse him of casting out demons in the power of the prince of demons (Matt. 12:24-37). Cf. Mark 3:22-30 and Luke 11:15:23. Luke has 'finger' in v. 20 instead of 'spirit'.

48. See also Matt. 10:20 (cf. Luke 12:11-20).

49. The theme is especially prominent in passages which Matthew does *not* share with Mark, e.g., 5:27-30; 7:1-5, 13-27; 10:15; 11:20-24; 13:24-30, 36-43, 47-50; 18:23-35; 22:1-14; 23:1-39; 25:1-46.

50. Matt. 3:10, 12; 5:22; 7:19; 13:40, 42, 50; 18:8, 9; 25:41.

to the stress throughout his Gospel on the future judgement by the Son of man. For him, 'baptism with fire' appears to lie in the future.[51]

Nevertheless, Matthew has retained Mark's account of the confrontation between Jesus and the Pharisees (Matt. 12:22-32//Mark 3:20-30). Indeed, he has strengthened it, since he has added to it the saying, 'But if it is by the Spirit of God that I cast out demons, then the Kingdom of God has come upon you' (12:28). Moreover, the incident is introduced with a quotation of Isaiah 42 which includes the words 'I will put my Spirit upon him' (12:18). Intriguingly, it is followed by sayings about the fruit of good and bad trees and the words 'You brood of vipers!' (12:33-34), echoing John's words in 3:7-10 and suggesting that what Jesus is doing 'by the Spirit of God' is seen as the fulfilment of John's promise that he would baptize 'with the Holy Spirit and fire', bringing both salvation and judgement. The continuity between John and Jesus is seen in the fact that both proclaim the same message (3:2; 4:17).

IV. The Fourth Gospel

Finally, we turn to the Fourth Gospel, where John's ministry of baptism is mentioned only incidentally. The Evangelist's emphasis is on the Baptist's testimony to the one who follows him. Twice in the Prologue, John testifies: first to 'the light' (1:6-9), then to the one who comes after him, but who ranks before him (1:15). When the narrative begins, in 1:19, it is with 'the testimony of John' to 'priests and Levites from Jerusalem'. His three negative answers to their questions emphasize the fact that he is merely the witness to the one who follows him. In the Fourth Gospel it is the Baptist, not the Evangelist, who applies the words of Isa. 40:3 to himself: he is simply 'a voice crying out in the wilderness', preparing the way of the Lord (John 1:23). Questioned by those who had been sent to interrogate him[52] as to why he is baptizing, he says merely that he baptizes with water, but immediately goes on to speak of the coming one who is already present, though unrecognized, whose sandal thong he is unworthy to untie (John 1:24-27). John's words seem a strange answer to the question, but they once again serve to emphasize his witness to Jesus.

51. Ulrich Luz, *Matthew 1–7: A Commentary* (Eng. trans.; Edinburgh: T&T Clark, 1990), pp. 171-72, maintains that Matthew distinguished between 'baptism by the Spirit' and 'baptism by fire'.

52. These people are described as having been sent 'from the Pharisees' (1:24). Either the Evangelist was confused about the beliefs of the Pharisees and has used 'Jews' (1:19) and 'Pharisees' interchangeably, or he was thinking of *another* group of interrogators and *not* the 'priests and Levites' referred to in 1:19.

On the following day, Jesus was identified by John as 'the Lamb of God' and as the one who ranks ahead of him because he was before him (1:29-30). This is the Johannine equivalent of the Synoptic saying about the coming one who is *stronger* than John. Its relevance to the rest of the Gospel is clear. It has been used already, in 1:15, to remind us that John's witness was to the pre-existent and incarnate Word, and it will be echoed later in the story.[53] Once again John speaks of his baptism: he 'came baptizing *with water in order that* [the one who ranks before him] might be revealed to Israel' (1:31). The sole purpose of John's baptism in the Fourth Gospel appears to be to provide the back-drop for John's testimony: 'I saw the Spirit descend like a dove from heaven and rest on him. I myself did not know him, but he who sent me to baptize with water said to me, "The one on whom you see the Spirit descend and rest, he it is who baptizes with Holy Spirit". I myself have seen and bear witness that he is the Son of God' (vv. 32-34). On the third day John sees Jesus again and repeats his testimony that he is the Lamb of God. The disciples who are with John then follow Jesus (1:35-37).

The way in which the fourth evangelist has used the tradition suggests a very different understanding of John's baptism from the one we find in the Synoptics. He has emphasized the role of John as witness to Jesus to the extent that his baptism no longer has any purpose in itself except to provide the setting for the revelation of Jesus' identity.[54] The Baptist himself denies that he is to be seen in the role of Elijah or 'the prophet', since he is only a voice bearing witness to his successor. Mark's comparison between the two baptisms, already separated in Matthew and Luke, is now pulled even further apart, so that John's statement that he baptizes with water occurs on the *first* day (1:26), his declaration that Jesus baptizes with the Holy Spirit on the *second* (1:33). The other two sayings comparing John with Jesus, which are closely linked in the Synoptics, are also divided between these two days.[55]

How did the fourth evangelist understand this baptism with the Holy Spirit? Like Luke, he seems to look forward to the future gift of the Spirit to Jesus' disciples. In 7:39, the enigmatic remark that 'there was as yet no Spirit' is explained by the context, which shows that he is thinking of the gift of the Spirit to believers, something that could not take place until Jesus was glorified. It may well be significant, then, that when Jesus dies — or, in Johannine terms, is glorified — he 'gives up his spirit' (19:30). Certainly he is said, after the resur-

53. John 8:58; 17:5.

54. The two baptisms are thus neither compared (as in Mark) nor contrasted (as in Matthew and Luke) but simply referred to. It is perhaps for this reason that John refers later to Jesus himself baptizing (3:22, 26) — although in 4:1-2 he indicated that it was his disciples who did so, not Jesus himself.

55. Cf. Matt. 3:11//Mark 1:17//Luke 3:16 with John 1:30, 27.

rection, to have breathed on his disciples and to have said, 'Receive the Holy Spirit' (20:22). Interestingly, the fourth evangelist apparently links *this* 'baptism' with the authority to forgive sins (20:23).

We find an echo of the Baptist's testimony in 3:5, where it is said that no one can enter the kingdom of God unless they are born of water and spirit.[56] Although John's water baptism is important for those who wish to be born from above, water is not mentioned again in this passage, and its significance is apparently subsumed in Spirit baptism. It is *the Spirit* who gives life (6:63).

In the Fourth Gospel, water is an image of the 'living water' that gives life to the believer (John 4:1-30); it is used in this sense as an analogy for the future gift of the Spirit in 7:37-39. The spring of water provided by Jesus (4:14; 7:38) brings renewal and life.

The work of the Spirit is described in chs. 14–16. The Spirit — or παράκλητος — is a Spirit of truth (14:16-17; 15:26; 16:13) who will teach (14:26) and guide (16:13-15) the disciples. The Spirit will also convict *the world* of sin, of righteousness, and of judgement (16:7-11). In this last passage we see the *negative* aspect of the Spirit's coming. How will this work be done? It will be done *through the disciples,* to whom the Spirit will be sent (16:7). This promise is fulfilled in John 20:21-23, when Jesus tells the disciples that he is sending them, *as the Father sent him,* breathes on them, and says, 'Receive the Holy Spirit: whoever's sins you forgive will be forgiven; whoever's you retain will be retained.' Although John, like Luke, sees 'baptism with the Holy Spirit' as something experienced by the disciples after Jesus' resurrection, for him (as for Luke) that baptism means that the disciples are *to continue the work that Jesus himself has done,* leading men and women into the truth and bringing forgiveness to some, condemnation to others (3:16-19). In other words, *receiving* the Spirit will enable them to *baptize* with the Spirit.

Conclusion

All our sources refer to John's baptism as a 'baptism with water', and to the expected baptism as a 'baptism with the Holy Spirit'. If any reliance can be placed on the criterion of multiple attestation, it would seem that the earliest form of the saying referred to πνεῦμα ἅγιον, not to πνεῦμα. Although 'wind and fire' are associated in Jewish thought as purifying agents, there is evidence that the

56. This is the natural interpretation of 'water' here, especially in view of the references to the Baptist in 3:22-24. The suggestion that it refers to physical birth seems inappropriate, since the Evangelist goes on to contrast flesh and Spirit.

Spirit of God could also be expected to purge and punish. 'Wind' and 'fire', then, are metaphors that spell out part of what the 'Holy Spirit' might be expected to do. The fact that the 'Q' tradition links the Spirit with fire demonstrates that this interpretation of what 'baptism with the Holy Spirit' signified is an early one, whether or not it was part of the original saying.

All our sources see *some* link between John's baptism and the baptism which Jesus himself is expected to carry out. For all the Evangelists, John's primary function was to be the witness to Jesus, but by the time we come to the Fourth Gospel, this is his only function, and the only purpose of his baptism is to identify Jesus.

The striking differences in these accounts leave us with difficulties, however. Firstly, there is the obvious tension in Luke-Acts between the context of the saying — prophecies of judgement and of punishment — and its interpretation as a promise of the gift of the Spirit to Jesus' disciples at Pentecost. For Matthew this is not a problem because he has concentrated on the theme of judgement, while the fourth evangelist has taken the alternative route and omitted any reference to judgement, interpreting John's words as a promise that Jesus would give his followers the Spirit. Mark's enigmatic version has neither the 'Q' context suggesting judgement nor a Pentecost experience at the end of the Gospel to explain how he interpreted it.

Secondly, there is an anomaly in Matthew and Luke in the fact that the recipients of John's baptism on the one hand and of Jesus' on the other are all addressed as ὑμᾶς.[57] In Matthew, it is apparently those who are baptized with water 'for repentance' (Matt. 3:11), 'confessing their sins' (3:6), who can expect to be baptized 'with the Holy Spirit and fire', and who will therefore experience judgement and punishment! The 'Q' context of the saying suggests that the logion *ought* to read, 'I have baptized you with water *lest* you are baptized with holy Spirit and fire' — that is, 'Repent, while you have time, lest you receive condemnation'. Luke, in spite of his use of the Q material, nevertheless suggests that many who came for baptism were repentant (Luke 3:10-15), and describes John's message as 'good news' (3:18). There is still an anomaly, however, since those who are baptized with water in Luke 3:16 are not the people who receive the gift of the Spirit in Acts 2. Why, then, is ὑμᾶς used in both halves of the saying? In other words, the form of the saying does not fit the Evangelist's interpretation, either in Matthew or in Luke. For the fourth evangelist there is no problem, since ὑμᾶς is missing: there is no indication as to *who* is baptized, whether with water or with the Holy Spirit.

57. This point is stressed by J. D. G. Dunn, 'Spirit-and-Fire Baptism', *NovT* 14 (1972): 81-92.

In Mark, too, the word ὑμᾶς is used twice, addressed to the crowds who come to John for baptism. Is the baptism with the Holy Spirit that John announces expected to bring judgement, or is it an eschatological gift? In the absence of the context provided by Q, emphasizing judgement, and of any 'Pentecost' scene, we have only Mark's own narrative to guide us. Are the two interpretations offered by Matthew and Luke perhaps *partial* understandings of the significance of John's baptism? And is it possible that in Mark the ὑμᾶς who are baptized with water are identical with the ὑμᾶς to be baptized with the Holy Spirit?

As we have seen, there is good evidence that first-century Judaism would have understood the pouring out of God's Spirit as an eschatological gift which would renew creation: Joel 2:28-29, the passage quoted by Luke in Acts 2:16-21, is an obvious example. We have seen, too, that there was an expectation that God would purge his people from their sins by a spirit of judgement and a spirit of burning (Isa. 4:4).

The fact that all our Evangelists preserve the link between the two baptisms suggests that John himself saw his baptism as a prophetic drama signifying baptism with the Holy Spirit. What he was expecting was an outpouring of God's Spirit, bringing judgement and destruction to the unrepentant,[58] forgiveness and renewal to those who responded.[59] In the words of Professor Dunn:

> What John held out before his hearers was a baptism which was neither solely destructive nor solely gracious, but which contained both elements in itself. . . . the repentant would experience a purgative, refining, but ultimately merciful judgement; the impenitent, the stiff-necked and hard of heart, would be broken and destroyed.[60]

'Q' emphasized the latter, and this influenced the way Matthew understood the tradition, while Luke balanced it with the more positive interpretation in Luke 4–11. The author of the Fourth Gospel stressed the *future* work of the Spirit. *All* our Evangelists portray Jesus as bringing both salvation and judgement to Israel

58. Cf. 1 Cor. 10:1-5, where Paul refers to baptism into Moses and links it with drinking from the spiritual rock (i.e., Christ), which makes one liable to judgement. He uses a similar idea of the Eucharist in 1 Cor. 11:29.

59. Cf. 1 Cor. 6:11.

60. 'Spirit-and-Fire Baptism', p. 86. All our Gospels portray Jesus as offering the choice to his hearers at the very beginning of his ministry — in Mark, in the parable of the Sower (Mark 4:1-20); in Matthew, in the Sermon on the Mount (Matthew 5–7; see esp. 7:13-27); in Luke, in the Sermon on the Plain (Luke 6:20-49). In John the choice is set out in 3:16-21.

in the course of his ministry, and *all* suggest that Jesus handed on the task of baptizing with the Holy Spirit to his disciples, who will extend his mission to the world.[61] Although Luke correctly understood 'baptism with water' to point forward to 'baptism with the Holy Spirit', he has misled us by *identifying* the enabling of a small company of disciples at Pentecost with the baptism itself. For John, and for Jesus, it was far more than this. Just as John's whole mission was to point forward to Jesus, so his baptism was intended to point forward to the baptism which Jesus would carry out. Behind *all* our traditions we can discern the powerful symbolism of a baptism with water that was intended to be a dramatic representation of a baptism with the Holy Spirit, bringing forgiveness of sins, renewal, and judgement. If we want to see how this baptism with the Holy Spirit was effected, we need look no further than to the ministry of Jesus himself.

61. Matt. 28:19; Mark 13:10; Luke 24:46, 49; John 20:21-23; Acts 1:8.

IV Covenant and Spirit: The Origins of the New Covenant Hermeneutic

Scot McKnight

The Miracle of Pentecost

For once again we stand at a watershed in salvation-history, the beginning of the new age and new covenant, not for Jesus this time, but now for his disciples. What Jordan was to Jesus, Pentecost was to the disciples. As Jesus entered the new age and covenant by being baptized in the Spirit at Jordan, so the disciples followed him in like manner at Pentecost. With the wider enjoyment of the messianic age made possible by Jesus' representative death, so at Pentecost the new covenant, hitherto confined to the one representative man, was extended to embrace all those who remained faithful to him and tarried at Jerusalem in obedience to his command.

JAMES D. G. DUNN[1]

The topic of 'Covenant and Spirit' is too large for a Festschrift study but, inasmuch as my *Doktorvater* is keen on sweeping studies that avoid the fate of Icarus, as well as keeping the big picture in mind so that theological and ecclesial implications can gain their hearing, I shall 'Dunn' this topic and hope to fill in details over time. On a positive front, we ask, where and when did early followers of Jesus begin to understand the relationship of Israel's heritage (Scriptures, salvation history, and tradition) to their 'Christian' experience of the Spirit in terms of an 'old' and 'new' covenant? When did some begin to recognize that what they had found in Christ and in the Spirit was the antici-

1. *Baptism in the Holy Spirit* (Philadelphia: Westminster, 1970), p. 40.

pated expectations of Jeremiah (and Ezekiel)? On a more negative front, when did some begin to exercise a cutting covenant hermeneutic that relativized, or even denigrated (*Barnabas* is a notable example), the Mosaic covenant as a result of a conviction of its completeness in the new age inaugurated by Jesus and the gift of the Spirit? In short, we are face-to-face again with one of those early partings of the way into two major paths. A covenant parting, to be sure, that can be profitably explored today to bandage and heal time-torn Jewish-Christian relations.[2] This study will look briefly at Paul, Hebrews, and Jesus, and then suggest an origin of the 'new covenant' hermeneutic. It does so, not so much as a message from a Gabriel, but as a *Talmid* who extends the tradition of the *Rabbi.*

Let me set my offering in a brief context: Knut Backhaus' *Habilitationsschrift* is perhaps the finest study available on the emergence of covenant thinking among the earliest Christians.[3] He studies the use of the term from John O'Groats to Land's End and concludes that the term 'covenant' was 'transformed' at the hands of the early Christian theologians who are now found in noncanonical sources (and he studies in particular *Barnabas* and Justin Martyr). Backhaus's judicious study also contends that this later transformation has been (too frequently) read back into the last supper traditions, the Pauline evidence, and especially the evidence now found in Hebrews. A fundamental conclusion of Backhaus is that 'covenant' is not *ipso facto* a 'salvation-historical category or scheme'; instead, there is one covenant, and time is not central to New Testament statements about the 'new covenant'. A reading of Galatians, 2 Corinthians 3, and Hebrews alongside *Barnabas* makes the contrast rather obvious. While I have certain misgivings about an occasional piece of exegesis he offers in Paul and Hebrews, his line of thinking is undoubtedly right-headed and takes us farther than we have been before. If the concern of this essay is not so much the exegesis of Paul or Hebrews but instead the origins of covenant thinking, the essay nonetheless builds on Backhaus as a point of departure.

2. On which, cf. J. D. G. Dunn, 'Two Covenants or One? The Interdependence of Jewish and Christian Identity,' in *Geschichte — Tradition — Reflexion: Festschrift für Martin Hengel zum 70. Geburtstag* (eds. H. Cancik, H. Lichtenberger, and P. Schäfer; Tübingen: J. C. B. Mohr, 1996), 3:97-122.

3. K. Backhaus, *Der neue Bund und das Werden der Kirche: Die Diatheke-Deutung des Hebräerbriefs im Rahmen der frühchristlichen Theologiegeschichte* (NTAbh n.f. 29; Münster: Aschendorffsche, 1996).

I. (New) Covenant Hermeneutics in Paul and Hebrews

Outside the last supper tradition found now in Mark 14//Luke 22 and 1 Corinthians 11 (see below), the earliest record we have of early Jesus–following Israelites sorting out their theology and experience of Christ and the Spirit in covenant[4] terms is most likely Gal. 4:24, a line embedded in Paul's infamous allegory on Hagar and Sarah that says these two women are two covenants.[5] One covenant, originating in the promise to Abraham with Sarah in their son Isaac (cf. Gal. 3:15-25), leads to Christ and the Spirit, to justification by faith and forgiveness of sins (cf. Rom. 11:27), and not to the 'works of the law';[6] the other covenant, originating in Abraham and Hagar and their son Ishmael, leads to Moses and the 'works of the law' and to the Judaizers, but not to 'faith', or 'justification', or 'life' (3:21). For Paul, no Hamlet when it comes to hermeneutics, one must learn to read the Bible (i.e., develop a hermeneutic) in terms of *Abrahamic promise* and not in terms of *Mosaic law:* there is *covenant promise* with Abraham and *covenant law* with Moses.[7]

Paul's next instance of a covenant hermeneutic can be found in his midrash of Exod. 34:29-35 in 2 Corinthians 3, which moves along the salvation-

4. On 'covenant', from a plethora of studies, the following are important: E. P. Sanders, *Paul and Palestinian Judaism: A Comparison of Patterns of Religion* (Philadelphia: Fortress, 1977); *Judaism: Practice and Belief, 66 BCE–66 CE* (Philadelphia: Trinity Press International, 1992), pp. 241-78, esp. pp. 262-75; C. Levin, *Die Verheißung des neuen Bundes in ihrem theologiegeschichtlichen Zusammenhang ausgelegt* (FRLANT 137; Göttingen: Vandenhoeck & Ruprecht, 1985); S. Lehne, *The New Covenant in Hebrews* (JSNTSup 44; Sheffield: JSOT, 1990), pp. 35-59 with nn.; F. Avemarie and H. Lichtenberger, *Bund und Tora: Zur theologischen Begriffsgeschichte in alttestamentlicher, frühjüdischer und urchristlicher Tradition* (WUNT 92; Tübingen: J. C. B. Mohr, 1996); R. Rendtorff, *The Covenant Formula: An Exegetical and Theological Investigation* (Edinburgh: T&T Clark, 1998). The general impression one gets from the Second Temple period is that the term functions, with varying degrees of emphasis, on three fronts: (1) the elective and establishing covenant with Abraham, (2) the law-revealing instructions of the Mosaic covenant [e.g., Exodus 19–24], and (3) the inviolability of a Davidic presence as specified in 2 Samuel 7. In this wider sense, one is quite justified in speaking of the 'Old Testament concept of the covenant.'

5. See C. K. Barrett, 'The Allegory of Abraham, Sarah, and Hagar in the Argument of Galatians,' in his *Essays on Paul* (Philadelphia: Westminster, 1982), pp. 154-70; Lehne, *The New Covenant in Hebrews*, pp. 65-68.

6. On which cf. J. D. G. Dunn, 'Works of the Law and the Curse of the Law (Gal. 3.10-14),' in his *Jesus, Paul and the Law: Studies in Mark and Galatians* (Louisville: Westminster John Knox, 1990), pp. 215-41; but see also M. Abegg, 'Paul, "Works of the Law" and MMT,' *BAR* 20 (1994): 52-55, 82.

7. J. D. G. Dunn, *The Epistle to the Galatians* (BNTC; Peabody, Mass.: Hendrickson, 1993), p. 249.

historical plane to create a past of promise and a present of fulfillment, with a special emphasis on *ministries.*[8] It is the 'new covenant' that is 'of the Spirit' and 'gives life', while the old was of 'letter' (i.e., the written law of concrete demands that could not give life) and therefore 'kills' (3:6). The clinching covenantal claim is that YHWH is now experienced[9] for messianic Israelites in the Spirit (3:17),[10] and where that YHWH-immanent-in-Christ-as-Spirit[11] is present there is a beholding of the 'glory of the Lord' that creates freedom — from the law, from sin, and from the flesh — and transformation (3:17-18). What the law did not, indeed could not, do (bring life and overcome sin), the Spirit now can do. We are led to two critical conclusions: for Paul, the *New Covenant is a pneumatic experience or an eschatological existence,* and the *New Covenant is rooted in the Abrahamic promise of justification by faith.* We should also say, however, that for Paul 'covenant' was not the central category used for perceiving God's work in history.

One who did sift that reality with covenant was the author of Hebrews, whose provocative work and singular perception of the relationship of Jesus Christ to Israel's heritage, especially its cult, contributed in no small measure to the gold letters on the Christian Bible. First, Jesus (not Moses; cf. Exod. 19:1-6, 9; 24:2, 12, 15-18; 32:9-14, 30-34; *As. Mos.* 1:14; 3:12; Gal. 3:19-20), as the 'firstborn son' with a superior 'name' (cf. 1:4, 6), is the mediator of a 'better covenant' (8:6; cf. 1 Tim. 2:5), which is in fact the 'new covenant' (8:8) because it has been 'enacted through better promises' (8:6; cf. 9:15). This 'new covenant' is Jeremiah's (as understood by the author of Hebrews), and it makes the first covenant 'antiquated' and, therefore, 'obsolete' (8:13; cf. 9:15; 10:9) and ready for an imminent disappearance (8:13). Second, Christ entered into the Holy Place (a) as a Melchizedekian priest (cf. 2:17-18; 7:1-28), (b) 'through the eternal Spirit' (9:14), (c) with his own blood (d) to obtain eternal redemption (9:12). Here we have covenant categories more centralized to the theology of an early messianic Israelite, but this time in the direction of *the eschatological effectiveness of sacrifice in the complete forgiveness of sins to enable purified worship.*

8. See J. D. G. Dunn, '2 Corinthians 3:17 — "The Lord is the Spirit,"' in *The Christ and the Spirit: Collected Essays of James D. G. Dunn* (2 vols.; Grand Rapids: Eerdmans, 1998), 1:115-25; C. F. D. Moule, 'II Cor. iii.18b, καθάπερ ἀπὸ κυρίου πνεύματος,' in *Essays in New Testament Interpretation* (Cambridge: Cambridge University Press, 1982), pp. 227-34. See also N. T. Wright, 'Reflected Glory: 2 Corinthians 3:18,' in *The Glory of Christ in the New Testament: Studies in Christology in Memory of George Bradford Caird* (ed. L. D. Hurst and N. T. Wright; Oxford: Clarendon, 1987), pp. 139-50.

9. For one example of the emphasis given to experience in early Christian theological developments, cf. J. D. G. Dunn, '1 Corinthians 15:45 — Last Adam, Life-Giving Spirit,' in *The Christ and the Spirit,* 2:154-66.

10. Dunn, '2 Corinthians 3:17,' pp. 122-24.

11. So Moule, 'II Cor. 3:18b.'

In the exegetical workshop of the earliest Jesus movement, then, the tool of 'covenant' became a way of sifting the relationship of believers in Jesus Christ to the scriptural revelation of the Torah and its people, Israel. For Paul, it was a tool that separated the Mosaic covenant from the New Covenant, primarily by recognizing the significance of the Holy Spirit. For the writer of Hebrews, it was a tool that separated the old system from the new system, primarily by recognizing the effectiveness of the forgiveness of sins through the sacrifice of Jesus Christ and his intercessory powers. If Paul crossed the threshold by sorting out the relationship of the old to the new in terms of covenant, the author of Hebrews set up shop and made the category his home to an unprecedented degree. For some this strategy on the part of early Christians to co-opt covenant is, to borrow an expression from Robert Louis Stevenson, 'a worm i' the bud',[12] but I would argue that covenant was an enduring, road-savvy category that could actually contain the newly shaped faith of the followers of Jesus.

This leads to a historically significant question: When and where did that tool come out of the box to be used by early messianic Israelites? Where do we find the origins of the use of 'covenant' as a hermeneutic for sifting the realities of this faith? And an attending question also is formed: Was it always a 'tool of separation' so that it was used for the 'parting of the ways'? These sorts of questions lead us directly to the traditions of the last supper. Is it possible that Jesus used the term 'covenant'? If so, what did it mean for him? And if not, where do we find its most likely origin?

II. Jesus and a (New) Covenant Hermeneutic

If one were tempted to think 'covenant' unimportant to earliest Christian reflection on the relation of followers of Jesus to their ancient heritage because the term occurs in only three writings, Galatians, 2 Corinthians (but not Romans!), and Hebrews, that temptation can be resisted by reminding ourselves that the early Christian eucharistic celebration almost certainly contained the term: Mark 14:24//Matt. 26:28//Luke 22:20 and 1 Corinthians 11:25. Even if the category was not central to Paul, it was central to those who developed the eucharistic traditions, and we should perhaps remind ourselves of the cruciality of liturgical ritual for both expressing and shaping the beliefs of a community.[13]

12. 'Crabbed Age and Youth,' in *The Lantern-Bearers and Other Essays* (ed. J. Treglown; New York: Cooper Square, 1999), p. 66.

13. On this, cf. A. F. Segal, 'Covenant in Rabbinic Writings,' *SR* 14 (1985): 53-62, here pp. 56-62.

If we take the tradition of the new covenant hermeneutic as prior to Paul, how early might this tradition be? The question is best answered by inquiring into the most reconstructable original form of the last supper words, even though Kähler's students get their knickers in a twist when such questions are posed. In speaking of an original reconstructable form of the words, however, we should recognize, along with Knut Backhaus, that it is highly unlikely that the earliest Christians would have fundamentally altered the intentional direction of what Jesus was all about, even if the specific term 'covenant' is in dispute.[14] Here are the four principal texts over the wine, four texts that are almost certainly somewhat independent:[15]

Mark 14:24	This is my blood of the *covenant*, which is poured out for many.
Matt. 26:28	This is my blood of the *covenant*, which is poured out for many for the forgiveness of sins.
Luke 22:20	This cup that is poured out for you is the ***new** covenant* in my blood.
1 Cor. 11:25	This cup is the ***new** covenant* in my blood.

There are four elements here: A. blood, B. (new) covenant, C. pouring out, and D. forgiveness of sins. What matters here are the literary allusions to ancient traditions. The last supper words over the cup ('this is my blood'), as printed above, may be alluding to one or more of the following four texts: (1) Jer. 31:31, (2) Exod. 24:8, (3) Zech. 9:11, (4) Isa. 53:12. For reasons we are not able to spell out here, we should omit Jeremiah and Isaiah because the evidence pointing to them appears to be later Christian interpretation.[16]

14. 'Hat Jesus vom Gottesbund gesprochen?' *TGl* 86 (1996): 343-56, here p. 347. He concludes: 'Daher erscheint es sachgemäß, in der gemeinsamen Überlieferungssubstanz der neutestamentlichen Einsetzungsberichte den Grundzügen nach die historische Selbstdeutung Jesu zu vermuten' (p. 347). Backhaus is the most recent and complete defense of Jesus' use of 'covenant' in the last supper. He disagrees with numerous German scholars (cf. pp. 347-48 n. 21).

15. So K. Backhaus, 'Hat Jesus?' pp. 352-53.

16. See my forthcoming study on Jesus and his death. When K. Backhaus appeals to the connection of eschatology with covenant under the category of the criterion of dissimilarity, he fails to observe that 'new' is hardly integral to the Jesus traditions; instead, it appears in the Lukan-Pauline tradition alone. And one should not make an immediate connection of 'eschatology' with 'new.' Furthermore, his strong contrast of John and Jesus (over the image of God; hence Jesus' 'newness') is suspect. Neither does this constellation make for as easy a connection to 'covenant' as he suggests (pp. 354-55). Nonetheless, Backhaus's contention that the presence of a covenant motif in the last supper traditions witnesses to a theme that is not common in the early Christian tradition is important and insightful (pp. 353-54).

The critical expression for determining whether our text appeals to Zechariah or Exodus, or not, is the term 'covenant' (cf. Gen. 12:1-3; 15:1-6; 17:1-8; Exodus 19–24; 2 Samuel 7).[17] The question is simple: Did Jesus use this term in the last supper?[18] Or is the term a *Lorelei?* Should it not be the Q.E.D.?

We should place on the table the following important observation, even if often neglected: the Passover event (Exod. 12) and the covenant-establishing ceremony (Exodus 24) are not one and the same; nor are they naturally connected in the Passover week celebration. In fact, Jewish history reveals that 'covenant renewal' is connected with *Pentecost* (cf. 2 Chron. 15:8-15; *Jub.* 6:15-31) and not with *Passover.* To be sure, in the 'grand story' or 'myth dream' of Israel, Passover and the covenant ceremony are integral parts of the story of redemption from Egypt (e.g., Hos. 2:15-18; Jer. 31:31-40; possibly Isa. 42:6), and Pentecost is the fitting completion of Passover, but the two events are nonetheless distinguished even in liturgy. Further, the commonality of 'blood' (smeared at Passover; tossed in the ceremony; even if later tossed in the slaughtering of the Passover victim in the Temple) does not make the *functions* or the *effects* of the blood the same. Nor is the major theme of the two founding events the same: deliverance and liberation (Passover) as compared to relationship-establishment, threat of punishment, and commitment (covenant). Being covered by blood at Passover differs functionally and effectively from being splashed with blood at the covenant ceremony. In one the person is protected from YHWH's wrath; in the other, a person becomes a covenant member and is warned of extirpation if the covenant terms are ignored.

If there is any place where the later *Passover Haggadah,* which could be a good test case of how Passover was understood, can aid these concerns with Jesus and first-century practice, it is at the level of *theologizing.* And one thing is clear: the later *Passover Haggadah* is not about covenant establishment. I find the term 'covenant' only one time in the *Haggadah:* when the *barekh* (the grace) is recited, all participants remember the history of God's working with Israel and, in so doing, they express thanks 'for thy covenant which thou hast sealed in our flesh' (an allusion to circumcision). Liberation and redemption and circumcision are everywhere; political vision and national hopes are as well. But covenant establishment is simply not the way these Jews reflected on

17. See above, n. 3. Cf. also H. Lichtenberger, '"Bund" in der Abendmahlsüberlieferung,' in Avemarie and Lichtenberger, *Bund und Tora,* pp. 217-28.

18. See esp. Backhaus, 'Hat Jesus?'; see also D. C. Allison Jr., 'Jesus and the Covenant: A Response to E. P. Sanders,' *JSNT* 29 (1987): 57-78, esp. pp. 65-66, where Allison, in a flourishing insight, contends that John the Baptist denied the efficacy of the Abrahamic covenant, that the early Christians at a very early date thought in terms of covenant, and that Jesus had an eschatological outlook that implied the downfall of the Mosaic dispensation.

the significance of Passover. The following arguments, leaning as they do on the distinction between Exodus 12 and Exodus 19–24, lead me to conclude that Jesus probably did not use the term 'covenant' to explain his death at the last supper.

First, the term 'covenant' is attributed to Jesus in the entire tradition (including John) only in the last supper text, a text crystallizing a tradition that itself became a fundamental liturgical expression in earliest Christianity, but which also shows several variations and developments to make it more expressive of early Christian theology. It is not circular to hold up a warning flag to authenticity because the term is not found elsewhere in the Jesus traditions; it is, in fact, an argument based on a consistent pattern of language for Jesus.[19] Second, central to Jesus is the term and category 'kingdom,' and it is that term around which Jesus oriented his mission and vision for Israel, not 'covenant'. And the more one finds Jesus to fit into the mould of 'prophet', the less explicable it becomes why he avoided the term 'covenant', for that is a characteristic term of the prophetic vision[20] — unless we recognize that he chose other terms to express his vision. Third, it follows that in no place in the teachings of Jesus is 'kingdom' coupled with 'covenant'. Fourth, very importantly but without the details that could be provided, the last supper betrays, apart from the wine (= blood), few signs of a covenant ceremony reestablishment, for, regardless of how one understands a covenant, the ceremony inevitably spells out the human obligations required to maintain that covenant.

Fifth, this means that 'covenant' renewal or reestablishment, especially in the sense of a 'new covenant', is not a category used by Jesus for his mission; for Jesus to have suddenly switched his vision to 'covenant' establishment would be an unprepared-for innovation in the final week. Accordingly, Jesus probably said only 'this is my blood' — a tidy parallel to 'this is my body'.[21] Sixth, what we do have is a Jesus who identifies the wine of the meal with his blood, and this affirmation must be the bedrock upon which covenant theology eventually builds its structures. In fact, that statement of his pollulated in the earliest churches and produced a variety of saving metaphors for Jesus' death.

There are clear steps that we can now trace from 'my *blood*', in the context of a *Pesah* week meal, to 'my blood of the *covenant*' and then to 'the *new* covenant in my blood'. But it appears that it was some early followers of Jesus who

19. Contra Backhaus, 'Hat Jesus?' p. 352.

20. So Backhaus, 'Hat Jesus?' pp. 344-45.

21. Justin, *Apology* 1.66 (ANF 1.185); Justin anchors his eucharistic practices in the 'memoirs of the apostles' in the two words of Jesus: 'this is my body' and 'this is my blood'. These may have been the words he heard in his community before AD 155, but it needs to be remembered that his origins are Palestinian.

took those steps.[22] In fact, it can be argued that 'covenant' and 'kingdom' are alternative hermeneutical categories — categories useful to Jews who are trying to get a handle on the diverse theological expressions of Jewish tradition as well as to find a grip around Jewish history. Inasmuch as Jesus chose 'kingdom', 'covenant' appears to be left to the side for others to use. (It is not that 'covenant' and 'kingdom' do not overlap semantically; nor would I claim that Jesus *could* not have used such a term. It remains a good Jewish category. The evidence, however, is such that we should be very careful in claiming that Jesus' mission was about the 'covenant' formation, even if in retrospect it seems to us to be a useful way of summing up his mission.)

III. New Covenant in the Early Christian Hermeneutic

If it is unlikely that Jesus used 'covenant' or 'new covenant' as a hermeneutical tool to sort out the realities of God's saving work in his mission, then it remains for us to ask the further question of where it got its start. In light of what has been sketched above, we can say that the category is used at least as early as the earliest Pauline churches but sometime after the last supper and Easter. A critical tool allowing us to sort out the data can be found in examining the evidence from Jeremiah and Ezekiel (Jer. 31:31-34; Ezek. 11:14-21; 34:25-31; 36:16-28; 37:20-28; cf. also Hos. 2:20, 25), for it is here that the 'New Covenant' gets its definitive shape (as understood by the early followers of Jesus).

First, there is the expectation of a *restoration of the twelve tribes*, which according to Ezekiel's vision will result in a total realignment of the land of Israel (Jer. 31:27-30; 32:44; 33:26; 50:4-7; Ezekiel 47-48!). This restoration theme is connected, of course, to the inviolability of the covenant (cf. Isa. 54:10; 55:3; 61:8). Second, the 'new' covenant will prove to be *unbreakable* (Jer. 31:32; 32:40), implying that the former covenant (of Moses) was breakable and had been broken so often that God had to send his people into exile as punishment and purgation (cf. Jer. 7:21-26; 11:1-13; Deuteronomy 28). Third, when the 'new covenant' is finally established, it will be *internal*, a knowledge-embedded-in-the-heart (cf. Jer. 24:7; Deut. 30:6) rather than an external relation or ritual enactment (cf. Jer. 31:33; 32:39).[23] That is, it will be an inwrought work of the Spirit or, differently expressed, the result of God's gracious care in once again taking Israel's hand in his (Jer. 31:32; cf. Isa. 32:15; 34:16-17; 59:21; Joel 2:28-32; Ezek. 11:17-21; 36:22-38;

22. Cf. E. Kutsch, 'Von der Aktualität alttestamentlicher Aussagen für das Verständnis des Neuen Testaments,' *ZThK* 74 (1977): 273-90; here pp. 286-89.

23. Cf. C. Levin, *Die Verheißung des neuen Bundes*, pp. 257-64.

37:4-14). This *interiority* is how most of scholarship perceives the blunt force of the expectation of exiled Judeans like Jeremiah, but most fail to perceive its original context: an antipriestly/scribal strain (cf. Jer. 8:7-9), or an anti-traditional theology (as narrated in Job!), or the expectation of a new Temple, or a connection with the proximity of God's (written) Word (cf. Jer. 30:2) in synagogal readings of Torah, the practice of phylacteries, and family instruction (cf. Deut. 6:6-8; 11:18; 30:11-14; Isa. 51:7; 59:21; Psalm 119). Fourth, the final covenant will be *democratic* in contrast to the royal and hierocratic priestly system (Jer. 31:34; cf. 36:20-31).

Fifth, the 'new covenant' will result in *forgiveness of sins*, which means the covenant will be restored, the people will inhabit their land, the Temple will be functioning properly with YHWH present, and Israel will enjoy peace *because YHWH will choose to forget Israel's history of covenant-breaking and consider its time of punishment, or exile, over* (Jer. 31:34; 33:8; 36:3; 50:20; cf. also Isa. 40:1-2; 55:7; Ezek. 16:63; Dan. 9:16-19). Sixth, the *former covenants* will find their consummation in the new covenant (Jer. 14:21; 32:40; 33:15, 20-21, 23-26; Ezek. 16:60; 34:23). Seventh, the covenant of the future will result in *peace* (Isa. 11:6-9; Ezek. 34:25, 27; 37:26, 28; cf. Mal. 3:2b-4, 12). Finally, if the covenant's restoration looks forward to the restoration of the twelve tribes, a more universal outlook is in view (Isa. 42:1-6; 49:6; 55:3-5; 56:6; Ezek. 16:61). At any rate, there is an expectation of a twelve-tribe restoration as the 'new seed' of the 'new covenant' days (Jer. 31:27-30).

It is not possible here to enter into a vigorous discussion of the evidence of the Second Temple period. Instead, I shall simply state my conclusion that the covenant theme is understood in that period as a Moses-like (Abraham is at times mentioned; cf. CD 12:11) covenant, and this covenant for at least the Qumran community is somewhat of an extension of the Book of the Covenant (Exodus 19–24) and Deuteronomy (12–26). More broadly, the 'covenant' of the Second Temple period is by and large the Mosaic covenant of obligation to keep the Torah — especially its flash-point regulations in circumcision, Sabbath, and food laws — in order to secure the blessings of YHWH for the people of Israel (e.g., Sir. 39:8).[24] But, for most, when the term 'new' is connected to 'covenant', it not so much the expectation of Jeremiah being realized as it is the revitalisation of the Mosaic/Sinaitic covenant.

To *that* fulfilment one must point to the early Jerusalem church's definitive visionary, missionary, and glossolalic (cf. 2:9-11) experience, and more

24. On this see J. D. G. Dunn's Rembrandt, *The Partings of the Ways between Christianity and Judaism and Their Significance for the Character of Christianity* (Philadelphia: Trinity Press International, 1991), pp. 23-31.

broadly to point to this messianic community that found its *pneumatic* experiences[25] to be a lever to pull down with such force that it erupted into a movement (Jerusalem: Acts 2; 8:14-17; 9:26-29; Damascus: Acts 9:17; Galilee: Mark 16:7; Pauline churches: Rom. 8:4-27; Gal. 3:1-5).[26] They were firmly convinced it was on the day of Pentecost[27] that the fulness of God's work in Jesus Christ was completed (cf. Acts 2:17-21's use of Joel 2:28-32). Put differently, the soteriological Spirit who is also the Spirit of prophecy was at work at the end of times in order to enable God's Word to be heard with power.[28]

The evidence is deep and wide to support the following claim: *the new covenant hermeneutic owes its origins to the pneumatic experiences of early Jerusalem-based followers of Jesus.* Before outlining this suggestion, however, we need to observe that one of the earliest hermeneutical reflections on the Pentecostal experience derived from Joel 2 and not from Jeremiah 31[29] or Ezekiel, even though the absence of Jeremiah/Ezekiel reflection is often missed in scholarship. Now to eight suggestions for a Pentecostal origin for the new covenant hermeneutic.[30]

25. In general, see J. D. G. Dunn, *Unity and Diversity in the New Testament: An Inquiry into the Character of Earliest Christianity* (2d ed.; Philadelphia: Trinity Press International, 1991), pp. 174-202.

26. On this, cf. Dunn, *Unity and Diversity,* pp. 38-54; *Jesus and the Spirit* (Philadelphia: Westminster, 1975), pp. 135-56; 'Pentecost,' in *The Christ and the Spirit: Collected Essays of James D. G. Dunn,* vol. 2: *Pneumatology* (Grand Rapids: Eerdmans, 1998), pp. 210-16; *The Acts of the Apostles* (Valley Forge, Pa.: Trinity Press International, 1996), pp. 22-23. For a judgment of Acts 2 as having less historical value, cf. J. A. Fitzmyer, *The Acts of the Apostles* (AB 18C; New York: Doubleday, 1998), p. 232; Levin, *Die Verheißung des neuen Bundes,* pp. 265-79, who observes that early Christian 'new covenant' thinking was the result of an experience and was also an exegetical looking-back. Further, he questions the exegesis of earliest Christianity in its use of 'new covenant' language.

27. Cf. C. F. D. Moule, 'The Post-resurrection Appearances in the Light of Festival Pilgrimages,' *NTS* 4 (1957-58): 58-61; Dunn, *Jesus and the Spirit,* pp. 139-42; 'Pentecost,' in *The Christ and the Spirit,* 2:210-15.

28. J. D. G. Dunn, 'Baptism in the Spirit,' in *The Christ and the Spirit,* 2:222-42.

29. This lack of reflection of Jeremiah 31 in Acts 2 confirms our proposal above on the absence of 'new covenant' language in the original last supper event. Even more, it is somewhat astonishing that Luke omits reference to Jeremiah 31 in Acts 2 after his 'new covenant' language of the last supper (Luke 22:20).

30. So also at this point I intervene to express the fundamental debt *Neutestamentlers,* as Jimmy Dunn is prone to call us, owe to him for, among other things, his early and discipline-shaping work on the pneumatic experience of earliest Christianity. More than one of his studies has become a cornucopia, served to others on a table with nectar. In the next few paragraphs that debt will be obvious, but it will be for me an apparatus of appreciation to a teacher who, both personally and professionally, has been a friend and mentor to many, not the least of whom is a group of his students who gather with him, in Aristotle's friendship between the

First, its concern with 'twelve', an expectation of Jeremiah and Ezekiel, continues the community focus of the historical Jesus (cf. Mark 3:13-19; 6:7-13, 30) as it reappoints a successor to Judas (Acts 1:12-26). This story, told in such fulness and detail, gives one pause to think it is a later fiction.

Second, if the claim is that the 'new covenant' will be unbreakable (Jer. 31:32; 32:40), there is evidence in the Ananias and Sapphira story to see that 'unbreakable' means 'immediate punishment' (Acts 5:1-11), and one is then tempted to think in terms of the community rules at Qumran and the Essene quarter in Jerusalem (1QS 6:20, 24-25).[31] An elaboration of this theme is carried out in the warning passage of Hebrews as an instance of the gravity of sin for those who voluntarily embrace the covenant.

Third, the *interiority* of the 'new covenant' finds its solid basis in the early experience of endowment and indwelling of God's Spirit (Acts 2:1-41, esp. vv. 3, 4, 33, 38b), a theme carried out quite remarkably in Paul's theology of the indwelling Christ and Spirit (cf. Gal. 5:13-26; 2 Cor. 3:18). Paul's theology was heavily anchored in the new-age significance of the gift of the Spirit.[32] More importantly, one of the (neglected) themes of the Peter speech is the democratization of the spirit of prophecy, and this democratization can be quite naturally connected to the knowledge-embedded-in-the-heart of Jer. 31:33-34. If some think the Peter speech is contrived, the polemical focus embedded in the early chapters of Acts confirms the democracy: strife with the priests, temple authorities, and the Temple itself (cf. Acts 3:1–4:22; 5:17-42; 6:8–8:1, etc.). We have reason to think that the democratization process was very early.

Fourth, the expectation of Jeremiah that God's Torah would be kept by all, from the youngest to the oldest, and that teaching one another would not be needed, finds its fulfilment (a) in the appeal to Joel 2:28-32 in Acts 2:17-21, (b) in Paul's theology of the democracy of charismatic gifts (1 Corinthians 12–14), (c) in the nonhierocratic nature of the Jesus movement, and (d) in the 'untrained' nature of their teachers (Acts 4:13). In fact, the idealized account of the church in the early chapters of Acts evokes the expectation of Jeremiah that the law would be written in the heart and from there would become a source of

---

'good' (ἡ τῶν ἀγαθῶν φιλία καὶ κατ' ἀρετὴν ὁμοίων; *Nic. Eth.* 8.3.6), annually over dinner at SBL for the Dunn Students reunion. Among whom I proudly number myself — and whom I imitate in style in this incomplete-but-meaningful-sentence!

31. Dunn, *Jesus and the Spirit,* p. 166; cf. B. J. Capper, 'The Palestinian Cultural Context of Earliest Christian Community of Goods,' in *The Book of Acts in Its Palestinian Context* (The Book of Acts in Its First Century Context 4; ed. R. Bauckham; Grand Rapids: Eerdmans, 1995), pp. 323-56.

32. For an important clarification by Dunn, cf. his 'Baptism in the Spirit,' in *The Christ and the Spirit,* 2:242.

democratic teaching ministry. It is likely that this pneumatic, democratic experience was in part responsible for the community of goods in the early Jerusalem church and its developing ethic of reciprocity.[33] In other words, the democratic interiorization vision of Jeremiah was a springboard for action in the Jerusalem-based churches.

Fifth, the emphasis on 'forgiveness' in early messianic theology (Acts 2:38; 5:31; 10:43; 13:38) could easily have led to the 'new covenant' theology of the early Jerusalem community, even if forgiveness is understood in more than individualistic terms in the prophetic expectations. One might just as easily suggest that the early preaching of Peter on forgiveness is more than individualism; in fact, that Peter sees in this new body of pneumatic eschatological followers of Jesus the core of the restored people of Israel so longed for by Jeremiah and Ezekiel.

Sixth, what occurs at Pentecost is later considered to be the fulfilment of the promises — probably those given to Abraham, Moses in the deuteronomic tradition (cf. Deut. 30:6), David, and the prophets to relay to Israel (Acts 1:4; 2:33, 38-39; Gal. 3:6-14). And, if Paul's theology clearly moves in the direction of replacing the Torah with the Spirit (Gal. 3:6-14; 5:1-26), he is at least suggesting Pentecost as the date when the salvation-historical clock struck daybreak, since it was at Pentecost that the Jews remembered the giving of the Torah (cf. Exod. 19:1; 2 Chron. 15:8-15; *Jub.* 1:1; 6:17-31; 14:20; 22:1-16; 1QS 1:8–2:25; *b. Pesah.* 68b).[34]

Seventh, Ezekiel declared that the final covenant would bring 'peace'. If this theme is not characteristic of Jeremiah's expectations (where it functions as the empty promises of the false prophet), neither is it the focus of the early messianic experience (but cf. Acts 10:36) nor of its imminent transnational movement![35]

Finally, the restoration of the twelve tribes surely looked forward to a larger Israel; perhaps an Israel that would transcend its national limitations. If so, then the preaching of the gospel to all at Pentecost evokes the universal expectations of ancient Israel. Fundamentally, under all these experiences that led to a new covenant hermeneutic is the belief that God's Spirit had empowered and indwelt the little community of Jesus' followers in Jerusalem (Acts 2) and elsewhere.[36]

33. See B. J. Capper, 'The Palestinian Cultural Context of Earliest Christian Community of Goods'; 'Reciprocity and the Ethic of Acts,' in *Witness to the Gospel: The Theology of Acts* (ed. I. H. Marshall and D. Peterson; Grand Rapids: Eerdmans, 1998), pp. 499-518.

34. Dunn, *Jesus and the Spirit,* pp. 140-41.

35. Dunn, *Baptism,* pp. 48-49.

36. J. D. G. Dunn, 'Spirit and Holy Spirit in the New Testament,' in *The Christ and the Spirit,* 2:3-21.

Conclusion

In a study of this length, it is impossible to tie up all loose ends and to defend each point made. But a sketch of a solution to the origin of the 'new covenant' hermeneutic has been provided, and the evidence suggests that it was the Pentecostal experience of the early Jerusalem followers of Jesus that provided the foundations for a complete reflection on the significance of Jesus of Nazareth. For it is here that one finds a constellation of factors that correlates substantially with Jeremiah's prediction of a 'new covenant'. Sometime *after* Pentecost (note that Joel's text is remembered as the focus there) and probably by someone other than Peter, an early Christian came to the conviction that the pneumatic experience of Pentecost was in fact what was expected by Jeremiah and Ezekiel. Therefore, it was inferred that messianic Israel has entered into the new covenant. Whoever it was, that person bequeathed to early Christians a category of wide-ranging implications, for it quickly became attached to the last supper tradition and found its way into the Pauline circle as well as the hermeneutic of the author of Hebrews.

Some early follower of Jesus had the insight to connect that belief in the 'new covenant' to the last supper tradition, for many of the themes above are also redolent in the early Jesus traditions. When Jesus sat at table over that last supper and spoke of his 'blood' as a Passover-like event, it would only be a few furious months before his followers would see, as a result of their pneumatic life, in that blood the very reconstitution of God's new covenant with Israel. That which is anachronistic is often what is also the historic.

Pentecost

The already established link between Pentecost, covenant renewal, and the giving of the Law probably prompted the first believers to interpret their experience of the Spirit as the fulfillment of the promise of a new covenant, as the Law written in their hearts (Deut. 30:6; Jer. 31:31-34; Ezek. 36:26-27; 37:14; cf. Acts 2:38-39; 3:25; 1 Cor. 11:25; Heb. 10:15-16, 29). But the implications of this insight for continuing faith and conduct were not recognized and elaborated until Paul (Rom. 2:28-29; 7:6; 2 Corinthians 3; Gal. 3:1–4:7; Phil. 3:3; Col. 2:11; 1 Thess. 4:8).

JAMES D. G. DUNN[37]

37. 'Pentecost,' in *The Christ and the Spirit*, 2:213.

V Spiritual Remembering: John 14.26

Peter Stuhlmacher

I. John's Gospel's Claim to Truth

How does St John's Gospel relate to the Synoptics? How shall we handle the astonishing freedom with which this Gospel treats the (Jesus-) traditions available to him? These questions have occupied exegesis since the times of the earliest church. The judgement of Clement of Alexandria is especially instructive. John, 'recognizing that the "outward facts" had been already set out in the [Synoptic] Gospels, urged on by his disciples and inspired by the Spirit, wrote a "spiritual" gospel (πνευματικὸν εὐαγγέλιον)'.[1] This early attempt to determine the particular character of the Fourth Gospel does have its attraction.

For the second Paraclete-saying, John 14.25-26, in fact shows that Clement had addressed an important point: the Fourth Gospel sets out the inherited memory of the mission and teaching of Jesus, in the shape in which it was formulated and handed on by the pupils of the 'disciple whom Jesus loved' (John 13.23; 19.26; 21.7, 20). The picture which the Fourth Gospel provides of this disciple is enveloped in an aura of idealism. That is why it remains unclear to this day whether we are dealing with a fictional or a historical figure:[2] the 'disciple

1. Quotation from Helmut Merkel, *Die Pluralität der Evangelien* (Traditio Christiana 3; Bern: Peter Lang, 1978), p. 7.

2. Martin Hengel, *Die johanneische Frage* (WUNT 67 Tübingen; Mohr [Siebeck], 1993), pp. 275ff. goes so far as to identify the disciple historically with the presbyter named John by

---

This essay has been translated from the original German by the Rev. Canon Dr. Martin Kitchen, Vice-Dean of Durham Cathedral.

whom Jesus loved' is not only the author and guarantor of the Gospel (John 21.24) but also the one μαθητής who in faith and believing insight surpasses Peter and the rest of the Twelve. He alone remains true to Jesus until the cross and is appointed protector to his mother (John 19.26-27). He saw with his own eyes that blood and water flowed from the side of the Crucified, and his testimony to this event supports the faith of the disciples in the foundation of baptism and the Lord's supper in the sacrifice of Jesus (cf. John 19.34-35 with 1 John 5.6). The 'disciple whom Jesus loved' believes in the resurrection of Jesus before Peter (John 20.8) and on the evening of Easter Day receives from the risen Christ, with the rest of the Twelve, the commission, the gift of the Holy Spirit, and the so-called power of the keys (John 20.21-23). This threefold gift enables and authorizes him to give testimony to the tradition as it is established in the Fourth Gospel and to stand at the head of a circle of adherents. John's Gospel presents itself to its readers and hearers as the inspired testimony of 'the disciple whom Jesus loved'. It offers the 'memory' of the person and teaching of Jesus which has been revealed to the disciple by the Spirit-Paraclete. This memory is of post-Easter origin, because the Spirit was given to the disciples by Jesus only after the resurrection (John 20.22). Therefore the Johannine *anamnēsis* is stamped with the confession that Jesus was, is, and remains the Logos, and as such the royal (messianic) representative of God and witness to the truth of God (John 1.1-18; 19.37). The recollection of this 'disciple whom Jesus loved' corresponds with Jesus' own testimony to the truth and can only be understood by believers who have been reborn through baptism (John 1.12-13; 3.5-6).

II. Synoptic and Johannine Testimony to Jesus

The Fourth Gospel's high claim to truth is linked with its understanding of the Paraclete, who is named in John 16.13 the 'Spirit of truth' and in John 14.26 the 'Holy Spirit'. According to John 14.26 the Paraclete facilitates and determines the memory of 'everything' that Jesus taught his disciples. The Paraclete also shapes contemporary testimony to Jesus within the Johannine circle over against the unbelieving world; this testimony is the subject of John 15.26-27 and 16.8-11.

The particular nature of Johannine memory of the teaching of Jesus becomes clearer when we attempt to clarify the relationship between John and the Synoptics. Since this relationship has been contested ever since the time of the early church, we restrict ourselves to the following four observations:

Papias, whereas Ulrich Wilckens sees in him an 'ideal representative of all disciples of the whole church of all times', in which the Evangelist conceals himself.

(1) The Evangelist and his circle of pupils grew out of the synagogue, but they were expelled from it (John 9.22; 12.42; 16.2). So we have to guard against tackling our question with modern criteria for contradictions and coherences. The Johannine community thought of itself in Jewish, or Jewish-Christian, terms. With respect to Old Testament and Jewish texts it is always surprising to note their readiness and capacity for placing different traditions alongside one another and to regard as complementary the differing viewpoints they offer.[3] The possibility, considered by Hans Windisch in his day, that John's Gospel was intended to replace the Synoptics does not arise in these circumstances.[4]

(2) With careful judgement one can say 'that the Fourth Gospel was written, not for a Johannine community isolated from the rest of the early Christian movement, but for general circulation among the churches in which Mark's Gospel was already being read'.[5] With regard to the contacts between the Fourth Gospel and the Lukan tradition, one may dare to extend Bauckham's judgement and also presuppose knowledge of Luke on the part both of the Evangelist and his addressees.[6]

(3) Since Mark, Luke, and John in common used the *Gattung* 'Gospel', the composition of all three Gospels is based upon the conviction that the one gospel of God concerning Jesus Christ has its decisive basis and content in the history and teaching of Jesus, but may be attested in a variety of narrative forms. This insight corresponds with the manner in which all the apostles bore witness to the one gospel.

(4) The common use of the *Gattung* 'Gospel' demonstrates, moreover, that the Gospels of Mark, Luke, and John were composed together in the spirit of memory of the person, teaching, and history of Jesus. In the case of Mark and Luke this anamnetic impression, however, is not so thoroughly reflected yet as it is in John.[7] Mark and Luke (and Matthew) are concerned with the transmission of the sayings tradition which goes back to Jesus himself as well as to the common tradition of Jesus's mighty acts and passion which is dependent

3. Cf. Emma Brunner-Traut, *Frühformen des Erkennens: Aspekte im Alten Ägypten* (Darmstadt: Wissenschaftliche Buchgesellschaft, 2nd ed. 1992) and my essay, "Anamnese — Eine unterschätzte hermeneutische Kategorie", in Peter Stuhlmacher, *Biblische Theologie und Evangelium* (WUNT 146; Tübingen: Mohr [Siebeck], 2002) pp. 191-214.

4. Hans Windisch, *Johannes und die Synoptiker* (UNT 12; Leipzig: Hinrichs, 1926).

5. Richard Bauckham, "John for Readers of Mark", in Richard Bauckham (ed.), *The Gospels for All Christians* (Grand Rapids and Cambridge, U.K.: Eerdmans, 1998), p. 171 (pp. 147-71).

6. Cf. C. K. Barrett, *The Gospel according to St John* (London: SPCK, 2nd ed. 1978), pp. 42-54.

7. In any case, the Lucan prologue, Luke 1.1-4, is evidence of an express historical consciousness and an equally clear image of the development of the Gospel tradition. The special Lucan tradition of the Passion displays particular christological emphases also.

upon Peter and the other disciples. The Fourth Gospel presupposes parts of the Synoptic tradition,[8] but it represents Jesus' mission in the way that it 'must have' proceeded according to the Johannine view (see below).

III. Spirit-borne Remembering of the Words of Jesus

Following Rudolf Bultmann,[9] the Spirit-Paraclete is often understood as the power of the contemporary Johannine proclamation of the Word. This proclamation includes the Jesus tradition as it is represented in the Fourth Gospel. Christian Dietzfelbinger, for example, says of John 14.26, 'The Paraclete will . . . teach after Easter what Jesus taught before Easter. But where will the teaching of the Paraclete be heard? There can be only one answer: in the community, that is, in the teaching and the proclamation of the community in which the Paraclete is at work. The Paraclete will ensure that the proclamation of Jesus finds its continuation in the proclamation of the community'.[10] To some extent this understanding is correct, on the basis of John 15.26-27; 16.7-15; but it is too restrictive. It neither takes into account the observation of Günther Bornkamm that all the Evangelists wish consciously to place their readers back to the time of Jesus,[11] nor does it allow John and his pupils to be the Jewish Christians that they were.[12] Jewish and Jewish-Christian memory of God's saving acts in his-

8. Cf. the lists of the contacts between John and the Synoptics provided by Udo Schnelle, *Einleitung in das Neue Testament* (Uni-Taschenbücher 1830; Göttingen: Vandenhoeck, 3rd ed. 1999), pp. 506-7.

9. In particular, Rudolf Bultmann, *Theologie des Neuen Testaments* (Uni-Taschenbücher 630; Tübingen: Mohr [Siebeck], 9th ed. 1984), p. 421: "The witness of the community is the witness of the Spirit which is given to it, who represents the position of Jesus as 'the ἄλλος παράκλητος (14.16); and if the Spirit 'reminds' the community of everything that Jesus said (14.26), then this reminding is not representing in the sense of historical reproduction, but in the sense of the eschatological event which broke into the world with him (16.8-11). And if the Spirit "leads into all truth" (16.13), that means that he teaches how to understand the present, whatever present that may be, in the light of this event.'

10. *Das Evangelium nach Johannes* (ZBK IV/2; Zürich: Theologischer Verlag, 2001), p. 67.

11. 'A particular feature of the Gospels, as opposed to the post-Easter *kerygma*, is the fact that they give the word back to the pre-Easter, historical Jesus and leave it there . . . they bring the hearers back to the beginning and lead them into a meeting with Jesus as on the first day, when he met his contemporaries with appeal and address, with the call to repentance and good deeds, demanding their response. . . . They encourage the hearers at a later stage to understand themselves as the original hearers, tax collectors, and prostitutes, the just and the unjust, the Pharisees and the "people of the land", in a situation in which the death and resurrection of Jesus are still in the future' ("Geschichte und Glaube im Neuen Testament", in Günter Bornkamm, *Geschichte und Glaube* (Gesammelte Aufsätze III; BevTh 48; München: Kaiser, 1968), p. 24 (pp. 9-24).

12. As long as twenty years ago James D. G. Dunn pleaded that John should be allowed to

tory was (and is) orientated to the basic assumption that the deeds of God depicted in a particular form in the Bible must be not only remembered and handed on but also and at the same time commemorated.[13] So Ulrich Wilckens is right to say that by drawing attention to the fact that, once Jesus has departed the Paraclete will remind the disciples 'of his words and deeds' (John 14.26), John is applying an elementary experience of Israel to the post-Easter church. Since God proves himself to be the God of his covenant people by his saving acts, these 'wonders' are not elements of the past. Insofar as Israel 'recalls' them, it maintains a share in them — for all time'.[14] Wilckens adds, 'Even in the word 'teaching' there is some continuity with Judaism: for in Judaism every exegesis of Torah is teaching in the sense of binding validation of the covenant will of God as it is expressed in and established on the basis of Scripture. The teaching of Jesus is God's teaching (7.16-17; 8.28); and what the 'Advocate' will teach after Easter is the representation of this teaching with an authority corresponding to that of Jesus in his time'.[15] The teaching which the Paraclete imparts extends beyond that which the earthly Jesus said (John 16.12-14). However, through the reminder of 'everything that I have said to you' it remains firmly bound up with what Jesus said as 'Lord and Teacher'.[16] When one evaluates from a Jewish-Christian standpoint the verbs used in John 14.26 — remind [ὑπομιμνῄσκειν]

---

be the man he was historically. Cf. his essay, "Let John Be John — A Gospel for Its Time", in Peter Stuhlmacher (ed.), *Das Evangelium und die Evangelien* (WUNT 28; Tübingen: Mohr [Siebeck], 1983), pp. 309-39.

13. The Jewish celebration of Passover is determined by the assumption that the meal will be celebrated as a commemoration: "In every generation all are obliged to regard themselves as though they were brought out of Egypt."

14. Ulrich Wilckens, *Das Evangelium nach Johannes* (see n. 2) p. 232.

15. Wilckens, *Das Evangelium nach Johannes,* p. 232.

16. James D. G. Dunn, *Jesus and the Spirit* (London: SCM, 1975), p. 351, speaks with good reason of a careful 'balance . . . between the continuing revelatory work of the Spirit and the revelation already given.' On the other hand, Hans Christian Kammler rejects the view that the 'office of the Spirit-paraclete' consists in 'assisting the historical memory of the disciples and so assuring the continuity of tradition.' The recollection brought about by the Spirit is achieved, according to Kammler, precisely the other way round in the formation of *new* words of Jesus, indeed of whole speeches of Jesus (Hans Christian Kammler, "Jesus Christus und der Geist-Paraklet", in Otfried Hofius and Hans Christian Kammler, *Johannesstudien* [WUNT 88; Tübingen: Mohr (Siebeck), 1996], p. 111 [pp. 87-190], italicized in Kammler. He draws attention to Johannes Schneider, *Das Evangelium nach Johannes* [THKNT Sonderband, 3rd ed. 1985], p. 264). Kammler works with a distinction between recollection of the words of the earthly Jesus and the formation of new sayings and speeches of Jesus through the Paraclete, which contradicts the Jewish-Christian concept of recollection along with the concern of the Evangelist not to dissolve his testimony from the history of the Logos. Moreover, he pins Schneider down to a contrast which he did not establish.

and teach [διδάσκειν], then it becomes clear not only why the evangelist and his disciples gave the form of a Gospel to their Jesus tradition but also why their gospel was not regarded as a replacement of Mark and Luke, but had to be placed alongside them: John's Gospel completes the other two Gospels in the light of the full truth of the Christ event that was revealed by the Paraclete.

This process has a Jewish analogy. The precise dating of the Temple Scroll from Qumran (11Q19 and 20) remains contested.[17] However, what is not contested is that it represents a daring continuation and completion of Deuteronomy. In the Temple Scroll the commands of God, which in the biblical original are formulated in the third person singular, are frequently translated into divine 'I-words', so that the whole appears as directly applicable Torah. For the Essenes the Temple Scroll was as valuable as Deuteronomy. In a similar way the Johannine circle sets its Gospel alongside the Synoptics and completes what they say. It sees in Christ Jesus the preexistent divine Revealer and has him speak in the first person even the fulfilment of scriptural passages such as John 19.28 (cf. Ps. 69.22). In the (absolute) 'I-am' sayings of Jesus the very Old Testament revelatory formula 'I am' occurs on the lips of the Son (cf. Deut. 32.29; Isa. 48.12; 51.12; 52.5, etc. with John 8.24, 28, 58; 13.19). Jesus and the Father are one (cf. John 10.30). In this way God's word sounds from the mouth of Jesus. If one assumes with Martin Hengel that the Evangelist may well spring from among Jerusalem priestly circles,[18] the striking analogies between the Temple Scroll and the Fourth Gospel may not simply be fortuitous.

IV. Characteristics of the Johannine *anamnēsis*

Franz Mussner,[19] Klaus Haacker,[20] and Andreas Obermann[21] have drawn attention to the fact that Spirit-effected memory has fundamental significance for the Fourth Gospel. In connection with Mussner, Udo Schnelle even sees in the anamnesis a programmatic basis of Johannine thought: 'The *post-Easter retrospective* is for John equally a theological program and a narrative perspective; it makes it possible for the fourth evangelist to transform theological in-

17. Cf. Johann Maier, *Die Tempelrolle vom Toten Meer und das 'Neue Jerusalem'* (Uni-Taschenbücher 829; München: Ernst Reinhart, 3rd ed. 1997), pp. 47ff., and Armin Lange and Hermann Lichtenberger, "Qumran", *TRE* 28, pp. 52-53 (pp. 45-79).

18. *Die johanneische Frage* (see n. 2), 306ff.

19. *Die johanneische Sehweise* (QD 28; Freiburg: Herder, 1965), pp. 45ff.

20. *Die Stiftung des Heils* (AzTh I/47; Stuttgart: Calwer, 1972), pp. 75, 86, 151-55.

21. *Die christologische Erfüllung der Schrift im Johannesevangelium* (WUNT 83; Tübingen: Mohr [Siebeck], 1996), pp. 399-408.

sights into narrated history. Certainly, all the Gospels were written from the perspective of hindsight, but John is the only evangelist expressly to thematize this viewpoint and hold it up as the key to understanding the whole work.' Schnelle adds, 'The understanding and the unfolding of the Christ-event are carried out as Spirit-wrought post-Easter anamnesis (cf. John 2.17, 22; 12.16; 13.7; 20.9)'.[22] In the light of these clear observations, we need only to draw attention to a few characteristics of the Johannine anamnesis which are important in our context.

Formulation in Johannine Technical Language

John and his disciples were bold enough to transfer into the language of their circle the whole of the Jesus tradition which was available to them; moreover, they amplified it on a grand scale. Much has been said about Johannine language that does not need to be repeated here.[23] For our purposes only the following points are important: The language of the Johannine circle departs from the Synoptic tradition. From the linguistic point of view John may be compared only with Matt. 11.28-30, and this comparison allows the two sources to be identified, from which the Johannine idiom is fed: Old Testament–early Jewish Wisdom tradition (cf. Matt. 11.28-39 with Sir. 51.23-27) and (possibly) Wisdom modes of expression in the circle of disciples in the time of Jesus.

Thanks to its extensive new formulation, the Fourth Gospel appears to be so uniform in its linguistic dress that any attempt to distinguish between pre-Johannine tradition and Johannine redaction remains hypothetical. The same must be said of thoroughgoing literary-critical work on the texts. We have to read St John's Gospel as a mature whole which was published by his pupils after the death of 'the disciple whom Jesus loved' (John 21.24-25). Textual criticism has established without doubt that the story of the adulteress, John 7.53–8.11, was added subsequently to the Gospel. Also, there are in the available texts repeated glosses and commentaries (cf., e.g., John 2.21; 11.51; 18.14; 19.35). The composition of the book demonstrates surprising breaks,[24] and John 21 has the

22. Both quotations in Udo Schnelle, *Das Evangelium nach Johannes* (THKNT 4; Leipzig: Evangelische Verlagsanstalt, 1998), p. 21. Schnelle's italics.

23. Cf. Eugen Ruckstuhl, *Die literarische Einheit des Johannesevangeliums* (NTOA 5; Fribourg: Universitätsverlag/Göttingen: Vandenhoeck, 1987), and Eugen Ruckstuhl and Peter Dschulnigg, *Stilkritik und Verfasserfrage im Johannesevangelium* (NTOA 17; Fribourg: Universitätsverlag/Göttingen: Vandenhoeck, 1991).

24. Cf. the old question whether John 5 and 6 must be reversed, along with the 'insertion' of John 14.1–16.33 + 17.1-27 between 13.38 and 18.1.

effect of an appendix. The Gospel has therefore evidently been composed and edited.[25] Nevertheless the texts resist the modern distinction between 'genuine' and 'false', 'traceable to Jesus' and 'secondary'.[26] The authenticity of John's Gospel rests on the spiritual anamnesis of 'the disciple whom Jesus loved'. In its execution he assimilated the whole Jesus-tradition to the idiom which was current in his school. The Fourth Gospel is therefore accessible only to such readers and hearers as are intimate with the language of the Johannine school.

Completion and Making More Precise the Synoptic Tradition

According to Heinrich Schlier, Johannine spiritual remembering embraces a threefold movement: 'first a re-presentation, . . . second an exposition . . . , and third a leaving to experience'.[27] This movement can be recognized in the way in which John has woven a kind of counterbalance to his linguistic appropriation of the tradition. He repeatedly gives hints which demonstrate the trustworthiness of his (eye-)witnesses (19.35; 21.24): through the mention of three celebrations of the Passover (John 2.13, 23; 6.4; 11.55; 12.1; 18.28) he makes it clear that the activity of Jesus continued not just for one year, as the Synoptists suggest, but longer than two. John reports more accurately than they that the Kidron was a winter torrent and Gethsemane a garden alongside it (John 18.1). The evangelist gives an insight into the architecture of the High Priest's house in the upper town of Jerusalem (John 18.27-55). He calls the spot *lithostrotos* (i.e., *Gabbatha*) at which Pilate condemned Jesus (John 19.13) and notes that Jesus was laid in a (new) rock-tomb, which was in a garden (19.41; 20.15). The Johannine special traditions of the miracle of turning water into wine at the marriage in Cana of Galilee (John 2.1-12), of the witness of John the Baptist 'at Aenon, near Salim' (John 3.22-30), of the conversation of Jesus with the Samaritan woman at Jacob's well near Sychar (John 4.1-42), of the healing of the lame man at the (correctly described) pool of Bethesda (John 5.1-9), of the activity of Jesus at the Feast of Tabernacles and of the Dedication of the Temple in Jerusalem (John 7.2; 10.22), and so on, may all be added to the list. The observations

25. The whole phenomenon and problem is precisely described in Hartwig Thyen's article "Johannesevangelium", *TRE* 17, pp. 203-8 (pp. 200-225).

26. It is a puzzle to me how the Jesus Seminar could overlook this fact and say that the Fourth Gospel could provide no assistance for understanding the historical Jesus (cf. Robert W. Funk and Roy W. Hoover, *The Five Gospels* [New York: Macmillan, 1993], pp. 401-70).

27. "Zum Begriff des Geistes nach dem Johannesevangelium", in Heinrich Schlier, *Besinnung auf das Neue Testament* (Exegetische Vorträge und Aufsätze, 2; Freiburg: Herder, 2nd ed. 1967), p. 267 (pp. 264-71).

show that the Evangelist was well informed — in chronological, geographical, and topographical detail — about the whole appearance of Jesus. He was obviously concerned to leave the ministry of Jesus its special historical place.

Christological Exegesis of Scripture

John 14.26 has an interesting parallel in 1 John 2.27.[28] Along with the Second and the Third Letters of John, the First is probably also written by the Elder (John). He writes in 1 John 2.27, 'The anointing (τὸ χρῖσμα) that you received from him abides in you, and so you do not need anyone to teach you. But everything that his anointing teaches you is true and not a lie, and just as you have been taught, so abide in him.' The Elder establishes here the fulfilment of Jeremiah 31.34: 'The teaching role of the Spirit is seen as a fulfilment of Jer. 31.34'.[29] The same thanksgiving for fulfilment might also stand behind John 6.45. If we start with the experience of the fulfilment of Jer. 31.31-34 in the Johannine circle, then the sayings about understanding and expositing Scripture which belong to our context — John 2.17, 22; 12.16; 20.9 — become easier to understand. The Scriptures provide basic testimony to Jesus (John 1.45; 5.39); their sayings are inviolable (John 10.35) and must be fulfilled (John 19.28). But the full christological sense of the scriptural testimony is opened up by the Spirit to the disciples only after Easter (John 2.22; 12.16; 20.9). In the memory of the sayings of the Scriptures — as it is carried by the Spirit — and in their christological understanding an active and a passive movement come together: the attempt on the part of the disciples to understand the way of Jesus in the light of the Scriptures meets words of Scripture and is guided by them in a particular direction.[30] With the help of the Spirit the disciples recognize that, long before the incarnation of the Logos, the Scriptures spoke of his divine sonship, his mission, and his fate, so that even Isaiah glimpsed the glory of the Lord in the Jerusalem temple (cf. John 12.41 with Isa. 6.1); but this hermeneutical insight is of post-Easter date.

28. Cf. Kammler, "Jesus Christus und der Geistparaklet" (see n. 16), p. 113.

29. Dunn, *Jesus and the Spirit* (see n. 16), p. 352.

30. Cf. Obermann, *Die christologische Erfüllung der Schrift im Johannesevangelium* (see n. 21), p. 400.

The Words of Jesus of Equal Importance as the Words of Scripture

From John 2.22 and 18.9, 32 it is clear that John equates the words of Jesus with the words of Scripture. The word of Jesus and the word of Scripture must be fulfilled in the same way. 'This equal treatment of the words of Jesus with the self-fulfilling words of Scripture demonstrates the high regard of the Evangelist for the Jesus tradition, as well as the relevance for his theology which he accords both to Scripture and to the words of Jesus'.[31] From these results we may conclude that John also has the greatest respect for the Jesus tradition which was available to him and which had been disclosed by the Spirit. So it is not possible to accuse the Evangelist of any lack of disloyalty with regard to the Jesus tradition. However, since we know the tradition of the words and deeds of Jesus only as they are reproduced by him, and must remain in the dark about their prior stages, it is very risky to deduce from John's respectful handling of Scripture his faithfulness towards the sources from which his Jesus tradition originates.[32] The high regard for Scripture and the Jesus tradition neither hindered the Johannine circle from interpreting the Old Testament christologically, nor did it keep them from having Jesus speak in a manner very different from that in which the Synoptics do.

The Johannine circle transmits words and speeches of Jesus which have no models in Mark and Luke, and these new sayings, as we read them today, were clearly formulated only after Easter. In the Fourth Gospel the readers and hearers hear Jesus speak as the Paraclete revealed to the Evangelist and his followers. Yet we must note one thing: while we today are accustomed to see the witness of John and the words of the 'Johannine Jesus' in a direct line, the Evangelist and his pupils distinguished between the words of Jesus and their own teaching. As the Johannine Epistles show, the teaching of the Elder (John) was contested in his own community. But concerning the Paraclete and his teaching, the Gospel says that the Spirit who is sent to the disciples from the Father in the name of the Son will not speak on his own authority, but will impart what he has heard (from Jesus) (cf. John 16.23-24). The Paraclete thus takes his sayings from Jesus and shares them with the Evangelist and his disciples. This sharing proceeds in the form of the memory 'of everything that I have said to

31. Obermann, *Die christologische Erfüllung*, p. 389.

32. Cf. Peter W. Ensor, *Jesus and His 'Works'* (WUNT 85; Tübingen: Mohr [Siebeck], 1996), p. 83: '. . . the author's handling of his Old Testament quotations offers us a unique paradigm of the way he handled a source which he believed expressed the word of God, and as such it offers a clue to the way he may well have handled the tradition of the sayings of Jesus which he possessed.'

you' (John 14.26). The words of Jesus, as they are heard by the Spirit and handed on by the Evangelist, are revelatory words of Jesus and not simply Johannine teaching, concerning which there might be controversial discussion. The words and the speeches of Jesus in the Fourth Gospel have a status equal to the gospel of God which was revealed by the risen Jesus to Paul outside Damascus (cf. Gal. 1.11-12). The Johannine *anamnēsis* has an inspirational character, and from the 'I am' sayings as well as from the revelatory discourses which the Gospel offers, one can read what an astonishing christological result this inspiration had.[33]

The Writing of History according to the Divine Standard

If the words and speeches of Jesus which we find in John are taken from the possession of the risen Christ after he has completed his earthly mission, an essential characteristic of the Johannine Gospel writing is set out, which is at variance with modern historical remembrance. John and his disciples ventured to rewrite the story of Jesus within the parameters of their own christology. The classical example of this is to be found in the Johannine Passion chronology. It is indeed preferred by the distinguished historians of primitive Christianity to that of the Synoptists,[34] but it is probably an anamnetic construct.

According to John 19.14, the Good Friday on which Jesus was crucified was only the 'preparation day' for the Passover festival, that is, 14 Nisan and not 15, of which the Synoptists speak. On the afternoon of 14 Nisan the Passover lambs were slaughtered in the Temple, and this happened exactly when Jesus died on the cross of Golgotha outside the walls of Jerusalem as the Lamb of God who takes away the sin of the world.[35] In favour of this view John departs

33. The comparison of the Johannine 'I-am' sayings with Mark 13.36 and Matt. 24.5 on the one hand and the 'I-am' sayings of the risen Christ in the Apocalypse on the other makes highly probable the prophetic origin of these sayings; cf. my *Biblische Theologie des Neuen Testaments* (Göttingen: Vandenhoeck, 1999), 2:228-32.

34. Cf., e.g., Bo Reicke, *Neutestamentliche Zeitgeschichte* (Berlin: de Gruyter, 3rd ed., 1982), pp. 180ff., and Gerd Theissen and Annette Merz, *Der historische Jesus* (Göttingen: Vandenhoeck, 1996), pp. 375-76.

35. In the Johannine language of the 'lamb of God' (ὁ ἀμνὸς τοῦ θεοῦ), who takes away the sin of the world (John 1.29), and in the identification of the Passover lamb with the Crucified in John 19.36, several traditions come together: of Jesus as the servant of God (Isa. 53.7); of Christ as the sacrificial lamb (Num. 28.3-8), which seems to lie behind the reference to Christ as the ἀρνίον in the Apocalypse, and the identification of Christ as the Passover lamb which was already known to Paul (cf. 1 Cor. 5.7) On this still unexplained fusion of traditions cf. Thomas Knöppler, *Die theologia crucis des Johannesevangeliums* (WMANT 69; Neukirchen: Neukirchener, 1994), pp. 91ff.; idem, *Sühne im Neuen Testament* (WMANT 88; Neukirchen: Neukirchener,

not only from the Synoptic Passion chronology. Certainly he enriches the report of the final meal of Jesus with the tradition of the footwashing (John 13.3-17); but he removes the meal from its original framework in the Passover.[36] At the same time he has already made the 'bread discourse' in the synagogue at Capernaum the place for setting out the meaning of the Lord's Supper (cf. John 6.51-59).

How are these considerable interferences in the existing tradition to be explained? If one accepts that the Evangelist is a Jewish Christian — as he was — then the story of Jesus 'had to' run in a way that corresponded to the essence of Jesus as Logos and Lamb of God.[37] The Gospel speaks in all clarity of the divine δεῖ which determines the life of Jesus (John 3.14, 30; 9.4; 10.16; [12.34]; 20.9), and the Evangelist kept to this 'must'. Ernst Käsemann accused John of seriously mistreating the tradition available to him. The Evangelist is said to have been the first in history to have 'used the earthly life of Jesus only as the foil of the divine Son who strides through the world and as the locus of the breaking in of heavenly glory', and by means of this representation to have promoted a Docetic christology.[38] This objection was not plucked out of thin air. It exaggerates, however, the Johannine representation and overlooks the fact that John followed the example of the kerygmatic representation of history in the Jewish tradition. In telling the history of the exodus and of the possession of the land which is constitutive of the religious self-understanding of Israel we stumble across a phenomenon which is quite similar to that of John: the Old Testament's narratives maintain how both events have impressed themselves upon the collective memory of Israel. Only in the modern era has it become clear that the history of its deliverance from Egypt and its entry into the promised land as it is remembered by Israel in no way accords with the facts of contemporary

2001), pp. 237-38; Peter Stuhlmacher, "Das Lamm Gottes — Eine Skizze", in Hermann Lichtenberger (ed.), *Geschichte — Tradition — Reflexion: Festschrift für Martin Hengel* (vol. 3; Tübingen: Mohr [Siebeck], 1996), pp. 529-42; and Jörg Frey, "Die 'theologia crucifixi' des Johannesevangeliums", in Andreas Dettweiler and Jean Zumstein (eds.), *Kreuzestheologie im Neuen Testament* (WUNT 151; Tübingen: Mohr [Siebeck], 2002), pp. 208-9 (pp. 169-238).

36. Joachim Jeremias and Karl-Theodor Kleinknecht have shown that an ancient account of Jesus' farewell meal was available to the Evangelist. Cf. Joachim Jeremias, *Die Abendmahlsworte Jesu* (Göttingen: Vandenhoeck, 4th ed. 1967), pp. 35-78, esp. pp. 73ff.; and Karl-Theodor Kleinknecht, "Johannes 13, die Synoptiker und die 'Methode' der johanneischer Evangelienüberlieferung", *ZThK* 82 (1985): 381-88.

37. Herein lies also the motive for depicting the Passion of Jesus as a victory procession and the cross not as the site of the greatest humiliation (cf. Phil 2.8), but as the exaltation of the Son of God (cf. John 3.16; 8.28; 12.32).

38. Ernst Käsemann, *Jesu letzter Wille nach Johannes 17* (Tübingen: Mohr [Siebeck], 3rd ed. 1971), p. 35.

critical-historical research and archaeology.[39] It is the same with John. The evangelist and his addressees knew Mark (and Luke) (see above). But because John followed the divine δεῖ and the truth of the mission of Jesus as it was revealed to him by the Spirit, he has consciously taken into account the contradiction between his own representation of the teaching and history of Jesus and that of the two other Evangelists. Nevertheless the Johannine circle did not do away with the Gospels according to Mark and Luke. On the contrary, it simply invited the readers and hearers of its own Gospel to hold to the anamnetic representation of the way of Jesus by 'the disciple whom Jesus loved'. It did so because this presentation helps in a particular way to understand Jesus and to open the way to faith in Jesus Christ (cf. John 20.31). The Fourth Gospel's intention is to surpass christologically the representation of Mark and Luke.

V. Correct Handling of the Johannine *anamnēsis*

John's Gospel draws attention to the fact that the message of Jesus is directed to those who have been born again by grace and can only be understood by them (John 1.12-13; 3.5). This shows how the Johannine representation is to be handled. Like the (biblical) texts recited in the celebration of the Passover, this tradition is intended for the community and its liturgical use. The Fourth Gospel is to be read in the assembly of the community as it gives thanks to the one God for the mission of the Logos and acknowledges him as the only begotten Son (of God). Since this community possessed (a certain) knowledge of the Synoptic tradition, it was able to relate the Johannine representation of Christ with the witness of the Synoptics and, for example, to plumb the deep dimensions of the various representations of the crucifixion in Mark 15.20-32, Luke 23.26-49, and John 19.16-37. The readers of the Gospel are led by the Evangelist to set against the Jewish accusation that Jesus died on the cross under the curse of God (cf. Deut. 21.23)[40] the narrated confession of the victorious raising of Jesus

39. Norbert Lohfink, a recognized expert on Deuteronomy and Joshua, sums up the critical consensus of Old Testament scholarship concerning Israel's occupation of the land: "An occupation" such as the book of Joshua depicts it "never took place. One can say that again in spite of the new controversies which are coming to the boil concerning the early history of Israel. The excavations of archaeologists prove it." ("Einzug ins verheißene Land", in *HEUTE in Kirche und Welt* 2 [Bad Tölz: Verlag Urfeld, 2002], p. 3). Also, the biblical accounts of the escape from Egypt cannot be confirmed in detail from history and archaeology.

40. Justin still had to answer the question from the Jew Trypho, whether it was necessary for Christ to die in such a humiliating way on the cross, for "according to the law [Deut. 21.23], whoever is hung on a cross is cursed" (*Dial.* 89.2).

from the dead and to meet their risen Lord in the word of the witness who was loved by Jesus (cf. John 20.28; 21.24). When John additionally calls for abiding in the word of Jesus which he received by the Paraclete (cf. John 1.38-39 with 8.31; 1 John 2.24, 27-28), and for obedience to this word (cf. John 8.51; 14.15, 21; 15.10; 17.6; 1 John 2.3, 5; 3.22, 24; 5.3), he commands the community — in good Jewish and Jewish Christian fashion — to learn the words of Jesus (by heart) and so make of them an inner possession which will determine their whole manner of witness. The *Sitz im Leben* of the Fourth Gospel is the liturgy and catechesis of the believing community.

This conclusion does not close scientific exegesis of the Fourth Gospel. It does, however, make clear that such research cannot on its own sound the depths of the spiritual profundity of the Gospel. With St John's Gospel in hand one may certainly search for the pool of Bethesda and the stations of the Passion in Jerusalem. That is important. But one only approaches the incarnate, crucified, and raised Logos as one meditates at these places upon the Johannine Prologue, the words of Jesus, and John 19.30 as well as 20.19. The words of Jesus as they were recalled by the Paraclete to the memory of 'the disciple whom Jesus loved' can only be sounded by spiritual *anamnēsis.* Heinz Schürmann correctly called this *anamnēsis* a 'basic practice' in the life of the church.[41] The judgement of Clement of Alexandria which was quoted at the beginning thus remains an important index for relevant exegesis of the Fourth Gospel within the church.

41. "Anamnesis als kirchlicher Basisvorgang", in Heinz Schürmann, *Wort Gottes und Schriftauslegung,* ed. Knut Backhaus (Paderborn: Schöningh, 1998), pp. 55-61.

VI The Breath of Life: John 20:22-23 Once More

Marianne Meye Thompson

When he had said this, he breathed on them and said to them, "Receive the Holy Spirit. If you forgive the sins of any, they are forgiven them; if you retain the sins of any, they are retained."

Much ink has been spilled in an effort to settle the interpretation of this passage in the Gospel of John. The issue which perhaps has drawn the most attention is the apparent tension between the events described in John 20 and Acts 2, inasmuch as each narrative presents the giving of the Holy Spirit without any acknowledgment of the event recorded in the other narrative. Various proposals have been advanced in an effort to preserve the integrity of each narrative, but also to allow the narratives to be harmonized with each other. To be sure, some commentators have denied the possibility of historical harmonization of the two incidents.[1] Others have suggested that this account is John's version of Pentecost, shaped so as to make the point that the departure of Jesus and coming of the Spirit are chronologically and theologically bound together.[2] Because the events in John 20 and Acts 2 are pictured so differently, still other commentators propose that John describes a "symbolic promise" or "acted parable" which prefigures the actual gift of the Spirit as recorded in

1. So C. K. Barrett, *The Gospel according to St. John* (2nd rev. ed.; Philadelphia: Westminster, 1978), p. 580.

2. So George Beasley-Murray, *John* (2nd ed.; WBC; Nashville: Thomas Nelson, 1999), pp. 381-82.

Acts 2.[3] But Rudolf Schnackenburg resists the tendency to make the "Lukan Pentecost" the starting point of interpretation, arguing that it "ought to be regarded not as a norm but as an exception, namely, as a special manifestation of the Spirit, which assisted the primitive Church in Jerusalem to make a break through."[4]

Whether or not one accepts Schnackenburg's argument, he does call attention to the extent to which the Lukan presentation of Pentecost in Acts 2 has served as norm for the interpretation of John 20. Virtually all interpretations of these two accounts assume that the New Testament speaks of one definitive gift of the Holy Spirit to the church. In Acts 2 the disciples receive the the Spirit to empower them as witnesses of the risen Lord "in Jerusalem, and in all Judea and Samaria, and to the ends of the earth" (Acts 1:8). As Peter's sermon at Pentecost and the subsequent narrative of Acts demonstrate, that commission is carried out primarily in the proclamation of the Word of God. Even so, a venerable tradition of interpretation holds that the means through which sins are forgiven and retained, according to the commission given by Jesus in John 20, is the proclamation of the Word. Calvin puts it most sharply: "The only subject handled here is the preaching of the Gospel."[5] Although Calvin's foil was the Roman Catholic use of John 20:22-23 as a scriptural proof for the sacrament of penance, the tradition that forgiveness of sins is mediated specifically through the preaching of the Word continues to find supporters.[6] Whatever might be said in its favor, this interpretation does facilitate harmonization with Acts 2. Since the apostles are depicted in Acts chiefly as those who, under the power and inspiration of the Spirit, proclaim the word of the Lord (Acts 4:31; 6:2; 8:14; 11:1; 12:24; 13:5, 7, 14; 17:13; 18:11), it is not surprising that the commission in John 20:23 has been read as a charge to preach the gospel. Such an interpretation explains the parallelism in the sending of Jesus, a "prophet mighty in word and deed" (Luke 24:19) anointed with the Spirit (3:22; 4:18-20), to proclaim "the word of God" (5:1; 8:1; 11; 11:28), and the apostles: both preached the Word of God, calling for repentance and offering forgiveness.

Among those who follow in Calvin's footsteps and see in the commission

3. D. A. Carson, *The Gospel according to John* (Leicester: Inter-Varsity; Grand Rapids: Eerdmans, 1991), pp. 651, 655.

4. Rudolf Schnackenburg, *The Gospel according to St. John* (3 vols.; New York: Seabury, 1980-1982), 3:325.

5. John Calvin, *The Gospel according to St. John* (2 vols.; trans. T. H. L. Parker; Grand Rapids: Eerdmans, 1959), 2:204.

6. John 20:23 is cited in the canons and decrees of the Council of Trent as warrant for the sacrament of penance; for an English translation, see H. J. Schroeder, *Canons and Decrees of the Council of Trent* (Rockford: Tan Books, 1978), pp. 39, 89.

in John 20:23 a charge to proclaim the gospel is Herman Ridderbos. Briefly entertaining a different viewpoint — namely, that Jesus' breathing of the Spirit recalls texts such as Gen. 2:7, Ezek. 37:9, and Wisd. 15:11, which refer to God's life-giving breath — Ridderbos comments, "If the reference to these texts were direct, then the meaning would be that just as in the beginning God breathed a living spirit into humankind, so in this moment of the new creation Jesus breathes the Holy Spirit into the disciples and so grants them eternal life."[7] Ridderbos rejects this interpretation, favoring instead the view that in giving the Spirit, Jesus equips the disciples for the work assigned to them.

However, it is worth reconsidering the possibility that the description of the "breathing" of the Spirit in John 20 deliberately evokes the creation of humankind in Genesis: just as God breathed the breath of life into humankind, so now Jesus "breathes" the divine breath of life into the disciples, representative of God's renewed people, the "children of God" who are born by "water and Spirit" (1:12-13; 3:3, 5). Although John does not use the word "baptize" in ch. 20, it is likely that this scene narrates the fulfillment of the promise that Jesus will baptize with the Holy Spirit (1:33), since Jesus has been glorified (7:37-39) and the Spirit has been sent; thus new birth by the Spirit (3:3, 5) is now possible. This understanding of John 20:12-23 is not new, having been suggested previously by Rudolf Schnackenburg as well as by the honoree of the present volume, J. D. G. Dunn. In his *Baptism in the Holy Spirit,* Professor Dunn suggests that John's use of ἐνεφύσησεν ("he breathed") recalls Gen. 2:7, Ezek. 37:9, and Wisd. 15:11, in which the divine breath brings life to that which was otherwise a corpse. In this way, "John presents the act of Jesus as a new creation: Jesus is the author of the new creation as he was of the old."[8]

This lead is worth following. To it we may add the observation that, by presenting Jesus as the author of the new creation, John adds one more stroke to his portrait of Jesus as the Son who, in union with the Father, exercises divine prerogatives, particularly the prerogative of giving life. According to John 20, Jesus "breathes" the Spirit. The Greek word ἐνεφύσησεν ("he breathed") is the same word found in the Septuagint of Gen. 2:7, 1 Kings 17:21, Ezek. 37:9, and Wisd. 15:11, where the context has in view not only divine breath, but the divine breathing of the Spirit to impart life. The points of contact between John and these Septuagintal passages are thus not based simply on the word "he breathed" but on the contexts of these passages as well. The text which provides the pattern for

7. Herman Ridderbos, *The Gospel of John: A Theological Commentary* (Grand Rapids: Eerdmans, 1997), p. 643.

8. J. D. G. Dunn, *Baptism in the Holy Spirit: A Re-Examination of the New Testament Teaching on the Gift of the Spirit in Relation to Pentecostalism Today* (Philadelphia: Westminster, 1970).

the others is Gen. 2:7, where God "breathes" (but here, πνοήν, "breath," rather than πνεῦμα ζωῆς, "spirit of life") into Adam, formed from the earth, so that Adam becomes "a living being."[9] Echoing this passage, Ezekiel promises that God will cause his divine "breath" to enter into his people in order to bring them — symbolized by the desiccated bones — to life again.[10] Through this life-giving act, God's people shall come to know and confess that "I am the LORD" (37:6). God's restoration of his people out of the hands of their enemies and to their land is further described as God's opening of the graves and raising his people up from them, again leading to the confession of God as the Lord (37:12-14). Moreover, God's life-giving act involves the gathering together of Israel, uniting them into one people under one king, the new David (37:21-22, 24). As the people gathered together by God, they shall be cleansed from idolatry and worship God rightly: "they shall be my people, and I shall be their God" (37:23). Thus in Ezekiel 37, God's life-giving breath restores the people to life as well as to their proper relationship to and acknowledgment of their God.

Although the explicit reference to God's "breathing" into his people is missing from Ezekiel 36, a number of the same themes appear there as well. God vindicates his people by gathering them together and restoring them to their land (36:23-24), so that "the nations" shall know that "I am the Lord" (36:23). At this time, Israel will be restored, cleansed from all its uncleanness and idolatry, and endued with a new heart and a new spirit (36:25-26; cf. 11:18-20). In fact, God will put his own Spirit within them, so that they will walk in the ways of God. As a result, "you shall be my people, and I will be your God" (36:27-28). This passage thus links together God's sanctification of his name, the gathering together of God's people, their obedience to his commands, and the renewal of their relationship with him. These realities are brought about by God's gift of the Spirit or his "breath," which, in the subsequent chapter, is pictured on analogy with the creating Spirit of Genesis. In Ezekiel 36, then, God's gift of the Spirit results in cleansing, renewal, and obedience, while in Ezekiel 37 the Spirit gives life to the dead. These are not, however, competing images; both show the state of God's people apart from his life-giving work: unclean in their idolatry, dead in the graves of sin, they need both the cleansing and life-giving Spirit of God.

9. For other instances in the Old Testament of "breath of life" see Job 33:4; Isa. 57:16; cf. Mal. 2:15.

10. Elsewhere in the Old Testament, the Spirit is the life-giving power of God. In Gen. 6:3, e.g., the Lord says, "My spirit shall not abide in mortals forever, for they are flesh; their days shall be one hundred twenty years." Of note here is that it is God's spirit which gives mortals life; otherwise they simply remain "mortal" and "flesh," a point also made in John 3:6, "That which is born of the flesh is flesh, that which is born of the Spirit is spirit."

Similar passages are found throughout Isaiah, where the outpouring of the Spirit effects eschatological re-creation and renewal.[11] In Isa. 32:15-17, God pours out the life-giving Spirit so that the "wilderness becomes a fruitful field," with the result that justice, righteousness, and peace govern the life of God's people. In 44:3-6, God pours out the Spirit as water on a thirsty land, an act which testifies to God's identity. The one who gives the water that brings life to the thirsty land is the "Redeemer, the Lord of hosts: 'I am the first and I am the last; besides me there is no god.'" Isaiah pictures the Spirit as life-giving water; the pouring out of God's spirit again leads to the revivification of God's people, who acknowledge that there is no god besides the Lord (Isa. 44:6).[12]

In light of these Old Testament texts, which point to the Spirit's life-giving and renewing work, we may look briefly at three texts of Second Temple Judaism which also speak of the giving of God's Spirit as purifying God's people, leading to their renewed obedience. In *Jubilees*, God warns Moses that the people will be taken into captivity among the nations (1:13-14), but promises that they shall eventually be delivered and gathered together by God, who will build his sanctuary among them and dwell in their midst. Although Moses entreats God to create for his people "a pure heart and a holy spirit" so that they will not be enticed by sin away from the paths of righteousness (1:20-21), the Lord warns that first there will come a time of sin and stubbornness. However, after that time, God promises that he will restore the people:

> I shall create for them a holy spirit, and I shall purify them so that they will not turn away from following me from that day and forever. . . . And they will do my commandments. And I shall be a father to them, and they will be sons to me. And they will all be called "sons of the living God . . ." and I am their father in uprightness and righteousness. And I shall love them. (*Jub.* 1:23-25)

The eschatological horizon of God's promise of a holy spirit and of the purification of the people also entails their deliverance from exile and their gathering, God's dwelling among them in a renewed or new sanctuary, and their steadfast obedience.

One also reads in the Dead Sea Scrolls of the hope for eschatological renewal, including the cleansing or purification of God's faithful people by God's

11. On this point see also Dunn, *Baptism in the Holy Spirit,* p. 192.

12. In the book of Wisdom, the man who was formed from the dust in turn forgets the one who "breathed into him a living spirit" and fashions idols out of the elements of the earth (15:8-11). Thus he fails to acknowledge God as creator and God as the one Lord (cf. Job 33:4).

Spirit, resulting in a renewed relationship with God and their renewed obedience. In 1QS 4:20-22, we read of this hope for God's refining Spirit to be given to the covenant community:

> God will refine, with his truth, all human deeds . . . cleansing him with the spirit of holiness from every irreverent deed. He will sprinkle over him the spirit of truth like lustral water (in order to cleanse him) from all the abhorrences of deceit and from the defilement of the unclean spirit. In this way the upright will understanding knowledge of the Most High, and the wisdom of the sons of heaven will teach those of perfect behavior.

In the meantime, however, there is deceit and injustice, because the spirits of truth and injustice are at war within the hearts of humankind. "For God has sorted them into equal parts until the appointed end and the new creation." The community also expects some divine action with respect to the temple, apparently the construction of a new, eschatological temple that will replace the present Jerusalem temple.[13]

In *Joseph and Aseneth,* the work of God's Spirit is portrayed as life-giving, but the emphasis falls on the present and personal aspect of the Spirit's revivifying work because the issue is the conversion of a Gentile rather than the eschatological renewal and gathering of God's people. God's Spirit "renews" Aseneth through an act of re-creation, forming her anew and making her alive, even as God made Adam a living being out of the dust of the earth. The entire prayer reverberates with echoes of the story of creation, and particularly of the creation of humankind, in Genesis.

> Lord God of my father Israel,
> the Most High, the Powerful One of Jacob,
> who gave life to all (things)
> and called (them) from darkness to light,
> and from error to the truth,
> and from death to life,
> you, Lord, bless this virgin,
> and renew her by your spirit,
> and form her anew by your hidden hand,
> and make her alive again by your life,

13. Some of the relevant passages from the Scrolls are 1QS 5:5-7; 8:4-10; 9:3-6, 26; CD 3:18–4:10; 1QH 20:3; 4QFlor (4Q174). The Temple Scroll offers a "blueprint" for the new temple; see James C. VanderKam, *The Dead Sea Scrolls Today* (Grand Rapids: Eerdmans, 1994), p. 59.

> and let her eat your bread of life,
> and let her drink your cup of blessing,
> and number her among your people
> that you have chosen before all (things) came into being,
> and let her enter your rest
> which you have prepared for your chosen ones
> and live in your eternal life for ever (and ever).

As a result of Aseneth's renewal by God's Spirit, she is formed anew, made alive, and numbered among the people of God who are destined for eternal life.

These three texts show various ways in which the account of God's creation of humankind through the Spirit was reinterpreted to apply to the people of Israel and to individuals in acts of divine re-creation. As God creates humankind by breathing into them the Spirit, the breath of life, so God will re-create his people by cleansing them of impurity and idolatry, restoring them out of their exile, and renewing them in a right relationship to him. Thus the act of physical creation provides the language to describe the moral and spiritual re-creation of God's people. Even when the object of the Spirit's work is a Gentile rather than Israel, the imagery is much the same: the Spirit effects cleansing and renewal, so that God's true people, including proselytes, may be gathered in obedience.

We may then briefly bring these observations from the Old Testament and later Jewish texts to bear on the interpretation of John 20:22-23, noting three points in particular. First, the actual wording of Jesus' charge to his disciples — "If you forgive the sins of any, they are forgiven" — is striking because "forgiveness of sins" does not play a prominent role in the Gospel of John. In fact, this is the only place in the Gospel where the phrase occurs. Elsewhere it is said that the Lamb of God "takes away the sin of the world" (1:29); the man at the pool is told to "sin no more" (5:14); and "the Jews" are told that they will "die in their sins" unless they believe (8:24). The point is not that Jesus' ministry and work have no relationship to the removal of sin, but rather that, unlike the Synoptic Gospels, Jesus does not tell anyone that their sins are forgiven (Mark 2:10; Luke 7:48), nor does he instruct his disciples that they are to forgive others (e.g., Matt. 6:12-15; 18:21-22). In light of the relatively minimal role that the theme of the "forgiveness of sins" plays in the Johannine narrative of Jesus' ministry, it is therefore all the more significant that Jesus commissions his disciples with a charge couched in terms of the forgiveness of sins. While one might account for this relatively common Christian topos by any number of means, it may well be that John's point is that it is precisely the giving of the Spirit which makes possible the forgiveness of sins, thus also engendering the transition from death to life as portrayed in Ezekiel and elsewhere. The coming of the Spirit, which happens only upon Jesus' death and return to the Father, makes available the benefits of Jesus' death to all, including the new birth (3:3, 5) and freedom from sin and death (8:24, 33-36). They are the first to receive the forgiveness of sins and the purification which the Spirit effects, and to be set into the renewed and right relationship to God characterized as the "birth from above," enabling them to be God's children (3:3, 5; 1:12-13). In other words, they receive the Holy Spirit not simply as the power for mission or evangelism, but as the life-giving power which renews and purifies them for obedience and worship. Indeed, this must happen first, before there is any possibility of their going out in response to Jesus' statement that he is sending them as the Father had sent him.

Second, the scene narrated in John 20 is first of all a resurrection appearance of Jesus to his disciples. While commentators often seek to reconcile it chronologically and theologically with Acts 2, in fact it is a parallel to the resurrection scene as recounted in Luke 24:36-40. As the second appearance, John 20:19-23 has been preceded by an appearance to Mary at the tomb, and will be followed by the appearance to Thomas and the others, and eventually by the appearance on the shore of the sea of Galilee. At a minimum, these appearances bear witness that Jesus is alive. But as the Gospel has so often made clear, Jesus does not first gain eternal life through the resurrection, but returns to the life and glory which he had with God "before the foundation of the world" (1:1-4, 10; 8:58; 17:5). In other words, Jesus does not now go to his Father for the first time, but returns to a previous state of union in life with God. The Johannine resurrection appearances bear witness that Jesus is alive with the eternal life of God, and they therefore bear witness to Jesus' divine identity.[14]

Thus while the scene in John 20:19-23 features a commission to the disciples, it focuses attention not only on what the disciples are to do but also on the one who empowers and charges them to do it. Throughout the Gospel, Jesus' various signs point to his life-giving power. Just as God promised his people that he would breathe the breath of life into them and raise them from the graves (Ezek. 37:12-14), so Jesus has the power to call people forth from the graves to resurrection, from death to life (5:21, 28). In so doing, he exercises a divine prerogative. He is the bread of life given by God; the messianic shepherd who leads people into rich pastures of life (Ezek. 37:21-22, 24); the gateway to life; the very source of resurrection and life (Ezekiel 37); and the vine who

14. This phrase comes from Richard Bauckham's *God Crucified: Monotheism and Christology in the New Testament* (Grand Rapids: Eerdmans, 1998), p. 7. For further discussion see also Marianne Meye Thompson, *The God of the Gospel of John* (Grand Rapids: Eerdmans, 2000), pp. 46-48, 106, 187.

nourishes his people with life (Ezekiel 15, 17, 19). The life he provides bears witness to his identity not only as the one sent by God, but indeed as the Son who is one with the Father. A crucial passage at this point is John 5:26: "For as the Father has life in himself, so he has granted the Son to have life in himself." What peculiarly characterizes God, namely, life "in himself" and the power to give life to others, as in Genesis 2, also characterizes the Son of God (see 1:1-3; 8:58; 17:3).

John focuses particularly on the Spirit as the agent through whom God imparts life to others. Hence the Spirit of God effects the new birth from "above" (3:3, 5); the Spirit gives life, and Jesus' words are "spirit and life" (6:63); and Jesus breathes the life-giving Spirit to his disciples (20:23). Inasmuch as the risen Jesus here gives the Holy Spirit, there can be little doubt that this is yet one more Johannine narrative in which Jesus is shown to have and exercise divine prerogatives, namely, that of the divine creative power, narrated in Genesis 2, and of the divine re-creating power, promised in Ezekiel and other prophetic books. The resurrection appearances testify not only that Jesus is alive but also that he is united with the Father. United with the Father, he has both the power to give life and the authorization to bestow the Holy Spirit, which marks the time of eschatological renewal and fulfillment of God's promises to his people. As one who carries out these unique activities of God, the Son has the unique identity of God. Not surprisingly, then, the appearance to Thomas leads to the climactic confession, "My Lord and my God!" As a resurrection appearance of Jesus, the scene in John 20:19-23 does as much to testify to the power and status which the risen Lord now has with God as it does to set out a "mission mandate" for his disciples. Indeed, it is in the very fact that Jesus has the power to send out his disciples that his authority is seen. Even as God had sent him out, now he will bestow upon the disciples the new life through the Spirit, and send them out as bearers of and witnesses to this life that is received through faith in him.

Finally, while all the Gospels assert that Jesus will baptize with the Spirit, John's Gospel contains more promises than any other regarding the coming of the Spirit. In John 1:33 we read the promise that Jesus will baptize with the Holy Spirit; in John 3:3 and 5, Jesus alludes to the "birth by water and Spirit" without which one cannot enter into God's kingdom; and in the Farewell Discourses, Jesus promises that the Spirit will be sent — either by the Father or by him (14:26; 15:26; 16:7). None of this can happen until Jesus' death and glorification (7:37-39), so that even though in the Gospel Jesus speaks about the realities of new life and birth, those realities lie in the future with respect to his earthly ministry. But now that Jesus has returned the life and glory he had before the world was made, all of these promises can — and will — be fulfilled. Specifically, when set against the backdrop of the passages cited earlier from both the Old Testament and Jewish literature, the imagery of Jesus' "breathing" the Spirit suggests that this is the moment in which the eschatological re-creation and renewal of God's people, as promised in Ezekiel and Isaiah and anticipated throughout John, takes place. Now that the Spirit is given (7:37-39), people may be born, not of flesh (1:12-13; 3:6), but from above, of Spirit and water (3:3, 5). Jesus' death has served to inaugurate the "gathering together of the children of God who are scattered abroad" (11:48-53) as the Good Shepherd gathers his wandering people and brings them to the safety of the fold and the sustenance of the pasture (10:1-18; Ezek. 36:23-24; 37:21-24). These are a people who acknowledge "the one true God" (John 17:3; Isa. 44:6; Ezek. 36:27-28, 37:6), now revealed in glory through the incarnation of the Word who "dwelt among us." They are raised from death to life, and freed from sin to enter into the new life (Isa. 32:15-17; Ezek. 37:9, 12-14). The Spirit also empowers true worship (4:23-24), which takes place without reference either to the temple in Jerusalem or the one in Gerizim, but rather in and through the temple of the risen Lord (2:21-22; Ezek. 37:23). God has vindicated his people and glorified his name (Ezek. 36:21-23). In short, Jesus' death and resurrection are the occasion for the Spirit's eschatological work of the recreation, renewal, cleansing, and restoration of God's people as described in the prophetic visions of Ezekiel and Isaiah as well as in later Jewish works.

In conclusion, the suggestion offered in this paper is that John presents the prophetic expectations of the work of God's life-giving and renewing Spirit as brought to fruition in Jesus' breathing on his disciples the Spirit, the breath of life. In doing so, John not only presents Jesus as the agent of both God's creation and re-creation, but also as the one who has the Spirit of life within him and so can bestow it to his followers. The Spirit "re-creates" or renews the people of God, granting them new life so that they may know God truly and walk according to God's commands. These are the primary and necessary preconditions for them to be sent as those who embody God's love and bear witness to the truth, thus mediating God's forgiveness to those who come to believe that Jesus is the Christ, the Son of God (20:30-31). It is only as the renewed people of God, given new life and new birth by the Spirit, that Jesus' disciples can serve as witnesses and ambassadors of the One through whom God gives life to the world (6:51). Just as Jesus embodies the truth, grace, love, and life of God, so his disciples, renewed by the Spirit he breathes in them, are to embody the truth, grace, love, and life of the Son of God. As the one who has "life in himself" (5:25), he now breathes that Spirit of life from within to the disciples, who have their life always derived from and in dependence upon him. John 20:22-23 narrates the giving of the Spirit, as promised in the Gospel, so that Jesus' life-giving work is sealed to his disciples, and so that they may, through whatever means, serve as witnesses of the life that God gives through his Son.

VII Initiatives Divine and Human in the Lukan Story World

Beverly Roberts Gaventa

One of the many pleasures that derive from researching and teaching devoted to the Acts of the Apostles, and one which our honoree has surely enjoyed, is the opportunity to engage in conversation with Christians from various traditions about their understanding of the Holy Spirit. If some traditions seem uncomfortable with Luke's frequent references to the Holy Spirit, fearing that they depict a rather passive humanity, others appear to have rendered the Holy Spirit's gifts into an achievement to be acquired by means of human endeavor. Oddly enough, many of these conversations across the spectrum share the assumption that human beings are the real actors in Luke-Acts, that they are the ones who shape the agenda and its outcomes. This is the assumption that I wish to address in this essay.

Three recent studies of Luke-Acts are helpful in introducing the problem. The first is Mary Rose D'Angelo's influential article, "Women in Luke-Acts: A Redactional View." D'Angelo contends that Luke depicts women in a way that would minimize the risk of offending the Roman Empire, with the result that women have "limited and conventional" roles in Luke-Acts.[1] Luke has heroes, Jesus as well as others, but women are not among them. Women carry out ministry, but it is a ministry of service rather than a ministry of leadership. Although D'Angelo does not explicitly contrast women's roles with those of men, it seems clear that the standard she employs is the ministry of men, whom she understands to be leaders and decision makers. The men are

1. Mary Rose D'Angelo, "Women in Luke-Acts: A Redactional View," *JBL* 109 (1990): 441-61, citation on p. 448.

the initiators, and Luke confines women within roles that will not give offense to outsiders.

The second study, undertaken by Daniel Marguerat, concerns the presentation of God in the book of Acts.[2] Marguerat importantly distinguishes between implicit and explicit discourse about God in Acts: "implicit" language occurs in the narration through God's mediators or mediating events (such as angels, visions, and miracles), and "explicit" language occurs in the speeches as the characters refer to God by name as the agent who is directing events. Having identified these two major ways in which God's activity is described, Marguerat moves in the second part of his essay to consider the relationship between God and human history (or the divine will and human freedom). He proposes a kind of cooperation between implicit and explicit discourses. In the implicit discourse the narrator reveals God's plan through events, and in the explicit discourse it is left to the human witnesses to interpret those events. The witnesses on their own decide what to say in their speeches about God. In addition, Marguerat identifies the freedom of those who refuse to listen to the witnesses and also the freedom attributed to the reader, who must discern certain of the signals imbedded in the narrative. He concludes, "Luke succeeds in aligning the omnipotence of God and human freedom, without the one eliminating the other, without providence crushing the individual's responsibility."[3]

The most recent study is that of Robert Wall in the *New Interpreter's Bible* commentary on Acts.[4] Wall's introduction to the theology of Acts begins with God as the initiator of a plan of salvation, yet Wall elsewhere highlights human leadership. Luke portrays "human leaders" in a way that underscores their "authority" and the importance of their traditions.[5] The title of Luke's second volume identifies it with "those heroes of the faith whose special status and divinely ordained destiny ensures the salvation of all who submit to their spiritual authority."[6] With this view in place, Wall suggests that Acts has canonical significance as a biographical introduction "to the implied authors of the letters that follow."[7]

These studies differ from one another in method, scope, and perspective,

2. Daniel Marguerat, "The God of the Book of Acts," in G. J. Brooke and J.-D. Kaestli (eds.), *Narrativity in Biblical and Related Texts,*" (BETL 159; Leuven: Leuven University Press, 2000), pp. 159-81.

3. Marguerat, "The God of the Book of Acts," p. 179.

4. Robert Wall, "Acts of the Apostles," in Leander E. Keck et al. (eds.), *The New Interpreter's Bible,* 12 vols. (Nashville: Abingdon, 2002), 10:3-368.

5. Wall, "Acts of the Apostles," 10:8.

6. Wall, "Acts of the Apostles," 10:29.

7. Wall, "Acts of the Apostles," 10:31.

and all of them contribute to our understanding of Luke-Acts. However, along with most work on Luke-Acts, they all assume that Luke-Acts is shaped both by God's initiatives and by those of human beings who are presented in the narrative as rightly acting out of their own judgments and concerns. If we speak of the narrative development in Luke-Acts in Luke's own terms as the growth of the Word of God, the assumption I am articulating is that the Word grows through a form of cooperation between God's large initiative and the smaller initiatives of human beings.

For Marguerat this assumption is explicit, as he speaks about the movement from God's originating action (e.g., Pentecost) to the human interpretation of that action (e.g., Peter's speech), which he takes to reflect the character's own conclusions — in Marguerat's view, an expression of human freedom. Wall is perhaps more typical of the scholarly tradition, in that he initially presents God as the central feature of the Lukan story and yet turns quickly to focus on the human figures and their authority and the traditions they underwrite. D'Angelo appears to endorse this same view, although to be sure she finds fault with Luke for his silencing of the leadership of women. All three reflect an assumption that pervades scholarship on Luke-Acts, and especially Acts, *an assumption that results in reading the story through its human leaders and to the neglect of God's role.*

In this paper I want to problematize that understanding, arguing that the story Luke tells concerns initiatives that come from God. When Luke shows *human beings* taking the initiative, that human initiative frequently has a negative function, usually in opposition to the gospel. There is, for Luke, a role for human responsibility, but that responsibility consists of aligning oneself with God's own initiatives — in shorthand, it consists of obedience to God.

The language I am using is admittedly slippery, so a few words about terminology are in order. I am preferring to speak of initiative rather than agency or responsibility, both of which are ambiguous for my purpose. Paul can be (and is in Luke-Acts) an agent of God in the sense that God uses Paul to do things without his having independent agency of his own, but we often use "agency" to refer to someone who acts independently. Similarly, I do think that humans in Luke-Acts have a kind of responsibility, but it is the responsibility to be obedient to God, not responsibility in the sense of responsibility for planning events or deciding on strategies. With the word "initiative," I refer to the power to make events occur, including matters of leadership, of decision making, and of authority.

When referring to the initiatives of God, I will include the actions attributed to God, the Holy Spirit, and Jesus. To be sure, some passages in Luke-Acts appear to lend themselves to neat distinctions among the roles of these three, such as Peter's Pentecost speech, which declares Jesus to have been God's agent (Acts 2:22-24) and the Spirit to be poured out by the exalted Jesus (Acts 2:33). Such boundaries disappear elsewhere, however. Peter first accuses Ananias of lying to the Holy Spirit and then accuses him of lying to God, without suggesting that the two are distinct from one another (5:3-4). In 13:1-3, the Spirit is not only the empowering agent but the director of events. Paul's address to the Ephesian elders refers to the actions of the three in ways that surely move in the direction of trinitarian thought.[8]

I. Divine Initiative in Luke-Acts

The claim that God is the overarching initiator of the action in Luke-Acts would seem to need no defending. In an article that has become a standard point of reference, Charles Cosgrove argued that the divine δεῖ ("it is necessary" or "it must," often obscured in English translations) in Luke-Acts concerns God's ancient plan as expressed in Scripture, as carried out by human agents of God's plan, and as guaranteed by God.[9] In his dissertation on the divine plan in Luke-Acts, John Squires demonstrated that the notion plays a central role in Luke-Acts and serves to confirm the reader's faith and encourage readers as witnesses and respondents to criticism of the faith.[10] Yet there is a curious gap in the literature as scholars salute the general observations made by Cosgrove and Squires, but do not carry those observations over into the actual interpretation of texts. When it comes to the interpretation of texts, the activity of God appears to yield rather quickly to the discussion of human agents as decision makers and leaders.

8. For a more extensive treatment of Acts 20, see Beverly Roberts Gaventa, "Theology and Ecclesiology in the Miletus Speech: Reflections on Content and Context," *NTS* 50 (2004): 36-52; and on the question of Luke's presentation of God, Jesus, and the Holy Spirit, see Gaventa, *The Acts of the Apostles* (Abingdon New Testament Commentary; Nashville: Abingdon, 2003), pp. 28-39.

9. Charles Cosgrove, "The Divine ΔΕΙ in Luke-Acts," *NovT* 26 (1984): 168-90.

10. John Squires, *The Plan of God in Luke-Acts* (SNTSMS 76; Cambridge: Cambridge University Press, 1993). Even Squires and Cosgrove eventually qualify their observations in such a way as to protect human freedom and responsibility, in part to distinguish Luke's position from an impersonal sense of fate.

The Case of Acts 13:1-3

Acts 13:1-3 will serve as a test case with which to illustrate both the pervasive character of divine initiative in Luke-Acts and the problem in the secondary literature. Perhaps it is obvious that the real test for my thesis derives from Acts, for it is Luke's second volume that so often funds notions of the church's leadership, of successors to Jesus, of the apostles as heroes, and other forms of human initiative.

Acts 13:1-3 stands at the beginning of the movement of the witnesses Barnabas and Saul from the Antioch church to Cyprus and then into Pamphylia and Pisidia. This passage is usually referred to as the beginning of the first missionary journey. Joseph Fitzmyer, for example, comments that this is the beginning of "the first missionary journey of Saul, who becomes the hero of the second part of Acts."[11] C. K. Barrett describes this journey as "deliberately planned," with "two associates of the local church" who are "to execute it."[12] F. Scott Spencer describes Saul as the "dominant protagonist in the narrative and the chief engineer of the Gentile mission."[13] Were we reconstructing the event from these remarks, we would imagine that the church at Antioch *decided* to start a mission and then *elected* Barnabas and Saul as the best representatives for *their* new work.

Luke's presentation of the story, however, begins elsewhere: "There were in Antioch, in the church there, prophets and teachers — namely, Barnabas and Simeon called Niger and Lucius of Cyrene, Manean a member of the house of Herod the tetrarch, and Saul" (13:1; author's trans.). In other words, v. 1 describes the presence of prophets and teachers in Antioch, prophecy having been clearly established already as a gift of the Spirit (Acts 2:1-4, 14-21, esp. v. 16). Verse 3 summarizes the response of this group in carrying out the directive of the Spirit: "Then fasting and praying and laying hands on them, they sent them on their way" (author's trans.). Between these two summary statements stands v. 2: "While they were worshiping the Lord and fasting, the Holy Spirit said: 'Now! Set aside for me Barnabas and Saul, for the work to which I have called them'" (author's trans.). By placing the Spirit's order in the form of direct ad-

11. Joseph A. Fitzmyer, *The Acts of the Apostles* (AB 31; New York: Doubleday, 1998), p. 494.

12. C. K. Barrett, *The Acts of the Apostles I–XIV* (ICC; Edinburgh: T&T Clark, 1994), p. 599. Similarly, Ben Witherington describes this as "the inaugural efforts by a church at planned evangelism of Gentiles as well as Jews" (*The Acts of the Apostles: A Socio-Rhetorical Commentary* [Grand Rapids: Eerdmans, 1998], p. 390).

13. F. Scott Spencer, *Acts* (Readings; Sheffield: Sheffield Academic Press, 1997), p. 131. Spencer does at least go on to say that Paul's role is "tempered by the affirmation that the Gentile mission . . . is supremely *God's doing*. . . ."

dress ("Set aside") and locating it between the two summary statements of v. 1 and v. 3, Luke draws attention to the fact that the initiative for this movement comes from the Spirit rather than from the church at Antioch or even from this group of human beings.

This group Luke describes as "worshiping the Lord and fasting" when the Holy Spirit speaks. In the context of the church's devotion to God, the Spirit speaks, ordering that Barnabas and Saul be set apart. The importance of this instruction is clear from the fact that the Spirit nowhere else in Acts directly orders the church to take a particular action (as distinct from directing the actions of an individual; see 8:29; 10:19-20; 21:22; 28:25-27). Despite the manifold ways in which Luke conveys the work of the Spirit and the divine will as guiding events, this is the only time in Acts that the Spirit issues a direct command to the church.

The wording of the Spirit's demand further enhances its significance. The particle δή ("now") signals that the matter is an urgent one (cf. Luke 2:15; Acts 15:36, where the same word appears for heightened emphasis). The exact nature of the "work" (see 14:26; 15:38) for which Barnabas and Saul are set apart remains unspecified, although Paul's vocation has been announced to Ananias in 9:15-16. *In response to this demand,* the community fasts and prays and sends the two away with the laying on of hands. That this commissioning continues to be God's rather than the church's is clear in that the laying on of hands comes in the context of invoking God's presence and will through fasting and prayer (cf. 6:6). Lest the community's role be misunderstood, v. 4 provides further evidence that the initiative for this journey lies with God, since it is the Holy Spirit that sends the pair on its way ("Having been sent out by the Holy Spirit, they went into Seleucia . . ."). This scarcely provides evidence that the church has planned the mission or that Paul is the narrative's hero.

Additional examples might be adduced, but this sliver of text and commentary may serve as representative both of Luke's insistence on God's role in events and of the scholarly insistence on making human beings the focal point and parsing God out of the action.

II. Human Initiative in Luke-Acts

That is not to deny the role of human initiative in Luke-Acts. Luke does provide stories of human beings who act on their own initiative. For example, in Luke 7, an unnamed woman lavishes both her tears and a jar of extravagant oil on Jesus' feet. In Luke 8, both Jairus and another unnamed woman initiate contact with Jesus when they seek healing.

In these and other instances, Luke presents actions of human beings that are lauded by Jesus, but *the most striking instances of human initiative are those that produce disaster.* In the Gospel, a variety of persons, especially religious leaders who oppose Jesus, take responsibility for putting devious questions to him and initiate plans to have him killed (e.g., Luke 6:1-11; 20:20-26, 27-40). Under the influence of Satan, Judas takes a kind of initiative by consulting the authorities about betraying Jesus (Luke 22:3-4). Most especially, for Luke the crucifixion is an instance in which human beings act on their own, refusing to recognize God's chosen.

Acts continues the thread in which various Jerusalem leaders undertake opposition to the witnesses to Jesus, but they are not the only initiators of events. Ananias and Sapphira take initiative in their stewardship, producing judgment on themselves (5:1-11). Simon Magus seeks to purchase the power to bestow the Holy Spirit (8:14-24). Herod Agrippa might be said to act on his own initiative when he kills James and confines Peter to prison with the intention of having him executed (Acts 12). Human initiative prompts the quarrel at the beginning of Acts 15, when unidentified persons from Jerusalem arrive in Antioch to insist that Gentiles must follow the law of Moses; here, importantly, Luke says nothing about the Spirit sending them out (by contrast with Acts 13). In Acts 19 the Ephesian Demetrius demonstrates leadership by apprising his fellow citizens of the disaster that Paul's preaching may inflict on their city and its god.

Satan plays a notable role in several of these instances, as when Satan "enters" Judas before his betrayal of Jesus (Luke 22:3) and when Peter identifies the action of Ananias and Sapphira as Satan "filling" their hearts (Acts 5:3; see also 13:10). Susan Garrett has convincingly demonstrated the association Luke makes between Simon Magus and other practitioners of magic and the influence of Satan.[14] The role of Satan in these stories suggests that the conflict may not be simply between God and human beings who wish to take their own initiative, but between God and Satan, each of whom holds human beings in a realm of power. The last of Paul's defense speeches makes this point explicit, when Paul describes the Lord's charge to him as that of turning people "from the power of Satan to God" (26:18).

III. Apparent Exceptions: Peter, Paul

I have deliberately set aside the two humans whose leadership, authority, and initiative play a prominent role in many treatments of Luke-Acts: Peter and

14. Susan R. Garrett, *The Demise of the Devil: Magic and the Demonic in Luke's Writings* (Minneapolis: Fortress, 1989).

Paul. Interpreters routinely identify them as heroes of Luke's story, as leaders of the church, as major figures. In a narrow, technical sense, of course, Peter and Paul are Luke's heroes, in that they, their words, and their actions appear extensively in the text. Yet they are not heroes in the more customary sense in which they dominate the plot with their bravery and leadership (which is the sense being applied to them in the literature, so far as I can determine).[15] Luke carefully insists that both Peter and Paul, when they are doing what they are supposed to do (which is not always!), are acting on God's instructions, not their own. Nor is there some algebraic formula according to which God takes a certain amount of initiative and Peter or Paul takes a certain (presumably lesser) amount.

Peter

The prominence of Peter in much of the first half of Acts causes most readers to identify him as the leader of the Jerusalem community, the one who makes decisions and who bears central authority. It is Peter who announces the need to identify a replacement for Judas, who delivers the programmatic sermons of the early chapters of Acts, who responds to the Jerusalem authorities when arrested, and who ventures to Samaria to baptize those who have been convinced by the preaching of Philip. It is also Peter who is called to the house of Cornelius and must defend his actions in Jerusalem.

That way of describing the events overlooks some important counterevidence, however.[16] Preceding all of these events is the comment of Jesus at the last supper: "'Simon, Simon, look! Satan has demanded to have you in order to sift you like wheat. But I have prayed for you that your faith may not fail. And you, when you return, strengthen your brothers'" (Luke 22:31-32). Satan and Jesus have engaged in a contest regarding the disciples, with Peter as the focal point. That Satan scores a temporary victory seems clear from his humiliation in the presence of a female slave, to whom he denies Jesus three times. The Peter who appears in Acts 1 as the spokesman is the one who has been delivered from Satan's grasp, from denial, and restored by Jesus himself as the one who should strengthen others. In addition, when Peter speaks at Pentecost, it is because he, in common with the others gathered together in Jerusalem, has been filled with the Spirit. His speech is proof of the Spirit's action, not of his own clever theologizing.

15. On the many uses of the term, see Dean A. Miller, *The Epic Hero* (Baltimore: Johns Hopkins University Press, 2000), esp. pp. 1-69.

16. Peter does show initiative at the Transfiguration, of course, but again it is initiative of the wrong sort (Luke 9:33).

Outside of Pentecost, the most significant story involving Peter is that of the so-called conversion of Cornelius in Acts 10 and 11, where Peter plays catch-up with God's initiative. Luke takes great pains to make it clear that going to Cornelius's house, speaking with Cornelius, and certainly baptizing Cornelius are not Peter's ideas. And Peter himself repeats that point in Acts 11 and acknowledges it in Acts 15 ("God chose among you that through my mouth the Gentiles would hear the word of the gospel and believe"). Peter's unexplained departure to another place following his deliverance from Herod's prison in Acts 12 and his subsequent disappearance after Acts 15 further undermine any notion of Peter's significance as leader of the community. The fact that Peter simply slips away from the narrative suggests that the focus of Luke's story lies elsewhere.

Paul

Similar problems plague the characterization of Paul as the hero of the second half of Acts. He is at center stage for much of the second half of Acts; from the beginning of his custody in Jerusalem (21:27-36) he is virtually isolated from other believers, so that the reader's attention naturally focuses on Paul. And treatments of the voyage and shipwreck in Acts 27–28 have emphasized his power as lord of the ship, the director of action, the central figure in the exchange with the residents of Malta.

Yet again there is counterevidence that must amend this picture of Paul as Luke's great hero, even as θεῖος ἀνήρ ("divine man"). The most compelling evidence comes in the repeated stories of Paul's persecution of believers. Luke's elaborate introduction of Saul/Paul as the archenemy of the church does not simply fade away (Acts 7:58–8:1; 9:1-2). The elaboration and repetition of this story in Acts 22 and 26 serve to interpret Paul as the one who initially resisted the gospel and simultaneously as the one whom the Lord delivered and sent on his way. In his speech to the Ephesian elders Paul identifies himself as bound by the Spirit (20:22) and as carrying out the role he received from the Lord (20:24). The climactic speech of Acts 26 reinforces this notion, since Paul describes himself, not as a leader, but as obedient to God's own command.

Regarding not only Peter and Paul but others among the apostles and elders, it may be thought that Acts 15 offers important evidence of human initiative. After all, James does declare, "I have decided about such and such. . . ." And he appears to formulate the content of the decree quite independently of divine instruction. The Council's seeming independence is contradicted by several factors, however. First, the entire scene serves as the outworking of God's actions in Acts 10–11 and needs to be understood in relationship to those actions.[17] Second, Acts 15 is replete with references to God's shaping of events. As noted above, Peter specifies that God chose him as the means of proclamation to the Gentiles, Barnabas and Paul report on what God has done through them, and James interprets Scripture as an indication of God's plan. There is little here that speaks of human initiative.

IV. How to Speak of Human Figures?

Students of Acts may want to reflect on the reasons for this distortion in the scholarly literature — the preoccupation with human initiative to the virtual exclusion of the roles of God, Jesus, and the Spirit. One contributing factor may well be the preoccupation of scholarship with the historical development of Christianity. When Acts is read primarily as an account (reliable or otherwise) of the early decades in the life of the church, then interpreters automatically look for human figures through whom to trace affiliations, developments, and leadership. An examination of New Testament scholarship through the lenses of cultural criticism may eventually suggest yet another factor, namely, the preoccupation of modernity with the freedom and independence of the individual human being, a preoccupation that Luke does not share.

If identifying the human characters in Luke-Acts as leaders, heroes, or initiators of events falls so far from the mark, it remains to ask how they might rightly be identified. Luke signals the answer to that question in the birth narrative, when Mary identifies herself as the δοῦλη ("slave") of the Lord. In this programmatic scene, where Gabriel announces that "nothing will be impossible with God," Mary offers an equally programmatic response. Those who consent to God's plan, who trust in it (as Elizabeth says of Mary in 1:45), are joined to God's household.

Does this mean that Ernst Haenchen was right to complain that there is little role for human beings in Acts apart from the "twitching of human puppets"?[18] Haenchen's criticism of Luke's human characters is based on the assumption that the only alternative is free or not free human beings, but Luke does not appear to hold that assumption. For Luke, the question is not whether humans have freedom, but under whose power they reside, which Lord they

17. On Acts 15 as the denouement to the Cornelius story in 10:1–11:18, see Beverly Roberts Gaventa, *Acts of the Apostles*, pp. 54-56, 210-12.

18. Ernst Haenchen, *The Acts of the Apostles* (14th ed.; Philadelphia: Westminster, 1971), pp. 362-63. Haenchen faults Luke for presenting such an unrealistic notion, asserting that "Luke has forsaken the dimension of reality in which the genuine decisions of faith are taken" (p. 363).

obey. To draw attention again to Paul's final declaration of his vocation in Acts 26, Luke understands that God's desire is to liberate humanity from the power of Satan (26:17). For Luke, human salvation consists of being delivered from the grasp of Satan and being installed among those who declare, with Mary, that they are δοῦλοι (slaves") in God's household.

VIII Rome's Victory and God's Honour: The Jerusalem Temple and the Spirit of God in Lukan Theodicy

Bruce W. Longenecker

I. The Sovereignty of God and the Destruction of Jerusalem

Among the earliest Christian thinkers, the third canonical Evangelist ranks as one who preeminently rooted the narrative of Jesus' life within the ongoing narrative of the Jewish people and their God. The salvation-historical accent of Luke's depiction of Jesus and of the movement that arose in his wake is clear from start to finish. Luke upheld the undivided relationship of the past activity of the God of the Jews and the present activity of that same God within Christian communities around the Mediterranean basin of the first century. Already in the first verse of his Gospel Luke describes the narrative that follows as 'an orderly account of the events that have been *fulfilled* among us' (1:1).[1] Throughout the rest of his work he depicts the Christian movement as the full-flowering of the ancient Jewish religion, imbued with the best of Jewish heritage and spirituality,[2] regardless of how the Christian message was being received within Jewish synagogues.[3]

1. L. Alexander (*The Preface to Luke's Gospel: Literary Convention and Social Context in Luke 1.1-4 and Acts 1.1* [Cambridge: Cambridge University Press, 1993], p. 113) writes: 'The reader in the know, that is, the Christian reader, might well see in this a covert allusion to the fulfilment of prophecy, but it is unlikely that anyone less privileged would have grasped the allusion.' I take it, however, that Luke is writing principally for 'the reader in the know'.

2. See esp. D. P. Moessner (ed.), *Jesus and the Heritage of Israel: Luke's Narrative Claim upon Israel's Legacy* (Harrisburg, Pa.: Trinity Press International, 1999).

3. Like the honoree of this Festschrift, I continue to think of Acts as 'the second of a two-volume work' (J. D. G. Dunn, *The Acts of the Apostles* [Valley Forge, Pa.: Trinity Press International, 1996], p. x).

This narrative feature was more than just a theological necessity for Luke. For many of his first-century readers, this salvation-historical accent would have offered Luke's narrative a rhetorical advantage that it might not otherwise have had. By establishing the Christian movement as a religion with long-established roots, Luke endows it with an antiquarian respectability. Since what is ancient has by definition not undermined society and has proved to be of value and benefit, Luke strengthens the rhetorical force of his narrative for his first-century contemporaries by establishing beyond doubt the antiquarian and honorable roots of the Christian movement.[4]

But if this salvation-historical accent served an important rhetorical role in Luke's narrative and was a theological imperative, it also created a theological problem. That problem involved the reputation of the God of the Jews, who had suffered a setback in honor in the events of 70 CE. The ancient world was largely dominated by social codes of honor and shame that governed much of the interaction between human players in agonistic contests for prestige and influence, as well as encompassing the gods with whom those humans aligned themselves. Luke's decision to showcase the Christian God as the God of the Jews involved significant risk in his context, writing in the immediate aftermath of the destruction of Jerusalem and its temple in 70 CE.[5]

In the ancient world, the reputation of a particular god had a reciprocal relationship to the reputation of that god's temple(s).[6] On those occasions when one god's territory was conquered by military forces loyal to other deities, it did not take a wise man to assess the situation in favor of the strength of the conquering divinity/divinities. The destruction of the Jerusalem temple was a clear indicator of the subordination of the God of the Jews to Rome's gods. This 'fact' was advertised throughout the Roman Empire in Roman coinage depicting Judaea in chains — a feature that cannot be underemphasized since coins of this kind were minted repeatedly by Rome, and in widespread contexts, in the aftermath of Jerusalem's defeat. The subjugation of the Jews by Rome, and consequently of their God by the gods of Rome, found expression in economic terms by means of the *fiscus iudaicus* imposed on Jews throughout the empire,

4. Cf. P. F. Esler, *Community and Gospel in Luke-Acts* (Cambridge: Cambridge University Press, 1987), pp. 201-19.

5. I date Luke's narrative at around 90 CE.

6. The construction and renovation of temples were big business in the ancient world. City officials were constantly mindful of their city's comparable status with rival neighbouring cities — status that had much to do with their reputations in the business of divinity worship. See B. W. Longenecker, 'Rome, Provincial Cities and the Seven Churches of Revelation 2–3', in P. J. Williams et al. (eds.), *The New Testament in Its First-Century Setting*, Bruce Winter Festschrift (Grand Rapids: Eerdmans, 2004), pp. 281-91.

in which their donations previously used to support the Jerusalem temple were now redirected to promote the high god of the Roman Empire through financial support of Jupiter's temple in Rome. Roman dominance over Judaea was advertised in the enslavement of many Judaean Jews. As the victor in the war, Rome extracted for itself a magnificent booty from the spoils of war, part of which went for the construction of the Colosseum in Rome, on which was emblazoned a large notice indicating that it had been built 'out of the booty from the Jewish war'.[7] Such things served as empire-wide reminders of where the power of world supremacy lay. For many of Luke's contemporaries, then, the destruction of Jerusalem signaled indisputably that the Jewish God was deficient in competence and honor in the face of the gods of Rome.

This estimate had precedent on previous occasions when the national fortunes of the Jews had suffered a setback at the hands of other nations. On the most serious of those occasions, the God of the Jews was thought to be impotent, his name being dishonored, 'despised', and 'profaned among the nations' (e.g., Isa. 52:4-5; Ezek. 36:20-23). A significant amount of Jewish prophetic, wisdom, and historical literature is given over to countering estimates of this kind, of course. Throughout Jewish history, potential blows to the reputation of the Jewish God had repeatedly been explained by means of a theodicy of divine displeasure. In theodicy of this kind, God is said to have permitted disasters to fall on God's people as a means of disciplining them, since God had grown dissatisfied with their infidelity as a covenant people.[8] On occasion, Jewish theodicy included also an element of divine conscription, in which the Jewish God was said to have made use of the forces of Israel's enemies to discipline the people of Israel.[9] So

7. See G. Alföldy, 'Die Spur der Steine: Eine Bauinschrift enthüllt: Das von Vespasian und Titus erbaute Colosseum wurde aus der Jerusalemer Kriegsbeute finanziert', in *Frankfurter Allgemeine Zeitung*, 15 March 1995. The notice, reconstructed from metal pegs fastened to a marble block on which letters were hung, read: I[mp(erator)] Caes(ar) Vespasi[anus Aug(ustus)]/ amphitheatru[m novum?]/[ex] manubis [fieri iussit]. The square brackets enclose the parts that have been damaged but are still 'readable'; the round brackets enclose the remainder of the abbreviated forms; the slash represents line breaks. Later a 'T' was added before Caesar, to include Vespasian's son Titus within the notice.

8. This kind of theodicy is also evident in a variety of Mesopotamian traditions. See D. I. Block, 'Divine Abandonment: Ezekiel's Adaptation of an Ancient Near Eastern Motif', in M. S. Odell and J. T. Strong (eds.), *The Book of Ezekiel: Theological and Anthropological Perspectives* (Atlanta: Society of Biblical Literature, 2000), pp. 15-42. For a survey of the same in the literature of Early Judaism, see H. Lichtenberger, 'Der Mythos von der Unzerstörbarkeit des Tempels', in J. Hahn (ed.), *Zerstörungen des Jerusalemer Tempels: Geschehen, Wahrnehmung, Bewältigung* (Tübingen: Mohr [Siebeck], 2002), pp. 92-107.

9. For the motif of divine conscription, see Isa. 10:1-7 (Assyria); Jer. 25:1-11 (Babylon); Isa. 44:28; 45:1-13 (Persia); 2 Macc. 6:12-17 (Antiochus Epiphanes).

whether through theodicies of divine displeasure or divine conscription, long-established Jewish traditions countered the implication that the God of the Jews was not the sovereign God who controlled the course of world history.

In the aftermath of national disasters that had beset the Jewish people centuries earlier, the issue of the honor of their God needed to be addressed. This applies also to many Jewish and Christian writers of Luke's day. For many of his Graeco-Roman contemporaries (most of whom would have been unfamiliar with the rich theodical tradition within Jewish literature), the destruction of the Jerusalem temple in 70 CE was yet another indicator that, when forced to compete with the gods of mightier forces, the God who had overseen Jewish history was clearly an inferior god. Consequently, if his narrative was to achieve maximal effect, Luke would need to surmount a significant hurdle. In the course of his narrative he would need to shore up the reputation of the God of the Jerusalem temple, which now lay in ruins through the overpowering force of Rome, the 'eternal city' and seemingly blessed by her own gods. Luke could not hope to satisfy the theological interests of many of his readers[10] if he failed to include within his historical monograph a strong current of theodicy defending not simply the Christian movement itself but specifically, and most importantly, its God. Even if this is not an articulated feature of Luke's narrative, it was nonetheless a pressing issue that needed to be addressed.[11] This is especially the case since Luke presents this God as the sovereign God without equal (e.g., Luke 10:17-20), in whose hands lies the course of world history (e.g., Luke 21:25-36).

Luke is not alone in including theodicy within the theological concerns of his literary enterprise in the aftermath of Jerusalem's destruction. Theodicy is at the forefront of a variety of post-destruction Jewish texts. This is true for the famous and extensive Jewish apocalypses of the late first century CE (i.e., *4 Ezra*, *2 Baruch*, *Apocalypse of Abraham*),[12] which ponder extensively the sovereignty

10. The issue of God's reputation in light of the destruction of the Jerusalem temple might have been predominantly a concern of 'outsiders' to the Christian community, but not exclusively so. Christian readers of Luke's Gospel (for whom Luke predominantly wrote) would have included many former 'pagans' unfamiliar with the rich theodical resources of Jewish tradition. Even those immersed in those resources would likely have wanted to see how the issue was managed in the Lukan narrative, not least as an example of how they might also address the matter themselves for those 'outsiders' with whom they interacted.

11. The issue might be especially pressing for Christians living in Rome, who, if Loveday Alexander is correct (*A Commentary on the Acts of the Apostles* [London: Continuum, forthcoming]), were Luke's intended audience (at least initially).

12. See P. F. Esler, 'God's Honour and Rome's Triumph: Responses to the Fall of Jerusalem in 70 CE in Three Jewish Apocalypses', in P. F. Esler (ed.), *Modelling Early Christianity* (London: Routledge, 1995), pp. 239-58. My title for this essay imitates Esler's.

of the God of the Jews in light of earthly events that seem to suggest otherwise.[13] And it is also true for the preeminent Jewish historian of the day, Josephus. In Josephus's works, the God of the Jews is shown to have already departed from the Jerusalem temple before the forces of Rome attacked it, leaving it as a 'sitting duck' for the invaders.[14] So, for instance, we read the following in *War* 6.293, 295-96 (as translated in Loeb):

> the eastern gate of the inner court [of the temple] — it was of brass and very massive, and, when closed towards evening, could scarcely be moved by twenty men; fastened with iron-bound bars, it had bolts which were sunk to a great depth into a threshold consisting of a solid block of stone — this gate was observed at the sixth hour of the night to have opened of its own accord. . . . The learned understood that the security of the temple was dissolving of its own accord and that the opening of the gate meant a present to the enemy, interpreting the portent in their own minds as indicative of coming desolation.

Elsewhere in Josephus we read: 'God Himself . . . turned away from our city . . . because he deemed the temple to be no longer a clean dwelling place for Him' (*Ant.* 20.166; cf. *War* 5.19).

Moreover, according to Josephus, whatever victory the Roman forces might have claimed for themselves was in fact a victory for the Jewish God, since that God had chosen to favor Rome by conscripting it as the instrument of God's own reign for the time being (e.g., *War* 5.412; cf. 4.323; *Ant.* 20.166). According to Josephus, then, the destruction of the Jerusalem temple occurred not because the forces of Rome had overpowered the God of the Jews but because that God had vacated the temple precinct and desired to oversee world history temporarily through Rome. Here then is a theodicy that includes motifs of both divine displeasure and divine conscription.

Similar undertakings in theodicy are evident in the writings of Christians who wrote in a post–70 CE context, providing their own explanations for the fall of Jerusalem. In the Matthean Gospel, for instance, the 'divine presence' theme that animates the narrative from start to finish (explicitly in Matt. 1:23; 18:20; 28:16-20)[15] has a doubly polemical edge to it. Not only does it have clear

13. I was privileged to work on *4 Ezra* as a PhD student under my esteemed mentor, Professor James Dunn, resulting in B. W. Longenecker, *Eschatology and the Covenant: A Comparison of 4 Ezra and Romans 1–11* (Sheffield: Sheffield Academic Press, 1991).

14. Cf. a similar narrative in *b. Yoma* 39b.

15. See D. D. Kupp, *Matthew's Emmanuel: Divine Presence and God's People in the First Gospel* (Cambridge: Cambridge University Press, 1996).

implications for the synagogue down the street that Matthew has his sights on, but it also counters a theology of divine presence associated with the now destroyed Jerusalem temple. In Matthew Jesus claims that 'something greater than the temple is here' (Matt. 12:6) precisely because in Matthew's view 'Jesus and his followers are the true temple'.[16] But Matthew does not just redefine divine presence; he also offers an explanation for the fall of the temple, which is evident in the parable of the marriage feast. In that parable, the king's invitation to join a wedding feast is repeatedly rejected by the invited guests, the result being that 'the king was angry and sent his troops and destroyed those murderers and burned their city' (Matt. 22:7). This highlights the destruction of Jerusalem in 70 CE, allegorically explained in terms of divine wrath for the killing of God's emissaries (recalling the infamous phrase 'His blood be on us and on our children' in Matt. 27:25). In this way, an event that was potentially devastating to the reputation of the Jewish God is shown to be in complete accord with God's will, to the extent that even the forces of Rome are said to be 'his troops' (cf. Josephus's theodicy of conscription).[17]

In similar fashion, in the Johannine Passion narrative 'the Jews' are asked by Pilate, 'Shall I crucify your king?' — a question that, in the context of a fiercely nationalistic Passover celebration, goes directly to the heart of Jewish hopes for the dissolution of Roman reign over them. Their famous reply, 'We have no king but Caesar' (John 19:15), is suggestive of a disavowal of the kingship of their God and their resignation to Rome's imperial lordship. The consequent destruction of Jerusalem and its temple is hardly surprising, then, even apart from any christological redefinition of divine presence and temple imagery (e.g., 1:51; 2:13-22).

Sketches of this sort can also be extended to include Christian literature in the period immediately following the Bar Kochba revolt of 132-35 CE (e.g., 5 Ezra),[18] but the point is clear enough without further demonstration: Christian theologians in a post–70 CE context, like their non-Christian Jewish counterparts, found it necessary in some manner to engage in theodicy to maintain the honor of the God of the Jews in light of the destruction of the Jerusalem

16. Kupp, *Matthew's Emmanuel*, p. 225; cf. pp. 240 and 243.

17. Cf. the undeveloped insight of J. K. Riches (*Conflicting Mythologies: Identity Formation in the Gospels of Mark and Matthew* [Edinburgh: T&T Clark, 2000], p. 214): 'The conversionist turn it [i.e., Matthew's community] was already displaying might further suggest that its sense of marginality was not so much to the Jewish community as to the wider world of the Roman principate.' See further W. Carter, *Matthew and the Margins: A Socio-Political and Religious Reading* (Sheffield: Sheffield Academic Press, 2000), pp. 36-43.

18. On *5 Ezra*, see G. N. Stanton, *A Gospel for a New People* (Edinburgh: T&T Clark, 1992), pp. 256-77; B. W. Longenecker, *2 Esdras* (Sheffield: Sheffield Academic Press, 1995), pp. 114-20.

temple. In the remainder of this essay, Luke's attempt at a post–70 CE theodicy will be outlined, not least with regard to its emphasis on the Spirit of the God who has overseen Jewish history.

II. From Divine Abode to Divine Abandonment: The Temple in Luke's Gospel

In view of the pressing matter of theodicy outlined above, it is not surprising that Luke has the Jerusalem temple firmly in view when writing his first volume. This is evident from a number of narrative features that are distinctively Lukan. For instance, events in the temple form a literary *inclusio* around the Lukan Gospel (1:8-22; 24:53). Luke alone includes a story of Jesus' involvement in the temple as a youth (2:22-24, 41-51). In the temptation narratives that Luke shares with Matthew (cf. Luke 4:1-13; Matt. 4:1-11), Luke's sequence of events culminates in Satan's tempting Jesus on the highest point of the temple (4:9-12), unlike Matthew's sequence (Matt. 4:5-7). Luke, more than any Evangelist, makes it clear that, after his dramatic actions in the temple, Jesus taught in its precincts every day prior to his arrest (19:47–20:1; 21:37).

Other features regarding the temple deserve to be noted in this overview, also being distinctively Lukan emphases. The Jerusalem temple is initially depicted as the place of abode for Israel's sovereign God. This is the assumption, for instance, of several characters that appear early on in the Lukan gospel. So, Zechariah serves as priest 'before God' in 'the temple of the Lord' (ἔναντι τοῦ θεοῦ . . . τὸν ναὸν τοῦ κυριοῦ, 1:8-9). Anna the prophetess does not depart from the temple (οὐκ ἀφίστατο τοῦ ἱεροῦ, 2:37), where she worships, fasts, and prays, presumably in the belief that the temple is the earthly dwelling place of the God of the Jews. In neither of these cases does Luke attempt to avoid or correct this belief that the God of the Jewish people has his earthly abode in the Jerusalem temple. In fact, the two distinctively Lukan narratives concerning Jesus' early years each assume the validity of this belief. At his 'dedication', Jesus is brought to the Jerusalem temple to be presented 'to the Lord' (2:22-24). Twelve years later, while he is in the temple, Jesus himself speaks of being ἐν τοῖς πατρός μου (2:49), a phrase which, even if it carries broader reference than the temple (e.g., 'about my Father's interests'), includes the temple within its scope.

But Luke's narrative also demonstrates that all is not well in the temple. In the middle of the Lukan Gospel Jesus forewarns of the destruction of Jerusalem and/or its temple: 'Behold, your house is forsaken' (13:35).[19] Various Lukan nar-

19. The fact that all is not well with Jerusalem may well be intimated as early as the Lukan

rative features bring the destruction of Jerusalem and its temple to the fore in a manner not already evident in Mark's Gospel, one of Luke's main narrative sources. For instance, whereas in Mark Jesus refers simply to the future destruction of the 'wonderful buildings' of Jerusalem (13:1-2), in Luke Jesus focuses exclusively on the impending destruction of the temple itself (21:5-6). Moreover, Luke includes four oracles about the despair that will befall Jerusalem in the future, the last three of which are distinctively Lukan: 13:32-35; 19:41-44; 21:20-24; 23:27-31. Two of these three additional Lukan oracles seem explicitly to highlight not only the destruction that came on Jerusalem in 70 CE but also the manner in which that destruction was carried out. So Jesus weeps over the city when envisaging the impending humiliation of the city of the God of the Jews: 'Your enemies will cast up a bank about you and surround you, and hem you in on every side, and dash you to the ground' (19:43-44). And again, whereas the Markan text spoke of the 'desolating sacrilege' that is to come upon Jerusalem (13:14), Luke speaks of Jerusalem being 'surrounded by armies' (21:20), just as Luke's Gospel alone prophesies that Jerusalem is to be 'trodden down by the gentiles' and its inhabitants 'led captive among all nations' (21:24). These details, some more specific than others, correspond to Josephus's depiction of Jerusalem's destruction in 70 CE (cf. Josephus, *War* 5.491-501; 6.413-19; 7.1-4).[20]

In these distinctive narrative features we see Luke highlighting the issue discussed at the outset of this essay. Within these idiosyncratic features of Luke's narrative lie evidence of Luke's own awareness of the need to address the matter of the reputation of the God of the Jewish people in light of the destruction of the Jerusalem temple by the forces of Rome. If Jesus' Father was known to be resident in the Jerusalem temple at the time of Jesus' youth, Jesus himself foresees the day when his Father's house will be devastated and laid to waste. This does not undermine Jesus' own confidence in the supremacy of his Father's reign, and the reader who is sensitive to the issues of post-70 theodicy is alert to discover the basis for Jesus' unswerving confidence in his Father's reign.

---

temptation narrative (cf. also 18:9-14). So H. Conzelmann (*Die Mitte der Zeit: Studien zur Theologie des Lukas* [Tübingen: J. C. B. Mohr (Paul Siebeck), 1954]) argued that, due to the ordering of Luke's temptation narrative, Satan is shown to remain a force within Jerusalem, waiting 'until an opportune time' to strike (cf. 4:9, 13). This might help to explain how it is that the temple can be depicted in the early chapters as the dwelling place of God and how, as early as Luke 13, Jesus can predict a fateful outcome for Jerusalem.

20. Since circumvallation (cf. 19:43), burning (cf. 19:44), and enslavement of a city's inhabitants (cf. 21:24) were an unlikely combination of events in the siege against and overtaking of a city in the ancient world, and since these features correspond precisely with Josephus's depiction of the overthrow of Jerusalem by Roman forces in 70 CE, Luke appears to have updated Mark's narrative with those events in mind.

On this Luke does not disappoint. But whereas the events of 70 CE had prompted the need for theodicy, Luke's own attempts at a positive theodicy have little to do with those events themselves. Luke does not attempt to interpret the destruction of Jerusalem and its temple as an ironic moment of divine sovereignty. He did not, for instance, entertain a theodicy of conscription, suggesting (as Josephus and Matthew had already suggested) that in the events of 70 CE the sovereign God had made use of the forces of Rome to carry out the divine will.[21] Unlike some of his Jewish and Christian contemporaries who grappled with urgent theological issues in a post–70 CE context, Luke did not seek to reinterpret the events of 70 CE in some novel or ironic fashion in order to maintain the sovereignty of God contrary to appearances. For Luke the events of 70 CE cannot be incorporated within a satisfactory positive theodicy. For those whose confidence in the God of the Jews is associated with that God's presence in the Jerusalem temple, the events of 70 CE have nothing to offer but despair (cf. 23:28-31). Luke's attempt at a positive theodicy lies in other narrative strands, bypassing the destruction of Jerusalem and its temple.

This is qualified, however, by one small but significant narrative feature. While Luke did not share the view that Rome's forces had acted as the instruments of God, he did share the view that God's presence had left the temple, leaving it unprotected and vulnerable to any who sought its overthrow. This remains the best interpretation of Luke's use of the tradition that he inherited from his Markan source regarding the rending of one of the curtains in the temple (Luke 23:45; cf. also Matt. 27:51 and Mark 15:38). The curtain Luke has in mind might be the outer curtain separating the temple from the outer court (according to Josephus, it was a tapestry of eighty-two and a half feet in height and thirty feet in width, *War* 5.211-14) or the inner curtain protecting the Holy of Holies. Either way, the point would seem to be the same: the God of the temple had departed from its precincts.[22] This feature, then, is the theological equivalent of Josephus's account of the mysteriously opening gates in the temple's inner court (cited above). In each case, the subsequent destruction of the

21. P. W. Walasky (*'And So We Came to Rome'* [Cambridge: Cambridge University Press, 1983], p. 47) argues differently: 'Rome is the chosen instrument of God which, having once had its own justice thwarted at the trial of Jesus, is thereby ordained to destroy the city and those institutions that stand in the way of justice.' This is an intriguing interpretation, but it assumes a posture towards Rome of which I remain sceptical (see n. 23 below). Moreover, such an interpretation has little merit when applied to other cases in Acts of miscarriages of justice within the Roman legal system.

22. The departure of the divine presence from the temple does not, of course, prevent Paul from having a vision in its precincts (Acts 22:17-21). Nor is the full significance of God's departure evident to the characters in the narrative; cf. Acts 21:17-31 contra Acts 7:48 and 17:24.

temple is the natural and inevitable result of its God's prior decision to depart from the temple of his own accord. In effect, both Josephus and Luke viewed the destruction of the Jerusalem temple as a simple matter of pushing over a collection of stones that had no internal coherence. Such an event, then, can hardly be an advertisement for the almighty and sovereign power of Rome. Consequently neither can it be taken as a serious blow to the honor of the God who had associated himself with the Jewish people and now, according to Luke, was working particularly within the movement of those who follow Jesus.

III. The Spirit of God in Lukan Theodicy

Luke does more, of course, than just prevent the reputation of the God of the Jews from being tarnished by the events of 70 CE. He also depicts the same God as being in the process of accomplishing an almighty and universal victory — not a victory along the lines of Rome's military victories in Jerusalem, Judaea, and throughout the Mediterranean basis, but a victory of an altogether different sort. Just as Rome aspired to rule the whole of the civilised world and to gather all peoples together in a single diverse but unified society of concord, so too this God would be content with nothing short of a victory 'to the ends of the earth', affecting the whole of the created order and unifying the diverse nations of the world. But the means by which this God accomplishes victory is not the means whereby Rome accomplished her numerable and 'impressive' victories. The victory of the God of the Jews is being accomplished, contends Luke, through the working of God's Spirit — specifically as the Spirit guides the followers of Jesus into ever-new configurations of identity and service. The earliest episodes of that victory after Jesus' ascension are narrated in Luke's second volume — sometimes referred to as the 'Acts of the Spirit', since it repeatedly highlights ways in which the corporate life of Christian communities is sustained by the influence of the Spirit (explicitly in, e.g., Luke 3:16; 11:13; 12:12; 24:49; Acts 1:4-5, 8; 2:1-42; passim; implicitly or at key structural points throughout Acts).

But Luke's depiction of the Spirit in the second volume of his historical monograph is simply a continuation and extension of his depiction of the Spirit's influence at a defining moment in Jesus' ministry in the first volume. If volume two is the continuation of 'all that Jesus began (ἤρξατο) to do and teach' in volume one (Acts 1:1), the narrative that it tells is itself the full flowering of the Spirit's own leading in the life and work of Jesus. If Acts narrates the working of the Spirit in the life of the church, the lens through which to interpret the Spirit's work is found especially in the Nazareth incident of volume one

(Luke 4:16-30). This incident, which Luke showcases at the very start of Jesus' public ministry (contrast Mark 6:1-6; Matt. 13:53-58), includes Luke's clearest articulation of the Spirit's significance and stands over the whole of the two volumes as the programmatic key for understanding the Spirit's work. In Luke's account, Jesus applies the prophetic words of Isaiah to himself and thereby reveals his own awareness of being driven by the Spirit towards certain ends (4:18-19; cf. Acts 1:1-3; 10:38): "He [the Spirit] has anointed me to bring good news to the poor. He has sent me to proclaim release to the captives and recovery of sight to the blind, to let the oppressed go free, to proclaim the year of the Lord's favour."

In Luke's view, the Spirit's empowering of Jesus (cf. 4:14) is good news for those who found themselves despised within the ancient system of honor and shame that had entrenched much of the Graeco-Roman world. In Jesus' ministry the empire of the Jewish God was becoming enlivened by means of the Spirit of that God, and the coming of that empire included a substantial critique of cultural norms of honor and shame (propped up by the systems of the Graeco-Roman world). As a consequence of Jesus' Spirit-filled ministry, however, those who were thought to be deficient in honor were becoming honorable citizens of God's sovereign and eternal empire, whatever their standing might be within the empire of Rome.[23]

The Spirit of God had empowered Jesus to bring and incarnate the empire that benefits 'the poor'. The term 'the poor' includes those who are lacking in material security, those who are insecurely placed within the severe socio-economic systems that operated throughout much of the agrarian Mediterra-

23. I find Luke to be less positive about Rome and its empire than many scholars do. Throughout his Gospel, especially, one finds repeated challenges to the pervasive system of honour and shame that animated Graeco-Roman culture and that the elite within that culture frequently used to their own advantage. Luke is walking a difficult tightrope. On the one hand, he depicts Christianity as a powerful and peaceful force for good that should be welcomed and promoted. On the other hand, he depicts it as challenging the premises upon which the social, economic, and political edifices of the Graeco-Roman world were based. (Was Luke crossing his fingers when he penned Luke 4:5-6, itself an intensification of Matt. 4:8-9?) Individual elites may frequently be depicted favorably in Luke's work, but they are participants in a system that Luke often challenged (e.g., 6:27-36; 14:7-33; 22:24-30; etc.) — a situation that may well resonate with contexts well beyond the first century.

A refreshing voice on this is that of J. B. Green (*The Theology of the Gospel of Luke* [Cambridge: Cambridge University Press, 1995], pp. 119-21, here pp. 119-20): 'To a degree not often recognized, the values and behaviour for which Jesus calls in Luke are contrary to and even put in question the existence of the Roman Empire in his day. . . . The message of Jesus in Luke violates the sacred political order of the Roman world. What is more, it does so on the basis of a clash of kings and kingdoms.'

nean basin in Jesus' day (and throughout much of human history). That Luke has his eye on the materially impoverished is clear from the manner in which he highlights their plight repeatedly through Jesus' words about and interaction with them (e.g., 6:20-26; 10:29-37; 12:13-34; 14:7-35; 16:19-31; 18:1-8, 18-30; 21:1-4). But Luke seems to understand 'the poor' in relation to wider categories as well, including in their number not only those who had been overcome by the severity of the economic system but also those with illnesses and physical disabilities, those who had entered into despised professions, those excluded from the normal definition of the 'people of God', those possessed by evil spirits, and any others that found themselves marginalised, the object of derision, or simply in need (not least, needing forgiveness). They are among those that Luke considered 'poor', the blessed ones to whom the empire of God belongs (6:20).[24]

The initial enactment of this reconciliation of the needy, the marginalised, the despised, and the forlorn within the empire of God is narrated within Luke's two volumes, an enactment orchestrated by the Spirit that empowered both Jesus and those who followed in his name. For Luke, the Spirit of God is instrumental and essential in bringing all varieties of needy people into the empire of God — embodied most clearly in Christian communities of goodness, generosity, and service.

This Spirit-driven process, Luke is convinced, cannot be stopped. This is briefly indicated within the Nazareth incident itself, when a mob of Jesus' fellow Nazarenes lead him out of the village to the brow of the hill in order to throw him down and stone him to death. Luke 'undernarrates' the outcome of this scene: 'But he passed through the midst of them and went on his way' (4:30). This rather surreal occurrence is played out time and time again in the narrative of Acts, in which obstacles to the progress of God's empire are shown to arise repeatedly but are overcome inevitably. Whether complications and adversities arise from within Christian communities or beyond them, and no matter their nature or severity, the empire of God progresses steadily and surely, ultimately surmounting all barriers and impediments, as ever-new permutations of Christian community become established throughout the world.[25] Luke's narrative demonstrates the way Paul brings his gospel into the

24. See J. B. Green, 'Good News to Whom? Jesus and the "Poor" in the Gospel of Luke', in J. B. Green and M. Turner (eds.), *Jesus of Nazareth: Lord and Christ* (Carlisle: Paternoster, 1994), pp. 59-74; M. Wenk, *Community-Forming Power* (Sheffield: Sheffield Academic Press, 2000), pp. 212-18.

25. Cf. D. Marguerat (*The First Christian Historian: Writing the 'Acts of the Apostles'* [Cambridge: Cambridge University Press, 2002], p. 108): 'The irony of God consists in integrating even the actions of his enemies in order to make them contribute to the advancement of the Word "to the ends of the earth".'

very heartland of the Roman Empire through the guidance and efficacy of the Spirit (19:21). So the very last verse of his two-volume work depicts Paul in Rome 'preaching the empire of God [τὴν βασιλείαν τοῦ θεοῦ] . . . with boldness and without hindrance' (28:31). This is not a God subjugated to the gods of Rome, nor an empire humbled by the empire's forces, but a God whose empire has no geographical boundaries, no temporal end, and no limitation of resources because of the empowering of the Spirit. Gamaliel speaks the Lukan viewpoint when he notes that if the God who had overseen Jewish history supports the expansion of Christianity, it will not be possible to restrain that expansion (Acts 5:39).

If Luke's theodicy is played out in this narrative about the expansion of Spirit-filled communities, that theodicy is rooted in and interpreted by the Nazareth incident of Luke 4 in which the Spirit of the God of the Jews is said to empower Jesus' own ministry in certain directions. In the long term, those directions do not involve the temple of Jerusalem (cf. Luke 23:45), and consequently the honor of the God of the Jews cannot be evaluated in relation to the destruction of the Jerusalem temple. Instead, that God has staked his honor to Jesus' proclamation that 'the Spirit of the Lord is upon me to proclaim the good news to the poor'. For Luke, the victory of God is becoming manifest as Jesus' Nazareth proclamation becomes embodied within Christian communities for and beyond the margins. In such communities Luke finds the sovereignty and honor of God affirmed and advertised.

We have seen that, in the decades immediately after the temple's destruction in 70 CE, any theology animated by a salvation-historical continuity involving the God of the Jews needed to include a strong dose of theodicy, defending that God's reputation in light of the destruction of the Jerusalem temple. Luke's narrative engages in just such a theodicy. The focus of his theodicy is the unconquerable Spirit of God who encourages ever-new configurations of Christian community among 'the poor', both during and beyond the first decades of the Christian movement.[26]

26. I am indebted to the Alexander von Humboldt Stiftung for providing the funding for a research period during which this article was written.

IX The Spirit and Salvation in Luke-Acts

Max Turner

If we have important consensus on major points concerning the nature of the gift of the Spirit in Luke-Acts, there nevertheless remains fundamental disagreement on perhaps the cardinal issue raised by Professor Dunn's magisterial *Baptism in the Holy Spirit,* that is, the precise relation of the Spirit to soteriology.[1] In a nutshell, Dunn argued that in Luke-Acts (as with Paul and John) the gift of the Spirit is essentially soteriological in that it brings the presence of God's kingdom, cleansing, new covenant life, and eschatological sonship, and is thus essential to authentic Christian existence, and necessarily granted in "conversion-initiation." Dunn did not wish to deny that Luke emphasized the Spirit as prophetic empowering, and that aspect became increasingly clear in his later writings. He was, however, resolutely challenging the Pentecostal interpretation that for Luke the gift of the Spirit was exclusively a *"donum superadditum,"* that is, nothing but a "second blessing" of prophetic empowering, *additional* to the grace of salvation.

Pentecostal respondents increasingly worried about his arguments on Luke-Acts, claiming that Luke had a quite *distinct* charismatic/prophetic pneumatology from Paul and John; one from which basic soteriological actions — those that undergird and establish ordinary Christian faith and life — were largely or wholly excluded. In this Dunn's respondents could claim to stand in the mainline of critical interpretation of the Spirit in Acts stretching from

1. J. D. G. Dunn, *Baptism in the Holy Spirit: A Re-Examination of the New Testament Teaching on the Gift of the Spirit in Relation to Pentecostalism Today* (London: SCM, 1970), esp. chs. 2–9.

Gunkel (1888) through Schweizer (1950s) to Haya-Prats (1975).[2] The most vigorous and able argument for this position has been presented by R. P. Menzies. His doctoral thesis was published in 1991, and it prompted the bulk of Dunn's response to Pentecostal scholars written two years later.[3]

Dunn's response conceded that his earliest work had perhaps not given enough attention to Luke's portrayal of the promise of the Spirit as characteristically, preeminently and paradigmatically Joel's "Spirit of prophecy" (Acts 2). Nevertheless, he maintained, the gift is not *exclusively* so, "as though, in effect, the Spirit of prophecy was a different Spirit from the Spirit of salvation."[4] Luke may be especially struck by the tangible effects of the Spirit inspiring various forms of "prophetic" speech, but that does not mean he *limited* the Spirit to this. If Luke clearly specifies the reference to "the promise of the Father" (Luke 24.49; Acts 1.4) as *Joel's* promise of the Spirit (cf. Acts 2.17, 33, and 38-39), that promise was itself soteriological in force (cf. Joel 2.28-32), and Luke will have understood it to embrace the related Old Testament promises of the Spirit (*inter alia*, Isa. 32.15; 44.3; Ezek. 36.26-27; 39.29; Zech. 12.10), where the soteriological force is also transparent. Dunn then provides an argued exegesis of passages where he thinks Menzies has it wrong, and where the Spirit's soteriological role is clear (mainly Luke 1.35; Acts 2.38-39; and 10.43-48 [with 11.14-18 and 15.7-9]); after further considerations of the Spirit as the eschatological Spirit and of the close relation between the Spirit and faith (especially with *initial* faith), he concludes that the gift of the Spirit of prophecy to a person in conversion-initiation must at once be *both* soteriological *and* empowering for mission. And as Luke knows only of a single "gift of the Spirit" to any individual, the Pentecostal interpretation of it as a *"donum superadditum"* risks reducing it to a "dispensable extra" and thereby tends to "diminish the weight and force of Luke's pneumatology."[5] In short, if Pentecostals are right, *Luke has left or even pushed the Spirit out of the center of his theology of salvation.*

In works initially published in 1996,[6] I argued the mediating position that

2. For a history of the debates, see Max Turner, *Power from on High: The Spirit in Israel's Restoration and Witness in Luke-Acts* (Sheffield: Sheffield Academic Press, 1996), chs. 1–2.

3. Robert P. Menzies, *The Development of Early Christian Pneumatology with Special Reference to Luke-Acts* (Sheffield: Sheffield Academic Press, 1991); James D. G. Dunn, "Baptism in the Spirit: A Response to Pentecostal Scholarship on Luke-Acts," *JPT* 3 (1993): 3-27.

4. Dunn, "Baptism," p. 9.

5. "Baptism," pp. 25-26. Against the occasional view that Luke thinks there are actually *two* theologically distinct gifts of the Spirit — one for conversion/salvation and the other (= baptism in Spirit) for mission — see Max Turner, "Interpreting the Samaritans of Acts 8: The Waterloo of Pentecostal Soteriology and Pneumatology?" *Pneuma* 23, no. 2 (2001): 265-86, esp. pp. 265-68.

6. Turner, *Power;* idem, *The Holy Spirit and Spiritual Gifts in the New Testament Church*

for Luke it is precisely *as* "the Spirit of prophecy" — that is, *by* giving various types of revelation, charismatic wisdom, and inspired speech — that the Spirit *both* performs God's soteriological functions *and* enables the church's prophetic/missiological roles. In rejoinders to Dunn and me, however, Menzies has firmly but eirenically demurred,[7] insisting that "[t]he Spirit in Luke-Acts is *never* presented as a soteriological agent," and defining the gift rather as "a prophetic enabling that empowers one for participation in the mission of God" — specifically and exclusively "nonsoteriological (or charismatic)," "prophetic," and "missiological."[8]

The purpose of this essay is not to reexamine the texts in detail — impossible within the space allowed — but to tease out some of the central issues that divide interpretation.

Defining the Principal Issue at Stake

The present consensus on Luke's pneumatology covers at least five points: (1) the essential background for Luke's pneumatological material is Jewish, deeply rooted in the Old Testament; (2) the Spirit is the uniting motif and the driving force within Lucan salvation history, and provides the legitimation of the mission to which this leads; (3) for Luke the Spirit is largely the "Spirit of prophecy"; in Acts especially as an "empowering for mission"; (4) correspondingly Luke shows relatively little interest in the Spirit as the power of spiritual, ethical, and religious renewal of the individual; (5) Luke's pneumatology develops beyond Judaism in giving the Spirit christocentric functions: the Holy Spirit is now the "Spirit of Jesus" too (Acts 16.6-7).[9] There is also near consensus on a sixth point: that Luke expects the Spirit "normally" or "ideally" to be given at, or in close temporal proximity to, conversion-initiation.

Within the context of that consensus, it is evidently the fourth point which most concerns us. Menzies represents a line of interpreters (not just Pentecostals) for whom "relatively little" shrinks to "virtually none" (while nevertheless recognizing that inspired speech might challenge and shape communi-

---

and Today (Carlisle: Paternoster, 1999), esp. chs. 1–3. NB: the page numbering of earlier editions (1996/98) of *Spirit* differ.

7. Robert P. Menzies, "Luke and the Spirit: A Reply to James Dunn," *JPT* 4 (1994): 115-38; idem, "The Spirit of Prophecy, Luke-Acts and Pentecostal Theology: A Response to Max Turner," *JPT* 15 (1999): 49-74. Both have been revised in W. W. Menzies and R. P. Menzies, *Spirit and Power* (Grand Rapids: Zondervan, 2000), chs. 5 (vs. Dunn) and 6 (vs. Turner).

8. Menzies, *Spirit*, pp. 89-90.

9. For elaboration of the consensus, see my *Spirit*, ch. 3.

ties in a positive way[10]) — unlike Paul, Luke does not think that the Spirit is given to have a *direct* effect on the moral, ethical, and personal-religious life of the individual: the gift is essentially "*non*-soteriological." By contrast, those at the other end of the interpretive spectrum (including Dunn and me) freely agree that Luke *demonstrates relatively* little interest in the interior soteriological functions of the Spirit but understand the import of that for Luke's theology quite differently. In a work essentially portraying the confirmation of the gospel in its surprising expansion across the known world and in the unexpected way it included Gentiles, we might anticipate the emphasis to fall largely on how God orchestrated, empowered, and legitimated this remarkable progression and development, that is, through the Spirit.[11] If the soteriological functions of the Spirit receive much less explicit emphasis, they are still there at crucial points, and, more important, it may be argued that they are central to the *coherence* of Luke's soteriology. What principally divides Menzies from Dunn and me are that (1) we are tacitly working with essentially incongruous concepts of "salvation"; (2) we understand the central transitional passages (Luke 24/Acts 1–2) quite differently; (3) we disagree fundamentally on what we mean by the "Spirit of prophecy," and (4) especially on whether Luke restricts it to *Amtscharisma* for the benefit of others rather than for the recipient too. These are the issues we shall examine in the following sections.

I. Issues of Difference over What Is Meant by "Salvation."

For Menzies (and Stronstad), "Luke does *not* present reception of the Spirit as necessary for one to enter into and remain within the community of salvation."[12] That is because for Menzies salvation essentially *means* justification (or "forgiveness of sins"), cleansing, and incorporation into the church. In his terms, the disciples clearly are already the community of the "saved" well before Pentecost. Men and women enter salvation by believing the good news, repent-

10. Menzies, *Spirit*, p. 89 (and references there). That he has underestimated this dimension is argued by Pentecostal scholar Matthias Wenk, *Community-Forming Power: The Socio-Ethical Role of the Spirit in Luke-Acts* (Sheffield: Sheffield Academic Press, 2000).

11. For these perspectives see esp. John T. Squires, *The Plan of God in Luke-Acts* (Cambridge: Cambridge University Press, 1993); W. Shepherd, *The Narrative Function of the Holy Spirit as Character in Luke-Acts* (Atlanta: Scholars, 1994); Ju Hur, *A Dynamic Reading of the Holy Spirit in Luke-Acts* (Sheffield: Sheffield Academic Press, 2001).

12. *Spirit*, p. 89. R. Stronstad glosses salvation as "regeneration, initiation and incorporation" (*The Prophethood of All Believers: A Study in Luke's Charismatic Theology* [Sheffield: Sheffield Academic Press, 1999], p. 121).

ing, and submitting to baptism (whether John's or the Christian sacrament). They are cleansed by their faith (Menzies appeals especially to Acts 15.9) — but such faith does not itself require the gift of the Spirit (as in Paul and John), but always precedes it (paradigmatically at 2.38-39; cf. Acts 8.14-17). Repentance and "forgiveness of sins" are rather given "directly" by the risen Lord or by God himself (Acts 5.31-32; 11.18),[13] while the spiritual wisdom/understanding required for obedient Christian life falls within ordinary unaided human capabilities (the Spirit being required only for more esoteric wisdom).[14] Hence the Spirit is "nonsoteriological." Luke believes there can be pious Christians without the Spirit (just as there had been pious Jews before Christ) — the charismatic Spirit is just for mission.

For Dunn and me, however, this analysis seems to miss the most important point. At the center of gravity of Luke's multifaceted view of "salvation" is God's invasive dynamic presence in strength (kingdom of God), powerfully transforming Israel into a community of radical filial obedience (sonship), joyful worship, and witness. More specifically, the "salvation" Luke is talking about is now widely becoming recognised as a christocentric version of Isaianic New Exodus hopes for Israel's restoration, based largely (but not exclusively) on Isaiah 40–55.[15] Within this, salvation begins with that forgiveness of Israel's sin which terminates God's historical chastisement of the nation (cf. Isa. 40.1-11) and allows Yahweh's "return" to Zion as peace-bringing restorer king, liberating forlorn Israel from her national and spiritual doldrums, and restoring her as a light to the nations. We do not know how widely such hopes were actually held in Judaism, but certainly *Luke* regards them as central. Mary (Luke 1.47-55), Zechariah (1.68-79), and Simeon (2.29-34, using Isa. 40.5 and alluding to 42.6; 49.6, 9) each prophesy their fulfillment. In Luke's view they are also cardinal for John the Baptist's understanding both of himself (cf. Luke 3.4-6, quoting Isa. 40.3-5) and of the one to come, who will "baptize/cleanse" Israel with the fiery Spirit (3.16-17). And, most important, Jesus clearly announces himself in such terms (4.18-21, using Isa. 61.1-2; 58.6), and the rest of his ministry is a call to all Israel to participate in this "good news" of God's transforming reign.

However, as all know, the high expectations of Luke 1–4 and of Jesus' subsequent preaching are not met within the period of the Gospel. A number experienced a variety of aspects of the salvation announced — through the mes-

13. *Spirit*, p. 86 n. 49.

14. *Spirit*, pp. 91-94.

15. For both the history and a development of this view, see David W. Pao, *Acts and the Isaianic New Exodus* (Tübingen: Mohr/Siebeck, 2000).

siah of the Spirit — but the hopes of Luke's opening chapters might seem to the unwary reader to lie in tatters before the cross. Israel remains largely untouched; the kingdom of God seems to have fizzled out.

Noting the way Luke centers God's reign so closely on Jesus, Conzelmann concluded that with the removal of Jesus through the ascension, the presence of "salvation" is indeed largely withdrawn until the distant end.[16] If so, Menzies' account could easily be right. If salvation in the period of the church means little more than knowledge that forgiveness is available through Christ, submitting to baptism, "keeping in" by conformity to the teaching of Jesus, and hoping for the return of the messiah, then it is not at first clear why Luke should think receiving the Spirit necessary for ordinary Christian life and piety. Conzelmann's interpretation, however, appears to be the reverse of Luke's understanding. For him the time of the church is a period in which the kingdom of God/salvation become *more strongly present,* not less. For Luke, the extensive community around the Twelve represent the core of the Israel of fulfillment. The picture of the Jerusalem church in Acts 2–8 (especially the summaries in 2.43-47; 4.32-35; 5.12-16) appears calculated to portray it as an almost paradisal community;[17] a genuine (if not yet complete) fulfillment of the hopes announced in Luke 1–4, and one that fits the shape of Jesus' own teaching, but *one that shows a presence of saving transformation that goes well beyond anything we meet in Jesus' earthly ministry.* Not surprisingly, by Acts 15 James can interpret Amos 9.11-12 to mean that the forlorn house of David has now been sufficiently restored under the messiah's rule (in the churches of believing Jews) that the "rest of men" (probably including as-yet-unbelieving Jews, but contextually emphasizing *Gentiles*) may be expected to flock to it (Acts 15.16).[18]

If the above is along the right lines, then clearly Pentecostal Lucanists are working with much too narrow a conception of salvation, and this is skewing the debates. But if salvation for Luke centers on the experience of the dynamic, self-manifesting, transforming presence of God and of Christ, then how does he think it is brought to the communities of Acts? Dunn has provided what for many would be the obvious answer: the Spirit at Pentecost. The occasional alternative explanations at present on offer — that salvation is present directly from God or immediately from Jesus, or that it is mediated through "the name"

16. H. Conzelmann, *The Theology of Saint Luke* (London: Faber, 1960), ch. 4. Conzelmann understood the Spirit as a partial substitute for Christ's presence (*Theology,* p. 204), but failed to grasp the import of this for the presence of "salvation" in the church.

17. Cf. B. Capper's essay in I. Howard Marshall and David Peterson, eds., *Witness to the Gospel: The Theology of Acts* (Grand Rapids: Eerdmans, 1998), ch. 24, and the literature there.

18. Turner, *Power,* passim (and esp. ch. 13)

or the "word" — all seem to be based on flimsy exegetical evidence and/or lead to eccentric theologies.[19]

But *could* Luke have provided the answer Dunn offers? Menzies replies to the contrary: the Spirit in Acts is merely *Amtscharisma,* prophetic empowering for mission/witness. This claim rests partly on his understanding of the very nature of the Spirit of prophecy and partly on his understanding of the transitional passages of Luke-Acts. For convenience, we shall consider these in reverse order.

II. The Spirit at the *Literary* Center of Luke-Acts

What light do the end of Luke and the beginning of Acts shed, especially the redactional transitional passages (Luke 24.44-52; Acts 1.1-11)? Menzies recognizes in them a number of the key allusions to Deutero-Isaiah and to Israel's restoration, including the references to Isa. 49.6 in Luke 24.47 and Acts 1.8. But he takes these in their co-text (i.e., the literary *text* of Luke and Acts, viewed as a united discourse) simply to mean that the church will be endowed with the Spirit of prophecy as the Isaianic servant *to witness.* He understands the Baptist's promise (Luke 3.16-17) to mean that the messiah, mightily empowered by the Spirit, will cleanse Israel simply by sifting her (cf. Isa. 4.4), that is, by promoting belief and allegiance to himself in those who become gathered into the church, while leaving the unbelieving chaff outside this "Israel of restoration," awaiting destruction. Jesus then is to fulfill the Baptist's promise more comprehensively than hitherto through the apostles' Spirit-inspired witness (Acts 1.5-8).

There is of course an important measure of truth in this construction. The apostolic witness continues radically to sift/divide Israel, and it indeed provides a light to the nations (cf. Paul's use of Isa. 49.6 at Acts 13.47). But the division itself is only the initial part of the restoration of Israel, and cannot explain Luke's understanding of the Baptist's promise. Luke has Jesus say, "Before many days *you* will *be* baptized with the Holy Spirit" (specifically referring to Pentecost: 1.5). As the second person plural passive refers to the apostles, not Israel, this cannot mean the apostles will sift Israel (requiring an active), nor can Luke possibly mean that the Twelve themselves will be sifted. He means instead either that they will be "deluged/overwhelmed with Spirit" or, more probably, that they will be "cleansed/purified by the Spirit" (and the two ideas are not necessarily exclusive). The latter fits better (a) with the Baptist's original contrast of water and Spirit in 3.16 (the water cleansed, not overwhelmed); (b) with

19. See Turner, *Power,* pp. 418-27.

the following interpretive logion about the messiah *cleansing* his threshing floor (3.17);[20] and (c) with the Cornelius story where the descent of the Spirit evokes Peter's memory of the Baptist's promise (11.15), is interpreted co-textually as evidence of the cleansing of the hearts of these Gentiles (15.8-9; most probably an allusion to Ezek. 36.25-27), and provides the rationale for adding them by baptism to the messianic restoration of Israel.[21]

One of the key Isaianic New Exodus allusions that Menzies fails to treat, however, is Luke's use of the language "Spirit/power from on high" (Luke 24.49; Acts 1.8), a clear allusion to Isa. 32.15. The point of both Isa. 32.15-20 and the related 44.3-5 is that Israel will remain in her exile/desert condition until God pours his Spirit on her to transform her in righteousness, peace, and life, just as his gift of rain transforms the parched wilderness into flourishing existence. *So Luke appears to be pointing readers back to Isaiah himself for any answer to the question of by what power Israel's New Exodus eschatological restoration/salvation becomes richly present to the post-ascension community.* If he focuses primarily on the actions of the Spirit of prophecy inspiring the witness and preaching which extends the Gospel through the then known world, that is not at the expense of viewing it as the transforming power of God in the community (a point made well by Wenk) and in the individual.

Other factors in the broader literary center of Luke-Acts point in the same direction. Luke has carefully prepared his reader to understand that Jesus' death will be the blood of the new covenant (22.20; assuming the longer reading), the Passover is soon to be fulfilled in the kingdom of God (22.14-16), and the Twelve are soon to rule over the twelve tribes of restored Israel (22.29-30). All this suggests an imminent intensification of God's messianic reign; accordingly (23.42), the co-crucified criminal understands that Jesus is soon to come into his kingdom, while in 24.26 Jesus' death/resurrection is nothing less than his (prophesied) "entry into glory." But given that the ascension will remove Jesus from the scene, how are these hopes to be fulfilled? Acts 1–2 essentially provides the striking answer that Jesus begins to exercise his rule as messiah and Lord — with its correlate in Israel's restoration, transformation, refreshment (cf. 3.19), and mission — *from the heavenly throne at God's right hand* rather than from one in Jerusalem: Acts 2.32-36 (answering to Luke 1.32-33). But since this last passage is Peter's interpretation of the Pentecost event, the reader will

20. Cf. *Power,* ch. 4 and cf. pp. 341-47. The Baptist thought the sifting of Israel was virtually complete through his own ministry: the messiah comes climactically to deal with the resultant divisions, restoring the one and destroying the other. But Luke knows things turned out rather differently (even leading the Baptist to doubt: 7.18-23). Menzies (*Spirit,* pp. 93-96) unfortunately misrepresents my position when he simply conflates the two different perspectives.

21. For some of the subtleties, see my *Power,* pp. 378-88.

surely assume that this reign is achieved precisely by pouring out from the Father the gift of the Spirit of prophecy promised by Joel (Acts 2.33, cf. 16-21) and Isaiah. The reader will be strengthened in this understanding both by the mutually interpretive oscillation between Kingdom and Spirit in Acts 1.1-8,[22] and, even more importantly, by the Pentecost account as a whole, with its rich tapestry of Sinai imagery.[23]

We may agree with Gunkel and his heirs when they insist that Luke does not explicitly attribute the immediately following transformation in the communities to the Spirit. But given the above, why would he need to say it *explicitly:* it would be assumed. And Judaism already understood the Spirit to be the basis of transformed life, especially in and through the Spirit of prophecy.

III. Issues of Disagreement concerning the "Spirit of Prophecy"

While virtually all Lucan scholars agree that Luke understands the Spirit as the "Spirit of prophecy," this term of convenience (*not* found in Luke) is being used in quite different ways by the protagonists. As we have seen, Dunn uses the term to refer to some broad and inclusive Old Testament promises of the Spirit, not merely Joel 2.28-32.[24] For him, this gift is only the "Spirit of prophecy" in the sense that Luke has a special (but not exclusive) interest in the Spirit's relatively dramatic and concrete workings, especially in various forms of inspired speech. By contrast, Menzies (following Schweizer and Haya-Prats) understands the term "Spirit of prophecy" as defining the *very essence* of the gift — it is simply prophetic *Amtscharisma* of inspired speech, charismatic wisdom, and revelation; neither more nor less.[25] He argues that this is how virtually *all* Jewish in-

22. Cf. Turner, *Power,* pp. 294-303.

23. Menzies denies such imagery on the grounds that (a) the purported parallels in Philo and *Targum Pseudo-Jonathan* are not unique to Sinai but more general theophanic language, and (b) there is no mention of Moses and the law (*Spirit,* p. 98). But I think he misses too many of the allusions. If one were to ask a contemporary Jew what significant moment in salvation history contains the following elements: "There is an assembly of the people of Israel. There is a mysterious noise from heaven, wind and a rush of fire. The leader of Israel has ascended on high to receive a foundational gift from God, and he then gives it to the people. God's word is divided to the nations and begins to reach to the end of the earth. The day all this happens is the feast of weeks?" the confident answer would be "Moses at Sinai." But these elements are all in Acts 2. And Luke, of course, is not describing Sinai itself but an event he thinks transcends it. Cf. Turner, *Power,* ch. 10.

24. "Baptism," pp. 9, 21-22.

25. Cf., more recently, Stronstad, *Prophethood;* but cf. Max Turner, "Does Luke Believe Reception of the 'Spirit of Prophecy' Makes All 'Prophets'? Inviting Dialogue with Roger Stronstad," *Journal of the European Pentecostal Theological Association* 20 (2000): 3-24.

terpreters of our period took it (excepting only Wisdom, Philo, and 1QH),[26] and that those Old Testament passages on which Dunn wishes to base a broader, more soteriological understanding of the Spirit (such as Isa. 44.3; Ezek. 36.26-27, etc.) were in fact consistently interpreted by first-century Judaism in the narrower and exclusive sense of the "Spirit of prophecy."

From a slightly different perspective again, in my own work I have used the term "Spirit of prophecy" merely functionally to designate a pneumatology for which five types of closely associated charismata are *prototypical* (i.e. *normally* associated with the gift): charismatic revelation, charismatic wisdom, invasive prophetic and invasive doxological speech, and (less certainly) deeds of power.[27] It will be noted that this definition — also based primarily on a discussion of Jewish interpretation of the Old Testament — is both flexible (allowing many different configurations of the "Spirit of prophecy") and neutral with respect to whether the gift includes soteriological functions. For example, 1QH, *Joseph and Aseneth*, Paul, and John each in very different ways evince a soteriological pneumatology, but they still regard the Spirit as a form of the "Spirit of prophecy"; for each it is largely through the prototypical charismata (especially revelation and wisdom) that the Spirit is experienced as the presence of the God of salvation.[28]

Menzies is right to claim that the majority of Jewish texts treat the Spirit as a *donum superadditum* — but that is simply because that majority relates to figures within the biblical history of Israel, or to contemporaries in an age when the Spirit was considered the special endowment of the few, and even as a reward for righteousness (rather than a cause of it). But Menzies does not take into sufficient consideration two related factors: (1) in a great many Jewish texts the Spirit of prophecy *is a transformative power whose revelation and wisdom stimulate and enable a new quality of spiritual life* before, and intimacy with, God;[29] and (2) new covenant and/or eschatological existence was anticipated as

26. *Spirit*, p. 76.

27. See esp. *Power*, chs. 3–5.

28. For Qumran and Paul, see Turner, *Spirit*, pp. 16-19 and chs. 7, 8, and 15; for *Joseph and Aseneth* see Moyer V. Hubbard, *New Creation in Paul's Letters and Thought* (Cambridge: Cambridge University Press, 2002), ch. 4; for John see esp. Cornelis Bennema, *The Power of Saving Wisdom: An Investigation of Spirit and Wisdom in Relation to the Soteriology of the Fourth Gospel* (Tübingen: Mohr, 2002).

29. These include the LXX, targums of Isa. 11.1-2, Ezek. 36.25-27, and Zech. 12.10; regular rabbinic interpretations of Ezek. 36.27 (*b. Ber.* 31b; *b. Suk.* 52b; *Tanḥuma* (Buber) Addition to חקת; *Deut. Rab.* 6.14; *Num. Rab.* 9.49; *Midr. Ps.* 14.6), but also *Tg. Ps.-J. Gen.* 6.3; Philo (numerous passages, but esp., e.g., *Gig.* 55; *Virt.* 217; *Somn.* 2.252; cf. *Op. Mund.* 144); Sir. 39.6; Wis. 9.17(?); *Test. Jud.* 24.2-3; *Test. Simeon* 4.4; *Test. Benj.* 8.1-3; *Test. Levi* 2.3B7-8, 14; 18.7-8; *Jos. and As.* 4.4; 8.9(10); 19.1; *1 Enoch* 49.2-3; 61.11-12; 62.1-2; 67.10; *Ps. Sol.* 17.37; 1QH (numerous passages);

a special form of such "higher life," so that what a Jew might have regarded as the Spirit's "second blessing," and occasional enhancement of life, in *this* age could be expected to become virtually a norm and *prerequisite* for the fuller righteousness/life of the age to come. It is hardly surprising that Ezek. 36.25-27 was regularly read this way,[30] and much Jewish tradition saw the messianic figure of Isa. 11.1-2 as a prime exemplar of such. The Targum renders the passage: "And a *king* shall come forth from the *sons* of Jesse, and *the Messiah* shall *be exalted* from *the sons of* his *sons.* And upon him shall rest *the* spirit *of prophecy,* a spirit of wisdom and understanding, a spirit of counsel and might, a spirit of knowledge and the fear of the LORD." Here the Spirit is not merely the messiah's *Amtscharisma* — though the Spirit is certainly that — but *also the basis of his redoubtable righteousness and intimate life with God.* It is this combination that informs the varied "messianic" portraits in *1 Enoch* 49:2-3; 62:1-2 (where the Spirit is actually called "Spirit of righteousness"!); *Ps. Sol.* 17:37; 18:7; 1QSb 5.25; 4Q215 iv.4; 4QpIsa[a] 7-10 iii.15-29; 4QMess ar (= 4Q536) 3 i.4-11; *Test. Levi* 18.7-8, and so on.

Given the wide diversity of Jewish material we have just referred to, it is rather surprising to be told that because Luke seeks to recover the Jewish concept of the Spirit of prophecy he would not be able to attribute the transformed life of the communities to the Holy Spirit. One would rather expect the opposite. And, of course, his allusion to Isa. 32.15 at Acts 1.8 offers strong confirmation of this, especially when we note that he has already given this same Isaianic Spirit/"power from on high" decisive ethical import when he presents it as the grounds of the Son of God's own unique holiness (Luke 1.35).[31]

1QS4.21-22; 1QSb 5.24-25; 4Q504, etc. The main texts are discussed in Turner, *Power,* ch. 5; but see now also John R. Levison, *The Spirit in First-Century Judaism* (Leiden: Brill, 1997).

30. In addition to the texts specifically interpreting Ezekiel 36 (see previous note), note also especially *Jub.* 1.22-25. Menzies thinks that rabbinical Judaism understood Ezekiel to mean that the decisive soteriological event is performed by the removal of the stony heart/evil *yeṣer.* The Spirit of prophecy is then given as a *donum superadditum.* This reading seems improbable; rather, the two complement each other to ensure a new life of radical obedience. See *Power,* pp. 129-32.

31. Luke 1.35 alludes to both Isa. 32.15 and Exod. 40.35: here Jesus is to be the very impress of the 'power from on high' that will bring about Israel's awaited salvation/restoration; cf. *Power,* pp. 153-62. Menzies wonders why I am willing to concede that Luke portrays Jesus' baptismal reception of the Spirit almost exclusively as an empowering for mission, yet affirm that the Pentecostal gift is not merely that, but soteriological too (*Spirit,* p. 92). The simple answer is that the disciples have no counterpart to Luke 1.35, except through the gift at Pentecost interpreted in the light of Isa. 32.15.

IV. Differences concerning the Intended Beneficiaries of the Spirit of Prophecy

For Menzies, "the Spirit comes upon the disciples to equip them for their prophetic vocation (i.e., for their role as "witnesses"). The disciples receive the Spirit *not* as the essential bond by which they (each individual) are linked to God; indeed, *not primarily for themselves.* Rather, as the driving force behind their witness to Christ, *the disciples receive the Spirit for others.*"[32] Again, "The Spirit . . . is not given principally for the benefit of the recipient; rather, it is directed towards others."[33] This latter quotation is part of a deliberate modification of his earlier somewhat misleading claim that the Spirit in Luke-Acts is "exclusively" empowering for mission; a modification that more explicitly recognizes the community-oriented dimension of the Spirit's work. If Menzies' statement were simply a way of saying that the majority of Luke's references relate to public actions inspired by the Spirit — but that he allows that the Spirit may be anticipated to have a profoundly transforming effect on the *internal* life of the individual who receives it too — then we could agree. But Menzies appears to wish to deny that the Spirit is necessary to sustain the individual's own spiritual life; for him reception of the Spirit is *not* necessary as the source of the believer's "righteousness, intimate fellowship with and knowledge of God,"[34] and *not* "the essential bond by which they (each individual) are linked to God," (indeed his whole point has consistently been that it is wrong merely to claim that Luke has some "special emphasis" on the Spirit as empowering for mission, while also allowing a broader view). But this is puzzling. One would have thought that "intimate fellowship with and knowledge of God" required some self-manifesting presence of God/Christ and involved ongoing contextualized spiritual understandings of the gospel, spilling over into joyful doxology. But that is exactly what we would expect the prototypical gifts of the Spirit of prophecy to afford, and intimacy with God is precisely what Judaism regularly attributes to the Spirit![35] And if the Spirit is *not* the relational link between the believer and the Lord, then what is? And why are two *different* means required for essentially the same functions?

32. *Development,* p. 207 (my italics).

33. *Spirit,* p. 90.

34. *Spirit,* p. 89.

35. See perhaps esp. Philo, *Virt.* 217; *Op. Mund.* 144; 1QH 9.32; 12.11-13; 14.12b-13; 16.6-7, 11b-12; and the traditions based on Isa. 11.1-2. The widespread hope that at the end all will have the Spirit of prophecy probably reflects a general understanding that the prophets have intimate knowledge of God.

As we have seen, Menzies hints that the risen Lord may perform soteriological roles (such as forgiveness) "directly," on the basis that this role is attributed to him without qualification in Acts 5.32. Similarly one might find evidence that the Lord gives wisdom to his persecuted disciples "immediately" on the basis of Luke 21.15; heals as-yet-unbelievers (on the basis of Acts 9.34), and so forth. But Luke only means that the enthroned Lord is the *author* of such activities, not that he is "directly" omnipresent and pan-active, apart from the Spirit. Initial assurance of his forgiveness is mediated through the Spirit-anointed preaching or teaching of his disciples, not by the Lord directly, and that would suggest that it is the same Spirit — received in conversion-initiation — who brings ongoing assurance of such. Similarly healings in Acts so regularly comes through his Spirit-filled spokesmen that it is difficult to believe that Luke attributes them to Christ *directly,* rather than to the power of the Spirit. And, clearly, despite the impression Luke 21.15 may give, Luke knows that Jesus does not himself come to the persecuted disciple to give him the words of his defense: Christ does that "mediately" through the Holy Spirit (cf. Luke 12.10; Acts 6.10), now acting as the Spirit of Christ (cf. Acts 16.7).

It is perhaps just *possible* that Luke believed that God and/or the risen Lord gave the soteriologically oriented gifts of self-revelation and transforming spiritual wisdom and inspired the believers' joyful worship, while the Spirit gave a perfectly congruent set of gifts whenever the purpose was missiological instead. But the more obvious solution is that the Spirit of prophecy is as much for the benefit of the believers who receive it as it is for the community and mission in which they serve.

Conclusion

I suspect Professor Dunn understood better than many of his critics that for Luke "salvation" was the dynamic *experience* of God's promised transforming and empowering reign. He understood that with the ascension of Christ, the gift of the Spirit would become the key to the ongoing presence and *intensification* of the salvation/kingdom of God which the disciples began to experience through Jesus' ministry. In that sense he saw that for Luke, as much as for Paul, the *whole* of Christian life — not merely the church's mission — was essentially what we might broadly call "charismatic." That, he argued, was *why* Luke anticipated that the Spirit of prophecy would be given within the somewhat elastic process of conversion-initiation. And Dunn's still remains a more satisfying explanation of that anticipation than those which claim that Luke thought converts should receive the Spirit as soon as possible merely because they need the gift to empower their mission. Luke does not think the majority of converts become actively involved in verbal witness/mission to outsiders;[36] he does, however, believe that all need the empowering presence of God to participate in the vibrant life of the Israel of restoration.

36. Cf. Max Turner, "Every Believer as a Witness in Acts? — In Dialogue with John Michael Penney," *Ashland Theological Journal* 30 (1998): 57-71.

x The Role of Charismatic and Noncharismatic Factors in Determining Paul's Movements in Acts

Robert Banks

Throughout his scholarly career, the recipient of this Festschrift has exhibited a continuing interest in the presence and significance of charismatic phenomena in earliest Christianity. Here I would like to focus on a particular aspect of this issue, one he has considered but not systematically explored. How, according to Luke, did Paul and his colleagues make decisions about where to evangelize and plant churches? What inclined him to go to one place instead of another, take one route rather than an alternative, and stay in one locale for a longer or shorter period? In general, Dunn regards Luke as being "a valuable but undiscriminating guide" in asking questions about the religious experience of the early Christians, "giving full attention to the ecstatic and eye-catching manifestations of the Spirit, and too little attention to others." [1]

I will first offer four general comments: (1) In the long-standing debate over the historical reliability of Acts, I am inclined to side with those who have a high estimate of its trustworthiness and a strong inclination to view Luke as the author. As I do not have the space to argue this in relation to individual passages, I will give supportive arguments in the literature below.[2] (2) In regard to

1. J. D. G. Dunn, *Jesus and the Spirit: A Study of the Religious and Charismatic Experience of Jesus and the First Christians as Related in the New Testament* (London: SCM, 1975), p. 195.

2. For the most detailed defense of "the general reliability" of Luke's narrative and for its "ostensible chronological framework," through "the details so intricately and so often unintentionally woven into that narrative," see especially C. J. Hemer, *The Book of Acts in the Setting of Hellenistic History* (Winona Lake, Ind.: Eisenbrauns, 1990). He indicates the impressive degree of specific local, as well as general and specialized, knowledge the author displays in his account of Paul's major journeys (pp. 101-58), as well as other historical corroboration (pp. 183-89). From all

Luke's general view of the Spirit, there is a scholarly consensus that the Spirit is the primary agent legitimating the mission, that in Acts it is largely the Spirit's prophetic work, which involves an "empowering for witness," that dominates, and that Luke shows little interest in the Spirit as the source of spiritual, moral, or religious renewal in the individual as such.[3] (3) According to a major study of the broader and distinctively Lucan theme of God's providential plan in Acts, God is the primary actor who directs the Gentile mission, granting epiphanies that guide the events of history and fulfilling prophecies and foreordained necessity in the missionary deeds of the apostles.[4] (4) Though the journey motif in Acts (13:1–21:26) as well as the Gospels, which amounts to approximately a third of both volumes, has a basis in his traditions, Luke has heightened its visibility and importance.[5] In the light of these considerations, what are we to make of the specific decisions the apostles make about the direction and destination of their missionary endeavors?

I. Guidance of the Apostles in Acts

More than a century ago, William Ramsay concluded that Luke finds "the justification of all Paul's innovations on missionary enterprise in the guiding hand

---

this he concludes that Luke's composition of the "we-passages' in the volume and authorship of the overall work are "not unlikely" (p. 414). In many respects this follows the earlier conclusions of A. Harnack, *The Acts of the Apostles* (London: Williams and Norgate, 1909), nearly a century earlier. This is different from the conclusion of G. Lüdemann, *Early Christianity according to the Traditions in Acts* (London: SCM, 1989), which appeared too late to be included in Hemer's work. Since he does not regard Luke as a witness of any of the events described in Acts, and sees him as mainly dependent on tradition, Lüdemann finds only an intermittent historical basis for Paul's movements and at points detects Lucan invention and chronological manipulation. He also rejects any miraculous or supernatural reports. A carefully reasoned and comprehensive challenge to Lüdemann's conclusions has since come from R. Riesner, *Paul's Early Period: Chronology, Mission Strategy, Theology* (Grand Rapids: Eerdmans, 1998), especially in the sections on the sequence (pp. 137-227), stages (pp. 229-323), and pace (pp. 307-17) of Paul's journeys respectively.

3. See M. Turner, "The 'Spirit of Prophecy' as the Power of Israel's Restoration and Witness," in *Witness to the Gospel: The Theology of Acts*, ed. I. H. Marshall and D. Peterson (Grand Rapids: Eerdmans, 1998), pp. 328-30.

4. John Squires, *The Plan of God in Luke-Acts* (Cambridge: Cambridge University Press, 1993), pp. 2-3, who throughout considers similarities and differences with phenomena described in Hellenistic writings.

5. So I. H. Marshall, *Luke: Historian and Theologian* (Exeter: Paternoster, 1970), especially pp. 148-53. The most recent analysis of the role of travel in Acts, which focuses on literary rather than historical concerns, is in D. Marguerat, *The First Christian Historian: Writing the Acts of the Apostles* (Cambridge Cambridge University Press, 2002), pp. 231-56. While he finds many parallels with relevant Graeco-Roman sources, he also finds many distinctive elements.

of God."[6] Is this the case and, if so, in what sense? Does Luke provide only a general justification of God's role in Paul's movements or particular expressions of that for each significant stage of his journeys? When divine involvement is mentioned, is particular reference made to the role of the Father, Jesus, or the Spirit? Whatever the case, how is their involvement described — the providential arrangement of circumstances, personal revelation, a form of charismatic direction, an unusual chain of events, spiritual conviction, or a miraculous intervention? Or do we find reference to factors of what might be termed a more "natural" or "human" kind that Luke does not connect to divine activity, such as patterns of transport, climatic conditions, strategic planning, or common sense? When guidance came, was it to individuals, groups, or churches, or some combination of these? Is it correct to refer to the "extraordinary combination of strategic planning and keen sensitiveness to the guiding hand of the Spirit of God, however that guidance was conveyed — by prophetic utterance, inspired prompting, or the overruling of external circumstances"?[7] Did Luke, then, have an overarching pneumatological interpretation of the different types of divine activity outlined above, or did he theologically distinguish between them, and did personal planning fall into a different category? These are the kinds of questions to keep in mind as we track through the main sections in Acts recording Paul's apostolic movements.

Interestingly, Luke's preface to all Paul's journeys (Acts 13:1ff.) begins with a clear reference to the Spirit. The latter declares through the prophets and teachers in the church at Antioch that Barnabas and Saul should be set aside "for the work to which I have called them" (Acts 13:2). This is confirmed and sealed through fasting and prayer, along with the laying on of hands (Acts 13:3).[8] We note here that the Spirit speaks *a word from God* (Acts 13:2). Presumably this takes place through one of the prophets who are mentioned. This word is *directive:* "set apart"; it is *specific:* "Barnabas and Paul." It is *purposive:* "for the work"; and, unlike the self-effacing character of the Spirit in John, it is *self-referential:* "for me."[9] It is also *evaluated,* through "fasting and prayer." The

6. *Paul the Traveller and Roman Citizen* (London: Hodder & Stoughton, 1898), p. 140.

7. As does F. F. Bruce, *The Book of the Acts* (rev. ed.; London: Marshall, Morgan and Scott, 1998), p. 306.

8. As H. Conzelmann, *A Commentary on the Acts of the Apostles* (Philadelphia: Fortress, 1987), p. 99, notes, this is more a blessing than an ordaining of the two being set aside, and it does not suggest a difference in rank between them and others.

9. On the Spirit as a major actor in the account of the mission in Acts, see W. H. Shepherd, *The Narrative Function of the Holy Spirit as a Character in Acts* (Atlanta: Scholars Press, 1994), especially pp. 209-38 and now J. Hur, *A Dynamic Reading of the Holy Spirit in Luke-Acts* (Sheffield: Sheffield Academic Press, 2001).

mission to which these men are called (cf. Acts 13:41; 14:26; 15:38) is clearly an aspect of the Spirit's activity. As Dunn suggests, there follow not so much three missionary journeys as three stages of a "sustained mission around the coasts of the Aegean Sea," beginning under the superintendence of Antioch but changing partway into an independent activity.[10]

Initial Journey (Acts 13:4–14:28)

At the start of the journey itself we have a further reference to the Spirit sending Barnabas and Saul on their way (Acts 13:4). Though sometimes regarded as simply another way of describing the prophecy just uttered, use of the verb ἐκπέμπω suggests something more, echoing the use of ἀπολύω to describe the action of the prophets and teachers in the previous verse but associating the Spirit with this act of commissioning.[11] As the story continues, however, it is neither stated nor inferred that the Spirit indicated the direction and destination of their journey.[12] The two missionaries headed toward Cyprus by way of Antioch's port, Seleucia, half a day's walk from the city, and the island's most direct entry port, Salamis (Acts 13:5). Though Luke does not tell us specifically why they chose this route, given Barnabas's leadership at this stage, his origin in Cyprus (Acts 4:36), and his sense of strong obligation to his homeland (Acts 15:39), beginning in Cyprus (part of which was even visible from the mainland) makes good sense. The presence of Jewish synagogues there (Acts 13:5),[13] and a few Christians (Acts 11:19-20 and later 21:16),[14] could also have been factors in the decision. Though the duo travelled from one end of the island to the other, the two places in which they spent most time were the leading trade (Salamis) and civic (Paphos) centers. In Luke's brief description of their movements on the island, the Spirit is mentioned only in connection with Paul's encounter with the sorcerer Elymas, whom he describes as "a child of the devil" (Acts 13:10) and prophetically predicts is "going to be blind" (Acts 13:11). In view of Luke's penchant for parallelism, his reference to a confronta-

10. So, rightly, J. D. G. Dunn, *The Acts of the Apostles* (Peterborough: Epworth, 1996), pp. 171, 213.

11. Compare the translation by Bruce, *Book of Acts,* p. 246.

12. Cf. W. J. Conybeare and J. S. Howson, *The Life and Epistles of St. Paul* (Grand Rapids: Eerdmans, 1856), p. 110.

13. Cf. 1 Macc. 15:23 and Philo, *Ad Gaium* 282.

14. Though E. Haenchen, *The Acts of the Apostles: A Commentary* (Philadelphia: Westminster, 1971), p. 402 regards this as an incorrect inference.

tion with evil powers immediately after mention of empowerment by the Spirit could well be intentional.[15]

We then read that the two missionaries, plus some other companions now mentioned for the first time, sail on to Perga, the seat of government, in Pamphylia (Acts 13:13). Though, according to Munck, "the journey might have been guided by the Holy Spirit,"[16] as he notes, Luke gives no explanation as to why they chose this course. There were significant racial, commercial, and political connections between these two ports, and presumably Barnabas and Paul would also have known that Jews had settled in areas to which Pamphylia was the gateway. However, Luke's lack of reference to any preaching in Perga itself suggests that their real destination lay elsewhere.

They travel north to Antioch in Pisidia (Acts 13:14).[17] While Luke gives no reason for their taking this route, commentators have suggested a number of possibilities. Was it due to Paul's falling ill and his need to repair his health in the mountains? Did they reach Perga at a time when, because of the weather, many customarily made this journey? Had Sergius Paulus, during their time in Paphos, mentioned political links he would have had with the Roman colony there? More simply the answer probably lies in the recent discovery, well known to Luke, that the paved Roman road, the *Via Sebaste,* started at Perga, went up to Antioch, and then curved to Iconium and beyond. This made it "the easiest, most convenient and perhaps the only route into Asia Minor,"[18] and explains the course of both the outward and return parts of the journey. When the two travellers reach Antioch, they continue their practice of going to the synagogue (Acts 13:14), where, following Paul's preaching, there is an encouraging response (Acts 13:44-45 and 48). Though this leads to their persecution and expulsion, the believers they leave behind are said to be "filled with joy and the Holy Spirit" (Acts 13:52).

There is no reference to divine guidance of any kind concerning the three days' journey from Antioch to Iconium.[19] This took the two preachers further along the *Via Sebaste* into an outlying city in the same district that was the center of the surrounding region and possessed a synagogue (Acts 14:2). Luke refers

15. So L. T. Johnson, *The Acts of the Apostles* (Collegeville, Minn.: Liturgical Press/Michael Glazier, 1992), p. 373.

16. J. Munck, *The Acts of the Apostles* (New York: Doubleday, 1967), p. 122.

17. Though, as Hemer, *Acts,* p. 110, notes, at the time this was really part of Phrygia, even if it guarded the Pisidian border.

18. D. French, "Acts and the Roman Roads of Asia Minor," in *The Book of Acts in Its First-Century Setting,* vol. 2: *The Book of Acts in Its Graeco-Roman Setting,* ed. D. W. J. Gill and C. Gempf (Grand Rapids: Eerdmans, 1994), pp. 55-56.

19. For Dunn, *Acts,* p. 186, the absence of detail and time notes in this section raises questions about the quality of Luke's sources for this part of the journey.

to their boldness of speech and to miraculous signs and wonders (Acts 14:3), no doubt inferring if not explicitly noting their source in the Spirit. Fleeing from a Gentile and Jewish plot to injure them, Barnabas and Paul head further down the road to the Roman colony of Lystra, about a day's walk away, and then on to the frontier city of Derbe, in Lycaonia.[20] This leads them for the first time into more remote places where there are no synagogues.

At this point the group decides to retrace some of its steps rather than traveling on through the Taurus mountains to their starting point in Syria. Traveling further would have brought them into non-Roman territory where they had less protection.[21] The explanation for returning over the route they had already come lay, as Luke tells us, in their pastoral concern for "strengthening the disciples and encouraging them to remain true to the faith" (Acts 14:22). This involved confirming elders in the churches they had founded, with prayer, fasting, and commendation to the Lord (Acts 14:23). Then they headed back down to Perga, this time preaching in the city, and went on to Attalia, from where they sailed back to their starting point in Antioch (Acts 14:24-25). As their work was now "complete(d)" (Acts 14:26), and God's purpose at the beginning of the journey to take the message to the Gentiles fulfilled (Acts 14:27), they decided to settle down there for a time (Acts 14:28). All in all, as I. Howard Marshall observes, apart from their initial identifying and commissioning by the Spirit "there is no reference to spiritual guidance at any point on this missionary tour,"[22] at least in the sense of any direct external or internal divine indication.

2. *Follow-Up Journey (Acts 15:36–18:22)*

Sometime after their visit to the Jerusalem Council on behalf of the church at Antioch — within which they refer to God's gift of the Spirit to the Gentiles (Acts 15:8) — Paul suggests to Barnabas that the two of them "go back and visit [or inspect][23] the brothers in all the towns where we preached the word of God and see how they are doing" (Acts 15:36). A secondary motive is also mentioned, that of delivering "the decisions reached by the apostles and elders in Jerusalem" (Acts 16:4). However, Paul and Barnabas go their separate ways, and Silas

20. The phrase "and to the surrounding countryside" probably refers to the outskirts of these cities. Otherwise this marks the first time Paul works outside larger or smaller urban areas, which just could be the case, as the urban areas themselves, uncharacteristically for him, contain no synagogues.

21. First noted by Ramsay, *Paul*, p. 112, who argued that for this reason Paul never saw such places as falling within his missionary responsibility.

22. Marshall, *Acts*, p. 220.

23. So Johnson, *Acts*, p. 282.

joins the group, so that it is now Paul who is chiefly responsible for determining their itinerary. Without explaining why, Luke reports their taking a land route through Syria and Cilicia directly to Derbe and Lystra. This may have been through the Cilician Gates, or it could have been a more westerly route.[24] Here Timothy was also drawn into the team, and then they moved on, most probably to Iconium (Acts 16:2-3).

They move on to Phrygia and Galatia, the exact territory envisaged here having occasioned much debate. Most probably we should follow the so-called South Galatian hypothesis for determining its location. Instead of continuing from here, as one would expect, to the east coast of the Aegean with its main metropolis Ephesus,[25] they found themselves "kept by the Holy Spirit from preaching the word in the province of Asia" (Acts 16:6). We are not told how this took place. However, it is the first reference to the Spirit's role in guiding the apostle's movements, even if, both here and in the next verse, the Spirit forbids only heading in a direction: no positive indication is given as to where they should go. They then seem to have assumed that God wanted them to head north toward the Greek cities on the Bosporus, a quite natural direction to take given its highly civilized character and Jewish settlements. Riesner suggests a different reason, that Paul was influenced by the prophetic promise in Isaiah 66:19-20 that God's glory would extend to Asis (Lydia), Mysia (Meshech), and Bithynia (Tubal).[26] Whatever the case, "when they came to the border of Mysia, they tried to enter Bithynia — the Spirit of Jesus would not allow them to" (Acts 16:7). The attribution to Jesus here indicates that he continues to play an active role in the apostolic story (cf. 7:56; 9:5). It probably also suggests here a prophetic utterance given in his name (cf. generally Acts 20:23; 21:4, 11), perhaps through either Paul or Barnabas, who are themselves prophets (Acts 13:1; 15:32).[27] In neither reference to the Spirit's activity is any reason given for the prohibition.[28]

24. See further French, "Roads," p. 56, who explains that the dating for the roads through this area at that time is still unclear. Once off his previous route beyond Iconium, Paul would almost certainly have been traveling on unpaved roads and tracks.

25. B. Witherington III, *The Book of Acts: A Socio-Rhetorical Commentary* (Grand Rapids: Eerdmans, 1997) p. 473, following J. Murphy-O'Connor, "On the Road and on the Sea with St. Paul," *BR* 1, no. 2 (1985): 6, suggests that traveling in this area at that time of the year may have involved delays. But the main, if implicit, emphasis seems to lie elsewhere, on focusing Paul's options beyond Asia.

26. Riesner, *Paul,* pp. 251ff.

27. Dunn, *Acts,* p. 217, interprets these two incidences of the Spirit as "an inner conviction" (217) and "common conviction or sense" (p. 218) respectively, but certainly for the second this seems unlikely. See more generally "The Spirit and Jesus," in *The Christ and the Spirit: Collected Essays,* vol. 2: *Pneumatology* (Edinburgh: T&T Clark, 1998), pp. 329-42.

28. F. Scott Spencer, *Acts* (Sheffield: Sheffield Academic Press, 1997), p. 162. To speculate,

Instead they took a route, probably passing through rather than by Mysia,[29] whose details are unknown, that brought them to Troas, an important center in the imperial system of communications, on the coast (Acts 16:8). Here the previous prophecy is completed by Paul's vision of "the man from Macedonia" pleading with him to "come over . . . and help us" (Acts 16:9). Though the author of the vision is not designated, since in the following comment it is said that "God had called us" to preach the gospel in this new setting (Acts 16:10), it is most likely God rather than Jesus or the Spirit who is in mind.[30] Though some have suggested that the vision came in a dream, this is not explicitly stated[31] (and, given the "we-passage" starting here from Acts 16:12, possibly Luke was the person who appeared).[32] It is through a vision (which does not mention God but is clearly understood to be divine in origin) that information is given about the direction the missionaries should take, though it is only a region, not city or cities, that is identified. Luke, however, presents it in a rather understated way (minus the usual supernatural accompaniments of a vision) and stresses the role of the team in evaluating and confirming the vision's message (Acts 16:10).[33] The wider significance of this passage is that, according to Luke, both the beginning of Paul's missionary work and this critical shift of focus from Asia to Europe require more than the usual decision-making approaches.[34] In this section, which William Ramsay described as "in many respects the most remarkable paragraph in Acts,"[35] divine action is mentioned no fewer than three times in four verses.

From Troas Paul sails across the northern tip of the Aegean for the port city of Neapolis and immediately on to Philippi, the leading city in that part of Macedonia and a Roman colony. Interesting and perhaps indicative of Paul's intentions is the fact that these two features of the city are expressly mentioned by Luke, the first only here in his writings (Acts 16:12). On the other hand, it would be hard to bypass Philippi, which was the gateway to Macedonia.

---

as French, "Roman Roads," p. 57 does, that this prohibition by the Spirit was a periphrasis for discretion, circumspection, trepidation, or even irresolution in the face of possible trouble with the Roman authorities in either north or west Asia is unnecessary.

29. Cf. C. K. Barrett, *Commentary on Acts XV-XXVIII* (London: T&T Clark, 1998), 2:770.

30. Three of the other five references to visions in Acts are from "the Lord" (Acts 9:10; 10:3; 18:9; 22:17), and two are associated with "an angel of God" (Acts 10:3; 27:23).

31. As J. Calvin, *Acts* (Wheaton: Crossway, 1995), p. 276, long ago pointed out.

32. As Dunn, *Acts,* p. 218, and many others have suggested.

33. On both of these, see further Porter, *Paul,* pp. 51-52.

34. It is better to see the turning point as here rather than, as with M. Goulder, *Type and History in Acts* (London: SPCK, 1964, p. 105), in the Spirit's preparation for this in the preceding verses.

35. Ramsay, *Paul,* p. 198.

Though there was no synagogue in the city, just outside it there was a place of prayer (Acts 16:13). After an eventful stay, including conversions, exorcism, and persecution, the band now minus the author of the "we-passages" passes through Amphipolis and Apollonia), perhaps overnight stops on the hundred-mile journey to Thessalonica (Acts 17:1).[36] Again Luke does not tell us why they chose this destination and route, but Thessalonica was the leading city in its part of Macedonia and again had a Jewish settlement. Once again Paul is following his general practice of focussing on the principal cities and starting with the synagogue within them. Their stay in Thessalonica was also highly eventful, and is followed by one of the few times Luke provides a reason for the group's moving on to another place.

Their hasty exit to Beroea, some sixty miles away, where there was also a synagogue, was organized by the Thessalonian Christians themselves (Acts 17:10). Similarly, their exit from Beroea to the coast and on to Athens — whether by sea or, as in the Byzantine reading and since Luke usually mentions the port of embarkation, by land — for which they were also supplied escorts (Acts 17:14-15). Though Luke says nothing about it, this double shift of direction may have distracted Paul from an original intention to continue on the *Via Egnatia* to its Adriatic terminus in Rome itself (see Rom. 1:13; 15:22).[37] Athens was not only the leading city in the area, as well as in Greece as a whole, but it also possessed a synagogue (Acts 17:17). Paul's well-known encounter with the city's idols and address on Mars Hill follow. No reason is given for his decision to go to the nearby port city of Corinth, though its commercial importance and proconsular status (Acts 18:12), the presence of a synagogue (Acts 18:4), and proximity may all have been factors. Interesting here, however, is the eventual move from a synagogue to a home base for the mission (Acts 18:7-8). It is in Corinth that Paul experiences another vision in which "the Lord [presumably this time Christ; cf. Acts 18:8] spoke" to him. Its contents were first to allay any fear he might have about his safety if he continued to preach, and second to assure him that a number of people in the city would respond to the gospel (Acts 18:9-10).[38] This means that, at least by implication, it is an encouragement to stay rather than to move on, and as a consequence Paul remained in Corinth for a full eighteen months (Acts 18:11).

36. In relation to this verse as well as to others such as 17:1; 19:1; 20:15; 21:16, W. A. Strange, *The Problem of the Text in Acts* (Cambridge: Cambridge University Press, 1992), pp. 42-27, 150-153, proposes reasons for the variants in the Western text.

37. W. P. Bowers, "Paul's Route through Mysia: A Note on Acts XVI.8," *JTS* n.s. 30 (1979): 511.

38. On the title "Lord" in Luke's second volume more generally, see J. D. G. Dunn, "KYRIOS in Acts," in *The Christ and the Spirit*, vol. 1: *Christology* (Edinburgh: T&T Clark, 1998), pp. 241-53.

Without explanation, Paul and his entourage then begin their return trip to Syria. The specific reference to the fact that Paul "left" the believers and set out "for Syria" (Acts 18:18, probably referring to Syria proper as in Acts 15:23, 41; 21:3) suggests for Luke that Paul sensed it was time to report back to the church at Antioch. Their choice was to travel by boat, first from nearby Cenchrea to Ephesus, the capital of the province of Asia, taking the most common sea voyage across the Aegean. There they stayed only briefly, visiting the synagogue (Acts 18:19), but promised "if it is God's will" to return (Acts 18:20).[39] After the usual trip around the coast of Asia Minor they landed at Caesarea, from which they may have visited Jerusalem (note "went up and greeted the church" and then returned to Antioch (Acts 18:22).[40]

Farewell Journey (Acts 18:23–21:15)

Paul completes his first two journeys with a third that "tak[es] in the whole sweep of the Aegean mission."[41] This trip adds only a little to the picture so far. As at the start of his previous journey, Luke says that the motivation for this trip was "strengthening the disciples" (Acts 18:23). Presumably Paul follows approximately the same route from Antioch to southern Galatia as during his previous journey, though this time Luke does not identify any particular locations but says only that Paul went "from place to place."[42]

Next Paul "took the road through the interior and arrived at Ephesus" (Acts 19:1), a route whose location we do not precisely know.[43] This was the more direct, though not necessarily the main, route. In both cases Luke gives no reason for the particular route taken by Paul; presumably it flows from the reason for the journey. Heading for Ephesus itself — the main center in this whole

39. The Western text makes it explicit here that Paul was anxious to reach Jerusalem for a feast, presumably the Passover, in the short time available after the start of the sailing season.

40. If there was a visit to Jerusalem, as R. Pesch, *Die Apostelgeschichte* (Zurich: Benziger/Neukirchener, 1986), 2:157-58. and others suggest, it would support the view of C. H. Talbert, *Reading Acts: A Literary and Theological Commentary on the Acts of the Apostles* (New York: Crossroad, 1997), p. 146, that the first two journeys have a similar structure, namely, commissioning, outreach, Jerusalem visit.

41. So Dunn, *Acts*, p. 265.

42. Only in the D revision of Acts is there a reference to the Spirit's role in Paul's movements here. The scribe assumed that the church in Acts 18:22 was the one at Caesarea, and inserted an interpolation to explain why Paul did not — as in his version of the previous verse — fulfill his intention to go to Jerusalem. He did this by attributing the change of direction, as in Acts 16:6ff., to the Spirit's intervention.

43. French, "Roads," pp. 56-57.

region — springs, however, from Paul's promise to return made during his previous passing visit (Acts 18:21). Then follows Paul's encounter with a dozen disciples whose understanding of Christ is derived from a knowledge of John's baptism only. He has to educate them further about the Holy Spirit, who, in keeping with two of the key related roles of the Spirit elsewhere in Acts, is described as the giver of prophecy and glossolalia (Acts 19:2, 6; cf. 2:4; 10:44ff.). The combination of the reference to "twelve men" here and the strategic importance of "Ephesus" may indicate "another decisive moment in the missionary history."[44] If this is the case, we have here a link between the Spirit and the ongoing work in a whole region, but not with any specific movements to one place or another.

Paul then begins a three-month period of teaching about "the kingdom of God" in the synagogue (Acts 19:8), followed by daily instruction in the Hall of Tyrannus for a further two years (Acts 19:9-10). Paul's performing miracles and an exorcism there most likely implies the work of the Spirit, as its being done in "the name of the Lord Jesus" and reference to the "power" with which the Word of God spreads (Acts 19:11-17) suggest. In the wake of this, Luke tells us that Paul "purposed in the [or his] Spirit," after traveling first further west through Macedonia and Achaia, to return to Jerusalem, and then go on to Rome (Acts 19:21). If the reference is to the Holy Spirit, it would be the first reference to a positive instruction by the Spirit regarding the direction he should take. If the reference is to Paul's resolution within his own spirit, it gives us a small glimpse into the inner mechanism by which Paul made decisions about such matters. Since there is precedence here for a reference to a person's spirit (Acts 7:59; 17:16; 18:25) and the key verb here implies Paul's action rather than his being acted upon, as is characteristic of reference to the Spirit elsewhere, it is preferable to opt for the second interpretation.[45] Although Paul's reason for wanting to return to Jerusalem is not given here, later in his defense before Felix he does mention the collection for the poor in Jerusalem (Acts 24:17).

Having sent off Timothy and Erastus to prepare for his trip across the Aegean, Paul stays on "a little longer" in the province of Asia (Acts 19:22), after which he bids farewell to the disciples there and sets out for Macedonia, presumably by sea. There he continues to fulfill his purpose of strengthening the believers with "many words of encouragement" (Acts 20:2). Then he goes on to Greece, the more popular name for Achaia, for three months and is about to

44. See already E. Käsemann, "The Disciples of John the Baptist in Ephesus," in *Essays on New Testament Themes* (London: SCM, 1964), pp. 136-48.

45. Barrett, *Commentary*, 2:919, finds supporting evidence for this from several Greek sources.

begin his return journey to Jerusalem by sea to Syria when local opposition forces him to go back by the landward route through Macedonia, perhaps retracing their steps.[46] Following on the start of a new "we-passage" (Acts 20:5), after celebrating the Feast of Unleavened Bread, Paul and his company take ship "at Philippi" (Acts 20:6; actually the port Neapolis) and begin the long sea journey home. Again, this is the quickest and most obvious route to take, and it is interrupted by a brief visit to the church at Troas (Acts 20:7-12), where others who have gone on ahead are awaiting them. This is followed by a short road trip by Paul to Assos (Acts 20:13-15), which Paul had independently arranged for reasons Luke does not mention.[47]

Having bypassed Ephesus to avoid getting distracted from his desire to reach Jerusalem by Pentecost (Acts 20:16), at Miletus he sends for and speaks with the Ephesian elders. He makes mention of his being "compelled by the Spirit," without mentioning how this took place, to head toward Jerusalem (Acts 20:22). He also refers to the Holy Spirit's having made them guardians of God's flock (Acts 20:28). After the timely discovery at Patara of a ship following the main coastal route toward Phoenicia (Acts 20:1), there is a further meeting with believers at Tyre where, paradoxically, they urge Paul "through the Spirit" not to go up to Jerusalem. This is not a contradiction since, a few verses later, it is the danger awaiting Paul in Jerusalem that is stressed by the visiting prophet Agabus (Acts 21:11), and it is most likely the believers' desire that Paul not be harmed that is in mind. Finally, the group reaches Jerusalem, accompanied by a wider group of Jewish disciples (Acts 21:15-16). In a small but interesting footnote to all his missionary journeys, he stays at "the home of Mnason . . . a man from Cyprus and one of the early disciples" (Acts 21:16). In the presence of this believer, one of the earliest in Jerusalem who had a connection with the place associated with Paul's first missionary endeavour, Paul's work has come full circle.

Concluding Reflections

Looking over all the material surveyed, Luke explicitly records the following purposes for Paul's journeys: (1) *undertaking evangelism and church planting,* both from the start of and throughout the initial journey and midway through its follow-up (Acts 13:5; 16:10, etc.); (2) *strengthening disciples and leadership* on the return portion of the initial journey and from the beginning of the follow-

46. Codex D again highlights the work of the Spirit here.

47. Conzelmann, *Acts,* p. 171, rightly says that all explanations given for this by the commentators are "purely speculative."

up and farewell journeys (Acts 14:22; 15:36; 18:23; 20:2, etc.); (3) *developing inter-church links and support,* as with passing on the decisions of the Jerusalem Council (Acts 16:4) and in supporting the church in Jerusalem at the conclusion of his final journey (Acts 20:16; 24:17).

At the end of the initial and follow-up journeys, Paul reports to his sending church (Acts 14:26-27; 18:22). These varying but complementary purposes lead automatically to his visiting or revisiting certain cities and regions, as well as simply passing through others because they were not central to his purposes or because he did not have time at the moment to adequately fulfill his mission there (Acts 20:16).

As for the extent of charismatic guidance of Paul's movements, this appears to have taken place only a few times in the many visits Paul and his colleagues made during his various journeys: (1) *a divine vision or word* (Acts 16:9; 18:9), confirmed by group endorsement (Acts 16:10); (2) *the Spirit's largely general — or negative — guidance* (Acts 13:2, 4; 16:6-7; 20:22; 21:4, 11), though these tend to occur at critical points such as at the beginning of the journeys, before a crucial new direction and at its culmination.

While references to the Spirit in these chapters are mostly related to other activities (Acts 13:9; 15:8; 19:2ff.; 20:28), the fewer references after the initial missionary journey could be due to the fact that by that point "Luke has in essence accomplished his literary purpose." [48] It is interesting that, as the predictions about Paul's fate in Jerusalem indicate (Acts 19:21; 20:22-23; 21:4), recipients can be divided over how to interpret prophetic utterances of the Spirit, suggesting that defining God's will on such occasions is not always straightforward.

Other, seemingly noncharismatic, reasons mentioned by Luke for Paul's taking or not taking a particular route include: (1) *his personal resolution* (Acts 15:36; 19:21; 20:3, 13); (2) *the presence of a synagogue* (Acts 13:4, 13; 14:1; 15:17; 17:1, 10; 18:4, 19), especially during the initial and follow-up journeys; (3) *the city's status and significance* from a Roman or Hellenistic vantage point (Acts 16:12; 19:21); (4) *a colleague's connection* (Acts 13:4; cf. 4:36); (5) *local believers' decision* (Acts 17:14-15); (6) *fulfilling a promise to return* (Acts 18:21 and cf. 21:14), recognizing that, according to the reference to "God's will" in these latter passages, Paul seems to have had a general awareness of all his movements, whether guided by charismatic factors or not, being "entirely at God's behest."[49]

At other times, only with hindsight can we see how Paul's movements were determined by the main land routes or regular sea lanes that appeared before him. Looking back, we can also take note of the fact that he always seems to

48. Shepherd, *Narrative,* p. 219.

49. Squires, *Plan,* p. 176.

work within territory governed by Rome, only passing through other regions not under its protection.[50]

This investigation confirms Dunn's general comment that Luke presents us with a variety of forms of spiritual experience present among the early Christians, including Paul and his colleagues. But if we keep in mind that Luke is primarily interested in the missionary expansion of early Christianity, not the personal religious experience of its adherents or even leaders, we should not find him wanting in paying less attention to the latter. In addition, Luke often prefers simply to state the facts about Paul's movements rather than formally articulate the principle behind them, leaving the reader to infer this from the general drift of the narrative or, at times perhaps, from their general topological knowledge. If we keep his purpose and approach in mind, we can say that Luke highlights the more charismatic forms of general guidance that occur at a few pivotal points in Paul's journeys, but depicts in greater detail how much their specific progress, even at such moments, sprang from a range of more personal or circumstantial factors.[51]

50. Cf. Ramsay, *Paul,* pp. 110-13, though he thinks that this was implied in what Luke wrote.

51. This is close to the general approach of I. H. Marshall, "Luke's Portrait of the Pauline Mission," in *The Gospel to the Nations: Studies in Honour of P. T. O'Brien,* ed. P. Bolt and M. Thompson (London: Inter-Varsity Press, 2000), p. 102.

XI Paul as Mystic

Ulrich Luz

Is Paul a mystic? This question has occupied my mind again and again since my theological beginnings in Japan, and I should like to develop some reflections upon it. My interest in this question has to do with the *religion* of Paul. Protestantism, at least in Switzerland, but perhaps also in other countries in Europe, finds itself in the remarkable situation in which a separation has taken place between the paths of religion and those of the Protestant Church and theology. At the start of the last century the fathers of Dialectical theology came to the definitive conclusion that Christian faith was not a religion, but rather the end of all human religion.[1] Now we worry about the fact that living religion has to a large extent emigrated from the mainstream churches and flourishes elsewhere: in the kaleidoscope fields of New Age, in living communities of neocharismatic groups, in colourful open-air meetings, and so on. In ways different from those of Dialectical theology, we have to take into account today the fact that the future belongs to religion and not to the traditional Christian churches.

I. On the Definition of 'Mysticism'

Exegesis has persistently explored the *theology* of Paul; but his religion, his piety, and his religious experiences have been of less interest to it. I should there-

1. The programmatic title of §17 of Karl Barth's *Church Dogmatics*, I/2 (Edinburgh: T&T Clark, 1956), reads, "The revelation of God as the abolition of religion".

This essay has been translated from the original German by the Rev. Canon Dr. Martin Kitchen, Vice-Dean of Durham Cathedral.

fore like to pose the question concerning the *'mysticism'* of Paul as a way into the question of his 'religion'. Rather than dealing with the question that is at the forefront in the Protestant theology of the Word concerning the action of God *extra me,* I should like to pose the question of the action of God *in me.* This question is important if theology, religious experience, faith, and piety are to remain together.

'If' — with Jacques Waardenburg[2] — 'we understand by mysticism in the widest and most general sense of the word the significance and cultivation of particular experiences of the absolute . . . ', then Paul is certainly a mystic. The *religionsgeschichtliche Schule,* which understood Paul again and again as a mystic, did this because his piety is shaped by his experience of the Spirit. For Wilhelm Bousset, the 'Christ-piety of Paul' is determined by 'his intense feeling of personal belonging and his spiritual bonding with the risen Lord'. Paul's Christ is 'the supernatural power which carries his whole life and fulfils it with its presence',[3] that is, the Lord himself, the Spirit (2 Cor. 3.17). Albert Schweitzer understood the Spirit in basically the same way, 'as a manifestation of the being-in-Christ'.[4] Paul as a mystic — this great theme of the *religionsgeschichtliche Schule*[5] — had only a minor influence on Protestant interpretation of Paul. The reasons are well known and extend far back into the history of Protestantism. At the time of the Reformation the rejection of any form of spiritualism and enthusiasm was particularly strong. It was important not to allow Spirit and faith to become independent over against the divinely instituted external guidelines of Word and sacrament. In the twentieth century, the 'No' of Dialectical theology to mysticism has had far-reaching consequences.[6] That the

2. Jacques Waardenburg, *Religionen und Religion* (Berlin and New York: de Gruyter, 1986), p. 221.

3. Wilhelm Bousset, *Kyrios Christos* (FRLANT 21; Göttingen: Vandenhoeck & Ruprecht, 2nd ed. 1921), p. 304.

4. Albert Schweitzer, *The Mysticism of Paul the Apostle* (1931; Baltimore and London: John Hopkins University Press, 1998), p. 166: 'For being in the Spirit is only a form of manifestation of the being-in-Christ.'

5. Cf., in addition to Bousset and Schweitzer, esp. Adolf Deissmann, *Paulus: Eine kultur- und religionsgeschichtliche Skizze* (Tübingen: Mohr Siebeck, 2nd ed. 1995). Important latecomers in the *religionsgeschichtlich* field of Pauline interpretation are Martin Dibelius, 'Glaube und Mystik bei Paulus' (1931), in *Botschaft und Geschichte* (Tübingen: Mohr [Siebeck], 1956), 2:94-116; idem, *Paulus und die Mystik* (1941), ibid., pp. 134-59; Alfred Wikenhauser, *Die Christusmystik des Apostels Paulus* (Freiburg: Herder, 2nd ed. 1956).

6. Emil Brunner interpreted it as 'experience' and 'intensity of feeling'; *Die Mystik und das Wort* (Tübingen: Mohr [Siebeck], 1924), p. 4. Friedrich Gogarten spoke of the 'endlessness of the mystic-moral task(!) of self-annihilation'. Mysticism is that part of religion which is the attempt to attain to God by human action (*Die religiöse Entscheidung* [Jena: Diederichs, 1921], pp. 64, 66). Rudolf Bultmann interpreted mystical ecstasy as 'a goal in itself and enjoyment'

representatives of the *religionsgeschichtliche Schule*, above all Albert Schweitzer, could seek to relativize Paul's theology of justification on the basis of his mysticism[7] strengthened Protestant rejection of it still more. Even today, in spite of the very great interest in mysticism in our society, the question is not a lively one in Protestant exegesis. In the face of the flood of literature on Paul, the number of works which deal with this issue is relatively small.

Caution reigns. Romano Penna understands Pauline mysticism not on the basis of ecstatic experiences, but as 'knowledge of and communion with God that is out of the ordinary'.[8] He thus understands the whole fullness of the Pauline experience of participation in Christ as 'mysticism'. Alan Segal interprets the call of Paul and his experiences of transformation (e.g., 1 Cor. 15.49; 2 Cor. 3.18; Gal. 4.19; Phil. 3.21) against the background of Jewish-apocalyptic mysticism.[9] In his lucid essay Daniel Marguerat retains the term 'mysticism' only when, on the one hand, the Christocentricity of Pauline mysticism and, on the other, the connection with the Pauline experiences of suffering are admitted.[10] Samuel Vollenweider speaks in his excellent essay, "The Spirit of God as the Self of the Believer", of 'indwelling' and 'participation', but only in passing of a 'Christ-mysticism' in Paul.[11] The Heidelberg dissertation of H.-C. Meier[12] starts from the ecstatic experiences of Paul. The honoree of this Festschrift expresses himself in appropriately cautious fashion when he says, in his major work on Paul the Apostle, that although 'study of the participation in Christ leads more directly into the rest of Paul's theology than justification', it is only with great caution that Paul can be described as a mystic: 'It is hard to avoid talk of something like a mystical sense of the Divine presence of Christ within and without'.[13]

(*Theologische Enzyklopädie;* Tübingen: Mohr [Siebeck], 1984, p. 115). Similarly also Fritz Neugebauer, *In Christus* (Berlin: EVA, 1961).

7. Schweitzer, *Mysticism* (n. 4, above), p. 220.

8. Romano Penna, 'Problems and Nature of Pauline Mysticism', in *Paul the Apostle: Wisdom and Folly of the Cross* (Collegeville, Minn.: Liturgical Press, 1996), pp. 235-73, quotation from p. 271.

9. Alan Segal, *Paul the Convert* (New Haven/London: Yale University Press, 1990) esp. pp. 58-71; cf. idem, 'Paul's Thinking about Resurrection in Its Jewish Context', *NTS* 44 (1998): 400-419.

10. Daniel Marguerat, 'La mystique de l'apôtre Paul', in Association Catholique Française pour l'étude de la Bible (ed.), *Paul de Tarse* (LD 165; Paris: Cerf, 1996), pp. 307-29, esp. p. 329.

11. Samuel Vollenweider, 'Der Geist Gottes als Selbst der Glaubenden: Überlegungen zu einem ontologischen Problem in der paulinischen Anthropologie' (1996), in *Horizonte neutestamentlicher Christologie* (WUNT 144, Tübingen: Mohr [Siebeck], 2002), pp. 163-92, esp. p. 175. Cf. idem, 'Grosser Tod und Grosses Leben: Ein Beitrag zum buddhistisch-christlichen Gespräch im Blick auf die Mystik des Paulus' (1991), in *Horizonte,* pp. 215-35.

12. Hans-Christoph Meier, *Mystik bei Paulus* (TANZ 26; Tübingen: Francke, 1998).

13. James D. G. Dunn, *The Theology of Paul the Apostle* (Edinburgh/Grand Rapids: T&T Clark/Eerdmans, 1998), pp. 395-401.

The reluctance of scholarship to describe Paul as a 'mystic' has its basis in the lack of clarity as to what counts as mysticism. 'Mysticism' is a phenomenon which only since the eighteenth century has come to be seen as an independent form of piety, and that on the basis of the increasing individuation of piety. 'Mysticism' is a modern term which has come into existence through the formation of a noun from the Greek adjective μυστικός, which in late ancient and medieval theology was mostly associated with θεολογία (μυστική θεολογία).[14] It would almost be possible to see in it the fate of modernity in the field of intellectual history: the concept of 'mysticism' (cf. μυστική) arose as a result of a particular type of piety's gaining independence over against the transcendent basis which carried it, namely, θεολογία. Only one who knows that the question is anachronistic can enquire into 'mysticism' in the case of Paul. According to the definition of mysticism presupposed,[15] Paul is completely, partly, or, at the extremes, not at all a mystic. The choice of a definition of mysticism is therefore not objective, but based on personal preferences. My interest lies in the link between theology and religious experience in Paul; in dogmatic terms, that is in the relationship between the *Christus pro nobis* and the *Christus in me.*

In the case of Paul a fruitful understanding of mysticism makes connections with the *cognitio divinae bonitatis . . . affectiva seu experimentalis* (Thomas Aquinas) and thus the experience of divine love.[16] Here mysticism is primarily understood as 'experience of God' or, more specifically, the experience of the overcoming of distance, the *unio,* the *communio,* or *connection* with God. Mysticism as direct relationship with the divine[17] signifies the overcoming of distance to the divine.[18] I speak deliberately not simply of *unio mystica,* for I think

14. On this cf. particularly Alois Haas, 'Was ist Mystik', in idem, *Gottleiden — Gottlieben: Zur volkssprachlichen Mystik im Mittelalter* (Frankfurt: Insel, 1989), pp. 23-44, esp. pp. 32-36, and Bernhard Neuenschwander, *Mystik im Johannesevangelium* (Biblical Interpretation Series 31; Leiden: Brill 1998), pp. 11-15.

15. A good overview of the basic types of mysticism is provided by Neuenschwander, *Mystik,* pp. 16-20.

16. Thomas, *STh* 2/II.97, art. 2; cf. Bonaventura, *De perfectione Evangelica,* I, concl. = Opera omnia 5 (*Ad Claras Aquas* [Quaracchi]: Typographia Collegii S. Bonaventurae, 1891), p. 120 *(cognitio causarum altissimarum et primarum . . . per motum cognitionis . . . saporativae et experientalis)* (for this reference I am grateful to Prof. A. Haas, Zürich). Cf also Hans Urs von Balthasar, *Pneuma und Institution* (Skizzen zur Theologie 4 (Einsiedeln: Johannes, 1974), p. 302; Alois Haas, 'Die Problematik von Sprache und Erfahrung in der deutschen Mystik', in W. Beierwaltes u.a., *Grundfragen der Mystik* (Einsiedeln: Johannes, 1974), pp. 75-76.

17. As emphasized by Daniel Marguerat, *Mystique* (above, n. 10), p. 311 in his definition: 'an immediate mode of perception of the divine, which seeks and activates an intimate consciousness of the presence of transcendence'.

18. Adolf Deissmann also advocated a broad understanding of mysticism, for which the mystic *union* is not the only essential element. Cf. his *Paulus* (n. 5), pp. 118-19. Mysticism is for

that the experience of the overcoming of distance includes not only the form of fusion with the divine,[19] but also the form of the communion with it, as well as the form of the vision the contemplation of the divine can have.

With respect to Paul, an understanding of mysticism which understands mysticism as the opposite of the prophetic is not very helpful.[20] Also not very fruitful is an understanding which — in a good modern way — understands 'mysticism' primarily as the piety of the individual, which deepens the traditional myths, teachings, rites, or practices of a religion by their own meeting with God.[21] For the purposes of my research, also less fruitful is the definition of mysticism as a transreligious phenomenon, as in the classic definition of Evelyn Underhill, who understands mysticism as 'the expression of the innate tendency of the human spirit towards complete harmony with the transcendental order, whatever be the theological formula under which that order is understood'.[22] The leading interest for her is specifically the discovery of convergences between religions.

---

him 'every piety which finds its way to the divine directly through inner experience, without rational mediation. . . . The immediacy of the communion with the Divine is essential.' Even broader is Meier's definition, *Mystik* (above, n. 12) p. 20: Mysticism is 'immediate experience of divine reality.' In this definition mysticism becomes a general term for all forms of religious experience.

19. In Friedrich Heiler fusion is in the foreground: 'Mysticism is that form of immediate relation with God by which the world and the Ego are radically denied, by which human personality is dissolved and destroyed and sinks in the eternal One of the godhead' (*Das Gebet;* München: E. Reinhardt, 2nd ed. 1920, p. 249).

20. Friedrich Heiler, *Das Gebet* (above, n. 19), pp. 248-83; cf. Gustav Mensching, *Vergleichende Religionswissenschaft* (Heidelberg: Quelle-Meyer, 1949), pp. 155-57. The juxtaposition of the prophetic and the mystical can be justified neither by early Jewish texts such as, e.g., The Wisdom of Solomon or Philo, nor by early Christian prophets speaking as the mouth of the risen Christ.

21. Thus, more or less, Ernst Troeltsch, *The Social Teaching of the Christian Churches* (Chicago/London: University of Chicago Press, repr. 1976), 2:730. According to Troeltsch, characteristic of mysticism is 'the insistence upon a direct inward and present religious experience' either as a 'reaction' against the growing rigidity of traditional religion in the institutionalization and objectification of religion, or as a 'supplementing of traditional forms of worship by means of a personal and living stimulus'. In a similar way Gershom Scholem understands mystical piety as 'the revival of mythical thought' in a situation in which older religions have become torpid and new religions are not available. Mystical piety attempts to 'transform the God whom it encounters . . . from an object of dogmatic knowledge into a novel and 'living experience and intuition' (*Major Trends in Jewish Mysticism* [New York: Schocken Books, repr. 1961], pp. 8-9). Pauline mysticism, however, consists not primarily in the renewal of an old religion, and certainly not in its individualization, but it represents a *new* religious starting point and is primarily community oriented.

22. Evelyn Underhill, *Mysticism: A Study in the Nature and Development of Man's Religious Consciousness* (London: Methuen, 7th ed. 1918), p. xiv.

My question therefore concerns the religious experiences of Paul, which overcome the distance to the Divine and create a relationship with God. I want to show the particularities of these experiences in Paul. This attempt takes the form of a brief exegetical sketch, which consists of theses and explanations.

II. Six Theses on the Profile of Pauline Mysticism

1. 'Mystical'-sounding expressions in Paul occur, in my opinion, when he interprets the experience of the Spirit which is given to believers as experience of Christ. 'The Lord is the Spirit' (1 Cor. 6.17; 15.45; 2 Cor. 3.17), but at the same time the Lord is more than spiritual experiences which the Spirit brings about. There exists an identity of effect as between the 'Lord' and the 'Spirit' in Paul, inasmuch as the 'Lord' is effective as Spirit in the believers and becomes their new personal centre (Rom. 8.9-10; Gal. 2.20). Thus Paul knows not only the Christ 'extra nos' and 'pro nobis', and not only the 'verbum alienum' of God, but also the actually experienced Christ 'in nobis' and the presence of God effective *in* human hearts.

The identification of the risen Lord with the Spirit is in my view a basic axiom of Pauline theology. 1 Cor. 15.45 is not the only example of that.[23] 2 Cor. 3.17 is also testimony, in my view, to this identification. In my view, it is hardly possible to interpret the 'turning to the Lord' (v. 16) other than as conversion to the Lord Christ, to whom Israel should in fact turn. ὁ δὲ κύριος τὸ πνεῦμά ἐστιν is thus a continuation and an exegetical remark which harks back to v. 6 and which presupposes the identity of the Lord and the Spirit. Certainly this identity is not a static identity, understood substantially — which is already excluded by πνεῦμα κυρίου — but an identity of effect; to that extent I agree with J. Dunn.[24] Also, 1 Cor. 6.17 is intelligible only if 'linking himself with the Lord' is understood as unity of the Spirit.

Only on the basis of this identity of effect of the Lord and the Spirit do those 'indwelling statements' of Rom. 8.9-11 become intelligible, in which one after another the dwelling of the 'Spirit of God', of 'Christ', and of 'the Spirit of him who raised Jesus from the dead' are referred to. Again the emphasis lies not on the definition of identity but on effect: through it arises life in dead, that is, in mortal, bodies.[25] Christ is spoken of, who is 'in you'. On the other hand, the ecclesiological dimension of the Pauline 'mystical' statements also becomes intelligible. Christ is one

23. Contra Dunn, *Theology* (above, n. 13), p. 262.

24. Cf. Dunn, *Theology*, p. 264: 'Christ is not conceived of as working separately from the Spirit.'

25. Cf. 1 Cor. 15.45: the second Adam became a life-giving Spirit (εἰς πνεῦμα ζῳοποιοῦν).

Spirit, and thereby 'we' become one by incorporation into the body of Christ in baptism: πάντες εἰς ἓν σῶμα ἐβαπτίσθημεν (1 Cor. 12.13). The hearers of 1 Corinthians will have been reminded at this point of the πνευματικὸν πόμα which flowed from the 'rock' which was Christ (1 Cor. 10.4). Also here the Spirit is the direct means of Christ's working since the Spirit not only really binds believers to Christ in that they are baptized into his body, but he also binds them to each other: πάντες εἰς ἓν σῶμα ἐβαπτίσθημεν.[26]

In his presentation of Paul J. Dunn sets out three 'aspects' of the way in which Paul can interpret the beginning of redemption: the juridical as 'justification'; the 'mystical' as participation; and as third the 'gift of the Spirit'.[27] In the context of the heading 'participation' he discusses essentially only the formulas 'in Christ', 'with Christ', etc. For this reason his view of Pauline mysticism is both pale and divorced from experience. I wonder whether it is possible to separate the aspect of 'mysticism' from the 'gift of the Spirit'; on the contrary, the 'gift of the Spirit' seems to me to be the experiential basis of Pauline Christ-mysticism.

2. However central experiences of the Spirit may be for Pauline Christ-mysticism, it is not the many 'particular' charismatic experiences of Paul — such as speaking in tongues, prophecy, ecstasy, and miracles — that could be described as central to what counts as 'mysticism' in Paul.

That Paul was a very significant charismatic and worker of miracles can be seen most clearly in his relation to speaking in tongues. It might be embarrassing, or even alienating, when Paul says precisely to the Corinthians, in his characteristically modest immodesty, 'I thank God that I speak in tongues more than all of you' (1 Cor. 14.18). For the Corinthians, speaking in tongues was simply *the* expression of the Spirit (cf. 1 Cor. 14.37). They might have understood it as the speech of angels (1 Cor. 13.1; cf. *Test. Job* 48.3; 49.2; 50.2). Speaking in tongues may have been something similar to what in Philo is the experience of the Divine indwelling, in which the νοῦς is replaced by the divine spirit.[28] Paul evaluates it specifically lower than prophecy, which leaves the νοῦς not ἄκαρπος (1 Cor. 14.14). However, above all he does not raise it to the 'angelic' heights, but to the earthly depths. In Rom. 8.26-27 he points to speaking in tongues as the inarticulate sighing of unredeemed human

26. J. Dunn will excuse me if I am not happy with his description of the body of Christ as a 'theological image' (Dunn, *Theology*, p. 548). Of course one might discuss endlessly how the 'image' is participating in the 'matter'. By the real 'being made to drink' by the Spirit, which is Christ's method, incorporation in the body of Christ, in my view, is more than a theological image.

27. Dunn, *Theology*, §§14-16.

28. The basic text is Plato, *Ion* 533-34, in which the inspiration of the poet is addressed. Regarding inspiration in Philo, cf. Vollenweider, "Geist Gottes" (above, n. 11) p. 170, nn. 24-25.

beings. And precisely to this sighing, which does not yet approximate intelligible speech, comes the Spirit to help and stand before God for us.[29] Thus it is not the case that human language rises to the level of the divine Spirit or of angels; rather, the divine Spirit stoops to the lowest depths of human creatureliness and turns the call of the unredeemed into his own language.

A similar ambivalence concerning ecstatic phenomena can be seen in the report of his transport to heaven in 2 Cor. 12.2-4. Although it must have meant a lot to him, he distances himself from it in a particular way. He uses a form of speech which perhaps signifies distancing of the ecstatic from his own self.[30] He speaks of 'someone' and thus deliberately uses a form of speech which avoids self-glory. Paul is prepared to glory in this 'man', but he himself lives in his weaknesses, concerning which he gives no grounds for glory (v. 5). Even more strongly Paul distances himself from his journey to heaven by reporting a further experience of God, this time in the first person. 'Even considering the exceptional character of the revelations, therefore, to keep me from being too elated, a thorn was given me in the flesh, a messenger of Satan to torment me, to keep me from being too elated' (v. 7). Three times Paul appealed to the Lord about this, but he experienced no liberation. God's answer was, 'My grace is sufficient for you, for power is made perfect in weakness' (v. 9). This is a real counterexperience to the heavenly journey; it takes place not in heaven but on earth; it does not take place out of the body, but it penetrates the body. It does not end in inexpressible words but in clear speech. By means of the difference between Pauline weakness and the power of Christ an infinite qualitative difference between Paul and Christ becomes visible.

Such particular ecstatic experiences, which Paul had, clearly do not finally settle what is the centre of his 'mystical' experiences.[31] He reevaluates them, draws out their depths, and emphasizes the difference which exists between the heavenly Christ and the earthly pneumatic and thus the grace which is imparted to the person who lives in the depths of earth.[32]

29. I follow here the interpretation of Ernst Käsemann, *An die Römer* (HNT 8a; Tübingen: Mohr [Siebeck], 1973), pp. 229-31. James D. G. Dunn, *Romans 1–8* (WBC 38A, Dallas: Word, 1988), pp. 492-93, interprets similarly, but rejects a special reference to glossolalia.

30. Cf. Victor Furnish, *II Corinthians* (AB 32A; Garden City, N.Y.: Doubleday, 1984), pp. 543-44, and Bernard Heininger, *Paulus als Visionär* (HBSt 9; Freiburg, etc.: Herder, 1996), pp. 242-66.

31. Meier, *Mystik* (see above, n. 12) places vision, audition, *raptus*, glossolalia and prophecy in the foreground and simply handles the question of 'immanence' as one among others.

32. Deissmann, *Paulus* (above, n. 5), p. 119, sensitively described Pauline mysticism as 'katabatic' mysticism: 'There is an active mysticism and a reactive mysticism, anabatic and katabatic mysticism. The human comes to God, or God comes to the human. Mysticism of effort or mysticism of grace!' Paul is thus correctly characterized — but whether there exists anywhere in the world an 'active' mysticism, a mysticism of effort, must remain to be seen.

3. Consequently, the unique and special encounter with Christ that Paul experienced near Damascus is not in itself the centre of Pauline Christ-mysticism. Rather, it is so only insofar as it expresses something which is subsequently applicable to all Christians. It is true of all that they 'by the law are dead to the law', so that it is no longer they, but Christ, who lives in them (Gal. 2.19-20).

Paul interprets his Damascus Road experience not as an inner experience[33] but as prophetic empowering and commissioning. In Gal. 2.19-20 he starts from his Damascus Road experience again and interprets it in the sense of a change of ego. Through the law he died to the law and was constantly crucified with Christ, so that now after the death of his ego, Christ lives in him as his new personal centre. Verses 19 and 20 were again and again interpreted mystically — and rightly so.[34] The relationship with Christ could hardly be expressed more intimately than by this 'ego-change'.[35] At the same time, however, it seems clear to me that the ego here is typical and not merely an individual.[36] Exactly the same is true of Romans 7–8. Here Paul is saying first that the 'ego' has died to the law through the law (Rom. 7.14-24) and then that through the redemptive action of Christ (Rom. 8.3-4) believers have a new personal centre, namely, the Spirit of God, that is, Christ (Rom. 8.9-11). The 'ego' is the collective 'I' of Adam (cf. esp. Rom. 7.9-10).[37] Rom. 7.14–8.11 is nothing other than an extensive paraphrase of Gal. 2.19-20. Thus in Gal. 2.19, by means of his 'mystical' formulation, Paul derives from his own path to Christ what may be valid for all Christians. Paul's experience on the Damascus road is a fundamental mystical experience precisely as an experience which is typical for all Christians.

4. Pauline mysticism is a mysticism which is connected with the the community. It is not 'elitist' but 'democratic'.[38] In Paul experience of the Spirit is closely related to membership in the community, and the community is the

33. Cf. James D. G. Dunn, *The Epistle to the Galatians* (BNTC 9; Peabody: Hendrickson, 1993), p. 64: ἐν ἐμοί expresses the 'personal transformation' in the sense of 'transformation of purpose and commitment'.

34. Cf. Schweitzer, *Mysticism* (above, n. 4), p. 125; Dibelius, *Paulus* (above, n. 5), p. 151; Vollenweider, "Grosser Tod" (above, n. 11), pp. 367-69.

35. The formulation is not 'of course exaggerated' (J. Dunn, *Galatians* [n. 33], p. 145) but expresses a true mystical paradox.

36. *Pace* J. Dunn, *Galatians* (above, n. 33), pp. 143, 147. In the previous v. 18 the 'ego' *cannot* mean Paul, for he has not done what is described there. The soteriological saying in v. 20b must refer to all Christians.

37. In passing it might be said that Rom. 8.3-11 is to be distinguished from Galatians 3.20 by the fact that in place of 'I' a 'we' is to be found. This is significant, whether intentional or not. Christ lives not only 'in me' but 'in you' (plural!) (Rom. 8.9-10); that is, he is not only the individual but also the collective personal centre of the whole community, which is his body.

38. D. Marguerat (n. 10), p. 327, speaks of the 'democratization of mysticism' in Paul.

'body of Christ', 'into which' the believers have been baptized (1 Cor. 12.13). It is at baptism that they 'put on' Christ, and thereby they became 'one' (Gal. 3.27-28). 'Mystical' expressions are to be found in Paul where he interprets those experiences which are constitutive of the faith of *all* Christians, and not where he interprets the particular experiences of individuals which mark these out from other people.

The Pauline statements which the *religionsgeschichtliche Schule* particularly designated as 'mystical' are consistently statements concerning *all* Christians. That is true in the case of 'in Christ', a phrase rich in nuances, as much as for its reverse, 'Christ in you' (Rom. 8.10; 2 Cor. 13.3.5; Gal. 4.19). It is also true in the case of statements concerning the Spirit, who lives in believers (Rom. 8.9, 11; 1 Cor. 3.16; 6.19), and in a special way in the case of statements concerning the body of Christ. Such statements describe the reality of salvation, which *each* has experienced in the present. All Christians are mystics!

The most important experiential background for such statements is not constituted by the particular experiences of Paul the ecstatic but by the gift of the Spirit, which for all believers is bound up with baptism (1 Cor. 6.11; 12.13; 2 Cor. 1.22). In baptism they 'put on' Christ (Gal. 3.27; cf. Rom. 13.14). In the context of baptism Paul is able to accentuate the new centre of the person, which is Christ, not individually, as in Gal. 2.20, but collectively, 'You are all one in Christ Jesus' (Gal. 3.28).[39] On this basis, if one wants to speak of Paul as a mystic, it is not possible to understand this as a particular characteristic of the piety of the individual. It is precisely the foundational experience of baptism, which is common to all, not some ecstatic or charismatic experiences of perfection which is the basic experience that stands behind many 'mystical'-sounding phrases of Paul.

5. Pauline Christ-mysticism has as its aim the conformity of the believer with the Lord Jesus in his passion and in his resurrection glory. Characteristic of it is, on the one hand, a consequent holding fast to the body and to the community with Christ in his suffering. In particular the suffering of Christians becomes an epiphany of Christ in the present. It is not just once in baptism that Christians complete the imitation of the cross of Christ in the present, but also daily: 'For your sake we are killed all the day long' (Rom. 8.36).[40] If there is any-

39. εἷς in Gal. 3.28 is difficult. According to J. Dunn, *Galatians* (above, n. 33), pp. 20-21, it alludes to the σῶμα Χριστοῦ. But why the masculine, εἷς? In my opinion, εἷς is a concentrated formulation understandable from the context, which is to be understood on the one hand in opposition to Jew-Greek dualism, and on the other in opposition to πάντες . . . ὑμεῖς. The first opposition alludes to the thought of new creation, the second to the thought of the body of Christ.

40. Cf. the perfect συνεσταύρωμαι (Gal. 2.19).

where in Paul where the definition of mysticism as a deepening and interiorization of an existing religion has a moment of truth, it is here, in the Pauline passion-mysticism.[41] On the other hand, Paul is also aware of a conformity with the resurrection glory with Christ already now. In phrases which he extends to all Christians, Paul does not shrink from speaking of experiences which allow the believer to participate in God's glory here and now. The fear and panic at 'enthusiasm' and any *theologia gloriae* which marks out many Protestant theologians is unknown to Paul, for it is not a question of his own glory, but Christ's.

The body is a member of Christ, a temple of the Spirit (1 Cor. 6.15, 19). The body is the place in which precisely in human weakness the power of Christ shows itself strong (2 Cor. 12.9). The body is the 'earthen vessel' in which the treasure of the power of God is contained (2 Cor. 4.7ff.). In contrast to the Hellenistic mysticism of Philo or the Hermetic texts,[42] which emigrates out of the lower spheres of earthly existence, the power and the life of God are effective in the depths of bodily existence. In Phil. 3.10-11 Paul speaks of his desire 'to know Christ and the power of his resurrection and the fellowship of his sufferings, being conformed to his death'. According to 2 Cor. 4.10, we 'always carry about the death of Jesus in the body'. In 2 Cor. 1.5 he speaks of the abundance of the sufferings of Christ, in Gal. 6.17 of the stigmata of Jesus in his body. Here we recognize a mysticism which does not lead to an experience of union with Christ at the end of a long road of piety, but one which causes the whole painful and difficult life of Paul to become conformable to Christ. The fact that the suffering Christ transfers and re-forms Paul's life does not extinguish his personal existence, but forms it in an extremely demanding way. It is certainly not by chance that in the whole of the early period of Christianity, and, I think, in almost the whole religious history of antiquity, there is hardly a person who comes across to us as such an unmistakable individual as this Paul, although — or rather, precisely because — he himself no longer lives, but Christ lives in him.

On the other hand, in statements which he extends to all Christians, Paul speaks about experiences which allow believers to participate in the glory of God already now, for example, of a present 'transformation' from glory into glory (2 Cor. 3.18), of 'illumination', even of the 'lighting of God' in the human person (2 Cor. 4.6; cf. 5.17), of the renewal of the human by the resurrection (2 Cor. 4.11-12, 18), of the 'formation of Christ in us' (Gal. 4.19). The statement of glorification in Rom. 8.30 — in the aorist tense — is also significant. It is not a question simply of a merely verbal-radical announced consciousness of salvation[43] but of a mystical ex-

41. Cf. E. Troeltsch (above, n. 21).

42. Philo, *Op. Mund.* 69; *Her.* 69; *Cher.* 13.3.10.

43. The glorification that has already happened has either been labelled as 'anticipatory'

perience of the Spirit which makes believers now. Paul is a 'pneumatic'; Paul is an 'enthusiast'. Only this enthusiasm may not overstep the conditions of its being experienced through the body, through suffering and through love.

6. Pauline mysticism is open to ethics. 'Transformation' has an ethical aspect (cf. Rom. 12.2). Putting on Christ is at the same time putting on the 'armour of light' (Rom. 13.11-14). Life 'in the Spirit' means the rejection of slavery 'in the flesh' (Rom. 8.6–8.12-14). The 'body of Christ' is the locus of love (1 Cor. 12.12-31), which is the highest of all the spiritual gifts (1 Cor. 13.13). Pauline Christ-mysticism has a horizontal dimension, that of love; and that means not individual attachment to Christ but the κοινωνία of the community.

Gal. 2.20 speaks — immediately after the statement that 'Christ lives in me' — of life 'in the flesh', which is now determined by faith in Christ. According to Romans 8 the person who lives in Christ, that is, in the Spirit, can no longer live according to the flesh as debtor to the flesh (Rom. 8.12-13). The ethical dimension of communion with the Lord becomes clear in contrast with sexual intercourse with prostitutes in 1 Cor. 6.12ff. The body belongs to the Lord, and the Lord to the body (v. 13). That means a union similar to marriage, so that Paul can formulate a saying analogous to becoming one flesh in marriage: 'But anyone who unites himself with the Lord becomes one with him in spirit' (v. 17). The practical consequences of that mystical-sounding sentence are evident: sexual intercourse with prostitutes is excluded. The body is the place of the indwelling of Christ; Christ takes shape in bodily existence. In a similar way in 1 Corinthians 12 and 13 the experience which corresponds to a person's being made a member of the body of Christ, and his being baptized with the Spirit and made to drink of one Spirit, is quite earthly: that of good communal living, of love in the community. In this love the reality of Christ is experienced. For Paul, the 'union' with Christ, the immersion into his reality, does not take place just anywhere, but in the body. It signifies not a removal from the world, but a new praxis in the community.

III. Conclusion

The conclusion can be quite short. It has to answer two questions.

1. Is Paul a mystic? The question is an anachronism and cannot be an-

---

(thus, e.g., Wilhelm Thüsing, *Per Christum in Deum* [Neutestamentliche Abhandlungen, N.F., I/1; Münster: Aschendorff, 3rd ed. 1986], p. 278) or dismissed as 'enthusiastic baptism tradition', which has simply been taken over by Paul (thus Ernst Käsemann, *An die Römer* [see above, n. 29], p. 234). Paul was well aware of what he was taking over! His eschatology is in my view not basically to be distinguished from the 'present' eschatology of the Epistle to the Colossians.

swered. However, it must be reformulated. Properly put, the question is: Is the anachronistic question about the mysticism of Paul fruitful? The answer must be, Yes; for it allows sides of the great apostle to be brought into the light which have been suppressed in Protestant exegesis. It is important to protect Paul from the constraints of one's own church's tradition and thus discover him anew over against one's own established views. In this context belongs the new discovery of dimensions such as religious experience, participation, Christ as the living Spirit, and Christ 'in' us. Here belongs also the discovery that the religion of Paul was much more than a religion of the 'pure word'. Only when we discover what is new, strange, and other in the very familiar biblical text, and only when we allow ourselves to receive new insight from members of other confessions and religions, in order to discover new — and even surprising — things in the Bible, will our reading of the Bible have a future.

2. What can the study of Pauline piety and theology add to our understanding of mysticism? The argument is naturally circular. Only when the first question has been answered affirmatively can questions deriving from Paul concerning contemporary definitions of mysticism be addressed. If we start from a positive answer, the following may be said: Pauline 'mysticism' is a quite particular mysticism, a 'mysticism *sui generis*'. It is no proper basis for defining 'mysticism' as a general, human phenomenon common to all religions. Rather, it supports the thesis that 'mysticism' is only a 'mysticism of . . . ', that is, Christian mysticism, Islamic mysticism, Jewish mysticism, Buddhist mysticism.[44] Mysticism only exists with reference to particular, historically given and unmistakable religious traditions. Contrary to contemporary views of the relative autonomy of 'mysticism' over against 'theology', it is true that Paul's 'mysticism' is an expression of his experience *of Christ* and in particular of his participation in Christ. It is the expression of the living power *of Christ* which takes shape in Paul and in all Christians. It is *not* the expression of something common to all religions, corresponding to an anthropological or a theological basis which is the same in all religions. There is no interreligious 'mystical ecumenism' beyond religion. Such a thing would be no more than a human construct and would then in fact fall under the 'mysticism-verdict' of Dialectical theology. Rather, there exists only the possibility of asking members of other religions concerning *their* experiences of God, allowing them to tell them and thereby becoming observant of and grateful for what God has given to us — and at the same time thankful for what has been granted to other people by other religions.

44. Thus most decisively G. Scholem, *Jewish Mysticism* (above, n. 21), p. 6, 'There is no mysticism as such, there is only the mysticism of a particular religious system.'

XII Pauline Pneumatology and Pauline Theology

Alexander J. M. Wedderburn

Professor Dunn was a regular and prominent participant in the seminar of the Society of Biblical Literature which was for many years involved with the theme of "Pauline theology," a theme, however, which was beset from the start with the problem of defining what it meant by "Pauline theology." On the one hand, the insight gained ground that what the group was investigating was more a process or an activity of the apostle's, his "theologizing."[1] On the other hand, at least one contributor, Paul Meyer, argued, plausibly enough, that one should rather be looking for "the end-product and result, the *outcome* to which [Paul] arrives in the process of his argument, his 'hermeneutic', or his 'theologizing,'"[2] although he did at least agree that this "end-product" would be the result of a process. Rightly, too, the seminar stressed more than once how many factors must be borne in mind in evaluating that process: the convictions and assumptions which Paul brought to it (both those inherited from his pre-Christian past and those which he had sooner or later acquired as a result of his coming to belief in Christ), the ideas and assumptions current in his world, the beliefs and practices and problems which he found in the churches to which he wrote,

1. Cf. Jouette M. Bassler, "Paul's Theology: Whence and Whither?" in David M. Hay, ed., *Pauline Theology* 2: *1 and 2 Corinthians* (Minneapolis: Fortress, 1993), pp. 3-17, here p. 11, and a number of others following her, so that James D. G. Dunn ("In Quest of Paul's Theology: Retrospect and Prospect," in E. Elizabeth Johnson and David M. Hay, eds., *Pauline Theology*, vol. 4: *Looking Back, Pressing On* [Atlanta: Scholars Press, 1997], pp. 95-115, here p. 98) sees this as part of an emerging consensus within the seminar.

2. Paul W. Meyer, "Pauline Theology: A Proposal for a Pause in Its Pursuit," in Johnson and Hay, *Pauline Theology*, 4:140-60, here p. 150 (his italics).

and the views of those who opposed him — all of these contributed positively or negatively to his "theologizing," to the formation of his theological ideas.

The seminar adopted the not altogether unproblematic strategy of looking at the theology of each individual letter in turn; it is not unproblematic, in that for much of the content of the individual Pauline letters one can at most say that it is applied theology, theology applied to various concrete situations. In this chapter I want to adopt a different plan, following through a single theme, Paul's pneumatology, in his various letters, in the hope that this concrete example may throw some light not only on the process of Paul's "theologizing" but also on its outcome or, perhaps better, its results, for I will argue that in each letter this thought process is crystallized anew in response to a different situation. At the same time the subject matter itself will compel me, in my own theologizing, to react to Friedrich Wilhelm Horn's substantial monograph on the subject and to take up a position on the way in which Paul's pneumatology developed which differs in many respects from his.[3]

I

Horn traces a three-stage development in Paul's thinking on the Spirit: its role in (1) his earliest extant letter, 1 Thessalonians, in (2) his struggle with enthusiasts at Corinth in 1 Corinthians, and in (3) his struggles with a Jewish-Christian countermission in 2 Corinthians, Galatians, and Philippians (in that chronological order).[4]

(1) In Horn's eyes the Spirit is in 1 Thessalonians the Spirit of God, poured out in the last days as in the Old Testament, and is not brought into any direct relationship with Christ. Nor would one expect that to be the case, for the 'Lord' in this letter is not the exalted Lord active in his church in the present, but always the Lord who will come at his parousia.[5] If the coming Lord looms

3. Friedrich Wilhelm Horn, *Das Angeld des Geistes: Studien zur paulinischen Pneumatologie* (FRLANT 154; Göttingen: Vandenhoeck & Ruprecht, 1992).

4. Like so many attempts to trace "development" in Paul's thought, this one is beset by problems of chronology, particularly if one thinks it more likely that Galatians was written before 1 Corinthians: see my "Paul's Collection: Chronology and History," *NTS* 48 (2002): 95-110.

It is also striking how small a role Romans plays in Horn's whole account, despite the fittingness of James D. G. Dunn's description of ch. 8 as "Paul's great Spirit chapter" and of 8:1-27 as "unquestionably the high point of Paul's theology of the Spirit" (*The Theology of Paul the Apostle* [Grand Rapids: Eerdmans and Edinburgh: Clark, 1998], pp. 438, 423).

5. So Horn, *Angeld*, pp. 149, 151. There are, however, passages in the letter which make one hesitate to accept that argument: 1:1 and 3:11 (is Christ's lordship any less a present reality than that of God the Father?); 2:15 (clearly the crucified Jesus and therefore a reference to the past);

large in 1 Thessalonians, then that is in large measure due to the themes handled in the letter. Yet that does not alter the fact that the christological interpretation of the Spirit characteristic of the later letters is not to be found here. Horn's point here finds support in Thomas Söding's article on the development that has taken place between Paul's earlier preaching as represented in 1 Thessalonians and that attested by the *Hauptbriefe:* Söding attributes this shift to the various problems confronting Paul during the period of the later letters.[6]

(2a) It is above all in 1 Corinthians that the Spirit and possession of the Spirit are clearly a problem in the church. Horn regards these problems as a peculiarity of the Corinthian congregation, and it is correct that, as far as we can know for certain, they were only a feature of that church. However, even if the problem arose only in this church, that does not mean that Horn is right to say that the phenomenon whose misinterpretation (in Paul's eyes) led to the problem did not exist elsewhere, even if it was not present everywhere. It is not implausible that ecstatic phenomena of this sort had spread to Corinth from the earliest Palestinian community, even though one may question, as Horn does, the historicity of Acts' Pentecost account as it now stands.[7] For the choice is not between accepting the Pentecost account as it stands and dismissing the whole phenomenon as characteristic of Palestinian Christianity; in between lies the possibility that the author of Acts has encapsulated in a dramatic scene a far less spectacularly recurrent feature of the earliest church, a feature whose nature he himself, however, perhaps did not fully understand and has therefore represented in a somewhat confused and historically implausible way. And if glossolalia was no longer a phenomenon with which this author was himself personally familiar in the Christian circles in which he moved, must one not all the more seek to explain why he was convinced that such a phenomenon was a feature of the earliest Christian communities? To this consideration one may add two others. For in 1 Cor. 14:18 Paul speaks of his ability to speak in tongues more than all the Corinthians. Is one to assume that he did that only in Corinth? Is it

---

4:1-2 (as in later Pauline letters both ἐν κυρίῳ Ἰησοῦ and διὰ τοῦ κυρίου Ἰησοῦ seem to refer to the present authority of the Lord Jesus), 4:15a (whether ἐν λόγῳ κυρίου refers to an utterance of a Christian prophet or prophetess in the name of Jesus, to the authority in whose name Paul speaks or to an at least supposed saying of Jesus, this then again refers to a past or present Lord, not to the coming Lord as in v. 15b).

6. "Der Erste Thessalonicherbrief und die frühe paulinische Evangeliumsverkündigung: Zur Frage einer Entwicklung der paulinischen Theologie," *BZ* 35 (1991): 180-203 = *Das Wort vom Kreuz: Studien zur paulinischen Theologie* (WUNT 93; Tübingen: Mohr [Siebeck], 1997), pp. 31-56, here p. 191/43 (cf. p. 201/53).

7. Cf. Horn, *Angeld,* pp. 82-89; also my "Traditions and Redaction in Acts 2.1-13," *JSNT* 55 (1994): 27-54.

not altogether more likely that he, so to speak, brought this phenomenon with him to Corinth, having encountered and experienced it in the churches further east with which he had previously been associated? And, second, how does one explain the rise of the conviction that the promised eschatological outpouring of the Spirit had indeed been fulfilled in the early church? That is all the more difficult to explain if one were to accept, as Horn does, that it was widely believed that the Spirit had been quenched and that Palestinian Jews would have been reluctant to accept ecstatic phenomena as evidence of the activity of God's Spirit. And even if their belief that they possessed the Spirit were a theoretical deduction from their theology, as Horn claims, would such a deduction not rapidly have led to appropriate experiences of Spirit possession?

(2b) Horn believes that in the Corinthian church the functional aspect of the Spirit as an eschatological power had been overshadowed, at least in a part of the congregation, by conceptions of a present participation in a heavenly sphere of Spirit, in which the Spirit formed the substance of the new existence and made possible a way of life in which one deliberately shakes off the fetters of the fleshly sphere. Since baptism was the rite which bestowed the Spirit, some could designate themselves as "spiritual," particularly those whose Spirit possession manifested itself in glossolalia.

Now Paul, too, speaks of the Spirit in such a way that one could readily believe that he viewed it as something material; he speaks of it, for instance, as something which we were given to drink or with which we were watered (1 Cor. 12:13, ἐποτισθῆμεν). Yet before one concludes that Paul's views were those of the Corinthians in this respect, two things must be noted: in the first place, it would be very hard to conceive, let alone to speak, of spirit or the Spirit in a wholly nonmaterial fashion. And, second, the point at issue is not whether the Spirit is interpreted nonmaterially or not, but whether the possession of it, once one has been given it, is one's inalienable right and privilege and what powers that possession then gives one, or whether the gift can at any time still be withdrawn by the Giver or negated by the attitude and behavior of the recipient.

(2c) It is striking that Horn repudiates the view of Ernst Käsemann and Peter von der Osten-Sacken that Paul introduced a christological (re)definition of the Spirit as a corrective to the misuse and misinterpretation of their spiritual gifts by some Corinthians, and argues that the latter had already identified Christ and the Spirit.[8] The mainstay of such a claim must be the interpretation

8. Horn here follows Gerhard Sellin, *Der Streit um die Auferstehung der Toten: Eine religionsgeschichtliche und exegetische Untersuchung von 1. Korinther 15* (FRLANT 138; Göttingen: Vandenhoeck & Ruprecht, 1986), esp. p. 179.

The reference above is to Ernst Käsemann, *An die Römer* (HNT 8a; Tübingen: Mohr

of 15:46 as a correction of the order of two ἄνθρωποι, an earthly and a spiritual, in the beliefs of the Corinthians, but that is, to my mind, a misunderstanding of v. 46. At most one could infer from that verse a theory of two natures, not two ἄνθρωποι since τὸ πνευματικόν and τὸ ψυχικόν are neuters. But *does* Paul reverse an order held by the Corinthians? For it is he who has just spoken of two men, two Adams, in v. 45. And, in the light of a situation in which some Corinthians seem to have been prepared to claim too much (in his eyes) for their present, Spirit-endowed existence (4:8), it makes more sense to interpret v. 46, not as a reversal of an order in the thought of the Corinthians, but as a reminder that a fully spiritual existence is not yet possible as long as the last enemy, death, has not been destroyed for the individual (15:26) and as long as each is still a being of flesh and blood, as yet unfitted to inherit God's kingdom (15:50). In other words, a rather different translation of v. 46 is not only possible but also more probable: "But the spiritual does not come at first, but (rather) the *psychikon,* and (only) then the spiritual."[9]

In that case, it is Paul who is responsible for the apparent identification of Christ and the Spirit or, more precisely, of Christ and spirit (anarthrous πνεῦμα).[10] That he gives this impression is due, above all, to the influence of the scriptural quotation of Gen. 2:7 in v. 45: in contrast to the first ἄνθρωπος who received life and became a (not the) ψυχή, the last, the eschatological ἄνθρωπος, becomes a πνεῦμα which bestows life (on others). In this respect, at least, if not in others, the function of the risen Christ and that of the Spirit are similar: both give life. It would be unwise to expect greater precision on Paul's part in 1 Cor. 15:45, for he and the Corinthians are agreed that Christ gives life and that the Spirit gives life. What he needs to stress for them here is that their condition on this side of the grave is still that of all humanity, ψυχή, and it is to support this assertion that he quotes the Old Testament.

(3) Whether the controversies of 2 Corinthians, Galatians, and Philippians are all to be ascribed to a third phase after that of 1 Corinthians may be doubted, particularly if Galatians is to be dated before 1 Corinthians.[11]

[Siebeck], 1973, 4th ed. 1980), pp. 202-3; Peter von der Osten-Sacken, *Römer 8 als Beispiel paulinischer Soteriologie* (FRLANT 112; Göttingen: Vandenhoeck & Ruprecht, 1975), p. 320.

9. Cf. my "Philo's Heavenly Man," *NovT* 15 (1973): 301-26, here pp. 301-2.

10. Cf. also 2 Cor. 3:17, where, to some at least, Paul also seems to identify Christ and the Spirit.

11. See n. 4 above.

II

Over against Horn's thesis it is, therefore, to be considered more likely that Paul, sooner or later after his conversion, which in itself may well have been an ecstatic experience of some sort, and probably by no means the last in his life, found himself in a movement where ecstatic experiences were a recognized and established feature of its life. It is, accordingly, intrinsically probable that such phenomena were recurrent elements in his missionary work and in his founding of new churches. His earliest extant letter, 1 Thessalonians, presupposes that that church was acquainted with prophecy, even if its attitude to it may have been less than unreservedly positive (5:20), and there is little reason to restrict the immediately preceding and more general injunction not to quench the Spirit (5:19) to prophetic manifestations alone,[12] even if there is here no clear and specific reference to glossolalia. In Galatians, too, Paul presupposes that experiences of the Spirit had been familiar to his converts in Galatia from the beginning and that this experience forms a main plank in his argument against the claims of the Judaizers (3:2-5); it is the more convincing as an argument if he already presupposes that the manifestations of the Spirit included the invocation of God as "Abba, Father" (4:6). Then he could justly claim that this showed that the status of the Galatian converts as God's children was already secure and did not need to be further enhanced or undergirded by circumcision or obedience to the law. And in all probability this gift of the Spirit was associated by Paul and by much of earliest Christianity with the rite of baptism.[13]

In his letter to the Galatian churches Paul also addresses them without reserve as "spiritual" (6:1). That is something he can no longer do in 1 Corinthians (1 Cor. 3:1), and that fact, together with the existence of a query about spiritual gifts or spiritual persons among the problems about which the church has asked him (12:1), to which Paul must then devote three chapters, and possibly ch. 15 as well, as a response, shows how much the possession of the Spirit posed problems for the church there. The problems are all the more far-reaching if Paul's repeated use of the verb φυσιοῦν, "to puff up," is a veiled but scornful reference to the claimed spiritual endowment of some Corinthians. For then this is associated with the reaction of some to Paul's absence (4:18-19), with their complacency about the incestuous relationship of one of their number (5:2)

12. *Pace* Horn, *Angeld*, p. 129.

13. That is suggested by the very probably traditional formulation in 1 Cor. 6:11, as Horn sees (*Angeld*, pp. 142-47). Gerhard Barth's endorsement of the picture painted by the book of Acts (*Die Taufe in frühchristlicher Zeit* [2nd ed.; Neukirchen-Vluyn: Neukirchener, 2002], e.g., p. 58) is accordingly a plausible one, for early Christianity baptism and the receiving of the Spirit belong together.

and with their vaunted knowledge (8:1). The problem, however, which directly provokes the question of the Corinthians dealt with in chs. 12–14, if one may judge from the thrust of Paul's answer, seems rather to have been one about who can claim to be "spiritual," to have the Spirit, and 14:37, "if any one supposes that he is a prophet or spiritual . . . ," coming directly after a passage in which two spiritual gifts, prophecy and glossolalia, have been discussed, suggests that claiming to be "spiritual" was particularly associated with the latter gift. In other words, some seem to have monopolized the designation "spiritual" and, at least by implication, to have denied it to other members of the congregation, as well as alienating them by their use of this gift in the worship of the community. Such a position is perhaps most easily intelligible if the possession of the Spirit were measured solely by external factors, if it were held that the more overtly supernatural a spiritual endowment was, the more obvious it was that the person endowed was "spiritual" and belonged, perhaps inalienably, to the class of the "spiritual." The implications of that for those who did not manifest such phenomena were presumably clear to the Corinthians, prompting them to ask Paul about this matter (1 Cor. 14:1).

Against this attitude Paul makes a number of counterclaims, pointing to the spiritual endowment of the Israelites which had not spared them from God's judgment in the wilderness (10:1-13), but above all advancing a number of arguments in chs. 12–14 which together undermine the claims of glossolalia to be *the* preeminent spiritual gift, even if the analogy of the many limbs in the one body should, *in theory*, mean that it is equally valuable with the rest. Everyone who confesses Jesus as Lord shows thereby that he or she is led by the Spirit (12:1-3). All the varied, and often not at all spectacular, spiritual gifts are distributed by God the Lord and the sovereign Spirit, all for the common good of the community (12:4-7; cf. 12:28-30). For the collective body of the community, like the human body, depends on the cooperation and unity of its many parts, which complement one another (12:12-27).

It is at the start of ch. 12 that the christological definition of the Spirit's presence is most clearly visible: Paul contrasts the cursing of Jesus and the confession of Jesus as Lord (12:3). Although it has been hotly discussed who cursed Jesus and why, the reference is most easily understood as a contrast to the confession of him as Lord; it is not, however, purely hypothetical because it reflects the attitude of non-believing Jews who see in the crucified Jesus proof that he is accursed (cf. Gal. 3:13). All who confess Jesus as Lord, on the other hand, have the Spirit; it is the Spirit in them which enables them to recognize him as Lord. They *all* have the Spirit, and the possession of the Spirit is not limited to a small, elite group manifesting more spectacular and more overtly supernatural spiritual gifts.

In other words, just as Paul asserts the claim of the Christ who has died for the "weaker" sister or brother in order to persuade the Corinthian "strong" not to follow through their "knowledge" to its logical, practical conclusion, regardless of the impact which their behavior may have on others (1 Cor. 8, esp. vv. 9-12), so too Christology should control the Corinthians' assessment and use of their possession of the Spirit. That Spirit was given for and to all of the Corinthian community, and the exercise of spiritual gifts should serve the good of all and the upbuilding of the whole community (12:7; cf. 14:4-5, 12, 26).

This is not an argument which Paul uses in 1 Thessalonians, nor indeed for that matter in Galatians. But then it is not an argument which, as far as we can tell, was needed in either of these letters, for there is no sign that the possession of the Spirit was thus misused in these churches; in other words, the argument from silence may be correct, but it does not settle the matter finally. In Corinth, on the other hand, at least some members of the church had apparently developed their own interpretation of what the gift of the Spirit entailed, perhaps above all under the influence of views on ritual acts and their effects which were current in their world. For Paul's arguments in 1 Cor. 1:13-17 strongly suggest that baptism played an important part in the thinking of some Corinthians and encouraged the divisiveness to be found among them — perhaps particularly among the supporters of Apollos if 1 Cor. 3:6, ἐπότισεν, is a reference to Apollos's baptizing activity. It is likely, moreover, that baptism had long been associated with the giving of the Spirit (this may account for the use of the same verb, ποτίζω, in 12:13), and this is in turn may have led some Corinthians to attach particular importance to this rite, especially if it led to ecstatic manifestations of the Spirit, and to attach particular importance also to the person who had administered the rite to them.[14]

Whatever the origins of this interpretation of the Spirit by some Corinthians, it is probably the reason for a thoroughly unusual piece of terminology on Paul's part, his repeated contrast of πνεῦμα (and πνευματικός) and ψυχή (and ψυχικός) (1 Cor. 2:14-15; 15:44, 46). Paul's previous readiness to call Christians "spiritual" (Gal. 6:1) may well have led members of one of his churches to take this usage up and invest it with a meaning which the apostle now considers highly undesirable. This undesirability very probably first became apparent in the way in which it was used by some Corinthians, with potentially devastating consequences for the unity of that church. At the same time the contrast between πνεῦμα and ψυχή is a striking and unusual one, in that the latter term tended, if anything, to be used positively in Greek dualistic traditions, con-

14. Cf. further my *Baptism and Resurrection: Studies in Pauline Theology against Its Graeco-Roman Background* (WUNT 44; Tübingen: Mohr Siebeck, 1987), esp. pp. 234-49, 287-95.

trasted with the body as its prison or burden. On the other hand, the contrast may not be Paul's or the Corinthians' own invention, but may stem from Christian wisdom traditions. For Jas. 3:15 uses the adjective ψυχικός of a worldly, as opposed to heavenly, wisdom, and exponents of a Christian wisdom may well have felt the need to develop such a contrast to show the very different source and nature of competing wisdoms circulating in their world. Even if the Corinthians had learned from Paul that they were "spiritual," the wisdom traditions with which they had been in contact (thanks to the ministrations of Apollos?) may have taught them to distinguish between a heavenly, spiritual endowment and a purely natural one, which all possessed through their human ψυχή, and to despise the latter. This contrast is, however, a usage which Paul quite likely abandoned again once he was no longer confronted with aggressive claims to be wise and with a preoccupation with the theme of wisdom such as is reflected in 1 Corinthians 1–3.

III

This discussion of 1 Corinthians may have, however, presented a misleading picture of the development of Paul's thought if his letter to the Galatians in fact precedes the Corinthian correspondence, as I have already hinted.[15] Three considerations connected with Paul's pneumatology may in fact be more easily explained if Galatians precedes 1 Corinthians rather than the reverse:

1. As already noted, it is easier to see how Paul can uninhibitedly address the Galatians as πνευματικοί (6:1) if all the problems which this designation was to present in the Corinthian church had not yet confronted him.
2. The contrast of πνευματικός and σάρκινος in 1 Cor. 3:1, where one might have expected ψυχικός again, is the more readily intelligible if Paul, faced with opponents who demanded the literally fleshly sign of circumcision from his converts, has already developed the contrast between Spirit and flesh in Galatians.
3. If the misuse of the claim to have the Spirit led to a stress on the Spirit's connection to Christ as a corrective, then it is to be noted that the only passage linking the Spirit to Christ in Galatians is 4:6, and there it is not as a corrective, but rather to underline the status of the Galatians as God's

15. If exception should be taken to the controversial term "development," then some other wordier expression like "the cumulative but selective process of semantic redefinition and refinement" would be necessary.

children: having the Spirit (3:2-5), they already enjoy this status and need not therefore do anything further, such as obeying the law of Moses, to enhance their status or to reinforce what they have already received and already enjoy.

IV

One of the most important passages on Pauline pneumatology, if not the most important, is Romans 8, but it is disconcertingly difficult to see immediately why the theme of the Spirit is introduced at this point, unless it is that the possession of the Spirit by believers was one of those convictions which Paul could assume as common to the whole of early Christianity, like the fact of their baptism in ch. 6, and which thus provided him with a point of contact with this church. That could support the claims of those who view Romans as a résumé of the apostle's thinking in his earlier writings. Yet there is much in this chapter which is not really foreshadowed in any of the earlier letters which we possess, and, above all, in relation to Paul's pneumatology, the intercession of the Spirit with our spirits (8:16) and its assistance in our weakness (8:26). Furthermore, although the christological shape of Paul's pneumatology has been stressed in the writings of some who have written on this letter and this chapter,[16] it is arguable that the inseparable connection between the Spirit and Christology is far clearer in the earlier 1 Cor. 12:3. For although it is also clear in Romans that the Spirit is the Spirit of Christ (8:9b) and that its indwelling is tantamount to the indwelling of Christ (8:10), it is just as much, or even more, the Spirit of that God who raised Jesus from the dead (8:9a, 11, 14; cf. 5:5; 8:15, 27).

This is not the place for a full discussion either of this letter or of this chapter,[17] but it needs to be noted, first, that the chapter starts by filling a glaring gap in the anthropology of 7:7-25, where the Spirit is nowhere mentioned. Moreover, Romans 8 fills this gap by picking up from 7:21-23 the puzzling, allusive use of the word νόμος, which seems to refer now to the Mosaic law, now to some other "law" (expressly "another" law in 7:23 and, moreover, one to be found in the limbs of the body). But not only does the beginning of ch. 8 fill this gap left in ch. 7, but it also enables Paul to rebut once again a charge that has preoccupied him in various forms in the course of the letter, the charge of encouraging libertinism and antinomianism or, in the language of Romans,

16. See above (n. 8) on Käsemann and von der Osten-Sacken.

17. See further my *The Reasons for Romans* (Studies of the New Testament and Its World; Edinburgh: T&T Clark, 1988).

unrighteousness, a charge implicit in Rom. 3:8 and in the questions of 6:1 and 15. Against that charge Paul now stresses that those who walk according to the Spirit fulfill the δικαίωμα of the law (8:4); indeed, that is the only way to fulfill it, for it is impossible if one lives according to or in the flesh (8:5-8). It is in fact the Spirit who enables the believer to put to death the deeds of the body (8:13).

There is, however, a further reason for speaking of the Spirit at this point. Paul has introduced the body of the letter with the assertion that he is not ashamed of his gospel (1:17). One reason for this assertion may well be a rebuttal of the charge that he should indeed be ashamed of it, for it depicts a God who has not treated the people of the promise, Israel, righteously, as well as its being a message which foments a libertine unrighteousness in its adherents. But another reason for this assertion is Paul's confidence of eschatological vindication, as is most clearly seen in the triumphantly defiant close of ch. 8 (vv. 31-39): at the end he and those who share his trust in this message will not be put to shame. He and they have confidence even amid present sufferings (5:3), and the mainstay of that confident hope is the outpouring of God's Spirit in their hearts (5:5), the presence in them of the power of a God who is love.

If chs. 5–8 form a ring composition, as many think, then it is only to be expected that these themes from the first part of ch. 5 should return and be developed in ch. 8. Indeed, the theme of confidence amid suffering, based on the present experience of the Spirit's presence, reappears there and is elaborated on at greater length. It is from its presence now that we eventually expect life for our mortal bodies (8:11). Of that coming redemption the present Spirit is the first fruits, sustaining those who groan as they await their adoption as God's children (8:23). In this groaning weakness we are sustained by the Spirit interceding for us (and within us?) with "unutterable groans," and in a fashion that reflects God's perspective and will (8:26-27).

In that case, then, the theme of the Spirit is here developed in a way that is closely related to the whole apologetic thrust of Paul's argument in his letter to the Romans. On the one hand, the Spirit is invoked to ward off the criticism that Paul's gospel is an incitement to immorality; instead Paul insists that those who are led by the Spirit fulfill God's will through God's powerful and loving Spirit dwelling in them, even if not by conforming to an external norm. That retort is already anticipated in the dry comment that there is no law prohibiting any of the fruit of the Spirit in Gal. 5:23, but now that line of argument is taken further, in a way that is also echoed in Gal. 5:14 (as well as again in the similar Rom. 13:8-10): a life according to the Spirit fulfills the δικαίωμα of the law (8:4). On the other hand, Paul stresses more clearly here than elsewhere the role of the Spirit as the first fruits of the still future redemption, although that theme was also foreshadowed in the similar image of the Spirit as a "pledge" in 2 Cor.

1:22; 5:5. Now that commercial metaphor has been replaced by the agricultural one of first fruits, an image that Paul has hitherto used for Christ, not the Spirit (1 Cor. 15:20, 23).

V

Were one, then, to ask, "What is Paul's teaching on the Spirit?" one would be faced with something of a quandary. For in each of the letters we have considered, different aspects of Paul's thinking on the Spirit emerge, reflecting in large measure his differing concerns in each letter. It is true that the apostle's thinking is in some measure cumulative, in the sense that later letters reflect insights gained in the particular situations with which he was dealing in earlier letters. Once, for instance, he has seen how closely linked to Christ the Spirit must be in order to avoid the situation that arose in Corinth, the Spirit remains the Spirit of Christ, as well as of God, in Romans. Even if, in the time between his conversion and the writing of 1 Corinthians, he could have thought of the Spirit apart from Christ, that was no longer possible for him, for the experience of the difficulties in that church had compelled him to make that connection explicit, for himself and for his converts, just as the encounter with opposition to his message for Gentiles which did not involve their becoming Jews in order to be saved very likely forced him to make explicit convictions that were hitherto only implicit in his life and work. But there are exceptions to this accumulation: the contrast between πνεῦμα and ψυχή, for instance, disappears again after 1 Corinthians, and this specialized usage seems to have no place in Paul's thought apart from this particular context. So should we take Romans as Paul's latest and most definitive statement on the matter, which defines what is to be retained and what can be and has in fact been discarded, like the πνεῦμα-ψυχή contrast? Yet *is* it in fact the latest of his extant letters? Even if Colossians was not written by Paul, what if Philippians were written from a later imprisonment in Rome? Yet Philippians adds little of importance to Paul's thought on this subject, and Colossians even less for that matter. The themes discussed in these letters do not seem to have necessitated recourse to pneumatology, whereas, as we have seen, that subject plays an important part in Romans. Yet can the teaching of Romans be considered "definitive," on this matter as on others, if the aspects of the subject treated there are so integrally linked to the apostle's particular concerns in framing this letter, and if aspects handled in earlier letters go unmentioned — not only the contrast with ψυχή but also, for instance, those enigmatic but important passages which may seem at first sight to identify Christ with the Spirit, 1 Cor. 15:45 and 2 Cor. 3:17a? The nearest to that which we have in Romans is the parallelism between the indwelling Spirit of Christ and the indwelling Christ in 8:9b and 10. If the statements in 1 and 2 Corinthians can be explained as produced by a particular argumentative situation, may that not apply equally strongly to Romans? That Paul has to explain and defend himself to a church which he has not yet visited may mean that he must expound things which he could otherwise simply assume his converts already knew, but that does not make the letter any less contextually determined; it is just a different context.

Is the apostle's thinking on this matter, then, to be considered episodic and, at the time of the writing of his latest letters, still incomplete, even if there are some aspects of his developing thought which may be regarded as having become constant features of it once they had developed? What his letters offer us are, in that case, a series of echoes, as it were, of his thinking, in part when the theme of the Spirit serves a purpose within his arguments relating to other issues, in part also, however, when he feels that the nature and role of the Spirit have been misunderstood, especially in the Corinthian church. It may even go beyond the evidence to assert that these echoes of his thinking all point in the same direction or are compatible with one another. On the matters of the relation between the Spirit and Christ and of the relation between the divine Spirit and the human spirit, at least, Paul's statements give a tantalizing and very inchoate impression. Yet part of their value may lie precisely in their nature as "unfinished business," which spurs us on to reflect further on this most mysterious and elusive reality, the Spirit of God and of Christ.

XIII Πνευματικός in the Social Dialect of Pauline Christianity

John M. G. Barclay

"It was generally recognized within the Pauline mission: that reception of the Spirit was the decisive and determinative element in the crucial transition of conversion; and that the presence of the Spirit in a life was the most distinctive and defining feature of a life thus reclaimed by God."[1] Thus Professor Dunn sums up one of the characteristic emphases in his research on early Christianity, a theme he has rightly highlighted throughout his extraordinary academic career. In tribute to a friend and scholar from whom I have learned so much, I offer here some reflections on early Christian Spirit-discourse. In particular, I wish to highlight the peculiarity of the adjective πνευματικός ("Spirit-related") as we find it in Pauline speech — a lexical oddity which could shed important light on the formation of early Christian identity.

I. Language and Social Dialect

Recent studies in the social formation of earliest Christianity have given rather little attention to the significance of its distinctive patterns of language. In analyzing "the language of belonging," Meeks rightly noted that "not just the shared content of beliefs but also shared forms by which the beliefs are expressed are important in promoting cohesiveness."[2] Noting some of the distinctive (though

1. J. D. G. Dunn, *The Theology of Paul the Apostle* (Edinburgh: T&T Clark, 1998), p. 425.

2. W. A. Meeks, *The First Urban Christians* (New Haven: Yale University Press, 1983), p. 93.

not wholly unique) jargon used by Pauline Christians, he remarked that much of this was inherited from Judaism and the "translation Greek" of the Septuagint, but that "very quickly the Pauline Christians developed their own slogans and patterns of speech that distinguished them from other Jewish groups as well as from the general environment."[3] This is an observation which invites much fuller investigation. Crucial to that study would be careful gathering of the linguistic data but also alertness to *patterns* and *networks* of speech (not isolated items of vocabulary); moreover, appropriate analytical tools are needed in assessing the data. Meeks's comments on this topic might suggest a rather straightforward relationship between groups, beliefs, and language: distinctive groups develop particular beliefs and then express these linguistically in forms which serve to reinforce group distinction.[4] But language can do more than just "express" beliefs: it can play a critical role in *shaping* ideas and identities since it does not just reflect, but in important senses *constitutes* the realities which we inhabit. In what follows, I will pursue Meeks's interest in early Christian language, and Dunn's interest in the Spirit, by examining one small, but significant, item in the "social dialect" of Pauline Christians, the adjective πνευματικός. I will also suggest how this peculiarity of language contributed to the "construction" of a world with a distinct though highly adaptable configuration, with important consequences for early Christianity.

The notion of "world construction" is drawn from the sociology of knowledge as developed by Berger and Luckmann. Among their many contributions to this field is their observation that "the most important vehicle of reality-maintenance is conversation."[5] As they point out, this is nowhere more evident than in primary socialization (childhood) and in those examples of "alternation" (such as religious conversion) in which an individual enters a new world and needs to acquire a new structure of plausibility. As a microsociety somewhat at odds with the taken-for-granted perspectives and practices of its environment (both Jewish and Gentile), the earliest Christian movement had to work hard to shape and maintain its own interpretation of reality; and one of its most important tools for this task was the very language it used. Conversation within such a group is of fundamental importance: that its members talk to one another, and how they do so, are both crucial in constituting the "world" they inhabit. Thus to become a convert was to acquire a new linguistic competence — not, of course,

3. Meeks, *First Urban Christians,* p. 94.

4. Note the statement cited above: the "beliefs . . . expressed are important in promoting cohesiveness." Meeks adds: "Every close-knit group develops its own argot, and the use of that argot in speech among members knits them more closely still" (*First Urban Christians,* p. 93).

5. P. L. Berger and T. Luckmann, *The Social Construction of Reality* (New York: Doubleday, Anchor Books edition, 1967), p. 152.

the acquisition of a whole new language but the ability to comprehend and to participate in the patterns of speech by which the Christian community described itself, its beliefs, its norms, and its social environment.

To this broad conceptual framework supplied by the sociology of knowledge, we may add some features of sociolinguistics.[6] Although early Christianity was not in all respects, or in all its manifestations, an "antisociety" equipped with an "antilanguage,"[7] we should expect some early Christian groups to display elements of a "social dialect" (or "sociolect") — special forms of speech which both reflect and shape their peculiar interpretations of the world.[8] In its fullest sense, a "dialect" typically encompasses distinctive patterns of pronunciation, vocabulary, and grammar, and we do not have evidence to suggest that Christians developed their own patterns of speech in all these respects; there is no hint, for instance, that they spoke in a distinctive "accent." But there were certainly some examples of unusual grammar in their texts (under the influence of the Septuagint), and many peculiarities in their vocabulary, not only in strange idioms like ἐν Χριστῷ ("in Christ") but also in the novel ways they used standard terms, such as ἐκκλησία ("church"), εὐαγγέλιον ("gospel"), and πνεῦμα ("Spirit"). Indeed, the characteristic linguistic innovation in early Christianity was not the coining of neologisms, but the special frequency and emphasis with which Christians deployed already existent terms which were used otherwise quite rarely, or rather differently, outside the circle of believers. As studies of social dialects indicate, what is particularly revealing in this regard is where particular terms come to prominence, and gain a stable meaning, in ways uncharacteristic of their normal usage outside the group.[9] If the in-group language is also in tension with its normal usage, producing meanings which strongly contrast with the usual senses outside the group, this could indicate a site of difference, one factor in constituting the "deviant" identity of the group concerned. The adoption of unusual self-labels can be particularly instructive

6. I am grateful to Dr. Edward Adams of King's College London for first pointing me in this direction while he worked on his innovative thesis, now published as *Constructing the World* (Edinburgh: T&T Clark, 2000). His advice has remained invaluable.

7. M. A. K. Halliday, *Language as Social Semiotic* (London: Edward Arnold, 1978), pp. 164-82.

8. Halliday, *Language*, p. 159: "A social dialect is a dialect — a configuration of phonetic, phonological, grammatical and lexical features — that is associated with, and stands as a symbol for, some more or less objectively definable social group."

9. Foundational here are a number of studies conducted in the 1960s and 1970s by Labov and his successors; see W. Labov, *The Social Stratification of English in New York City* (Washington, D.C.: Center for Applied Linguistics, 1966); L. Milroy, *Language and Social Networks* (Oxford: Blackwell, 1987); cf. J. Holmes, *An Introduction to Social Linguistics* (London: Longman, 2002), pp. 144-61, 202-8; J. K. Chambers, *Sociolinguistic Theory* (2nd ed.; Oxford: Blackwell, 2003), pp. 74-115.

in this regard. Once again the social dialect does not merely "reflect" or "embody" the distinct worldview of the group concerned; it also shapes that distinction since a worldview cannot be conceptualized and thus cannot take shape at all, except through language.[10]

II. The Peculiarity of πνευματικός

Early Christian experience of God did not come self-labeled as "the Spirit." While stressing the importance of post-Easter experience, we should note the very particular ways in which early Christians categorized this experience, as a mediation of divine presence or power specifically through "the Spirit." As Paige has recently insisted, the description of the personal presence of a deity as πνεῦμα was highly unusual in Greek-speaking antiquity everywhere except in Judaism.[11] Older *religionsgeschichtliche* scholarship appears to have been seriously misguided in its attempts to trace the "roots" of this language in Greek "mysticism" or "Gnosticism": it relied on later texts which were themselves influenced by Christianity, or it grossly exaggerated the significance of only vaguely parallel patterns of vocabulary. In this, as in much else, early Christians were drawing from a biblical and Jewish linguistic reservoir.[12] Even so, the prominence of their Spirit-language is unusual; perhaps only in the Dead Sea Scrolls is the Spirit such a frequent topic of discussion. And nothing that we know of Judaism prepares us for the significance of what we should consider a distinctly Christian adjective, πνευματικός.[13] Since it is in Pauline circles that we can trace the first uses of this term, we will focus our analysis there.[14]

10. The influence of the "linguistic turn" has certainly been felt in sociolinguistics. See the critique of older scholarship (on the basis of contemporary discourse theory) by G. Williams, *Sociolinguistics: A Sociological Critique* (London: Routledge, 1992). At a theoretical level, the field may be said to be highly unstable, or diversified, at present; see B. Carter and A. Sealey, "Language, Structure and Agency: What Can Realist Social Theory Offer to Sociolinguistics?" *Journal of Sociolinguistics* 4 (2000): 3-20.

11. T. Paige, "Who Believes in 'Spirit'? Πνεῦμα in Pagan Usage and Implications for the Gentile Christian Mission," *HTR* 95 (2002): 417-36. He describes the Jewish-Christian usage of πνεῦμα as "a kind of specialized religious dialect unfamiliar to most Greek speakers" (p. 434).

12. On the discourse about the Spirit in late Second Temple Judaism see J. R. Levison, *The Spirit in First-Century Judaism* (Leiden: Brill, 1997).

13. For its use in Philo, see below. Compared to its absence from the LXX and the tiny trickle of examples in Greek-speaking Judaism, the flood of occurrences of this adjective in early Christian literature is striking; see, e.g., G. Lampe, *A Patristic Greek Lexicon* (Oxford: Clarendon, 1961), s.v. πνευματικός.

14. Cf. J. D. G. Dunn, "Spirit (NT)," in C. Brown (ed.), *New International Dictionary of New Testament Theology* (Exeter: Paternoster, 1978), 3:693-707 (esp. pp. 706-7 on "spiritual").

Of the 24 uses of the adjective πνευματικός in the Pauline corpus, 15 occur in one letter alone, the first letter to the Corinthians (also the site of the abverb πνευματικῶς, 1 Cor. 2:13). In this letter Paul refers to "Spirit people" (πνευματικοί) on at least four occasions (1 Cor. 2:13, 15; 3:1; 14:37; possibly also in 12:1), but also uses the neuter plural to refer to "things of the Spirit" in several places (1 Cor. 2:13; 9:11; 12:1[?]; 14:1). The heaviest use of these terms (1 Cor. 2:6–3:4; 12–14) occurs in contexts which make clear that the adjective is strongly associated with, even coined from, the noun πνεῦμα, the name used by Paul for the eschatological gift of God's power and grace. Even if a parallel can be drawn with the human "spirit" at one point (1 Cor. 2:11), it is clear that the adjective πνευματικός is not in origin an anthropological but an eschatological term: it describes people not through analysis of their human constitution but in relation to their new status as graced by the Spirit of God. Thus the term is self-consciously new — not in the sense that it was wholly unprecedented in the Greek language (we shall note some examples below), but in the sense that Paul employs it to designate a reality not hitherto attested because it describes a state of affairs believed to be wholly without precedent. If this is true of the adjective as applied to people, it is equally the case with the neuter "things of the Spirit," which are said to be not generally understood (2:13-14) but which characterize the special work of Paul's preaching (9:11). Thus also when Paul refers to the πνευματικὸν σῶμα (1 Cor. 15:44, 46), this is a body which can be envisaged only as an eschatological reality. This form of body appears to be so labeled as energized by Christ, "the life-giving Spirit" (15:45), but the nature of the association with the Spirit is less clear where the adjective is applied to the food and drink consumed by Israel in the wilderness, and the rock which followed them (namely, Christ) in 1 Cor. 10:3-4.[15] Here pre-Christian realities are described in terms which seem self-consciously *transferred* from the Christian era, an exception which thus confirms the rule that Paul employs the adjective to interpret reality in specifically Christian terms. All these uses of πνευματικός derive from and embody a particular Christian hermeneutic.

That Paul can use this language without special explanation suggests that it is not a wholly idiosyncratic phenomenon, an "idiolect." Indeed, there are reasonable grounds for suspecting that this might be an item of vocabulary particularly common in the Corinthian church, even a favoured self-label employed by an "elite" group within it. Much scholarly attention has been paid to this possibility,

15. In the first two cases the adjective might be construed in the sense of "conveying the Spirit," but this is hardly the case with the third; see discussions in G. D. Fee, *The First Epistle to the Corinthians* (NICNT; Grand Rapids: Eerdmans, 1987), pp. 446-49; W. Schrage, *Der erste Brief an die Korinther* (EKKNT; Neukirchen-Vluyn: Neukirchener, 1995), 2:392-95. We are alerted already here to the elasticity of the term and its potential for adaptation.

in the hope of eliciting the theology of the Corinthian "enthusiasts" or "Gnostics." But much depends here on a subtle "mirror reading" which presumes that Paul's unusual vocabulary is explicable only if it is derived from the Corinthians' usage; and we know too little about the Corinthians to go much beyond speculation in these matters.[16] Nonetheless, even if we cannot delineate in detail what the Corinthians meant in employing these terms, they seem to have shared this vocabulary with Paul (while possibly disagreeing on its connotations). Whoever "coined" it, the term has become an important item in the social idiom of this particular network. What is more, its usage has set up binary oppositions, which provide an important means to categorize the world. If some people, but only some, are πνευματικοί, others have to be given another category label — either ψυχικοί ("soul-related," 1 Cor. 2:14; cf. 15:44, 46) or σαρκινοί/σαρκικοί ("flesh-related," 1 Cor. 3:1-3; cf. 9:11). In other words, this Christian network has developed an important linguistic tool with which to interpret social reality, a term which is fully comprehensible only within its own patterns of discourse.

It was not just Paul and the Corinthians who understood each other when they spoke in these terms. Although Paul uses πνευματικός much less frequently elsewhere, the fact that he does use it in other letters, without explanation, suggests that it had wide Christian currency. It appears that the Galatians could also appreciate the label πνευματικοί; Paul uses it also in writing to them (6:1), in line with his instruction on the importance of the Spirit as the defining characteristic of their lives (3:1-5; 5:13-25). Even in writing to the Romans, who had not encountered his speech patterns before, Paul employs the neuter adjective πνευματικά ("things of the Spirit") in referring to the gospel (Rom. 15:27; cf. the identical metaphor in 1 Cor. 9:11). He also deploys πνευματικός in the context of the Spirit-flesh antithesis (Rom. 7:14, of the law), but once adjoins it to the noun χάρισμα (Rom. 1:11) in an echo of 1 Corinthians 12–14. The adjective has clearly become part of Paul's vocabulary stock, and he assumes that it was generally comprehensible to other believers, whether or not he had previously met them. It continued to be used by his immediate successors, who referred to "spiritual" understanding (Col. 1:9), "spiritual" songs (Col. 3:16; Eph. 5:19), and "spiritual" blessings (Eph. 1:3; cf. 1 Pet. 2:5, "spiritual" sacrifices in a "spiritual" building). The term clearly became common currency in these Pauline circles; but that it could be used in Eph. 6:12 for malign "spiritual" forces shows how far it could stray from its originally close connection to the "Holy Spirit."

16. For just one recent example, see the careful investigation by F. W. Horn, *Das Angeld des Geistes* (Göttingen: Vandenhoeck & Ruprecht, 1992), pp. 180-201. He concludes that πνευματικός was an exclusive self-categorization of Corinthian glossolalists, who contrasted themselves with ψυχικοί and may have used the statement of 1 Cor. 2:15 as their watchword. All of this is possible, but it is dependent on a string of hypotheses which remain difficult to establish.

All of this stands in stark contrast to the rare and wholly different uses of the adjective in Greek outside early Christianity, both "pagan" and Jewish. Compared to its heavy usage in the Pauline epistles, πνευματικός is an extremely rare term in non-Jewish Greek. Where it occurs it generally has the sense of "gaseous" or "windy" since the normal sense of πνεῦμα is "wind" or "air." Thus, in Plutarch it can be used in reference to the airs or vapors that circulate through the body (e.g., *Mor.* 129c, 290a-b, 978e), while in Athenaeus's dinner talk it means "flatulent" (e.g., *Deipn.* 2.55b, 69e)![17] In such cases, even if the adjective has anthropological reference, it is never used in relation to some higher dimension of existence since πνεῦμα is very rarely employed to designate the highest human capacities.[18] We thus have no precursors to the Christian antithesis between πνευματικός and ψυχικός, and on the rare occasions where πνεῦμα is used in relation to divine influence (e.g., in poetic inspiration or prophecy) it is never prominent or distinctive enough to spawn the adjective πνευματικός for those who receive this divine "breath."[19] Indeed, the only context in which the adjective is deployed with frequency in non-Jewish Greek is in Stoic physics, where the significance of the πνεῦμα which circulates through the cosmos and binds it together makes it natural that the corresponding adjective should be used to describe those cosmic bonds. Although Stoic physics is also, in the broadest sense, "religious," the term is never used of *people* or of religious practices, and the Pauline sense of the term seems worlds apart from the Stoic notion that earth and water maintain their unity "by virtue of participation in a pneumatic and fiery power" (πνευματικῆς μετοχῇ καὶ πυρώδους δυνάμεως, Plutarch, *Mor.* 1085d).[20] The "Gnostic" sources sometimes cited as Pauline parallels clearly draw from early Christian usage and cannot be used to attest an independent linguistic tradition.

Scholarly discussion of the (possible) Corinthian use of the πνευματικός-ψυχικός antithesis turned in the 1970s from a "Gnostic" to a "Hellenistic-Jewish" background.[21] Since πνευματικός is absent from the LXX and occurs

17. I am grateful to Terence Paige for sending me the relevant portions of his Ph.D. thesis ("Spirit at Corinth: The Corinthian Concept of Spirit and Paul's Response as Seen in 1 Corinthians"; University of Sheffield, 1994), based on a Thesaurus Linguae Graecae search for πνευματικός; to his material one may add examples from the *Stoicorum Veterum Fragmenta.*

18. In Epictetus, *Diss.* 3.13.15, e.g., τὸ πνευμάτικον is just one of the four physical elements of the body which dissipate at death; it is not identified with reason, mind or soul.

19. See the discussion in Paige, "Who Believes in 'Spirit'?" The denigration of the category ψυχικός also seems to be unprecedented.

20. Thus, although Celsus tried to make sense of early Christian terminology by reference to Stoic notions of πνεῦμα, Origen rightly highlighted the gulf between the two linguistic traditions (*Cels.* 6.69-75).

21. The development can be traced in U. Wilckens, *Weisheit und Torheit: Eine exegetisch-*

nowhere in other Greek-Jewish literature except in Philo, the argument depends entirely on Philonic usage; this is sometimes claimed to suggest a stratification within humanity similar to that found in 1 Corinthians and to rest on an interpretation of Gen. 2:7 like that taken to be Paul's target in 1 Cor. 15:44-49. However, closer inspection of the Philo passages indicates that none of the elements of this argument are convincing, and especially not the supposed parallels to the use of πνευματικός.[22] This adjective occurs no more than nine times in the whole Philonic corpus, in many of which it echoes the Stoic sense of the "pneumatic bonds" which bind all matter (animate and inanimate) together (e.g., *Her.* 242; *Aet.* 86, 125; *QG* 2.3?). Where it is used of human beings, it is clear that the "pneumatic bonds" are not some "higher" feature but merely the ligaments which keep the body cohesive, in contrast to the virtues of the soul (ψυχή; e.g., *Praem.* 46). If πνεῦμα represents the life force or life breath, this is not the same as the "soul" or "reason" (*Opif.* 67). On the two occasions where the adjective is deployed to represent a superior form of materiality (that of angels), it stands not above but in parallel to the "soul-like" substance (ψυχοειδὴς οὐσία, *Abr.* 113; *QG* 1.92). Thus there is nothing in Philo to suggest the prominence of the adjective in the Pauline corpus and the peculiar antitheses it there spawns. Even when Philo interprets Gen. 2:7, he gives no special emphasis to the divine πνεῦμα, and appears to take the "inbreathing" in the account of human creation to represent the installation of the soul (ψυχή); the passage is never taken to signal a particular class of people or things.[23] As Theissen rightly concludes: "The fact remains that it has up to now been impossible to derive the

religionsgeschichtliche Untersuchung zu 1 Kor 1 und 2 (Tübingen: Mohr-Siebeck, 1959); M. Winter, *Pneumatiker und Psychiker in Korinth* (Marburg: Elwert, 1975); B. Pearson, *The Pneumatikos-Psychikos Terminology in 1 Corinthians* (Missoula: University of Montana Press, 1973); this remains the explanation of Corinthian vocabulary favored by Horn, *Angeld,* pp. 194-98.

22. For similar scepticism, see G. Theissen, *Psychological Aspects of Pauline Theology* (Edinburgh: T&T Clark, 1987), pp. 358-67. Note Theissen's conclusion: "If we read 1 Cor. 2:6-16 against the background of the Jewish Hellenistic wisdom tradition, then it is precisely deviations from this tradition which can best be explained by specifically Christian impulses" (p. 367).

23. From Josephus, *Ant.* 1.34, it is clear that it was possible to interpret what God breathed into humanity as πνεῦμα (cf. LXX Gen. 2:7: πνοὴ ζώης). But since the result of this inbreathing was to create the human being as a ψυχὴ ζῶσα, it is hard to see how an antithesis can be created from this verse between πνεῦμα and ψυχή. Philo normally cites this verse as the inbreathing of πνοὴ ζώης, but where he uses πνεῦμα he interprets this "divine breath" as the soul, even the "essence of the soul" (*Leg.* 1.36; 3.161; *Her.* 55–57; *Spec.* 4.123; *Det.* 80–84); even in *Opif.* 135 and *Plant.* 18, the "divine spirit" is not something distinct from, or higher than, the soul which is given to every person. The people Philo admires are those who cultivate the "soul" and "reason," not a special class of "Spirit-people"; and he never uses the adjective πνευματικός in connection with Gen 2:7. It thus greatly confuses the matter for Horn (and others) to use the term "Pneumatiker" as a label for Philo's highest achievers (*Angeld,* pp. 45-48).

opposition of *pneumatikos* and *psychikos* from pre-Pauline sources. The interpretation of the two creation accounts with these antonyms is a step beyond the known Hellenistic Jewish exegesis."[24]

III. Pauline πνευματικά and Their Semantic Potential

The remarkable frequency of πνευματικός in the Pauline Epistles is not difficult to explain. Once the new and overwhelming experience of God in early Christianity was interpreted as the presence of "the Spirit," it was natural that this term, and its adjectival derivative, would play a prominent role in Christian discourse. Since Paul places particular emphasis on "the Spirit" as the source of eschatological life, the medium of knowledge, and the criterion of morality, it is not surprising that he, and those influenced by his thought, should find themselves speaking of things which characterize their new life as πνευματικά. For those whose lives were dramatically redefined by this new reality, it was natural to consider themselves πνευματικοί. The adjective thus takes on a new and semitechnical sense within a particular religious network, a self-consciously novel family of churches. They did not coin the adjective — it was perfectly good Greek — but they used it with a frequency and an emphasis which mark it out as peculiar to their discourse. They also used it in senses it had not acquired before, since they deployed it within a web of associations (with experience and with other terms) which was unique to this new religious movement.[25] If they employed it in conversation with "outsiders," it would surely have caused puzzlement; used among themselves, it resonated with other elements in their discourse, notably their special understanding of "the Spirit." The term thus creates a linguistic distinction between "insiders" and "outsiders." This does not necessarily correlate with a social separation from non-Christians — indeed, if the Corinthian church used the term, it circulated among Christians who were relatively well integrated into their social environment.[26] But it is not surpris-

24. Theissen, *Psychological Aspects*, p. 363. Only in passing does Horn allow (*Angeld*, p. 200) that there might lie behind the Pauline usage a specifically Christian interpretation of the effusion of the Spirit.

25. On the importance of webs of association in determining meaning, as against persistent attempts to "derive" the meaning of terms from preceding linguistic traditions, see A. Millar and J. K. Riches, "Interpretation: A Theoretical Perspective and Some Applications," *Numen* 28/1 (1981): 29-53.

26. So I have argued in "Thessalonica and Corinth: Social Contrasts in Pauline Christianity," *JSNT* 47 (1992): 49-74. For the self-understanding of the Christians in Corinth, see now S. Chester, *Conversion in Corinth* (Edinburgh: T&T Clark, 2003).

ing that this unusual category of "Spirit things" and "Spirit people" should create a linguistic and conceptual distinction from "non-Spirit" phenomena and thus establish novel binary oppositions between πνεῦμα and σάρξ, or πνευματικοί and ψυχικοί. In other words, the use of this linguistic apparatus creates conceptual categorizations which serve to *constitute* the worldview of Pauline Christians: by referring to themselves and the things they held most precious with this adjective, Christians began to define reality in distinctive ways.

But if πνευματικός is of nodal significance in Pauline discourse, it also displays a degree of semantic indeterminacy which would enable it to be deployed richly, and variously, in later Christianity. As a label for "spiritual" people, the adjective creates a categorical distinction between Christians and "others," but the complexities and ambiguities of the key passage on this topic, 1 Cor. 2:6–3:4, leave unclear what it means to label the others as ψυχικοί and σαρκικοί, and indeed whether those constitute one category or two. Since those adjectives relate to familiar anthropological terms, the passage invites reflection on the constitution of human nature and what makes Christians distinct.[27] And since there could be doubt whether Paul considered all Christians to be properly labeled πνευματικοί (1 Cor. 3:1; 14:37; even Gal. 6:1), the term could be reserved for an elite, as by Valentinian Christians.[28] Paul's use of the neuter plural in relation to the proclamation of the gospel (1 Cor. 9:11; Rom. 15:27) also stands in an antithesis, with σαρκικά, but leaves unclear what these antonyms designate: Does the "fleshly" realm consist of material things (as against the immaterial), or ordinary human concerns (as against concerns of the "Spirit"), or "secular" affairs (as against the affairs of the church)? The flesh-spirit antithesis, so important and so slippery in Paul, could slot into a number of hermeneutical frameworks, in which "Christian" phenomena are variously defined and variously related to reality as a whole. Much will depend here on what nuance is given to the *relationship* between what is "fleshly" and what is "spiritual": Are these polar opposites or complementary realms, and if complementary, in what sort of hierarchical relationship do they stand to each other?[29]

27. For the passage and some chapters in its history of interpretation, see A. Thiselton, *The First Epistle to the Corinthians* (NIGTC; Grand Rapids: Eerdmans, 2000), pp. 276-86.

28. The label πνευματικός acquired particular significance in Valentinian circles, where it functioned within a threefold stratification of humanity; see Irenaeus, *Haer.* 1.5-9 and the *Excerpta ex Theodoto* (F. Sagnard, *Clément d'Alexandrie, Extraits de Théodote* [SC 23; Paris: du Cerf, 1970]). Cf. E. Pagels, *The Gnostic Paul* (Philadelphia: Trinity Press International, 1975).

29. Ignatius's particularly heavy use of the adjective πνευματικός nicely illustrates both the influence and the ambiguity of the Pauline legacy. As soon as he mentions the category distinction between πνευματικοί and σαρκικοί, Ignatius pulls back from allowing the two realms to

Even the Pauline application of the adjective to particular objects leaves many things unclear: if, for instance, some gifts or some songs are "spiritual" and others (implicitly) not (Rom. 1:11; Col. 3:16), does the adjective designate a special quality inherent within them, some special dimension to which they attain, or merely some Christian context in which they are used? Equally ambiguous, though of enormous long-term significance, is the way πνευματικός is used to reinterpret biblical objects (e.g., 1 Cor. 10:3-4; 1 Pet. 2:5; cf. Rom. 2:29); when this was combined with Pauline reflection on the role of the Spirit in "unveiling" Scripture (2 Corinthians 3), it enabled a Christian hermeneutic of Scripture to be termed "spiritual" and thus spawned a long tradition of allegorical exegesis under this label (cf. already Rev. 11:8).

Both the distinctiveness and the potential ambiguity of the label πνευματικός were thus of pivotal significance for early Christianity. Labeling themselves and their attributes in this unusual way, Pauline Christians constituted themselves a distinct phenomenon in their social and religious environment, and, through their textual legacy, invited early Christianity to both think and act in unprecedented ways. But what precisely it valued as "spiritual" could be variously understood by Christians of different strands and different epochs. The history of the term "spiritual" is thus one index of the multiple ways in which Christianity has construed its identity and significance.[30] That it began as a peculiarity in the social dialect of Pauline Christians both grounds and illuminates many aspects of that subsequent history.

---

separate: even what the former do κατὰ σάρκα is πνευματικά (*Eph.* 8.2). This, together with his strong emphasis on the "fleshliness" of Christ's life, passion, and resurrection (e.g., *Smyrn.* 3.2-3; 5.2; 12.2), reflects Ignatius's anxiety about Docetism; cf. W. R. Schoedel, *Ignatius of Antioch* (Philadelphia: Fortress, 1985), pp. 23-24, 64. Ignatius's almost obsessive use of σαρκικός and πνευματικός *together* (e.g., *Pol.* 1.2; 2.2; *Eph.* 10.3; *Magn.* 13.1-2; *Smyrn.* 13.2) recognizes the difference between the two "spheres" without allowing them to become separate or in conflict; in the process, the specific connection between πνευματικός and the Spirit is lost, and the meaning of "spiritual" becomes correspondingly thinned.

30. See the surveys and discussions by J. Leclercq, "Spiritualitas," *Studi Medievali* 3a, serie 3 (1962): 279-96; L. Tinsley, *The French Expressions for Spirituality and Devotion: A Semantic Study* (Washington, D.C.: The Catholic University of America Press, 1953). (I owe these references to Mr. Alan Brown, who is surveying this field in his Cambridge Ph.D.) The contemporary generalization of the term (to mean anything "religious," even anything "interior") reflects the dissipation of a specifically Christian meaning and makes Christians themselves uncertain how to use it. In recent discussions of the "spiritual" role of the elder in the Church of Scotland, it was clear that the term had become so imprecise and polysemous as to be practically valueless.

XIV Who and Where Is the 'Wretched Man' of Romans 7, and Why Is 'She' Wretched?

David Catchpole

It is a great personal delight to be able to offer this contribution to a richly deserved tribute to the achievements of a fine scholar and a valued friend. Almost exactly forty years ago we first met, coped with the unique regime of a truly amazing Cambridge landlady, shared the highs and lows of postgraduate existence, cut our teeth on biblical critical issues, and wondered what the future might hold. Only one shadow has been cast over the years during which the future became the present and then the past, namely, disagreement over a key issue in Pauline interpretation[1] in a dialogue we pursued with some doggedness! It may seem an outrageous piece of temerity for a non-Pauline specialist to make one last attempt to persuade a Pauline specialist to a different view, but for better for worse such is the aim of what follows.[2]

The proposal I wish to put forward in connection with Romans 7:13-25 involves above all taking account of how the structure of the letter to the Romans exposes the argumentative strategy. I want to urge that the ἐγώ of 7:13-25 is an Adamic person living in the sphere of Moses, trapped in era 1 and a stranger to era 2 of salvation history: s/he needs to pass through a corporate death, the characteristic and climactic experience of era 1, and to share in a corporate resurrection, the definitive and inaugural experience of era 2. In so doing I shall register my conviction that one should not be unnecessarily hesitant

1. See "Rom 7:14-25 in the Theology of Paul," *Theologische Zeitschrift* 31 (1975): 257-73; *Romans 1–8* (WBC 38A; Dallas: Word, 1988), pp. 374-413; *The Theology of Paul the Apostle* (Edinburgh: T&T Clark, 1998), pp. 94-100, 150-61.

2. I am grateful for stimulating conversation about this matter with my colleague David Horrell.

about recognising that the community of faith consists of those who have indeed already come to share in that corporate resurrection of Christ. To that end, I need to protect the argument about Romans from a sort of pincer movement represented by Paul's 'no problem' outlook of Phil. 3:4-6 and his critique of the 'already rich and reigning' outlook in 1 Cor. 4:8. On the former: if we had only Romans we would never dream that Paul would make the claim 'as to righteousness under the law, blameless', a claim which is in any case exaggeration[3] sharpened by polemic rather than detached appraisal. In other words, we should not interpret Romans by Philippians. On the latter: a sarcastic retort to those who embrace for themselves a wholly realised eschatology should not lead us instinctively to retreat into a wholly futurist eschatology for Paul himself: Does not the quest of the historical Jesus alert us to a third option, namely, inaugurated eschatology? So, in an attempt to work within parameters which recognise the distinctiveness and integrity of Romans, here goes.

I

The first major section of Romans consists, not of 1:18–5:21 but of 1:18–5:12. A clear dividing line should be drawn between 5:1-11 and 5:12-21, for the following reasons:

First, in 5:1-11 Paul reviews what has been achieved through and in Christ, and picks up key terms which have been part of the previous argument but which do not recur in what follows: the 'peace'/'reconciliation' which was hoped for in the future has now been achieved (5:1; cf. 2:10); appropriate, as distinct from inappropriate, 'boasting' can now be indulged (5:2, 3, 11; cf. 2:17, 23; 3:27); the 'glory' which had been missed has now become a matter of certain hope (5:2; cf. 3:23); and the confident affirmation that 'we shall be saved' (5:9, 10) brings us back to where we stood prior to the beginning of the argument (1:16). The language of 5:1-11 hooks that section into what precedes, and its perspective is aligned to the future. What has happened in the past logically implies that the community of faith is safe in the future.

Second, in 5:12-21, not only is there a distinct change in characteristic language but in thought we go back to the beginning — to Adam and to his successor Moses, as well as to Adam's counterpart, Christ. It is as if the story needs to be told again from the beginning using different parameters, and the drama needs to be played out again from the first act with new *dramatis personae,*

3. We may compare the apologetically motivated and one-sided claims for the 'blamelessness' of Abraham, Israel *(sic!)* and Moses (Wis. 10.5, 15; 18.21).

Adam for the first time (5:14), and Moses for the first time (5:14), before we dwell on Adam's counterpart, Christ. The personalised and transcendent power Sin, mentioned only once before in a passing allusion (3:9), now scarcely leaves the stage and dominates the mythological scheme which controls the second telling of the salvation-historical epic. In short, while the past is remembered, it is the future towards which we are pointed in 5:1-11. And while the future is not forgotten in 5:12-21, it is the past and indeed the very beginning of everything towards which we turn. So 5:1-11 closes one section, and 5:12-21 starts another.

II

The argument of 1:18–5:11 is determined and controlled by 1:18-32, which is in turn determined and controlled by 1:18-23. This is evident from the fact that the three subsections which begin διὸ/διὰ τοῦτο/καθὼς παρέδωκεν αὐτοὺς ὁ θεός (1:24, 26, 28) do not constitute a trio in which each builds logically on its predecessor. On the contrary, the content of any one subsection is in essence the same as that of any other, so the three are equivalent to one another. Therefore with typical Jewish exploitation of the unqualified forcefulness of threefold repetition, Paul is causing the three subsections to reinforce one another almost unbearably. Content-wise, the three present the extremely daring proposition that a life of sinning does not just *lead to* God's judgement; it *is* God's judgement. He is also indicating that structurally 1:23 is the climactic high point of the controlling unit 1:18-23. And that would not have made congenial reading for any non-Christian Jew. For however vital the *adapting* of the text of Ps. 106:20 may be — and it is very vital indeed — it is the *adopting* of that text that really, as one might say, 'puts the boot in'. It is the supreme incidence of idolatrous apostasy in the history of the *Jewish* people (Exodus 32) which Paul invokes. That being so, the penny drops in our minds and we understand a surprising deviation in 1:18-23 from the 'background' text of Wisdom 13–14: Whereas Wisdom gives credit to those Gentiles who search for God on the basis of creation, but apportions blame because of their not carrying the process through to completion, Paul assigns blame for the rejection of the creation-based knowledge which has been made available, recognized, and rejected. In other words, he assimilates the Gentile situation to that of the Jewish people, and vice versa: their problem, the problem of the Jewish people, is not that they do not possess the knowledge of God, but that they do have it and then turn from it. Used to targeting others, they themselves are the real targets. They are inextricably implicated in what Günther Bornkamm described as 'the anti-divine revolt of mankind'. That is the central thrust of the argument.

Confirmation of this very specific argumentative tendency is provided in 2:1-16, 17-29, where the judging tendency of the covenant-conscious and repentance-resisting outlook of the *Jewish* people is exposed and then subjected to searing criticism and dire warning. Two subunits of argument illustrate the point.

First, held within the *inclusio* formed by 'he will repay according to each person's deeds' and 'God shows no partiality' (2:6, 11; cf. 2 Chron. 19:7), there is set a chiastic a-b-b′-a′ structure in which the a/a′ elements speak of future bliss for those who do good (vv. 7, 10) and the b/b′ elements of judgement for those who do evil and disobey the truth (vv. 8-9; cf. 1:18). Significantly, in b′-a′, in each case the second of the paired and antithetical statements, that is, where the emphasis is normally placed, the formula 'the Jew first and also the Greek' is set, so the priority of the Jews is just as much a priority under judgement as it is a priority in receipt of life and glory. That, rather than anything said about the plight and predicament of Gentiles, would be what a Jewish reader would find very hard to take, and is therefore the main thrust of the argument.

Second, the main thread of the concluding subsection (2:12-16) can be discerned as 'All who have sinned apart from the law will also perish apart from the law, and all who have sinned under the law will be judged by the law; for it is not the hearers of the law who are righteous in God's sight, but the doers of the law who will be justified . . . on the day when, according to my gospel, God, through Jesus Christ, will judge the secrets of humankind' (vv. 12-13, 16). Within the flow Paul pauses, as it were, to open up the genuine prospect of the telling testimony of Gentile obedience bringing security before the God of the world — and thus implicitly undermining once again the tacitly encouraging notion of Jewish specialness.

From this devastating first part of the argument of the letter to the Romans we can see how certain extremely awkward questions could not but arise. The first question concerns how now to define the 'people of God' in the light of the levelling down of the special status of the Jews. When Paul goes on (3:27-31) to insist that the inclusive God of undivided humankind is the God who has opened up and offered the relationship of righteousness on the basis of faith in Jesus Christ, and that alone, the awkwardness of the question is increased exponentially. Only an extended coverage of all the issues will suffice, coverage to which Paul gets around in Romans 9–11. The second question concerns the *prima facie* precarious position of the law, not just in respect of the boundary-marking 'works of the law' but also in terms of behavioural guidance and sanctions within a scheme where God's faithfulness and truth prevail over all human faithlessness and truthlessness. It is all very well to throw terse one-liners at critics (3:1-8) or to assert that 'we do not overthrow but rather uphold the law' (3:31): more needs to be said, and to be said at length, about the consequences for law of daring to characterise what God has done in and through Christ by the catchphrase χωρὶς νόμου (3:21). Only extended coverage will do, which Paul moves to first of all in 5:12–8:39, the section of the letter dominated by 5:12-21.

III

Within 5:12-21 the primary parameters of the argument are provided by (i) v. 12, where ὥσπερ . . . οὕτως establishes 'sin → death' parallel for Adam and for humankind, a parallelism qualified only by the fact of Adam's responsibility for the introduction of personified Sin into the world while for humankind thereafter Sin was already there; and (ii) vv. 15, 16-17, where two οὐχ ὡς . . . statements, bolstered by quality-driven *a minore ad maius* reasoning, set out the antithetical consequences of the two εἷς . . . πολλοί/πάντες regimes. The remaining material concerned with those same themes (vv. 18-19, 21) adds nothing but restatement (v. 18: ἄρα οὖν . . .) with minor clarification. On this basis we can see that the law-focused statements (vv. 13-14, 20) are in a sense superimposed upon, and secondary in relation to, the primary scheme. They exhibit a carefully crafted balance. If we think the thoughts of a Jewish listener to this argument, then vv. 13-14 would strike a wholly acceptable chord. The essence of the argument is that the Sin/death problem of humankind antedates Moses and the arrival of his law: Sin was there throughout the pre-Moses period, and the coming of the law merely enabled Sin to be recognized and held responsible (by discerning human beings; cf. already 3:20b: διὰ νόμου ἐπίγνωσις ἁμαρτίας). There is clear space between Sin/death and the law. Thus far Paul is protecting the law. But our hypothetical Jewish listener would find the chord struck by v. 20 anything but acceptable. Here at the heart of the presentation of the achievement of the eschatological Adam-type figure (cf. v. 14b), that is, the definitive solution to the universal problem, the law is not just assigned a position which is secondary (παρεισῆλθεν; cf. v. 13) but assigned a role which makes it part of that problem rather than any kind of solution to the problem: 'the law came in alongside, with the result that the trespass multiplied'. The law, not by design but certainly by effect, did not make the problem better — it made it worse, but fortunately not so much worse that χάρις could not cope.

There are three minutiae within 5:12-21 over which it may be helpful to pause:

First, when describing the era in the experience of humankind brought about by the second εἷς figure Paul adjusts the terminology ever so slightly as he goes along — from τὸ χάρισμα (= χάρις//δωρεὰ ἐν χάριτι) in vv. 15, 16 to χάρις/ /δωρεὰ τῆς δικαιοσύνης in v. 17, to δικαίωσις ζωῆς in v. 18 and the all-embracing formula combining all the terminology in v. 21: ἡ χάρις βασιλεύσῃ διὰ δικαιοσύνης εἰς ζωὴν αἰώνιον. Those who belong to the community of faith, to era no. 2, to sphere no. 2, already belong to the sphere of grace; they look forward to the ultimate fulfilment of all that it means to be 'righteoused', yet they are already just as aptly designated/constituted as δίκαιοι as those in era no. 1, sphere no. 1, are designated/constituted as ἁμαρτωλοί . . . (v. 19); they look forward to the final perfection of eternal life, but they already participate in that life which *is* righteousness (v. 18).

Second, when talking about the two contrasting orders of existence, Paul makes much of two contrasting kingly figures, as it were — death (vv. 14, 17) or, which comes to the same thing, Sin in death (v. 21a) *versus* grace (v. 21) — but, very significantly at one point, the kingship is the possession not of grace but of the recipients of grace: 'those who receive the abundance of grace . . . exercise kingship in life' (v. 17). Kingly prerogatives are of the essence of where they are by virtue of 'the one person Jesus Christ'!

Third, in somewhat the same vein, we notice that the all-embracing formula in v. 21 expands christologically to διὰ Ἰησοῦ Χριστοῦ τοῦ κυρίου ἡμῶν. To be sure, that phrase is used frequently and sometimes somewhat formally by Paul. In principle it could be no more than formal here, but it is safer not to assume so but rather to allow Paul to use even a formula with maximum theological intent. At the beginning of this letter, in the first half of which this formula is used infrequently, Paul dropped the heaviest of hints. Before quoting the pre-Pauline tradition in Rom. 1:3b-4a he indicated in v. 3a that it was really only the resurrection-based Sonship in which he was interested theologically, and which he saw as the heart of the gospel. Immediately afterwards the matter was put beyond all doubt by the attachment of Ἰησοῦ Χριστοῦ τοῦ κυρίου ἡμῶν (v. 4b). Similarly, the two διὰ τοῦ κυρίου ἡμῶν Ἰησοῦ Χριστοῦ references which form an *inclusio* in 5:1-11 have been given an unmistakable resurrection conditioning by the preceding definition of God in 4:24 as 'the one who raised Jesus our Lord [*sic*] from the dead'. Although the point cannot be pressed at this stage, it looks as if the ground is being prepared for the affirmation that the *risen* Christ is the eschatological Adam, the embodiment of the new order. His death may be (certainly is) important, but his resurrection is for the purpose of the present argument mega-important.

IV

Sensitivity to the extremely risky proposition concerning the law in 5:20 is evident in the bipartite section which follows, first 6:1-11 plus 6:12-14 and then 6:15-23 plus 7:1-6. The parallelism between and complementariness of these two subsections, and their shared dependence on 5:12-21, emerge clearly from certain structural features:

First, both begin with more or less the same question: 'Shall we continue in sin that grace may abound? . . . Shall/should we sin because we are . . . under grace?' The term χάρις occurs in this section, leaving aside the thanksgiving formula (6:17), only in 6:1, 14, 15 and directs our attention back to what precedes.

Second, both follow the same strategy as 5:12-21 vis-à-vis the idea of νόμος, that is, a primary exposure of the two eras scheme has at the end, almost 'tacked on', as it were, something about the law. All of a sudden, out of the blue, almost unnecessarily in view of what has been said in 6:1-14a, we are told in 6:14b, οὐ γάρ ἐστε ὑπὸ νόμον ἀλλὰ ὑπὸ χάριν. Similarly, after a careful exposure of the two-eras scheme in 6:15-23 we are launched on an intense argument about the law in 7:1-6. There is agreement between 6:14b and 7:1-6 in a radical clarification of 5:20, namely, that the law does not just have an unfortunate effect in Adamic era 1 but *actually belongs exclusively within that era.*

Third, both focus on the transitional experience of Christian initiation, viewed from two complementary perspectives, as inherently laying the foundation of era 2–type holy living. In the one case, it is baptism — a participatory sharing in the death *and therefore, logically, a sharing in the resurrection,* of Christ (6:3-4). In the other case, it is a matter of being committed (by God) to the obligation articulated in the gospel of grace: ὑπηκούσατε . . . εἰς ὃν παρεδόθητε τύπον διδαχῆς (v. 17).

Fourth, the dominant motif in each paragraph matches the selected aspect of Christian initiation while at the same time showing an awareness of the complementary motif. Thus, in 6:1-14, given the focus on baptism, the dominant motif is incorporation into Christ, solidarity, participation; in 6:15–7:6, given the focus on obedience to a gospel of demanding grace, the dominant motif is that of lordship. Just as lordship/obedience appears as a subordinate motif in 6:1-14 — see v. 6 on serving Sin, v. 9 on death's exercising lordship, v. 12, 14 on Sin's reign/lordship — so also solidarity/incorporation, that is, all that the term ἐν Χριστῷ Ἰησοῦ conveys, appears as a subordinate motif in 6:15–7:6 — see 6:23 on the prospect of eternal life, and 7:4 on the shared death within the body of Christ which brings about a whole new experience of belonging.

Fifth, with 7:5b, 'while we were living in the flesh, our sinful passions, *aroused by the law,* were at work in our members to bear fruit for death', we are essentially back at 5:20a. And with 7:6a, 'now we are discharged from the law', we are essentially back at 6:14, 'you are not under law'. Similarly, with 7:6, 'so that we might serve ἐν καινότητι πνεύματος', we are doubtless intended to recall 6:4, with its only other allusion to καινότης in this letter, 'just as Christ was raised . . . so we too might walk ἐν καινότητι ζωῆς'.

Structurally, then, it is important to see the major controlling section, 5:12-21, being amplified and protected from what Paul would regard as misunderstanding in two parallel supporting sections, 6:1-14 and 6:15–7:6. Theologically, what is the main thrust of these two complementary subsections? If the key demand is for the readers to get their minds straight, what firmly understood insights would make their minds truly Christian?

First, there are only two spheres/eras of existence, and one is either in one sphere/era or in the other. Death is the exit experience from sphere/era 1 at the conclusion of era 1: Christ has died, moved out of that sphere/era, and by virtue of baptism, so, too, have Christians. Resurrection is the entry experience into sphere/era 2: Christ has been raised and become alive, and the logical implication is that participation in him, the once-for-all dead but now raised and living corporate person, means that so, too, have Christians been raised and now live. Resurrection life is not something that they merely imitate in the present and hope to share in the future. That interpretation could appeal to the future tenses of the verbs in 6:5, 8 (ἐσόμεθα . . . συζήσομεν), but this would be to straightjacket logical futures into eschatological futures;[4] it would fail to take sufficiently seriously the summarising commentary on 6:4-11 provided by 6:13, 'present yourselves to God ὡσεὶ ἐκ νεκρῶν ζῶντας'; it would require an inexplicable shift from participatory involvement in 6:4a to pattern-type imitation in 6:4b, an inexplicable lurch in logic from ethics to eschatology within the same sentence, and a curious *non sequitur* in 6:10-11, where 'dead to Sin . . . alive to God' is a matter of both pattern (οὕτως καὶ ὑμεῖς) and participation (ἐν Χριστῷ Ἰησοῦ). So resurrection experience is not something for which they only wait

4. Already in Rom. 3.3 we have had an εἰ + verb in past tense (ἠπίστησάν), . . . verb in future tense (καταργήσει) formulation, where the future tense is plainly logical rather than temporal. Two formulations in 2 Corinthians (3.7-9; 4.16) are comparable: 'If the ministry of death . . . came in glory . . . , how much more will the ministry of the Spirit come (ἔσται) in glory? For if there was glory in the ministry of condemnation, much more does the ministry of righteousness abound (περισσεύει: *sic*) in glory.' The parallelism in the sense of the two sentences demonstrates the equivalence of the future and the present verbal forms. And in the argument that 'if our outer person is wasting away, our inner person is being renewed (ἀνακαινοῦται) day by day' (4.16), the overall flow of the logic — apostolic experience of suffering is an experience of participation in Christ's death, but one within which paradoxically the experience of resurrection is to be detected — as well as the emphatically present 'day by day', demonstrates again that a future form conveys present reality.

until the final completion of the salvation-historical plan of God. If that were so, let it be emphasised, the question about their present ethical stance would simply not have been answered. No, 'walking' ἐν καινότητι ζωῆς (6:4) is living in every sense in the resurrection. Living for God is what the risen Christ does; living for God in Christ Jesus is what Christians can and must do. *En passant,* one might observe that even if this sounds a little like the thought of Colossians 2:12-13, that should not in principle be a problem, for as Jimmy Dunn indicates frequently in his *Theology of Paul,* the deutero-Pauline writers sometimes, even if certainly not always, understood Paul correctly!

Second, all life is an experience of lordship and therefore obedience. No one can serve two lords. The alternatives are stark: *either* Sin *or* God/righteousness. To suppose that sinning is an option for the baptised and death-and-resurrection-incorporated Christian is to suppose that one can receive and respond to orders from lord no. 1 when one has truly moved out into the sphere of authority of lord no. 2. To speak by way of analogy, it is as if one moved out of a contractual relationship with the Vice-Chancellor of the University of Nottingham (or Lancaster) into a contractual relationship with the Vice-Chancellor of the University of Durham (or Exeter), and then quite illogically, when committed to the second vice-chancellor, accepted illegitimate demands from the first. The nonnegotiable *brutum factum* of the matter is that a both/and relationship is impossible, and should be recognised as such: only an either/or relationship will do. The old relationship has been severed once and for all: the new is all there is.

Third, as already indicated in 5:12-21, the transfer experience is a matter of being righteoused (6:7; note the perfect tense of δεδικαίωται) as well as being freed. Being the beneficiary of a righteous-ing transference means that one is committed to a life of righteousness. Being must arise from, and be a behavioural projection of, one's having become.

Fourth, if belonging to the risen Christ and moving out of the sphere of law are equivalent, then the very serious theological problem of the law cannot any longer be bypassed. The law is not just an agent of intensification of the human problem; it belongs inseparably within the Sin/death complex, which is no longer a reality governing the Christian's existence. But what about the content of the law — that surely cannot be devalued or denied? Probably not, but we haven't yet listened to the arguments or heard the precise relationship between the law and Sin/death defined, or for this purpose revisited the one and only context, sphere/era 1, within which the Sin/death/law relationship can be measured.

Fifth, out of the blue in 7:5-6 the loaded term σάρξ appears, more heavily loaded indeed than in any previous allusion in this letter (neutral references to physicality or humanness). The term is much more loaded than what might at first sight seem an equivalent term, τὰ μέλη, but this apparent equivalence is severely qualified: τὰ μέλη can be, and indeed once were, submitted to Sin but they can in principle be submitted to God/righteousness in a way that σάρξ cannot (6:13, 19, 20; 7:5). They, τὰ μέλη, are throughout, whether in sphere/era 1 or sphere/era 2, the department of human existence where either pattern of lordship/obedience may be played out. But σάρξ is different: it stands for something that once was true but is no longer true: 'While we were living ἐν τῇ σαρκί . . . νυνὶ δέ . . .'. And that is crucially significant, for the last piece in the jigsaw of pre-Christian, law-defined sphere/era 1 existence *(sic)* is now in place, and the picture is ready to be turned into a verbal self-definition: "I am fleshly, a slave of Sin, a captive of the law, a candidate for death."

V

Just as 6:1-14 and 6:15–7:6 exhibited parallelism and complementarity with one another in responding to 5:20, so, too, do 7:7-12 and 7:13-25 in responding to 7:5. In spite of registering in 7:6 awareness of the new freedom and the new Spirit-driven obedience which characterises sphere/era 2, Paul recognises that some further clarification is needed when law has been so closely associated in sphere/era 1 with, first, Sin, and, second, death. So, with the questions, 'Is the law Sin?' and 'Did [the law] become death to me?' he proceeds to a twin-track analysis of the Adamic/Mosaic era and, in effect, a defence of law. That the analysis is twin-track, and the two paragraphs, vv. 7-12 and vv. 13-25, parallel and complementary, is of the utmost importance.

Less controversy attends the first than the second, though this should not be so. That 7:7-12 projects on the small screen of individual experience the big scheme of 5:12-21 is clear. There are all the key features: the Adamic paradigm, an original absence-of-law phase succeeded by a presence-of-law phase, the law's articulation of what *must* be a good principle — 'you shall not covet', a shortened and therefore generalising version of Exod. 20:17/Deut. 5:21 (cf. 4 Macc. 2:5) — but the law's *de facto* provocation of sinful behaviour and therefore of submission to Sin. The new element is the inherent goodness of the commandment, which Paul takes to be self-evident, serving to show that ultimate responsibility rests with personified Sin. That snake in the grass, as it were, may use the commandment, but that is as close an association as may be inferred. Sin may frustrate the intended purpose of the law ('life'; cf. Lev. 18:5) by using the law as an instrument, but specifically within sphere/era 1 the gap between law and Sin in respect of both content and intention works to the advantage of the law. It is worth noting Paul's choice of the specific law, Οὐκ ἐπιθυμήσεις, and that in this connection (i) 1:24 already, and again 6:12, have signalled abandonment to ἐπιθυμίαι as the epitome of judgement-effecting abandonment of and by God; and (ii) biblical tradition is so regular in using ἐπιθυμία to describe a shift from loyalty to the one and only God towards allegiance to another, which is the essence of the accusation of 1:18-23. It is also worth noting (i) that the projection of the general Adamic/pre- and post-Mosaic situation is throughout set out in ἐγώ-speech — not for the first time in Romans (cf. 3:7); and (ii) that the speaker can view himself as *already having died* at the moment when Sin was able to impose its authority — three times in 7:10-11, and, by the way, not at all irrelevant to the debate about whether life/resurrection is *already* effected at the moment of transference ἐν Χριστῷ Ἰησοῦ into sphere/era 2.

It is with 7:13-25 that the defence of law and the attribution to Sin of responsibility for the whole sorry human situation reaches its conclusion. Again the key to the argument is to be found in the structure.

First, working with a sharp πνεῦμα versus σάρξ antithesis (v. 14ab), Paul sets out in vv. 14b-17 and vv. 18-20 two matching units of argument. Each consists of (i) a σάρξ statement, introduced by οἴδαμεν/οἶδα, in vv. 14ab, 18a; (ii) a description of inner conflict, with special emphasis on the will as against the deed, in vv. 15-16, 18b-20a; (iii) a concluding (νυνὶ δὲ) οὐκέτι ἐγὼ κατεργάζομαι αὐτὸ ἀλλὰ ἡ οἰκοῦσα ἐν ἐμοὶ ἁμαρτία, in vv. 17, 20b.

Second, in relation to one another these two units of argument exhibit no progression at all: νόμος appears explicitly in the first, defined twice synonymously as πνευματικός/καλός in vv. 14a, 16, but in the second the ἀγαθός/καλός versus κακός antithesis does duty for νόμος. Paul therefore says the same thing twice, the effect being to make the two units stand out from their context while, of course, hooking up with the repeated ἀγαθός language about the law in v. 13 (cf. also v. 12).

Third, the essential thrust of the initial answer in v. 13b to the question of v. 13a is to be found in the phrase ἵνα φανῇ ἁμαρτία: in a setting defined by the two synonymous phrases διὰ τοῦ ἀγαθοῦ and διὰ τῆς ἐντολῆς, something has to become evident. That 'something' is what vv. 17, 20b articulate as the certain inference from the analysis of the conflict experience. Consequently, v. 13b, which can in any case scarcely function by itself as an adequate answer to the question set, should on no account have vv. 14-20, let alone vv. 14-25, separated from it.

Fourth, there follow on from the two subunits two repetitive restatements (cf. ἄρα, vv. 21, 25b) of the inference which is drawn within them. In the first ἄρα-complex, the conclusion (Εὑρίσκω . . .) is stated in v. 21 and the supporting argument in vv. 22-23. The conclusion says nothing new; the supporting argument says nothing new and merely varies the terminology: the term ὁ ἔσω ἄνθρωπος for the term νοῦς (for their equivalence, cf. Rom. 12:2// 2 Cor. 4:16), the term (ἕτερος) νόμος τῆς ἁμαρτίας for ἁμαρτία, and the rather vigorous verbs ἀντιστρατεύομαι and αἰχμαλωτίζω to portray the conflict and its consequences. At the end of v. 23 we are still, as it were, at the end of v. 20.

Fifth, in v. 25b nothing has changed, and we are still where we were in vv. 21-23. That is actually rather crucially important. If nothing has changed between the situations before and after vv. 24-25a, then v. 25b cannot document any change and certainly cannot be the answer to the problem of the ταλαίπωρος ἐγὼ ἄνθρωπος, that is, the unliberated typical human person in all her/his distressing and alienated humanness. Doubtless Paul was aware that in using the term ταλαιπωρία he was tapping into a stream of thought in which again and again it was used of that condition of disobedience to God which brings judgement in its wake (cf. Amos 3:10; 5:9; etc.), or of the judgement itself and the condition of those who stand under it (cf. Jer. 6:26; 10:20; 12:12; etc.), or of the situation of oppression under alien powers (cf. Tob. 13:10; Josephus, *Ant.* 11.1, in both of which cases the word is synonymous with αἰχμαλωσία), or as part of a personal cry of lamentation in circumstances of suffering and judgement (cf. Jer. 4:13, 20; Tob. 7:7), or in association with the promise of divine rescue (cf. Pss. 16[17]:9; 37[38]:6). No wonder he found it serviceable here! Consequently, vv. 24-25a must be an anticipatory and celebratory parenthesis, reminding us that what has been under scrutiny is a situation of 'this death' (v. 24, looking back to 'death' language in v. 13ab), looking forward to the sphere/era 2 situation of freedom, but at the same time not in the least intended to distract from the conclusion, the quite vital conclusion, articulated in v. 25b. That conclusion is the final statement of the evidence which permits Paul to open up clear space between the law and the experience of death and therefore to answer the question of v. 13.

VI

The ground is now clear for the liberation described in Romans 8 to be a true liberation. In the setting of salvation history the law belonged to sphere/era 1, the sphere of σάρξ-type existence and slavery under the lordship of Sin and death. That era is emphatically past — 'of that there is no manner of doubt, no probable, possible shadow of doubt, no possible doubt whatever' (W. S. Gilbert). But the law was inherently good in moral terms even if weak in transformation-cum-obedience terms. Weakness was in fact its only defect, but if that could be compensated, it would come into the reckoning so that through the Spirit those who 'walk not according to the flesh' might fulfil the law's true δικαίωμα. If only the existence of sphere/era 2 ἐν Χριστῷ Ἰησοῦ is allowed to come into view and be realised through the power of that divine Spirit, unqualified and unspoiled by an interpretation of Rom. 7:13-25 which superimposes upon it the obsolete parameters of sphere/era 1, then the newness of the gospel can be appreciated. More than that, in Paul's view, it can be experienced by the community of faith if they follow the injunction to 'become what they are', that is, persons who shared *in the past and once for all* the death of the corporate Christ, and who have shared and do share, *in the past, in the present, and on into the future,* his resurrection.

XV The Contrite Wrongdoer — Condemned or Set Free by the Spirit? Romans 7:7–8:4

Peder Borgen

Introduction

In the exegesis of Rom 7:7–8:4 scholars realize that Paul, in addition to citing the commandment against covetousness (Exod 20:17/Deut 5:21), also draws on the story of Adam and Eve in Genesis 2–3.[1] As for Paul's quotation of the tenth commandment, J. A. Ziesler and others have examined the understanding of covetousness in Jewish sources. He concluded that covetousness was widely regarded as a basic sin.[2]

Scholars have brought in Jewish and non-Jewish texts as background for some of the ideas in the section. Thus H. Hommel and others have examined parallels to Paul's statement that a person does not do what he wants to do.[3] E. W. Smith and other scholars look to *Jos. As.* 6:1-18 and other texts to illustrate the lament in Rom 7:24.[4] As shown by H. Braun, several of the an-

1. See J. D. G. Dunn, *The Theology of Paul the Apostle* (Edinburgh: T&T Clark, 1998), pp. 98-100; C. E. B. Cranfield, *The Epistle to the Romans* (ICC; Edinburgh: T&T Clark, 1975), 1:350-53, and other commentaries.

2. J. A. Ziesler, "The Role of the Tenth Commandment in Romans 7," *JSNT* 33 (1988): 41-56. See also G. Theissen, *Psychologische Aspekte paulinischer Theologie* (Göttingen: Vandenhoeck & Ruprecht, 1983), pp. 204-13, and H. Lichtenberger, *Studien zur paulinischen Anthropologie in Römer 7, Habilitationsschrift* (Typewritten; Tübingen: Eberhard-Karls-Universität, 1985).

3. H. Hommel, "Das 7. Kapitel des Römerbrief im Licht antiker Überlieferung," *Theologia Viatorum* 8 (1962): 90-116; Theissen, *Psychologische Aspekte*, pp. 213-23; Lichtenberger, *Studien*, pp. 192-201.

4. E. W. Smith, "The Form and Religious Background of Romans VII 24-25a," *NovT* 13

thropological and hamartiological ideas are similar to ideas in the Qumran writings.[5]

These texts illuminate parts of Rom 7:7–8:4, but it would be desirable to find parallel texts to the flow of ideas in the paragraph as a whole, texts which can contribute to determining its form. In his essay "Gattung, Adressaten und Intention von *Philos In Flaccum*," M. Meiser lists some texts which look promising.[6] These texts contain a cluster of similar ideas and notions, although formulated in a variety of ways. Meiser called them "Rede eines gezüchtigten Gottesfeindes." The texts are Herodotus (5th cent. B.C.), *Hist.* 9.116-20; Sophocles (5th cent. B.C.), *Antigone;* Diogenes Laertius (early 3rd cent. A.D.), *Lives of Eminent Philosophers* 4.54-57, and Philo (ca. 15 B.C.–ca. A.D. 45) *In Flaccum* 154–91. Other relevant texts are parts of *Joseph and Aseneth* (written somewhere between ca. 200 B.C. and ca. A.D. 100) and LXX Genesis 2–3 (translated in the 2nd cent. B.C.). In the story about Artaÿctes Herodotus, *Hist.* 9.120, refers to what was told by the inhabitants of Chersonesus. Likewise Diogenes Laertius in *Lives* 4.54 refers to what was told by the people of Chalcis where Bion died. Thus these stories seem to reflect a traditional form which could occur in oral as well as in written versions.

The section Rom 7:7–8:4 has the form of biography, and even of autobiography in the first person singular. W. G. Kümmel has argued that Paul's use of the first person here is rhetorical.[7] G. Theissen agrees with Kümmel that Rom 7:7 is not a biography of Paul, but he maintains that the text has a biographical background. What Paul in a general and typical way says about man under the law has its "Sitz im Leben" in Paul's own experience.[8] The present author agrees with Theissen that Rom 7:7-25 has its background in biography, not in Paul's own experiences, but in a biographical presentation of a wrongdoer who admits his misdeed, affirms the authority of the law/the divine rule, reacts existentially, and faces punishment or/and deliverance. The thesis is that Rom 7:7–8:4 contains sufficient numbers of similarities with the Jewish and Greek texts listed so as to make a comparison fruitful.

(1971): 127-35; J. D. G. Dunn, *Romans 1–8* (WBC 38; Dallas: Word, 1988), p. 396; Lichtenberger, *Studien*, pp. 185-88.

5. H. Braun, "Römer 7:7-25 und das Selbstverständnis des Qumran-Frommen," *ZThK* 56 (1959): 1-18; also in *Gesammelte Studien zum Neuen Testaments und seiner Umwelt* (3rd ed.; Tübingen: Mohr [Siebeck], 1971), pp. 100-119.

6. M. Meiser, "Gattung, Adressaten und Intention von *Philos In Flaccum*," *JSJ* 30 (1999): 421 n. 21.

7. W. G. Kümmel, *Römer 7 und das Bild des Menschen im Neuen Testament* (München: Kaiser, 1974), pp. ix-160, reprint of *Römer 7 und die Bekehrung des Paulus* (Leipzig: Hinrich, 1929).

8. Theissen, *Psychologische Aspekte*, pp. 181-82.

I. Supernatural Revelation and/or Other Special Experiences Bring the Wrongdoer to Admit His/Her Misdeed and to Recognize the Divine Authority

Some observations on Rom 7:7–8:4 should be given at the outset. In 7:7-13 Paul's argument has the form of a biographical report in the past tense. The law, *in casu* the tenth commandment (Exod 20:17 and Deut 5:21), spoke and made the person recognize the crime and admit that sin had been committed: "But I would not have known what sin was except through the law. For I would not have known what it is to covet if the law had not said, 'Do not covet'. . . . In the absence of law I was once alive, but when the commandment came, sin became alive and I died" (Rom 7:7-9). The active revelatory function of the law is evident. The person recognized the authority of the law that had spoken to him. The lasting revelatory function of the law is seen in 7:14 where the law is characterized as "spiritual" (πνευματικός).[9]

As mentioned above, Paul draws on the story of Adam and Eve. According to Genesis 2–3 God gave the commandment not to eat of the tree in the midst of the garden. When he later came to them and unveiled their disobedience, Adam and Eve admitted their misdeed. In some Jewish traditions God's commandment in the garden of Eden anticipated the Mosaic law.[10]

A corresponding active role played by supernatural interventions is seen in Sophocles' *Antigone*, in the Jewish writing *Joseph and Aseneth*, and in Philo's *In Flaccum*.

The tragedy *Antigone* centers around a conflict between the divine laws and a provocative decree of King Creon in the case of the burial of Polyneices. King Creon decreed that he was not to receive a burial since he had been a traitor. Antigone followed the divine laws, defied Creon's edict, and said, ". . . nor did I think your proclamations strong enough to have power to overrule, mortal as they were, the unwritten and unfailing ordinances of the gods" (ll. 453-55).[11]

9. So far the phrase ὁ νόμος πνευματικός has not been found elsewhere. See Lichtenberger, *Studien*, p. 150. P. Stuhlmacher, "Klage und Dank: Exegetische und liturgische Überlegungen zu Römer 7," *Jahrbuch für Biblische Theologie* 16 (2001): 61-62, suggests that relevant background ideas are seen in Sir 24:23 and Wis 7:22-27. It should be added that the phrase πᾶσα γραφὴ θεόπνευστος in 2 Tim 3:16 may also be drawn into this discussion. The word θεόπνευστος describes the Old Testament writings that have divine authority. The stress is on the work of Scripture.

10. See, e.g., Dunn, *Romans 1–8*, pp. 378-79.

11. Sophocles, *Antigone, The Women of Trachis, Philoctetes, Oedipus at Colonus* (ed. and trans. H. Lloyd-Jones; Loeb; Cambridge, Mass.: Harvard University Press, 1994), p. 45. This translation is used throughout the essay.

King Creon condemned Antigone to be immured in a rock-hewn chamber. The divine intervention came through the seer Teiresias. He went to King Creon and predicted doom. The prediction was based on bad omens: wild cries by birds and refusal by the gods to accept sacrificial offerings. Teiresias admonished Creon to repent (*Antigone*, ll. 998-1090). Creon now recognized the authority of the divine ancient laws about the burial of the dead (ll. 1111-14): "Since my decision has been thus reversed, I who imprisoned her [Antigone], shall myself be present to release her! I am afraid that it is best to end one's life in obedience to the established laws (τοὺς καθεστῶτας νόμους)." King Creon went to release Antigone.

In the case of Aseneth, too, there was a marked dividing line between the time before and after a revelation was received. The revelation had the dual form of the epiphanic appearance of Joseph and that of his blessing of Aseneth.[12] Upon Joseph's coming she understood that he was a son of God and God's elect one, and she admitted that out of ignorance she previously had insulted him, thinking that he was just a shepherd's son from Canaan and an adulterer. Joseph blessed Aseneth and prayed for her conversion, and she recognized the name of God Most High and repented (μετανοεῖν)[13] of the gods she used to worship (*Jos. As.* 8:9–9:2). As a guest in the pagan home of Aseneth, Joseph observed the Jewish law and made clear that he worshipped the living God (7:1–9:2).

Within the context of the Roman political and legal system, Flaccus was arrested, had to face trial in Rome, was condemned (*Flacc.* 108-15, 125-27, and 146-51), and was exiled to the island of Andros. Although these penalties were put into effect outside of the actual jurisdiction of the Jewish law, Flaccus came to realize that they were measured out within the context of God's providential care for the Jewish people and their rights. In Corybantic frenzy he offered a prayer to God in which he admitted his crimes: ". . . all the acts which I madly committed against the Jews I have suffered myself." (*Flacc.* 170).[14]

In a different way the supernatural intervention took place in the case of

12. Concerning *Joseph and Aseneth*, see C. Burchard, "The Present State of Research on Joseph and Aseneth," in J. Neusner, P. Borgen, E. S. Frerichs, and R. Horsley (eds.), *New Perspectives on Ancient Judaism, 2: Religion, Literature, and Society in Ancient Israel, Formative Christianity and Judaism* (Lanham, Md.: University Press of America, 1987), pp. 31-52.

13. M. Philonenko, *Joseph et Aséneth* (Studia Post-Biblica 13; Leiden: Brill, 1968), p. 160. If not stated otherwise, the translation used in the essay is that of C. Burchard, "Joseph and Aseneth," in J. H. Charlesworth (ed.), *The Old Testament Pseudepigrapha* (Garden City, N.Y.: Doubleday, 1985), 2:177-247.

14. See P. Borgen, "Philo's *Against Flaccus* as Interpreted History," in K.-J. Illman et al. (eds.), *A Bouquet of Wisdom*, K.-G. Sandelin Festschrift (Aabo: Aabo Academy, 2000), pp. 50-52.

the Persian governor Artaÿctes.[15] He was given permission by Xerxes to rob the sanctuary of the Greek hero Protesilaus in Elaeus, since it had been the house of a Greek man who had fallen in the war. Later Artaÿctes was conquered by the Greeks, and as a prisoner of war he experienced that the divine Greek hero Protesilaus intervened in his situation by means of an amazing event. Artaÿctes was frying dried fishes, and they began to leap as though they were fish newly caught. Artaÿctes interpreted it in this way: ". . . it is to me that Protesilaus of Elaeus would signify that though he be dead and dry, he has power given him by the gods to take vengeance on me that wronged him" (Herodotus, *Hist.* 9.120).[16] In his interpretation of this incident Artaÿctes (seemingly) admitted his crime and said that he recognized the authority of the hero, an authority given by the gods.

As for Bion, his deadly illness caused him to repent from his atheism. He confessed his sin and said, "I have transgressed (ἤλιτον), pardon (σύγγνωτε) the past." By his confession he indirectly testified to the divine authority and laws (Diogenius Laertius, *Lives* 4.54-57).[17]

Thus the interventions related to divine laws and divine authority brought a change in the lives of the persons Adam and Eve, Aseneth, Creon, and Flaccus, and (seemingly) also to Artaÿctes.

Correspondingly in Rom 7:7-13, the divine intervention when the law spoke marked a change in the biography of the person "I." Thus the Pauline passage fits into the kind of biographical statements found in these parallel texts.

II. Further Existential Reactions in Words or/and Behavior

In Rom 7:7-13 past tenses are used, while vv. 14-25 have the present tense. This shift indicates that Paul moves from a biographical story to more existential reflections made by the person "I."[18] One observation should be made at this point. In Rom 7:7-13(14) it is made clear that the person "I" admitted his wrongdoing and recognized the authority of the law. In vv. 15-23 this dual perspective is internalized existentially in two ways: (a) the person confesses that he does what he does not want to do. Thereby he agrees that the law is good. The (per-

15. See *Herodotus with an English Translation,* by A. D. Godley (Loeb repr.; Cambridge, Mass.: Harvard University Press, 1981), 4:295-99.

16. Herodotus, *Hist.* 9.120. I translate πρὸς θεῶν as "by the gods."

17. *Diogenes Laertius, Lives of Eminent Philosophers with an English Translation,* by R. D. Hicks (Loeb; Cambridge, Mass.: Harvard University Press, 1980), 1:423-33, esp. p. 433.

18. See Lichtenberger, *Studien,* pp. 147 and 173-75.

sonalized) sin that dwells in the person acts, not he himself; (b) there is a war between the law of the person's mind and the law of sin which dwells in his members.

Existential struggles are also expressed by the person(s) concerned in some of the other texts examined. Since the cases differ, the existential reactions differ as well.

King Creon issued a royal decree which made him breaker of eternal laws. When he heard the seer Teiresias's prediction of doom, he experienced an inner conflict: "I know it myself, and my mind (φρήν, midriff, heart, mind) is disturbed! For to yield would be terrible, but if I resist, my will may run into the fowler's net of disaster" (*Antigone,* ll. 1095-97). King Creon repented, but too late. He found lying side-by-side Antigone, who had hanged herself, and her fiancé, Creon's son Haemon, who had also committed suicide. Returning to the palace, he found his wife, who, when learning of her son's death, had stabbed herself to death. Against this background the laments and woes express Creon's reaction to his own wrongdoings and to his fate. No indications of hope are added to the laments. Creon exclaims:

"Woe (ἰώ) for the errors of my mistaken mind . . ." (ll. 1261-62). "Alas (οἴμοι), I have learned, wretched [my trans.] (δείλαιος) as I am . . ." (ll. 1271-72). "Ah, ah (φεῦ φεῦ), woe (ἰώ) for the sad troubles of men" (l. 1276). "Alas, alas (αἰαῖ αἰαῖ)! My mind leaps up with fear! Why has no one struck me to the heart with a two-edged sword?" (ll. 1307-9). Wretched [my trans.] I am (δείλαιος ἐγώ), alas (αἰαῖ), and miserable the woe with which I am compounded" (ll. 1310-11). The expression of lament in Rom 7:24, ταλαίπωρος ἐγὼ ἄνθρωπος, "wretched man I am," has a parallel in *Antigone,* l. 1310, "Wretched I am (δείλαιος ἐγώ)."

Both in Romans 7 and in *Antigone* the laments are followed by questions. To King Creon the tragedy is final and closed. He therefore asks questions of "why."

In *Antigone* ll. 1283-85 King Creon laments and asks:

> "Woe, woe (ἰώ ἰώ), all-receiving Hades, never to be appeased.
> Why (τί), why do you destroy me?"

Likewise in ll. 1307-9:

> "Alas, alas (αἰαῖ αἰαῖ)! My mind leaps up with fear!
> Why (τί) has no one struck me to the heart with a two-edged sword?"

The person "I" in Rom 7:24 is also wretched, but the question raised expresses hope of deliverance:

"Wretched man I am!
Who (τίς) will deliver me from this body of death?"

Also in *Joseph and Aseneth* 6, exclamation of lament is followed by a question, as noted by E. W. Smith. Smith used the text of M. Philonenko, but included in brackets words from the longer text of P. Batiffol.[19] The term ταλαίπωρος, used by Paul in Rom 7:24, is found in *Joseph and Aseneth* 6. In this longer text two sections begin with the exclamation οἴμοι τῇ ἀθλία, which functions in the same way as Paul's ταλαίπωρος ἐγὼ ἄνθρωπος· In Smith's translation parts of *Joseph and Aseneth* 6 read:

"[Woe to me the miserable one (οἴμοι τῇ ἀθλίᾳ)!]
Whither (ποῦ) [now] shall I [the miserable one] depart?
And where shall I flee from his face?
Or how (πῶς) will Joseph the son of God look upon me,
Because I have spoken evil things about him?
[Woe to me the miserable one (οἴμοι τῇ ἀθλίᾳ)!]
Whither shall I flee and hide, because he sees every hidden thing,
[and knows everything,]
and nothing hidden has escaped him,
because of the great light which is in him?"

A prayer addressed to God follows:

"And now be merciful to me, God of Joseph,
because I have spoken evil words of ignorance [against him].
What then shall I the wretched one see?"

Paul in Rom 7:24 has a prayer in the form of a question, "Who will deliver me from this body of death?" The words of thanks in v. 25a, "Thanks be to God through Jesus Christ our Lord," tell implicitly that God is the addressee of the question. Correspondingly, Aseneth is bewildered and asks where to go and to flee, and then moves into a prayer addressed to God. In chs. 12–13 she continues praying to the Lord God. She confesses her sins and asks again for pardon. In this prayer she repeats that she is a wretched person.

Aseneth's prayer of pardon leads in 14:1 to a report on her deliverance and

19. E. W. Smith Jr., "The Form and Religious Background of Romans VII 24-25a," in *NovT* 13 (1971): 128-30; Philonenko, *Joseph et Aséneth*, pp. 148-50; J. Batiffol, *Le Livre de la Prière d'Aseneth* (SP 1-2; Paris: Leroux, 1889-90).

her transformation into a Jewish proselyte. A man from heaven came and announced Aseneth's acceptance with God and her marriage to Joseph. Then in 15:12-13 it is said that Aseneth rejoiced exceedingly, and fell down at the man's feet, and blessed God: "Blessed (εὐλογητός) be the Lord your God, the Most High, who sent you out to rescue me from the darkness and to bring me up from the foundations of the abyss, and blessed be your name for ever." This blessing is a parallel to the thanksgiving in Rom 7:25a: "But thanks (χάρις) be to God through Jesus Christ our Lord." Thus there are common features in Rom 7:7–8:4 and *Joseph and Aseneth* 6–15: Divine intervention causes persons to repent, to exclaim lament, to ask and pray for deliverance, and to offer thanks and blessing to God. In *Joseph and Aseneth* the thought pattern of crime and punishment/acquittal has been modified by the category of proselytism: a pagan person who confesses her/his sin and does penance is accepted as a Jewish proselyte.

The existential reactions of the governor Flaccus are next to be characterized. As punishment he was sent into exile on the island of Andros. When he approached the island, he let a stream of tears pour down, smote his breast with bitter wailing (*Flacc.* 157; cf. 168), and acted like a madman (§162). He was a wretched person (δείλαιος, §167). His limbs shivered and his soul was shaken (§176). He had no hope: "That their [those Jews whom he killed] avenging furies await me I know full well. The ministers of punishment are already as it were standing at the barriers and press forward eager for my blood; every day or rather every hour I die in anticipation and suffer many deaths instead of the final one" (§175).[20] Later the Emperor Gaius sent executioners to the island. They put him to death (§§185-91). Thus, instead of a question for a possible deliverer and words of thanks as in Rom 7:24, Flaccus has words about his fear of further punishments, even of the death penalty.

Genesis 2 and 3 must be included here. When Adam and Eve heard the sound of the Lord walking in the garden, they hid themselves. In answering the Lord God's question, Adam put the blame on Eve, and Eve on the serpent. They were still responsible for their disobedience, however. Correspondingly the person "I" in Rom 7:17 and 20 blames his evil actions on the personalized "Sin" which is pictured as an evil master who misuses his slave. Paul comes close to absolving the person "I" from responsibility. He does not go this far, however. The person "I" is involved in a battle in which he is made a captive to the law of sin (7:22). Thus the person 'I' is still responsible for his misdeed.

Thus, although there are differences among various cases, important similarities exist among the existential reactions of King Creon, Governor Flaccus,

20. *Philo with an English Translation,* by F. H. Colson (Loeb repr.; Cambridge, Mass.: Harvard University Press, 1960), 9:397.

and the person "I" in Rom 7:7–8:4, and even more extensive similarities are seen between *Joseph and Aseneth* 6–15 and Rom 7:7–8:4. These observations support the thesis that Paul consciously or unconsciously was following a common type of biographical story in which a wrongdoer admits his misdeed, reacts existentially, and faces punishment or is set free.

III. Jesus in the Likeness of Sinful Flesh and the Crime Story of the Person 'I'

Rom 8:1-4 is quite complex, and only a few points can be discussed in the present study. One such point is the phrase "in the likeness of sinful flesh" (8:3). Fitzmyer understands ὁμοίωμα, likeness, in this way: "He came in a form like us in that he became a member of the sin-oriented human race; he experienced the effects of sin and suffered death, the result of sin, as one 'cursed' by the law (Gal 3:13). Thus in his own self he coped with the power of sin. Paul's use of the phrase σάρξ ἁμαρτίας denotes not the guilty human condition, but the proneness of humanity made of flesh that is oriented to sin."[21]

Such theological formulations do need to be made, but at the outset it should be emphasized that Jesus was punished as a criminal. For those who executed him, he was punished for his own sins, or, to approach Paul's view, in the likeness of a person who was punished for his own sins.[22] There was, according to Paul, no basis for presenting Jesus' crime-story in the first person, however, since he was without sin (2 Cor 5:21). Instead the death penalty would have been a just verdict upon the lawbreaker "I" in Rom 7:7-25. Correspondingly, Artaÿctes was put to death by crucifixion, and Flaccus was executed by men sent by the Roman emperor Gaius.

Paul's use of first person singular here should be compared further with the use of first person in the parallel texts. In all of these the first person is used. Of special interest is the circumstance that Joseph and Aseneth and Adam and Eve are seen as model persons. Adam and Eve represent the collective of humankind, and Aseneth and Joseph are an ideal Jewish proselyte and an ideal Jewish man. As a model proselyte Aseneth is given the name "City of Refuge," for many nations shall take refuge in her, and within her walls those who give their allegiance to God in penitence will find security.

21. J. A. Fitzmyer, *Romans* (New York: Doubleday, 1993), p. 485.

22. Cf. P. Borgen, "Openly Portrayed as Crucified: Some Observations on Gal 3:1-14," in D. G. Horrell and C. M. Tuckett (eds.), *Christology, Controversy & Community* (Novum Testamentum Supplements 99; Leiden: Brill, 2000), pp. 346-51.

Against this background it is understandable that Paul could write the "biography" of the person "I," who represented the Jewish people as a collective under God's law, and Adam and Eve as humankind under God's law. Further studies on Rom 7:7–8:4 should enter more deeply into the question of the Torah as the law of the Jewish people and as the law of the world and of all of humankind.[23]

Thus, the present study has shown that Paul used the first person, "I," in Rom 7:7–8:4 under the impact of biographical crime stories told about contrite lawbreakers. In such stories the employment of first person was common.

IV. The Spirit: Some Observations

According to Paul, the death of Christ Jesus was a decisive intervention by God: God sent his Son in the likeness of a criminal, but actually as a condemnation of sin in the flesh (Rom 8:3). As a result there is no condemnation for those who are in Christ Jesus, and the law of the Spirit of life has set "me"/"you" free from the law of sin and death (8:1-2).[24] This deliverance made possible a life according to the Spirit as an alternative to a life according to the flesh.

It may be fruitful to compare the role of the Spirit in Romans 8 and in the case of Aseneth. In both places the Spirit brings about a fundamental change. Joseph prayed: "You, Lord, bless this virgin, and renew her by your Spirit, and form her anew by your hidden hand, and make her alive again by your life" (*Jos. As.* 8:9). Correspondingly, according to Paul the law of the Spirit of life has set the person free from the slavery of sin (Rom 8:2). While Aseneth's repentance and prayer for pardon made her acceptable for being transformed, Paul tied the condition for being set free to the Christ event. To Paul the transforming work of the Spirit in the believers has its basis in God's raising of Christ Jesus from the dead (8:11).

According to Philo of Alexandria, a similar role of the Spirit is seen in Abraham: Abraham, as a model proselyte, was transformed, for the divine Spirit which was breathed upon him from on high made his lodging in his soul (*Virt.* 218). Moreover, the proselytes joined a truly inspired and living commonwealth (πρὸς ἔμψυξον τῷ ὄντι καὶ ζῶσαν πολιτείαν, §219). Correspondingly, those who were delivered by being in Christ Jesus walk according to the Spirit (Rom 8:4). It is then worth exploring further the possibility that ideas about

23. Cf. J.-N. Aletti, "Rm 7:7-25 encore une fois: enjeux et propositions," *NTS* 48 (2002): 358-76.

24. Concerning the different readings in the textual witnesses, see Dunn, *Romans 1–8*, p. 414.

Gentiles entering the Jewish community as proselytes may (in the new eschatological situation) have been transformed into the context of the Christian community, into which both Jews and Gentiles entered by being in Christ.[25]

V. Stories Used by the Author to Serve Literary Aims

In their contexts the stories discussed may be used by the authors to serve literary aims, as seen in particular in Philo, *In Flaccum* and in Herodotus, *Hist.* 9.120.

Philo used the story of Flaccus, of his evil deeds against the Jews, and of his arrest, trial, and punishments as proof that God in his providence still cared for the Jewish people (*Flacc.* 191). As for the story of Artaÿctes, Herodotus emphasized that Artaÿctes was crucified by the Hellespontian shore where Xerxes had bridged the strait. Thus the fate of Artaÿctes served as a warning to all invaders of Greek territory.[26]

Also, the stories of King Creon and of Aseneth are understood within a larger literary context. Sophocles' aim in writing the story about Creon and Antigone was to demonstrate that reverence and obedience toward the gods and the divine laws must be inviolate (*Antigone*, ll. 1349-50).[27]

The aim of the part of *Joseph and Aseneth* which has been examined was to present the conversion of a model proselyte to Judaism, and thereby also to clarify the proper relationship between Jews and Gentiles. There may also be an apologetic tendency at work by which the author explains how it came to be that Joseph married a pagan woman.[28]

Against this background it is quite understandable that Paul has used the biographically shaped story of Rom 7:7–8:4 to serve larger literary purposes. In the context of the letter, this biographical kind of story is used in Paul's defence of the law.[29] Another aim of Paul is to demonstrate the person "I"s need for redemption, as told and developed in Rom 7:25–8:30. This perspective comprises the new life in the Spirit and the eschatological fulfillment (8:5-30).

25. See P. Borgen, "Jesus Christ, the Reception of the Spirit and a Cross-National Community," in J. B. Green and M. Turner (eds.), *Jesus of Nazareth, Lord and Christ* I. H. Marshall Festschrift (Grand Rapids: Eerdmans, 1994), pp. 227-29; also printed in P. Borgen, *Early Christianity and Hellenistic Judaism* (Edinburgh: Clark, 1996, repr. 1998), pp. 262-63.

26. *Herodotus with an English Translation* by A. D. Godley, 4:xvii.

27. See A. Lesky, *Greek Tragedy*, trans. from German by H. A. Frankfort (London: Benn, 1965), pp. 103-8.

28. Burchard, "The Present State," pp. 35 and 38.

29. Dunn, *Romans 1–8*, p. 376.

VI. Summary

The thesis of the present essay has been that the paragraph Rom 7:7–8:4 contains a sufficient number of similarities with some listed Jewish and Greek texts which center around the idea of a contrite wrongdoer as to make a comparison fruitful. Further analysis is needed to relate these observations to the various questions raised by scholars in the exegesis of this section of Paul's letter to the Romans. Similarities registered are:

(1) Divine interventions related to divine laws and divine authority brought a change in the lives of the persons dealt with in the texts: Adam and Eve, Aseneth, Creon, Flaccus and Artaÿctes. Similarily, the divine intervention by means of the spoken law, Rom 7:7-12, marked a dividing line in the biography of the person "I."

(2) Existential reactions are reported in all the texts. Moreover, in Romans 7, in *Antigone,* and in *Joseph and Aseneth* exclamations of lament are followed by questions, and in Romans 7 and *Joseph and Aseneth* also by thanksgiving/blessing.

(3) As in Rom 7:14-25 (and 8:2?), so also in the other texts, the first person singular is used. Thus Paul's use of the first person, "I," seems written under the impact of (auto)biographical crime stories told about contrite lawbreakers. Since the texts are spread out over some centuries, it is probable that such stories about contrite wrongdoers belonged to a traditional type which might also have been told orally.

(4) The Spirit was a transforming power when the Gentile Aseneth became a Jewish proselyte. According to Philo, *De Virtutibus* 217–19, a similar role of the Spirit is seen in the transformation of another model proselyte, Abraham. Moreover, according to Philo, the proselytes joined a truly inspired and living commonwealth. Correspondingly, those who are set free by the law of the Spirit of life are to walk according to the Spirit (Rom 8:1-4).

It is then worth exploring further the possibility that to Paul such ideas about Gentiles entering the Jewish community as proselytes may (in this new eschatological situation) have been transferred into the context of the Christian community, into which both Jews and Gentiles entered by being in Christ.

(5) In their contexts the stories discussed may be used by the author to serve special literary aims, as seen, for example, in Philo's *In Flaccum* and Herodotus's *Historiae* 9. Against this background it is quite understandable that Paul has used the biographically shaped story of Rom 7:7–8:4 to serve the larger literary purpose of being a defense of the law. At the same time Paul in 7:7-24 also demonstrates the need for redemption and new life, as outlined in 7:25–8:30.

XVI The Question of the "Apportioned Spirit" in Paul's Letters: Romans as a Case Study

Robert Jewett

The odd references to God's Spirit (πνεῦμα) as "mine" or "yours" within the Pauline letters remain puzzling, despite the exegetical efforts of the past century. The difficulty is intensified because several factors are ordinarily not taken into account in the discussions of commentators. The context of Pauline mysticism and charismatic group experiences tends to be sidestepped for various apologetic reasons.[1] In several of his early studies,[2] our honoree countered this tradition by taking the charismatic character of early Christianity seriously. In his more recent study, *The Theology of Paul the Apostle,* there are substantial discussions of mysticism and the gift of the Spirit that overcome traditional scholarly reluctance to honor this terrain.[3] These factors explain in part why contemporary scholars still have difficulty in accounting for the references to "your πνεῦμα" in Gal. 6:18; Phlm. 25; Phil. 4:23 and 1 Thess. 5:23; to "my πνεῦμα" in 1 Cor. 14:14; 2 Cor. 2:13 and Rom. 1:9; to "his πνεῦμα" in 2 Cor. 7:13; or to "our πνεῦμα" in Rom. 8:16. Equally puzzling (although more widely discussed as if perfectly understandable) is how Paul can speak of believers as "having," "receiving," or being "given" the Spirit (Gal. 3:2; Rom. 5:5; 8:10, 15), or of the Spirit

1. For example, F. W. Horn, *Das Angeld des Geistes: Studien zur paulinischen Pneumatologie* (Göttingen: Vandenhoeck & Ruprecht, 1992), p. 113: "Der Blick auf die frühesten ntl. Quellen zeigt zweifelsfrei, daß an keiner Stelle charismatische Phänomene den Ausgangspunkt darstellen, um aus ihnen die Gegenwart des Geistes zu folgen."

2. J. D. G. Dunn, *Baptism in the Holy Spirit* (London: SCM, 1970); "Jesus — Flesh and Spirit: An Exposition of Rom. 1.3-4," *JTS* 24 (1973): 40-68; *Jesus and the Spirit* (Philadelphia: Westminster, 1975).

3. Grand Rapids/Cambridge: Eerdmans, 1998, pp. 390-441.

"dwelling" in them (Rom. 8:9, 11; 1 Cor. 3:16). How can the divine Spirit become a human possession? Does the spirit in these passages refer to the new personality of the converted?[4] If so, how can the spirit continue to function as Christ, whose sovereignty is established in conversion? What is the significance of the participatory terminology developed especially in Romans: to co-witness (συμμαρτυρέω), to stand alongside (συναντιλαμβάνομαι), to intercede (ὑπερεντυγχάνειν), and to work alongside of (συνεργεῖν)?

Within the confines of this article, I concentrate on some of the references in Romans, which as Paul's final letter seems to provide his most mature view. While moving beyond Jimmy Dunn's analysis in some particulars, the thesis that I intend to document in the sections below follows his lead in appreciating the communal, charismatic, and mystical experiences of the Spirit that marked the early Pauline congregations. The various expressions in Romans for joint participation between the Spirit and believers offer a hitherto unexplored clue to understanding the apportioned Spirit.

I

Serving God "in my πνεῦμα in the gospel of his Son" (Rom. 1:9) is one of the "most complex uses of πνεῦμα in the Pauline corpus," as Gordon Fee observes.[5] It is an unparalleled expression of Paul's self-identity, and in view of the connection with the verb 'to serve' (λατρεύω), the parallel with Phil. 3:3 strongly suggests that as one of the believers "who serve by the Spirit of God" Paul wishes to emphasize the source of his calling and effectiveness.[6] In view of his premise that the "spirit of man" is incapable of understanding God (1 Cor. 2:11) and his insistence later in Rom. 8:9 that those lacking the Spirit of God do not belong to him, it is difficult to understand why he would wish to discredit his calling in Rom. 1:9. He makes plain in Rom. 8:26 that genuine prayer derives from God's Spirit, a premise developed in 1:8 where he describes his thanksgiving for the Roman believers "through Jesus Christ." An allusion to his "individuelle Lebenskraft und zugleich Sitz von Gefühlen,"[7] incapable of genuine prayer or service to the gospel, is precisely what he would not want to stress

4. See Samuel Vollenweider, "Der Geist Gottes als Selbst der Glaubenden," *ZThK* 93 (1996): 163-92.

5. G. D. Fee, *God's Empowering Presence: The Holy Spirit in the Letters of Paul* (Peabody, Mass.: Hendrickson, 1994), pp. 484-85.

6. See Fee, *Empowering Presence*, pp. 485-86.

7. Hans-Christoph Meier, *Mystik bei Paulus: Zur Phänomenologie religiösen Erfahrung im Neuen Testament* (TANZ 26; Tübingen/Basel: Francke, 1998), p. 252.

here. Instead, as part of laying out his credentials and clarifying the purpose of his letter, Paul emphasizes that his advocacy of the gospel derives from the apportioned Spirit, whereby God directly participates in his ministry.

The gift of the Spirit places Paul in the structure of obedience to the gospel; although the Spirit is given to him in his conversion in such a manner that he can refer to it as "mine," he remains in dialogue with God's "witness" and he remains a servant to the Lord into whose service his conversion called him. The peculiar kind of co-participation in charismatic activity visible later in his letter emerges here.

II

Romans 8:9 opens the argument that belonging to Christ involves possession of the Spirit. Their being is shaped by πνεῦμα rather than flesh because their conversion sets them free from the compulsion to conform to the world's method of gaining honor through competition with others or by reliance on some allegedly superior status. While they remain human and therefore vulnerable, they are no longer "in the flesh" (ἐν σαρκί) in the sense developed since Rom. 7:5. The formulation simply assumes that all of the Christians in Rome, in contrast, are ἐν πνεύματι,[8] implying an undeniably charismatic description of the community.[9]

Whether the next clause, "if indeed/since indeed God's Spirit dwells within you" (8:9) is intended as a warning, a condition, or as assurance has long been debated.[10] The conjunction εἴπερ can be read either as "since" or "if indeed."[11] Since those who see a warning or condition[12] are unable to explain why the verb οἰκεῖ is in the indicative rather than the subjunctive,[13] and why Paul did not select εἴγε rather than εἴπερ.[14] Consequently Paul's formulation is more

8. See W. Sanday and A. C. Headlam, *A Critical and Exegetical Commentary on the Epistle to the Romans* (Edinburgh: T&T Clark, 1902), p. 197; C. K. Barrett, *A Commentary on the Epistle to the Romans* (London: Black, 1957), p. 158.

9. See Fee, *Presence*, p. 547; J. A. Fitzmyer, *Romans* (New York: Doubleday, 1993), p. 490; Dunn (*Romans 1–8, 9–16* [WBC; Waco, Tex.: Word, 1988], p. 428) attempts to qualify the "enthusiastic" dimension of this distinction by insisting that "the flesh is still a factor."

10. See O. Kuss, *Der Römerbrief übersetzt und erklärt* (Regensburg: Pustet, 1957-78), 2:500-501 for a listing of patristic and more recent views.

11. See BAGD, p. 200, §11; BDF §454.2.

12. For example, Dunn *Romans*, p. 428.

13. See Kuss, *Der Römerbrief*, 2:501.

14. See F. Godet, *Commentary on St. Paul's Epistle to the Romans* (New York: Funk & Wagnalls, 1883), p. 304.

likely intended to provide assurance.[15] A translation with "since indeed" is also more consistent with the formulation of 8:9a which flatly states that Christians "are" in the Spirit. That God's Spirit dwells "among" or "within" (ἐν) the congregation, rather than merely within the heart of individuals,[16] seems likely in view of the second person plural address that matches Paul's reference in 1 Cor. 3:16 to what was apparently a typical component in early catechesis,[17] "Do you not know that you [plural] are God's temple and that God's Spirit dwells in you [plural, ἐν ὑμῖν οἰκεῖ]?" It is likely that Paul's conceptual framework and that of early Christianity in this regard were drawn from Judaism. The Hebrew text of Exod. 29:45-46 has Yahweh promise, "And I will dwell among the people of Israel, and will be their God . . . that I might dwell among them; I am the LORD their God." This theme reappears in the *Test. Levi* 5:2, where God promises, "I shall come and dwell in the midst of Israel (κατοικήσω ἐν μέσῳ τοῦ Ἰσραήλ)." It is consistent with this tradition that Paul refers here, for the first time in Romans, to "God's Spirit," which is identical with the "Spirit of Christ" because of its strict parallelism in 8:9b. The idea of the Spirit dwelling in the midst of the Christian community was widely shared,[18] reflecting a charismatic view of the church (1 Corinthians 12–14), whose common life featured Christ as the Lord of the love feast, ushering in God's kingdom by granting God's Spirit to all believers.

In contrast to the assuring, collective language of 8:9a-b, Paul refers to the antithetical circumstance in 8:9c with an impersonal, individual expression: "but if anyone" does not have the Spirit, that person does not belong to Christ. In contrast to later, noncharismatic understandings of the church, Paul here clearly states that possession of the Spirit is a *sine qua non.* He does not hesitate to use the language of "possession," employed both for demonic forces and for the Spirit of God.[19] A striking feature of this formulation is the mutuality of possession: the person not having the Spirit is therefore not had by Christ: οὗτος οὐκ ἔστιν αὐτοῦ. This language reflects Paul's charismatic view of the faith, as Käsemann explains:

15. Kuss (*Der Römerbrief,* 2:501) cites others who see assurance for other reasons.

16. The individualistic construal is widely represented in the commentaries: C. E. B. Cranfield, *A Critical and Exegetical Commentary on the Epistle to the Romans* (Edinburgh: T&T Clark, 1975-79), p. 388; U. Wilckens, *Der Brief an die Römer* (Zürich: Benziger; Neukirchen-Vluyn: Neukirchener, 1978-82), 2:131; D. J. Moo, *The Epistle to the Romans* (Grand Rapids: Eerdmans, 1996), p. 490.

17. See O. Michel, "οἰκέω," *TDNT* 5 (1967), p. 135.

18. H. Paulsen, *Überlieferung und Auslegung in Römer 8* (Neukirchen-Vluyn: Neukirchener, 1974), p. 50.

19. See Meier, *Mystik,* pp. 259-60.

> Nevertheless the reciprocity in the use of the formulae makes sense only if they are derived from pneumatology and understood in the light of it. By the Spirit Christ seizes power in us, just as conversely by the Spirit we are incorporated into Christ.[20]

Although many exegetes remain uncomfortable with this dimension, Paul's language throughout this passage is charismatic and "mystical";[21] it reflects a collective type of charismatic mysticism in which God's Spirit was thought to enter and energize the community as well as each member. Its primary arena of manifestation, in contrast to most later Christianity, was not individual devotion but social enthusiasm: speaking in tongues, prophecy, and joyous celebration in the context of the common meal that united the formerly shamed from different families and backgrounds into a single family honored and chosen and hallowed by God.[22]

The "but if" that opens 8:10 stands in antithesis to 8:9c and picks up the tone of assurance from 8:9a-b.[23] Christ is in fact "among/in the midst of you [pl.]" (ἐν ὑμῖν), again with the collective connotation most likely. Although many scholars are uncomfortable with the seeming identification of Christ and the Spirit of God reflected in this parallel use of ἐν ὑμῖν in 8:9-10, since it raises problems for later trinitarian thought,[24] there seems little doubt "that Christ and Spirit are perceived in experience as one"[25] in the circle Paul represents. In the overpowering enthusiasm of the love feast in which the Spirit was perceived to be ushering in God's new age, the sharp distinctions made by later christological controversies were not necessary.

The final "if" formula opens 8:11 in a parallel manner to 8:10, reiterating the presence of the Spirit ἐν ὑμῖν. That it is once again conceived as God's Spirit as in 8:9 is evident in the christological formula that Paul cites twice in this verse. The Spirit of God is the "one who raised Jesus from the dead," or in the second version, clearly with a Pauline formulation not found elsewhere in the tradition, "the one raising Christ Jesus from the dead." Here the Spirit of God

20. E. Käsemann, *Commentary on Romans* (Grand Rapids: Eerdmans, 1980), p. 222; see also Dunn, *Romans*, pp. 429-30.

21. See F. J. Leenhardt, *L'Épître de Saint Paul aux Romains* (2nd ed.; Geneva: Labor et Fides, 1981), p. 208; M. Black, *Romans* (2nd ed.; Grand Rapids: Eerdmans, 1989), p. 112.

22. See Robert Jewett, *Paul the Apostle to America: Cultural Trends and Pauline Scholarship* (Louisville: Westminster/John Knox, 1994), pp. 73-86.

23. See Dunn, *Romans*, p. 430.

24. See Kuss, *Der Römerbrief*, 2:502; Cranfield, *Romans*, p. 389; Fee, *Presence*, pp. 548-49.

25. Dunn, *Romans*, p. 430.

that resurrected Jesus is not only the very Spirit animating the churches in Rome, but also the basis of their future hope.[26]

The reference to "being led" by the Spirit in 8:14 is a distinctively Pauline formulation, found in Gal. 5:18, reflecting an "enthusiastic" understanding of believers being "carried away" by a spiritual force.[27] In 1 Cor. 12:2 Paul uses the same verb (ἄγω) to refer to the pagan experience of being carried away by "dumb idols," which reflects the sense dominant in the Greco-Roman world of spiritual forces overpowering humans and leading them this way and that. It is therefore appropriate to explain Paul's formulation of being led by the Spirit as "being constrained by a compelling force, of surrendering to an overpowering compulsion,"[28] which implies divine intervention into the decision-making process of the community, led by inspired leaders, and tested by the inspired and transformed minds of the members (Rom 12:1-2). Interpreters are usually skittish about this language and seek to rein it in by insisting on the non-compulsory decision of believers to follow Christ and that Paul does not issue a "license for uninhibited ecstasy,"[29] but no such reminders are actually included here. The suspicion of charismatic excess typical of the modern interpreter has no part in this letter.

The declaration in 8:15 that "you received a spirit producing sonship" appears to reflect a widely available concept of adoption. The charismatic Spirit in the familial community of the early church produces adoption as "sons" and "children" of God. The confirmation of this extraordinarily high status granted to believers is drawn from the widely shared experience of charismatic language being used in the early house and tenement churches. Just as in Gal. 4:6, Paul refers to an acclamation which "we cry out" (κράζομεν), apparently referring "to a worship situation"[30] in which unison prayer is heard. Such prayer is thought to be an indication of the presence of the Spirit, which explains the formulation ἐν ᾧ κράζομεν. The verb is similar to the English word "croak," implying "a rough or raucous sound,"[31] with a semantic range from "cry out, scream, shriek" to "call out."[32] This potentially "violent verb"[33] leads some interpreters

26. See Paulsen, *Überlieferung,* p. 53.

27. H. D. Betz, *Galatians* (Philadelphia: Fortress, 1979), p. 281; see also T. Zahn, *Der Brief des Paulus an die Römer* (Leipzig: Deichert, 3rd ed. 1925), p. 392. The classification of this usage as "figurative" by BAGD (p. 14) is apparently intended to prevent this enthusiastic reading.

28. Dunn, *Romans,* p. 450.

29. Dunn, *Romans,* p. 450; see also L. Morris, *The Epistle to the Romans* (Grand Rapids: Eerdmans, 1988), p. 313.

30. See Käsemann, *Romans,* p. 272; H. Fendrich, "κράζω," *EDNT* 1 (1990), p. 313.

31. W. Grundmann, "κράζω κτλ," *TDNT* 3 (1965), p. 898.

32. BAGD, pp. 447-48; see also Paulsen, *Überlieferung,* pp. 94-96.

33. Barrett, *Romans,* p. 164.

to think of the words "Abba, the Father" as an ecstatic "acclamation,"[34] which seems highly likely.[35] The question of the original setting of the acclamation has been taken up by Henning Paulsen, who concludes that the translation suggests a setting in "Hellenistic Jewish Christianity," and that the connection both with Spirit and sonship found in Galatians and Romans was probably derived from that setting.[36] Since the Spirit impels believers to utter their prayers directly to their Abba, this is a powerful, experiential confirmation of their status as children of God. Since the Spirit confirms that they belong to God, there is no longer any basis for anxiety about their status. Their need for honor has been fully met.[37]

Romans 8:16 amplifies the relational implications of the congregations' charismatic experience. The lack of a particle or conjunction between 8:16 and the preceding verse indicates, in Godet's words, "profound emotion,"[38] while making clear that this verse reiterates and clarifies the thought of the preceding verse.[39] The expression "that very Spirit" (αὐτὸ τὸ πνεῦμα) has a resumptive sense, referring with emphasis to the theme of the preceding sentence. The Abba cry is confirmation of sonship, not merely in the reception of the "Spirit producing sonship" but in the actual status as sons and daughters of God.

Paul's choice of the verb συμμαρτυρέω in connection with "our spirit" has occasioned considerable discussion.[40] If "our spirit" is understood as the human spirit in an anthropological sense,[41] then it would have no independent knowledge of divine destiny (see 1 Cor. 2:11); but if this is the "apportioned Spirit" of God granted to believers,[42] then the verb seems to imply the theologically awkward conundrum that God's Spirit witnesses to himself. Some commentators have avoided such problems by following Hermann Strathmann in eliminating the συν- component of the verb and translating it simply as "bear witness."[43]

34. Käsemann, *Romans*, p. 228; C. H. Dodd, *The Epistle of Paul to the Romans* (London: Hodder & Stoughton, 1932), p. 145; Paulsen, *Überlieferung*, pp. 90-91, 95.

35. See W. A. Meeks, *The First Urban Christians* (New Haven: Yale University Press, 1983), p. 88.

36. Paulsen, *Überlieferung*, p. 92.

37. See Jewett, "Honor and Shame in the Argument of Romans," in A. Brown, G. F. Snyder, and V. Wiles, eds., *Putting Body and Soul Together: Essays in Honor of Robin Scroggs* (Valley Forge, Pa.: Trinity Press International, 1997), pp. 257-72.

38. Godet, *Romans*, p. 310.

39. See Kuss, *Der Römerbrief*, 2:604.

40. See H. Strathmann, "μάρτυς κτλ," *TDNT* 4 (1967), p. 509.

41. See Dunn, *Romans*, p. 454; Fee, *Presence*, p. 568; Moo, *Romans*, p. 503.

42. See M.-J. Lagrange, *Saint Paul: Épître aux Romains* (Paris: Gabalda, 1931), p. 202; Robert Jewett, *Anthropological Terms* (Leiden: Brill, 1971), pp. 198-99.

43. Strathmann, "μάρτυς κτλ," *TDNT* 4 (1967), p. 509.

This is inadmissible because this verb is in fact typically used to depict co-witnessing of some sort. Others suggest that Paul really meant to say that God's Spirit witnesses *to* our spirit, which also effectively eliminates the element of co-witnessing.[44] In view of the fourfold reiteration of the συν- component of verbs in these two verses, revealing explicit authorial intent to emphasize the mutuality produced by the Spirit, it is inappropriate to reduce the semantic range of συμμαρτυρέω for apologetic reasons. It is preferable to accept Paul's idea that both the apportioned Spirit granted to believers and the "Spirit itself" confirm that believers are "children of God,"[45] despite the "logical difficulties in conceptualizing this in modern terms."[46] If the participatory orientation of Paul's gospel that is so often overlooked in Pauline studies were allowed to play its central role in Pauline scholarship, this interplay between divine and human responsibility would not seem so strange.

III

In 8:26-27 the role of the Spirit in co-participation with believers is introduced by the active verb συναντιλαμβάνεται,[47] which occurs elsewhere in the New Testament only at Luke 10:40. The Spirit "in a similar way also" stands alongside the saints as they persevere in prayer. While this verb is used in the LXX to refer to humans taking up a portion of each other's work (Exod. 18:22; Num. 11:17), there is a close parallel to Paul's expression in Ps. 89:21, where Yahweh offers to provide aid to his people, Israel: ἡ γὰρ χείρ μου συναντιλήψεται αὐτῷ.

For Paul, the necessity of such aid is described by the phrase "in our weakness," referring to the vulnerable position of believers caught between the two ages and thus involved in the "suffering" referred to in 8:18. They know enough of the coming new age to yearn for it, along with the rest of the creation, but they continue to be assaulted by the principalities and powers of the old age of the flesh. Given the use of the derogatory term "weak" to refer to groups of Roman Christians, it is significant that Paul attaches the possessive pronoun to this term in 8:26 ("in *our* weakness"), making clear that he and all

44. See Godet, *Romans,* p. 311; Leenhardt, *L'Épître,* p. 215; Cranfield, *Romans,* p. 403.

45. See Black, *Romans,* p. 114.

46. Jewett, *Anthropological Terms,* p. 199.

47. A. Deissmann (*Light from the Ancient East* [trans. Lionel R. M. Strachan; Grand Rapids: Baker, 1965], p. 83) refers to the use of this verb in the LXX, in Josephus, and in inscriptions such as in the temple to Apollo at Delphi, "to lend assistance (συναντιλήψεσθαι) in things profitable unto the city."

other Christians share this vulnerable status. He refuses to accept the premise held by some in the early church that the gift of the Spirit lifts believers above weaknesses, and thus above each other. All believers participate in the groaning of 8:23.

In 8:26b-c, Paul explains how the Spirit lends assistance to believers caught between the two ages. The two lines need to be kept together as a coherent antithesis because 8:26b taken by itself is so sweepingly stated that serious misunderstandings have arisen.[48] The phrase καθὸ δεῖ is associated with the verb "we pray" and is best translated "as we ought,"[49] referring to divine compulsion. The resultant translation of 8:26b, "What are we to pray for, as we ought? We do not know!" helps to clarify the exegetical options. It is not that Christians are fundamentally incapable of praying,[50] are too ignorant to pray as particular exigencies demand,[51] or lack the visionary capacity to see into the eschatological future.[52] When the second half of the antithesis in 8:26c is taken into account, referring explicitly to the Spirit's prayerful intercession on behalf of Christians, Paul's view may be seen as consistent with his premise of co-responsibility with the divine Spirit as the mark of proper discipleship. "I will pray with the Spirit, but I will pray with the mind also" (1 Cor. 14:15); "for it is God who is at work in you, enabling you both to will and to work for his good pleasure" (Phil. 2:13; also 1 Cor. 12:6, 11; Gal. 3:5). It would be consistent to maintain, therefore, that even Christians, who have the Spirit, cannot pray without the Spirit; yet with the Spirit, they have aid, as 8:26a asserted. They do not pray alone, but the "Spirit himself intercedes (ὑπερεντυγχάνει)" on their behalf. Paul apparently coined this word by adding the prefix ὑπέρ to the familiar word ἐντυγχάνειν since the first appearance of this double compound verb within Greek writings is in this pericope. It conveys his distinctive view of the Spirit as both apportioned out to believers and as the Spirit of God and/or Christ acting within them and beyond them.[53] Paul re-

48. See Käsemann, *Romans,* pp. 239-40.

49. See Godet, *Romans,* p. 320 and BAGD, p. 172, option 2.

50. See K. Niederwimmer, "Das Gebet des Geistes, Röm 8:26f.," *Theologische Zeitschrift* 20 (1964): 255-56. G. Harder (*Paulus und das Gebet* [Gütersloh: Bertelsmann, 1936], p. 161) posited a cultural crisis in the Greco-Roman world that followed the breakup of a naive believe that the gods answer prayer.

51. See J. Murray, *The Epistle to the Romans* (Grand Rapids: Eerdmans, 1975), p. 311; and Morris, *Romans,* p. 327.

52. See W. Bindemann, *Die Hoffnung der Schöpfung: Römer 8:18-27 und die Frage einer Theologie der Befreiung von Mensch und Natur* (Neukirchen-Vluyn: Neukirchener, 1983), p. 80; followed by R. Gebauer, *Das Gebet bei Paulus: Forschungsgeschichtliche und exegetische Studien* (Giessen: Brunnen, 1989), p. 167.

53. See Jewett, *Anthropological Terms,* pp. 172-200, 451-53.

mains "the first to speak clearly of the Spirit as an intercessor. . . ."[54] It is clearly "a Pauline novelty."[55]

There is widespread disagreement about the reference to the στεναγμοῖς ἀλαλήτοις by which the Spirit conveys its intercession. Käsemann[56] has popularized the idea suggested by Origen and Chrysostom[57] that this expression refers explicitly to the kind of glossolalia evident in 1 Corinthians 14,[58] while others suggest that it refers to the "inarticulate aspiration" of believers.[59] The most appropriate explanation is offered by Roland Gebauer: "In this passage the Spirit comes before God with a sigh that requires no language . . . because God as the one who knows both the human heart and the impulse of the Spirit, receives and understands the sighs of the Spirit without language."[60] The Spirit of God interacts with the inner sighs (8:23) in the human heart (8:27), bringing them before God in unspoken intercession.

Paul is clearly suggesting that the "weakness" of believers is addressed and sustained by the Spirit's intervention, so it is fair to conclude that he understands all prayer as arising from an inarticulate realm that expresses human vulnerability at its depth.[61] Glossolalia could well arise from such experience, but there is nothing like an explicit polemic here against either the practice or the theology of speaking in tongues. His point is a positive one, that the inarticulate groans of believers, whether of glossolalia, frustration, or pain, are taken up by the Spirit's silent intercession on behalf of the children of God whose dominion over a fallen world is not yet fully realized. By associating charismatic experiences with human weakness rather than strength, it "becomes a vehicle to make one sensitive to the sufferings of all creatures" while impeding grandiosity on the part of charismatics.[62]

That the Spirit's intercession, even in the most unintelligible form, is un-

54. E. A. Obeng, "The Origins of the Spirit Intercession Motif in Romans 8:26," *NTS* 32 (1986): 630.

55. Fitzmyer, *Romans,* p. 518.

56. Käsemann, *Romans,* pp. 240-41.

57. Cranfield (*Romans,* p. 423) provides the references: Origen, *PG,* col. 1120; Chrysostom, *PG,* col. 533.

58. A charismatic construal of "inexpressible groans" is also favored by Zahn, *Der Brief,* pp. 412-13; Paulsen, *Überlieferung,* pp. 122-23; G. Theissen, *Psychological Aspects of Pauline Theology* (trans. J. P. Galvin; Edinburgh: T&T Clark, 1987), pp. 315-20.

59. Dodd, *Romans,* p. 135; Godet, *Romans,* p. 321; H. Schlier, *Der Römerbrief* (Freiburg: Herder, 1977), p. 269.

60. Gebauer, *Gebet bei Paulus,* p. 169.

61. See E. Gaugler, "Der Geist und das Gebet der schwachen Gemeinde: Eine Auslegung von Röm. 8,26-27," *IKZ* 51 (1961): 69-80.

62. Theissen, *Psychological Aspects,* pp. 339-40.

derstandable by God provides the conclusion of Paul's argument in 8:27. He resorts to typical Old Testament usage in referring to God[63] as ἐραυνῶν τὰς καρδίας. The potentially threatening invasion of divine oversight is transformed here by a penetrating grace that accepts and sustains the deepest levels of human consciousness and unconsciousness. What God knows is τί τὸ φρόνημα τοῦ πνεύματος, which should be translated as "the Spirit's intention," "the Spirit's thinking," or "the Spirit's aspiration."[64] The intentionality and *modus operandi* of the Spirit are in view here, not the objective content of its "mind,"[65] because the context deals with the Spirit's activity within the human heart. With a line of thought similar to 1 Cor. 2:11 ("no one understands the things of God except the Spirit of God"), Paul is insisting not only that God knows and intercedes at the point of the deepest human confusion[66] but also that God communicates with God's self[67] through the groans that humans share with the rest of the fallen creation. To place this in the context of the argument beginning in 8:18, even the "sufferings" that cause human groaning are being drawn by the Spirit into "the glory about to be revealed to us," the glory of a dialogue within deity itself. That glory also discloses itself in ecstatic language such as glossolalia,[68] where the weakness and vulnerability of the creature expresses itself with sounds that only the Spirit can interpret. This is a "cognitive restructuring of ecstatic experience" as "an impulse toward human transformation."[69] The holiness of believers thus entails an ongoing intervention of the Spirit, maintaining their relationship as children of God through the inarticulate groans they utter as well as their "Abba" acclamations as described in 8:15-16.

63. G. W. MacRae's proposal ("A Note on Romans 8:26-27," *HTR* 73 [1980]: 227-30) that "spirit" rather than "God" is the antecedent for the verb "search" reduces the complexity of communication within aspects of divinity but provides a poor basis to understand the reference to the interceding before "God" in 8:27b.

64. BAGD (p. 866) refers to classical and intertestamental references as well as to Josephus, *J.W.* 1.204 and 4.358, where the expression φρόνημα ἐλευθερίου appears. See Godet, *Romans*, p. 321, and Dunn, *Romans*, p. 479.

65. The translation "mind" is found in the RSV and NRSV as well as in many commentaries.

66. See Käsemann, *Romans*, p. 242.

67. See O. Michel, *Der Brief an die Römer* (Göttingen: Vandenhoeck & Ruprecht, 1978), p. 273; Dunn, *Romans*, pp. 479-80.

68. See Käsemann, *Romans*, p. 242.

69. Theissen, *Psychological Aspects*, pp. 337, 320.

IV

As one can infer from the density of text-critical variants,[70] the theological comment in 8:28, πάντα συνεργεῖ εἰς ἀγαθόν in 8:28b, has long provoked difficult translational and interpretive problems. Given the text-critical likelihood of the shorter text being original, there are three options in translating this clause. If πάντα is understood as the subject of the verb (i.e., "all things cooperate for good"),[71] Paul is turned into an advocate of what Dodd aptly described as a congenial modern theory that the universe contains "a natural tendency towards progress."[72] While it seems more appropriate on substantive grounds to construe πάντα as an accusative of specification, "in all things,"[73] it remains unclear why Paul did not provide a preposition such as κατὰ πάντα, which would have removed all possibility of ambiguity. If the translation "in all things" is followed, there are two options for construing the subject of the verb. The path most frequently taken is to supply "God" as the subject, which follows the logic of the early textual variant that added ὁ θεός.[74] This is stylistically awkward because the immediately preceding clause ends with the word "God" in the accusative, τὸν θεόν,[75] and it requires an unexplained and unstated change of subject from "the Spirit," which was the subject of the third person singular verbs since the beginning of 8:26.

The most likely option is that Paul intended τὸ πνεῦμα to be supplied by the reader in 8:28b,[76] because this requires no change of subject from the end of 8:27. This option is strongly suggested by the repetition of the prefix συν- in συνεργεῖ, following συναντιλαμβάνεται in 8:26 where the subject "the Spirit" is explicitly supplied. The same subject is also stated for the next verb in 8:26, ὑπερεντυγχάνει, and must be supplied for the final verb in the immediately preceding 8:27, ἐντυγχάνει.

The use of the verb συνεργεῖν brings Paul's formula close to the apocalyptic

70. See the extensive discussion of the eight interpretive options involving both the shorter and longer readings in Cranfield, *Romans*, pp. 425-29.

71. This option is favored by the KJV and AV, and by a variety of modern commentators, e.g., Barrett, *Romans*, p. 169; Käsemann, *Romans*, p. 243; Wilckens, *Römer*, 2:163; Dunn, *Romans 1–8*, p. 481.

72. Dodd, *Romans*, p. 138.

73. Cranfield (*Romans*, p. 427) says that Baur cites Alexander Aphrodisiensis, *De fato* 31 for πάντα used as an accusative of respect; on pp. 632-33 of BAGD other instances are cited but not this particular one.

74. This is found, e.g., in RSV, NIV, NJB; Byrne, *Reckoning*, p. 173; Paulsen, *Überlieferung*, pp. 152-54.

75. See Black, *Romans*, p. 118.

76. This option is followed by the NEB; Black, *Romans*, p. 118.

perspective of the *Testament of the Twelve Patriarchs*,[77] but I have been unable to find any parallel that matches the precise thrust of Paul's compressed formula. It claims a divine-human synergism in the midst of disadvantageous circumstances, because the Spirit works "with" those who love God. In the tangled discussion about the translation and appropriate parallels for 8:28, the συν- of the verb συνεργεῖν has tended to drop out of consideration.[78] Paul's wording implies divine and human co-responsibility in the face of adversity, and in the context of this letter, the "good" to be accomplished by this co-operation includes the daily work and congregational formation on behalf of the Roman house and tenement churches as well as the risky mission to Spain that they will be asked to support.[79] The thrust of the argument is encouraging: despite adversity and the ongoing weakness of the congregation, the Spirit labors alongside believers in such tasks.

V

The theme of charismatic cooperation is taken up again in Romans 12. The three exhortations in Rom. 12:11 would seem to begin with a tautology except for the context of a charismatic ethic as established in 12:3-8. Translators overcome this in part by selecting verbal forms like "flagging"[80] for the noun ὀκνηρός, the antithesis of σπουδή.[81] The premise of the exhortation is an already active enthusiasm that derives from an extrahuman stimulus, but which can be stifled or allowed to become inactive. This is countered by an exhortation phrased with a term typically used to warn against worthless indolence on the part of slaves or employees.[82] Paul's striking juxtaposition of indolence and

77. See Dunn, *Romans*, p. 481, who refers to *T. Iss.* 3:7 ("And the Lord increased the good things through my hands; and also Jacob knew that God worked together with my integrity"); also *T. Reub.* 3:6; *T. Dan* 1:7; *T. Gad* 4:5, 7.

78. Cranfield (*Romans*, p. 428) explicitly repudiates the translation "work together with" in favor of the more bland translation "assist, help on, profit," which is consistent with a Calvinist perspective hostile to synergism.

79. See Jewett, "Paul, Phoebe, and the Spanish Mission," in *The Social World of Formative Christianity and Judaism: Essays in Tribute to Howard Clark Kee* (ed. P. Borgen et al.; Philadelphia: Fortress, 1988), pp. 144-64.

80. The RSV selects this term.

81. See G. Harder, "σπουδάζω κτλ," *TDNT* 7 (1971), p. 566, who interprets this reference in terms of "holy zeal . . . full dedication to serving the community." He shows (p. 561) that this usage derived from Hellenistic political and military contexts where serious, expeditious engagement was demanded.

82. F. Hauck, "ὀκνηρός," *TDNT* 5 (1967), pp. 166-67. Matt. 25:26 uses this term to refer to a "slothful slave."

diligence serves notice that the energies of love, stimulated by the Spirit, must be allowed to flow freely or be lost.

The spiritual basis of this "diligence" is reiterated in the middle phrase of the verse. It has been suggested that τῷ πνεύματι ζέοντες is a unique, early Christian expression.[83] The verb means to bubble, boil, ferment, or seethe, and was frequently used in a metaphorical sense to describe high emotion.[84] The use of this precise expression in a traditional description of the preacher Apollos (Acts 18:25) leads one to infer that it was probably developed by the first generation of charismatic Christianity.[85] That the apportioned Holy Spirit was in view in this expression is generally assumed.[86] This is consistent with the subsequent clause, "serving the Lord." For Paul the Spirit was the Lord's presence among and within believers, evoking obedience.[87] The admonition calls for believers to participate in this charismatic effervescence of which God's Spirit is the source. Co-participation requires assent and issues in obedience. The wording of Rom. 1:9 and the exhortation of Romans 6 are reflected here, with the community of believers being urged to exercise its gifts of love within the context of the lordship of Christ. Taken as a whole, 12:11 reveals that for Pauline ethics, service is the natural expression of spiritual enthusiasm, not the consequence of dutiful obedience to moral obligations or a violation of freedom.[88] The task of Christian ethics is to keep the spiritual current flowing in responsible channels. The intent of that current is not merely to uplift believers with an exalted mood, but rather extends the Lord's rule over a formerly disobedient creation. The reference to "serving the Lord" at the end of the verse brings the discussion of ethical guidelines within the parameters of the general thesis of the letter concerning the "righteousness of God." This verse thus closes the circle that we have followed since 1:9, linking the experience of the Spirit with the theme of obedience and thus defining the self and the community in co-participation with Christ.

83. A. Oepke, "ζέω κτλ," *TDNT* 2 (1964), p. 876.

84. See BAGD, p. 337; Dunn, *Romans*, p. 742.

85. See E. Käsemann, "Die Johannesjünger von Ephesus," *ZThK* 49 (1952): 150; in contrast, Horn, *Angeld*, 373 argues that Paul intended no link between this formulation and "ekstatisch-enthusiastische Äußerungen."

86. See Käsemann, *Romans*, p. 330; Cranfield, *Romans*, p. 634; Barrett, *Romans*, p. 240.

87. See Rom. 6:12-23; 1 Cor. 3:17.

88. See F.-J. Ortkemper, *Leben aus dem Glauben: Christliche Grundhaltungen nach Römer 12–13* (Münster: Aschendorff, 1980), pp. 94-96.

XVII The Holy Spirit in 1 Corinthians: Exegesis and Reception History in the Patristic Era

Anthony C. Thiselton

I. "Spirit" and "Spiritual" in Pauline Texts and Their Posthistory

During a class in 1958 one of my fellow students asked, "Dr. Simon, what is a 'Festschrift'?" Never one to lose a chance for a touch of irony, Ulrich Simon replied (best subvocalized with a mildly Germanic accent): "When you are old, and have lost all interest in your subject, they give you a book of essays about those things concerning which you no longer wish to know."

James Dunn has never lost his infectious zest and enthusiasm for Pauline theology and exegesis. Nevertheless, lest there could be even the smallest grain of truth in Ulrich Simon's ironic comment, this chapter is not only about the Holy Spirit in 1 Corinthians but also about the posthistory of Pauline texts in patristic writings. A little seasoning may be added by seeking to identify two points of tentative reservation concerning James Dunn's claims about the Holy Spirit in 1 Corinthians, alongside my admiration for, and agreement with, his work on this subject in general.

My first reservation concerns the use of such terms as "supernatural," "miraculous," and "spontaneous" to describe of some of the gifts and work of the Holy Spirit in 1 Corinthians. Is it true, to cite one example, that prophetic speech in 1 Corinthians is necessarily "a spontaneous utterance"?[1] Second, can we not find in Paul the foundations of a trinitarian *theology* or *ontology*, which a number of the later church fathers believe they find in 1 Corinthians? Dunn

1. James D. G. Dunn, *Jesus and the Spirit* (London: SCM, 1975), p. 228.

concedes that "there is what might be called *a 'Trinitarian' element in the believer's experience* . . . (Rom. 8:15f.; 1 Cor. 12:3)" (his italics).[2] But later attempts to trace ontological or metaphysical dimensions on the basis of this Christian experience may do "more to retard the Gospel than to advance it."[3] The subject index to *Jesus and the Spirit* contains only a single reference to the Trinity (namely, that just cited), while that of Dunn's *The Theology of Paul the Apostle* appears to contain none, even if half a page addresses the actualization by the Spirit of the *Kyrios* confession (1 Cor. 12:3) and the cry "Abba, Father" (Rom. 8:15).[4] Discussions of the theme "God is one" focus more especially upon possible christological ramifications apparently without reference to the Spirit.[5]

Like Dunn himself, however, many of the church fathers draw on 1 Corinthians to engage with issues of exegesis that have remained central for the Christian church over the centuries. First, many are well aware of the very varied semantic and lexicographical range of πνεῦμα and πνευματικός, and of the need to identify instances where these terms distinctively denote the Holy Sprit or what characterizes the actions of the Holy Spirit. Dunn reflects a growing consensus when he rightly insists that "Πνευματικός . . . expresses so clearly the sense of belonging to the Spirit, embodying Spirit, manifesting Spirit, of the essence or nature of Spirit."[6] Cyril of Jerusalem and Augustine provide striking examples here. Cyril writes, "For many things are called spirits. Thus an angel is called 'spirit'; our soul is called 'spirit'; the wind that blows is called 'spirit'. . . . Beware, therefore, . . . such is not the Holy Spirit. . . . He comes to save and to heal . . . , to enlighten the mind."[7] Augustine distinguishes between the meaning of "spirit" in Rom. 12:2 (the spirit of your mind) and 1 Cor. 14:14 (my spirit prays) from that of "Spirit" as denoting "the Holy Spirit," and from spirit-as-soul, or from the breath of life in created beings of various orders.[8]

Similarly both Dunn and many patristic writers address the difficulty of how to be clear about whether Paul's description of certain gifts of the Spirit actually corresponds with what later generations claim as "the same" gifts or experiences under the same name. Augustine, for example, is so convinced, at

2. Dunn, *Jesus and the Spirit*, p. 326.

3. Dunn, *Jesus and the Spirit*, p. 326.

4. James D. G. Dunn, *The Theology of Paul the Apostle* (Edinburgh: T&T Clark, 1998), p. 264.

5. Dunn, *Theology*, pp. 31-50, 252-65, 272-93; and *Jesus and the Spirit*, pp. 318-26.

6. Dunn, *Jesus and the Spirit*, pp. 207-8. On the history of interpretation of πνεῦμα (mainly on "human spirit"), see Robert Jewett, *Paul's Anthropological Terms* (Leiden: Brill, 1971), pp. 167-200 and 451-53.

7. Cyril of Jerusalem, *Catechetical Lectures* 16:12-16.

8. Augustine, *On the Trinity* 14:22; see also *On the Soul and Its Origin* 4:36:22.

least in some later writings, that "glossolalia" does not necessarily entail a miraculous ability to speak some other "language" that he reserves the term *jubilatio* to describe the phenomenon to which Paul alludes in 1 Cor. 14:2-27, leaving others to use glossolalia to denote the popular understanding of what many then and now believe that it denotes. Augustine anticipates the view of "wordless praise" advocated by Stendahl, Theissen, Macchia, and (since 1979) regularly by the present writer as a more adequate account of the phenomenon in 1 Corinthians.[9] Augustine writes, "In jubilatione cane. . . . Quid est in jubilatione canere? . . . Verbis explicare non posse quod canitur corde; . . . in verbis canticorum exsultare laetitia, veluti impleti tanta laetitia, ut eam verbis explicare non possint, avertunt se a syllabis verborum, et eunt in sonum jubilationis. . . . Et quem decet ista jubilatio, nisi ineffabilem Deum? Ineffabilis enim est, quem fari non potes . . . ut gaudeat cor sine verbis. . . . Bene cantate ei in jubilatione."[10]

That 1 Corinthians provokes these reflections more than any other Pauline Epistle is not surprising. In practice the term πνεῦμα and its cognate adjective and adverb πνευματικός and πνευματικῶς occur here more frequently than in any other Epistle: some 52 times, as against 35 in Romans, less than half that number in 2 Corinthians and in Galatians, and less than half-a-dozen times each in Philippians, Colossians, and 1 and 2 Thessalonians. Yet word frequency alone is an unreliable guide. It is more significant that in 1 Corinthians Paul goes out of his way to correct and to redefine his readers' understanding of πνευματικός, "spiritual," for example, in 1 Cor. 3:1-3. More than this, Paul takes pains to underline the "otherness" and transcendence of the person and work of the Holy Spirit (1 Cor. 2:10-16) as well as the christological criticism of the

9. Anthony C. Thiselton, "The 'Interpretation' of Tongues in 1 Corinthians 14:13: A New Suggestion in the Light of Greek Usage in Philo and Josephus," *JTS* 30 (1979): 15-36, and idem, *The First Epistle to the Corinthians: A Commentary on the Greek Text* (NIGTC; Grand Rapids: Eerdmans, and Carlisle: Paternoster Press, 2000), pp. 1094-1111; K. Stendahl, "Glossolalia," in *Paul among Jews and Gentiles* (London: SCM, 1977), pp. 109-24; G. Theissen, *Psychological Aspects of Pauline Theology* (Edinburgh: T&T Clark, 1987), pp. 59-114 and 292-341; and F. D. Macchia, "Sighs Too Deep for Words: Toward a Theology of Glossolalia," *JPT* 1 (1992): 47-73.

10. Augustine, *Expositions on the Book of Psalms* 32: *enarratio* ii, *sermo* 1; 8 [on v. 3], *CC,* 38:254. The Latin exposition on wordless praise is omitted from the English Post-Nicene Library Series 1, 8:71, but can be found in J.-P. Migne, ed., *PL,* vol. 36 (1861), col. 283. An English translation might run: "Sing in jubilation. . . . What is it to sing in jubilation? . . . It is to be unable to explain in words what is sung by the heart; . . . to exult with joy in the words of a song, just as it is to be filled with so great a joy that they cannot set it forth with words, and turn away from the syllables of words to pass to the sound of 'jubilation'. . . . And to whom is this jubilation fitting, unless to the God who is ineffable? For he is ineffable whom you cannot grasp by word . . . so that the heart rejoices without words. . . . 'Sing well and in jubilation'" (Ps. 32:3).

Spirit's authentic action (also 12:1-8); he redefines their questions about spiritual gifts (or "spiritual" people, περὶ δὲ τῶν πνευματικῶν, 12:1) in different terms as a matter of διαιρέσεις δὲ χαρισμάτων (12:4) and χαρίσματα (12:9, 18, 30, 31); he insists on the holiness of the Holy Spirit (3:16-17; 6:19-20); and he prepares the way in earlier argument (2:10-16; 3:1-3; 12:1-3) for the definition of the σῶμα πνευματικόν in 15:44 on the resurrection as deriving its semantic and theological force by its contrast with ψυχικόν (v. 44, twice) and the christological association (15:44-49). All of these seminal thoughts and watersheds feature among patristic writers, as we observe below.

In practice virtually all the main classic patristic sources on an explicit theology of the Holy Spirit tend to select the same eleven passages from 1 Corinthians as a basis for their reflection on this subject. Among the classic sources, in addition to earlier scattered references from Irenaeus, Clement of Alexandria, and Tertullian, we include: Origen, *On First Principles* 1:3; Cyril of Jerusalem, *Catechetical Lectures* 4:16 and 17; Hilary of Poitiers, *On the Trinity* 2:29-35; Athanasius, *Letters to Serapion* 1–3; Basil of Caesarea, *On the Holy Spirit;* Gregory of Nazianzus, *Theological Orations* 5; Ambrose, *On the Holy Spirit;* Chrysostom, *Homilies on 1 Corinthians;* and scattered sections from Augustine, *On the Trinity,* especially 2:5-7; 5:11-15 and 15:17-27. These writers repeatedly cite, discuss, and develop the following eleven passages from 1 Corinthians as seminal texts (the final seven being less directly but also of importance): 1 Cor. 2:4; 2:9-12; 2:15-16; 3:16-17; 8:6; 12:3; 12:4-7; 12:8-11; 12:13; 14:2, 14-25; and 15:44-50.[11]

11. On 1 Cor. 2:4, see, e.g., Athanasius, *Letters to Serapion* 1:17; Greek, J.-P. Migne, *PG,* vol. 26, cols. 569-71; critical English text, C. R. B. Shapland, *The Letters of Athanasius concerning the Holy Spirit* (London: Epworth, 1951), pp. 103-6; Cyril of Jerusalem, *Catechetical Lectures* 4:16, 17; Gregory Nazianzus, *Theological Orations* 5:32.

On 1 Cor. 2:9-12, see Irenaeus, *Against Heresies* 1:9:1; 5:8:4; Clement, *Stromata* 5:5; Tertullian, *Against Marcion* 5:6; Origen, *On First Principles* 1:3:4-5; Cyril, *Catechetical Lectures* 4:16-17; Athanasius, *Letter to Serapion* 16:38; 19:50; 24:56; Basil, *On the Holy Spirit* 16:38, 40; 19:50; 24:56. See also Chrysostom, *Homilies on 1 Corinthians* 7:6-9.

On 1 Cor. 2:15-16, see Clement, *Stromata* 5:5; Origen, *On First Principles* 4:1:11 and "Fragments on 1 Corinthians," sects. 11 and 17, *JTS* 9 (1908): 240-41; Cyril, *Catechetical Lectures* 17:1; Athanasius, *Letter to Serapion* 1:22, 25, 26; Ambrose, *On the Holy Spirit* 2:9:99; 2:11:122; and 3:3:16; cf. Chrysostom, *Homilies in 1 Corinthians* 7:8-12.

On 1 Cor. 3:16-17, see Irenaeus, *Against Heresies* 5:6:2; Athanasius, *Letters to Serapion* 1:19, 20; 3:3; Ambrose, *On the Holy Spirit* 3:12:90; Augustine, *On the Trinity* 7:3:6.

Although 1 Cor. 8:6 does not mention the Spirit, the monotheistic creedal form plays a vital role in the discussion; see, e.g., Ambrose, *On the Holy Spirit* 1:3:32; 3:11:84; Athanasius, *Letters to Serapion* 3:1 and *Against the Arians* 3:16. A second "indirect" passage is 1 Cor. 10:2-4, where the phrase πνευματικὸν ἔπιον πόμα is related to the "procession" of the Spirit (e.g., Basil, *On the Holy Spirit* 14:31-32).

On 1 Cor. 12:3, see Tertullian, *Against Marcion* 5:8; Origen, *On First Principles* 1:3:2; 3:7;

Depending, then, on what we seek in considering the "posthistory" or *Wirkungsgeschichte* of these texts in the patristic church, a dialogue between their exegesis and their reception may perhaps be of value.

II. "Posthistory," "Wirkungsgeschichte," or "Rezeptionsgeschichte"?

The ways in which patristic writers "received" Pauline texts and allowed them to provoke fresh, creative reflection provide instances of what has widely come to be known as the *Wirkungsgeschichte* of the text. However, this is different from simply "a history of interpretation" of the text. Three terms are often used interchangeably, but in more technical uses they may not strictly denote the same agenda. In my commentary I used the most general term, "the posthistory" of the text.[12] This carries perhaps the least explicit theoretical commitments. Wolfgang Schrage regularly uses the phrase *Auslegungs- und Wirkungsgeschichte.*[13] Ulrich Luz uses *Wirkungsgeschichte* alone in his commentary on Matthew, which his translator, Wilhelm C. Linss, consciously and deliberately translates "history of influence."[14] However, Luz comments in his Introduction

---

Basil, *On the Holy Spirit* 11:27; 16:38; 18:47; Ambrose, *On the Holy Spirit* 1:4:56; 1:11:124; 3:11:20; Augustine, *On the Trinity* 1:8:18; 5:14-16.

On 1 Cor. 12:4-7, see Tertullian, *Against Marcion* 5:8; Cyril of Jerusalem, *Catechetical Lectures* 16:1-4 and 16:12; Athanasius, *Letters to Serapion* 1:31 and 3:5-6; Basil, *On the Holy Spirit* 16:37; cf. Chrysostom, *Homilies on 1 Corinthians* 29:1-6.

On 1 Cor. 12:8-11, see Clement, *Stromata* 4:21:134; 5:13:89; Tertullian, *On the Soul* 9:3-6: Origen, *On First Principles* 1:3:7; Cyril, *Catechetical Lectures* 16:12, 23, and 25 and 17:2; Basil, *On the Holy Spirit* 16:37 and *Against Eunomius* 3:4; Ambrose, *On the Holy Spirit,* 1:1:18; 2:12:139-41; 2:13:143, 152; 3:6:38; Augustine, *On the Trinity* 15:19:34.

On 1 Cor. 12:13, see Athanasius, *Letter to Serapion* 1:19-20; Basil, *On the Holy Spirit* 10:26; Ambrose, *On the Holy Spirit* 1:3:45; Augustine, *On the Trinity* 15:19:33.

On 1 Cor. 14:2, 14-25, see Basil, *On the Holy Spirit* 16:37; Ambrose, *On the Holy Spirit,* 2:12:131; 3:11:70; Gregory Nazianzus, *Theological Orations* 5:12.

On 1 Cor. 15:44-50, see Irenaeus, *Against Heresies* 5:7:1-2; Tertullian, *Against Marcion* 5:9-10; Chrysostom, *Homilies on 1 Corinthians* 41:4-8.

12. Thiselton, *First Epistle to the Corinthians,* pp. 196-204, 276-86, 330-44, 479-82, 531-40, 658-61, 908-1026, and 1306-14.

13. Wolfgang Schrage, *Der erste Brief an die Korinther* (4 vols.; EKKNT; Zürich: Benziger and Neukirchen-Vluyn: Neukirchener, 1991, 1995, 1999 and 2002), 1:163-65, 190-203, 218-22, 236-38, 269-78, 284-86, 317-18, 327-29, 350-51, 365-67 (simply up to 4:21 alone by way of example).

14. Ulrich Luz, *Matthew 1–7: A Commentary* (Edinburgh: T&T Clark, 1989), p. 11; cf. pp. 95-99; and *Matthew 8–20* (Philadelphia: Fortress, 2001); trans. from *Das Evangelium nach Matthäus* (EKKNT; Zürich: Benziger and Neukirchen-Vluyn: Neukirchener, 1990).

that the term denotes "history, reception and actualising of a text *in media other than a commentary,* e.g., in sermons, canonical law, hymnody, art, and in the actions and sufferings of the church" (my italics).[15] Here "actualization" or "appropriation" plays a part, in life as well as in thought; and Luz implicitly alludes to "Reception Theory" or to reception history *(Rezeptionsgeschichte).* These terms come out of a similar but nevertheless distinct intellectual matrix or background from that of *Wirkungsgeschichte.* Hence some clarification of these terms may be needed.

The term "*Wirkungsgeschichte*" derives most typically from within philosophical hermeneutics, especially from Hans-Georg Gadamer (1900-2002). In the first English edition of *Truth and Method* (1975 from German, 2nd ed. 1965, 1st ed. 1960), Garrett Barden and John Cumming translated the German as "*effective history.*"[16] In the improved second revised English edition (1989 and 1993), from the German fourth edition (and from *Gesammelte Werke*), Joel Weinsheimer and Donald G. Marshall translate the German as "*history of effects.*" More significantly the earlier translation of *wirkungsgeschlichtliches Bewusstsein* as "effective historical consciousness" has been replaced in the revised edition (after careful discussion) by "*historically effected* consciousness" (my italics).[17]

This change from the active (effective) to the passive (effected) denotes "a consciousness that is doubly related to tradition, at once 'affected' by history (Paul Ricoeur translated this term as 'consciousness open to the effects of history') and also itself brought into being — 'effected' — by history and conscious that it is so."[18] We shall shortly note how closely this relates to a hermeneutic of question and answer, as dialectic.

The term *Rezeptionsgeschichte* primarily derives from Hans Robert Jauss and the literary theorists of the University of Constance. Wolfgang Iser and his reader-response theory contributed to the notion of a *potentiality* of textual effects. Drawing on Husserl and Roman Ingarden, Iser drew on the analogy of "filling in," or "completing," what perception did not directly apprehend but could be presupposed. Jauss's Inaugural Lecture at the University of Constance in 1967 was later published as *Literaturgeschichte als Provokation*

15. Luz, *Matthew 1–7,* p. 95.

16. H.-G. Gadamer, *Truth and Method* (1st Eng. ed.; London: Sheed & Ward, 1975), pp. 267-74, 305-10, and 324-25.

17. H.-G. Gadamer, *Truth and Method* (2nd rev. Eng. ed.; London: Sheed & Ward, 1989 and 1993), p. xv; cf. also pp. 300-307, 341-46, and 377-78. Gadamer, *Gesammelte Werke* (10 vols.; Tübingen: Mohr, 1985-95), contains the 5th ed. of *Wahrheit und Method* as vol. 1 and its supplementary essays in vol. 2 (both 1986).

18. Gadamer, *Truth,* 2nd Eng. ed., p. xv.

für die Literaturwissenschaft.[19] Reception Theory, then, emerged as a subgenre of *reader-response theory,* while *Wirkungsgeschichte* emerged from *philosophical hermeneutics.*

Gadamer shows the limitations of abstract, reflective reason, which supposedly has no grounding or contingent situatedness within history and traditions.[20] Experience *(Erfahrung)* embodies a dialectic, which "leads on," enabling an appropriation of yet further experience. Yet "every experience worthy of the name thwarts an expectation. . . . [It] involves an escape from something that had deceived us and held us captive."[21] Genuinely "hermeneutical experience" entails "openness to tradition" and especially *"openness to the other . . .* recognizing that I myself must accept some things that are against me. . . . This readiness is what distinguishes historically effected consciousness *(wirkungsgeschtliches Bewusstsein)* (my italics).[22]

Neverthless we cannot have experiences, Gadamer claims, "without asking questions."[23] We must respect "the priority of the question."[24] He declares, "That a historical text is made the object of interpretation means that *it puts a question to the interpreter*" (my italics).[25] In Gadamer's view, this *"logic of question and answer"* (exemplified in R. G. Collingwood) differs in kind from the notion of *solving "problems"* (exemplified in Kant). "The identity of the problem is an empty abstraction."[26] However, if this emptiness is recognized, a process of questioning may be begun which arises "out of the motivated context of questioning from which it receives . . . its sense."[27] Gadamer invites us to provide a critique of the concept of *"problem"* and thereby "to destroy the illusion that problems exist like stars in the sky. Reflection on hermeneutical experience *transforms problems back to questions that arise and derive their sense from their motivation*" (my italics).[28]

To trace the formulations, modifications, and reformulations of ongoing *agenda* yields an appreciation of the distinctiveness of that of each generation.

19. Hans Robert Jauss, *Toward an Aesthetic of Reception* (Minneapolis: University of Minnesota Press, 1982), pp. 3-45.

20. Gadamer, *Truth* (2nd Eng. ed.), pp. 341-46.

21. Gadamer, *Truth,* p. 356.

22. Gadamer, *Truth,* pp. 361-62.

23. Gadamer, *Truth,* p. 362.

24. Gadamer, *Truth,* p. 363.

25. Gadamer, *Truth,* p. 369.

26. Gadamer, *Truth,* p. 375. On this aspect of Gadamer's thought, see also Brook W. R. Pearson, *Corresponding Sense: Paul, Dialectic and Gadamer* (Leiden, Boston, and Cologne, 2001), pp. 93-97.

27. Gadamer, *Truth,* p. 376.

28. Gadamer, *Truth,* p. 377.

But it yields more, namely, an appreciation of the dialectic of continuities and discontinuities that form the ongoing agenda of history. Further, *to ask how the text questions each agenda that is brought before it* in turn tells us more about the Pauline text and its effects than defining a one-dimensional set of "problems" reconstructed as if from some supposed Archimedean point *outside* history. To recognize the priority of the question over dehistoricized "problems" may provide a useful hermeneutical resource. It may also provide a constructive approach (which I am currently exploring) to a "hermeneutics of doctrine," designed to avoid the regrettable dichotomy between biblical interpretation and "systematic theology" as it is too often practiced. "History" and the interpreter's own historical situation color the agenda brought *to* the text; but the text itself also *shapes successive agenda by and through the effects that it produces.*

Thus, for Athanasius and for Basil of Caesarea Paul's language about the Holy Spirit of God in 1 Cor. 2:6-16 demands that they "hear" how it shapes questions and answers about the deity and personal agency of the Holy Spirit, as well as questions more explicitly asked by Paul about revelation, wisdom, and divine transcendence.[29] 1 Cor. 12:3-7 *demands* that questions and answers relating to God as Trinity be addressed in the light of these verses. The successive readings of 1 Cor. 1:18-25 over generations establish a dialectic of continuity and contrast about *how* the proclamation of the cross involves what Gadamer calls "accepting some things that are against me." What "folly" and false "wisdom" amount to may not be exhaustively defined by a single generation.[30]

Jauss, no less than Gadamer, perceives texts of literature as "existing" in the process of their collective interpretation of successive generations of readers, and in the textual *effects,* or *actualizations,* of hitherto potential meaning by these successive generations. Each generation (or, more strictly, each "audience") interacts with the text in terms of a different "horizon of expectations" *(Erwartungs-horizont).* Like Gadamer, Jauss regards the text as "potential" until it is "performed," like a script or score that finds its "reality" in the play or the concert which performs it interactively with an *audience* as an *event.* He declares, "The coherence of literature as an event is primarily mediated in the horizons of expectation of the . . . experience of contemporary and later readers, critics and authors."[31] Further, "A literary event can con-

29. For example, esp. Athanasius, *Letters to Serapion;* and Basil, *On the Holy Spirit,* on which cf. Michael A. G. Haykin, *The Spirit of God: The Exegesis of 1 and 2 Corinthians in the Pneumatomachian Controversy of the Fourth Century* (Leiden, New York, and Köln: Brill, 1994), pp. 59-169.

30. Cf. Ulrich Wilckens, *Weisheit und Torheit: Eine exegetisch-religionsgeschichtliche Untersuchung zu 1 Kor. 1 und 2* (Tübingen: Mohr, 1959), pp. 5-41 and 205-24.

31. Jauss, *Towards an Aesthetic of Reception,* p. 22.

tinue to have an effect only if those who come after it still, or once again, respond to it."[32]

Jauss sets out seven "theses." Thesis 1 explicitly endorses Gadamer's rejection of "historical objectivism," and develops an emphasis on question and answer. "The dialogical character of the literary work . . . establishes why . . . understanding can exist only in a perpetual confrontation with the text."[33] It is not enough to establish past "facts" about the text once for all; it requires successive engagements with successive readers to bring out its potential meaning in interaction with a series of horizons. Like Iser and Eco, Jauss sees this eventfulness in terms of "productivity" and "completion" of meanings.

Theses 2 and 3 explicate this principle further. Only in interactions between texts and readers does a "directed perception come into play whereby the text may be comprehended according to its constitutive motivations and triggering signals. . . ."[34] A horizon of expectation, built up from earlier texts, may become "varied, corrected, altered," although it may also be "just reproduced."[35] Reception can result in a "change of horizons." Jauss expresses in *literary* terms a parallel with the observations of Luther, Calvin, and Bonhoeffer about the word of God as "our adversary" which, in turn, recalls Paul's assertions in 1 Cor. 1:18-25 about the cross. When the text blandly accords with readers' prior assumptions, it is like what Jauss dismissively calls "culinary" (i.e., like a mere kitchen recipe) or "chat" texts *(Unterhaltungskunst)*.[36] By contrast a capacity to satisfy, surpass, disappoint, or refute the expectations of its first audience provides a positive criterion of "its aesthetic value."

Theses 4-7 highlight the value of reception theory for offering "controls" in understanding the text and for the *formation* of understanding. Texts are "socially formative."[37] Jauss not only addresses issues about the creative and formative potential of texts but also seeks to offer constraints on the historical relativity of the "latest generation" of interpreters. He also explores the difference (so relevant to the reading of the Bible as scripture) between an *initial* reception of a text and a "retrospectively interpretive reading."[38]

Jauss draws on Thomas S. Kuhn's well-known concept of "paradigms" in *The Structure of Scientific Revolutions.* As history and experience advance, the

32. Jauss, *Reception,* p. 22.

33. Jauss, *Reception,* p. 21.

34. Jauss, *Reception,* p. 23.

35. Jauss, *Reception,* p. 23.

36. Jauss, *Reception,* p. 25.

37. Jauss, *Reception,* pp. 32, 36 and 45; and pp. 32-45 throughout.

38. H. R. Jauss, "The Poetic Text within the Change of Horizons of Reading," in *Reception,* pp. 139-85, where he selects Baudelaire's "Spleen II" as a textual example.

emergence of *more complex issues and agenda* call for fresh conceptual schemes. These may generate fresh paradigms. The "older" paradigm may still serve the earlier agenda that the text addressed, and which may still arise; but new paradigms also expand the ground beyond the capacities of earlier paradigms to address in full. This is precisely the conceptual and hermeneutical frame within which questions arise about a trinitarian *ontology* when this has been placed on the agenda. Does this not "arise" from Pauline texts? Jauss here begins to explore "change in belief" and "liberation . . . of mind" produced by shifts in norms.[39] However, the confines of space prohibit further discussion of Jauss.

III. Semantic Strategies for Maintaining Contrasts within Polysemic Meaning: πνεῦμα as the Transcendent Holy Spirit

Eugene Nida regularly argued that in modern lexicography we should begin not with polysemic meaning, that is, with the different meanings of single words as such, but with the paradigmatic relations between different words (very frequently in semantic opposition) that attach to each separate instance of meaning conveyed by the single word.[40] Thus, to take a familiar example, rather than comparing simply the different meanings of the English word "run" in such examples as "run a race," "run a business," and a "run on a bank," in the first instance "run" stands in opposition to "walk" or "crawl"; in the second instance it stands in contrast to "direct" or "participate in"; and in the third instance it may stand in paradigmatic relation to "an acquisition of new securities." My collaboration with James Dunn (and one of the editors) began not less than thirty years ago in 1973, when we produced a volume on New Testament interpretation in which I included a semantic tree diagram of uses of πνεῦμα in the New Testament.[41]

In 1 Corinthians Paul is careful to disengage his uses of πνεῦμα to denote the Holy Spirit from these other meanings conveyed by the same Greek word. In 1 Cor. 2:12 he uses the device familiar in modern semantics under the term "safe-

39. H. R. Jauss, *Aesthetic Experience and Literary Hermeneutics* (Minnesota: University of Minnesota Press, 1982), p. 92. See further *Question and Answer: Forms of Dialogue Understanding* (Minnesota: University of Minnesota Press, 1989).

40. E. A. Nida, "The Implications of Contemporary Linguistics for Biblical Scholarship," *JBL* 91 (1972): 85; cf. 73-89.

41. A. C. Thiselton, "Semantics and New Testament Interpretation," in I. Howard Marshall (ed.), *New Testament Interpretation* (Exeter: Paternoster, 1977), pp. 75-104; tree diagram on p. 91; cf. J. D. G. Dunn, "Demythologizing . . . ," pp. 285-307; and G. N. Stanton, "Presuppositions . . . ," pp. 60-74.

guards" in instances of polysemic meaning. One standard "safeguard" is clarification and explication by the addition of another word or phrase. Ullmann cites the example of the English word "fair."[42] This word may denote a measure of size or achievement that is not less than medium or average; or in other contexts, a judicious balance of assessment that is fair to all sides; or a color which stands in semantic opposition to "dark." By adding a hyphenated word to form a compound we may, for example, differentiate between fair-sized, fair-minded, and fair-haired. Thus in 1 Cor. 2:12 Paul anticipates this *semantic* device by a "safeguard" which would develop into a feature of profound *theological* significance for later Christian doctrine. In place of the simple genitive used to qualify πνεῦμα in the first half of the verse, οὐ τὸ πνεῦμα τοῦ κόσμου, he adds the preposition ἐκ, *from* or *out of*, to form an adjectival phrase to indicate a distinctive nuance of this use of πνεῦμα, namely, ἀλλὰ τὸ πνεῦμα τὸ ἐκ τοῦ θεοῦ. H. B. Swete compares the parallel notion of the Spirit's "going forth from" ἐκπορεύεται ἐκ God in John 15:26-27.[43] This coheres with Johannes Weiss's point about "the essential difference between the Stoa and Paul. The former thinks of an innate and inborn divine nature; the latter, of the divine, supernatural equipment given [by God]."[44] This stands in contrast to the immanental perspective of Epictetus: "Our souls are joined together with God as parts and fragments of him."[45]

While several patristic writers address the issue of semantic polysemy, many stress the transcendent character of the Holy Spirit as "Other" and distinctively "of God" on theological grounds. We have already drawn attention to the awareness of semantic polysemy shown by Cyril of Jerusalem. He adopts both approaches. Cyril opens *Lecture 16* by reminding his hearers of what is at stake in "blasphemy against the Holy Spirit," and asserts, "The Holy Spirit is a most mighty power, a Being divine."[46] The Spirit apportions grace and gifts as he wills (1 Cor. 12:11).[47] He then cites the range of *charismata* enumerated by Paul in 1 Cor. 12:7-11. In this context he introduces his warning against semantic confusion between different meanings of πνεῦμα.[48] In this context πνεῦμα emphatically does not denote the human spirit. Equally, πνεῦμα does not here denote simply that from which the physical or bodily is absent: "Such is not the Holy Spirit."[49] Cyril expounds those activities of the Spirit (comfort, enlighten-

42. S. Ullmann, *Semantics* (Oxford: Blackwell, 1967), pp. 158-80.
43. H. B. Swete, *The Holy Spirit in the New Testament* (London: Macmillan, 1909), p. 155.
44. J. Weiss, *Earliest Christianity* (New York: Harper, 1959), 2:512.
45. Epictetus, *Discourses* 1:14:6.
46. Cyril, *Catechetical Lectures* 16:1, 3.
47. Cyril, *Lectures* 16:12.
48. Cyril, *Lectures* 16:13.
49. Cyril, *Lectures* 16:15, 16.

ment, intercession for believers [Rom. 8:26]), which, he insists, underline his divine, rather than creaturely, agency. The climax of this part of the argument finds expression in an appeal to 1 Cor. 2:10, 11 and 12:11.[50]

The possibility of semantic confusion indeed found expression long before Cyril. Irenaeus discusses the differences between the human spirit, the Spirit of God, and that which is "spiritual" on the ground that "they ["spiritual people"] partake of the Spirit, and not because their flesh has been stripped off and taken away. . . . To be 'spiritual' is the handiwork of God, the Spirit of God."[51] Later, Gregory of Nazianzus urged the need to address "the task of examining carefully, and distinguishing, many senses of the word πνεῦμα . . . in holy scripture. . . . The combination of the two words . . . 'Holy Spirit' is used in a peculiar sense."[52] Gregory also calls attention to the transcendent divine agency which characterizes the Holy Spirit as Other. Commenting on prayer in the Spirit in 1 Cor. 14:15, he writes: "Therefore to adore or to pray to the Spirit seems to me to be simply Himself offering prayer or adoration to Himself [through us]. Who can disapprove of this because of the equality of honour and deity between the Three?"[53]

R. B. Hoyle traces the wide-ranging use of πνεῦμα in Hellenistic literature to convey the notion of a pervasive, animating, quasi-substance that permeates the world.[54] I discuss this background, together with 2:11, in my commentary, and conclude: "Paul's use of the phrase τὸ πνεῦμα τὸ ἐκ τοῦ θεοῦ, *the Spirit who issues from God,* thus stands in semantic opposition or contrast to *the spirit of the world.* . . . The divine Spirit comes from 'beyond' to impart a disclosure of God's own 'wisdom.'"[55] On v. 11 I urged that only a superficial reading could suggest that Paul "argues on the basis of a natural correspondence between human spirit/human person and divine Spirit/God, as if *Spirit,* πνεῦμα, embodied a natural continuity between the two instantiations of the term."[56]

Some patristic writers expound theologically the transcendence and "otherness" of the Spirit in 2:12 on the basis of the prepositional phrase, even if without semantic discussion. Athanasius rightly sees that v. 12 qualifies v. 11 and exclaims, "What kinship could there be, judging by the above [vv. 11 and 12], between the Spirit and the creatures? That which is from God (ἐκ τοῦ

50. Cyril, *Lectures* 16:25. See also 4:16-17.

51. Irenaeus, *Against Heresies* 5:6:1.

52. Gregory, *Theological Orations* 5:2.

53. Gregory, *Orations* 5:12.

54. R. B. Hoyle, *The Holy Spirit in St Paul* (London: Hodder & Stoughton, 1927), p. 219.

55. Thiselton, *First Epistle to the Corinthians,* p. 263; cf. pp. 257-64.

56. Thiselton, *First Epistle to the Corinthians,* p. 257.

θεοῦ) could not be from that which is not (ἐκ τοῦ μὴ ὄντος)."[57] We shall return to 2:12 in section 5 below. Meanwhile, Dunn fully addresses the semantic range of πνεῦμα and the transcendent power of the Holy Spirit.[58] The background of רוח in the Old Testament remains significant here. The adjectival πνευματικός also reflects this emphasis when it denotes that which is characterized by the Holy Spirit.[59]

IV. The Holy Spirit and "Miracles"?

Dunn speaks of "those charismata which are most obviously a display of divine power, that is, miracles." So in [1 Cor.] 12:10 we read, "To another is given the operation of miracles (ἐνεργήματα δυνάμεων). . . . *The charisma is the actual miracle, or the miracle-working power operating effectively in a particular instance*" (his italics).[60] To be sure, the NRSV, NJB, AV/KJV, C. K. Barrett, and, in effect, R. F. Collins translate the Greek phrase as "the working of miracles," while the REB, NIV, and Moffatt translate it as "miraculous powers." Yet I see no ground for Dunn's assumption that this is likely to denote primarily "a non-rational power."[61] In my commentary I have translated ἐνεγήματα δυνάμεων as "actively effective deeds of power" on the basis of a carefully argued case.[62] Calvin and Barth, it so happens, tend to view *power* (δύναμις) at least in this Epistle as denoting what is *effective* (since its semantic opposites include *weakness* and "*mere*" *word*) rather than what is necessarily miraculous or spectacular.[63] What lacks "power" is not the ordinary but what is ineffective, idle, or empty. As *BDAG* (Danker-Bauer, 3rd ed.) makes clear, "capability, . . . ability to carry out something . . . resource" denote the thrust of the term, even if "the power that

57. Athanasius, *Letters to Serapion* 1:22. Greek, Migne, *PG*, vol. 26, col. 58, and critical Eng. text, C. R. B. Shapland, *The Letters of Saint Athanasius concerning the Holy Spirit* (London: Epworth, 1951), p. 121 (including n. 1).

58. Dunn, *Jesus and the Spirit*, pp. 201-3.

59. See Dunn, *Jesus and the Spirit*, pp. 207-9, and further F. W. Danker and W. Bauer, *Greek-English Lexicon of the New Testament and Other Early Christian Literature* (BDAG) (Chicago: University of Chicago, 3rd ed. 2000), pp. 832-37; and G. W. H. Lampe, *A Patristic Greek Lexicon* (Oxford: Clarendon, 1961), pp. 1097-1105 (some 18 cols. of close print).

60. Dunn, *Jesus and the Spirit*, p. 210. Cf. further pp. 206-65; and cf. Dunn, *The Theology of Paul* pp. 554-59.

61. Dunn, *Jesus and the Spirit*, p. 210.

62. Thiselton, *First Epistle to the Corinthians*, pp. 952-56.

63. J. Calvin, *First Epistle to the Corinthians* (Edinburgh: Oliver and Boyd, 1960), p. 262; and Karl Barth, *The Resurrection of the Dead* (London: Hodder & Stoughton, 1933), pp. 18, 24, 26, 49, 52, 75, and 79-82.

works wonders" conveys a given nuance in specific contexts.[64] Do the contexts in 1 Corinthians demand this specific sense?

There are many levels of discussion at which this case may be pursued. One is that of lexicography and its contextual qualifiers. Another is that of Pauline theology and whether Paul differentiates between a "natural" and "supernatural" level of divine operation. Does this impose onto Paul an anachronistic worldview of largely post-Enlightenment thought? A third level or area invites a reevaluation of the probable semantic scope of each of the *charismata.* Dunn acknowledges, especially in his later *Theology of Paul,* that these "included more humdrum tasks and organizational roles, as well as eye-catching prophecy, tongues and miracles."[65] But were *even* these last three necessarily "eye-catching," and was "prophecy" necessarily "not . . . a previously prepared sermon . . . ," but "a spontaneous utterance . . . (14:3)" in *all* cases?[66]

I leave aside discussion of the exegetical details to be assessed in part by comparing these claims with the different ones proposed in my commentary. There I translated κυβερνήσις as "ability to formulate strategies";[67] and χαρίσματα ἰαμάτων as "gifts of various kinds of healings," where I argue for the generic use of the plural. This does not exclude Bengel's *"per naturalia remedia."*[68] I translate προφητεία as "prophecy," but this does not exclude the views of David Hill, Ulrich Müller, and T. W Gillespie that this would include applied, pastoral preaching;[69] and γένη γλωσσῶν as "species of tongues," which leaves room for at least some types to correspond with the "wordless praise" mentioned above in connection with Augustine, Stendahl, and Theissen. I render ἑρμηνεία γλωσσῶν as "intelligible articulation of what is spoken in tongues," which is what transposes otherwise wordless praise into public edification. There is no τις (someone) in 14:13 to denote an "interpreter" other than the speaker.[70]

I do not propose to repeat old arguments. I appeal, instead, to a fourth, fresh consideration that relates to patristic sources. A seminal paper by

64. *BDAG,* pp. 262-63. Cf., more strikingly, Lampe, *Patristic Greek Lexicon,* pp. 389-91 (six cols.).

65. Dunn, *Theology of Paul,* p. 556.

66. Dunn, *Jesus and the Spirit,* p. 228.

67. Thiselton, *First Epistle to the Corinthians,* pp. 1021-22.

68. Thiselton, *First Epistle to the Corinthians,* pp. 946-51; cf J. A. Bengel, *Gnomon Novi Testamenti* (Stuttgart: Steinkopf [1773], 1866), p. 652.

69. Thiselton, *First Epistle to the Corinthians,* pp. 956-65 and 1087-94 (two notes); cf. U. B. Müller, *Prophetie und Predigt im Neuen Testament* (Gütersloh: Mohn, 1975), and T. W. Gillespie, *The First Theologians: A Study in Early Christian Prophecy* (Grand Rapids: Eerdmans, 1994), esp. pp. 97-164.

70. Thiselton, "The 'Interpretation' of Tongues? . . . ," *JTS* 30 (1979): 15-36.

M. Parmentier concedes that in the patristic era "A distinction was often made between ordinary and extraordinary, inner and outer, normal and miraculous, gifts of the Spirit."[71] Everyday talents such as serving, teaching, and being a leader (as in Rom. 12:7-8) did not pose any problems, but "special," miraculous powers (as in 1 Cor. 12:8-10) did. Parmentier continues, "However, Paul himself does not make such a distinction anywhere, and he would surely have rejected it."[72]

Parmentier concedes that many of the early church fathers did understand the *charismata* in this way. Irenaeus argues that Christians perform miracles in the name of Christ for the well-being of other people, and that this vindicates certain christological claims. He adds that such miracles include foreknowledge, prophecy, healing the sick, and even raising the dead.[73] Tertullian also speaks of experiences of visions "in ecstasy, which means abeyance of mind, if there is added also an interpretation of the tongue."[74] He also describes a worship assembly in which *charismata* include experiences "in the Spirit" by ecstasy, converse with angels, and the hearing of mysterious things.[75] To be sure, matters seem to have changed by the fourth century, since Eusebius quotes Irenaeus as a witness to the possibility of the miraculous in the second century but also implies that this is no longer actual in his own day.[76] A number of patristic writers state or imply that certain "miraculous" gifts faded from view at an early date. Cyril of Alexandria and Chrysostom both appear to believe that glossolalia, as a gift of *languages,* existed in the early church but no longer now. This perspective finds clear expression in John Chrysostom. He writes, "For in truth the church was a heaven then, the Spirit governing all things. . . . But not so now: the present church is like a woman who has fallen from her former prosperous days and in many respects retains the symbols only of that ancient prosperity; displaying indeed the repositories and caskets of her golden ornaments, but bereft of her wealth."[77]

We have already noted above that Augustine distinguishes between "wordless jubilation" as "exceptionally suitable for the praise of God, who is ineffable," and as a permanent gift of the Spirit, and an earlier gift of "lan-

71. M. Parmentier, "The Gifts of the Spirit in Early Christianity," in J. den Boeft and M. L. van Poll–van de Lisdonk (eds.), *The Impact of Scripture in Early Christianity* (Leiden, Boston, and Köln: Brill, 1999), pp. 58-78.

72. Parmentier, "The Gifts of the Spirit," in *The Impact of Scripture,* p. 58.

73. Irenaeus, *Against Heresies* 2:32:4-5.

74. Tertullian, *Against Marcion* 5:8:12.

75. Tertullian, *On the Soul* 9:3-4.

76. Eusebius, *Ecclesiastical History* 5:7.

77. Chrysostom, *Homilies on 1 Corinthians* 36:7.

guages" for the initial gospel era.[78] Parmentier now makes his main point. This gift of the Spirit "is *a continuous phenomenon in Christian tradition, from the first Pentecost until now*."[79] He insists that it would be an un-Pauline reception of the texts to read them in such a way as to predispose later readers to perceive *earlier* experiences of the Spirit as somehow *more intense, or more authentic* than later, current ones. He then couples this with a closely related concern. Paul formulates a criterion for authentic activity of the Spirit not in terms of "miracle" or "power," but as a *christological criterion.* Thus in 1 Cor. 12:3 the confession Κύριος Ἰησοῦς is fundamental as a criterion of the Spirit's presence and activity, as well as of Corinthian claims to be πνευματικός. Parmentier observes, "John Cassian, who . . . knows powerful charismatic works from his own experience, shows clearly how miracles in themselves mean nothing, because Satan can work them also. What matters is love. The imitation of Christ does not consist in the imitation of his signs, but in the imitation of his patience and his humility."[80] This is why, I have argued, it is not only the case that ch. 13 on love illuminates everything about the gifts of the Spirit, but also that the chapters on these gifts form part of the long section on respect for the "other" in various contexts: that of food offered to idols (chs. 8 and 10), the principle of forbearance for the sake of others on the matter of patronage and apostolic stipend (ch. 9), mutuality between men and women (11:1-16), and love on the part of the "haves" for the "have-nots" at the Lord's Supper (11:17-end).

That an emphasis upon "miraculous" gifts might be pastorally unhelpful or distracting cannot of itself be determinative or even significant for exegesis. However, Parmentier's concerns suggest that our other arguments cohere sufficiently closely with Paul's pastoral and theological aims to be brought into play. At the very least, they suggest that the burden of proof may belong to claims that certain *charismata necessarily* have to be understood as "supernatural," "miraculous," "spontaneous," or "nonrational." This is not to limit divine sovereignty in any way at all. It is to affirm that the activity of the Spirit may be experienced in what theologians might describe as "incarnational" modes of ordinary human life, without prejudice to the precise "how" of divine agency.

78. Augustine, *On the Psalms,* 32, *enarratio* ii, *sermo* 1; 8 (see above, n. 10, for sources and texts).

79. Parmentier, "The Gift of the Spirit," in *The Impact of Scripture,* p. 73 (my italics).

80. Cassian, *Conlationes,* 15:1; Parmentier, "Gifts of the Spirit," in *Impact,* p. 78.

V. Trinitarian Experience — and Ontology?

James Dunn helpfully reminds us that the Pauline churches approached issues about the role of the Holy Spirit in relation to God in terms of "experience," not of theological theory, let alone theological polemic.[81] As a contributor to successive Reports of the Church of England Doctrine Commission, I identify with this approach. In such a Report we wrote: "The attempt has been to indicate an experience of prayer from which pressure towards Trinitarian thinking might arise. . . . We start with the recognition of a vital, though mysterious, divine dialogue within us . . . the flow of Trinitarian life."[82] Prayer prompted by the Spirit is typically prayer made *to* God as Father, offered *through* Christ, inspired *by* the Holy Spirit. The Report cites Pauline material, especially Rom. 8:15-16, 21-22, 26; 1 Cor. 2:9-16; 12:3; Gal. 4:6, but equally insists that Basil and other fathers combine experiential considerations with theological formulations designed to guard against invalid inferences.

In our discussion of *Wirkungsgeschichte* above, we noted that Paul's language in 1 Cor. 2:6-16 and 12:3-7 "demands" that Athanasius and Basil "hear" how these texts engage with questions and agenda of their day, as long as this does not obscure or distort Paul's immediate concerns. Michael Haykin observes, "Athanasius' argument for the divinity of the Holy Spirit . . . is coupled with the exegesis of the Corinthian correspondence . . . [especially] the concordance of . . . 1 Cor. 2:11-12, 12:11, 13, 6:11 . . . ."[83] Citing these texts from 1 Corinthians, Athanasius writes: "Why then do they [the Pneumatomachi of Thmuis] say that the Holy Spirit is a creature (κτίσμα), who has the same oneness (τὴν αὐτὴν ἔχον ἑνότητα) with the Son (πρὸς τὸν Υἱόν) as the the Son with the Father?"[84] If it were the case that the Spirit belonged to the created order, and was not God, "on this showing once again the Triad (δείκνυσι τὴν Τριάδα) is no longer one (ἕν) but is compounded of two differing natures (ἐκ δύο διαφόρων φύσεων).[85] This would run entirely counter to 1 Cor. 2:10-15; 8:6; and 12:4-6.

On the basis especially of these texts in 1 Corinthians Athanasius writes again, "The Spirit is not a creature (κτίσμα). . . . For if he were a creature, he would not be ranked with the Triad (οὐ συνετάσσετο τῇ Τριάδι). For the whole

81. Dunn, *Jesus and the Spirit*, p. 326 (cited above).

82. Doctrine Commission of the Church of England, *We Believe in God* (London: Church House Publishing, 1987), p. 111; cf. pp. 104-21, "God as Trinity: An Approach through Prayer."

83. Haykin, *The Spirit of God*, p. 67.

84. Athanasius, *Letters to Serapion* 1:2, Greek, Migne, *PG*, vol. 26, 533A; English, Shapland, *Letters*, p. 62.

85. Athanasius, *Letters to Serapion* 1:2; Migne, *PG*, vol. 26, 533A; and Shapland, *Letters*, p. 63.

Triad is one God (ὅλη γὰρ εἰς θεός ἐστι).[86] Again, this reflects 1 Cor. 12:4-6 as well as 8:6 and 2:12. The metaphors of "drinking," or being saturated by, the Spirit in 1 Cor. 12:13 (ἓν πνεῦμα ἐποτίσθημεν) resonate with τὸ πνεῦμα τὸ ἐκ τοῦ Θεοῦ in 2:12, and allusively with πνευματικὸν ἔπιον πόμα in 10:4. Hence, not surprisingly, Athanasius uses the image of a flowing fountain (πηγή) to denote the relation of the Spirit to God as Father and Source, from whom he flows or proceeds, but not as a created being. In *Letters* 1:19, he explicitly quotes 1 Cor. 12:13, and then in 1:20 comments, "Who can separate either the Son from the Father, or the Spirit from the Son?"[87] Athanasius insists that this qualitative difference between the Holy Spirit and "creatures" is warranted wholly by the Scriptures.[88]

Many patristic specialists would be reluctant to conclude that Athanasius fails to find an "ontology" in the texts of 1 Corinthians to which he appeals, even if the allusion to "flowing" is one short step away from exegesis. T. C. Campbell, for example, points out that Athanasius uses ὕπαρξις and ὑπάρχειν to characterize the actuality of the "Triad."[89] As Haykin observes, *Letters to Serapion* 1:22 discusses 1 Cor. 2:12 (ἐκ τοῦ Θεοῦ) precisely to explicate an ontology of the nature of the Spirit.[90] In 1 Cor. 6:11, and also 3:16, 17, the Spirit is uniquely the Spirit of holiness, who has no need of a derived holiness, but in whom "all the creatures are sanctified."[91] To be sure, we cannot impose all this onto modern exegesis uncritically, but when the related evidence of 1 Corinthians is viewed as a whole, is this "ontology" more than a logical explication of Paul's thought?

In Basil's *On the Holy Spirit* (especially 10-27) the basis for trinitarian theology again comes from 1 Cor. 2:9-16; 3:16-17; 8:6; and 12:3-7, 12-13. Basil cites 1 Corinthians 2:10-11 to urge that God as Father cannot be known except by the Son and the Spirit.[92] The Holy Spirit is divine because he shares in all the action properly ascribable only to God.[93] "The Spirit knows 'the deep things of God' [1 Cor. 2:10, 11]. . . . The Spirit gives life . . . raised Christ from the dead . . . comes 'that we might know the things freely given by God' [1 Cor. 2:12)]."[94] Basil turns

86. Athanasius, *Letters*, 1:17; Migne, *PG* 26, 569C; and Shapland, *Letters*, p. 103.

87. Athanasius, *Letters to Serapion*, 1:20; Migne, *PG*, vol. 26, 577A; Shapland, *Letters*, p. 113.

88. Athanasius, *Letters to Serapion*, 1:21; Migne, *PG*, vol. 26, 581A; Shapland, *Letters*, p. 120.

89. T. C. Campbell, "The Doctrine of the Holy Spirit in the Theology of Athanasius," in *Scottish Journal of Theology* 27 (1974): 408-40, esp. pp. 430-33.

90. Haykin, *The Spirit of God*, pp. 78-83.

91. Athanasius, *Letters to Serapion* 1:22-24, Migne, *PG*, vol. 26, 584A-C; Shapland, *Letters*, pp. 122-23 and 126.

92. Basil, *Against Eunomius* 1:14; Migne, *PG*, vol. 29, 544B.

93. Basil, *Against Eunomius* 3:4; Migne, *PG*, vol. 29, 664C.

94. Basil, *On the Holy Spirit* 24:56; Migne, *PG*, vol. 32, 172C.

especially to 1 Cor. 12:4-6 and 11 when he insists that "the Holy Spirit is inseparable and wholly incapable of being parted from the Father and the Son. . . . There are diversities of operations, but it is the same God who works . . ." (1 Cor. 12:4-6).[95] Basil pays particular attention to 1 Cor. 12:13, ἐν ἑνὶ πνεύματι ἡμεῖς πάντες ἓν σῶμα ἐβαπτίσθημεν, a passage on which Dunn has written most constructively.[96] Basil understands this verse to confirm the inseparability of Father, Son, and Holy Spirit. Once again we may concede that this is not Paul's first concern here, but since, in Dunn's words, "the baptism of the Spirit is what made the Corinthians members of the body of Christ," is it conceivable that Basil's point is not a Pauline presupposition?[97]

Gregory of Nazianzus, Ambrose, and Augustine maintain and develop these themes, but they also believe, no less than Basil, that these are founded on Pauline (and Johannine) exegesis, perhaps most especially on 1 Cor. 2:10-15. In his *Theological Orations* Gregory insists that a "swarm" of biblical passages point to the divinity of the Holy Spirit.[98] Gregory insists that the Holy Spirit is "not a creature, in that he proceeds from the Father."[99] His use of the Greek verb πορεύω (proceed, come forth) and the cognate noun ἐκπόρευσις (procession) may reflect John 15:26, but, as Haykin observes, "The use of the preposition 'from within' (ἐκ) instead of the Johannine 'from' (παρά) probably reflects the influence of 1 Corinthians 2:12."[100] The "procession" of the Holy Spirit from God the Father is parallel with, but not exchangeable with, the "generation" (γέννησις) of the Son. Both terms signify that neither the Son nor the Spirit shares the status of a merely created being. Gregory's use of the term "proceeds" (about A.D. 380) finds its way into the formulations of Constantinople in 381. In Gregory's view not only does the term "proceeds" rest on sound exegesis; the belief that the Spirit is no mere "creature" rests on a multiplicity of biblical passages.

Gregory of Nyssa shares many of the assumptions of his brother, Basil, even if he writes on the subject of the Holy Spirit less fully. In some ways he may be even closer to Paul since he believes that to call the Holy Spirit "God" relates primarily to divine activity. Gregory writes, "Being God, as says the apostle, he searches all things, even the deep things of God" (1 Cor. 2:10); but he is more hesitant than Basil or Gregory of Nazianzus to speak of the Holy Spirit as "one

95. Basil, *On the Holy Spirit* 16:37.

96. J. D. G. Dunn, *Baptism in the Holy Spirit* (London: SCM, 1970), pp. 127-31; cf. pp. 103-38; and Basil, *On the Holy Spirit* 12:28; Greek, Migne, *PG*, vol. 32, 117A.

97. Dunn, *Baptism*, p. 129.

98. Gregory, *Orations* 31:29.

99. Gregory, *Orations* 31:8.

100. Haykin, *The Spirit of God*, p. 217.

in being" or "essence" with God, on the basis of several Pauline texts, including 1 Cor. 2:11.[101] Nevertheless he believes that the divine character of the Spirit's activity demands that, together with the Father and the Son, the Spirit receives divine honour and glory in Christian worship.

These interpretations of passages in 1 Corinthians are not confined to the Cappadocian Fathers. In the West Ambrose and Augustine share this tradition. Ambrose's "On the Holy Spirit" probably also stems from 381. Citing 1 Cor. 8:6, Ambrose firmly asserts that God is one.[102] Nevertheless there are differentiations between divine agencies: the Holy Spirit reveals (1 Cor. 2:10) and gives such gifts as the word of wisdom (12:8), although "there is no distinction of the divine power that can arise. . . . No doubt all things are of him through whom all things are."[103] Ambrose draws a logical inference from an exegesis of 1 Cor. 2:11. He writes, "'No one knows the things of God except the Spirit of God'; not that he [the Spirit] knows by searching, but he knows by nature; not that the knowledge of divine things is an accident in him [the Spirit], but it is natural knowledge." Hence, Ambrose concludes, a oneness of nature and of knowledge holds between God and the Holy Spirit.[104]

Ambrose now goes further, but still in the belief that he does so on the basis of exegesis. He cites the diversity of the gifts of the Holy Spirit in 1 Corinthians 12:4, 5, 6, and 8-10, and, on the basis of 12:5, writes: "If the Holy Spirit is of one will and operation with God the Father, he is also of one substance, since the Creator is known by his works. So, then, it is the same Spirit, he [Paul] says, the same Lord, the same God. If you say 'Spirit', he is the same; and if you say 'Lord', he is the same; and if you say 'God', he is the same. Not the same, so that himself is Father, himself Son, himself Spirit, but because both the Father and the Son are the same power. He is, then, the same in substance and in power."[105] We do not suggest that all this is explicit in Paul. Nevertheless the inferences that Ambrose draws firmly discourage too much hesitancy in ascribing divinity to the Holy Spirit. Such hesitation seems to miss some of the logical implications of texts in 1 Corinthians. Ambrose also includes arguments of a less metaphysical and more practical nature. For example, he cites 1 Cor. 3:16, "You are the temple of God, and the Holy Spirit dwells in you," and comments, "Now . . . a creature has no temple. But the Spirit, who dwells in us, has a temple."[106]

Augustine is more complex, and draws on a wider and more general

101. Gregory of Nyssa, *Against Eunomius* 7:1.

102. Ambrose, *On the Holy Spirit* 2:9:85.

103. Ambrose, *On the Holy Spirit* 2:9:99-100; also 11:122-23.

104. Ambrose, *On the Holy Spirit* 2:11:127.

105. Ambrose, *On the Holy Spirit* 2:12:138-42.

106. Ambrose, *On the Holy Spirit* 3:12:90.

range of biblical passages than Athanasius, Basil, the Cappadocians, and Ambrose. However, in several places he appeals to the logic of 1 Cor. 2:11. Commenting on this verse in *City of God*, he notes the distinctive meaning "Spirit" as applied to the "*uncreated* Creator Spirit" (Lat. *non creatura, sed creator*). The Spirit to whom this verse alludes is "the Creator Spirit who in the Trinity is distinctively called the Holy Spirit," and "with whom is the Trinity, the Father and the Son and the Holy Spirit, . . . Creator *(cum quo est trinitas pater et filius et spiritus sanctus . . . creator)*."[107] Appealing elsewhere to the same verse, together with 1 Cor. 12:4-7, Augustine observes, "The Spirit is sometimes spoken of as if he alone were entirely sufficient [i.e., apart from the Son]."[108] In such cases, however, this cannot be taken to imply a "separation" within the one God. "For the Spirit of God is one: the Spirit of the Father and Son, the Holy Spirit, who works all in all" (1 Cor. 12:6; cf. vv. 4-7).[109] To be sure, Augustine also enters into metaphysical complexities that take us, arguably, far from Pauline exegesis; but we are *not* claiming that *all* material about the Holy Spirit in the patristic era contributes to a posthistory of the exegesis of 1 Corinthians.[110] Debates about οὐσία and ὑπόστασις take us well beyond Paul.

The varied agenda brought to our attention by *some* patristic writings may serve *to explicate what is often presupposed* in Pauline texts. This need not lead to imposing Greek metaphysics onto Paul in the interests of a later theology, although this risk must be kept in mind. The claim to explicate what may lie beneath Paul's conscious thought as a presupposition recalls Schleiermacher's maxim that interpretation may go beyond the conscious awareness of an author.[111] As one who believes, like James Dunn, that Pauline exegesis is rooted in "Pauline theology," I share serious caution about going beyond the mind of Paul. Yet Theissen's work *Psychological Aspects of Pauline Theology* illustrates something of the point (as well as limits) of Schleiermacher's maxim.[112] Theissen penetrates beneath the surface of Pauline texts to explore concepts of which Paul himself might scarcely have been fully conscious as conceptual tools or categorizations. Yet if he were given a retrospective understanding of modern notions of the unconscious and of related mechanisms of self-

107. Augustine, *The City of God* 13:24; cf. also 14:4.

108. Augustine, *On the Holy Trinity* 1:(8):18.

109. Augustine, *On the Holy Trinity* 4:(20):29.

110. One example would be Augustine, *On the Holy Trinity* 7:(6):11, on "essences."

111. F. D. E. Schleiermacher, *Hermeneutics: The Handwritten Manuscripts* (ed. Heinz Kimmerle; Missoula, Mont.: Scholars Press, 1977), p. 246 n. 12; and 112; and the more recent critical edition, *Hermeneutics and Criticism, and Other Writings* (ed. A. Bowie; Cambridge: Cambridge University Press, 1999).

112. G. Theissen, *Psychological Aspects of Pauline Theology* (Edinburgh: T&T Clark, 1987).

deception, might not Paul have said with reference to language about the human heart, "Yes, this is the kind of thing that I wish to convey."

Wrestling with *Wirkungsgeschichte* or reception history opens the door to exegesis as explication: an explication that permits us to see dimensions of meaning that *successive contexts of reading bring into sharper focus* for our attention. On the present subject I have suggested that, in the light of patristic exegesis, new contexts have sharpened many of the themes treated in James Dunn's exegesis of Pauline texts about the Spirit, in ways that fully cohere with Dunn's work. On two issues, however, I have also suggested that this posthistory may invite greater caution about speaking of "supernatural" gifts of the Spirit in this Epistle, and also a greater boldness to speak of an implied "trinitarian" theology in these texts.

XVIII The Spirit in 2 Thessalonians

Victor Paul Furnish

The present topic has been prompted by James Dunn's observation that "Paul's vision of charismatic community under the control of the Spirit" seems not to have outlived him. In this respect, Professor Dunn has noted, "Colossians and Ephesians take us to the very fringe of the genuine Pauline correspondence, if not beyond, and . . . the Pastorals belong to the next generation, at least."[1] The question taken up here is whether a similar fading of the Pauline vision is evident in 2 Thessalonians — which, to be sure, Professor Dunn himself judges to belong to "the genuine Pauline correspondence"[2] and does not hesitate to cite as representative of the apostle's thought.[3]

With few exceptions, interpreters are agreed that 1 Thessalonians antedates 2 Thessalonians, and that the latter, whether Pauline or deutero-Pauline, presupposes the existence of the former. Thus, for comparative purposes we must begin by considering what view of the Spirit is reflected in 1 Thessalonians. This will have to be accomplished in more or less summary fashion because primary attention needs to be given to 2 Thessalonians itself. We must try to understand this later writing on its own terms, without concern for whether its thought is authentically Pauline. Our exposition of the pertinent passages

1. James D. G. Dunn, *Jesus and the Spirit: A Study of the Religious and Charismatic Experience of Jesus and the First Christians as Reflected in the New Testament* (Philadelphia: Westminster, 1975), p. 346.

2. *Unity and Diversity in the New Testament: An Inquiry into the Character of Earliest Christianity* (2nd ed.; London: SCM; Philadelphia: Trinity Press International, 1990), p. 326; *The Theology of Paul the Apostle* (Grand Rapids: Eerdmans, 1998), p. 13 n. 39.

3. For example, *Theology of Paul*, pp. 301-5.

will therefore proceed without reference to the conception of the Spirit in 1 Thessalonians, lest we operate with expectations that are inappropriate to the particular aims and themes of 2 Thessalonians, or import meanings that are not there. Thus all comparisons of the two letters will be reserved until the end, when a few summary observations will be offered in response to the question with which we are beginning.

I. 1 Thessalonians

The word πνεῦμα appears five times in this letter, four times with a theological reference (the "Holy Spirit" in 1:5, 6; 4:8; simply the "Spirit" in 5:19) and once as an anthropological term (5:23). Taken together, the theological occurrences present a generally coherent understanding of the role of the Spirit.[4]

1 Thessalonians 1:2-10

Paul mentions the Spirit twice as he comments on his mission to Thessalonica and how his gospel was received there: "The gospel came to you not in word only, but also in power and in the Holy Spirit and with full conviction" (v. 5); and "in spite of persecution" the Thessalonians "received the word with joy inspired by the Holy Spirit" (v. 6).[5]

In the immediately preceding verses, the apostle has emphasized his gratitude to God for the congregation's faith, love, and hope (vv. 2-3). He now says that the twofold proof of their election by God (ἐκλογή, v. 4) is the manner in which the gospel came to them, and the joy with which they accepted it, even amid tribulation. The gospel had come not just as a message ("not in word only") but also in the powerful working of the Holy Spirit and in the "full conviction" which that instilled in the missionaries (v. 5).[6] Paul neither says nor implies anything about accompanying "signs and wonders."[7] Instead, he imme-

4. For an excellent discussion of pneumatology in 1 Thessalonians, see Friedrich W. Horn, *Das Angeld des Geistes: Studien zur paulinischer Pneumatologie* (FRLANT 154; Göttingen: Vandenhoeck & Ruprecht, 1992), pp. 119-57.

5. Except as noted, all biblical quotations are taken from the New Revised Standard Version.

6. The difficult phrase πληροφορίᾳ πολλῇ (NRSV, "full conviction") is perhaps best interpreted, "great fullness of divine working" (Gerhard Delling, *TDNT,* 6:311). It would appear that Paul is thinking of those who preached the gospel in Thessalonica (note v. 5b), not of those who accepted it.

7. Correctly, Horn, *Angeld,* pp. 122-23; Abraham J. Malherbe, *The Letters to the Thessalo-*

diately shifts the focus from how the gospel came to how it was received (v. 6). In spite of the persecution it brought to them, the Thessalonians had joyfully accepted it, and this, too, Paul attributes to the working of the Holy Spirit. One may infer that he understands the gospel to have disclosed to them "a living and true God" and a promise that the Son whom God had raised from the dead would return as their Savior (vv. 9-10). The credal statements about Jesus' death and resurrection that he cites later (4:14; 5:9-10) pointedly summarize the gospel in terms of Jesus' death and resurrection.[8]

Paul mentions the Thessalonians' response to his gospel again in 2:13. Speaking of it as "the word of God," he gives thanks that the gospel was accepted "not as a human word but as what it really is, God's word, which is also at work in you believers." This comment no doubt presupposes what he has said about the Holy Spirit empowering the proclamation and reception of the gospel. Moreover, his characterization of God's word as "working" in the believers (ἐνεργεῖται, present tense) presumes that the Spirit's activity among them is current and continuing, and thus points ahead to ch. 4.

1 Thessalonians 4:3-8

Whereas in ch. 1 the Holy Spirit is connected with the inception of faith, in ch. 4 it is connected with the continuing life of the believing community. Here Paul summons his congregation to holiness, using the *nomen actionis* ἁγιασμός, which denotes the state resultant upon an act of "consecration" or "sanctification" (as distinguished from ἁγιωσύνη, which denotes the ultimate or perfect holiness for which believers hope, 3:13). He identifies this holiness as both the essence of God's will (v. 3) and integral to God's call (v. 7). And reinforcing this, he warns that anyone who turns from holiness is therefore rejecting God, "who also gives his Holy Spirit to you" (v. 8).

The unusual formulation, "his Spirit, who is the Holy Spirit" (τὸ πνεῦμα αὐτοῦ τὸ ἅγιον), accents the idea of holiness. It is also striking that Paul speaks of the Holy Spirit as *given* to the congregation (τὸν [καὶ] διδόντα, present tense). The idea is reminiscent of Ezekiel, but the prophet speaks of a spirit that

nians: A New Translation with Introduction and Commentary (AB 32b; New York: Doubleday, 2000), p. 112. For the contrary view see, e.g., Robert Jewett, *The Thessalonian Correspondence: Pauline Rhetoric and Millenarian Piety* (Philadelphia: Fortress, 1986), p. 100; Gordon D. Fee, *God's Empowering Presence: The Holy Spirit in the Letters of Paul* (Peabody, Mass.: Hendrickson, 1994), p. 45.

8. Cf. Raymond F. Collins, "The Faith of the Thessalonians," in *Studies on the First Letter to the Thessalonians* (BETL 66; Leuven: Leuven University Press, 1984), pp. 209-29.

will be given (e.g., 36:26-27; 37:6, 14), while the apostle refers to it as already bestowed, and implies that it has a continuing presence within the believing community. The community itself is therefore both eschatological and charismatic.[9] Accordingly, and notwithstanding the importance that he places on the instructions they have received from him (4:1-2), Paul can refer to the Thessalonians as "taught by God" (θεοδίδακτοι, 4:9). He understands their formation in holiness to depend, finally, on the powerful, sanctifying work of God's Holy Spirit among them.

1 Thessalonians 5:19-22

The apostle's directives, "Do not quench the Spirit. Do not despise the words of prophets, but test everything" (vv. 19-21a), may reflect his knowledge that some in the congregation were seeking to stifle prophesying. But what the exact situation was, or whether Paul even has a particular situation in view, cannot be determined with any confidence.[10]

However, two things are clear about Paul's own thinking: he regards prophecy as a manifestation of the Spirit's presence, and believes that prophetic utterances may contribute to the congregation's life; but he also believes that all such utterances must be evaluated in order to determine which have merit and which do not.

It is impossible to say whether Paul knew of other spiritual gifts (an expression not used in this letter) that were being exercised in the congregation. One is also left wondering how he expected the "testing" (δοκιμάζειν) of prophetic utterances to be carried out. It is evident, however, that the apostle regards prophetic speech as an expression of the Spirit's continuing and creative presence within the believing community.

II. 2 Thessalonians

Two of the four occurrences of πνεῦμα in this letter are not pertinent to our topic. The suggestion that τὸ πνεῦμα in 2:8 does not mean "breath" ("whom the Lord Jesus will destroy with the breath of his mouth") but "the Spirit"[11] has

9. Cf. Horn, *Angeld,* pp. 125-26.

10. For example, Fee's reconstruction of the historical context (*Presence,* pp. 56-58) depends on 2 Thess. 2:1-2, and is therefore possible only if 2 Thessalonians is actually Paul's.

11. Charles H. Giblin, *The Threat to the Faith: An Exegetical and Theological Re-Examination of 2 Thessalonians 2* (AnBib 31; Rome: Pontifical Biblical Institute, 1967), pp. 91-95.

failed to gain assent.[12] Attempts to name the Holy Spirit as the power or person who is presently restraining the "man of lawlessness" (2:7) have been hardly more successful.[13] In addition to the objection that the author would have had no reason to speak of the Spirit so obscurely,[14] it is difficult to see how he could be thinking of the Spirit when he anticipates that "the one who now restrains [lawlessness]" will be "removed" (2:7). This leaves just two instances that must claim our attention.

2 Thessalonians 2:1-2

Introducing the topic which has moved him to write, the author admonishes his readers "not to be quickly shaken in mind or alarmed, either by spirit or by word or by letter, as though from us, to the effect that the day of the Lord is already here" (2:2). It is impossible to know exactly what was being claimed about the Lord's arrival, and by whom it was being claimed. It is clear, however, that the author wants to rule out every possible authorization of such a view.

The mention of a "letter" reflects his knowledge (or fear) that either 1 Thessalonians or some letter falsely claimed to be from the apostle has been used to support the aberrant teaching. If he is thinking of 1 Thessalonians,[15] then the ambiguous phrase ὡς δι' ἡμῶν is probably to be understood, "as though what is claimed represents our view [which it does not]." If he is thinking of a letter falsely attributed to Paul,[16] then the phrase is to be understood, "as though it were from us [which it is not]."[17] The "word" is doubtless to be

12. See the critique by Fee, *Presence*, p. 75.

13. This was the view of only a few patristic commentators (notably, Severian of Gabala), and is held by only a few modern interpreters, e.g., Robert L. Thomas, *1, 2 Thessalonians* (Expositor's Bible Commentary; Grand Rapids: Zondervan, 1978), pp. 227-337, here pp. 324-25; and Charles E. Powell, "The Identity of the 'Restrainer' in 2 Thessalonians 2:6-7," *BSac* 154 (July-September 1997): 320-32.

14. This point is made as early as Chrysostom, *Homily IV on 2 Thessalonians.*

15. For example, Malherbe, *Thessalonians*, p. 416, who attributes 2 Thessalonians to Paul; Wolfgang Trilling, *Der Zweite Brief an die Thessalonicher* (EKKNT 14; Zürich and Braunschweig: Benziger; Neukirchen-Vluyn: Neukirchener, 1980), p. 76, who regards 2 Thessalonians as pseudonymous.

16. For example, Earl J. Richard, *First and Second Thessalonians* (SP 11; Collegeville, Minn.: Liturgical Press, 1995), p. 325.

17. This interpretation would also apply if a pseudonymous author is alluding to 1 Thessalonians, intending that his own letter be accepted in its place; e.g., Andreas Lindemann, "Zum Abfassungszweck des zweiten Thessalonicherbriefes," repr. in *Paulus, Apostel und Lehrer der Kirche: Studien zu Paulus und zum frühen Paulusverständnis* (Tübingen: Mohr, 1999), pp. 228-40.

identified as Paul's oral presentation of the gospel, presumably as it had taken place in Thessalonica specifically (cf. 2:5).[18]

The first term, πνεῦμα, cannot be a reference to God's Spirit because it is scarcely conceivable that either Paul or a later Paulinist could have regarded God as responsible for the false teaching. In this context, πνεῦμα refers either to a spirit that is not from God (cf. 2 Cor. 11:4; 1 John 4:1-3; also 1 Kings 22:22-23) or, concretely, to an ecstatic utterance, something that has been spoken "in the spirit" (Rev. 1:10; 4:2). The latter is more likely, because it allows the preposition (διά) to function in the same way with all three terms, in each case identifying a particular *manner* or *mode* by which teaching is communicated.[19] Since the author is thinking of an intelligible utterance, he must not be referring to glossolalia, but to the spirit-driven speech of Christian prophets. Unlike the considered discourse of oral instruction and proclamation, such utterances would have been spontaneous, episodic, and generally confined to gatherings of believers.

There is no compelling evidence that the false teaching had its origin in some aberrant burst of spiritual frenzy, although this is often proposed.[20] There is no polemic in this letter against spiritual "enthusiasm," nor anything that resembles Paul's corrective teaching in 1 Corinthians about the gifts of the Spirit. The threefold reference to "spirit," "word," and "letter" is sufficiently explained as an effort to include every possible mode in which misunderstandings might be conveyed or deceit perpetrated.

2 Thessalonians 2:13-17

The only direct reference to God's Spirit occurs in the second statement of thanksgiving, 2:13-14 (cf. 1:3-4), which the author extends with a summary command (v. 15) and a benedictory prayer (vv. 16-17). The mention of the Spirit

18. If ὡς δι' ἡμῶν is to be taken also with "word," or — highly improbable — even with all three terms, including "spirit" (e.g., Ernest Best, *The First and Second Epistles to the Thessalonians* [Harper's New Testament Commentaries; New York: Harper & Row, 1972], p. 278; Charles A. Wanamaker, *The Epistles to the Thessalonians: A Commentary on the Greek Text* [NIGTC; Grand Rapids: Eerdmans, 1990], p. 239; Malherbe, *Thessalonians*, p. 417), one could still interpret it in either of the two ways indicated: those who have attributed the false teaching to Paul either misunderstand or intentionally misrepresent him.

19. Cf. BDAG, s.v. διά, A3b.

20. For example, Karl Paul Donfried, "The Theology of 2 Thessalonians," in *The Theology of the Shorter Pauline Letters* (New Testament Theology; Cambridge and New York: Cambridge University Press, 1993), pp. 81-113, here p. 103; Richard, *Thessalonians*, 359; Fee, *Presence*, p. 75.

comes as readers are advised of their obligation to give thanks: "because God chose you from the beginning[21] for salvation through sanctification by the Spirit and through belief in the truth" (v. 13b).

A few interpreters have held that the genitive in the phrase ἐν ἁγιασμῷ πνεύματος should be read as objective, so that the reference is actually to the human spirit (thus Moffatt's translation, "by the consecration of your spirit").[22] However, this expression, which was likely traditional, appears in an identical form in 1 Pet. 1:2, where it certainly refers to the Spirit of God, and where, as in the present instance, it is associated with the idea of divine election.[23]

Beginning with his description of the readers as "beloved by the Lord" (v. 13a) and continuing through his invocation of God as "our Father, who loved us" (v. 16), the author draws on biblical idioms which are associated with God's election and call of Israel (note, in the LXX, Deut. 33:12; Isa. 41:8; 44:2; Hos. 11:1, etc.). Although some scholars interpret the statements about God's love as implicit references to Jesus' saving death on the cross,[24] this is supported by nothing in the context or in the letter as a whole. In this context, the past event to which both love (vv. 13, 16) and grace (v. 16) refer is not the cross, but God's election of believers for salvation;[25] and in the letter overall there is not a single explicit reference either to Jesus' death or to his resurrection. Salvation itself (see also 2:10) is conceived wholly in terms of the future, like the punishment that will be visited upon those who afflict God's elect. For the elect, salvation will bring relief from afflictions (2:7; cf. vv. 9-10) and entry into the presence and glory of the Lord [Jesus Christ] (2:9, 14; cf. 1:9, "glorified . . . in him"; 1:5, entering into the "kingdom of God").

21. In spite of NA[27] and *GNT*[4] (see Bruce M. Metzger, *A Textual Commentary on the Greek New Testament* [2nd ed.; Stuttgart: Deutsche Bibelgesellschaft/United Bible Societies, 1994], p. 568), ἀπ' ἀρχῆς ("from the beginning") is to be preferred to ἀπαρχήν ("first fruits"). Those who argue for ἀπ' ἀρχῆς include Ernst von Dobschütz, *Die Thessalonicher-Briefe* (7th ed.; Kritisch-exegetischer Kommentar über das Neue Testament 10; Göttingen: Vandenhoeck & Ruprecht, repr. 1974), p. 298 n. 3; Beda Rigaux, *Saint Paul: Les Épîtres aux Thessaloniciens* (Études Bibliques; Paris: Gabalda, 1956), p. 682; Best, *Thessalonians*, p. 313; Trilling, *Der Zweite Brief*, pp. 120-21; Glenn S. Holland, *The Tradition That You Received from Us: 2 Thessalonians in the Pauline Tradition* (HUT 24; Tübingen: Mohr [Siebeck], 1988), p. 47; Judith M. Gundry Volf, *Paul and Perseverance: Staying In and Falling Away* (Louisville: Westminster John Knox, 1991), p. 17; Richard, *Thessalonians*, p. 356.

22. See esp. George G. Findlay, *The Epistles of Paul the Apostle to the Thessalonians* (CGTSC 13; Cambridge: Cambridge University Press, repr. 1911), pp. 189-90.

23. Thus, e.g., Best, *Thessalonians*, pp. 314-15; Richard, *Thessalonians*, p. 356; Fee, *Presence*, p. 78 n. 144.

24. For example, Maarten J. J. Menken, *2 Thessalonians* (New Testament Readings; London and New York: Routledge, 1994), pp. 123, 147; cf. Fee, *Presence*, p. 78.

25. Similarly, Ethelbert Stauffer, *TDNT*, 1:49; Gottlob Schrenk, *TDNT*, 4:184.

Election for salvation remains the theme as the author proceeds to speak of "sanctification by the Spirit" and "belief in the truth."[26] Apart from a reference to "the saints" (1:10), this is the only instance of "holiness" terminology in the letter. In this context, the Spirit's sanctifying activity (ἁγιασμός) is understood as the means through which the elect are set apart for salvation. Nothing, either in the immediate context or in the letter as a whole, supports the view, sometimes advanced (often with an appeal to 1 Thess. 4:3-8),[27] that the author is thinking of the Spirit's present and ongoing activity within the believing community.

Along with "sanctification by the Spirit," the author identifies "belief in the truth" (πίστις ἀληθείας, an expression unique to him) as instrumental to election. Although the two phrases are closely joined, there is no indication that he has reflected on how sanctification may be related to belief.[28] It is therefore impossible to know whether he may regard belief as engendered by the Spirit's sanctifying work, although some commentators suggest that the sequence of the phrases may imply as much.[29] The point being registered is something else — that salvation depends not only on God's decision and the Spirit's sanctifying work but also on a decision from the human side to believe.[30]

What it means to believe in "the truth" is evident from what has been said about "those who are perishing." Because they "refused to love the truth" and "have not believed the truth," they have been led to "believe what is false" and to "[take] pleasure in unrighteousness," for which they "will be condemned" (2:10-12). The falsehood is that the day of the Lord has already arrived (2:2), and the "truth" which stands over against this error is that "the rebellion" and the revealing of "the lawless one" must take place first (2:3). Accordingly, "belief in the truth" means embracing the true teaching which leads to salvation rather than the false teaching which leads to wickedness and condemnation. Thus "truth" remains a largely formal concept here, the opposite of error; the suggestion that it denotes "the revelation of God and his way of salvation imparted in the gospel"[31] endows it with a content to which nothing in the text specifically points.

26. This is overlooked when the phrases are taken with "salvation" only, as Findlay does (*Thessalonians*, p. 189); correctly, Malherbe, *Thessalonians*, p. 437.

27. For example, James E. Frame, *A Critical and Exegetical Commentary on the Epistles of St Paul to the Thessalonians* (ICC; New York: Scribner's, 1912), p. 281; Rigaux, *Thessaloniciens*, p. 684; Donfried, "2 Thessalonians," p. 103.

28. Correctly, Fee, *Presence*, p. 79.

29. For example, von Dobschütz, *Thessalonicher-Briefe*, p. 299; I. Howard Marshall, *1 and 2 Thessalonians* (NCB; Grand Rapids: Eerdmans, 1983), pp. 207-8; Gundry Volf, *Paul*, p. 20.

30. Cf. Rigaux, *Thessaloniciens*, p. 684.

31. Frederick Fyvie Bruce, *1 & 2 Thessalonians* (WBC 45; Waco: Word, 1982), p. 191.

Although there is no indication that the author thinks of the Spirit as empowering faith, we must consider whether he sees some such connection between the Spirit and the gospel. This question arises not only because Spirit and gospel are so closely linked in 1 Thessalonians. It is also the case that the one direct reference to the Spirit in 2 Thessalonians (2:13) is followed by a statement about the gospel (2:14).

"Gospel" in 2 Thessalonians

Although the word "gospel" (εὐαγγέλιον) occurs only twice (1:8; 2:14), three other expressions are used as virtual synonyms: "testimony" (μαρτύριον, 1:10), "truth" (ἀλήθεια, 2:10, 12, 13), and "the word of the Lord" (ὁ λόγος τοῦ κυρίου, 3:1). Moreover, the gospel is tied closely to the "tradition(s)" (παράδοσις, 2:15; 3:6).

In 1:8 the author speaks of the punishment that ultimately will be visited "on those who do not know God and on those who do not obey the gospel of our Lord Jesus." There is nothing here to indicate that two different groups are in view, because (as most interpreters agree) not knowing God and not obeying the gospel are simply parallel designations for unbelievers. The identification of the gospel with "our Lord Jesus" associates it above all with the expectation of his eschatological revealing (v. 7; cf. 2:8), the principal focus of the entire letter. Beyond this, one may perhaps infer from the parallelism that "the gospel" is understood to be the sum total of what is rejected by those who "do not know God."

Continuing, the author characterizes the punishment that awaits those who disobey the gospel as separation from the presence and glory of the Lord (v. 9), to which he adds that "on that day" the Lord will be glorified "by his saints and . . . among all who have believed" (v. 10a; again there is parallelism — the "saints" are those "who have believed"). An aside not only includes the present readers in this group but also indicates how they have come to be included: "because our testimony to you was believed" (v. 10b). It is evident that Paul's "testimony" is nothing else than his "gospel," for those who have believed that testimony are being distinguished from those who have not obeyed the gospel (v. 8). Moreover, there is a clear parallel in 2:14, where the readers are told that God has called them "through our proclamation of the gospel" (NRSV altered). Significantly, both of these formulations connect believing (the response to God's call) with Paul's gospel specifically.

Equally significant, in ch. 2 this Pauline gospel is closely linked with both the "truth" (vv. 10, 12, 13) and the "traditions" (v. 15). A close connection to the former is evident when the gospel is declared to be the way that God's call is made effective for the elect (v. 14), who are thereby summoned to "belief in the truth" (v. 13; cf. vv. 10, 12). This is consistent with the author's earlier characterization of the gospel as "testimony" (1:10b), and suggests that he understands it to have a critical evidential function. The gospel is regarded as enabling authentic belief by attesting to what is true, and therefore to what is essential for the elect to believe and obey.[32]

In concluding the discussion begun in 2:1-2, the author issues an appeal that is more comprehensive and fundamental than his initial warning about being swept away by the false teaching: "stand firm and hold fast to the traditions that you were taught by us, either by word of mouth or by our letter" (v. 15). As a call to embrace specifically the Pauline traditions (those "taught by us"), it corresponds to his linking of the gospel to his/Paul's testimony in particular. Indeed, it is clear that he understands those traditions to include his/Paul's gospel (v. 14), as found both in his preaching and in his letter(s).[33] However, because he now mentions only "word" and "letter," not also "spirit" (as he had in 2:2), he seems not to regard prophetic utterances as forming any part of those traditions.

The absence of even an indirect reference to the Spirit in 2:15 is consistent with the author's view of the tradition as a well-defined and stable body of teaching, which is true because it is Paul's and which therefore commands one's faithful adherence (see also 3:6). He no doubt expects his readers to accept both his eschatological instruction (1:5-12; 2:1-12) and his commands about work (3:6-12) as part of that tradition. Otherwise, however, he offers no indication, and certainly no summary formulation, of either the tradition as a whole or the gospel in particular.

The author employs one further expression for the gospel when he requests that his readers "pray for us, so that the word of the Lord may run forward and be glorified, just as it is among you . . ." (3:1; NRSV altered). Here, quite clearly, "the word of the Lord" (a LXX locution, e.g., 1 Kings 12:22; Ps. 32:4 [33:4]; Isa. 1:10) is Paul's missionary gospel (cf. 1:10; 2:14). This vivid portrayal of it as a word that energetically "runs forward" (cf. Ps. 147:4 LXX [147:15]) is striking in itself, and especially so when compared with the other references to the gospel in 2 Thessalonians, because this is the only place where one is led to think of the gospel as lively and dynamic. Overall, the author represents the

32. Cf. Wolfgang Trilling, *Untersuchungen zum zweiten Thessalonicherbrief* (ETS 27; Leipzig: St. Benno-Verlag, 1972), p. 111; Willi Marxsen, *Der zweite Brief an die Thessalonicher* (ZBK 11.2; Zürich: Theologischer, 1982), p. 71.

33. Interpreters differ on whether "our letter" refers to 1 Thessalonians, 2 Thessalonians, or even to all of Paul's letters (the singular standing for a plural).

gospel as unchanging and immovable, the truth that must be believed, and thus the critical component of the established traditions which believers have been taught, and according to which they must live.[34]

Concluding Observations

When our findings from 2 Thessalonians are compared with the understanding of the Spirit that is present in 1 Thessalonians, it would appear that the question posed at the outset of this essay needs to be answered in the affirmative. While it is not unimportant that the letter contains only one direct reference to God's Spirit, this in itself does not settle the matter, given the relative brevity of the letter and that it is devoted primarily to a single, special issue.[35] A few concluding observations, summarily stated, will highlight several other, weightier considerations.

1. In both 1 and 2 Thessalonians the Spirit is viewed as the agent of sanctification (1 Thess. 4:3-8; 2 Thess. 2:13), and in both (although more clearly in 1 Thessalonians) the Spirit is viewed as inspiring prophetic utterances (1 Thess. 5:19-22; 2 Thess. 2:2). The similarities on these points do not run deep, however, and in other respects there are significant differences in what these letters suggest, respectively, about the role of the Spirit.

2. In 2 Thessalonians the Spirit's sanctifying work is associated exclusively with God's choosing of the elect ("from the beginning") for future salvation (2:13). Apart from the mention of ecstatic utterances as a possible source of doctrinal error (2:2), nothing in this letter suggests an understanding of the Spirit as present with and for the believing community. In 1 Thessalonians, however, the Holy Spirit is understood to be a continuing, sanctifying presence in the lives of believers, forming them both individually and corporately according to the holiness in and for which God has called them (4:3-8).

3. That 2 Thessalonians lacks any specific affirmation of ecstatic utterances comparable to the one in 1 Thessalonians (5:19-20) is not in itself significant. It is significant, however, that 2 Thessalonians implicitly disallows a place for such utterances within the body of teaching that it commends as normative (2:2 + 2:15).

4. In 1 Thessalonians the Holy Spirit is represented as both empowering

34. Cf. Franz Laub, "Paulinische Autorität in nachpaulinischer Zeit (2 Thes)," in Raymond F. Collins, ed., *The Thessalonian Correspondence* (BETL 87; Leuven: Leuven University Press/Peeters, 1990), pp. 403-17, here pp. 413-14.

35. Cf. Philemon, where πνεῦμα appears only once (v. 25), and then as a reference to the human spirit.

the proclamation of the gospel and generating the faith which accepts the gospel as the word of God (1:5, 6; 2:13). In 2 Thessalonians there is no reflection on how the Spirit may be related to faith, and the gospel is not conceived in dynamic terms at all, but identified primarily with the truth that does not change and traditions that must be held fast (2:13-15).

Thus, even when 2 Thessalonians is compared only with 1 Thessalonians, it is evident that one must speak of a diminished sense of the role of the Spirit, not only in the ongoing life of the believing community but also in relation to the gospel itself. It is therefore not surprising that in 2 Thessalonians believers are described, not as "taught by God" (θεοδίδακτοι, 1 Thess. 4:9), but as instructed (ἐδιδάχθητε) by Paul concerning the traditions (2:15); it is according to those that they must live (3:6). Although any judgment about the authorship of 2 Thessalonians must take other factors into account, our present findings are consistent with viewing the letter as deutero-Pauline. As regards the role of the Spirit, its thought is more in accord with Colossians, Ephesians, and the Pastorals than with 1 Thessalonians.

XIX The Significance and Relevance of the Spirit in the Pastoral Epistles

Paul Trebilco

I. Introduction

It has often been noted that in the Pastoral Epistles we see a degree of institutionalization of the work of the Spirit. The Spirit is said to give gifts to leaders rather than to everyone, and the Spirit is connected with the institution of the church through the laying on of hands. But does this mean that, as the significance of "office" grows, the Spirit has become unimportant?

Here I will argue that the work of the Spirit is not such a neglected feature in the Pastorals as is often thought.[1] Rather, the Pastor relates the Spirit to crucial issues he faces, makes connections between the Spirit and other facets of his theology, and understands the Spirit's activity to involve new and different areas.[2] In order to show this, we need to ask why the Pastor wrote these let-

1. See, e.g., J. D. Miller, *The Pastoral Letters as Composite Documents* (Cambridge: Cambridge University Press, 1997), p. 143. M. A. G. Haykin, "The Fading Vision? The Spirit and Freedom in the Pastoral Epistles," *EQ* 57 (1985): 289-305 also challenges this view, but in a different way from that attempted here; see also J. D. Quinn, "The Holy Spirit in the Pastoral Epistles," in *Sin, Salvation and the Spirit* (ed. D. Durken; Collegeville, Minn.: Liturgical Press, 1979), pp. 35-68.

2. In my view the Pastorals are pseudonymous, and are probably to be dated in the generation after Paul's death.

I am enormously grateful to Jimmy for his friendship and his wise advice as my Ph.D. supervisor and in the years since then. I am delighted to be able to write this as a token of my appreciation.

ters and to outline some of his key theological themes. Then we can ask how the author saw the Spirit's activity in relation to these matters.

Two of the key aims the Pastor has as he writes are to combat opponents and, because of the opponents' activity, to advocate the appointment of certain types of leaders. Three key theological themes of these letters are salvation, the importance of living out the Christian life, and the significance of Christ. I will argue that, according to the Pastor, the Spirit has a significant part to play in relation to each of these aims and themes. If this is the case, then we are justified in claiming that the Spirit has a significant part in the overall theology of these letters.

II. The Spirit and the Pastor's Aims in Writing

The Spirit and Combatting the Opponents

There is widespread agreement that one of the key reasons the Pastor wrote these letters was to counteract the teachers whom we will call "the opponents." The exact nature of the opponents is not crucial for our discussion here. At this stage, we simply need to note that they have created a crisis for the Pastor. This can be seen from the number of passages in which he writes about the opponents[3] and their impact,[4] and the way, for example, he tells Titus that the opponents "must be silenced, since they are upsetting whole families by teaching for sordid gain what it is not right to teach" (Tit. 1:11).[5]

Given that one of the Pastor's key aims is to oppose these teachers, is the Spirit part of the solution to this crisis? If so, then this would be one way in which the Spirit is a significant part of his theology. I will argue that the Spirit features in three ways with regard to the opponents.

The Spirit's Prior Warning about the Opponents

In 1 Tim. 4:1 we read: "Now the Spirit expressly says that in later times some will renounce the faith by paying attention to deceitful spirits and teaching of de-

3. The Pastor writes about his opponents in 1 Tim. 1:3-7, 18-20; 4:1-7; 6:3-10, 20-21; 2 Tim. 2:14–4:5; Tit. 1:10-16; 3:9-11. On the opponents see F. Young, *The Theology of the Pastoral Letters* (Cambridge: Cambridge University Press, 1994), pp. 5-20; J. L. Sumney, *'Servants of Satan', 'False Brothers' and Other Opponents of Paul* (JSNTSup 188; Sheffield: Sheffield Academic Press, 1999), pp. 253-302.

4. See 1 Tim. 2:8-15; 5:13-15.

5. See also 1 Tim. 1:3; 6:2b-5, 20; 2 Tim. 3:5; Tit. 1:13; 3:10-11, which are all strongly worded; see also A. J. Malherbe, "'In Season and out of Season': 2 Timothy 4:2," *JBL* 103 (1984): 235-43.

mons." We do not know the details of how, when, or where the Spirit gave this message. Perhaps the prophetic Spirit spoke in the church through a prophet, or perhaps the Pastor is "claiming the Spirit as the authoritative source for his own words."[6] In any case, the present tense of λέγει indicates that the Spirit's speaking has present and ongoing significance.

According to the Pastor, the Spirit has said that people will renounce the faith in this way "in later times" (ἐν ὑστέροις καιροῖς). The passage does not state explicitly that the prophecy has now been fulfilled but that the Pastor thinks this is the case is shown by 1 Tim. 4:3-6, where he addresses the present situation on the basis of the prophecy, and urges Timothy to instruct the church in this regard now (v. 6). The opponents' teaching is regarded as a present danger by the Pastor, and he regards the "later times" as being a reference to his present.[7]

Because the Spirit has previously warned about such departures from the faith, the church is not caught unawares by the activity of the opponents. Seeing the opponents as part of events the Spirit predicted would occur means that their activity can be understood within the Pastor's theological framework; it is in accord with prophecy. Other features of the opponents' work can also be comprehended; as predicted by the Spirit about apostates in the last days, the opponents display, for example, the features of being scoffers and following ungodly passions.[8]

We can see, then, that the prophecy originating in the Spirit's activity helps the Pastor, and he hopes his readers, to understand the activity of the opponents. The Spirit is seen to be a guide to their current plight, and thus belief in the Spirit's work is intensely relevant.

The Spirit Guarding "the Deposit"

Faced with the challenge of the opponents, the Pastor is determined to ensure that the community adheres to what he regards as correct teaching, seen as a deposit to be protected and transmitted. Thus, for example, Timothy is exhorted to "guard what has been entrusted to you" (1 Tim. 6:20).[9] Related to this is the Pastor's emphasis on "sound teaching" or being "sound in the faith";[10] the

6. J. M. Bassler, *1 Timothy, 2 Timothy, Titus* (Nashville: Abingdon, 1996), pp. 78-79.

7. Other authors predicted a time of apostasy "at the end of days"; see 1QpHab. 2:5-6; Matt. 24:12; 2 Tim. 3:1; 2 Pet. 3:3-7; Jude 17-18.

8. 1 Tim. 1:6 and 2 Tim. 3:2-6; compare Jude 17-18.

9. See also 1 Tim. 1:11; 4:16; 2 Tim. 1:12; 2:2. παραθήκη is found in 1 Tim. 6:20; 2 Tim. 1:12, 14. 2 Tim. 2:2 uses παράθου.

10. See also 1 Tim. 1:10; 6:3; 2 Tim. 1:13; 4:3; Tit. 1:9, 13; 2:1, 2, 8.

deposit consists of "sound words." All of this is in contrast to the opponents, who can be spoken of as people "of corrupt mind and counterfeit faith" who "oppose the truth" (2 Tim. 3:8).[11] The Pastor is anxious that his readers do not go in the same direction, and so exhorts Timothy to "guard the deposit."

But for the Pastor, the Spirit also has a role in this guarding process. In 2 Tim. 1:14 we read: "Guard the precious deposit through the Holy Spirit who dwells in us." The deposit is here clearly the gospel. As we have noted in 1 Tim. 6:20, Timothy and, by implication, other leaders are told to "guard what has been entrusted to you." Yet in 2 Tim. 1:14 the Pastor states that they do so "through the Holy Spirit (διὰ πνεύματος ἁγίου) who dwells in us." This suggests that the Spirit is a key agent of this guarding activity, enabling leaders to remain faithful to the tradition in the face of the threat from the opponents.[12] Thus Timothy is exhorted to guard the gospel, but he will be able to do this through the Spirit given to him. The Pastor makes it clear that the leader can be enabled by the Spirit to guard the deposit because the Holy Spirit "dwells in us" (τοῦ ἐνοικοῦντος ἐν ἡμῖν).

We see, then, that in this crucial matter of guarding "the faith" in the face of the deceptions of the opponents, which is one of the Pastor's key concerns, the Spirit has a significant role to play.

The Spirit of Power, Love, and Self-Discipline

In 2 Tim. 1:6-7 the Pastor enlists the Spirit in the fight against the opponents. Here he writes: "For this reason I remind you to rekindle the gift of God that is within you through the laying on of my hands; for God did not give us a Spirit of cowardice but of power and of love and of self-discipline (δυνάμεως καὶ ἀγάπης καὶ σωφρονισμοῦ)." Before we discuss the passage in detail, we need to turn to three introductory issues.

First, is the Pastor speaking of the human spirit or the Holy Spirit here? The context of v. 6 is decisive: Timothy has been given "τὸ χάρισμα τοῦ θεοῦ" through the laying on of hands. The image of rekindling and so of fire, often used with the Spirit, the use of χάρισμα and πνεῦμα in close proximity,[13] and the use of δίδωμι, which is often used of God giving the Spirit,[14] strongly argue that πνεῦμα in v. 7 is a reference to the Holy Spirit.

11. See also 1 Tim. 1:6, 19; 4:1; 6:5.

12. On the Spirit's role as an enabler in the Pastorals see L. R. Donelson, *Pseudepigraphy and Ethical Argument in the Pastoral Epistles* (Tübingen: J. C. B. Mohr [Paul Siebeck], 1986), pp. 143-45, 184-86.

13. Cf. 1 Cor. 12:5, 7.

14. See Luke 11:13; Acts 5:32; 8:18; 15:8; Rom. 5:5; 1 Cor. 1:22; 5:5; Eph. 1:17; 1 Thess. 4:8;

Second, the Pastor begins by speaking of the gift given to Timothy through the laying on of hands, and then speaks of the Spirit given "to us" (ἡμῖν) in v. 7. It is most likely that the Pastor refers to the Spirit of power, love, and self-discipline as God's gift to all believers rather than using ἡμῖν with only leaders in mind. The Pastor affirms that all Christians receive the Spirit at conversion in Tit. 3:6-7. In 2 Tim. 1:14 we read: "Guard the precious deposit through the Holy Spirit who dwells in us." It seems unlikely that ἐν ἡμῖν here should be restricted to leaders; in 2 Tim. 1:14, after having given singular exhortations to Timothy in vv. 13-14 ("Follow the pattern (Ὑποτύπωσιν ἔχε) . . . guard the good treasure (τὴν καλὴν παραθήκην φύλαξον) the author writes: "through the Holy Spirit who dwells within *us* (ἐν ἡμῖν)." That the Pastor returns to the plural to speak of the Spirit suggests that he turns from thinking of Timothy to all Christians, emphasizing again that, for the Pastor, the Spirit indwells all Christians.[15] Further, as Marshall notes with regard to 2 Tim. 1:7, "The determining factor is that the qualities here associated with the Spirit are in no way peculiar to leaders. . . . [T]he gift of the Spirit given to all believers equips each for their particular needs."[16] We conclude, then, that, although the Spirit is here associated with leaders, the passage also speaks of all Christians having the Spirit of power, love, and self-discipline. Thus when the Pastor writes in 2 Tim. 1:7 that "God did not give (ἔδωκεν) us a spirit of cowardice, but rather a Spirit of power . . . ," the aorist ἔδωκεν refers to the action of God in giving the Spirit to the believer at conversion-initiation.[17]

Third, what does the Pastor mean by the genitive, πνεῦμα . . . δυνάμεως ("Spirit of power") and so on? Given that σωφρονισμός in particular is clearly a human characteristic, the meaning must be that the Spirit develops these characteristics in those to whom the Spirit is given.[18] That the Spirit develops these characteristics in Timothy and, by implication, others, is the overarching point in the context (2 Tim. 1:8-14).

The Pastor is saying, then, that the Spirit, whom God has given to "us"

---

cf. also 1 Tim. 4:14. That the Holy Spirit is meant is argued by G. W. Knight, *The Pastoral Epistles: A Commentary on the Greek Text* (NIGTC; Grand Rapids: Eerdmans, 1992), p. 371; cf. W. D. Mounce, *Pastoral Epistles* (WBC; Nashville: Thomas Nelson, 2000), pp. 477-78.

15. See L. Oberlinner, *Kommentar zum Zweiten Timotheusbrief* (HTKNT; Freiburg: Herder, 1995), p. 52. Note also the plurals in v. 9, which refer to Christians in general.

16. I. Howard Marshall, *A Critical and Exegetical Commentary on the Pastoral Epistles* (ICC; Edinburgh: T&T Clark, 1999), p. 699; see also Knight, *The Pastoral Epistles*, p. 371.

17. Thus in v. 6 we have a reference to Timothy's commissioning and the Spirit, and in v. 7 to conversion and the Spirit; the Pastor reminds the reader of the nature of the Spirit, whose gift is to be rekindled by recalling the nature of the same Spirit given at conversion.

18. Similar genitives are found in Rom. 8:2, 15; 11:8; 1 Cor. 4:21; 2 Cor. 4:13; Gal. 6:1; Eph. 1:17.

gives the Christian power, love, and self-discipline. In the context of the Pastorals, each of these three dimensions is significant, particularly in relation to the opponents, and will be dealt with in turn.

The Spirit of power The Spirit whom God has given to the readers is the Spirit of power (δύναμις), or, perhaps better, the empowering Spirit. In the Pastorals, δύναμις is found only here and in 2 Tim. 1:8 and 3:5. In 2 Tim. 1:8 the Pastor speaks of Timothy "relying on the power of God" as he testifies to and suffers for the gospel; we see here the relevance of the indwelling "Spirit of power" of 1:7. In 2 Tim. 3:5 the opponents are spoken of as "holding to the outward form of godliness but denying its power. Avoid them!" By contrast, believers should *not* deny the power of godliness, but rather be "empowered" by the Spirit.

On the other hand, the forcefulness of the opponents is at times emphasized in the letters. Note, for example, 2 Tim. 3:2-4 with reference to the opponents: "For people will be . . . abusive, . . . implacable, . . . brutes, haters of the good, treacherous. . . ."[19] Thus, although they deny the true power of godliness (since they have shipwrecked their faith), they operate in "powerful" ways. Hence, to counter this, the Spirit who gives power is needed. Empowering is also needed by Timothy and hence other leaders as they preach (e.g., 2 Tim. 4:2) and needed in other activities of leadership as a result of the opponents' activities (e.g., 1 Tim. 1:3; Tit. 1:11), although gentleness is at times also called for (e.g., 2 Tim. 2:25).

So we see that, for the Pastor, the "empowering Spirit" aids leaders and believers in general in the struggle against the opponents. Again, the Spirit is significant in this crucial situation facing the Pastor.

The Spirit of love The Spirit is also spoken of as the Spirit of love (ἀγάπη), the Spirit who gives love. A number of passages suggest that the behavior of the opponents has led to dissension and hateful actions and is disruptive of community. In 2 Tim. 3:2-5, which is clearly about the opponents (see v. 6), we read: "For people will be lovers of themselves, lovers of money, boasters, arrogant, abusive, disobedient to their parents, . . . slanderers, profligates, brutes, haters of good, treacherous, . . . lovers of pleasure rather than lovers of God. . . . Avoid them!"[20] It seems reasonable to suggest that for the Pastor, the Spirit who leads to love would be considered an antidote to opponents such as these.[21]

19. Note also 1 Tim. 4:4; 2 Tim. 2:18; 3:6; Tit. 1:10; see also 1 Tim. 4:1; 5:15; 2 Tim. 2:26.

20. See also 1 Tim. 6:4; 2 Tim. 2:14, 23-24; 3:13; Tit. 1:10-12; 3:9; cf. Tit. 3:3.

21. See Marshall, *The Pastoral Epistles*, p. 369.

We note also that the author often makes the exhortation to love,[22] and at times this is contrasted with the behaviour of the opponents.[23] We can suggest that, for the Pastor, at least one of the reasons the readers are able to love is that they have received the Spirit of love. In addition, the Spirit who gives love counteracts the disruption of the opponents and enables mutual love to be shown in the community. Again, then, the Spirit has a significant role in countering the opponents and counteracting the impact of their behavior.

The Spirit of self-discipline According to 2 Tim. 1:7, the Spirit is the Spirit of σωφρονισμός — moderation, self-discipline, or sound-mindedness.[24] The σώφρων word group and related concepts are very important in the Pastorals, with eight words and word groups being used in twenty-six references to express these ideas.[25] That the Spirit leads to self-discipline is thus very significant. But again we will ask if this role of the Spirit is related to the opponents.

The σώφρων word group, which is used ten times, is found, for example, in 1 Tim. 3:2 where we read that "a bishop must be above reproach, . . . sensible (σώφρονα), respectable. . . ." In Tit. 2:11-12 the Pastor states that the grace of God has appeared, training us "to live lives that are self-disciplined (σωφρόνως), upright, and godly." Σωφρόνως has become "a fundamental characteristic of the Christian life . . . [which] communicates in readily understandable terms the idea of 'a suitable restraint in every respect', a self-control which leads to behavior appropriate to the situation."[26]

The Pastor regularly calls for self-discipline, or related ideas, in leaders and in all believers. Although the readers, and leaders in particular, are called on to be "self-disciplined" (e.g., Tit. 1:8), the Spirit of σωφρονισμός, whom God has given to the readers, leads to this very quality. We can suggest, then, that the readers are implicitly encouraged to "give free course to the Spirit,"[27] who will enable them to show what the Pastor regards as the vital quality of self-discipline.

22. See also 1 Tim. 1:5; 2:15; 4:12; 6:11; 2 Tim. 1:13; 2:22; Tit. 2:2.

23. See, e.g., 1 Tim. 6:10-11; 2 Tim. 2:22-4; 3:10-13.

24. See BDAG, p. 987; G. D. Fee, *God's Empowering Presence: The Holy Spirit in the Letters of Paul* (Peabody, Mass.: Hendrickson, 1994), p. 785.

25. In addition to the σώφρων word group, note ἐγκρατής "disciplined" (Tit. 1:8), νηφάλιος "sober" (1 Tim. 3:2, 11; Tit. 2:2), νήφω "to be sober" (2 Tim. 4:5), ἀνανήφω "to become sober" (2 Tim. 2:26); σεμνότης "seriousness, respectfulness" (1 Tim. 2:2; 3:4; Tit. 2:7); σεμνός "worthy of respect, serious" (1 Tim. 3:8, 11; Tit. 2:2); see Marshall, *The Pastoral Epistles*, pp. 185-91.

26. Marshall, *The Pastoral Epistles*, p. 184. All the occurrences of the word group are in 1 Tim. 2:9, 15; 3:2; 2 Tim. 1:7; Tit. 1:8; 2:2, 4, 5, 6, 12.

27. Marshall, *The Pastoral Epistles*, p. 700.

But, given the activities of the opponents, we can see the need for this quality of self-discipline. Note again the behavior of the opponents, spoken of in 2 Tim. 3:2-5: "For people will be . . . proud, arrogant, abusive, disobedient to their parents, . . . inhuman, implacable. . . ."[28] This is clearly behavior that the Pastor could describe as "out of control". Note also that the Pastor sees the opponents as involved in foolish discussions, profane chatter, and speculative controversies.[29] The call to self-discipline, sobriety, and seriousness is clearly responding to this situation.

In this context it is significant that the Pastor has said that the Spirit given to the community by God is the Spirit who leads to σωφρονισμός. Again the Spirit is seen to be counteracting the activities of the opponents, as well as crucial for the believer in living the Christian life.[30]

The Spirit and Leadership

One of the Pastor's responses to the opponents was to develop a certain style of leadership in the community. It is clear, firstly, that some of the opponents had been leaders in the community since some of those with whom the Pastor disagrees are said to have been involved in teaching,[31] an activity which for the Pastor is clearly the preserve of leaders.[32] We can understand, then, why one facet of the Pastor's response is to write at length about the sort of people who should be leaders. In this he is attempting to bring stability to the community and to its faith. Leaders are to "guard the deposit" of "sound teaching," which we have already discussed, and in which the Spirit has a role. Another facet of the Pastor's response is to provide lists of qualifications for leadership; the Pastor is seeking to bring stability through the appointment of what he regards as competent and respectable leaders who will protect the

28. See also 1 Tim. 2:8; 6:4-5; 2 Tim. 2:14, 23-24; 3:13; Tit. 1:10-12; 3:9-10.

29. 1 Tim. 1:3-7; 4:7; 6:4-5, 20; 2 Tim. 2:16, 23; 4:3; Tit. 1:10-14; 3:9-10. The suggestion of J. M. Ford, "A Note on Proto-Montanism in the Pastoral Epistles," *NTS* 17 (1970-71): 342-44 that the stress on sobriety is responding to the ecstatic prophecy of the opponents is unlikely. See also R. J. Karris ("The Background and Significance of the Polemic of the Pastoral Epistles," *JBL* 92 [1973]: 557-58), who argues that there is no clear evidence that the opponents claimed to be specially endowed with the Spirit. Accordingly, there is no indication that the Pastor played down the role of the Spirit because of the opponents' views.

30. 2 Tim. 3:16 says that Scripture is "God-breathed" (θεόπνευστος), but it is not clear that the Spirit is necessarily in view here. If there is an allusion to the Spirit here, then it is clear that the Scriptures are useful against the opponents; see 1 Tim. 2:13-14; 2 Tim. 3:5-9, 16.

31. See 1 Tim. 1:3, 7; 6:3; 2 Tim. 3:6-7.

32. See 1 Tim. 3:2; 5:17-18; Tit. 1:9.

"household of God."[33] It is within this whole context that we can understand what the author says about the Spirit, laying on of hands, and leadership.

In three passages we read about the Spirit, or the Spirit's activity of prophecy, in connection with the establishment of leadership. For example, in 1 Tim. 4:14 we read: "Do not neglect the gift that is in you, which was given to you through prophecy by the laying on of hands by the council of elders."[34] 1 Tim. 4:14 and 2 Tim. 1:6-7 envisage the bestowal of a gift which is seen as a gift of the Spirit; this is clearest in 2 Tim. 1:6-7, where the Pastor speaks of a gift bestowed through the laying on of hands, and then, in a more general way, of God giving "πνεῦμα," which we have already argued is a reference to the Spirit. The mention of prophecies in the other two passages also suggests a connection with the Spirit, and indicates that it is the Spirit's gift that is in view.

In these three verses the Spirit's gift is closely tied to the organization of the church. It is not as if the Spirit "blows where he wills," but rather that a gift of the Spirit is associated with the laying on of hands by the council of elders (1 Tim. 4:14) or by an individual in authority (Paul in 2 Tim. 1:6; Timothy in 1 Tim. 5:22). Care is also to be exercised about this, and some form of testing is implied in 1 Tim. 5:22;[35] this is a sign of an increasingly ordered group. Thus the Spirit is related to the organizational structure of the church,[36] although the Spirit itself is not restricted to leaders.[37]

However, this connection between a gift of the Spirit and church structure does not mean that the Spirit is *necessarily* less important. It is clear in these verses that the Spirit has a role vis-à-vis leaders, even if it is a different role from that in the undisputed Paulines. The Spirit *remains* significant in relation to the establishment and enabling of leadership. This can be seen in the following ways.

First, what "charisma," which is always in the singular, does the Pastor envisage as given by the Spirit to Timothy and hence to leaders? The context of 1 Tim. 4:13-16 is helpful: "Give attention to the public reading of scripture, to exhorting, to teaching. Do not neglect the gift that is in you. . . . Pay close atten-

33. See M. Y. MacDonald, *The Pauline Churches: A Socio-historical Study of Institutionalization in the Pauline and Deutero-Pauline Writings* (SNTSMS; Cambridge: Cambridge University Press, 1988), p. 220.

34. See also 1 Tim. 1:18; 2 Tim. 1:6-7.

35. See MacDonald, *The Pauline Churches,* p. 213; see also 1 Tim. 3:10.

36. See in particular E. Käsemann, *Essays on New Testament Themes* (London: SCM, 1964), pp. 86-89; J. D. G. Dunn, *Jesus and the Spirit* (London: SCM, 1975), pp. 347-50.

37. See 2 Tim. 1:7, 14; Tit. 3:6. Note also that we cannot say that all believers do not receive gifts just because the Pastor is silent on the matter; nor should we think that the Spirit is active only in those appointed to office.

tion to yourself and to your teaching." This suggests that teaching, and perhaps ministry more generally, is a gift from the Spirit, and so is related to the Pastor's emphasis on teaching sound words and on protecting and guarding the faith.[38]

Second, it is said that Paul is entrusting the charge to Timothy "according to the earlier prophecies made concerning you" (1 Tim. 1:18). This suggests that Spirit-inspired prophecies pointed to Timothy as having this role of leadership. Similarly, what is envisaged in 1 Tim. 4:14 is that the prior, Spirit-inspired prophecy pointed to Timothy, and thus indicated on whom the council of elders should lay their hands. The result was that Timothy was given a special gift, probably a gift for ministry.[39] Both 1 Tim. 1:18 and 4:14 imply that the Pastor envisages the prophetic Spirit having a role in indicating who should lead the contemporary community.[40] Does this suggest that the Spirit will guide current leaders to other leaders? Yes, although we might then expect some reference to the leading of the Spirit in the discussions of the appointment of leaders and of qualities required for leadership (1 Tim. 3:1-13; Tit. 1:5-9).[41] But perhaps these lists are to be read in conjunction with our three passages which mention prophecy and the laying on of hands in connection with the gift of the Spirit and leadership. This would suggest that, for the Pastor, selection of leaders involved not only "testing" and examining personal qualities of a potential leader, but the prophetic Spirit also had a role in indicating who should lead the community; then the laying on of hands (1 Tim. 5:22) involved the Spirit giving that person the gift for ministry. In any case, these verses suggest that the prophetic Spirit had a part in appointing leaders.[42]

38. Given that in 2 Tim. 1:8 the author goes on to write about "testifying to our Lord," the gift in vv. 6-7 is probably again teaching and preaching; see also v. 13. In 1 Tim. 5:22 the context is leadership, and the concern is that a leader be compromised by a wrong choice of successor. Fee ("Pauline Literature," in *Dictionary of Pentecostal and Charismatic Movements*, ed. S. M. Burgess et al. [Grand Rapids: Zondervan, 1988], p. 673) suggests that the gift "refers first to the Spirit (2 Tim. 1:6-7) but is also broadened to refer to the gift for ministry that came by the Spirit (1 Tim. 4:14)."

39. Alternatively, the prophecy could confirm prior giftedness by the Spirit, and the laying on of hands would involve recognition by the community (see Fee, *Empowering Presence*, pp. 773-76). It is unlikely that these verses relate only to the past; Timothy here functions as a paradigm for contemporary leaders.

40. This is taking what is said about Timothy here as paradigmatic for leaders in the present, which seems the most likely way to read it, rather than as simply historical notes about Timothy's past.

41. And note the idea of aspiring to office in 1 Tim. 3:1.

42. N. Brox, *Die Pastoralbriefe* (RNT; Regensburg: Friedrich Pustet, 1969), p. 180, notes "die Propheten an der Auswahl des Kandidaten bzw. an der Anordnung seiner Ordination maßgeblich beteiligt waren." See also A. T. Hanson, *The Pastoral Epistles* (NCB; Grand Rapids: Eerdmans, 1982), pp. 38, 94.

Hence the Pastor believes the Spirit has a role in the establishment of leaders and gives a gift for ministry to contemporary leaders. Given the huge importance of leadership and teaching for the Pastor, the Spirit was in this way playing a significant role. Although we see a connection between the Spirit and church structure, this does not mean that the Spirit has become unimportant, least of all in relation to leadership. Rather, as we have sought to show, in a new situation, different activities of the Spirit (prophecy indicating who should lead, and the Spirit's gift [singular] for ministry), mediated in different ways (through the laying on of hands), have become valued.

III. The Spirit and Key Theological Themes

The Spirit and Salvation

We will now discuss briefly three of the Pastor's key theological themes and seek to show how each is related to the Spirit.

A strong case can be made that salvation is at the center of the Pastor's theology or, at the very least, is a crucial theme.[43] His belief about salvation is expressed in passages such as 1 Tim. 1:15; 2:3-7; 3:16; 4:10; Tit. 2:11. That the Spirit is related to this theme is highlighted by Tit. 3:4-7. There we read: "But when the goodness and lovingkindness of God our Savior appeared, he saved us, not because of any works of righteousness that we had done, but according to his mercy, through the water of rebirth and renewal by the Holy Spirit. This Spirit he poured out on us richly through Jesus Christ our Savior, so that having been justified by his grace, we might become heirs according to the hope of eternal life. The saying is sure."

In this passage, the Spirit has a crucial role in the work of salvation, for it is the Spirit who "washes," bringing about rebirth and renewal,[44] and thus implements or effects the work of Christ, the one mediator (1 Tim. 2:5-6), in the life of the individual. Salvation is therefore appropriated through the regenerating work of the Spirit, the agent of rebirth and transformation. That the Spirit

43. See MacDonald, *The Pauline Churches,* pp. 231-34; P. H. Towner, *The Goal of Our Instruction: The Structure of Theology and Ethics in the Pastoral Epistles* (JSNTSup 34; Sheffield: JSOT, 1989), pp. 75-119.

44. "Through the water of rebirth and renewal by the Holy Spirit" is almost certainly a reference to one event, since if it was to be a reference to two events, we would expect διά to be repeated before ἀνακαινώσεως. Further, we do not need to decide if Tit. 3:5 is a reference to water baptism or to the washing away of sin since, as Fee ("Pauline Literature," p. 675) notes, "In any case, the final genitival phrase, 'of the Spirit,' is the key to the whole."

can do this for the individual is shown by the fact that the Spirit has been "poured out on us richly" by God.[45] The lavishness of the outpouring of the Spirit means that there is no question that the Spirit can bring about the washing. In this crucial matter of salvation, the Spirit has a key role to play.

The Spirit and Living Out the Christian Life

The author regularly calls for "good works,"[46] or expresses the hope that believers may lead lives which are "godly and respectful in every way";[47] he also gives lists of virtues sought for in leaders, or all believers.[48] Tit. 2:14 is characteristic; Jesus is said to have given himself for the readers to "redeem us from all iniquity and purify for himself a people of his own who are zealous for good deeds."[49] We will show the connection between this key theme of "a godly life" and the Spirit by looking again at Titus 3.

At the beginning and end of Tit. 3:1-8 we see a stress on a life of "good deeds"; at the heart of the passage, and indicating how the change happens, is the Christ event (vv. 4-5). But the agent through whom this change is effected in the individual is the Holy Spirit — it is "through the water of rebirth and renewal by the Holy Spirit" (v. 5). This activity of the Spirit forms the theological foundation for living out the "newness" of the Christian life, here contrasted with how people once lived (v. 3).

We thus see the connection between the Spirit and the importance of a certain way of living. We also note the emphasis in vv. 1-2 and v. 8 on some crucial ethical themes of the letters, including good deeds, submission, obedience, no evil speaking, avoiding quarreling, gentleness, and perfect courtesy. We can suggest that all of these attributes are enabled in the individual's life by the agency of the Holy Spirit.[50]

45. The phrase draws upon Joel 2:28 and thus underlines the fulfillment of prophecy. An allusion to Pentecost is also likely; see J. D. G. Dunn, *Baptism in the Holy Spirit* (London: SCM, 1970), pp. 165-70; Fee, *Empowering Presence*, pp. 755-95.

46. See 1 Tim. 2:10; 5:10, 25; 6:18; 2 Tim. 2:21; Tit. 2:7; 3:1, 8, 14.

47. 1 Tim. 2:2; see also 1 Tim. 4:7-8; 5:4-8; 6:3, 5, 11, 14; Tit. 1:1; 2:11-12.

48. For leaders, e.g., 1 Tim. 3:1-13; Tit. 1:5-9; for all believers, 1 Tim. 5:3-16; Tit. 2:1-10.

49. This sort of new life is also strongly contrasted with the action of the opponents; see, e.g., 1 Tim. 5:20; 6:4-5; 2 Tim. 3:1-5; Tit. 1:10-16; 3:9-11.

50. Note again a link with the opponents (spoken of in 3:9-11) in this passage. The implication of Tit. 3:1-11 is that if the individual is washed by the Spirit, then he or she will avoid all the actions of the opponents spoken of in vv. 9-11.

The Spirit and Christ

There is no doubt about the centrality of the Christ event for the Pastor. This is clear in 1 Tim. 3:16, for example, which is a key doctrinal statement in hymnic form, which undergirds the statement of purpose of the letter and the call for appropriate behavior in 1 Tim. 3:14-15. But the importance of the Christ event comes through on many occasions.[51] Since Christ is so crucial for the author, the links between Christ and the Spirit that we will outline reinforce the significance of the Spirit.

First, we have suggested that there was a connection between the work of Christ and the work of the Spirit in Tit. 3:6-7. The Pastor first of all makes it clear that God has saved the believer and is thus the ultimate cause and initiator of salvation: "But when the goodness and lovingkindness of God our Savior appeared, *he saved us* . . . according to *his mercy*." The use of the word "appeared (ἐπεφάνη)" with reference to God's goodness and lovingkindness is clearly a reference to the Christ event, often spoken of in the Pastorals by the use of the concept of epiphany.[52] But Christ's work is said to be actualized in the community by the work of the Holy Spirit — it is "through the water of rebirth and renewal by the Holy Spirit."

Second, we note Tit. 3:6: "This Spirit he poured out on us richly *through* Jesus Christ (διὰ Ἰησοῦ Χριστοῦ) our Savior." God is the one who poured out the Spirit, but this is "through" Jesus Christ. Here, then, Christ is the agent of God's action of giving the Spirit.

Third, the activity of Christ and the Spirit are connected in 2 Tim. 1:12 and 14. In 2 Tim. 1:12 we read: "For I know the one in whom I have put my trust, and I am sure that he is able to guard until that day what I have entrusted to him." But is it God or Christ in whom "I have put my trust" and who is said to guard here? Given the context of "the appearing of our Savior Jesus Christ" and Paul's appointment as an apostle (vv. 10-11), which is elsewhere an appointment made by Christ,[53] Christ is clearly included in the reference to guarding in 2 Tim. 1:12.[54] This is significant because in 2 Tim. 1:14 we go on to read: "Guard the good treasure entrusted to you, with the help of the Holy Spirit living in us." This means that in v. 12 Christ is the agent of guarding, while in v. 14 guarding is said to be "through the Spirit." In each case, φυλάσσω

51. See 1 Tim. 2:5-6; 3:16; 2 Tim. 1:10; Tit. 2:13-14.

52. See A. Lau, *Manifest in Flesh* (WUNT 2.86; Tübingen: Mohr [Siebeck], 1996); H. Stettler, *Die Christologie der Pastoralbriefe* (WUNT 2.105; Tübingen: Mohr [Siebeck], 1998), pp. 135-49, 330-31.

53. 1 Tim. 1:12; 2 Tim. 1:10-11.

54. See Marshall, *The Pastoral Epistles*, p. 710.

and παραθήκη are used. Here, then, we have Christ and the Spirit being involved in the same activity.

Given the significance of Christology for the Pastor, it is noteworthy that the author makes these connections between Christ and the Spirit.[55]

IV. The Pneumatology of the Pastor and of Paul

Fee argues that the Pastorals "clearly reflect Pauline ideas throughout; this is especially true in their use of Spirit language."[56] We are now in a position to suggest briefly that the situation is more complex than Fee suggests, although we cannot discuss Paul's pneumatology in depth.

There are indeed some features that the Pastor and Paul share. We can note the importance of the Spirit at conversion,[57] the concept of the indwelling Spirit,[58] the Spirit and living the Christian life,[59] the Spirit and power,[60] the Spirit and love,[61] the Spirit and eschatology,[62] and the connection between Christ and the Spirit.[63]

Other features of Paul's view of the Spirit are absent in the Pastorals. Perhaps this is due to the subject matter of the Pastorals, and we must of course always be wary of an argument from silence, given the contextual, occasional nature of both Paul's writings and the Pastorals. The features of the pneumatology of the undisputed Paulines which are absent from the Pastorals include the Spirit-flesh contrast with regard to the Christian,[64] the Pauline emphasis on the Spirit granting revelation and understanding,[65] the Spirit and worship,[66] and the Spirit and community/unity.[67]

55. The new spiritual realm, the realm of the Spirit, entered by Christ through his resurrection, is spoken of in the hymn of 1 Tim. 3:16; on the much-debated passage see Fee, *Empowering Presence,* 761-68.

56. Fee, "Pauline Literature," p. 666.

57. Rom. 5:5; 8:9, 15-17; 1 Cor. 2:12; 6:11; 12:13; Gal. 3:2-4; 4:4-6; 1 Thess. 1:5-6; Tit. 3:5-6.

58. Rom. 8:11; 2 Cor. 6:16; Col. 3:16; 2 Tim. 1:6-7, 14; Tit. 3:5-6.

59. Rom. 12:9-11; 14:17; 15:13, 19; Gal. 3:3; 5:13–6:10; Col. 3:12-13; Tit. 3:1-8.

60. Rom. 15:13, 18-19; 1 Cor. 2:4-5; Phil. 1:19-20; 1 Thess. 1:5; 2 Tim. 1:7.

61. Rom. 5:5; 15:30; Gal. 5:22; Col. 1:8; 2 Tim. 1:7.

62. Rom. 8:23; 2 Cor. 1:21-22; 5:5; Gal. 3:14; 1 Tim 4:1; Tit 3:7.

63. Rom. 8:9, 15-17; Gal. 4:4-6; Phil. 1:19; 1 Tim. 1:12-14; Tit. 3:6-7.

64. See Rom. 8:3-17; Gal. 4:29; 5:13–6:10; Phil. 3:3. This absence in the Pastorals is interesting since the opponents could clearly be regarded as living in the flesh, in Paul's terms. The Spirit-flesh contrast is found in the Pastorals of Christ in 1 Tim. 3:16, the only time σάρξ is used.

65. See 1 Cor. 2:6-16; 14:24-25; cf. 2 Tim. 2:7; Tit. 2:11-12.

66. See Rom. 12:1-2; 1 Cor. 14:6, 24, 26; Phil. 3:3.

67. See 1 Cor. 12:13; 2 Cor. 13:13; Phil. 2:1.

But most significantly, there are features of the Pastor's theology of the Spirit which are not found in Paul, and are *new within the Pauline tradition.* We note the connection with "guarding the deposit" so that we can speak of the guarding Spirit, the Spirit leading to self-discipline or sound-mindedness,[68] the Spirit working through the organizational structure of the church in the laying on of hands and giving a gift for ministry through this action,[69] and Spirit-inspired prophecy pointing toward leadership,[70] again with an organizational connection. This means that Fee's view — that the Pastorals are totally Pauline in their pneumatology — is difficult to sustain. While, as we would expect, they share much with Paul's letters, at places they go beyond Paul.

What this means is that the Pastorals show continuity with Paul but also demonstrate both development and creativity. In particular, the Pastor sees the Spirit's activity as relevant to the new situation faced by the community. Because this situation has some new dimensions in comparison to that faced in the Pauline letters,[71] the Pastor's pneumatology shows development from Paul's pneumatology. Although the point is perhaps more obvious with Christology, where the Pastor develops his epiphany Christology, here with regard to the Spirit the Pastor again shows himself to be a creative, contextual theologian, while also being committed to the Pauline tradition. Thus he has discerned certain new dimensions or facets of the Spirit's work which are not found in Paul, new dimensions which are clearly relevant to the new situation the author and his community face. The "deposit of the faith" is not passed on unchanged. In the new situation he faces, the Pastor discerns new dimensions of the Spirit's work, which means that the Spirit remains relevant to the new day.

68. Paul does speak of self-control (ἐγκράτεια) as a fruit of the Spirit (Gal. 5:23; cf. 1 Cor. 7:9; 9:25). However, Marshall (*The Pastoral Epistles,* p. 186) notes that the focus of ἐγκράτεια is on self-control of the body and desires (as is shown by the negative list of works of the flesh in Gal. 5:17-21, which concentrate on bodily passion, and by 1 Cor. 7:9; 9:25, which concern restraint of sexual and bodily desire), "whereas σωφροσύνη would appear to be more concerned with sobriety in one's thinking and in the resulting behavior. It has more the nuance of acting thoughtfully and wisely." The Pastorals in their understanding of σωφροσύνη thus show development from the idea of ἐγκράτεια in the undisputed Paulines and clearly take the idea of "self-discipline" to a different level.

69. On the Spirit, gifts, and ministry in Paul see Rom. 12:6-8; 1 Cor. 11:4-5; 12:8-10, 28-30; 14:29; 1 Thess. 5:20.

70. The Spirit is not explicitly said to have this role in the undisputed Paulines, whereas it is a significant dimension in the Pastorals.

71. Paul faced opponents often enough, but here the new dimension is created by the nature of the opponents and the fact that they are actual leaders of the community who have had a considerable impact. Further, new developments relate to a more structured and regulated leadership, the greater concern to avoid scandalizing outsiders by living "sober" lives, and the content of the faith.

V. Conclusion

I have argued that when we consider the Pastor's aims in writing and his key theological themes, the Spirit does feature significantly. The Spirit is seen to have a role in many of the crucial issues that concern the Pastor, and we also see strong connections between the Spirit and key theological themes. Thus, although we see a growing connection between the Spirit's role and the organizational structure of the church in comparison with the undisputed Paulines, this does not mean that the Spirit is no longer important. Far from it! But the Spirit's role is one that is relevant for the situation of crisis faced by the author. For the author, the Spirit's role is not static, as if the Spirit could only do exactly what the Spirit had done a generation earlier in the Pauline churches. Rather, in the next generation in which the Pastor lived, facing new and equally challenging issues, the Pastor discerns that the Spirit takes on a modified role, with some features being continuous with those of the past (e.g., the Spirit of new life), some fading (e.g., the Spirit and revelation), but with new roles emerging (e.g., the Spirit as guarding the deposit) as needed for the life and health of the new community. So the Spirit remains significant, but, while seen as retaining some of its previous work, the Spirit is significant in some new and different ways and by undertaking some new roles. For the Pastor, the Spirit is the relevant, creative Spirit who remains significant for the life of the community.

XX The Holy Spirit in the Pastoral Epistles and the Apostolic Fathers

I. Howard Marshall

Attempts to plot the place of the Pastoral Epistles (PE) in the development of early Christian theology will naturally compare them not only with the other writings in the Pauline corpus but also with other Christian writings that may come from the end of the first century and the beginning of the second. In a famous exercise P. N. Harrison argued that the vocabulary of the PE was closer to that of the Apostolic Fathers (AF) and the Apologists than to that of Paul.[1] But what now of a theological comparison? In this essay we shall confine ourselves to a comparison with the role of the Holy Spirit in the AF.[2]

1. P. N. Harrison, *The Problem of the Pastoral Epistles* (Oxford: Oxford University Press, 1921). See, however, D. Guthrie, *The Pastoral Epistles and the Mind of Paul* (London: Tyndale, 1956).

2. On the Spirit in the Pastoral Epistles see P. Trebilco, "The Significance and Relevance of the Spirit in the Pastoral Epistles," in this volume, and the literature cited there.

On the Spirit in the AF see H. B. Swete, *The Holy Spirit in the Ancient Church* (London: Macmillan, 1912); J. E. Morgan-Wynne, "The Holy Spirit and Religious Experience in Christian Literature c. 90-200 AD" (Ph.D., Durham, 1987); G. F. Hawthorne, "Holy Spirit," in R. P. Martin and P. H. Davids (eds.), *Dictionary of the Later New Testament and Its Developments* (Downers Grove/Leicester: InterVarsity Press, 1997), pp. 489-99.

Except where otherwise indicated, biblical quotations are from the NIV. I used J. B. Lightfoot and J. R. Harmer, *The Apostolic Fathers: Revised Greek Texts with Introductions and English Translations* (Grand Rapids: Baker, 1984 repr.).

I. The Spirit in the Pastoral Epistles

The term πνεῦμα occurs only seven times in the PE. One reference is in a benediction that the Lord will be with Timothy's own spirit (2 Tim. 4:22). Another is to deceitful spirits associated with demons (1 Tim. 4:1b). Significantly this occurs in a prophecy attributed to the Spirit (1 Tim. 4:1a), although the mode of the Spirit's communication is not stated: the activity of a Christian prophet or a private revelation to the implied author (Paul) is meant.[3] This reference fits in with the fact of continued prophetic activity in the church (1 Tim. 1:18; 4:14).

In a key passage there is reference to the way in which God saved the readers through a washing of rebirth and of renewal by (lit. of) the Holy Spirit (Tit. 3:5). The piling up of nouns in the genitive case produces a text that is ambiguous. Even if only 'renewal' is directly linked with the Spirit, it is probable that the Holy Spirit would have been regarded as active in the whole process. Whether or not an allusion to water baptism is intended,[4] the primary referent is the inward, spiritual process of cleansing and renewal. The reference to the Holy Spirit being poured out richly is reminiscent of the Pentecost event (Acts 2:17, 18, 33; 10:45; *1 Clem.* 2:2; 46:6; *Barn.* 1:3).

The Holy Spirit, thus conveyed to believers, does not produce bad effects like cowardice but is rather the source of power, love, and self-control (2 Tim. 1:7). While the context of a letter to a Christian leader dictates that the thought is especially of his divine equipment for his task, the qualities conveyed are those that are to be found in all believers, and therefore the reference is to a gifting that is common to all believers and manifests itself in supplying their individual needs. Thus equipped, Timothy is exhorted to guard the good deposit 'with the help of the Holy Spirit who lives in us' (2 Tim. 1:14); again the focus is on the specific task of Timothy as a leader, but the 'us' can scarcely be restricted to leaders. Nevertheless, Timothy was set aside to his task through the laying on of hands by Paul (2 Tim. 1:6) and the elders (1 Tim. 4:14) and received his charisma for that task. To some extent, then, there is a gift of the Spirit for ministry which is conferred on those whom God calls to this task.

Finally, in the ambiguous text 1 Tim. 3:16 Christ 'was revealed in flesh, vindicated in spirit' (NRSV; mg.: 'by the Spirit'). The contrast with 'flesh' strongly suggests that 'spirit' refers to the spiritual mode or sphere of Christ's vindication by God (through his resurrection and exaltation) rather than to the

3. There is scarcely any direct quotation of the Old Testament in the PE (1 Tim. 5:18; 2 Tim. 2:19), but the Scriptures are described as "God-breathed" (θεόπνευστος), a term which might arouse echoes of πνεῦμα for readers.

4. See esp., J. D. G. Dunn, *Baptism in the Holy Spirit* (London: SCM, 1970), pp. 168-69.

activity of the Spirit, but the association elsewhere in the New Testament of the Spirit with the resurrection of Jesus prevents us from ruling out the possibility that the activity of the Spirit as the agent of vindication is present here.

II. The Spirit in the Apostolic Fathers

1 Clement

Clement shares the common view that the words of Scripture were said by the Holy Spirit (*1 Clem.* 13:1; 16:2; 22:1). The Scriptures, which are true, were given through the Holy Spirit (*1 Clem.* 45:2).[5]

Similarly, Paul gave instruction 'spiritually' in 1 Corinthians (*1 Clem.* 47:3). The writer himself claims that what he writes is done 'through the Holy Spirit' and therefore deserves obedience (*1 Clem.* 63:2). God's ministers spoke through the Holy Spirit about repentance (*1 Clem.* 8:1). The apostles were 'confirmed in the Word with full assurance of the Holy Spirit' and went out to evangelise (*1 Clem.* 42:3); they appointed the first converts, when they had proved them by the Spirit, to be bishops and deacons (*1 Clem.* 42:4).

The gift of the Spirit is universally bestowed on believers. An abundant outpouring of the Spirit fell upon all the readers (*1 Clem.* 2:2). Christians have 'one God and one Christ and one Spirit of grace that was shed upon' them (*1 Clem.* 46:6). This trinitarian statement is matched by the oath 'as God lives, and the Lord Jesus lives, and the Holy Spirit, who are the faith and hope of the elect' (*1 Clem.* 58:2).[6] Swete notes that these statements have implications for the threatened unity of the church.[7]

1 Clement does not go beyond the New Testament but lacks teaching on baptism and the gifts of the Spirit.[8]

5. The Holy Spirit is mentioned in the lengthy citation of Psalm 51 in *1 Clem.* 18:11-12 (cf. 21:2; 28:3). There are also references to the contrite human spirit in the citations from Ps. 51:19 in *1 Clem.* 18:17; 52:4 and to angels as spirits in *1 Clem.* 36:3.

6. God is the benefactor of all spirits and God of all flesh (*1 Clem.* 59:3a; cf. 59:3b; 64:1).

7. Swete, *Spirit,* pp. 11-12.

8. A. Lindemann, *Die Clemensbriefe* (Tübingen: Mohr, 1992), p. 21. J. D. G. Dunn, *Jesus and the Spirit* (London: SCM, 1975), 267-68, speculates as to whether the younger members of the church in Corinth were overvaluing the "charismata of speech and knowledge."

2 Clement

The author is referring to the incarnation of a preexistent being when he states that 'Christ the Lord who saved us, being first spirit, then became flesh' (2 *Clem.* 9:5).[9]

A major passage is 2 *Clement* 14. Here the author works with three pairs of concepts. First, he makes a contrast between a sinful community, apparently a corrupt church, and the 'first', spiritual church. Those who do God's will belong to the spiritual church, whereas those who do not do his will belong rather to its evil counterpart. Second, he compares the church and Christ. Just as Christ was spiritual and then manifested to save us, so too the first church was spiritual and was created before the universe. It is the church of life and is the body of Christ. Indeed, the church was made manifest in the flesh of Christ. With this comment the author introduces his third pair of concepts, making a contrast between the flesh and the Spirit. Whoever guards the church in the flesh and does not defile her will receive the church again in the Spirit. The flesh is the counterpart of the Spirit. So those who defile the flesh cannot receive the Spirit. The author then states that the flesh is the church and the Spirit is Christ; therefore, those who insult the flesh insult the church and so will not share in the Spirit which is Christ. The flesh can receive life and immortality if the Spirit is joined to it. The development of the thought is not entirely coherent.

Ignatius

For Ignatius the conception of Jesus in the womb of Mary was not only of the seed of David but also of the Holy Spirit (Ign. *Eph.* 18:2; cf. *Rom.* 1:3).

He can use the terminology 'flesh and spirit' to cover the whole of human nature, both terms being used positively (Ign. *Eph.* 10:3; *Magn.* 13:1; *Trallians*, Preface; *Romans*, Preface; *Smyrn.* 13:2; *Pol.* 1:2; 5:1). He also has a tripartite formula of 'flesh and soul and spirit' (Ign. *Phld.* 11:2). In a form of self-reference he can say, 'My spirit salutes you', along with the love of the churches that received him (Ign. *Rom.* 9:3; cf. *Smyrn.* 10:2). Similarly, his spirit is 'made an offscouring for the cross' (Ign. *Eph.* 18:1; cf. *Trall.* 13:3).

The flesh can also be a negative concept (Ign. *Magn.* 6:2). Those of the flesh cannot do the things of the Spirit, and vice versa (Ign. *Eph.* 8:2). Consequently, Jesus is the physician 'of flesh and of spirit' (Ign. *Eph.* 7:2). Those who

9. A human spirit that is not righteous is overtaken by divine judgment (2 *Clem.* 20:4).

tried to deceive Ignatius after the flesh were not able to do so, for 'the spirit is not deceived, being from God' (Ign. *Phld.* 7:1).

There is a contrast between the outward visible person and the inward, invisible spiritual person when Ignatius comments that after the resurrection Christ ate with his disciples 'as one in the flesh though spiritually he was united with the Father' (Ign. *Smyrn.* 3:3).[10] He prays that in the churches there may be 'the union of the flesh and of the spirit which are Jesus Christ's, . . . a union of faith and love, . . . a union with Jesus and with the Father' (Ign. *Magn.* 1:2). Similarly, he wants his readers to prosper in all that they do 'in flesh and spirit, by faith and love, in the Son and Father and in the Spirit'; they are to be obedient, 'that there may be both fleshly and spiritual union' (Ign. *Magn.* 13:1-2).

The church at Smyrna is 'in a blameless spirit and in the word of God' (Ignatius, *Smyrnaeans,* Preface). It is not lacking in any gift (χάρισμα; cf. Ign. *Pol.* 2:2). Here the boundary between the human spirit and the divine Spirit may well be fuzzy. Ignatius can also say that believers possess 'a steadfast spirit, which is Jesus Christ' (Ignatius, *Magnesians* 15).

The activity of the Spirit in the prophets (Ign. *Magn.* 9:3) and in church leaders is also mentioned. The leaders of the church at Philadelphia were confirmed and established 'by his Holy Spirit' (Ignatius, *Philadelphians,* Preface). Ignatius is conscious of his own inspiration by the Spirit; what looks like a prophetic utterance was 'the preaching of the Spirit who spoke in this way' (Ign. *Phld.* 7:2). Conversation with a good bishop can thus be not human but spiritual (Ign. *Eph.* 5:1).

In a vivid extended metaphor or analogy he sees the temple of God the Father being built up as the stones are hoisted by the engine (the cross of Jesus Christ) using the rope (the Holy Spirit) and the windlass (the faith of believers; Ignatius, *Ephesians* 9). The death of Christ cannot affect people without the work of the Spirit.

Polycarp

Polycarp echoes Galatians 5 with his statement that 'every lust wars against the Spirit' (Pol. *Phil.* 5:3). He also cites the Gospel saying that 'the spirit is willing, but the flesh is weak' (Pol. *Phil.* 7:2).

10. Ignatius can refer to his bonds as his "spiritual pearls" (Ign. *Eph.* 11:2), thus describing what they "really are."

Martyrdom of Polycarp

Polycarp associates the anticipated resurrection of his soul and body to eternal life with 'the incorruptibility of [conveyed by] the Holy Spirit' (*Mart. Pol.* 14:2). This fits in with the Pauline link between the Holy Spirit and the resurrection of Christ and of believers. He associates the Holy Spirit with God and Jesus Christ in what is said to be the earliest trinitarian doxology (*Mart. Pol.* 14:3; similarly in the closing comment by Pionius, *Mart. Pol.* 22:4).[11]

Barnabas

The activity of the Spirit in prophetic insight and activity comes over strongly. Abraham was able to look forward in the Spirit to Jesus (*Barn.* 9:7). Likewise Jacob saw 'in the Spirit' a type of the people who would come afterwards (*Barn.* 13:5). It was the Spirit who spoke into the heart of Moses and directed him to lift up his arms when he prayed, thus making a type of the cross (*Barn.* 12:2). Moses received 'the two tables which were written by the finger of the hand of the Lord in the Spirit' (*Barn.* 14:2). Moses gave his commandments in the Spirit (*Barn.* 10:2), and some of his teaching had a spiritual sense which went beyond the literal (*Barn.* 10:9). Ezekiel through the Spirit of the Lord foresaw those whose hearts would be changed (*Barn.* 6:14).

Similarly, Barnabas recognises that his readers are people on whom the Spirit has been poured out richly so that they have an innate gift of the Spirit (*Barn.* 1:2-3; cf. 19:7, where those who are called by the Lord are those whom the Spirit has prepared). He refers to them as spirits to whom he ministers, the impression being that they have a developed spirit because of the activity of the Holy Spirit (*Barn.* 1:2, 5; cf. 19:2). In his benediction the Lord will be with their spirit (*Barn.* 21:9; cf. Gal. 6:18; 2 Tim. 4:22).

In an unusual phrase the Son of God offered the vessel of the Spirit[12] as a sacrifice for our sins (*Barn.* 7:3). Similar language is used of believers in *Barn.* 11:9. In the context of baptism this indicates that (like the Lord) believers become the bearers of the Spirit; it is 'in the Spirit' that, coming up from the water, they have fear and hope in Jesus (*Barn.* 11:11).[13] They are to 'strive to be spiritual, a perfect temple for God' (*Barn.* 4:11).

11. Swete, *Spirit,* p. 12.

12. The parallel in *Barn.* 11:9 ("his spirit") shows that he probably means "the vessel of the Spirit" rather than "the vessel of his spirit."

13. But perhaps we should take this as "in the spirit" (Swete, *Spirit,* p. 19).

Didache

In the *Didache* God calls people whom the Spirit has prepared (*Did.* 4:10; *Barn.* 19:7), the implication being that the Spirit is no respecter of persons (whether masters or slaves). Baptism is administered in the threefold name (*Did.* 7:1, 3), but the writer can also refer simply to being baptised 'in the name of the Lord' (*Did.* 9:5). In the thanksgiving that follows the congregational meal there is reference to spiritual food and drink and eternal life granted through Christ (*Did.* 10:3; cf. 1 Cor. 10:3-4).

Various people claim to speak in the Spirit; the words of prophets who do so are to be accepted, but nevertheless not all who do so 'have the ways of the Lord' and are genuine, especially those who look for their keep or who make requests 'in the Spirit' for money (*Didache* 11).

Hermas

Although in much of *Hermas* there is silence regarding the Spirit, there are a number of passages where considerable attention is paid to the Spirit. Initially Hermas is carried off by a spirit[14] into the wilderness to receive revelations (*Herm. Vis.* 1:1:3; 2:1:1).

Mandate 5 is specifically about the way in which people may be inhabited by the Holy Spirit and/or by one or more evil spirits. There appear to be several evil spirits associated with specific evil desires, but Hermas regards the spirit of evil temper as the worst. It is powerful enough to drive out the 'delicate' Holy Spirit from people who are not 'full in the faith' and do not have the power of the Lord to withstand it. Similarly, 'double-mindedness is an earthly spirit from the devil' (*Herm. Man.* 9:11), but faith has greater power than it and can overcome it. In *Mandate 10* sorrow is also said to be more evil than all the other spirits and can crush the Holy Spirit in a person (*Herm. Man.* 10:1:2). Believers must put aside their sorrow lest this grieves and afflicts the Holy Spirit, which is a cheerful spirit, and it leaves them (*Herm. Man.* 10:2-3).

In *Hermas, Mandate* 11 Hermas contrasts false and true prophets and shows how to test a person who claims to be moved by the spirit (πνευματοφόρος). True prophets have the divine Spirit (τὸ θεῖον πνεῦμα or τὸ πνεῦμα τῆς θεότητος) and are gentle and humble; they speak spontaneously when they are in a company of people who have faith in the Spirit. This is contrasted with the earthly spirits of the devil which look for money and seek out

14. Πνεῦμα is anarthrous, but the Holy Spirit may well be meant. Cf. Acts 8:39.

unspiritual people. Therefore, true and false prophets are distinguished by their works.

In *Herm. Sim.* 5:6 Hermas is instructed about the Son of God. The holy, preexistent Spirit who created the whole world was made by God to dwell in the flesh that he desired. And so this flesh lived honourably and purely. It laboured and cooperated with the Spirit, and so God made it a partner with the Spirit. Therefore the Son was taken along with the angels as God's advisers as some kind of reward. This point is then generalised to the effect that all flesh in which the Holy Spirit dwells and which remains undefiled will receive a reward. And then it is particularised in an exhortation to Hermas himself (*Herm. Sim.* 5:7). He is not to defile his flesh (because he thinks that it is perishable) since to defile the flesh is to defile the Spirit.

In *Herm. Sim.* 9:1 Hermas learns that the instruction that he had received came from the Holy Spirit, who spoke with him in the form of the church, and this Spirit is now identified as the Son of God. Instruction given by an angel is likewise through the same Spirit. In the ensuing allegory of the tower and the virgins, the virgins are identified as holy spirits (plural! but cf. the use of the singular in *Herm. Sim.* 9:24-25) and powers of the Son of God; those who want to be in the kingdom of God must clothe themselves with these spirits or their garments (*Herm. Sim.* 9:13). The various garments are given names similar to those of the fruit of the Spirit in Galatians 5 (*Herm. Sim.* 9:15). The general implication is that 'a person must first be good in order for the Spirit to come and do a sanctifying work'.[15]

Brox holds that a distinction must be made between the 'Holy Spirit', who is associated with Christ, and the 'holy spirit' or 'holy spirits', who are powers that dwell in believers.[16]

III. Assessing the Evidence

We can now attempt a summary of the various references to the Spirit and the spiritual in the texts. The danger with such a summary is that it may be misinterpreted as an attempt to set out a coherent, underlying theology of the Spirit as held by the several writers in the corpus, and therefore it needs to be emphasised that this is nothing more than a categorised listing of the various statements that we have observed.

15. Hawthorne, "Holy Spirit," p. 495.

16. N. Brox, *Der Hirt des Hermas* (Göttingen: Vandenhoeck and Ruprecht, 1991), pp. 323-24, 541-46.

1. There is a dualism of flesh and spirit in human beings, these two terms covering the whole of human nature (Polycarp; though the trichotomy of flesh, soul, and spirit also occurs; Ignatius). 'Flesh' can be used neutrally (including use as a self-reference) or negatively (*2 Clement;* Ignatius). But 'spirit' can also be used to refer to persons (Ignatius, *Barnabas*) and to supernatural beings (frequently).
2. The Spirit was active before and in the creation of the world *(Hermas).*
3. The Spirit was active in the prophetic activities of Old Testament persons and the writing of Scripture *(1 Clement;* Ignatius; *Barnabas).*
4. The Spirit was active in the incarnation and birth of Jesus (Ignatius). The Son of God, who was spirit, became flesh *(2 Clement).* In his human form he was a vessel for the Spirit *(Barnabas;* just as are believers, *Barnabas;* cf. *Hermas).*
5. The church is likewise preexistent, being created before the universe and is spiritual, like Christ. Although, therefore, it is of the flesh, it can be of the Spirit *(2 Clement).*
6. God's building is being built up on the basis of the death of Christ by the conjoint activity of the Spirit and the faith of those who believe (Ignatius). The Lord calls those whom the Holy Spirit has prepared *(Didache; Barnabas).* The Holy Spirit is active in Christian baptism *(Barnabas).* Baptism may be administered in the threefold name *(Didache).* The Spirit is poured out abundantly on believers *(1 Clement; Barnabas).*
7. The Holy Spirit is active in the lives of believers *(Barnabas).* They have the Spirit dwelling in them *(2 Clement).* But there can be conflict between the Spirit and other powers or desires in believers (Polycarp, *Philippians*). In *Hermas* the Spirit is opposed by other evil spirits which may drive out the Holy Spirit, but believers are exhorted not to let this happen.
8. The union of the Spirit with the flesh leads to life and immortality *(2 Clement).*
9. The Holy Spirit is similarly active in the prophets and writers of the New Testament *(1 Clement; Didache; Hermas)* and in the writers of the texts themselves (*1 Clement;* Ignatius). But prophets may be inspired by the Holy Spirit or by evil spirits, and discernment is needed before accepting their messages. In general the test of character is applied to them, greed for money being a conspicuous sign of false prophets *(Didache; Hermas).* The Spirit can carry people away to receive revelations *(Hermas).*
10. Church leaders are confirmed and established by the Spirit (*1 Clement;* Ignatius). They speak through the Holy Spirit *(1 Clement).*

11. At the Lord's Supper there is spiritual food and drink *(Didache).*
12. The resurrection of believers takes place by the instrumentality of the Holy Spirit, who conveys incorruption *(Martyrdom of Polycarp).*
13. There are specifically trinitarian statements where Father, Son, and Spirit appear alongside each other in formulaic fashion (baptism; doxology; oath; *1 Clement;* Ignatius; *Martyrdom of Polycarp; Didache*). But the Spirit is sometimes added rather hesitantly,[17] and there can be some tendency to identify the Son as the Spirit (Ignatius; *Hermas*), or even to speak of holy spirits *(Hermas).*

Morgan-Wynne sums up one of the findings of his thesis by commenting:

> The truth lies somewhere between the impression created by the letters of Paul that true Christianity is experience of the Spirit of Christ and the assumption made by many writers that experiences of the Spirit were much rarer even by the end of the first century, never mind the second century. If we do not live in the atmosphere of the Pauline letters, nor do we descend to the impoverished level painted by some. The literature surveyed leaves us with a variegated picture and in that at least it probably faithfully reflects second-century Christianity.[18]

There is in fact a much broader development of teaching about the Spirit in the AF when compared with the PE, although this is only to be expected in a larger corpus of generally longer documents. At the same time, some aspects of the teaching in the PE do not reappear in the AF. The Spirit's prior warning about opponents and the importance of guarding the deposit are peculiar to them. There is no indication that the AF were significantly affected by the PE in their understanding of the Spirit, even if some of them were acquainted with them.

Major aspects of the work of the Spirit reappear, particularly the key role of the Spirit in conversion and the Christian life and in the equipping of the church's leaders.

We have a developing concept of the work of the Spirit in the pre-Christian era. The Spirit was active at creation, no doubt on the basis of Gen. 1:2. But there is nothing of this in the PE. Equally, there is no reference in the PE to the relationship of the Spirit to Christ except in 1 Tim. 3:16, and nothing about the identification of the Spirit with Christ or with the church.

17. E. Schweizer, *TDNT,* 6:451 n. 842.
18. Morgan-Wynne, "Holy Spirit," p. 427.

The repeated references to the Spirit inspiring the Old Testament prophets link up with the concept of Scripture as θεόπνευστος in 2 Tim. 3:16. Although this term signifies 'God-breathed', the relation of -πνευστος to πνεῦμα encouraged recognition of the activity of the Spirit in the inspiration of the writers (Mark 12:36 par.; Acts 1:16; 4:25; Heb. 3:7; etc.).

The outpouring of the Spirit on all believers is paralleled. There is surprisingly little stress in the AF on the activity of the Spirit in church leaders.

In other ways the AF go beyond the PE. There is a developing vocabulary of ways of referring to or describing the Spirit in the AF. Hawthorne lists references to the Spirit as 'Spirit', 'the Spirit', 'the Holy Spirit', and infrequently as 'the Spirit of God', 'the Spirit of the Lord', 'the Spirit of truth', and, in new formulations, 'the blameless Spirit' (Ignatius), 'the delicate Spirit' *(Hermas)*, 'the Spirit of the Godhead' *(Hermas)* and 'the divine Spirit' *(Hermas)*, 'the Spirit of Jesus Christ' (Ign. *Magn.* 1:2; cf. Acts 16:7; 1 Pet. 1:11), 'the Spirit . . . who is Christ' (Ign. *Magn.* 15:1); further 'the Spirit is Christ' (2 *Clem.* 14:4), 'the Holy Spirit . . . is the Son of God' (*Herm. Sim.* 9:1:1).[19]

There is nothing like this in the PE. Nor is there any use of the flesh/spirit contrast (except in 1 Tim. 3:16). There is no development of trinitarian formulae.

There is certainly a diversity of teaching in the AF, with some statements that are peculiar to individual writers and at times idiosyncratic. The PE show none of these developments. On the whole, it would seem that they are as close, if not closer, to Paul than they are to the AF.

In his brief treatment of the Spirit in the AF, E. Schweizer recognised that the New Testament kerygma still retained its force but concentrated on noting three dangers that he found to be present in the development of doctrine. These are: (1) a stress on the idea of spiritual substance in the preexistent Lord and on the union of flesh and spirit in Christ, making the resurrection of believers possible; (2) a confusion of the Spirit with unusual psychic phenomena; and (3) the conferral of the Spirit on those ordained to office rather than the choice of those endowed with the Spirit to minister.[20]

This is a rather negative estimate of the situation. The New Testament asserts that God is Spirit, and any development of the belief that the Saviour was preexistent would necessarily think of him also as Spirit. Certainly the language of flesh and spirit in the believer is characteristic of Ignatius, but his teaching is similar to that of Paul. The belief that the Spirit could initiate unusual psychic experiences is also not foreign to the New Testament, as in the

19. Hawthorne, "Holy Spirit," pp. 490-91.

20. E. Schweizer, in *TDNT,* 6:451.

case of Philip in Acts 8 and John the Seer. Neither of these points happens to occur in the PE.[21]

More importance attaches to the question of the Spirit and ministry. Here Schweizer's view of ministry and leadership in the New Testament reflects an estimate of the situation that has now become somewhat outmoded. The broad tendency in his time was to view the church as originally charismatic, with ministry being carried out spontaneously by those whom the Spirit gifted to do so (Romans; 1 Corinthians; 1 Thessalonians). Charisma then gave way to office, and the activity of the Spirit tended to be confined to those who were ordained to office and received the charisma by the laying on of hands. Such a development was traced in the later documents of the New Testament, and not least in the PE.

It is now recognised that this picture is a considerable simplification of a more complex phenomenon.[22] From the start we can trace a system of leadership and oversight alongside the tasks of ministry (1 Thessalonians; 1 Corinthians), and there is overlap in that some leadership is more by appointment (e.g., apostleship and local eldership), whereas other leadership is more charismatic. The picture in Acts 6 is of the recognition and appointment of people already specially endowed with the Spirit. In the PE those to be appointed are already godly people, although there is no specific mention of spiritual endowment. Perhaps this is taken for granted since the Spirit is generously poured out on all believers (Titus). Certainly there is prayer for fresh endowment on leaders.

In Ignatius the essential role of a three-level leadership is strongly emphasised, and it is 'confirmed and established by his Holy Spirit'. In *1 Clement* church leaders are established by the Spirit and speak by the Spirit, but this is in a context of upholding their authority over against opposition. The church leaders appointed by the apostles were the 'first fruits' (cf. 1 Cor. 16:15). The activity of prophets, who are almost by definition not 'official' appointees, is reflected in the *Didache* and *Hermas*. Otherwise, there is little if any reference to ministry (as distinct from leadership) by other members of the congregation at

21. Dunn, *Jesus*, 347-50, sets out this view of the subordination of the charismata to office, ritual and tradition in the PE (see also J. D. G. Dunn, *Unity and Diversity in the New Testament: An Enquiry into the Character of Earliest Christianity* [London: SCM, 1977], pp. 196-98; idem, *The Christ and the Spirit*, vol. 2: *Pneumatology* [Edinburgh: T&T Clark, 1998], pp. 18-19, 252-53). He appears to be critical of the way in which the Spirit is associated more with the passing on and preservation of tradition than with new revelations; but may it not be that in the context of developing error this was precisely the route that the church had to take?

22. A. D. Clarke, *Serve the Community of the Church: Christians as Leaders and Ministers* (Grand Rapids: Eerdmans, 2000). Cf. Trebilco, "Significance."

large. There is thus rather more stress on the church leaders in some of the AF, especially *1 Clement* and Ignatius, but this is not accompanied by a significant development in the tying of the work of the Spirit to the appointed leaders.

The result of this survey is to demonstrate that the PE represent a stage on the way to the AF, in which, although the endowment of all believers with the Spirit is strongly affirmed, there is less attention to the role of the Spirit in ministry in the congregation and more on the Spirit's role in relation to leaders. At the same time the PE do not develop the more speculative ideas that we find in some of the AF. It is probably fair to say that the PE stand closer to Paul and to the rest of the New Testament than they do to the AF, and, for what it is worth, this may be another pointer to an earlier date for them.[23]

23. It is a privilege to be invited to share in this conversation with Jimmy on an aspect of the understanding of the Holy Spirit in the New Testament and to be given the opportunity to thank him for his stimulating insights and to express my good wishes for his continuing scholarly work.

XXI The Spirit of God in Us Loathes Envy: James 4:5

Richard Bauckham

It is understandable that the letter of James hardly ever appears in the discussion of New Testament pneumatology. The word πνεῦμα occurs only twice (2:26; 4:5), and only one of these references could conceivably refer to the Holy Spirit or Spirit of God. But whether the words τὸ πνεῦμα in Jas. 4:5 refer to the divine Spirit or to the/a human spirit is only one of the many debatable aspects of this verse and cannot be decided without discussion of other controverted issues. According to most, though not all interpreters, the reference to τὸ πνεῦμα occurs in a short quotation from Scripture (ἡ γραφή), but the quotation is not to be found in any of our Hebrew or Greek texts of the Bible. Perhaps it is from an apocryphal work no longer extant. But the quotation also presents a series of problems of translation which together make a whole series of proposed translations apparently possible. Deciding between such proposed translations is not easy.[1] In this essay we shall review the proposed translations of the verse, finding none of them wholly satisfactory, and then offer a new proposal. It is this proposal, which takes τὸ πνεῦμα to be the Spirit of God, that justifies the inclusion of this essay in the present volume. The new proposal for translating the verse will then lead to a suggestion about the source from which James drew this quotation.

1. W. Popkes, *Der Brief des Jakobus* (THKNT 14; Leipzig: Evangelische Verlagsanstalt, 2001), pp. 269-71, considers the problem insoluble.

I. The Problem of Translation

(1) In the first place, we must note a text-critical issue. The readings κατῴκισεν ('he made to dwell') and κατῴκησεν ('he took up residence') are both attested: in the former case the subject of the verb must be God (understood) while in the latter case it must be τὸ πνεῦμα. Nearly all modern scholars[2] prefer the former as the harder reading, both because scribes are more likely to have replaced the verb κατοικίζειν ('to make to dwell'), used only here in the New Testament, with the much more common κατοικεῖν ('to dwell'), than vice versa,[3] and because scribes who understood τὸ πνεῦμα to be a spirit of envy might wish to avoid the idea that God made such a spirit dwell in humans.[4]

(2) There is also a question about how to punctuate the verse. Most translations and scholars take ἡ γραφὴ λέγει ('the Scripture says') to introduce a scriptural quotation and take the rest of the verse (πρὸς φθόνον ἐπιποθεῖ τὸ πνεῦμα ὃ κατῴκισεν ἐν ἡμῖν) to be that quotation. However, since these words cannot easily be understood as a quotation from the known text of the canonical Jewish scriptures, various other ways of punctuating and interpreting the verse have in the past been proposed, sometimes involving taking πρὸς φθόνον with λέγει, often involving treating the second part of the verse, along with the opening words of the next verse (μείζονα δὲ δίδωσιν χάριν: 'but he gives greater grace'), as a parenthesis, such that ἡ γραφὴ λέγει in v. 5 refers to the quotation from Prov. 3:34 in v. 6.[5] The version of this view that has been advocated by some recent scholars is that which reads v. 5 as two rhetorical questions: 'Or do you think that the Scripture speaks in vain? Does the spirit that he [God] made to dwell in us desire enviously?' According to Sophie Laws, who pioneered this interpretation in recent scholarship,[6] the second question alludes indirectly to scriptural passages, while according to others both questions refer forwards to

2. One exception is J. Adamson, *The Epistles of James* (NICNT; Grand Rapids: Eerdmans, 1976), p. 165.

3. B. M. Metzger, *A Textual Commentary on the Greek New Testament* (Stuttgart: United Bible Societies, 1975), p. 683.

4. R. W. Wall, *Community of the Wise: The Letter of James* (New Testament in Context; Valley Forge, Pa.: Trinity Press International, 1997), p. 203.

5. For references to and arguments against such proposals, see J. B. Mayor, *The Epistle of James* (2nd ed.; London: Macmillan, 1897), p. 136; J. H. Ropes, *A Critical and Exegetical Commentary on the Epistle of St. James* (ICC; Edinburgh: T&T Clark, 1916), pp. 262-63; M. Dibelius and H. Greeven, *James* (trans. M. A. Williams; Hermeneia; Philadelphia: Fortress, 1975), pp. 221-22.

6. S. Laws, 'Does Scripture Speak in Vain? A Reconsideration of James iv. 5,' *NTS* 20 (1974): 210-15; S. Laws, *A Commentary on the Epistle of James* (BNTC; New York: Harper & Row, 1980), pp. 176-79; followed by T. C. Penner, *The Epistle of James and Eschatology* (JSNTSup 121; Sheffield: Sheffield Academic Press, 1996), p. 152.

the scriptural quotation in v. 6.[7] The plausibility of such an interpretation will be discussed below.

(3) Besides punctuation there are a series of other issues about the translation of the second part of the verse.[8] The main issues are: (a) Does πρὸς φθόνον indicate the goal of the action of the verb ἐπιποθεῖ ('longs for envy') or should it be understood adverbially, as equivalent to φθονερῶς ('enviously'). (b) Does φθόνον have a bad sense ('envy') or a good sense ('jealously' in a good sense)? (c) Is the subject of ἐπιποθεῖ God (understood), making God the subject of both verbs, or τὸ πνεῦμα? (d) Is τὸ πνεῦμα the divine Spirit or the human spirit (understood as either good or bad)? Different answers to these questions in different combinations account largely for the differences of translation of the second part of the verse. We shall consider first the main translations offered of the second part of the verse by those who consider it a quotation introduced by ἡ γραφὴ λέγει, and then the translations that treat it as a question.

(3.1) Among scholars over the last century, the most popular option has been the translation: 'He [God] longs jealously for the spirit he has made to dwell in us.'[9] Among major English translations, this is adopted by the RSV and the NRSV (and cf. the RV margin). This translation takes πρὸς φθόνον adverbi-

7. L. T. Johnson, *The Letter of James* (AB 37A; New York: Doubleday, 1995), pp. 280-82; Wall, *Community of the Wise*, pp. 202-4. Johnson's earlier study ('James 3:13–4:10 and the *Topos* περὶ φθόνου,' *NovT* 25 [1983]: 330-31, 346) follows Laws in general but does not make clear what he takes to be the referent of ἡ γραφὴ λέγει in v. 5.

8. There have also been proposals to amend the text, though these do not seem to have appealed to any recent scholars; cf. J. A. Findlay, 'James iv.5, 6,' *ExpTim* 37 (1926): 381-82 (θόνον for φθόνον); some earlier attempts at emendation are listed in H. Coppieters, 'La Signification et la Provenance de la Citation Jac. iv,5,' *Revue Biblique* 12 (1915): 38.

9. For example, F. J. A. Hort, *The Epistle of St. James* (London: Macmillan, 1909), pp. 93-94; Ropes, *A Critical and Exegetical Commentary*, pp. 262-65; J. Moffatt, *The General Epistles* (Moffatt New Testament Commentary; London: Hodder & Stoughton, 1928), pp. 60-61; J. Marty, *L'Épître de Jacques* (Paris: Félix Alcan, 1935), pp. 159-60; H. Windisch and H. Preisker, *Die katholischen Briefe* (3rd ed.; HNT 15; Tübingen: Mohr [Siebeck], 1951), pp. 26-27; C. Spicq, ''Επιποθεῖν, Désirer ou Chérir?' *Revue Biblique* 64 (1957): 189-91; J. Jeremias, 'Jac 4 5: ἐπιποθεῖ,' *ZNW* 50 (1959): 137-38; F. Mussner, *Der Jakobusbrief* (HTKNT 13/1; Freiburg: Herder, 1964), pp. 181-82; C. L. Mitton, *The Epistle of James* (London: Marshall, Morgan & Scott, 1966), pp. 154-56; Dibelius and Greeven, *James*, pp. 223-24; P. Davids, *The Epistle of James* (NIGTC; Exeter: Paternoster, 1982), 163-64; D. J. Moo, *The Letter of James* (Tyndale New Testament Commentary; Leicester: Inter-Varsity Press/Grand Rapids: Eerdmans, 1985), pp. 144-46; H. Frankemölle, *Der Brief des Jakobus* (Gütersloh: Gütersloher, 1994), pp. 602-5; M. Klein, *"Ein vollkommenes Werk": Vollkommenheit, Gesetz und Gericht als theologischen Themen des Jakobusbriefes* (Beiträge zur Wissenschaft vom Alten und Neuen Testament 17/19; Stuttgart: Kohlhammer, 1995), pp. 112-15; D. J. Moo, *The Letter of James* (Pillar New Testament Commentaries; Grand Rapids: Eerdmans/ Leicester: Apollos, 2000), pp. 188-90.

ally, gives φθόνον a good sense ('jealousy'), takes God to be the subject of ἐπιποθεῖ (it is, in fact, the only proposed translation that does), and understands τὸ πνεῦμα to be the human spirit (given in creation, as in Gen. 2:7). Its appropriateness to the context in James can be defended, as recently by Moo, for whom this is the decisive criterion for preferring this translation, given the inconclusive nature of other criteria in his view.[10]

However, this translation founders on its need to understand φθόνον in a good sense, as the divine jealousy (or zeal) frequently attributed to God in the Scriptures and in Jewish literature. The Greek word for this positive divine quality is always ζῆλος. The use of φθόνος in this sense is unattested and hardly conceivable, since in Hellenistic moral philosophy, while ζῆλος can be a vice or a virtue, φθόνος is always a vice.[11] For this reason Jewish writers, while frequently using ζῆλος of God, consistently avoid using φθόνος of God. The fact that φθόνος was often used of the gods of Greek mythology[12] in 'the true Greek sense of a spiteful god's envy of man'[13] would certainly not have recommended it to a Jewish writer wishing to speak of the God of Israel; indeed, the opposite would more likely be the case.[14] That the two words φθόνος and ζῆλος are often linked and can be used virtually synonymously (e.g., 1 Macc. 8:16; *1 Clem.* 3:2; 4:7; 5:2) is not a basis for thinking that James could, exceptionally, have used φθόνος positively of a divine attribute,[15] since the two words are used synonymously only in a bad sense, not in the good sense of ζῆλος. Moreover, even if we could think of James (or his source) inappropriately and incompetently using φθόνος of divine jealousy, it is scarcely credible that he could have done so *in this context.* James has used ζῆλος in a bad sense in 3:14 and the cognate verb ζηλοῦν also in a bad sense in 4:2. Luke Johnson has shown that themes common to the ancient moral *topos* on envy run through 3:13–4:10.[16] If James had wanted to distinguish the positive divine quality in v. 5 from the negative human qual-

10. Moo, *The Letter of James* (2000), p. 190.

11. Johnson, 'James 3:13–4:10,' p. 335 (and see the whole article); Johnson, *The Letter of James*, p. 281.

12. For example, Mayor, *The Epistle of James*, pp. 136-37.

13. Adamson, *The Epistle of James*, p. 171.

14. Davids, *The Epistle of James*, p. 163, is mistaken in claiming that G. W. H. Lampe, ed., *A Patristic Greek Lexicon* (Oxford: Oxford University Press, 1961), cites three passages in the Alexandrian fathers where φθόνος is used of God. On the contrary, these deny that God acts out of envy (φθόνος) and echo Plato's famous statements (*Phaedr.* 247a; *Tim.* 29e) that envy is absent from the divine realm; cf. P. W. van der Horst, *The Sentences of Pseudo-Phocylides* (Studia in Veteris Testamenti Pseudepigrapha 4; Leiden: Brill, 1978), pp. 163-64.

15. Davids, *The Epistle of James*, pp. 163-64; R. P. Martin, *James* (WBC 48; Waco, Tex.: Word, 1988), p. 150; Moo, *The Letter of James* (2000), p. 190.

16. Johnson, 'James 3:13–4:10,' pp. 327-47.

ity in the preceding passage, he should have used ζῆλος in v. 5 and φθόνος/φθονεῖν in the other cases. But even this might not have served the purpose of contrasting the two terms. In a passage so heavy with resonances of envy and using both terms, they are most likely both to be read in the same negative sense that is the only sense in which they are synonymous.

(3.2, 3.3) There are two translations which give a similar sense in English but differ at just one point in how they understand the Greek: (3.2) 'The spirit he [God] made to dwell in us longs for envy';[17] (3.3) 'The spirit he [God] made to dwell in us longs enviously.'[18] Among major English translations, 3.2 is adopted by the NEB ('The spirit which God implanted in man turns towards envious desires'), while 3.3 is apparently adopted by the REB ('The spirit which God implanted in us is filled with envious longings') and the NIV ('The spirit he caused to live in us envies intensely'). Both translations give φθόνον a bad sense, take τὸ πνεῦμα to be the subject of ἐπιποθεῖ, and understand τὸ πνεῦμα to be the human spirit. They differ in that 3.2 understands πρὸς φθόνον as the goal of the action of the verb, while 3.3 understands the phrase adverbially as equivalent to φθονερῶς. 3.2 is the less plausible of these options. Although the use of πρὸς after ἐπιποθεῖ,[19] as proposed by this translation, can be paralleled (LXX Ps. 41[42]:1: ἐπιποθεῖ ἡ ψυχή μου πρὸς σέ, ὁ θεός), it is hard to make much sense of 'longs for envy,' and advocates of this meaning often give ἐπιποθεῖ the reduced sense of 'tends, inclines,' which does not seem to be paralleled. The verb always refers to strong desire.

However, there is no such difficulty in understanding πρὸς φθόνον as an adverbial phrase equivalent to the adverb φθονερῶς (cf., e.g., similar phrases in Josephus, *B.J.* 2.534; *Ant.* 7.195; 12.398), as translation 3.3 does. It is true that the verb ἐπιποθεῖν generally has a good sense in the biblical literature,[20] but it certainly can have a bad sense when its object or some other aspect of the context implies that (e.g., Sir. 25:21; Ezek. 23:5, 7, 9 Aquila). An entirely possible translation of πρὸς φθόνον ἐπιποθεῖ would be 'lusts enviously.'

17. For example, Coppieters, 'La Signification,' pp. 35-50; Adamson, *The Epistles of James,* pp. 171-73; J. Marcus, 'The Evil Inclination in the Epistle of James,' *CBQ* 44 (1982): 608-9 n. 7, 621; L. J. Prockter, 'James 4.4-6: Midrash on Noah,' *NTS* 35 (1989): 625-26; C. Burchard, *Der Jakobusbrief* (HNT 15/1; Tübingen: Mohr [Siebeck], 2000), pp. 171-74.

18. For example, J. Chaine, *L'Épitre de Saint Jacques* (Études Bibliques; Paris: Gabalda, 1927), pp. 101-3; A. Meyer, *Das Rätsel des Jacobusbriefes* (Giessen: Töpelmann, 1930), p. 258; J. Michl, 'Der Spruch Jakobusbrief 4,5,' in J. Blinzler, O. Kuss, and F. Mussner, ed., *Neutestamentliche Aufsätze,* Festschrift for J. Schmid (Regensburg: Pustet, 1963), pp. 167-72; E. M. Sidebottom, *James, Jude and 2 Peter* (NCB; London: Nelson, 1967), pp. 52-53.

19. One would expect a direct object or ἐπί.

20. Spicq, ''Επιποθεῖν,' pp. 184-95.

If this phrase has a bad sense, as it does for both translations 3.2 and 3.3, then clearly τὸ πνεῦμα must be the human spirit. The most plausible account of the meaning, in that case, is that which sees here the Jewish idea of the 'evil inclination' (יצר),[21] which was based on Gen. 6:5; 8:17 and is well illustrated by Sir. 15:11-20.[22] This shows that the evil inclination was understood to belong to the created nature of humans, but that this did not make God directly responsible for evil, since humans have the choice whether to yield to the inclination or to resist it. Jas. 1:13-15 is very close to this passage of Sirach and certainly reflects a similar notion of the evil desire, which James there calls ἐπιθυμία. There are two difficulties about finding the same idea in Jas. 4:5. One is the word πνεῦμα. Can this be equivalent to ἐπιθυμία ('desire') in 1:14-15? It is true that in the Qumran literature רוח ('spirit') is used in a somewhat similar sense: Abraham 'did not choose according to the will of his own spirit (ברצון רוחו)' (CD 3:2-3; cf. the use of יצר in 2:16), and the well-known passage about the 'two spirits' God placed in humanity, to one of which, 'the spirit of deceit,' sin is attributed (1QS 3:17–4:26).[23] But even these passages use 'spirit' for the evil inclination only with some further specification. James's own anthropological use of πνεῦμα in 2:26 certainly does not have this sense. Secondly, while this translation of Jas. 4:5 fits well with the succeeding context (which would mean that for those who wish to resist the evil inclination God's grace is available and proves stronger), it does not follow so well from the preceding context. In what sense might those whom James has been attacking in the preceding verses think that the sentence quoted in v. 5 had been spoken 'in vain'? By simply acknowledging their envy as deriving from the inclination God placed in them at creation what does it say to counter their behaviour or their ideas? In spite of these difficulties, 3.3 is probably the most satisfactory of the translations that have been proposed.

(3:4) 'The Spirit he [God] made to dwell in us longs jealously': this translation, advocated by Mayor,[24] was adopted by the JB ('the spirit which he sent to live in us wants us for himself alone'), and is also given in the RV margin and the NIV margin. It gives φθόνον a good sense, understands πρὸς φθόνον adverbially, takes τὸ πνεῦμα to be the subject of ἐπιποθεῖ, and understands τὸ πνεῦμα

21. See esp. Marcus, 'The Evil Inclination,' pp. 606-21, for an account of this idea in Second Temple Jewish sources and in James.

22. But note that Di Lella in P. W. Skehan and A. A. Di Lella, *The Wisdom of Ben Sira* (AB 39; New York: Doubleday, 1987), pp. 271-72, understands יצר in 15:14 as free will. On the relationship of James to Sir. 15:11-20, see H. Frankemölle, 'Zum Thema des Jakobusbriefes im Kontext der Rezeption von Sir 2,1-18 und 15,11-20,' *Biblische Notizen* 48 (1989): 21-49.

23. But cf. also the two spirits in some passages of *Hermas:* O. J. F. Seitz, 'Two Spirits in Man: An Essay in Biblical Exegesis,' *NTS* 6 (1959-60): 82-95.

24. Mayor, *The Epistle of St. James*, pp. 136-40.

to be the divine Spirit. It also requires something to be understood as the object of ἐπιποθεῖ (Mayor interprets: 'The Spirit which he made to dwell in us jealously yearns for the entire devotion of the heart'). But it is untenable primarily for the same reason as translation 3.1: φθόνον cannot have a good sense.

(3.5) Ralph Martin offers this translation: 'The Spirit God made to dwell in us opposes envy.'[25] Of all the translations offered, this provides the best fit with the context, both preceding and following, but unfortunately it is hard to see how the Greek can mean this. Martin writes: 'The meaning must be that God's jealous yearning over his people is set over against (πρός + accusative) their "jealousy"; hence our rendering, admittedly more a paraphrase.'[26] But can πρὸς φθόνον ἐπιποθεῖ really mean 'opposes'? Mayor is surely right to object: 'πρὸς can only mean "against" when joined with a word that implies hostility: it cannot have this force when joined with a word which implies strong affection like ἐπιποθεῖ.'[27]

(3.6, 3.7) We turn finally to proposals to translate the verse, not as containing a quotation, but as two rhetorical questions. One such proposal (3.6) translates the whole verse thus: 'Or do you think that scripture speaks to no effect? Does the spirit which he made to dwell in us long enviously?'[28] This adopts the translation given above as 3.3, but turns it into a question. The scholars who propose this translation understand it as a question expecting the answer 'no.' The spirit is not the evil inclination, but the good spirit given by God, and so the reader is expected to respond, 'No, of course the spirit given by God does not envy!' This avoids the difficulty about the use of the word πνεῦμα which was raised in our discussion of translation 3.3. There is, however, a grammatical difficulty in that a question expecting a negative answer should include the particle μή, as Johnson admits.[29] This problem is avoided if the question is understood to expect an affirmative answer, as in Robert Walls's proposal to translate the verse (3.7): 'Or do you think that Scripture says foolish things? Does the spirit that God made to dwell within us incline us intensely towards envy?'[30] He takes τὸ πνεῦμα to be the evil inclination, and apparently thinks

25. Martin, *James*, p. 140.

26. Martin, *James*, p. 141.

27. Mayor, *The Epistle of St. James*, p. 138. Mayor is responding to older interpreters who took πρός to have the sense of 'against.'

28. Laws, 'Does Scripture Speak in Vain? A Reconsideration of James iv. 5,' pp. 212-15; idem, *A Commentary on the Epistle of James*, pp. 176-79; L. T. Johnson, 'James 3:13–4:10 and the *Topos* περὶ φθόνου,' pp. 330-31, 346; idem, *The Letter of James*, pp. 280-82; Penner, *The Epistle of James and Eschatology*, p. 152. The translation given is by Laws; Johnson translates similarly.

29. Johnson, *The Letter of James*, p. 282.

30. Wall, *Community of the Wise*, p. 202.

that the second question expects the answer yes, by contrast with the first question.[31] This translation is therefore subject to the same objections we made to translations 3.2 (of which this is the interrogative version) and 3.3. Moreover, all proposals to treat the latter part of this verse as other than a quotation face the objection that the formula ἡ γραφὴ λέγει elsewhere directly introduces a quotation (John 19:37; Rom. 9:17; 10:11; 1 Tim. 5:18), even when it is used interrogatively (Rom. 4:3; Gal. 4:30; cf. Rom. 11:2).

II. A New Proposal for Translation

Since none of the proposals reviewed above is entirely satisfactory, it is appropriate to offer a new proposal. This postulates that the quotation in Jas. 4:5 is taken from an apocryphal text originally written in Hebrew (and the Greek translation in Jas. 4:5 either taken by James from an already existing Greek translation of the apocryphal work or made by James himself).

The verb ἐπιποθεῖν is used 12 times in the Septuagint and renders no fewer than eight different Hebrew verbs in those occurrences which have an extant Hebrew *Vorlage*. One of these is תאב ('to long'), used in Ps. 118(119):174 ('I have longed for your salvation, O LORD'). This verb is rare in the Hebrew Bible. It occurs also in Ps. 119:40, and the cognate noun תאבה is used in Ps. 119:20. The only other occurrence of תאב is in Amos 6:8, where the Pi'el is used with God as the subject. This is problematic because the context here requires the verb תעב, a more common verb which in the Pi'el means 'to regard as an abomination, to abhor, to loathe' (with God as subject: Pss. 5:7; 106:40; with a human subject: Deut. 7:26; Pss. 5:7; 107:18; 119:163; Amos 5:10; Mic. 3:9). In Amos 6:8 the Septuagint has βδελύσσειν, indicating either that the *Vorlage* had מתעב instead of מתאב, or that the translator understood מתאב to have the same meaning as מתעב. Modern scholars and lexicographers regard מתאב in Amos 6:8 as a scribal error or a deliberate alteration replacing an original מתעב.[32] But it may be that some ancient Hebrew speakers thought of the two verbs תאב and תעב as the same verb with two different meanings: 'to long for' and 'to regard as an abomination.' Both meanings entail intense feeling, positive in one case, negative in the other.

The Hebrew original of the quotation in Jas. 4:5 may have used תעב/תאב

31. Wall, *Community of the Wise*, pp. 202-4.

32. W. R. Harper, *A Critical and Exegetical Commentary on Amos and Hosea* (ICC; Edinburgh: T&T Clark, 1905), p. 153 n.; J. L. Mays, *Amos* (Old Testament Library; London: SCM, 1969), p. 117 n.

in the sense of 'to abhor,' giving the meaning of the sentence: 'The Spirit [or spirit] God made to dwell in us abhors envy.' The translator used ἐπιποθεῖ πρός, which would appropriately translate תעב/תאב in the sense of 'to long for.' He attributed to the Greek verb ἐπιποθεῖν the same range of meaning as he attributed to תעב/תאב. He meant ἐπιποθεῖ πρός to mean 'abhors, is intensely opposed to,' but unfortunately ἐπιποθεῖν has the positive sense of תאב but not the negative sense of תעב. To extend the range of meaning of a word in one language to match the range of meaning of a word in another language is a natural error in translation.[33]

The translation, 'The Spirit [or spirit] God made to dwell in us abhors envy', is close to translation 3.5 above ('The Spirit God made to dwell in us opposes envy'), which we observed would, of the proposals hitherto made, make best sense in the context, but which seemed impossible as a rendering of James's Greek. The new proposal explains how such a meaning could have been intended owing to the improper use of ἐπιποθεῖν to translate תאב in this sentence. If the quotation is read attributing to ἐπιποθεῖ the strong meaning of the Hebrew תעב — 'the Spirit [or spirit] regards envy as an abomination, something to which God is implacably opposed' — it follows very well not only from 3:13–4:3, where envy is the theme, but also from 4:4, with its sharply dualistic correlation between friendship with the world and enmity with God. The quotation in 4:5 provides the scriptural basis for this by pointing out God's enmity towards envy. This contextual consideration makes it much more likely that, if this proposal for translation is correct, then τὸ πνεῦμα refers to the divine Spirit rather than the human spirit. A reference to the human spirit here would be an unnecessarily indirect way of pointing out God's own opposition to envy.

If we are correct in finding a reference in Jas. 4:5 to the divine Spirit indwelling Christians, is this a unique reference to the Holy Spirit in James? It has sometimes been observed that the way in which Jas. 3:13-18 speaks of the wisdom that 'comes down from above' and produces the fruits of ethical qualities in Christians resembles the Pauline understanding of the Holy Spirit, especially in Gal. 5:22-23,[34] where there is a contrasting list of works of the flesh (5:19-21) comparable with many of the vices James attacks in 3:14–4:3. Understanding James as deploying here a wisdom pneumatology (cf. Wis. 1:3-8; 7:7, 22-25; Sir.

33. Cf. J. M. Voelz, 'The Language of the New Testament,' in W. Haase and H. Temporini, eds., *Aufstieg und Niedergang der Römischen Welt*, pt. 2, vol. 25/2 (Berlin/New York: de Gruyter, 1984), pp. 957-58, for Greek words whose meaning was extended by their Jewish and Christian use to correspond to Semitic terms.

34. For example, Windisch and Preisker, *Die katholischen Briefe*, p. 26; Davids, *The Epistle of James*, p. 154.

24:3)[35] fits very well with our proposed understanding of the quotation in 4:5. Both the wisdom from above of 3:13-18 and the Spirit of 4:5 are opposed to envy.

III. The Source of the Quotation

We need not here review the many suggestions as to the source of the quotation in Jas. 4:5 which find some kind of basis for it in the Hebrew Bible, since our new proposal for translating the quotation provides a fresh starting point for considering this question.

One of the very few passages in the Hebrew Bible which could be understood as a warning against envy is the story of Eldad and Modad in Num. 11:25-30. It speaks of the Spirit that rested upon the seventy elders, with the result that they prophesied (11:25), and also upon Eldad and Modad, who were outside the camp at the time and also prophesied (11:26). Because this was anomalous, Joshua protested to Moses, asking him to stop Eldad and Modad from prophesying. Moses replied, 'Are you jealous (המקנא; LXX: μὴ ζηλοῖς) for my sake? Would that all the Lord's people were prophets, and that the Lord would put his Spirit on them' (11:29).

The reference to jealousy is picked up in an interesting way in Pseudo-Philo's *Biblical Antiquities*, where the content of Eldad and Modad's prophecy is said to have been that after Moses' death the leadership would pass to Joshua:[36] 'And Moses was not jealous *(zelatus)* but rejoiced when he heard them' (20:5). Despite the usually positive word *zelatus*, it is clear that jealousy here has a bad sense. The theme of jealousy is also taken up in a quite different way in Midrash *Num. Rab.* 15:19, where Moses, commanded by God to appoint seventy elders (Num. 11:16), wondered how to select this number from the twelve tribes without taking more from one tribe than from another, with the result that 'I will introduce jealousy between one tribe and another.' These examples illustrate how Jewish exegesis of this passage could seize on the reference to 'jealousy' (Num. 11:29) and develop it as a quality to be avoided.

35. J. A. Kirk, 'The Meaning of Wisdom in James: Examination of a Hypothesis,' *NTS* 16 (1969): 24-38, argues that wisdom in James functions in some respects as the Spirit does in other Jewish and Christian literature, and cites much evidence for the association of the Spirit with wisdom.

36. Cf. *Sifre Num.* 95: 'And what did they [Eldad and Modad] say as their prophecy? "Moses will die and Joshua will bring Israel into the Land"'; similarly *b. Sanh.* 17a; *Tg. Ps.-Jon. Num.* 11:26; *Tg. Neof. Num.* 11:26; *Num. Rab.* 15:19. All of these sources, apart from *Sifre,* also attribute to Eldad and Modad a prophecy about Gog and Magog (a tradition doubtless intended to explain Ezek. 38:18).

It is not difficult to imagine how a Jewish retelling of the story of Eldad and Modad could have expanded Moses' words to Joshua (Num. 11:29) and included the sentence: 'The Spirit God made to rest on us (dwell in us) abhors envy.' But where might James have found such a retelling of the biblical story? There was an apocryphal book of Eldad and Modad to which the ancient canonical lists refer, and of which we have only one explicitly attributed quotation. *Herm. Vis.* 2:3:4 reads: '"The Lord is near to those who turn to him," as it is written in the book of Eldad and Modad, who prophesied to the people in the wilderness.' That this quotation occurs in the *Shepherd of Hermas* is significant, because it is also in *Hermas* that a remarkable parallel to Jas. 4:5 is found: 'the Spirit which God made to dwell in this flesh' (τὸ πνεῦμα ὃ ὁ θεὸς κατῴκισεν ἐν τῇ σαρκὶ ταύτῃ)' (*Mand.* 3:1; cf. also *Mand.* 5:2:5; 10:2:6; 10:3:2). There is a similar passage, though with reference to the flesh of Jesus, in *Sim.* 5:6:5: 'The Holy Spirit which goes forth, which created all creation, God made to dwell in the flesh (κατῴκισεν ὁ θεὸς εἰς σάρκα) that he willed.' These three passages (Jas. 4:5; *Herm. Mand.* 3:1; *Sim.* 5:6:5) contain the only occurrences of the verb κατοικιζεῖν in Christian literature before Justin.

Other resemblances between James and *Hermas* have often been noticed.[37] Most significant of these is the word δίψυχος (Jas. 1:8; 4:8), a New Testament hapax, which occurs 19 times in *Hermas,* who also uses the verb διψυχεῖν 20 times and the noun διψυχία 16 times. This vocabulary also appears in a quotation from an unknown apocryphal work (called ἡ γραφή in *1 Clement* and ὁ προφητικὸς λόγος in *2 Clement*) which appears in both *1 Clem.* 23:3 and *2 Clement* 11:2 (δίψυχοι). Otherwise this vocabulary (completely unattested in non-Jewish, non-Christian Greek) is found in Jewish and early Christian literature before Clement of Alexandria only in *1 Clem.* 23:2; *2 Clem.* 11:5 (both with reference to the quotation); 19:2 (διψυχία); *Did.* 4:4; and *Barn.* 19:5 (both διψυχεῖν).[38] It has sometimes been suggested that the apocryphal quotation in *1 Clem.* 23:3 and *2 Clem.* 11:2 comes from the *Book of Eldad and Modad,*[39] and it

37. For example, Laws, *A Commentary,* pp. 22-23.

38. For the usage in the Fathers, see S. E. Porter, 'Is *dipsuchos* (James 1,8; 4,8) a "Christian" Word?' *Biblica* 71 (1990): 484-96. O. F. J. Seitz, 'Antecedents and Signification of the Term ΔΙΨΥΧΟΣ,' *JBL* 66 (1947): 218-19, shows that the title given to a fragment of Philo — περὶ δειλῶν καὶ διψύχων — does not imply that Philo actually used the word δίψυχος.

39. For example, J. B. Lightfoot, reported in M. R. James, *The Lost Apocrypha of the Old Testament* (London: SPCK, 1920) pp. 39-40; James himself thinks the apocryphal *Ezekiel* a more likely source of the quotation. O. J. F. Seitz, 'Afterthoughts on the Term "Dipsychos,"' *NTS* 4 (1958): 332-34, agrees with Lightfoot and goes on to speculate that the Book of Eldad and Modad might actually be the 'little book' which *Herm. Vis.* 2 describes and that Hermas himself was instrumental in the publication of the *Book of Eldad and Modad.*

has also been argued quite cogently that the work from which this apocryphal quotation was drawn was also the source of *Hermas*'s use of this very distinctive vocabulary.[40] We should note that one of the two occurrences of δίψυχος in James (4:8) is in close proximity to the quotation in 4:5. There are also other striking resemblances to *Hermas* in this immediate context (Jas. 4:7: cf. *Herm. Mand.* 12:5:2; Jas. 4:12: cf. *Herm. Mand.* 12:6:3). Finally, also in this immediate context James even has a quite close parallel (4:8: ἐγγίσατε τῷ θεῷ καὶ ἐγγίσει ὑμῖν) to the one explicit quotation we have from the Book of Eldad and Modad (*Herm. Vis.* 2:3:4: Ἐγγὺς κύριος τοῖς ἐπιστρεφομένοις).

We can conclude that there is considerable probability that the quotation in Jas. 4:5 comes from the apocryphal *Book of Eldad and Modad*, which was also well known in the Roman church,[41] quoted by *Hermas*, and described as ἡ γραφή in *1 Clement* (23:3) and ὁ προφητικὸς λόγος in *2 Clement* (11:2).

40. O. F. J. Seitz, 'Relationship of the Shepherd of Hermas to the Epistle of James,' *JBL* 63 (1944): 131-40. S. E. Porter, 'Is *dipsuchos*,' maintains that James is the source of all other occurrences of δίψυχος and its cognates, but can do so only by apparently just denying that *1 Clem.* 23:3 and *2 Clem.* 11:2 do quote an apocryphal source. While he recognizes that '*1* and *2 Clement* are not apparently directly summarizing or paraphrasing James at this point' (p. 476), it is wholly unclear what he thinks they are doing.

41. S. S. Marshall (subsequently S. Laws), 'Δίψυχος: A Local Term?' *Studia Evangelica* 6 = *Texte und Untersuchungen* 112 (1973): 348-51, argues that δίψυχος was a local term used in Jewish and Christian circles in Rome and may have been coined in a Greek-speaking Jewish community in Rome. On the relationship of the letter of James to the Roman church, see R. Bauckham, *James: Wisdom of James, Disciple of Jesus the Sage* (New Testament Readings; London/New York: Routledge, 1999), pp. 18, 23.

XXII Faithful Witness in the Diaspora: The Holy Spirit and the Exiled People of God according to 1 Peter

Joel B. Green

Writing for the expanded English edition of *Theologisches Begriffslexikon zum Neuen Testament*, James D. G. Dunn wrote of the Spirit in 1 Peter,

> 1 Peter's understanding of the Spirit is nicely typical of the NT — the Spirit of prophecy (1 Pet. 1:11), the inspirer of mission and the power of the gospel (1 Pet. 1:12), the power that sets men [*sic*] apart for God (1 Pet. 1:2) and transforms into the image of God's glory through suffering and persecution (1 Pet. 4:14), the mode of existence in the life beyond death. (1 Pet. 3:18; 4:6)[1]

Dunn's assessment of the pneumatology of 1 Peter echoes a common view of the thought of this letter more generally — namely, that it lacks a distinctive theology. Some, including Dunn himself, interpret this in positive terms, casting Peter in the role of mediator among early Christian theologians.[2] My own sense is that the essential coherence between the theology of this letter and the

1. James D. G. Dunn, "Spirit, Holy Spirit (NT)," *NIDNTT*, 3:693-707 (p. 705); repr. as "Spirit and Holy Spirit in the New Testament," in *The Christ and the Spirit*, vol. 2: *Pneumatology* (Grand Rapids: Eerdmans, 1998), pp. 3-21. Similarly, Ralph P. Martin, "The Theology of Jude, 1 Peter, and 2 Peter," in *The Theology of the Letters of James, Peter, and Jude*, by Andrew Chester and Ralph P. Martin (New Testament Theology; Cambridge: Cambridge University Press, 1994), p. 119.

2. James D. G. Dunn, *Unity and Diversity in the New Testament: An Inquiry into the Character of Earliest Christianity* (Philadelphia: Westminster, 1977), pp. 384-85; cf., e.g., F. F. Bruce, *Peter, Stephen, James, and John: Studies in Early Non-Pauline Christianity* (Grand Rapids: Eerdmans, 1979), pp. 42-43.

work of, say, Paul and James represents a strategic theological move on the part of Peter.[3] The challenges of pluralism outside the church and the experience of hostility in the larger empire more generally provide Peter an occasion for reflecting on and articulating what is common ground within the church. Challenges to the church from the outside provide the occasion for solidifying the church's roots in the ancient purpose of God, drawing out the continuity from Israel of old to the contemporary life of God's people, and remembering that the primary orientation of faithful life is the God and Father of our Lord Jesus Christ. Hence, the rhetoric and message of 1 Peter are inscribed deeply into the saga of Israel and so participate fully in the emerging Christian consensus, as Peter explores the significance of the great mural of Israel's story, interpreted now through the pivotal events of Jesus' life, death, and resurrection, and emphasizes the common ground of the faithful as they look for places to secure their feet in the struggle for faithful witness.

Even if the pneumatology of this letter is typical of the larger witness to the Spirit characteristic of the New Testament documents, the important question remains how pneumatology functions in this instance of Petrine theological discourse. How has Peter deployed a theology of the Spirit in this letter? What role does pneumatology serve in this Epistle concerned with the identity, constitution, and faithful witness of God's people in a world marked by hostility to Christian faith and life? These questions set our agenda.

I. Strangers in a Strange Land

Peter deploys a range of images to characterize his audience, to map their identity, so to speak. Among these, the one we might be tempted to read in the most literal fashion is the list of geographical locations enumerated in 1:1: "Pontus, Galatia, Cappadocia, Asia, and Bithynia." A straightforward reading is not without its problems, however, since the first and last names in the sequence, Pontus and Bithynia, had by the time of 1 Peter long been a single province, having been combined under Pompey in 63 BCE. The whole area to which Peter refers would have marked out the northern half of Asia Minor, but there is little suggestion in historical reminiscence, and even less within the letter itself, regarding the significance of this particular collocation of regions. The diversity oth-

3. Although I regard the apostle Peter as the author of this letter (see Paul J. Achtemeier, Joel B. Green, and Marianne Meye Thompson, *Introducing the New Testament: Its Literature and Theology* [Grand Rapids: Eerdmans, 2001], pp. 519-21), and will refer to the author as Peter, my argument does not depend on this attribution.

erwise characteristic of this part of the empire — the degree of Hellenization, the latitude in natural and economic resources, and the extent of Roman administrative and military presence, for example — was well on display in these environs. Given that geography is socially defined space, it is important to push further, though, to inquire into the role of this locale (these locales) within Peter's rhetoric. One observation of interest would be the *inclusio* constructed between the opening and closing of the letter: 1:1-2 (to the elect of Pontus, Galatia, Cappadocia, Asia, and Bithynia) and 5:13 (from the fellow elect of Babylon) — a connection that captures our attention all the more through the fact that Babylon is the only other geographical locale named in the letter. That Babylon functions at one and the same time to designate the city from which this letter is posted, Rome, and to identify the author and his faith community as dwelling in exile,[4] underscores what is already clear from the letter's opening. This is that the regions of Pontus, Galatia, Cappadocia, Asia, and Bithynia designate venues where Peter's audience is "not at home."

The location of Peter's readers as strangers in a strange land is a leitmotif of this letter. Linguistically, it is marked by such terms as παρεπίδημος (1:1; 2:11), διασπορᾶς (1:1), and πάροικος (2:11). In an interesting study, Troy Martin highlights the importance of this concept by identifying it as the "controlling metaphor," and this evaluation finds resonance in the work of Reinhard Feldmeier and Miroslav Volf.[5] Even if Martin's is an exaggerated assessment, as we shall see momentarily, this emphasis presses us appropriately to map Peter's readers further, both in terms of their social location and with regard to their theological habitation within the narrative of God's project. These come into focus in the experience of exile.

In what sense are Peter's model readers "exiles"? The antecedents are many: the expulsion of Adam and Eve from Eden (Gen. 3:24) and Abraham's life among the Hittites as "a stranger and alien" (Gen. 23:4), for example, as well as Babylonian exile in more recent memory, and, contemporarily, the realities of Jewish life under Roman rule.[6] Negatively, Peter's audience does not share

4. ἡ συνεκλεκτή is found only here (5:13) in the Greek Bible. Its connection with the opening ἡ ἐκλεκτός (1:1; cf. 2:4, 6, 9) is obvious. On the dual association of Babylon with Rome and, more generally, with "alienation or displacement," cf. J. Ramsey Michaels, *1 Peter* (WBC 49; Waco, Tex.: Word, 1988), p. 311.

5. Troy W. Martin, *Metaphor and Composition in 1 Peter* (SBLDS 131; Atlanta: Scholars, 1990): Reinhard Feldmeier, *Die Christen als Fremde: Die Metapher der Fremde in der antiken Welt, im Urchristentum and im 1. Petrusbrief* (WUNT 64; Tübingen: J. C. B. Mohr [Paul Siebeck], 1992); Miroslav Volf, "Soft Difference: Theological Reflections on the Relation between Church and Culture in 1 Peter," *Ex Auditu* 10 (1994): 15-30.

6. For evidence of the understanding that Israel's exile was still in progress in the first

with their forebears in Israel the experience of exile in the sense of their having been forcibly removed from their homes. Nor is there any hint in 1 Peter that the status of Peter's readers as exiles rested on their lack of faithfulness to the covenant. The opposite is closer to the mark: their election by God serves as the theological basis of their life as aliens.[7] Nevertheless, they identify, or are called upon to identify, with Israel-in-exile. And, borrowing the language and promise of Exodus and New Exodus, Peter sets before them the hope of salvation that marks exile's end.

Thus, although those believers to whom Peter addresses this letter have not been drawn into a new geographical space, they have been born anew (1:23) within the space they had previously inhabited. They belong, but they do not belong. As Volf helpfully observes, "Christians do not come into their own social world from the outside seeking either to accommodate to their new home (like second generation immigrants would), shape it in the image of the one they have left behind (like colonizers would), or establish a little haven in the strange new world reminiscent of the old (as resident aliens would)."[8] Peter's exiles are not "Jews" living among "Gentiles" in the expected sense of these terms, then, as though the author were concerned with their ethnic or nationalistic status, at least as such status was normally construed. Attempts to find in Peter's descriptive terms a reference to his readers' economic status[9] founders similarly on a problem of category. One's social status was a product of numerous, intersecting considerations, relative income or access to the means of production being only one of them. In fact, there is no basis within the letter itself for suggesting that Peter's audience occupied any rung on the ladder of economic measurement other than would have been characteristic of the broad spectrum of people living in Asia Minor, sans persons of the ruling elite.

John Barclay has analyzed the way in which Diaspora Judaism responded to its environment with reference to assimilation (i.e., a measurement of social integration, including social interaction and practices), acculturation (i.e., the degree of linguistic, educational, and ideological achievement), and accommodation (i.e., the practical utility of acculturation, whether to embrace or resist

---

century CE, see the convenient survey of relevant materials in Craig A. Evans, "Jesus and the Continuing Exile of Israel," in *Jesus and the Restoration of Israel: A Critical Assessment of N. T. Wright's "Jesus and the Victory of God"* (ed. Carey C. Newman; Downers Grove, Ill.: InterVarsity, 1999), pp. 77-100.

7. Georg Strecker, *Theology of the New Testament* (New York/Berlin: Walter de Gruyter; Louisville: Westminster John Knox, 2000), p. 637.

8. Volf, "Soft Difference," pp. 18-19.

9. As in, say, John H. Elliott, *A Home for the Homeless: A Sociological Exegesis of 1 Peter, Its Situation and Strategy* (Philadelphia: Fortress, 1981).

one's surrounding culture).[10] We may gather from this sort of analysis that identity and boundary maintenance were pivotal to exilic life: Who are *we* in relation to *them?* What is the basis of *our* constitution as a community? What are *our* characteristic practices? By what strategies are these maintained? The metaphorical world within which Peter's model readers dwell is qualified, on the one hand, by the temporal nature of the experience of diaspora in which the people of God are depicted as a journeying people (e.g., 1:3-12); and, on the other, as a people confronting the perennial challenges of the possibility and threat of assimilation and defection.[11]

We find ample evidence within this letter that Peter has addressed these sorts of questions and concerns, encouraging his audience to the sort of faithfulness that had traditionally attached itself to discourse in the Jewish diaspora. To take a single, though important case in point, in his biblical theology of exile, Smith-Christopher observes that "a stronger sense of 'community identity' arises under circumstances of minority, stateless existence."[12] A survey of descriptive language in 1 Peter bears this out.

Members of Peter's audience of Christian followers are epitomized with familial/household language and terms of endearment: "children" (1:14; 3:6), "infant" (2:2), "son" (5:13), "family" (lit. "brotherhood," 2:17; 5:9), "house/household" (2:5; 4:17), "servant/slave/household servant" (2:16, 18; 4:10), and "beloved" (2:11; 4:12). Given the prominence of familial language, the relational language used of God, "Father" (1:2, 3, 17), should not be overlooked as further evidence of this motif. Other appellatives Peter uses for his audience include "aliens/exiles" (1:1; 2:11), "chosen" (1:2; 2:9), "holy nation" (2:9), "God's (own) people" (2:9, 10), "priesthood" (2:5, 9), and "Christian" (4:16). These descriptors — some of which serve as direct address forms, others indirect — both estab-

10. John M. G. Barclay, *Jews in the Mediterranean Diaspora: From Alexander to Trajan (323 BCE to 117 CE)* (Hellenistic Culture and Society; Berkeley: University of California Press, 1996), pp. 92-102. The need for the sort of nuance Barclay introduces into the discussion is observable in the competing perspectives on Jewish response to Hellenism represented by Martin Hengel, *Judaism and Hellenism: Studies in Their Encounter in Palestine during the Early Hellenistic Period* (2 vols. in 1; Philadelphia: Fortress, 1974); and Louis H. Feldman, *Jew and Gentile in the Ancient World: Attitudes and Interaction from Alexander to Justinian* (Princeton, N.J.: Princeton University Press, 1993). Concerning the Jewish experience of the diaspora in this period, see also, e.g., John J. Collins, *Between Athens and Jerusalem: Jewish Identity in the Hellenistic Diaspora* (New York: Crossroad, 1983); Irina Levinskaya, *The Book of Acts in Its Diaspora Setting* (Acts in Its First-Century Setting 5; Grand Rapids: Eerdmans, 1996); James M. Scott, ed., *Exile: Old Testament, Jewish, and Christian Conceptions* (JSJSup 56; Leiden: Brill, 1997); Daniel L. Smith-Christopher, *A Biblical Theology of Exile* (OBT; Minneapolis: Fortress, 2002).

11. Cf., e.g., Martin, *Metaphor and Composition*, pp. 150-61.

12. Smith-Christopher, *Biblical Theology of Exile*, p. 141.

lish, assert, and uphold relationships between speaker/writer and readers/auditors, and instantiate a strong semantics of solidarity within the communities of the letter's destination.[13] In the context of the ancient Mediterranean, we might expect metaphors of household and family to signal relations of status and power, but this is not the case here, where all are children and servants in the household of Father God.[14] It is true that Peter refers to himself as "elder," potentially suggesting his authority in a hierarchical pattern of relationships, but he immediately relativizes his own position by referring to "elders among you," by insisting that the work of an elder is aimed at the benefit of others rather than self-aggrandizement,[15] by rejecting lordly behavior while countenancing humility, and by a reminder that the true leader, the Chief Shepherd, will come in judgment (5:1-5).

If not to establish relations of status between sender and receiver, how do these descriptors function? They serve as identity markers for persons whose experiences of opposition in the larger world of northern Asia Minor would have undermined any conventional claim to status before God and possibly would have splintered their experience of oneness. For example, John Elliott associates ἡ ἐκλεκτός with ἡ ἀδελφότης in this letter[16] — the latter term appearing in the New Testament only in 1 Pet. 2:17; 5:9, and in the LXX in 1 Macc. 12:10, 17; 4 Macc. 9:23; 10:3, 15; 13:19, 27. The potential association with 4 Maccabees is especially interesting since not only the sense of "(the character and heritage of) the family of believers" but especially "the family of believers called to faithful testimony in the face of hostility" would be suggested. In a world that honored deep roots of tradition, many of these appellations anchored Peter's audience in the solid granite of Israel's ancient story — giving them both a strong sense of identity in unbroken connection to the distant past and, because it is especially the Israel of Exodus and New Exodus with whom they are encouraged to identify, the sure hope of liberation. As exilic identity is a matter of disciplined life oriented toward survival as a distinct people, so, in the present, they are to embody the call to Israel in Exodus and Exile to be holy. As a priestly people, a holy nation, they would embrace the

13. Cf. Ralph Fasold, *Introduction to Sociolinguistics*, vol. 2: *Sociolinguistics of Language* (Language in Society 6; Cambridge: Blackwell, 1990), pp. 1-38.

14. More generally, cf. Eva Marie Lassen, "The Roman Family: Ideal and Metaphor," in *Constructing Early Christian Families: Family as Social Reality and Metaphor* (ed. Halvor Moxnes; London: Routledge, 1997), pp. 103-20.

15. προθύμως, used only here in the New Testament: "eager to meet the needs of others rather than seek gain for themselves" (BDAG, p. 870).

16. John H. Elliott, *1 Peter: A New Translation with Introduction and Commentary* (AB 37B; New York: Doubleday, 2000), pp. 880-82.

missional vocation to be "holy" — that is, "different" or "distinctive" — in the midst of the Gentiles (e.g., 2:9-12).

Thus, on the positive side of the ledger, dispositions and behaviors encouraged throughout the letter are grounded in these forms of address, in this identity, while, on the negative side, these very dispositions and behaviors had become the impetus for the hostility with which Peter's model readers were by now intimate. Transformed allegiances and practices located them on the margins of honorable society. They had become the victims of social ostracism, their allegiance to Christ having won for them slander, animosity, reproach, scorn, vilification, and contempt. In the household of the Roman Empire, status was achieved via conformity to dispositions that had become so conventional that they were largely unspoken, "what everyone knows"; noncompliance and other forms of social distinctiveness were valued negatively. Within the empire, Peter envisions an audience that lives as though they belonged to another household, one headed by God the Father (1:1-2; 1:13–2:10). If "glory" or "honor" (δόξα) was the fundamental social currency of the Roman world, Peter's audience seems to have experienced bankruptcy. As with Israel in the diaspora,[17] then, these persons whom God has made "a people" are bonded through a combination of ancestry (in this case, their lineage in a shared story as heirs of Israel) and shared dispositions and characteristic behaviors.

As important as it is for Peter that his auditors identify themselves with Israel, so that "the language and hence the reality of Israel pass without remainder into the language and hence the reality of the new people of God,"[18] it is even more important that we grasp that the narrative of Israel is itself determined by the story of Jesus and by the soteriological journey and eschatological hope it engenders. The Israel into whose history Peter writes his audience is *Israel as interpreted* by the suffering, death, resurrection, ascension, and pending revelation of Jesus Christ. Similarly, although Peter sketches a number of characteristic dispositions and behaviors for his readers, it is of real significance that his concern is not so much to segregate Christian communities from the larger world as it is to tie them firmly to their center. Peter does not engage in invective rhetoric against "the world at large," as though Christian identity and behavior were fundamentally defined in oppositional terms over against non-Christians. Nor does he counsel retreat from the world, as though the demands of holiness might necessarily be parlayed into patterns of isolation.[19] His audi-

17. Cf. Barclay, *Jews in the Mediterranean Diaspora*, pp. 402-13.

18. Paul J. Achtemeier, *1 Peter* (Hermeneia; Minneapolis: Fortress, 1996), p. 69.

19. Indeed, their lives in the world were to be such that others would be won over (e.g., 2:9, 12, 15; 3:1-2; cf. 3:18).

ence is to work out the nature of holiness as aliens in this world. Christian identity and practice are not defined negatively vis-à-vis those who reject the ways of Yahweh, but positively in relation to the way of Jesus Messiah. Indeed, the logic of Peter's Christology is grounded in and oriented toward the new lives of those who are enabled and called to follow Christ.

To put it differently, Peter works less to construct a perimeter as to define a center, and he does this by locating his audience geographically — not at the most basic level as persons of the diaspora, but rather as persons "in Christ." Alien status or diasporic life do not constitute the "controlling metaphor" for Peter's message in 1 Peter. That designation belongs to another point of orientation by which Peter has mapped the location of his readers. Peter's model readers certainly comprised "a stateless minority in the context of a massive empire,"[20] but, for Peter, the lives of these followers of Christ are determined decisively not by their location in the empire but by their habitation of a space he designates in 3:16; 5:10, 14 as "in Christ."

Given that Peter prioritizes his description of his audience as aliens, strangers, outsiders, the ostracized, we might justifiably ask, Where might they be "at home"? Ultimately, of course, one might reply that Peter locates the "inheritance" of his readers "in heaven" (1:4). Certainly, he disallows any suggestion that they might find a home or gain their bearings ἐν τοῖς ἔθνεσιν (2:11-12), as it is such people whose lives are characterized by "licentiousness, passions, drunkenness, revels, carousing, and lawless idolatry" (4:3) as well as "excesses of depravity" and blasphemy (4:4). Indeed, reference to "in" (ἐν, referring to boundedness within a container, whether spatial, temporal, or a state or condition) implies an "out," and ἐν τοῖς ἔθνεσιν may designate "the outside" — or, perhaps better, serve well as a précis of that place within which those who follow Christ can only be strangers. Just as the letter begins by declaring model readers as strangers of the diaspora, so it ends with a climactic declaration of their true domicile; their life is "in Christ" (5:10, 14) — a life defined, then, throughout the letter in christological terms with particular reference to the redemptive and exemplary journey of Jesus through suffering and death to his exaltation. The passion of Christ, Peter affirms, was both atoning and exemplary: "Christ suffered on your behalf, leaving you a pattern so that you might follow in his footsteps" (2:21).

20. So Smith-Christopher characterizes the Hebrews in exile (*Biblical Theology of Exile,* p. 144).

II. Spirit and Exile

How are these ruminations apropos the pneumatology of 1 Peter? We have identified and may now explicitly surface two major, interrelated challenges of diasporic living, according to 1 Peter: the threat of assimilation and the concomitant need to pursue a holy life; and the need to give meaning to the struggles of life in the diaspora. The pneumatology of 1 Peter is oriented to both concerns. Since the Spirit is the divine agent of sanctification and the enabler of charismatic (or inspired) exegesis, his work is, in 1 Peter, intimately tied to faithful life as strangers in a strange land. A brief examination of those texts in 1 Peter in which the Spirit appears will undergird this thesis.

1 Peter 1:1-2; 4:12-14

In the Epistle's opening address, Peter qualifies the status of his audience as "elect strangers" with three, parallel, prepositional phrases:

κατὰ πρόγνωσιν θεοῦ πατρὸς
ἐν ἁγιασμῷ πνεύματος
εἰς ὑπακοὴν καὶ ῥαντισμὸν αἵματος Ἰησοῦ Χριστοῦ

The first, with its reference to election "according to the foreknowledge of God," is more straightforward than the second and third, the relationship of which is debated. εἰς, taken in its telic sense, would relate the second and third clauses as cause and effect — that is, the sanctifying work of the Spirit is for the purpose of obedience and sprinkling of blood. This view falters on the question, What would it mean to say that sanctification results in "the sprinkling of the blood of Jesus Christ"? Drawing on the background of the notion of "sprinkling of blood" in Exod. 24:3-8, Achtemeier ingeniously theorizes that Peter refers to "the sanctifying action of the Spirit to the end that they be the people of a new covenant, which like the covenant of Israel entails obedience and sacrifice, in this case the sacrifice of Christ."[21] This requires that we relate "obedience" to the elect as subject but blood sprinkling to Jesus Christ as subject, a reading that would be confusing grammatically; or that we take "obedience" absolutely, without reference to Christ. If we follow the grammatical work of Francis Agnew, a more ready solution is at hand.[22] Taking εἰς as causal rather

21. Achtemeier, *1 Peter,* p. 89.

22. Francis H. Agnew, "1 Peter 1:2: An Alternative Translation," *CBQ* 45 (1983): 68-73.

than telic and Ἰησοῦ Χριστοῦ as a subjective genitive yields the translation, "because of the obedience and sprinkling of blood of Jesus Christ." This reading coheres with Peter's larger emphasis on the exemplary and redemptive faithfulness of Christ, demonstrates the interrelation of Christology and pneumatology in Peter's theology, and underscores the balance in these three phrases, which then focus on the activity of God, the Spirit, and Jesus Christ. That the Spirit's work here is for the purpose of the believer's obedience is widely held.[23] The exegesis adopted here does not vacate Peter's letter of this notion, but instead asserts from the very beginning the basis of the life of the elect in the life of Christ.

Here, as in 4:12-14, the Spirit is identified as the agent of God's power. In this case, the Spirit is oriented toward the work of "making holy" — a motif of significance elsewhere in the letter (1:15, 16, 19, 22; 2:5, 9; 3:15). Of special interest is the exegesis of scriptural material in 2:4-10, where holiness is collocated with human rejection but divine election. Evidently, the antidote to the threats of exilic life is the empowering work of the Spirit, who enables God's people not only to survive as a distinct people but to embody the call to Israel in Exodus and Exile to be holy. This way of thinking surfaces in 4:11-14, where Christian speech in the midst of testing draws on "the strength that God supplies," "because the spirit of glory, which is the Spirit of God, is resting on you" (cf. Isa. 11:2).

As a corollary to this way of thinking, it is worth asking whether the preposition ἐν (in the phrase ἐν ἁγιασμῷ πνεύματος [1:2]) ought to be read, as is typical, as instrumental. If we recall the Petrine concern to locate his readers on the map, so to speak, we might press for a reading of "in the sanctification of the Spirit" as a close semantic cousin of that other "place," "in Christ." To put it differently, "because of the obedience and sprinkling of blood of Jesus Christ," Peter's auditors have been relocated in a new space: "in the realm of holiness engendered by the Holy Spirit."[24]

Peter's theology at this juncture resonates with that of another wilderness community: Qumran, whose *Rule of the Community* has it that the Spirit is integral to cleansing and holiness (e.g., 1QH 3.7-8; 9.3-4; 14.13-14; 16.15-20). In other early Jewish texts, too, sanctification is tied to the reception and activity of the Spirit.[25]

23. For example, David Peterson, *Possessed by God: A New Testament Theology of Sanctification and Holiness* (New Studies in Biblical Theology; Grand Rapids: Eerdmans, 1995), pp. 64-65.

24. Thus, taking πνεύματος as a genitive of production; for this construction, cf. Daniel B. Wallace, *Greek Grammar beyond the Basics: An Exegetical Syntax of the New Testament* (Grand Rapids: Zondervan, 1996), pp. 104-6.

25. See the discussion in John R. Levison, "Holy Spirit," in *Dictionary of New Testament Background* (ed. Craig A. Evans and Stanley E. Porter; Downers Grove, Ill: InterVarsity, 2000),

1 Peter 1:10-12; 4:12-14

Although the general sense of 1:10-12 is easy enough to grasp — the prophets of old and the gospel messengers of the present were both directed by the Spirit — one phrase remains especially controversial. Does πνεῦμα Χριστοῦ refer to the Spirit testifying concerning the Messiah or to the preexistent spirit of Christ? It is not clear that a choice between these two options is necessary since Christ was destined before the foundation of the world (1:20) and Peter has it that Jesus Christ is the one of whom the ancient prophets spoke. What is most crucial for our purposes here is that Peter thus determines how the Scriptures of Israel must be read — as testifying "in advance to the sufferings destined for Christ and his subsequent glory" and in continuity with the faith communities comprising Peter's audience, a continuity guaranteed by the Holy Spirit.[26]

Why is this important? It is increasingly clear from neurobiology that meaning making is central to our day-to-day experience, and that we will go to great lengths to construct stories that provide a context for understanding and interpreting our perceived realities. My "perception" of the world is based in a network of ever-forming assumptions about my environment and in a series of well-tested assumptions, shared by others with whom I associate, about "the way the world works." We typically explain our behaviors through the historical narratives by which we collaborate to create a sense of ourselves as persons. Memory, then, is not passive retrieval of information but active reconstruction, through which we seek coherence. Because we are intensely social beings, the stories we tell about ourselves, through which we construct our sense of self, are woven out of the threads and into the cloth of the stories present to us in our social world and communal traditions. Consequently, embodied, social, human life performs like a neurohermeneutic system, locating (and, thus, interpreting) current realities in relation to our grasp of the past and expectations of the future.[27] How do we con-

---

pp. 507-14 (pp. 513-14); Matthias Wenk, *Community-Forming Power: The Socio-Ethical Role of the Spirit in Luke Acts* (JPTSup 19; Sheffield: Sheffield Academic Press, 2000), pp. 102-5.

26. Henry Barclay Swete anticipated much of the discussion on the use of Scriptures of Israel by New Testament authors when he wrote, "This context is the *locus classicus* for the New Testament doctrine of Messianic Prophecy" *(The Holy Spirit in the New Testament: A Study of Primitive Christian Teaching* [London: Macmillan, 1919], p. 261). Thus, emphasis would fall on proof of Jesus' messiahship grounded in scriptural prophecy (classically, Barnabas Lindars, *New Testament Apologetic: The Doctrinal Significance of the Old Testament Quotations* [Philadelphia: Westminster, 1961]). This interest is misplaced, however, since Peter is not working to prove Jesus' messiahship (which he and apparently his audience take for granted — 1:1) but to show how to read the Scriptures ecclesiologically — that is, so as to legitimize and direct the life of God's people.

27. Cf. Daniel J. Siegel, *The Developing Mind: How Relationships and the Brain Interact to Shape Who We Are* (New York: Guilford, 1999); Stephen P. Reyna, *Connections: Brain, Mind, and*

strue the past and future, by which we make sense of the present? More particularly in this context, how might Peter's audience give significance to day-to-day experience when daily living can be cast under the heading of "suffering as a Christian" (cf. 4:16)?

What Peter's readers require is a way to locate their present, difficult circumstances within a web of meaning that would encourage persistent fidelity. Ready to hand were ways of construing the world that undermined any notion of their status as God's elect: How could they attract hostility and rejection if they were blessed with divine honor? Required is an alternative narrative, which Peter provides. Most basically, it is a particular way of articulating the beginning, middle, and end of the biblical story. The story of salvation is this: the prophets who prophesied in advance testified to the sufferings destined for Christ and the subsequent glory. How do we know this is the "true" story? How do we know that this reading of the story is true? They prophesied through the Spirit, and the gospel message, which embodies this story, was brought by means of the Spirit. In short, Peter presents the Holy Spirit as the enabler of authentic exegesis of Israel's story, Israel's Scriptures.

This exegesis functions, first, to tie the exemplary and salvific life of Jesus Christ into the ancient purposes of God found in Scripture, and, then, to tie the lives of these "aliens and strangers" into the life of Jesus Christ. As the fate of Christ is tied to that of the Christian readers of Peter's letter, so they can be assured that their suffering will have a redemptive effect and will lead to glory and honor from God just as Jesus' did.[28] This is the interpretation of things inspired by the Spirit.

1 Peter 4:12-14 provides a case study in this sort of exegesis. Taking up again the direct address "beloved" (see 2:11), Peter grounds his exhortation in the shared identity of his audience, then proceeds to shape the theological imagination of his readers. First, he interprets their suffering as a participation in the messianic woes of the end time. Although no biblical text is cited, Peter's thesis nevertheless represents a rather developed exegesis, along christological lines, of the scriptural expectation of the calamities that would accompany the advent of the age of salvation.[29] Second, Peter borrows the language of Isa. 11:2 to insist that suffering for Christ is the occasion of the anointing of the Spirit.

Culture in a Social Anthropology (London: Routledge, 2002); Joseph LeDoux, *Synaptic Self: How Our Brains Become Who We Are* (New York: Viking, 2002).

28. Cf. Barth L. Campbell, *Honor, Shame, and the Rhetoric of 1 Peter* (SBLDS 160; Atlanta: Scholars, 1998), pp. 55-56.

29. See Ezekiel 38–39; Joel 2; Zechariah 11–14; etc. On varieties of interpretation of this motif in Second Temple Judaism, see Dale C. Allison Jr., *The End of the Ages Has Come: An Early Interpretation of the Passion and Resurrection of Jesus* (Philadelphia: Fortress, 1985), pp. 5-25.

There was already a tradition of interpreting Isa. 11:2 with reference to a messianic figure, and here Peter appropriates the Isaianic text with reference to the suffering, messianic community. This is unsurprising, given his having already conjoined Jesus as messiah with the suffering Servant of Yahweh, and his interpretation of the character of Christian discipleship within the pattern of Isaiah's Servant of Yahweh (cf. 1 Pet. 2:22-25). In this way, hostility and suffering ("the fiery ordeal") are set within a narrative determined by an exegesis that writes the way of suffering for the sake of Christ into the way of Isaiah's messianic ruler. Rather than allowing the probable view that suffering and dishonor contravened the status of the elect before God, this exegesis appropriates the promise of the Spirit to rest on the believer precisely in the midst of distress.

Again, Peter's pneumatology at this point is not without precedent. Repeatedly in the literature of Second Temple Judaism — in Josephus, at Qumran, in Sirach, in Philo, and more — the Spirit of God is associated with the ability to appropriate the Scriptures.[30]

1 Peter 3:18; 4:6

These two texts stand in parallel and can be taken together. Whether either refers to the Holy Spirit is debated. Speaking against this reading is the parallel σαρκί — πνεύματι, which appears in both texts. How can Jesus be raised to life *by* the Spirit if he is put to death *in* the flesh (3:18)? (The same question is present with regard to 4:18, where "the dead" are in view.) Does not the balance of these two terms in the dative require symmetry in grammatical function?[31] One might answer in the affirmative, but construe the death-giving agent as human beings and the life-giving agent as the Spirit.[32] Alternatively, one might take one's cue from 4:1-2, wherein Peter juxtaposes suffering "in the flesh" with living "by the will of God" (σαρκί — θελήματι), which speaks against the need for simple grammatical balance. In any case, with regard to its contribution to our concerns, the primary import of the juxtaposition of these two texts is how they cement the motif of continuity between Christ and Christians: so in suffering and death, so in life and vindication. And this contributes to the larger motif in the letter, whereby Peter clothes his readers in the robes of the suffering and glory of Jesus Christ.

30. Levison, "Holy Spirit," pp. 512-13; idem, *The Spirit in First-Century Judaism* (AGJU 29; Leiden: Brill, 1997), pp. 254-59.

31. So, e.g., Elliott, *1 Peter*, p. 645.

32. As in Achtemeier, *1 Peter*, p. 250.

III. Conclusion

There is no reason to doubt the valuation of James Dunn that Peter's pneumatology is nothing but traditional. What is more, along the way I have hinted that the Spirit's work, as this is articulated in 1 Peter, is very much at home in the wider thought-world of Second Temple Judaism. But this sort of commonality does not detract from the further observation that the pneumatology of 1 Peter is deeply contextualized in the realities of the diasporic life of Peter's model readers. Peter wants his audience to find their true home "in Christ" rather than "among the Gentiles," and a rather conventional pneumatology is mobilized to that end. On the one hand, the Spirit guides the appropriation of the Scriptures, with the result that one embraces a christological hermeneutic that finds in its pages the suffering, death, and glorious vindication of Christ. In this way, Peter's model readers are given the wherewithal to locate their own suffering in the grand story of Israel, now comprehended christologically, and therefore they have reason to imagine that their own suffering will lead to redemption and vindication. On the other hand, the Spirit is the enabler of faithful living in the present. Given the pressures of exilic living, holiness — engagement in the world of nations as the people belonging uniquely to Yahweh and therefore representing his character and ways — is possible though the agency of the Spirit. Christians making their lives in the diaspora thus find themselves living in the realm of holiness effected by the Spirit.

XXIII "Test the Spirits": God, Love, and Critical Discernment in 1 John 4

R. W. L. Moberly

The first letter of John contains some of the most famous words of the whole Bible, so famous that they are regularly taken as a freestanding axiom that epitomizes Christian faith — "God is love" (1 John 4:8, 16). My purpose in this essay is to seek, if possible, to shed a little fresh light on what is, and is not, meant by these famous words.

The argument will revolve around the time-honored principle that one should not take words out of context, a principle sometimes easier to acknowledge than to observe. The tendency to take the Johannine "God is love" as a freestanding axiom with disregard for the exposition of which it forms a part is, I suspect, matched only by the comparable tendency to take the other most famous words about love in the New Testament, the Pauline "hymn to love" in 1 Corinthians 13, in isolation from their context of argument (1 Corinthians 12–14). Yet surely it is hardly accidental that each of these famous statements about love is situated within a similar context of concern for spiritual discernment (1 John 4:1; 1 Cor. 12:1-3). Attention to this contextual concern may enable a better understanding and use of what the New Testament has to say about love.

I am grateful to Marianne Meye Thompson for numerous improvements to a draft of this essay.

I. Introduction

First, although John's[1] purpose in writing has been characterized in many ways, I suggest that it may best be characterized as *articulating a critical theological epistemology* — or, in John's own, more straightforward, terminology, the key issue is, How can we know that we know God?[2] As John puts it at an early stage (2:3), "By this we know that we know him: . . . ," and his criterion is a demanding one, ". . . by keeping his commandments." The criteria for knowledge of God are, however, easily misrepresented ("I write this to you about those who would lead you astray," 2:26), and so toward the end John states his positive overall purpose, "I write this to you that you may know that you have eternal life . . ." (5:13).[3] John's concern is intrinsic to any form of Christian faith. For where notions of divine self-revelation and corresponding human knowledge of God play a crucial role, possibilities of error and the deception of either self or others abound. If faith in God in and through Jesus is in some way the key to human existence — as the Prologue to John's Gospel puts it — then there is a need for criteria not only to specify the content of this faith but also to determine when it is, and is not, truly present.

Secondly, the need to articulate such an epistemology is urgent since clearly some kind of schism had recently taken place within the community John addresses (2:18-19).[4] Yet although we might like to know more about the stance of John's "opponents," and although interpreters would be unwise to turn their backs on any source of illumination, in the case of 1 John we simply do not have any knowledge of context other than what may be gleaned from the

1. I use the conventional designation without prejudice to discussions of historical authorship.

2. The overall structure of the letter clearly indicates this concern ("the structure of the letter itself reproduces the process of self-analysis and testing"; Judith Lieu, *The Theology of the Johannine Epistles* [Cambridge: Cambridge University Press, 1991], p. 50). After the introduction (1:1-4), an affirmation about God (1:5) leads instantly into a series of denials and affirmations as to what human engagement with God entails (1:6–2:2), which then leads into the explicit statement of "knowing that we know him" (2:3-6). The letter concludes with a series of "we know" affirmations (5:18, 19, 20), which culminate in "We know that the Son of God has come and has given us understanding to know the one who is true . . . this is the true God and eternal life" and a corresponding warning to shun what is counterfeit and deceptive with regard to God, "Little children, keep yourselves from idols" (5:21).

3. The verbs γινώσκω (2:3) and οἶδα (5:13) are used interchangeably in the Gospel of John and 1 John. Likewise, "having eternal life" is not different from "knowing God" (cf. John 17:3).

4. Standard contextual proposals are conveniently set out with some preliminary evaluation in Ruth B. Edwards, *The Johannine Epistles* (New Testament Guides; Sheffield: Sheffield Academic Press, 1996), ch. 5.

letter itself (which is minimal). Whatever may have been affirmed or denied by others in John's context of writing, an understanding of the letter requires above all else *a grasp of the intrinsic logic of John's thought.*

Thirdly, John's pattern of thinking does not involve sequential logic in the manner of a conventional argument so much as the literary equivalent of musical variations on a theme — a constant circling around the basic issue, coming at it from a variety of angles, developing now this aspect and now that aspect, balancing one statement with another to clarify what is and is not entailed, returning to a point already made so that it may be seen afresh in the light of what has been said subsequently, and generally amplifying a basic conceptuality until he considers his exposition to be sufficient for conclusion to be appropriate.[5] Thus the parts and the whole need to be read in constant conjunction with each other. In other words, the statement that "God is love" must be related to the overall theme of critical testing or else its role within the letter will not be accurately grasped.

II. Translation[6] and Selective Exposition of 1 John 4

> 1Beloved, do not believe every spirit, but test the spirits to see whether they
> are from God; for many false prophets have gone out into the world. 2By
> this you know the spirit of God: every spirit which confesses that Jesus
> Christ has come in the flesh is from God, 3while every spirit which does not
> confess Jesus is not from God. And this is the spirit of the antichrist, of
> which you heard that it is coming, and now, already, it is in the world.
> 4Little children, you are from God, and you have enduring victory over
> them, for the one who is in you is greater than the one who is in the world.
> 5They are from the world; and so what they say is from the world, and the
> world heeds them. 6We are from God; whoever knows God heeds us, who-
> ever is not from God does not heed us. By this we know the true spirit and
> the spirit that leads astray.

John's concern is with the discernment of that which purports to belong to the realm of God, that is, "spirit(s)."[7] So his basic injunction is clear: "Do not be-

5. Thus seeming repetitiveness and lacunae need not give rise to the complex theories of composition that are sometimes proposed.

6. Although the translation is my own, my wording is often indebted to that of others.

7. The question as to when a Christian interpreter might appropriately capitalize "Spirit" in 1 John is difficult. My preference is for lower case as much as possible, for John is not speaking of the Holy Spirit in the mode of Luke or even Paul ([τὸ] ἅγιον πνεῦμα does not appear in

lieve every spirit," that is, do not be gullible, credulous, or unthinking in the spiritual realm, but rather "test the spirits" to see whether claims to be "from God" are indeed justified; they may well not be, for those who proclaim messages that purport to be from God but are not in fact from God are not isolated or occasional but rather numerous ("many false prophets").

The language of being "from God" (4:1, 2, 3, 4, 6) is contrasted with being "from the world" (4:5), and expresses a fundamental Johannine polarity between life responsive to and expressive of, and life estranged from and antipathetic toward, its Creator.[8] As in the Gospel,[9] this polarity can be expressed in a number of ways.[10] In our passage the parallelisms in 4:6a are illuminating:

> We are from God;
> whoever knows God heeds us,
> whoever is not from God does not heed us.

The second clause could presumably be equally expressed as "whoever is from God heeds us." Being "from God" is inseparable from "knowing God," though context and nuance may make difference of formulation appropriate. Thus the original injunction to "test the spirits to see whether they are from God" could be reexpressed as "test those who speak as prophets to see whether they know God" (δοκιμάζετε τοὺς ὡς προφήτας λάλουντας εἰ γινώσκουσι τὸν θεόν).

The logic of 4:6, that it is those who know God who heed those who are from (who know) God, makes knowing God a condition for knowing whether others know God — it takes one to know one. Such a circularity, which is characteristic of John, could appear to be vicious. Yet John regards the context within which the knowing person is located not only as open (people may leave or enter, 2:19; 3:14) but also as involving qualities capable of growth and diminution (love must grow to fullness, 4:12, 17-18). So the circle is not something

---

1 John), but rather of that realm which is both life-giving and destructive, whose accurate discernment is crucial.

8. This polarity, whose heuristic value is analogous to that of sociological ideal types, runs in one form or other throughout Scripture: in the Old Testament, the righteous and wicked, wise and foolish; in the New Testament, the believing and unbelieving, those being saved and those being lost.

9. The Gospel contrasts that which is "from God," "from above," "from heaven," "from the Spirit," "not from this world," with that which is "from the world/earth," "from the flesh," "from oneself" (see, e.g., John 1:12-13; 3:1-8, 31-32; 8:23, 28; 18:36-37).

10. 1 John, e.g., contrasts those who are "in the light," "in/have life," "in him [God]," "of God," "of the truth," "have overcome the evil one/the world," "do the will of God," with those who are "in darkness," "in death," "love the world," "are of the world," "of/in the devil/evil one" (1:5-7; 2:5, 9-11, 14, 15-17; 3:8, 12, 19; 5:4-5, 12-13, 19).

fixed but involves the dynamics of responsiveness and growth, and is more akin to a spiral.

Since John has made clear that claims to know God are testable, he specifies the communicable content of the knowledge of God and so enables testing to be carried out: every spirit which confesses that Jesus Christ has come in the flesh (ἐν σαρκὶ ἐληλυθότα) is from God. This poses four related interpretative problems. First, what is the best textual reading? Second, what is the precise meaning of this confession? Third, how does this confession relate to other confessions and statements of belief in the Johannine letters? Fourth, how does this confession relate to John's wider argument?

Textually, the variants mainly affect v. 3a and seem to be expansions of its summary restatement of v. 2, which make no real difference to the overall sense. Likewise, the Codex Vaticanus variant in v. 2, the perfect infinitive ἐληλυθῆναι in place of the perfect participle ἐληλυθότα, makes no difference in sense.

In terms of meaning, the perfect tense of ἐληλυθότα suggests "the enduring result of a past coming."[11] How far this should be pressed is open to dispute.[12] If it is given full weight, it suggests the continuing presence of Jesus in the (Johannine) Christian community, along the lines expressed in 3:24; 4:13, that is, the presence of God spiritually mediated — the very issue whose critical testing John is expounding. The precise force of ἐν σαρκί might be illuminated by a supposed alternative which is being denied, perhaps, for example, some docetic idea of (mere) "appearance."[13] But "anti-docetism" may well be a distracting imposition upon what is a convenient shorthand for the coming of Jesus on earth, that is, a shorthand for the importance of the foundational figure to whom John looks and directs his fellow believers. The concern is not that Jesus' mission on earth is *real* as opposed to *apparent,* but rather that it is *definitive* for knowledge of God.

Comparable confessions and affirmations of belief abound in the Johannine letters (1 John 2:22-23; 3:23; 4:14-16; 5:1, 5, 13; 2 John 7). All the formu-

11. Raymond E. Brown, *The Epistles of John* (AB 30: New York etc.: Doubleday, 1982), p. 493.

12. For example, Brown regards this as a temptation to be resisted, on the basis of 2 John 7, where a similar formula is used without the perfect (*Epistles,* 493), while Georg Strecker considers the choice of tense meaningful on the basis of comparable variations elsewhere (*The Johannine Letters* [trans. Linda M. Maloney; Hermeneia; Minneapolis: Fortress, 1996], pp. 134, 133 n. 12). I incline toward Strecker (one can regard 2 John 7 simply as a less precise formulation than 1 John 4:2).

13. As Jimmy Dunn puts it, "I John contests a docetic-like christology whose closest parallels are the earliest forms of Gnosticism proper which probably emerged round about the turn of the first century AD" (*Christology in the Making* [London: SCM, 1980], p. 31).

lations look to be variations on one theme — that in Jesus God's salvation/gift of life has come to the world, and this life is appropriated through responding to Jesus as the Son in whom God's nature and action are known (it is difficult not to appeal to a passage such as John 5:19-24 to spell out the underlying thought more fully). The precise wording of 1 John 4:2 is not making a different affirmation but expressing a particular nuance of the one core belief.

The fuller significance of this confession of 4:2 is not immediately spelled out because John's initial move is to stress the definitive nature of the confession as that which embodies the power of God to overcome the world and divides between the true spirit and the spirit which leads astray (4:4-6). But John has not finished with it yet.

> 7Beloved, let us love one another, for love is from God, and everyone who loves has been born from God and knows God. 8The one who does not love does not know God, for God is love.

John returns to the significance of the confession of 4:2 in 4:7 (it is unfortunate that so many commentators see 4:1-6 as a discrete section and 4:7 as the beginning of a new topic).[14] He reintroduces the theme of love (ἀγάπη), which has already been a concern earlier in the letter, and relates it specifically to critical discernment. First, he reiterates key terms and concerns:

> Beloved, let us love one another,
> for love is from God,
> and everyone who loves has been born from God
> and knows God.

We have already seen that "being from God" and "knowing God" mutually express the same reality. Now John specifies that love is also "from God," in such a way that the person who embodies love can be said to be "born from God" (a

14. For example, Brown lists numerous scholars who see no real link between 4:1-6 and 4:7ff., dissents from them, but himself sees the linkage in terms of 4:1-6 as an exposition of 3:23a while 4:7–5:4a expounds 3:23b and "praises" those who love (*Epistles*, pp. 542-43). Strecker classifies 4:1-6 as "dogmatic exposition" and 4:7–5:4a as "paraenesis" (*Letters*, p. xliv). I. Howard Marshall comments: "Somewhat abruptly John turns from his discussion of true and false spirits to present his readers with a further appeal to love one another" (*The Epistles of John* [NICNT; Grand Rapids: Eerdmans, 1978], p. 210). C. H. Dodd sees 4:1-6 as "in the nature of a parenthesis" (*The Johannine Epistles* [London: Hodder & Stoughton, 1946], p. 107). These all tend to expound "God is love" in more or less general terms (e.g., unity of doctrine and ethics); no one relates it directly to critical testing.

fuller formulation, applicable to persons, of the more common "from God"). At the end of the verse love is also linked to the overall key theme; "loving God" is thus added to "being from God" and "knowing God" as another variant of the same core reality (the variants connoting differing facets according to differing contexts).

The relationship of this to the task of critical discernment is instantly spelled out (4:8): "Whoever does not love does not know God, for God is love." This is the negative aspect of discernment, the importance of being able to know how to disqualify, and so not heed, those who might claim to know God (be from God, speak for God as prophets), since to credit unjustified claims could entail being led astray from what is true. The criterion is the absence of love. For just as the father is seen and known in the Son, who displays the qualities of the Father, so too believers, who become children of God (3:1-2), display the qualities of God their Father — supremely love (cf. 3:14, "We know that we have crossed from death to life, because we love the brothers; whoever does not love remains in the realm of death"). From this one may infer that the absence of love shows the absence of knowing God (being a child of God, being from God). The principle of 4:8 thus restates the negative aspect of discernment spelled out in confessional terms in 4:3. This suggests that the meaning of 4:8 is an "applied" way of looking at the confession of 4:2-3.

> 9The love of God has been revealed among us in this way: God sent his only son into the world so that we might have life through him. 10This is what love consists of: not that we have loved God but that he loved us and sent his son as an atonement for our sins. 11Beloved, if God so loved us, we also ought to love one another.

That 4:8 should be seen as a practical re-expression of 4:2-3 is indicated also by the specific form of the developing exposition. For John gives content to that love which God is by spelling out its revelation in Jesus, and the form this takes is the recitation of a summary account of the meaning of the life of Jesus (4:9-10).[15] This quasi-creedal recitation is an amplification of the earlier, summary formulation "Jesus Christ has come in the flesh," spelling out more fully what is the significance of Jesus. The consequence is that Christians, to be true to their calling, must reciprocate and replicate in their lives and their dealings with each other that same mode of being that characterizes God, that is, love (4:11).

15. That John is not thinking of "God is love" in generalizing or definitional terms is underlined by the aorist "God loved" as distinct from a present tense "God loves." God's love must be spoken of in terms of the particular person and mission of Jesus.

> 12Nobody has ever seen God. If we love one another, God abides in us, and
> his love is brought to fullness within us.

This love enables critical discernment to take place. This is the logic of 4:12a, which sometimes appears puzzling: Why specify that "nobody has ever seen God"? The point is that God is not a person or object within the world, of the kind where questions having to do with verification of claims to knowledge could in principle be resolved by conventional criteria. God is intrinsically Other (though John would express this in terms of πνεῦμα/spirit) in that he entirely eludes that sense of sight by which most people establish their understanding of the reality of what there is in the world. Hence the problem of verification with reference to God is important. Yet for John this Otherness of God in no way leads to undecidability (and ultimate meaninglessness) with reference to claims to know God as a reality.[16] Rather, John reworks (in a brief way, to be expanded later in 4:20-21) his principle that the presence of God's qualities in those who would know God/be of God demonstrates the validity of their claim (4:12b).

> 13By this we know that we abide in him and he in us: he has given us of his
> spirit. 14And we have seen and bear witness that the Father has sent the Son
> as savior of the world. 15Whoever confesses that Jesus is the Son of God,
> God abides in them and they in God. 16So we have come to know and come
> to believe the love which God has for us. God is love, and whoever abides in
> love abides in God, and God abides in them.

The concern for critical discernment is directly restated. Mutual abiding (another mode of knowing God) can be known through God's gift of his own spirit. This reiterates the earlier affirmation about God's gift of spirit (3:24). Just as that earlier affirmation led directly into the question of critical discernment and a christological specification, so here too (4:14-15) John complements the affirmation about the spirit with an affirmation about Jesus, comparable to 4:2. Knowing that one abides in God has as its corollary the presence of the spirit given by God. It equally has as its corollary that one confesses Jesus to be Son of God. Then in 4:16a the language of knowing and believing would most naturally be followed by some propositional content about Jesus. Instead the expressed object of knowledge and belief is love — the nature and meaning of which is to be found in the mission of Jesus to the world, as spelled out in 4:9-

16. Compare John 1:18 for the centrality of Jesus' role in making known the unseeable God.

10. This love which is encountered in the mission of Jesus is constitutive of God in the kind of way that enables critical discernment to take place: "God is love, and whoever abides in love abides in God, and God abides in them." One can know that one abides in God because of the spirit; one can know that one abides in God because of one's confession of Jesus; one can know that one abides in God because one shows that quality of love that is constitutive of God (and continues the presence of Jesus in the world). John rings the changes on his one theme: that one can know that one knows God only if the loving reality of God in Jesus is appropriated and demonstrated. The presence of God's spirit, confession of Jesus, and love are different facets of, or modes of expressing, the one rich reality of the knowledge of God.

> 17By this means love is brought to its fullness among us, and so we have confidence on the day of judgment; because as is he, so are we in the world. 18There is no fear in love, but love in its fullness expels fear; for fear has to do with punishment, and whoever fears has not grown to fullness of love. 19So let us love, because he first loved us.

One consequence of the mutual indwelling of believer and God is that love can reach its full fruition, with the further consequence that the future and God's final reckoning can be faced with confidence — because believers replicate the qualities of Christ (i.e., supremely love) within the world. A further mark of love reaching its full fruition is that it removes inappropriate fear, fear focused on punishment (4:17-18). These marks of mature love enable further critical discernment, though in this case less between true and false than between differing levels of true. A further incentive to grow in love is the reminder that it is a response in kind to the initiative which God has taken in the mission of Jesus (4:19); that is (in the language of 5:3), love is not burdensome but is continuing and growing in that reality which has constituted Christians as those who are from God in the first place.

> 20If anyone says "I love God" and hates his brother, he is a liar. For whoever does not love his brother whom he has seen, cannot love God whom he has not seen. 21So we have this commandment from him: whoever loves God must also love his brother.

John now amplifies the point expressed briefly in 4:12, the problem of testable knowledge when the reality in question, God, is invisible (and so not amenable to conventional forms of verification via the senses). John is not simply reaffirming the dominical double commandment to love God and neighbor (in his own particular form, with "brother" instead of "neighbor"), but is rather making a point about the nature of that which is visible and accessible to test claims to the invisible and (in conventional terms) inaccessible. His point is that the visible and accessible (and "moral") practice of love for brother (and, no doubt, sister) is what enables one to rebut, or confirm, claims to knowledge/love with regard to the invisible and otherwise inaccessible ("spiritual") reality of God. As in 4:3 and 4:8, the primary formulation is pointedly negative — this is how one can know whom to disregard; lack of love of the visible brother disqualifies claims to love the invisible God. Positively, those who love God must love their brethren also — where the point is that those who love are those who know God (4:7b). So the way to know that one knows God is to display that love for the brethren which is not only embodied by Jesus but also mandated by Jesus as the form that the knowledge of God must take.

III. Summary and Conclusion

One of the most damaging misunderstandings that has afflicted the Christian faith in modern times has been a tendency to understand "spirit"/"Spirit" as some kind of opposite to matter — an immaterial something or other, which somehow inhabits, perhaps animates, and may outlive, the material; except that scientific investigation of the material finds no need of such a hypothesis, which then falls victim to Occam's ever-active Razor. For John, by contrast, "spirit"/"Spirit" in its true (i.e., life-giving) form is marked by acknowledgment of Jesus as sent by the Father in a self-giving love which also comes to characterize those who respond. "Spirit" is a "moral" reality, constituted by Jesus, which enables human life to fulfill its divine purpose, and its opposite, which is also "spiritual," is sin, which chains human life to the realm of death.

In the context of John's exposition of critical discernment, the famous affirmation that "God is love" (just like its counterpart, "God is light," 1:5-6) is neither a freestanding axiom[17] nor a theoretical definition of deity in terms of a supreme human quality (which can give rise to Feuerbach's potent critique that

17. Systematic theologians regularly treat the text thus. So, e.g., Eberhard Jüngel, "What Does It Mean to Say 'God Is Love'?" in Trevor Hart and Daniel Thimell (eds.), *Christ in Our Place* (Exeter: Paternoster, 1989), pp. 294-312. Similarly, Trevor Hart, "How Do We Define the Nature of God's Love?" and Alan J. Torrance, "Is Love the Essence of God?" in Kevin J. Vanhoozer (ed.), *Nothing Greater, Nothing Better: Theological Essays on the Love of God* (Grand Rapids: Eerdmans, 2001), pp. 94-113, 114-37, each focus on the problem of analogical language with reference to God without bringing out that for John the problems in saying "God is love" are problems not of language but of discipleship.

the quality is more ultimate than the deity, and that to keep the quality, while disposing of the deity, is to hold firm to the one thing needful).[18] Rather, it is an indication of how, in a confusing world full of competing and misleading claims, people may rightly recognize that spiritual reality whose life-bestowing qualities, definitively enacted in the particular person and history of Jesus as recognized by his "witnesses," entail acknowledgment of that spiritual reality as the true God. This acknowledgment is inseparable from an appropriation and enactment of the reality which is acknowledged, that is, the (nonidentical) living out within the church of the Son's self-giving love in obedience to the Father. In short, John's concern is to enable recognition of God.

Finally, is John's argument a good one? A question like this cannot be answered in the abstract, without reference to the particular uses to which John's argument may be put. Does, for example, an argument which is for the most part expressed in absolute terms admit of exceptions and qualifications? Certainly, if we construe the Johannine polarity, "of God"/"of the world," as analogous to ideal types, then the language has a heuristic value that can help one to discern pattern and meaning in situations whose initial appearance may be more or less confusing; and the language also prescribes movement, and can help people to move, toward the life-giving pole.

Alternatively, many Christians often need, at particular times, a form of assurance that lays a greater emphasis upon divine grace and a lesser emphasis upon human obedience than characterizes John's text. This may be readily recognized without this being in any way a reason for setting John's text over against other (perhaps Pauline) texts. In any case, John's argument is less about individuals or pastoral psychology than it is about that discernment and demanding responsiveness which should characterize the Christian community as a whole.

Perhaps the hardest overall question is: How is one to understand people who live lovingly but who do not confess a Christian faith?[19] An answer in Johannine terms might draw upon John 3:19-21. This passage suggests an understanding of divine grace as present even when unrecognized. A Christian mission entrusted with the light of Christ should enable the real nature of "do-

18. See *The Essence of Christianity* (trans. George Eliot; with introduction by Karl Barth and foreword by H. Richard Niebuhr; New York: Harper, 1957), pp. 50-58, esp. pp. 52-53.

19. D. Moody Smith properly cautions, "These statements should not be taken out of context as if they were applicable universally apart from God's revelation in Jesus. They are addressed to the Christian community and are intended to be understood on the basis of God's revelation in Christ" (*First, Second, and Third John* [Interpreter's Bible Commentary; Louisville: John Knox, 1991], p. 106). Yet the question about the wider implications of what John says remains a legitimate one.

ing the truth" to be recognized, that what is done truly is done in God (as definitively understood in Jesus); and such recognition, which reconstitutes human self-understanding, should then enable the doing of the truth to flourish more fully than otherwise.[20]

In short, all legitimate concerns about possibly harmful use of the text need to be met by implementation of the principle that wise use of the text is not wooden use, and by real appropriation of that reality of love of which the text speaks.

It is a pleasure and a privilege to write in honor of Jimmy Dunn, who has written lucidly and engagingly about so much of the New Testament, who has served with outstanding, self-giving leadership within the Durham Department of Theology, and who has become a valued friend.

20. The interpretation offered here differs, I think, in some not insignificant ways from that of Jimmy Dunn, and I offer it in the spirit of "just raising one or two minor points." In his *Jesus and the Spirit* (London: SCM, 1975), p. 356, Dunn sees John as valuably "able to maintain the freshness of religious experience even when the eschatological tension is almost wholly slackened and forgotten" but at the cost of a "loss of Pauline realism about the divided state of the believer as one caught in the overlap of the ages, and a rather unyielding and unlovely self-assurance (I John 4.6)"; this latter point is surely a misconstrual of John's concerns by failing to relate his language sufficiently to its context of discernment. He continues, "In marshalling his various 'tests of life' (indwelling Spirit, love, obedience, right confession) John unfortunately did not conceive of the possibility that some might 'pass' on one while 'failing' on another. The case of an individual who, for example, displayed a Christ-like love (I John 4.7), but who made a wrong confession, is not envisaged in the Johannine either-or." For reasons given in my exposition and conclusion this does not quite capture the dynamic and heuristic nature of John's vision of faith.

XXIV The Holy Spirit in the *Ascension of Isaiah*

Loren T. Stuckenbruck

I. Introduction

During the past twenty-five years, the *Ascension of Isaiah* has been shown — especially by Italian scholars — to be a Christian composition which, though drawing heavily on Jewish tradition, cannot be traced back to a non-Christian Jewish source.[1] In this two-part Christian document, dateable in its present

1. See esp. Mauro Pesce, *Il "Martirio di Isaia" non esiste:* L'Ascensione di Isaia *e le tradizioni guidaiche sull'uccisione del profeta* (Bologna: EDB, 1984); Enrico Norelli, *L'*Ascensione di Isaia: *Studi su un apocrifo al crocevia dei cristianesimi* (Origini, n.s. 1; Bologna: EDB, 1994), *Ascensio Isaiae: Commentarius* (CCSA 8; Brepols: Turnhout, 1995), pp. 31-33 nn. 3 and 1-3 (hereafter *Commentarius*), and *L'*Ascensione di Isaia: *Studi su un apocrifo al crocevia dei cristianesimi* (Collata origini, n.s. 1; Bologna, Persiceto: EDB, 1994), pp. 45-49; Jonathan Knight, *The Ascension of Isaiah* (Guides to the Apocrypha and Pseudepigrapha 1; Sheffield: Sheffield Academic Press, 1995), pp. 25-26 and *Disciples of the Beloved One* (*Journal for the Study of the Pseudepigrapha* Supplement Series 18; Sheffield: Sheffield Academic Press, 1996); and Richard Bauckham, "The Ascension of Isaiah: Genre, Unity, and Date", in *The Fate of the Dead: Studies in Jewish and Christian Apocalypses* (Leiden: Brill, 1998), pp. 363-90.

Sections III and IV of this study represent a slight revision of my previous publication, "The Ascension of Isaiah: Monotheism and Christology," in James Davila, Carey Newman, and Gladys S. Lewis (eds.), *Monotheism and the Worship of Jesus: Papers from the Proceedings at the International Conference on the Origins of the Worship of Jesus in St. Andrews University* (Leiden: Brill, 1999), 70-89. Some of the adjustments and reformulations of the argument constitute an attempt to address some aspects of Richard Bauckham's response to that contribution.

form to at least the early part of the second century CE,[2] the Holy Spirit occupies a baffling, yet pivotal, conceptual position. It is the pneumatology of the *Ascension* which shall be the focus of my present reflections, which are dedicated to James D. G. Dunn, whose published works on the Spirit in the New Testament have long been an inspiration to me.

II. The Problem

On the one hand, above and in distinction from all other beings in the cosmos, the Spirit is aligned with both Christ 'the Beloved One' and God who is transcendent above the seventh heaven. This status of the Spirit is illustrated by the scene of the sixth heaven, where the seer 'Isaiah' joins the angels in praising the 'primal Father and the Beloved One and the Holy Spirit' (8:18). Moreover, aligned with Christ, the Spirit occupies a place on one side of God, with Christ on the right and the Spirit on the left; beside the divine throne they are in a standing position before Christ's descent to the earth (9:35), and after Christ's descent and exaltation they each take up a sitting position (11:32-33). With the transcendent God at the centre, the Spirit and Christ are given supportive, even subordinate roles. And so, at God's side, the Spirit joins Christ in worshipping God (9:40). Taken together, these ideas provide not only what may be our earliest explicit evidence for the notion of worshipping the Holy Spirit, but also reflect a significant model of emerging Christian trinitarian theology at an early stage.

On the other hand, in the textual traditions of the document the Spirit is distinguishable from Christ and God. The Spirit is the only one among the three to be explicitly designated as an 'angel'. This usually occurs within the phrase 'angel of the (Holy) Spirit' (7:23; 8:14–Eth. mss. A, C; 9:35-36, 39-40; 10:4; 11:4, 33; cf. 3:15 and 4:21).[3] Though Christ, too, is given such an association, this is much less direct.[4] This reticence to apply 'angel' to Christ in the same way as to the Spirit needs to be accounted for within the framework of the *Ascension of Isaiah* (cf. below). Since the term 'angel' is also applied not only to Isaiah's heavenly guide in the vision and to the angelic beings that populate the seven heav-

2. See esp. the discussions of Robert G. Hall, "The *Ascension of Isaiah:* Community Situation, Date, and Place in Early Christianity", *JBL* 109 (1990): 289-306; Knight, *Disciples of the Beloved One;* and Norelli, *Commentarius,* pp. 53-66.

3. On the other hand, while Christ is said to be *like* or *in the appearance of* an angel (9:30–Eth.), no straightforward identification of Christ as an angel is made in any of the versions.

4. In 9:30 (Eth.) Christ (here called 'Lord' — 9:32) is simply *likened* to an angel in appearance. In 9:35 the designation of the Spirit as 'the second angel' implies an understanding of Christ as the 'first'.

ens but also to Beliar,[5] the significance of the 'angel' terminology is not immediately clear. Furthermore, though worshipped with Christ and God in 8:18, the Spirit is left out of the equation on other occasions within the textual traditions (so especially in 7:17, 37 and 8:7-8, while in 8:13 only Christ is worshipped). Thus the purpose of this essay is to explore briefly the nature and function of the Holy Spirit in *Ascension of Isaiah*. To do so, we may pose the following questions: What accounts for the worthiness of the Spirit to be worshipped alongside God, and why is the Spirit nonetheless apparently assigned to a subordinate position, a position lower than that of Christ?

In a recent discussion of the theology of the *Ascension*, Darrell Hannah has stressed, as others before him, that the positions of Christ and the Spirit alongside and yet subordinate to God were inspired by Christian exegesis of Isaiah 6 preserved by Origen (esp. *Princ.* 1.3-4; *Cels.* 6.18), Irenaeus (cf. *Demonstration of the Apostolic Preaching* 10), *Revelations of Elchasai* (in Hippolytus, *Haer.* 9.13.2-3), and *Apostolic Constitutions* (8). According to such exegesis, Christ and the Spirit would have been identified, respectively, with the Cherubim and Seraphim (which, in turn, are understood as angelic beings), both of which are portrayed as worshipping God, as in *Ascension of Isaiah* 9:26-42.[6] Hannah rightly observes that if *Ascension of Isaiah* received such a tradition, then — along with, for example, Irenaeus — the author has corrected or modified it by placing the Spirit in a position subordinate to Christ. In this way, an apparently widespread reading of Isaiah 6 in Christian circles was being adjusted in the direction of a more 'orthodox' doctrine according to which the one worshipped in Isaiah 6 was interpreted as the Logos (i.e., in terms of Christology) instead of as God. Similar to *Ascension of Isaiah*, Irenaeus played down any association of Christ with an outright 'angel Christology'; however, Irenaeus went further than *Ascension of Isaiah* by distancing the Spirit from explicit 'angel' terminology as well. Thus, while the vision of the enthroned figure surrounded by Seraphim and Cherubim in Isaiah may help to explain the appearance of Christ and the Spirit (even in relation to angelology) in trinitarian fashion, it does not in itself explain why it is that Christ and the Spirit should be differentiated from one another in *Ascension of Isaiah*. In other words, if the *Ascension* is read on its own terms, the presentation of the Spirit by the author may be a deliberate innovation that was not necessarily modeled on contemporary exegetical traditions.

5. Only the Ethiopic and Greek (so-called 'Legend') versions preserve these verses of the *Ascension*. In 4:2 the Ethiopic mss. designate Beliar 'the great angel', while in 4:4 he is simply 'angel'. The Greek, however, has to be reconstructed, i.e. as [ὁ ἄρ]χων, i.e. 'ru]ler'.

6. See D. D. Hannah, "Isaiah's Vision in the *Ascension of Isaiah* and the Early Church", *JTS* 50 (1999): 80-101, esp. pp. 90-99.

Richard Bauckham has taken a different view of the matter, emphasising that, as with Christ, the Spirit is being included in the identity of God in the *Ascension.*[7] Although acknowledging the differences in terminology applied as well as the less clear formulations about the Spirit by the author, Bauckham argues that no 'ontological' status should be associated with the use or non-use of 'angel'. Instead, the use of the term 'angel' for the Spirit is to be understood as having been exegetically derived from a possible reading of the Hebrew to Isa. 63:9-11:[8] 'the angel of his (God's) presence' in v. 9 is referred back to in vv. 10-11 as 'his holy spirit'. For Bauckham, this derivation from interpretation of Scripture provides an argument against the notion that the Spirit is in any way subordinate, that is, considered lower than Christ and, as an 'angel', is to be thought of as a created being. The possibility that scriptural interpretation has led to the outright identification of the Holy Spirit as an 'angel' cannot be discounted. Indeed, this might be one way to explain why it is that the Spirit, and not Christ, is attached to such nomenclature. Bauckham is, in addition, no doubt correct in dissociating the application of 'angel' to the Spirit from the notion that the Spirit is thus to be understood as a created being (unlike other beings called 'angels').

However, for reasons that I hope to delineate below, it remains unclear that this exegetical background should be regarded as a key to the interpretation of the *Ascension*'s pneumatology. While Scripture interpretation would have fed the theological ideas of the author with terms and ideas within a prophetic visionary context, this does not mean that the author has not created a 'narrative world' in its own right. The tributary traditions and ideas were not merely fitted together in *Ascension of Isaiah* as pieces of a jigsaw puzzle. At times they could be interwoven in ways that continued to reflect the original literary and social contexts in which they had been embedded (as Bauckham has argued in relation to Isa. 63:9-11), while on other occasions the author will have created a new web of meaning on the level of the document. Thus the interpretation of the *Ascension of Isaiah* must ultimately go beyond a simple acknowledgement of the traditions and sources that inspired the author(s). However much the author was indebted to his visionary counterparts in Jewish (and Christian) traditions and even from the biblical Hebrew tradition of Isaiah, the

7. In addition to my comment at the bottom of the first page of this essay, see the bibliography in n. 1 above.

8. Whereas the LXX does not allow for such a reading of v. 9 (LXX: ἐκ πάσης θλίψεως οὐ πρέσβυς οὐδὲ ἄγγελος, ἀλλ' κύριος ἔσωσεν αὐτούς . . .), the Hebrew may be interpreted as either like the LXX ('. . . in all their trouble. It was no messenger or angel, but his presence that saved them') or to mean, 'In all their trouble he was distressed; and the angel of his presence saved them'.

product ultimately expressed something novel: a *creative fusion* of traditions that does not necessarily require an appeal to the traditions themselves in order to understand the new world of meaning created in the text.

III. Angels in *Ascension of Isaiah*

Given the close, even terminologically overlapping association between the Spirit and 'angel' in the *Ascension,* it is necessary to explore the degree to which the angelology of the document can inform us about the author's pneumatology. Beyond its application to the Spirit, the term 'angel' is used broadly within *Ascension of Isaiah* to refer to beings in service to God that populate each of the seven heavens. Less likely is the possibility that, in addition, the term is applied to Beliar in 4:2 ('the great angel') and 4:4 ('this angel'); the word takes an ambiguous form in the Ethiopic tradition and thus can also mean 'ruler' (as in the Greek version). If we restrict ourselves to the (good) angels in the seven heavens, two issues emerge that have already surfaced in the discussion above regarding the Spirit: (a) their status in relation to each other (cosmology) and (b) their involvement in the vision as both worshippers and, in a more restrictive sense, objects of worship. These points are interrelated and explored immediately below.

That angels in any Jewish document might in some, even limited, way become the object(s) of praise might at first seem surprising. However, according honour to angelic beings neither would have been unpredecented in Early Judaism nor would it have been irreconcilable within a monotheistic framework.[9] Thus, when the textual traditions are complex, one should beware lest one analyse them with an a priori assumption that such a phenomenon would, on theological grounds, have been unwarranted. The problem emerges in relation to the status of angelic figures located in the lower heavens of the vision.

9. So the 4Q400-403 passages cited in n. 11 below and 11QBer (= Milḥamah) ll. 4-5; Tob. 11:14-15 (esp. Codex Sinaiticus, but also Codexes A and B); *Jos. Asen.* 15:11-12. The passages in 11QBer and Tobit appear to have preserved a liturgical fragment from a common source which they, in turn, have adapted to very different literary contexts. Further evidence for angel veneration may arguably be found in the sapiential *Instruction* preserved in 4Q418 fr. 81, ll. 1-15 (esp. ll. 1-2; cf. 11-14?). Far from regarding praise towards God's angels as a threat to devotion to one God, the authors of these sources leave the monotheistic imprint on their theologies unmistakable. For a similar tendency to retain a monotheistic pattern despite inclusion of angels alongside God in the context of prayer, see Gen. 48:15-16 (LXX) and the inscriptions from Rheneia and Kalecik (discussed in Stuckenbruck, *Angel Veneration and Christology* [Tübingen: Mohr (Siebeck), 1995], pp. 67 n. 58 and 183-87).

At first, it appears that evidence to support the notion of angels being worshipped is hard to come by. Indeed, we might argue that angels in the *Ascension of Isaiah* are beings whose primary function is simply to worship God from their respective inferior positions in the heavens (7:17 [Eth.]; 10:1-6; cf. 9:40-42). Furthermore, the vision in two places has an anonymous *angelus interpres* reject the seer Isaiah's attempt to worship or honour angels (7:21-22; 8:4-5). While this angelic 'refusal tradition'[10] would seem to disallow the worship of angels from the start, traces of an angel 'veneration' on the level of the text can nevertheless be discerned in several versions of the seer's ascent. These become apparent if we ask why the seer wishes to worship angels at all. Is there any analogy between such worship and the worship accorded the Holy Spirit in the seventh heaven?

As Isaiah is escorted through the seven heavens by his angel guide, he is so overwhelmed by what he sees in the second heaven that he prostrates in an act of worship (7:18-23). Just what the seer is doing, however, is variously described in the versions corresponding to v. 21:

Latin (L^2)	Slavic (S)	Ethiopic (E)
And I fell on my face	And I fell on my face	And I fell on my face
in order to worship *him* . . .	wishing to worship *them* . . .	in order to worship *him* . . .

According to S, the seer is inspired in the second heaven by the quality of the angels' praise; their worship is superior to the worship he has encountered and observed in the first heaven (7:20). That the exemplary worship of angels can, in turn, inspire an attempt to worship them or at least to consider them praiseworthy would not be unusual against the background of Jewish apocalyptic tradition.[11] However, as far as the *Ascension of Isaiah* is concerned, the L^2 and E

10. As identified by Bauckham, "The Worship of Jesus in Apocalyptic Christianity", *NTS* 27 (1980-81): 322-41 and printed in revised form in idem, *The Climax of Prophecy: Studies on the Book of Revelation* (Edinburgh: T&T Clark, 1992), pp. 118-49; see further Stuckenbruck, *Angel Veneration*, pp. 75-103 and "An Angelic Refusal of Worship: The Tradition and Its Function in the Apocalypse of John", in *SBL Seminar Papers* (ed. Eugene Lovelace; Atlanta: Scholars Press, 1994), pp. 679-96.

11. As this passage shows, there could be a fine line between praising *with* angels and worshipping angels themselves. S to *Asc. Isa.* 7:21 may be an adjustment which combines these motifs. Though not in the context of a visionary journey, cf. 4Q400 fr. 2, ll. 1-2 (= 4Q401 fr. 14 col. i, ll. 7-8) and 4Q403 fr. 1 col. i, ll. 31-33, where a description of angels' praise is combined with an acknowledgement that they are "honored among all the camps of the *elohim* and revered by human councils"; *contra* the objections raised by C. H. T. Fletcher-Louis, *Luke-Acts: Angels, Christology and Soteriology* (WUNT II/94; Tübingen: J. C. B. Mohr [Paul Siebeck], 1997), p. 6 n. 23. I distinguish between honorific language accorded to angels *within a cultic setting* and an out-

versions, which otherwise often diverge in their readings, probably preserve the more original text.[12] In this case, Isaiah is described as wishing to praise a single figure who, endowed with superior glory, is seated on the 'throne' at the upper centre of the second heaven (7:19 [Eth.]).[13]

The text raises questions. It says nothing at this point about why Isaiah worships in this way, that is, whether he engages in the praise because of his participation in and joining with the worship of the other angels or whether he himself is inspired by the splendour of the enthroned figure. Moreover, and related to this, is that the text traditions of the ascent do not clarify whether the angels of the second heaven worship the enthroned figure in their midst or whether their activity is, strictly speaking, actually and ultimately directed towards God. A similar ambiguity is already apparent from the author's description of the first heaven (7:13-17): whereas the extant versions agree that the angelic worship there is directed towards God (7:17; esp. L² and S: "to the glory of God, who is above the seventh heaven . . . '; E: '. . . to the One who rests in the holy world') and that Christ, God's 'Beloved', is included alongside God as the object of worship,[14] another phrase — and this is retained only in the Ethiopic recension of 7:15 — describes the angels' activity as follows: '. . . and a throne was in the middle, *and they* [the angels on the right and on the left] *were glorifying it/him*'. Thus, in a way similar to L² and E in the second heaven (7:21), the E recension allows the angels' worship of the first heaven to be directed towards the throne or, if L² and S are consulted, to the angelic figure seated on this throne (cf. 7:14).[15] Since this reading might seem to be contradicted by the emphasis in 7:17 on the worship of God, Norelli recognises that the Ethiopic version of 7:15 constitutes the *lectio*

---

right *cultic worship* which focuses on angels as such (which cannot be infered from either 4Q400 or *Ps.-Philo* 13:6 without considerable qualification). Concerning the occurrence of angelic refusals of worship within the broad framework of a seer's observation of or participation in worship, see my *Angel Veneration*, pp. 84 n. 99 and 156-64 (discussion of Col. 2:18).

12. So Norelli, *Commentarius*, p. 400.

13. The antecedent of *eum* within the context of the L² version is not immediately apparent; Charles suggests plausibly (*The Ascension of Isaiah* [London: Adam and Charles Black, 1900], p. 109) that the object was probably omitted in the text at an earlier stage. S is, on the other hand, consistent in that the antecedent for *them* is the worshipping angels from vv. 19-20. In any case, the Ethiopic tradition makes sense as it stands.

14. Less transparent is E, in which the seer is initially told that the praise is directed 'to the glory of the seventh heaven'. While the text, as it stands, could have a larger circle of angels from the seventh heaven in view alongside God and the Beloved One, it is more likely that a reference to God has been omitted through *homoioteleuton* in the Greek *Vorlage;* cf. Norelli, *Commentarius*, pp. 395-96.

15. L² and S refer to 'an angel seated on it [the throne] in great glory'.

difficilior and, therefore, is to be preferred.[16] With respect to the third and fourth heavens — in which the ascending pattern of angels on the left and right and throne in the middle is continued — the author does not specify that the focus of the heavenly worship is on God (7:27, 29-30), while in the fifth heaven the angels (L^2 and S) or Isaiah (E) explicitly praises the transcendent God, who 'has given to angels such glory'.

Thus, while it is clear that the heavenly worship observed by the seer has God in view (7:17, 37 [L^2 = S]), there are sufficient traces in the *Ascension of Isaiah* to suggest that angels are being 'venerated' as well.[17] Due to the lack of evidence, we have to leave open the question of whether such traces betray attempts to remove such from the document at an early stage or whether the author of the vision has modified this aspect of a Jewish or Jewish-Christian apocalyptic tradition. The evidence reviewed, however, may shed some light on the nature of the angel's rebuke in 7:21-22; it is a proscription of the *seer's* activity and perhaps should not be read as a commentary on the angels' activity of praising the enthroned figure per se. In the context of the second heaven, then, Isaiah is dissuaded from worshiping angels on the grounds that he and the other righteous ones will be given a superior place in the seventh heaven after death (7:23; 8:11-14; 9:17-18; 11:32). According to the cosmological scheme of the vision, it is inappropriate for the inferior to be honored by the superior.[18]

If we are correct in suggesting that the *Ascension of Isaiah* allows for a certain degree of angel veneration, how is this to be interpreted in light of the worship of 'the angel of the Holy Spirit' in the seventh heaven? Three points may be made. First, the veneration of angels in the document is very limited in scope: (a) significantly, it is limited to language of praise; (b) the prostration referred to in 7:21 reflects position without bearing any connotation of sacrificial worship; (c) the venerative language does not serve the author's particular paraenetical concern to place those who are faithful in the seventh heaven, especially since it is through Christ (and not any of these angels; cf. 9:4-5) that

16. Norelli, *Commentarius*, p. 395. However, Norelli wishes to consider the *force* of the Ethiopic version as secondary; he emphasizes that '[i]n ogni caso, la quantità (non la direzione) della lode e della gloria traccia come una spirale ascensionale.'

17. I use here the term 'venerate' instead of 'worship' despite the fact that there is no attempt in any of the versions to make such a terminological distinction. Clearly the author does not consider the veneration of angels to be the equivalent to or rival of the worship of Christ or the Holy Spirit. Nevertheless, the presence of this veneration in the *Ascension of Isaiah* is conspicuous if one compares this to the absence thereof in the Apocalypse of John; cf. my *Angel Veneration*, p. 207.

18. The same emphasis is made by the angel guide's refusal to be called 'lord' by the seer in 8:4-5; cf. Stuckenbruck, "An Angelic Refusal of Worship", pp. 688-89.

their admission to the seventh heaven will be secured. Second, though the 'glory' of the angels would have been a factor in the seer's wish to worship them,[19] it is a feature derived from God, 'who has given such glory from heaven to heaven' (7:37).[20] The inspiring glory of the angels' appearance and activity was but a reflection of God and, as such, is not to be questioned. Third, to the degree that there is any veneration of angels in the *Ascension of Isaiah,* it is not of the kind that is understood to be in conflict with the worship of God.[21] This is broadly consistent with the pattern of such honorific language when applied to angels in early Jewish sources.

IV. The 'Angel of the Holy Spirit'

As we have noted at the beginning of Section II, whereas the seer is forbidden to worship other angels, in the seventh heaven the angel guide instructs him to worship the 'angel of the Holy Spirit' (9:36; cf. 8:18).[22] In the *Ascension of Isaiah* the consistent designation for the Holy Spirit as an 'angel of the (Holy) Spirit' reflects an 'angel pneumatology' in which the Holy Spirit is analogous, yet superior, to all the other angels.[23] In 7:23 Isaiah recognises that it is by means of 'the angel of the Holy Spirit' that those who love 'the Most High and His Beloved' will be able to secure their place (robes, crowns, thrones) in the seventh heaven. In this way, the Spirit may be represented as a guiding angel par excellence (7:21; 11:40; cf. 8:14–Eth. mss. A, C), that is, the 'angel' who will lead the faithful righteous to the seventh heaven when they die.[24] Furthermore, there

19. The different degrees of the angels' 'glory' is described throughout the vision: 7:15, 20, 27, 31, 34-36; 8:2. Furthermore, the angel companion who forbids the visionary to address him as 'lord' (8:4-5) is the object of the visionary's fascination at the beginning of the journey in 7:2: 'I saw a glorious angel; he was not like the glory of the angels . . . but he had great [L^1, S: and holy] glory. . . . I cannot describe the glory of this angel'. Similarly, the 'Greek Legend' (2:6): εἶδον θεοῦ ἄγγελον δεδοξασμένον· οὐ κατὰ τὴν τάξιν δὲ τῶν ἀγγέλων ὧν εἶδον τότε ἐγὼ ἔβλεπον νῦν, ἀλλὰ πλείονα καὶ περισσότεραν εἶχεν δόξαν.

20. On glory in the *Ascension of Isaiah* see Norelli, *L'*Ascensione di Isaia, pp. 249-52. Conspicuous is the degree to which the language of 'glory', in addition to describing the appearance of heavenly beings (7:2, 24–Isaiah; 9:21, 27, 33), is closely bound up with the quality of the heavenly worship (7:15, 19-20, 27, 30-31, 33-36; 8:2-3; etc.).

21. For this reason I think, e.g., that vv. 15 and 17 in ch. 7 (Eth.) are not irreconcilable positions for the author.

22. The Holy Spirit is already worshipped in the sixth heaven together with the Father and Christ in 8:18.

23. Except, of course, in those passages in which Christ is rendered as an angelic being (esp. 9:35; cf. 9:30).

24. It seems, therefore, that Isaiah's ascent through the heavens with the help of the guid-

seems to be some parity in the prophetic vision of 3:15-17 between the 'angel of the Holy Spirit' and Michael, 'the chief of the holy angels':[25] both are credited with having opened the grave at the resurrection, after which they emerge with the Beloved sitting on their shoulders.[26]

However, the Spirit's function in 3:15-17 does not fit well with the picture that emerges from the vision of chs. 6–11. Here it is important to distinguish between the versions. In contrast to the Ethiopic tradition, the Latin[2] and Slavic versions assign Michael to a prominent position in the seventh heaven (to 9:23, 29, 42). In 9:23 these versions identify Michael as the angel who shows the seer the heavenly books of 'the deeds of the children of Israel'; as such, he is an angel 'more glorious than the glory' of the *angelus interpres* (cf. 7:2).[27] Moreover, in 9:29 and 9:42, Michael is included among the list of those who worship Christ and God. However, and significant for the Latin[2] and Slavic text traditions, Michael is *not* explicitly mentioned as being among those who worship the Holy Spirit (9:34).[28] Thus, although the Latin[2] and Slavic versions for 9:23, 29, 34, 42 would be consistent with 3:15-17, they are nevertheless best explained as secondary additions to the text.[29] If this is the case, then ch. 3 contains the only refer-

ing angel is regarded as a temporary expedient which allows the visionary to see that which is promised in the future to those who remain faithful (8:14-15, 22-28).

25. Contra Knight, *Disciples of the Beloved One*, p. 153, who assumes '[t]he Spirit's apparent superiority to Michael in 3.16-17', a view which could be reached only if chs. 6–11 are considered as well.

26. This is similar to the *Gospel of Peter* 36, 39–40, in which two angels ('men') descend and enter the tomb, and then emerge from the tomb supporting Jesus in the middle ('three men'). Both the *Gospel of Peter* and the *Ascension of Isaiah* are developments of the earlier tradition associating two angels with the empty tomb (cf. Luke 24:4-7, though there are no signs of literary dependence; the *Gospel of Peter* seems dependent on Matthew 28), and the *Ascension of Isaiah* identifies one of these two angels as the Holy Spirit. Norelli (*Commentarius*, pp. 203-4 and n. 1) argues that 3:15-17 mark a development beyond the scope of chs. 6–11 (for Norelli, the earlier part of *Ascension of Isaiah*) in an attempt, based on the Christian tradition of two angels, to relate the Spirit's activity to the resurrection event. While I agree with Norelli's appeal to Christian tradition, the parity between Michael and the Holy Spirit in 3:15-17 is more difficult to fit into his thesis that chs. 1–5 presuppose chs. 6–11, for in the latter the Spirit's position *among those called angels* is unrivalled.

27. The interest of L^2 and S in Michael is further apparent in that Ethiopic's description of Christ in 9:27 ('whose glory surpassed all') is absent, while in 9:23, in contrast to Ethiopic, they add the reference to Michael, who is 'pre-eminent over all the angels in his glory'.

28. This point may require more analysis than is possible here. The question is whether one can infer from L^2 and S some sort of parity (perhaps on the basis of 3:15-17?) between Michael and the Holy Spirit.

29. So correctly Norelli, *Commentarius*, pp. 205-6 and 472-74. There would have been no apparent reason for removing the references to Michael once they had become part of the tradition.

ence to Michael in the entire *Ascension of Isaiah*. Whichever version is followed, it remains true that the Holy Spirit is superior, as nowhere is Michael said to be worshipped.[30]

The prominence of the Holy Spirit in the *Ascension of Isaiah* is linked closely to the author's understanding of his role as a prophet. Isaiah is commanded to worship 'the angel of the Holy Spirit', who is described as one 'who has spoken in you and also in the other righteous' (9:36). Just as the Holy Spirit had inspired the Scriptures of old (4:21-22; esp. the psalms and the prophets), so the prophetic community to which the seer belonged regarded its own activity as inspired by the Holy Spirit in a time when the apostles' teaching had been abandoned (3:21) and the numbers of true prophets were dwindling (so 3:26-27). The Holy Spirit, then, bridges the gap between the inspired message of the contemporary prophecy about Christ (3:13, 18-19) and the rewards which await those who believe in this message (7:22-23).

The description of the worship of the 'angel of the Holy Spirit' (9:33-36) is modelled on the preceding section in which Christ is worshipped (9:27-32).[31] In these scenes the angel guide gives Isaiah the command to worship (vv. 32, 36), a reversal of the warning not to worship in the second heaven (7:21).[32] Moreover, after Christ's ascent, he and the Holy Spirit are both enthroned at God's right and left respectively (11:32-33). The parallels between the Holy Spirit and Christ have led some interpreters to think that the *Ascension of Isaiah* gives expression to a trinitarian model in which Christ is represented as an angel as well (on Christology, see below).[33]

30. Some interpreters have suggested that Gabriel traditions underlie *Ascension of Isaiah*'s presentation of the Holy Spirit; so Jean Daniélou, *Théologie du Judéo-Christianisme* (Paris: Desclée, 1958), pp. 178-80. See, however, Bauckham, "The Worship of Jesus in Early Christianity", pp. 146-47 (esp. arguments a, c, and d). In addition, Charles, *The Ascension of Isaiah*, pp. 19-20, restored κ[αι Γαβριηλ] in a lacunae of the Greek P. Amherst 1 before 'the angel of the Holy Spirit' in 3:16; but there is no warrant within any of the text traditions to 3:15 or anywhere in the context of the *Ascension of Isaiah* to support this restoration-identification; cf. further Norelli, *Textus*, p. 143 and Verheyden, "L'Ascension d'Isaïe et l'Évangile de Mattieu", pp. 249-50. If there is a tradition-historical connection between Gabriel tradition in *2 Enoch* 22:3 (Recensions A, J) and the Spirit in 7:23, it has not contributed formatively to the trinitarianism of the *Ascension of Isaiah*.

31. See Bauckham, "The Worship of Jesus in Early Christianity", pp. 145-46. A similar pattern is adopted to express the worship of God in 9:40–10:6, though some elements are added (worship by Christ and the Holy Spirit, worship from the six heavens), and the explicit command to worship does not occur.

32. Bauckham, "The Worship of Jesus in Early Christianity", p. 145.

33. See Martin Werner, *Enstehung des christlichen Dogmas* (Berlin/Leipzig, 1941), pp. 327-28: Origen (*Princ.* 1.3.4) cited the view of his 'Hebrew teacher' that the two Seraphim on both sides of the throne in Isa. 6:2-3 (esp. in the LXX) are the 'only-begotten Son of God and the Holy

However, several indicators suggest that in the author's scheme the Holy Spirit does not share the privileges of Christ. First, this is indicated by the Holy Spirit's position to the left of God (9:36; 11:33). That being to the left implies a subordinate status is made plain in the description of the five lower heavens, each of which contains an explicit hierarchy of glory: first angels on the left, then angels on the right, and most glorious of all the angel enthroned in the middle (7:13-37).[34] Though the location on the left of the divine throne is attested for angelic beings in Jewish tradition (*2 Enoch* 24:1),[35] it is within the *Ascension of Isaiah* itself that its meaning is best inferred. As 10:14 makes clear, the author's emphasis is on Christology, which is illustrated by his use of Ps. 110:1 to depict the exaltation of Christ 'to the right hand of God' after his ascension.[36] In this aspect the pneumatology of the vision is a function of the author's Christology. Second, the Holy Spirit's subordinate position to Christ is implied

---

Spirit'; similarly, Georg Kretschmar, *Studien zur frühchristlichen Trinitätstheologie* (Beiträge zur historischen Theologie 21; Tübingen: J. C. B. Mohr [Paul Siebeck], 1956), pp. 62-124. Daniélou, *Théologie du Judéo-Christianisme*, pp. 189-92, argued that Irenaeus's view that the Son and Spirit are the Cherubim and Seraphim respectively (*Dem. Apost.* 10, extant in Armenian) must reflect the influence of the *Ascension of Isaiah*. In his contribution to the 1981 conference on the *Ascension of Isaiah*, M. Simonetti, "Note sulla cristologia dell'*Ascensione di Isaia*", in Mauro Pesce, ed., *Isaia, il Diletto e la chiesa* (Testi e richerche di scienze religiose 20; Brescia, 1983), pp. 188-93, detects the presence of two trinitarian models in the document, a 'triangular' one (Christ and Holy Spirit are paired on the same level as angels) and a scheme based on a 'Logos Christology' (Christ is superior to the Holy Spirit); for Simonetti, the latter has begun to displace the former in the *Ascension of Isaiah*. The notion that these two models stand in tradition-historical tension in the document has been rightly criticized by Norelli, *Commentarius*, pp. 484-85, and Knight, *Disciples of the Beloved One*, p. 152, who appeal *inter alia* to Philo's identification of λόγος, λόγοι with ἀρχάγγελος, ἄγγελος (cf. *Cher.* 3; *Fug.* 5; *Deus* 182; *Leg. All.* 3.177; *Conf. Ling.* 28 and 146; *Her.* 205; *Mut. Nom.* 87; *Abr.* 173; *Post. Caini* 91; *Somn.* 1.155; *Agr.* 51).

One may consider the possibility, of course, that the presentation of Christ and the Holy Spirit in the *Ascension of Isaiah* itself reflects a exegetical reading of the Seraphim (understood as angels) in Isa. 6:2; so, e.g., Hannah in his recent article cited in n. 6 above. If so, the passage from Isaiah may account for Christ and the Holy Spirit as worshippers of God; however, one would have to look elsewhere to explain why the *Ascension of Isaiah* has them being worshipped as well in the seventh heaven.

34. It is arguable that the stratification of the lower heavens is derived from the author's hierarchical arrangement of the Trinity.

35. The left of the throne is occupied by Enoch along with Gabriel, and nothing is said about anyone on the right.

36. The christological interpretation of Ps. 110:1 was of course widespread in early Christian circles. See Martin Hengel, "Psalm 110 und die Erhöhung des Auferstandenen", in Cilliers Breytenbach and Henning Paulsen (eds.), *Anfänge der Christologie: Festschrift für Ferdinand Hahn* (Göttingen: Vandenhoeck & Ruprecht, 1991), pp. 43-73. For a list of New Testament and other early Christian texts see Stuckenbruck, *Angel Veneration and Christology*, pp. 128-29 n. 208.

by the Spirit's absence in several formulae which mention only God and Christ (7:7-8, 17; 8:7, 25), while God and the Spirit do not occur together without Christ (7:23; 8:18; 9:40; 11:32-33). Third, in the context of being worshipped by the angels of the seventh heaven, the Holy Spirit, who stands on the left of Christ, is designated 'the second angel' (9:35-36).

V. Conclusion

The subordinate rank of the Holy Spirit in the *Ascension of Isaiah*, conveyed through symbolic language and spatial categories, should not be interpreted as a demotion of the Spirit vis-à-vis a "higher" pneumatology being corrected by the author. It is, after all, not in the area of worship that the Spirit's subordinate status is expressed. Much to the contrary, *Ascension of Isaiah* constitutes our earliest evidence of worship being rendered to the Holy Spirit alongside Christ and God.[37] From the above analysis it seems that this 'trinitarian devotion' is a Christian development. While the function of the Holy Spirit as 'a messenger' or 'angel' reflects a development from ideas contained in the Jewish scriptures and angelological traditions, the *worship* of 'the angel of the Holy Spirit' is ultimately discontinuous with the occasional notions of angel veneration in the document; this becomes clear when the position of the Holy Spirit is compared not only with angelologies of earlier and contemporary Jewish tradition but also, and especially, with the nature and function of angelic beings in the document itself. In the *Ascension of Isaiah*, while the equivocation of the Holy Spirit with 'angel' may ultimately derive from an exegetical tradition to Isa. 63:9-11 that allows for such a link, the document nonetheless goes well beyond the rubrics of such an interpretive tradition when it introduces the notion that this Holy Spirit is to be worshipped. As such, this worship is an extension of binitarian devotion which had become so characteristic of Christian faith.

37. Cf. Justin Martyr, *1 Apol.* 6.1-2: 'But we revere and worship [σέβομεθα καὶ προσκυνοῦμεν] that one [God] and the Son who came from him and who taught us these things, and the army of the other good angels who follow [him] and are made like [him], and the prophetic Spirit. And we give honor in word and truth, even handing on [the tradition] without envy to everyone who wishes to learn.'

XXV The Spirit in the Writings of Justin Martyr

Graham N. Stanton

Justin Martyr has often been chided for his alleged failure to set out clear and coherent teaching on the Spirit. But expressions of bewilderment have not deterred scholars from attempting to bring order out of chaos.[1] All too often, however, discussion of the teaching on the Spirit of this outstanding second-century Christian philosopher and martyr has been dominated by fourth-century rather than second-century agendas. Is Justin's theology binitarian? Does Justin understand the Spirit in personal terms? Does Justin conceive the relationship between Father, Son, and Spirit in triadic or embryonic trinitarian ways?

These important questions will be touched on in the pages that follow, but my own focus is rather different. I shall start by offering a brief reading of the important opening chapters of Justin's *Dialogue with Trypho;* here the references to the Spirit have regularly been overlooked. I shall then discuss Justin's favourite terminology for the Spirit, that is, the phrase 'the prophetic Spirit'. Only then will triadic passages be examined. Finally, I shall turn to Justin's comments on the gifts of the Spirit. The biblical and New Testament roots of Justin's understanding of the Spirit will be given more attention than its relationship to later patristic thought.

Given the theme of this Festschrift and the prominence of the Spirit (and especially Christian experience of the Spirit) in the writings of our distin-

1. See, e.g., E. R. Goodenough, *The Theology of Justin Martyr* (Jena, 1923; repr. Amsterdam: Philo Press, 1968), pp. 176-88. Eric Osborn, *Justin Martyr* (Tübingen: Mohr, 1973), p. 102, notes that Justin's doctrine of the Holy Spirit is difficult to understand.

guished honoree, there are several reasons for turning to the writings of Justin. Jimmy Dunn's exposition in his first book of Luke's understanding of the Spirit, *Baptism and the Spirit* (1970) is still at the centre of current discussion of this topic — and that is a quite remarkable achievement. But neither Jimmy Dunn nor more recent writers on the Spirit in Luke-Acts have stopped to consider Justin's comments on the Spirit, even though Justin clearly betrays the family likeness of his 'grandfather', Luke.

When Jimmy Dunn did discuss briefly the understanding of the Spirit found in second-generation writings in what I consider to be one of his finest books, *Jesus and the Spirit* (1975), he did so under the banner 'the Vision Fades'. He claimed that in order to extend his researches into the second generation, 'much chaff would have to be winnowed for a much poorer return of grain.'[2] But what of the third and fourth generations? Even more chaff? Perhaps we shall not have to wait long for the answers, for the third volume in Jimmy's trilogy *Christianity in the Making* will cover the period AD 70 to 150, now dubbed 'the second and third generations' of Christianity.[3] So we can hope that the role of the Spirit in Justin's writings will receive due attention in that volume. In the meantime, here is a starter.

I shall argue that if we refrain from reading Justin through Pauline or Johannine spectacles and give due weight to the setting and purpose of his writings, his understanding of the Spirit turns out to be rich and many-sided.

Justin's writings are lengthy, riddled with textual problems, and often difficult to interpret.[4] The *First Apology* was written very shortly after AD 150, the *Dialogue with Trypho* about 160. However it is unwise to try to trace development in Justin's thinking from the earlier writing to the later. Some sections of the *Dialogue* were almost certainly written before the *Apology* and inserted lock, stock, and barrel into Justin's account of his conversations with Trypho.[5]

2. *Jesus and the Spirit*, p. 345.

3. See *Jesus Remembered*, p. 7.

4. Quotations from Justin are taken from Miroslav Marcovich's critical editions of the Greek text, *Iustini Martyris Apologiae pro Christianis* (Patristische Texte und Studien 38; Berlin: de Gruyter, 1994) and *Iustini Martyris Dialogus cum Tryphone* (Patristische Texte und Studien 47; Berlin: de Gruyter, 1997). Marcovich regularly proposes additions and corrections to the Parisinus codex (dated 1363), the one surviving manuscript of any importance. Marcovich's editions provide a solid platform for fresh study of these fascinating writings; nonetheless they remind us that the text of Justin's writings is in a parlous state. Translations are my own.

5. See esp. O. Skarsaune, *The Proof from Prophecy: A Study of Justin Martyr's Proof-Text Tradition: Text-Type, Provenance, Theological Profile* (Leiden: Brill, 1987).

I. The Role of the Spirit in Justin's Conversion

There has been no shortage of scholarly comment on Justin's lengthy account of his initial conversation with his Jewish adversary Trypho 'in the cloisters of the colonnade'.[6] In the opening eight chapters of the *Dialogue* Justin regales Trypho and his friends with his quest for the truth via his participation in the most prominent philosophical schools of his day. The philosophical themes are of perennial interest, but for my present purposes Justin's encounter with a mysterious unnamed elderly man not far from the sea is especially important (*Dial.* 3.1). This encounter leads to Justin's conversion to 'philosophy safe and beneficial', that is, Christianity.

The old man rebukes Justin for his devotion to Plato, Pythagoras, and their ilk. 'A long time ago', he insists, 'there were men of greater antiquity than all these so-called philosophers. These men were blessed, righteous, and beloved of God. They spoke by the divine Spirit, and foretold things of the future which are now coming to pass. They are called prophets. . . . they were filled with the Holy Spirit' (*Dial.* 7.1). Here a prominent theme in the *Dialogue,* the role of the Spirit in the prophets' witness, is mentioned for the first time.

The writings of the prophets, which may be consulted by anyone, do not compel assent on account of the 'logical proof' they contain, but rather on the grounds that their prophecies have taken place and are now taking place (*Dial.* 7.2). In order to shore up his claims, the old man appeals to the prophets' miracles which glorified God and proclaimed Christ as his son. In stark contrast, he refers to 'the false prophets' who, filled with the seducing and unclean spirit, performed 'miracles' which amazed some and thus gave glory to the spirits of error and demons (i.e., they were magicians).[7] The clear implication is that the prophets were filled with God's Spirit (*Dial.* 7.3).

The old man disappears as mysteriously as he had appeared. Who is he? Proposals have ranged from 'a non-Christian barbarous stranger' to (most recently) the view that the old man is Christ himself.[8] In my judgement (shared

6. According to Eusebius (*H.E.* 4.18.6), this took place in Ephesus.

7. In *Dial.* 69.7 Justin claims that some of the contemporaries of Jesus considered him to be 'a magician and a deceiver of the people' rather than one who fulfilled the prophecies of Scripture. See further G. N. Stanton, 'Jesus of Nazareth: A Magician and a False Prophet Who Deceived God's People?" in my *Jesus and Gospel* (Cambridge: Cambridge University Press, 2004), pp. 127-47.

8. For the latter, see Andrew Hofer's intriguing but unconvincing claim in 'The Old Man as Christ in Justin's *Dialogue with Trypho*', *Vigiliae Christianae* 57 (2003): 1-21. Hofer offers a critical assessment of the main proposals concerning the identity of the old man. I am grateful to my colleague Dr. James Carleton Paget for drawing my attention to this article.

with variations by several scholars), the old man is simply a respected Christian whose witness to the prophets and to Christ triggered Justin's conversion. At an early point in his discussion with Justin, the old man shows his hand. 'Can man's mind ever see God if it not be adorned with the Holy Spirit (ἁγίῳ πνεύματι κεκοσμημένος) (*Dial.* 4.1)?[9] Surely this is a comment of a Christian! It foreshadows the old man's final recorded words to Trypho in which he insists that true insight is given only to those to whom God and his Christ give understanding (*Dial.* 7.3).[10]

Justin notes that immediately after the old man's disappearance, 'a fire was kindled in my soul (πῦρ ἀνήφθη), and a passionate desire possessed me for the prophets, and for those great men who are the friends of Christ' (*Dial.* 8.1). 'Fire' evokes the Spirit, as it does in Justin's account of the baptism of Jesus. Justin notes that when Jesus went down to the water, 'fire was kindled in the Jordan (πῦρ ἀνήφθη), and as he rose up from the water the Holy Spirit fluttered down on him, as the apostles of this our Christ have written' (*Dial.* 88.3). Justin is drawing in part on a non-Synoptic tradition, but the linking of fire and the Spirit in the context of baptism recalls the Q tradition, 'he will baptise you with the Holy Spirit and with fire' (Matt. 3.11 = Luke 3.16).

Elsewhere Justin emphasizes that baptism with the Holy Spirit is the initiatory rite for Christian believers; they have no need of 'that other baptism (i.e., circumcision)' (*Dial.* 29.1; cf. 14.1). Baptism with the Spirit is of the essence of being a Christian, hence Justin must have accepted that his own conversion was a baptism with the Holy Spirit, even though in his short account of his conversion he refers only to 'the kindling of fire' and not explicitly to the Spirit. The role of the Spirit in Justin's conversion is also implied by the reference to the 'passion' (ἔρως) with which he turned to Scripture.

Justin's conversion involves a radical change from a 'philosophy' based on intellectual and rational argument to a 'Christian philosophy' grounded in his personal experience of the writings of the prophets and 'the Saviour's words' (*Dial.* 8.2). The latter are said to evoke *profound awe* (δέος). Justin expands on these comments in a further appeal to Trypho in the very next chapter. He promises Trypho that he will show him that Christians do not believe in empty fables, or in words that cannot be proved (presumably philosophical arguments). Rather, Christians believe in 'words that are full of the Divine Spirit', and are 'gushing forth with power (δυνάμει βρύουσι), and teeming with grace'

9. κοσμέω does not seem to have been used by Christians prior to Justin to refer to the role of the Spirit. M. Marcovich notes (with references) that Irenaeus, Clement of Alexandria, and Origen use similar phraseology of the Spirit (*Iustini Martyris Dialogus,* p. 76).

10. Cf. Marcovich's comment on 4.1: 'inde apparet senem incognitum Christianum esse'.

(*Dial.* 9.1). From the context, the words in question are the words of the prophets and the words of the Saviour. The link between the Spirit, power, and the words of 'Scripture' is striking,[11] and it underlines the extent to which there is a very strong experiential basis to Justin's conversion.

Many scholars have been so bewitched by the possible literary parallels to the role played by the old man in the opening chapters of the *Dialogue* that they have sidestepped a basic question. Why does Justin include an eight-chapter account of his philosophical quest and his conversion to Christianity as the prolegomenon to his dialogue with Trypho? The remaining 134 chapters of the *Dialogue* focus almost exclusively on disputes between a Christian and a Jew concerning the interpretation of Scripture, not philosophical arguments. And unlike Justin himself, Trypho does not undergo a conversion to Christianity. At the close of two days of discussion Justin and Trypho go their own ways, agreeing to pray for one another.

I do not think that Justin's *main* aim was to 'win over' Jews such as Trypho. If that had been his hope and expectation, he would not have allowed Trypho to go his own way. Justin must have recognized that some Gentiles (such as Trypho's companions)[12] were so strongly attached to Judaism that their conversion was unlikely. So his primary appeal (via his Christian 'school') was to Gentiles who were broadly sympathetic to both Judaism and Christianity — Gentiles who did not appreciate the differences, Gentiles with a weak level of attachment either to Christianity or to Judaism.

In that context, Justin's account of his abandonment of the leading philosophies of the day and of his conversion to 'the true philosophy' is entirely appropriate alongside his extended discussions with Trypho. Justin records his own dramatic conversion experience in the hope that others will also follow this path. Hence his strong insistence that baptism with the Holy Spirit is the entry rite to 'the true philosophy', and not 'that other baptism', circumcision (*Dial.* 29.1).

11. I have argued elsewhere that for Justin the sayings of Jesus have the same standing as the words of the prophets. See G. N. Stanton, 'Jesus Traditions and Gospels in Justin Martyr and Irenaeus', in J.-M. Auwers and H. J. de Jonge, eds., *The Biblical Canons* (Leuven: Leuven University Press and Peeters, 2003), pp. 355-70; this article is now included in my *Jesus and Gospel,* pp. 92-109.

12. For a defence of the view that Justin's companions are Gentiles, see G. N. Stanton, 'Justin Martyr's *Dialogue with Trypho: Group Boundaries, "Proselytes" and "God-fearers,"* in G. N. Stanton and G. G. Stroumsa, eds., *Tolerance and Intolerance in Early Judaism and Christianity* (Cambridge: Cambridge University Press, 1998), pp. 263-78.

II. The Prophetic Spirit

In the preceding paragraphs attention has been drawn to Justin's insistence that the words of the prophets and the words of the Saviour are 'full of the Divine Spirit'. Justin refers to the prophets' experience of the Spirit repeatedly, normally using his favourite phrase 'the prophetic Spirit'.[13] This phrase is found 25 times in the two *Apologies*[14] and 12 in the much longer *Dialogue.*[15] The phrase is nearly always used in the context of the fulfilment of prophetic predictions: what the 'prophetic Spirit' predicted through Moses, David, Isaiah, or the other prophets has now been fulfilled.

Two passages may be mentioned as typical of many others. In *1 Apol.* 31.1 Justin notes that there were 'certain persons among the Jews who were prophets of God, through whom the prophetic Spirit announced beforehand things that were to come to pass before they happened.' In his first use of his stock phrase in the *Dialogue* (32.3) Justin notes that in the words of 'the blessed David' (in Psalm 110) Christ has been called Lord by 'the holy prophetic Spirit'.

There is a striking echo of Justin's stock phrase in the two most reliable recensions of the accounts of the martyrdom of Justin and his companions. Justin is asked by the prefect Rusticus to give an account of the doctrines he practises. In his reply Justin refers to his belief in God the Creator and in Jesus Christ, and then includes these words: 'I acknowledge the prophetic power (προφητικήν τινα δύναμιν), for proclamation has been made about him whom I have just now said to be the Son of God. For you know that in earlier times the prophets foretold his coming among men.'[16] Here the phrase 'the prophetic power' is used in a context very similar to Justin's repeated uses of 'the prophetic Spirit'. Since Justin's favourite phrase is not used in either the LXX or the New Testament (though the concept is undoubtedly present), and since it is not a stock phrase either in early Jewish or Christian writings, its use on the lips of Justin in the accounts of his martyrdom is not likely to be coincidental. Here is

13. Justin's favourite way of referring to the Spirit is echoed in the use of the phrase 'the Spirit of prophecy' by several writers as a shorthand term to sum up *Luke's* understanding of the Spirit. The debt to Justin's terminology goes unacknowledged! See, e.g., Max Turner, *Power from on High: The Spirit in Israel's Restoration and Witness in Luke-Acts* (Sheffield: Sheffield Academic Press, 1996); R. P. Menzies, *Empowered for Witness: The Spirit in Luke-Acts* (Sheffield: Sheffield Academic Press, 1994).

14. *1 Apol.* 6.2; 13.3; 31.1; 32.2; 33.2, 5; 35.3; 38.1; 39.1; 40.1, 5; 41.1; 42.1; 44.1, 11; 47.1; 48.4; 51.1; 53.4, 6; 59.1; 60.8; 63.2, 12, 14. If Marcovich's plausible conjecture at *1 Apol.* 35.5 is accepted, this is a further reference.

15. *Dial.* 32.3; 38.2; 43.3, 4; 49.6; 53.4; 55.1; 56.5; 77.3; 84.2; 91.4; 139.1.

16. For the Greek text and a translation, see *The Acts of the Christian Martyrs,* ed. H. Musurillo (Oxford: Clarendon, 1972), pp. 42-61.

one reason (and there are others) for accepting that authentic traditions lie behind the accounts of Justin's martyrdom.

It is not easy to uncover the roots of Justin's favourite phrase, though the *concept* of the Spirit's inspiration of the prophets is not hard to find.[17] In his voluminous writings Philo uses the phrase 'the prophetic Spirit' only twice (*Fuga* 186; *Vit. Mos.* 1.277). Although there are some similarities with Justin's use of the phrase, there is no question of literary dependence.[18]

In earlier Christian writings the only example of the phrase is in the *Shepherd of Hermas* 43.9 (= *Mand.* 11.9) in the context of a discussion on how one differentiates between true and false prophecy.[19] None of Justin's 37 uses of the phrase resembles this passage. So Justin may well have coined the phrase himself. Certainly his repeated emphasis on the fulfilment of the words of the prophets as the result of their inspiration by the 'prophetic Spirit' is the most prominent feature in his understanding of the role of the Spirit.

Several exceptions to this general way of using the phrase are noteworthy. (i) The phrase is used by Trypho in his objection to Justin's insistence that Elijah has already come as John the Baptist: 'It seems to me strange that God's prophetic Spirit which was in Elijah has also been in John' (*Dial.* 49.6). Justin has placed his favourite phrase in Trypho's mouth simply in order to allow Justin to press home his claim that as God transferred some of the Spirit that was in Moses to Joshua (Num. 27.18; Deut 34.9), so also God was able to cause Spirit from Elijah to come upon John. Here the bestowal of the Spirit is linked to leadership rather than to predictive prophecy.

(ii) At *Dial.* 55.1 Justin once again places his favourite phrase in the mouth of Trypho. Justin is challenged by Trypho to show that 'another God besides the maker of all things is accepted by the prophetic Spirit (ὑπὸ τοῦ προφητικοῦ

17. Eduard Schweizer's often quoted dictum is apt: 'Luke . . . shares with Judaism the view that the Spirit is essentially the Spirit of prophecy' (*TDNT,* 6:409). For recent discussion of Jewish evidence, and especially for a critical assessment of scholarly discussion on Luke's view of the Spirit, see Archie Hui, 'The Spirit of Prophecy and Pauline Pneumatology', *TynB* 50 (1999): 93-115.

18. There is a third reference at *Quaest. in Exod.* 2.105, extant only in Armenian: Aaron is possessed by God 'and by the prophetic Spirit'. See David T. Runia, *Philo in Early Christian Literature* (Assen and Minneapolis: Van Gorcum and Fortress, 1993), pp. 97-105, on Justin's knowledge of Philo. O. Skarsaune is very cautious about links between Justin and Philo; see esp. *The Proof from Prophecy,* p. 234, where he emphasizes the apologetic tradition of Hellenistic Judaism as the link. He also notes that there is still more work to be done in relating Justin to the whole scope of Jewish apologetic and missionary literature in Greek. Runia is in broad agreement, but notes that Hellenistic Judaism 'is more a supposition than a reality' (p. 104).

19. See Marcovich's references (in his note to l. 6 of *1 Apol.* 6.20, p. 40) to Athenagoras, *Leg.* 10.4; 18.2; Irenaeus, *Adv. Haer.* 1.13.4.

πνεύματος)'. Justin appeals to the appearance of God to Abraham at the oak of Mamre in the form of three men to support his view that there is a 'God and Lord other than the Maker of all things, who is also called "Angel" (ἄγγελος)' (*Dial.* 56.4; cf. Gen. 18.1-3). Justin claims that 'the holy prophetic Spirit' states (in Scripture) that God the Creator was one of three who appeared to Abraham (56.5). In both cases the phrase 'the prophetic Spirit' seems to mean no more than 'inspired Scripture'; there is a hint (as so often elsewhere) of predictive prophecy (cf. also 56.15). As the lengthy debate between Justin and Trypho concerning the identity of the three men unfolds, it becomes clear that Justin's primary focus is Christology. He does not claim that one of the three men is the Spirit; unlike *the Ascension of Isaiah,* he does not identify the Angel as the Spirit.[20]

(iii) In *1 Apol.* 63.2, 12, and 14 the prophetic Spirit *rebukes* 'the Jews' via Scripture. The same verb is used of Jesus Christ, who is said to have rebuked the Jews because they did not know the nature of the Father and the Son; a version of Matt. 11.27 = Luke 10.22 is then quoted. Justin brings this part of his argument to a climax by insisting that the Jews are rebuked 'both by the prophetic Spirit and by Christ himself, for they knew neither the Father nor the Son' (63.14). In each case the verb ἐλέγχω is used. *Dial.* 38.2 also refers to the role of the prophetic Spirit in rebuking Jewish teachers for their failure to interpret Scripture aright, though here textual disruption forces editors of the Greek text to propose emendations.

It is not easy to determine the precise nuance attached to ἐλέγχω by Justin. I have used 'rebuke' above in all five cases, though some translators prefer 'upbraid' or 'censure'. A judicial sense, 'convict', is probably not implied by Justin in any of the five passages. Hence one should be cautious about making a link between this aspect of the role of Justin's prophetic Spirit and the role assigned to the Paraclete in John 16.8-11 (cf. John 8.46). In John 16.8 the future tense is used (not the present, as in Justin), and a judicial sense is almost certainly present.

Although there are some interesting exceptions, as we have just seen, Justin's stock phrase is used in a rather wooden way. He insists that the prophetic Spirit enabled the prophets to predict what is now being fulfilled. Or, conversely, belief in the fulfilment of prophecy implies the inspiration of the prophetic Spirit. This theme lies at the heart of Justin's apologetic. Only rarely does Justin say more about the nature of that inspiration. In two passages he states explicitly that two prophets were in a state of ecstasy (Daniel, *Dial.* 31.7;

20. See Loren Stuckenbruck's fine study, 'The Holy Spirit in the *Ascension of Isaiah*', in this volume, pp. 308-20.

Zechariah, *Dial.* 115.3). If these two, then Justin may have envisaged that the presence of the prophetic Spirit led to ecstasy for the other prophets, but we cannot be certain about this.[21]

III. Father, Logos-Son and Spirit

In two passages in the *First Apology* 'the prophetic Spirit' is mentioned in yet another context, in 'triadic' statements concerning the Father, the Son, and the Spirit. In the first strong theological statement near the beginning of the *First Apology,* Justin is adamant that Christians are not atheists with respect to the most true God, the father of righteousness. 'We worship and adore (σεβόμεθα καὶ προσκυνοῦμεν) both him and the Son who came from him and taught us these things, *and the army of the other good angels, who follow him and are made like him,* and the prophetic Spirit; we give honour to him (the Father) in reason and truth. To everyone who wishes to learn (μαθεῖν) we willingly hand over (παραδιδόντες) what we have been taught' (*1 Apol.* 6.1-2).

The strong emphasis on *worship* of 'the father of righteousness', the Son, and the Spirit, as the context of this confessional statement is striking. This is among the earliest evidence we have for worship being given to the Spirit alongside Christ and God, though Justin does not elaborate on this.[22] Justin insists that the truths of the faith taught by Christ himself are to be transmitted carefully in his own day (cf. also 8.3). But it is of course the clause in italics in the quotation in the preceding paragraph which catches the eye, for it disrupts the triadic confession. For my present purposes I need not comment on the significance of the good, 'Christ-like' angels who are worshipped.[23] I need merely note that here, as elsewhere in Justin's triadic statements, the Spirit is referred to, but without comment or elaboration. This is in stark contrast to Justin's comments on God the Father/Creator and the Son/Logos.

21. See, less cautiously than above, R. M. Grant, *The Letter and the Spirit* (London: SPCK, 1957), p. 75. For a different view, see Osborn, *Justin Martyr,* p. 102, who suggests that as Justin nowhere uses the word 'ecstasy', it seems unlikely that he regarded this as the normal prophetic state.

22. Loren Stuckenbruck notes that the earliest evidence is in the *Ascension of Isaiah.* See his 'The Holy Spirit in the *Ascension of Isaiah*', in this volume, pp. 308-20.

23. In his fine study *Lord Jesus Christ* (Grand Rapids/Cambridge: Eerdmans, 2003) Larry Hurtado does not comment on this passage. But see L. W. Barnard's comments in his *Justin Martyr: The First and Second Apologies* (New York/Mahwah, N.J.: Paulist, 1997), p. 110. Barnard notes that this is one of the most enigmatic passages in *1 Apol.,* and rightly dismisses attempts to evade the clear sense of the text.

A reason for this imbalance emerges in an elaboration of this passage in ch. 13; here Justin's stock phrase 'the prophetic Spirit' is used once more. The context is once again worship and the transmission in Justin's day of Christ's own teaching. In this even more clearly credal and triadic passage, Justin notes that Christians are charged with madness (μανίαν) for giving to 'a crucified man second place after the unchangeable and eternal God, begetter of all things' (13.4).[24] Since opponents of Christians are ridiculing their christological views, it is not surprising that a full statement concerning Jesus Christ 'crucified under Pontius Pilate, procurator in the time of Tiberius Caesar' is included. Christian views on the Spirit were not the subject of ridicule, so elaboration was not called for.

In this passage, there is, however, a brief comment on the Spirit which must be noted. Christ is 'in second place (ἐν δευτέρᾳ χώρᾳ) to the true God himself' (13.3; cf. 12.7). The prophetic Spirit is in the third rank (ἐν τρίτῃ τάξει). Christ and the Spirit are clearly differentiated, though without implying different degrees of subordination. Although one might be tempted to see here a partial anticipation of later trinitarian formulations, Justin is not concerned with doctrinal precision, for this terminology is not repeated elsewhere in his writings. In the traditional doctrinal statements Justin has received from his predecessors, the Spirit is referred to *after* statements concerning 'the Maker of all things' and Jesus Christ, that is, in third position. For Justin, the Spirit and the gifts of the Spirit are given to Christian believers anew *after* the ascent of Christ to heaven (*Dial.* 87.5), so the Spirit's 'rank' is third. It is primarily a chronological position rather than one of subordination, though there does seem to be a hint of the latter.[25]

In Justin's further triadic statements in *1 Apol.* 61.3, 13; 65.2; 67.2 the terminology of rank is conspicuous by its absence (as is the phrase 'the *prophetic* Spirit'), thus confirming that Justin himself attaches little or no significance to his earlier comment that the Spirit is 'in the third rank'. In the first of these passages, Justin notes that Christian baptism is a 'washing in water' in the name of God, 'the Father of all and Master, and of our Saviour Jesus Christ, and of the Holy Spirit' (61.3; similarly 61.13). The phraseology is strikingly similar to Matt. 28.19, though perhaps not close enough to suggest direct literary dependence.

In the much-discussed account of the baptismal eucharist in *1 Apology* 65, the 'president' or 'ruler' sends up praise and glory to the Father of all, 'through

24. See M. Marcovich's list of later, similar accusations of Christian madness or folly, *Apologiae*, ad loc.

25. This point is made explicitly by Origen, *Cels.* 1.46: *after* the Saviour was sent by the Father, *then* the Holy Spirit was sent (by the Father).

the name of the Son and of the Holy Spirit, and offers thanksgiving at some length. . . .' Justin concludes his account of the baptismal eucharist with very similar phraseology: 'For everything we receive we bless the Maker of all through his Son Jesus Christ and through the Holy Spirit' (67.2).[26]

Justin's lack of precision concerning the role of the Spirit is nowhere clearer than in *1 Apology* 33 where Justin merges Matthean and Lucan traditions in his account of the annunciation of the birth of Jesus. Justin informs his readers that 'the power of God (δύναμις θεοῦ) overshadowed the virgin, and that the angel brought her good news: "You will conceive in the womb of the Holy Spirit and will bear a son . . ." (33.4-5). Justin then adds this surprising comment: 'Thus the Spirit and the Power from God cannot be understood as anything else than the Word (τὸν Λόγον), who is also the first-begotten (πρωτοτόκος) of God.' He then continues in similar vein by noting that the prophets are inspired by none other than the divine Word (33.9; cf. also 36.1) — not, as many other passages in Justin lead us to expect, by the prophetic Spirit. Here Justin seems to have grafted his convictions concerning the Logos rather awkwardly onto traditional phraseology concerning the role of the Spirit.[27]

Although some scholars have maintained that this passage confirms that for Justin the Spirit and the Logos were two names for the same person, E. R. Goodenough rightly insists that this conclusion outruns the evidence, for Justin is not making a general or formal statement.[28] When one considers all the references to the Spirit in the *Apology*,[29] traditional triadic formulations are more prominent than the apparent confusion between the Spirit and the Logos just noted. Justin attaches considerable importance to earlier Christian traditions and shows himself to be heir (however indirectly) to triadic passages such as Matt. 28.19 and 2 Cor. 13.14.

IV. The Gifts of the Spirit

In several passages in the *Dialogue* the role of the Spirit in the experience of Christian believers is emphasized. I have already drawn attention to the prominence of the Spirit in Justin's account of his conversion, and to his insistence

26. The traditional chapter division is misleading at this point; 67.1-2 belong with the preceding account of the baptismal eucharist and not with Justin's account of Sunday worship, which follows in 67.3-8.

27. Similarly, Osborn, *Justin Martyr*, p. 101. Osborn notes that the miraculous conception by the Word is a view which lingered on until the middle of the fourth century.

28. E. R. Goodenough, *Justin Martyr*, p. 181.

29. It is difficult to account for the absence of triadic formulations from the *Dialogue*.

that baptism with the Holy Spirit is the entry rite to 'the true philosophy'. In *Dial.* 54.1 Justin notes that the Holy Spirit is *continually* (ἀεί) present in those who receive the forgiveness of sins through baptism.

I shall now refer to several further passages in the *Dialogue* which refer to Christian experience of the Spirit. In 39.2 Justin refers to Jews who are becoming Christians in his own day; he claims that this is a daily occurrence. Having been enlightened (by baptism; cf. *1 Apol.* 61.12) through the name of Christ, they receive gifts (δόματα). 'For one receives the Spirit of understanding, one of counsel, one of strength, *one of healing, one of foreknowledge, one of teaching,* one of the fear of God' (*Dial.* 39.2). A similar list of the seven gifts of the Spirit is found at 87.2, where there is explicit reference to, and closer correspondence with, the list in Isa. 11.1-3. In Justin's first list of the sevenfold gifts in 39.2 the absence of a reference to Isaiah and the less close correspondence are not surprising, for three allusions to 1 Corinthians 12 are woven into the list: 'healing' recalls 1 Cor 12.9b; 'foreknowledge' is Justin's interpretation of 'prophecy' in 1 Cor. 12.10b; and 'teaching' alludes to 1 Cor. 12.28.[30]

These allusions strongly suggest dependence on 1 Corinthians (even if only indirectly). The sentences which follow leave no doubt at all about Justin's knowledge of Ephesians. Justin notes that it was prophesied (in Ps. 68.19, LXX) that after the ascent of Christ into heaven he would give gifts (δόματα), but the wording quoted in 39.4 is much closer to Eph. 4.8 than to Psalm 68, as it is also in Justin's second reference to this passage in 87.6.[31] From the immediate contexts of both passages, it is clear that the 'gifts' given by the ascended Christ are gifts of the Spirit, as in Acts 2.33.

Justin elaborates this point in *Dial.* 87.5-6 (cf. also 82.1). Immediately after the quotation of Ps. 68.19/Eph. 4.8, Justin refers to another prophecy: 'And it shall be that after these things I will pour out my Spirit on all people, and upon my servants both men and women, and they will prophesy.' The phrase 'after these things' is closer to Joel 3.1, LXX, than to Acts 2.17, but the addition of 'my' points to use of the version of Joel cited in Acts 2.17-18. O. Skarsaune suggests that this text may be the work of someone (perhaps prior to Justin) condensing the Acts testimony into a much shorter and tighter text, concentrating on the gift of prophecy.[32] I believe that this is undoubtedly the case, for immediately after the citation Justin comments on its continuing significance: he notes that 'among us', that is, in his own day, both men *and women* have been granted gifts

30. These allusions to 1 Corinthians 12 are missed by J. E. Morgan-Wynne in his helpful survey, 'The Holy Spirit and Christian Experience in Justin Martyr', *Vigiliae Christianae* 38 (1984): 172-77.

31. See the 'Synoptic' comparison set out by Skarsaune, *The Proof from Prophecy,* p. 100.

32. *The Proof from Prophecy,* p. 123.

(χαρίσματα) by the Spirit of God. Justin has in mind primarily the gift of prophecy, but the plural 'gifts' should be noted, as should the switch from the δόματα of Ps. 68.19, LXX/Eph. 4.8 to Paul's favourite word in 1 Corinthians 12, χαρίσματα.

Here is unexpected evidence for the continuance of gifts of the Spirit in Justin's day among both men and women, a decade or so before the emergence of Montanism. There is further evidence for the prominence of women in the church in Rome in Justin's day in *2 Apol.* 2.1-20.[33] An unnamed woman has become a Christian through knowledge of the teachings of Christ (as had Justin himself). Marital discord with her non-Christian husband incites him to press charges against Ptolemaeus, her Christian teacher. Ptolemaeus and two other Christians are condemned to death. Peter Lampe has shown that the unnamed woman was a Roman Christian woman of considerable status and cautiously identifies her as Flora, to whom the well-known *Letter of Ptolemaeus to Flora* was written.[34] Rather surprisingly, he does not refer to the further evidence from the *Dialogue* just noted which confirms that women were prominent in the church and exercised the gifts (χαρίσματα) of the Spirit.

In *Dialogue* 87–88 Justin develops his view of the gifts of the Spirit in another unexpected way. He reminds Trypho that one or two of the powers of the Spirit were given by God to the prophets, but they all found their resting place in Christ. 'The Spirit rested therefore, in other words ceased, when Christ came. . . . But after him, it was necessary that those gifts should cease (being among you) . . . and be given by the grace of the power of the Spirit to those who believe in him . . .' (87.5-6; cf. also 88.1).[35]

Justin claims that whereas Israel had experienced the gifts of the Spirit in a limited way before the coming of Christ, with his coming they ceased to be in evidence among the Jewish people and were given in full to Christian believers. The argument is taken further in *Dial.* 135.3-6. 'We, quarried from the bowels of Christ, are the true race of Israel.' On the basis of Isa. 65.9-12 and Isa. 2.5-6 Justin concludes that there are 'two races, two houses of Jacob, the one born of flesh and blood, and the other of faith and the Spirit.'

This stark contrast takes us to the heart of the rhetoric of the *Dialogue.* There is an allusion to the terminology of John 1.13 in the phrase 'flesh and blood'. Even more significant for our present purposes is the allusion to 1 Cor.

33. Eusebius was so impressed by the sorry saga that he quotes Justin's lengthy account in full (*H.E.* 4.17.1-13).

34. Peter Lampe, *From Paul to Valentinus: Christians at Rome in the First Two Centuries* (Germ. ed. 1989; rev. for Eng. trans.; Minneapolis: Fortress, 2003), pp. 237-40.

35. On 'the powers' and the gifts of the Spirit, see esp. C. Oeyen, 'Die Lehre der göttlichen Kräfte bei Justin', *SP* 11, ed. F. L. Cross (TU 108; Berlin: Akademie-Verlag, 1972), pp. 215-21.

12.9 and Gal. 3.14 in Justin's insistence that what differentiates Jews and Christians is faith and the Spirit.

Of course Justin's understanding of the Spirit is less profound than that found in the Pauline and Johannine writings. Nonetheless Justin's understanding of the role of the Spirit is much less wooden than his use of his stock phrase 'the prophetic Spirit' would suggest, for he refers to the Spirit in varied ways. Although his debt to Old Testament and to Jewish traditions is clear, he does develop distinctively Christian views.

Justin's claim that the prophets were inspired by the Spirit did not surprise Trypho, for Justin shared this conviction with Trypho and his fellow Jewish teachers. But Justin's insistence that the predictions of the Spirit-filled prophets have been fulfilled in the coming of Christ or were being fulfilled in his own day was unacceptable and incomprehensible to Trypho.

The distinctively Christian aspects of Justin's understanding of the Spirit have deep roots, primarily within the New Testament writings themselves. Echoes of Matthew, John, Luke-Acts, 1 Corinthians, Galatians, and Ephesians have been noted. Only in the case of 1 Corinthians 12 and Eph. 4.8 is direct literary dependence likely, but there is no doubt that in his understanding of the Spirit Justin has been influenced, however indirectly, by a wide range of New Testament passages.

Justin rarely goes further than his Christian predecessors. With the exception of his fleeting reference to worship of the Spirit in *1 Apol.* 6.2, his thought is no closer to later trinitarian doctrine than that of any of the New Testament writers. His occasional failure to differentiate sharply between Christ (or the Logos) and the Spirit has earlier precedents. In one important respect, however, Justin goes his own way. His double claim that among the Jewish people prophecy ceased with the coming of Christ and that the gifts of the Spirit were evident only among Christian believers strikes a shrill note. But even here Justin's views may be seen as a corollary (in the highly rhetorical context of the *Dialogue*) of his conviction that Christians are the true Israel (*Dial.* 11.5; 123; 135.3), a 'third race' — and that claim has earlier roots in passages such as Matt. 21.43, 1 Cor. 10.32, and Gal. 6.16.

XXVI The Transformation of Some New Testament Texts in Fourth- and Fifth-Century Disputes about Πνεῦμα: *Disputando Inclarescet Veritas*[1]

J. Lionel North

Πνεῦμα occurs 379 times in NA[27], a calculation making it the sixth most common noun after θεός, κύριος, ἄνθρωπος, πατήρ, and ἡμέρα. Πνευματικός/-κῶς occur 28 times. Examination of the fate of these three cognates, as recorded in the *apparatus criticus* of Tischendorf[8], revealed that in the first five hundred years of Christian history about one half became involved in textual alteration of one sort or another, trivial or significant, deliberate or not. Sometimes the definite article was omitted, sometimes added, similarly with ἅγιον and prepositions, particularly ἐν. Factors that led to deliberate alteration include the evolution of the Greek language and style and a developing religious sensitivity and theological sophistication; for example, in gospel exorcisms there was a tendency to downgrade even the unambiguous πνεύματα by substituting δαιμόνια or qualifying it with ἀκάθαρτα.

1. The Latin tag comes from a letter of Hugo Grotius to his brother Willem, dated 4 December 1638. Our theme does not appear to have been treated in the literature covered by Watson E. Mills, *The Holy Spirit: A Bibliography* (Peabody, Mass.: Hendrickson, 1988). The relevant pages in two classics, T. Schermann, *Die Gottheit des heiligen Geistes nach den griechischen Vätern des vierten Jahrhunderts* (STS 4/4-5; Freiburg: Herder, 1901), pp. 1-17, and H. B. Swete, *The Holy Spirit in the Ancient Church* (London: Macmillan, 1912), pp. 163-91, are equally silent on textual matters. Swete's silence is unexpected since his earlier book, *The Holy Spirit in the New Testament* (London: Macmillan, 1909), deals with them fully. Other studies merely mention disputed verses: F. Loofs, "Macedonianism", in *HERE* 8 (1915), p. 226b; M. Meslin, *Les Ariens d'Occident 335-430* (PS 8; Paris: Du Seuil, 1967), pp. 227-35; R. Gryson, *Scolies ariennes sur le Concile d'Aquilée* (SC 267.175-79); R. P. C. Hanson, *The Search for the Christian Doctrine of God: The Arian Controversy 318-81* (Edinburgh: T&T Clark, 1988), p. 770. On pp. 824-49, Hanson discusses "The Influence of Scripture" on the whole debate; cf. Maruta's biblicism below.

One factor especially contributing to the development of theologies of the Spirit was the part played by 'heretics' and their exegesis of Scripture. This starts some fascinating hares. From the 407 instances of πνεῦμα and its cognates I have selected for inevitably brief discussion seven verses where there is textual variation, of which both those dubbed Arians and Pneumatomachians ('Opponents of [claims for the divinity of] the Spirit') and the Nicene-Orthodox took advantage. The last five examples were also alleged to be the subject or result of wilful tampering. I do not invariably concern myself with the putative original, like Grotius finding more value in debates that clarify, to which Christians of many stripes can contribute.

Though Arius and the early Arians concentrated on the status of the Son, I include Arians because it is more than likely that 'Arian' (with 'Semi-Arian') was sometimes used to demonise the Pneumatomachians, the appropriate focus in this volume. This occurred not only because they were all thought, at this point incorrectly, to share[2] Arius's views about the Son, but because even early Arians had already begun to busy themselves with the status of the Spirit.[3] After all, this was the next logical step in their concern to protect the divine monarchy, a concern which lies no less at the heart of Pneumatomachianism.

I

Before we proceed to texts dealing specifically with πνεῦμα (§II), we should note the charges that were brought by their opponents against what they suspected to be Arian and Pneumatomachian text tampering, either with particular verses containing other subject matter or indiscriminately. I relegate accusations levelled explicitly against Arians to the shorthand of a footnote (not forgetting that 'Arians' may disguise Pneumatomachians),[4] and here deal more

2. On the origin of Pneumatomachianism in Arianism, cf. Basil, *Ep.* 125.3 (*PG* 32.549A = Courtonne 2.33); Damasus *ap.* Theodoret, *HE* 5.11 (*PG* 82.1221C = *EOMIA* 1.2.1.285 = GCS, N.F., 5.298); Photius, *Ep.* 8.10 (*PG* 102.637B).

3. For example, Arius himself, as reported by Athanasius, *C. Arian.* 1.6 (*PG* 26.24B); cf. Meslin, *Ariens*, pp. 320-24: "*L'Esprit*, in tertio loco".

4. In chronological order, Hilary, *Coll. Anti. Par.* (*PL* 10.559AB = CSEL 65.183); Marcellus(?), *De Sancta Ecclesia* 10 (*JTS*, n.s. 51 [2000]: 92), on John 1:18; Ambrosiaster, *QVNT* 91.11 (*PL* 35.2285[A] = CSEL 50.158-59), on John 1:1-2; Ambrose, *Fid. Grat.* 2.135; 5.193, on Matt. 24:36 (*PL* 16.587A; 688A = CSEL 78.104; 289) and *Acta Synodi Aquileiae* 36 (*PL* 16.927B = *PL* 62.442AB = CSEL 82/3.348 = SC 267.356), on John 14:28; Augustine, *Doctr. Chr.* 3.3 (*PL* 34.66[B] = CSEL 80.80 = CC 32.78), on John 1:1-2; Salvian, *De gub. Dei* 5.5-7 (*PL* 53.94C-96B = CSEL 8.102-3 = SC 220.314-16). Since Germanists seem to agree that Salvian is referring to the Gothic Bible, and Ulfilas, the bishop who translated it from Greek, was a Homoean Arian, I invite attention to this

fully with two explicit charges against the latter, where the evidence is much less familiar.

First, we have an early fifth-century catalogue of heresies, compiled in Syriac by Maruta, the orthodox bishop of Maipherkat (in eastern Turkey).[5] In order to draw contrasts, the heresiologist groups together Arians, Eunomians, and 'Macedonians'. These last derive their name from Macedonius, the Homoe(ousi?)an bishop of Constantinople who died ca. 362. Like 'Tropici' ('Allegorisers'), Athanasius's nickname for early Pneumatomachians, 'Macedonians' is another, perhaps inappropriate, nickname; hence our interest in Maruta's list. Though his triadic grouping is not peculiar to him,[6] here it serves to claim that while there were doctrines, not specified, which the three parties held in common, they could be distinguished, not only by their attitude towards the Son but by their treatment of the biblical text. The relevant paragraph reads, "In part they [the three heretics] overlap, in part they do not. Arius and Eunomius say that the Son is a creature; Macedonius says that the Son is of

greatest monument of Arian Christianity and to the question, Does it betray signs of bias? Salvian appears to have thought so, but the fragmentary form in which it has been transmitted allows at best only a couple of passages where interference has been detected, namely, 1 Cor. 15:25-27 and, the better candidate, Phil. 2:6 (*PL* 18.745-46; 807-8), but Gryson, *Scolies*, pp. 170-71, doubts even these. P. Heather and J. Matthews, *The Goths in the Fourth Century* (Liverpool: Liverpool University Press, 1991), chs. 5–7, provide up-to-date discussion and orientation.

5. A Syriac text became available in the 1890s, and a German translation was published by O. Braun in 1898 (p. 49 [page numbers in brackets refer only to the lines on Maruta's *Macedonians*]). Bibliographical details are scattered throughout Villecourt's edition (see below), pp. 597 nn. 3-4, 601 n. 7, 682 n. 1, with (incomplete) updating in J. W. Drijvers, "Marutha of Maïpherqat on Helena Augusta, Jerusalem and the Council of Nicaea", SP 34 (Leuven: Peeters, 2001), pp. 54-55 nn. 6-9. In the following year Harnack reprinted Braun's German along with a Latin translation of the anonymous Arabic version, published by Abraham Ecchellensis in Paris in 1645 (cf. TU 19/1b.11; 16-17) and reprinted in the great conciliar collections of Labbe (1671, 2.385E-86A [*sic;* really 387E-88A]), Hardouin (1728, 2.394CD), and Mansi (1759, 2.1059AB). Abu'l-Barakat's Arabic version was first edited and translated into French by L. Villecourt, with E. Tisserant and G. Wiet, as part of his *Livre de la Lampe des Ténèbres* (*PO* 20/4 [1928-29]: 691-92). Beneath this text Villecourt printed translations of parallels in the third version, 'Amr ibn Matta's *Book of the Tower* (p. 692). Other Syriac mss. have been edited by I. E. Rahmani in 1909, *Studia Syriaca* 4 (pp. 79 [Latin], 102* [Syriac]) and A. Vööbus in 1982, CSCO 439-40, *Script. Syr.* 191-92 (439/191.26 [Syriac]; 440/192.22 [English]). A different punctuation led Vööbus to translate the crucial sentence "Yet in the Scriptures they have not corrupted, though Arius and Eunomis and Maqedon have changed words of the New [Testament]". Though this does not alter my point about Pneumatomachian criticism, it undermines my view of Maruta's strategy (see below). I prefer to follow Braun, Rahmani, and Villecourt. There is an early Syriac redaction of Maruta's catalogue by Barhadbesabba 'Arbaïa, but it mentions only Arians in the equivalent paragraph; cf. *PO* 23/2 (1932): 196-97; cf. p. 199.

6. Cf. Loofs, "Macedonianism", p. 225a.

the same nature [as the Father] but that the Holy Spirit is a creature. Arius and Eunomius have falsified nothing in the Scriptures; on the other hand Macedonius has changed the words of the New [Testament]". There are at least three Arabic versions of Maruta's catalogue; one abbreviates and two expand. In the *Book of the Tower,* the fourteenth-century writer 'Amr ibn Matta makes no reference to any alteration of texts. The two expansions enlarge upon the substance of Macedonius's changes, reversing and conflating the accusations about Spirit and Scripture. The version incorporated into the work of another fourteenth-century writer, Abu'l-Barakat, reads, "He altered what was in the books of the New Testament and changed there what he found there on the Holy Spirit". The anonymous version embellishes even that: "He deleted all the passages in the Holy Scriptures which testify to the divinity of the Holy Spirit".

Maruta also was no stranger to embellishment. In view of the allegations reported in n. 4 about Arian tampering with Scripture, his exoneration comes as a surprise. But the reason for his strategy is not far to seek. It is driven by a deep pastoral anxiety about the way Scripture had been and could still be manipulated to the harm of the church, particularly its unity, through the rise of parties, schisms, and heresies (as numerous as bishops!), and he wants to measure the heresies known to him mainly against the yardstick of their treatment of Scripture: Do they corrupt it or not? Of the fifteen heresies Braun and Vööbus list, nine are appraised in this manner. Four have not corrupted it: Arians, Eunomians, Timotheanists (an ascetic group), and Cathari (= Novatianists). Five are guilty: Marcionites, Paul of Samosata, Cuciani (only the New Testament), Montanists and Macedonians.

While Arianism might now politically be considered a spent force, at least in the East, there remained its hydra offspring still to behead (cf. n. 2). In 381 Maruta had attended the Council of Constantinople with his friend John Chrysostom[7] and taken part in the condemnation of Pneumatomachianism. So the purpose of Maruta's unscrupulous rhetoric a generation later becomes clear: to continue to vilify the Pneumatomachians by claiming that they are worse than even the old Arians and Eunomians, and that their Nicene-Orthodox Christology cannot compensate for their high-handed treatment of Scripture, which even their dreadful predecessors had not dared to corrupt.

A second, much later witness to the textual interests of Pneumatomachians may be found in the accusation of the ninth-century churchman, Photius. In an appendix to *De Mystagogia Sancti Spiritus,* just after referring to "Macedonius's insanity" he slyly suggests, νενοθεύκασιν οἱ πνευματομάχοι τὰς τούτων συγγραφάς (*PG* 102.393A). The antecedent of τούτων, however, is not

7. For Maruta's association with John, cf. *PG* 47.236-37; 52.618[A].

New Testament writers but the Latin fathers, Ambrose, Augustine, and Jerome. Since it is improbable that fourth- and fifth-century Greek Pneumatomachians had ever been in a position to meddle with Latin texts, it seems more likely that the Pneumatomachians Photius really has in mind are his *contemporaries in the Lateran in Rome.* In his view they resist the Spirit by attributing 'its' origin to a double source, to the Son as well as the Father. By interpolating their texts with *Filioque* terminology they claim the support of three of the four doctors of the Latin church. But Photius's use of this accusation to describe contemporaries loses its polemical punch if he and his readers were unaware that the *first* Pneumatomachians also had been accused of falsifying Scripture in order to endanger the status of the Spirit (even though Maruta, the only other specific witness, had spoken of change understood as deletion, not interpolation).[8]

Even if some or all of these accusations, above and in n. 4, are well-founded, they prove to be of unequal weight concerning matters like punctuation (Ambrosiaster; Augustine), misquotation (Ambrose, *Acta Synodi Aquileiae*), interpretation (Ambrose, *Fid. Grat.* 2; Salvian), as well as definite tampering, by means of substitution of unsatisfactory alternatives (Marcellus[?]; Ulfilas on Phil. 2:6?) or interpolation (Hilary, *Coll.?;* Ambrose, *Fid. Grat.* 5; Salvian; Photius?), or omission (Maruta). (The following texts could be similarly classified.)

II

Luke 11:2 ἁγιασθήτω τὸ ὄνομά σου· **ἐλθέτω ἡ βασιλεία σου.** (NA[27])

For the origin of Gregory of Nyssa's alternative for the kingdom-clause we may have to go back to Marcion's version of the Lord's Prayer (of course the Lukan version), as far as it can be reconstructed from the comments of his opponent, Tertullian. Instead of the clause *Hallowed be thy name* Marcion appears to have read, *Let thy Holy Spirit come upon us* (*Adv. Marc.* 4.26.3-4 [*PL* 2.425BC = SC 456.332]). Sometime in the 380s Gregory preached a series of sermons on the Prayer, and in the third sermon commented on both *Hallowed be thy name* and *Thy kingdom come,* as found in Matthew, and then introduced his version of Luke into the comment: *Or perhaps, since the same thought is interpreted for us more clearly by Luke, he who thinks it right that the Kingdom should come summons the help of the Holy Spirit. For so he* [Luke] *says in that gospel, instead of Your kingdom come,* ἐλθέτω τὸ πνεῦμά σου τὸ ἅγιον ἐφ' ἡμᾶς καὶ καθαρισάτω

8. Photius was well informed about the first Pneumatomachians; cf. n. 2 and *s.vv.* Macédonios; Pneumatomaque in Photius, *Bibliothèque* (Budé, 1991), ed. J. Schamp, 9:179, 431.

ἡμᾶς. The clause in bold is quoted twice more, and very probably as though it were original (*PG* 44.1157CD; 1160D = Jaeger VII/2.39-40, 44). And when Gregory immediately goes on to ask, *What will those who brazenly sound off* (θρασυστομοῦντες) *against the Spirit have to say to this?* it is easy to see Pneumatomachians in these presumptuous men, especially as he specifically speaks of 'the madness of the Pneumatomachians' (*PG* 1160C = Jaeger, p. 43). Against them it looks as though Gregory has pressed into service and expanded an old Marcionite (or pre-Marcionite) variant or gloss for *Hallowed be thy name* to replace the *next* clause in the Prayer. By clarifying Matthew's βασιλεία, God's executive power, with Luke's πνεῦμα ἅγιον, Gregory would have no difficulty in demonstrating the Spirit's divinity.[9]

The clause was sufficiently plausible to shoulder its way into copies of Luke, where, probably following Gregory, it is read by 700 and, with unimportant differences, by Maximus the Confessor (also writing on the Lord's Prayer, *PG* 90.884B; cf. 885B = CCSG 23.41; cf. 43) and 162.

Luke 11:13 εἰ οὖν ὑμεῖς πονηροὶ ὑπάρχοντες οἴδατε δόματα ἀγαθὰ διδόναι τοῖς τέκνοις ὑμῶν, πόσῳ μᾶλλον ὁ πατὴρ [ὁ] ἐξ οὐρανοῦ δώσει **πνεῦμα ἅγιον** τοῖς αἰτοῦσιν αὐτόν

Debating in the anti-Arian interest and probably following Didymus the Blind (*De Spiritu Sancto* 11–13 [*PG* 39.1042D-46B = SC 386.152-54]; cf. Didymus(?),[10] *Trin.* 2.8 [*PG* 39.532A]), Ambrose notes from the parallel that his Matthew has *bona.* Since *bona* must have the same referent as the Lukan version, *spiritus sanctus,* he concludes that Matthew's *good things* are exemplified in Luke's *Holy Spirit.* Second, Ambrose shows himself aware that some [Lukan] mss. have *bonum datum* instead of Holy Spirit, but this does not disconcert him; the variant is gratefully incorporated into his theology of the Spirit. He conflates Matthew with both alternatives in Luke: the Spirit is both good and God-given, on *two* counts divine (*Sp. S.* 1.65-66 [*PL* 16.720CD = CSEL 79.42-43]).[11]

There are four variants for πνεῦμα ἅγιον, namely, πνεῦμα ἀγαθόν, ἀγαθὸν

9. James Dunn wrote on "Spirit and Kingdom," in *The Christ and the Spirit* (Grand Rapids: Eerdmans, 1998), 2:133-41, and enquired about the originality of the clause (p. 138; cf. p. 6). J. Delobel, "The Lord's Prayer in the Textual Tradition: A Critique of Recent Theories and Their View on Marcion's Role," in *The New Testament in Early Christianity,* ed. J.-M. Sevrin (BETL 86; Leuven: Leuven University Press, 1989), pp. 293-309, esp. 294-98, doubts both its originality and the importance of Marcion.

10. 'Didymus (?)' indicates the uncertainty about *De Trinitate;* see under Rom. 8:11 for details about the works attributed to Didymus.

11. Marcellus(?) similarly conflates; cf. *De Incarnatione et contra Arianos* 16 (*PG* 26.1012A).

δόμα, δόματα ἀγαθά, and simply ἀγαθά. *Good gift(s)* and *good things* are clearly harmonisations to or adaptations of either the parallel in Matt. 7:11b, ἀγαθά, or the first element in Luke's own *qal waḥomer,* δόματα ἀγαθά. But what of the two variants involving πνεῦμα? Πνεῦμα ἀγαθόν is particularly interesting because of (a) its earliness of attestation in P^{45} (ca. 225), and (b) its even earlier attestation in the LXX (2 Esdr. 19:20[= Neh. 9:20]; Ps. 142[143]:10), τὸ πνεῦμά σου τὸ ἀγαθόν.[12] Could it be original?[13] Πνεῦμα must be, and ἀγαθόν, qualifying πνεῦμα only here in Luke-Acts, both echoes δόματα ἀγαθά and has that antique Septuagintal patina about it which Luke emulated elsewhere. Though we cannot overlook the possibility of clerical error (ἈΓ . . . ON → ἈΓ . . . ON) or contamination from an identical error in both LXX passages, standardisation to ἅγιον, with πνεῦμα occurring 55 times in Luke-Acts, must have been irresistible.

John 1:3-4 καὶ χωρὶς αὐτοῦ **ἐγένετο οὐδὲ ἕν. ὃ γέγονεν** ἐν αὐτῷ ἐν αὐτῷ ζωὴ ἦν, . . .

Prima facie these verses do not involve Spirit, only a famous punctuation crux. Should we read . . . ἐγένετο οὐδὲ ἕν. ὃ γέγονεν . . . or . . . ἐγένετο οὐδὲ ἓν ὃ γέγονεν? The former, the earlier-attested form, had been prominent in Gnostic and Arian exegesis and therefore in their opponents', vis-à-vis the Son. But its adoption by the Pneumatomachians led the orthodox to embrace the latter form of punctuation, to exclude the Spirit from the created order. It was used first by Epiphanius (*Ancoratus* 74-75 [*PG* 43.156C, 157A = Holl 1.93-94], ca. 374) and then by John Chrysostom (in loc., *PG* 59.53, ca. 389). Strangely, neither labels his opponent since elsewhere both could be sharply specific; for example, Chrysostom could utter the warning, τὸ ἔνδυμα . . . μὴ Μακεδονικῇ πνευματομαχίᾳ φορέσῃς ('Don't dress up in Macedonius's Pneumatomachianism!', recorded by Anastasius of Sinai; *PG* 89.401B). But here Chrysostom speaks only of αἱρετικοί, and Epiphanius only of those who blaspheme the Holy Spirit. Labelling was left to the eleventh-century exegete Theophylact: οἱ . . . Πνευματομάχοι, later called οἱ περὶ Μακεδόνιον, punctuate the clause after ἕν in their wish to include the Spirit within the creation referred to in the sequel ὃ γέγονεν ἐν αὐτῷ ζωὴ ἦν, . . . (in loc., *PG* 123.1145AB). Theophylact is followed 250 years later by Constantine Harmenopulos, who, with a lawyer's conciseness, extracts the salient points from what his predecessor had said (*PG* 150.21A).

12. Without reference to 11:13 Didymus quotes the LXX examples and the variant in the Psalm (see below); cf. *Sp. S.* 232 (*PG* 39.1078A = SC 386.352-54).

13. W. Grundmann (in loc. [1971[6]], p. 235) and M. Turner, *Power from on High* (Sheffield: Sheffield Academic Press, 1996), pp. 340-41, esp. n. 61, think so.

Today the Gnostic-Arian punctuation is often accepted as John's original and the orthodox repunctuation seen as a nervous apologetic riposte.[14] But, as Ambrose twice insisted, apropos the Son, the proper response is sound exegesis of the earlier ambiguous punctuation, not rearranging it (*Ps.* 36.35 [*PL* 14.984BC = CSEL 64.98]; cf. *Fid.* 3.41-45 [*PL* 16.598A-99A = CSEL 78.122-24]).

John 3:6b καὶ τὸ γεγεννημένον ἐκ τοῦ πνεύματος πνεῦμά ἐστιν

et quod natum est ex spiritu spiritus est (Vulgate)
Latin mss., Hilary and Ambrose add ***quia deus spiritus est;***
cf. 4:24a, ***spiritus est deus*** (Vulgate)

Here for Ambrose was particularly clear evidence of Arian tampering with the text. At *Sp. S.* 3.59 (cf. §§59-63; 66 [*PL* 16.789C-92A = CSEL 79.174-76; 178]) Ambrose twice distinguished between *your* [Arian] *codices* and *those of the church (ecclesiastici)* and claimed that Arians in northern Italy and the Balkans had deleted the clause *quia deus spiritus est.*[15] Today, however, this clause is found in only five Old Latin mss. and one Vulgate ms. and cannot be regarded as original. So it is not the case that Arians deleted anything. John never wrote this, and it is Ambrose (with Hilary [see below]) who has based his argument on a strand of the textual tradition contaminated by orthodox interpolation with a *pre*-Arian history.

It is one of several supplements at 3:6, and first found among the fathers, as part of a longer supplement, in Tertullian, *quia deus spiritus est et de deo natus est* (*Carn. Chr.* 18.5 [*PL* 2.783C = SC 216.286]). It is found in the shorter form *(quia deus spiritus est)* in Hilary (*Trin.* 7.14, 30 [*PL* 10.210C-211A; 225B = CC 62.274, 297 = SC 448.304, 346]), and then in Ambrose, both now gratefully deploying its anti-Arian thrust. It may arise from 4:24a, πνεῦμα ὁ θεός = *spiritus est deus,* with the reversal of subject and predicate.[16] Ambrose's mistake infiltrated copies of John, as contained in the six Latin mss., and, along with the

14. K. Aland, "Eine Untersuchung zu Joh 13.4: Über die Bedeutung eines Punktes", *ZNW* 59 (1968): 174-209, esp. 199-204, concentrates on the Arian use of the verses, along with their opponents' punctuation, vis-à-vis the Son, rather than the contemporary Arian-Pneumatomachian use vis-à-vis the Spirit.

15. Ambrose had already quoted the interpolated verse at *Sp. S.* 2.63 (*PL* 16.756B = CSEL 79.111). Faller is mistaken in saying (CSEL 79.174n.) that in Ambrose's view the Arians had interpolated *quia deus spiritus est;* they had *deleted* it, and Ambrose rings the changes on *auferre, tollere, abolere, oblinire,* and *delere* to say so.

16. But Hilary can allude to or quote 4:24a as either *spiritus deus est* (four times) or *deus spiritus (est)* (five times); cf. *Trin.* 2.31; 4.8 (*PL* 10.71B-72B; 102A = CC 62.65-67; 109 = SC 443.324-26; 448.26). But *deus spiritus est* might be an ungrammatical reminiscence of 3:6.

slander, was still being peddled 500 and 650 years later, by two Gallic bishops, Hincmar (*PL* 125.527A; 126.351D) and Fulbert(?) (*PL* 141.197BC). This versatile *theologoumenon* was spliced onto 3:8 as read by Optatus of Milevis, ca. 365: *nam* ***spiritus deus est*** *et ubi vult aspirat et vocem eius audis et nescis unde veniat et quo eat* (2.7.1 [*PL* 11.959B-60A = SC 412.256]).

Romans 8:11 εἰ δὲ τὸ πνεῦμα τοῦ ἐγείραντος τὸν Ἰησοῦν ἐκ νεκρῶν οἰκεῖ ἐν ὑμῖν, ὁ ἐγείρας Χριστὸν ἐκ νεκρῶν ζῳοποιήσει καὶ τὰ θνητὰ σώματα ὑμῶν **διὰ τοῦ ἐνοικοῦντος αὐτοῦ πνεύματος ἐν ὑμῖν**

Will God make alive your mortal bodies ***through*** *his Spirit that dwells within you* or ***because of*** *his Spirit* . . . (διὰ τὸ ἐνοικοῦν αὐτοῦ πνεῦμα . . .)? Does διά take the genitive to express agency or the accusative to express cause? This is not a case where one reading is obviously orthodox and the other obviously heretical, though that differentiation did occur later on (see below). Both readings are within Paul's theological compass; both make good sense; both have early and good attestation; both have been declared original. To make a decision more difficult, I notice from Bauer that διά plus genitive can express cause and διά plus accusative agency, that is, in prescribed circumstances they are interchangeable.[17] But, either the genitive replaced the accusative in some mss.[18] or vice versa, and by the fourth century both readings were known and discriminated, and the distinction taken sufficiently seriously to be made to support different theologies of the Spirit.

This verse is one of the most interesting in our survey in that for it we have explicit documentation which shows that it figured prominently in debates between Nicene-Orthodox and Pneumatomachian Christians. Our three sources are perhaps all the work of Didymus, though uncertainty does not affect our results. There is no doubt about the authenticity of *De Spiritu Sancto* (extant only in Jerome's translation), some about *De Trinitate,* and more about the important third dialogue *De Sancta Trinitate,* printed among the *spuria* of Athanasius.[19]

17. *BDAG, s.v.* διά A5; B2, d, β; cf. H. G. Meecham, *The Letter of Aristeas* (Manchester: Manchester University Press, 1935), pp. 144-46.

18. P^{46} is not extant for this verse. το, the reading of TR, was favoured by B. Weiss as *'exegetisch nothwendig'* (TU 14/3.54-55). Could the syllable -του in αυτου have contaminated an original το, perhaps aided and abetted by -ου- in ενοικουν, with participle and noun then conformed to the dittograph? See n. 22.

19. Hanson, *Search,* pp. 654-57, shares the doubts about *De Trinitate,* but *cf. CPG* §2570 and Supplement. A. Heron leaves the authorship of the Dialogue open; cf. "The Two Pseudo-Athanasian Dialogues against the Anomoeans," *JTS,* n.s. 24 (1973): 122, n. 1.

De Spiritu Sancto, written ca. 375, contains no specific indication of an opponent. In §§177 and 193 Didymus calmly quotes the verse with the genitive, *per* in Jerome's Latin = *through* (*PG* 39.1067D [*propter,* wrongly[20]]; 1070A = SC 386.304-6; 316). But about ten years later, again with the genitive, Didymus(?) provides a context. His opponents, very probably Pneumatomachians, are οἱ αἱρετικοί κόρακες, unclean ravens who foul the divine words (see below on Phil. 3:3) and here exchange (ἐναλλάξαντες[21]) the genitive for the accusative, giving as their reason *lest* [the Spirit] *be shown to be life-giving and* [so] *a creator* (*Trin.* 2.11 [*PG* 39.664BC]; similarly *Trin.* 2.7.1; 2.7.3; 3.23 [560B, 568A, 933A]). Finally, in the third dialogue *De Sancta Trinitate,* between Orthodox and Pneumatomachian, we seem to have the record of a real debate or, as Heron puts it (n. 19, p. 101), "a point-by-point Orthodox refutation of arguments quoted from documents put out by the other side". The long passage in §20 deserves to be paraphrased (*PG* 28.1233BC). When asked for biblical proof that not only the Father and the Son raise the dead and give them life but that the Spirit also makes alive, 'Orthodox' quotes Rom. 8:9-11 with the genitive and is corrected: "Scripture reads the accusative not the genitive in v. 11, *because of,* not *through*". Then it is 'Pneumatomachian's' turn to be challenged: "If you were shown that the genitive is the correct reading, would you believe in the divinity of the Spirit?" He prevaricates, "Do you think you can persuade me by showing me one or two copies of Romans that you have corrupted (ἐσφαλμένον)?" 'Orthodox' replies with unscrupulous exaggeration: "All the old copies read the genitive"! Later in the Dialogue 'Pneumatomachian's' preference for the accusative is characterised as debasing theological coinage, counterfeiting a fully trinitarian gospel (παραχαράττοντες, §26 [1244B]).[22]

Philippians 3:3 ἡμεῖς γάρ ἐσμεν ἡ περιτομή, **οἱ πνεύματι θεοῦ λατρεύοντες** καὶ καυχώμενοι ἐν Χριστῷ Ἰησοῦ καὶ οὐκ ἐν σαρκὶ πεποιθότες
nos enim sumus circumcisio, ***qui spiritu deo servimus*** *et gloriamur in Christo Iesu et non in carne fiduciam habentes*

20. Cf. the editors' notes in *PG* 39.559-60 and SC 386.401.

21. Cf. τῶν νοθευθέντων τόπων and παραποιηθεῖσαι βίβλοι (665A).

22. Before the rise of Pneumatomachianism the orthodox had not found the accusative an embarrassment; e.g., Methodius (died ca. 311) used both cases in quoting this verse (*ap.* Epiphanius, *PG* 41.1160B; 1176B = GCS 31.484, 498). Even afterwards Ambrose used both *propter* (*Sp. S.* 2.31 [*PL* 16.749B = CSEL 79.98]) and *per* (*Sp. S.* 2.99; 3.149 [*PL* 16.764A; 811C = CSEL 79.125, 213]). Hilary used only *propter* (*Trin.* 2.29; 8.21 [*PL* 10.70A; 252B = CC 62.65; 62A.333 = SC 443.322; 448.410]).

NA[27] prints what may be Paul's original, and most commentators and translators, preferring θεοῦ and construing λατρεύοντες absolutely and πνεύματι as an instrumental dative, translate the Greek clause in bold *We who serve by the Spirit of God* (though *We who serve the Spirit of God* is possible; see [c] below). Transmission, however, has disturbed the clause in two ways: (a) θεῷ was substituted for θεοῦ,[23] and (b) P[46] reads neither. Then, (a) and (b) are complicated in that (c) λατρεύω takes the dative. These three factors set up five new possibilities that differently modify the syntax of the clause and our understanding of πνεύματι. (a) plus (c) allow *We who serve God by the Spirit* and *We who serve the Spirit who is God;* (b) plus (c) allow *We who serve by the Spirit, We who serve the Spirit,* and, in the more anthropological rendering of *NEB* (1961 and 1970[2], not repeated in *REB* [1989]), *We whose worship is spiritual.* The Greek mss. alone are witness to seven permutations and a real puzzle.

Three or four fathers quote this verse and show how their knowledge of some of these permutations could be used to reflect their own theological purposes and changing circumstances. First, at *Sp. S.* 249 (*PG* 39.1081B = SC 386.368), just before dealing with Rom. 8:11, Didymus loosely quotes our verse in the form *We are the circumcision, who serve the Lord by the Spirit (spiritu domino) and put no trust in the flesh.* Then, in *De Trinitate* Didymus(?) reads, *We who serve the Spirit of God* (πνεύματι θεοῦ), and says that it is heretical ravens who try to foul the divine words by reading, *We who serve God by the Spirit* (πνεύματι θεῷ) (2.11; 21 [*PG* 39.664B; 741B]). With a minimum of change (ὑπαλλαγή), just a single letter, θεοῦ → θεῷ, they achieve their purpose, to deny that worship is offered to the Spirit, to enable them to conclude that the Spirit is not divine. By providing λατρεύοντες with another object, πνεύματι can be construed differently, no longer object but agent. This reading is of course the one that Didymus had preferred ten years earlier.[24]

Since Ambrose and Augustine write in Latin, they introduce additional complications. Like λατρεύω, *servio* takes the dative, but, unlike Greek, their mother tongue has a fifth case, the ablative, which (a) can deal with agency and (b) in the second declension has a suffix identical with the dative (e.g., *deo*). The plot thickens!

Ambrose (*Sp. S.* 2.45-47 [*PL* 16.752B = CSEL 79.103-4], repeated at *Sp. S.* 3.77, 142; cf. 140) follows the Greek, which he quotes (πνεύματι θεοῦ) and translates *spiritui dei servimus, We who serve the Spirit of God;* his Latin can mean no

23. The dative, the reading of the TR, was defended by H. A. A. Kennedy in loc. (1910), adopted in their translations by J. Moffatt (1913) and W. Barclay (1969).

24. His editors comment on what they thought was the same author's abandonment of θεῷ; cf. *PG* 39.663 n. 1, 665 n. 4; SC 386.407.

other. But for anti-Arian reasons (see below) he chooses to concentrate on *serve.* Biblical monotheism implies that liturgical service, the specific force of λατρεύω, is acceptable only if it is offered to God; so Ambrose concludes that the Spirit, offered this service, must be divine. Arians are not specifically mentioned here, but, as we have seen on John 3:6b, they are mentioned later in *De Spiritu Sancto* (3.59), where they are accused of similar tampering; so when here in 2.45-47 Ambrose refers to unbelievers who falsified Latin mss. *(perfidi falsaverunt),* we can be confident he already has Arians in mind. Their falsification must have been to read *deo, We who serve God by the Spirit.*

Like many whose *oeuvre* extends over half a lifetime, Augustine is not embarrassed about retracting earlier views. He discussed this verse at least three times over twenty years. Early in his long work *De Trinitate,* begun in 399, Augustine reads *We who serve the Spirit of God* (*spiritui dei;* 1.13 [*PL* 42.828A = CC 50.43-44]). It has, he says, the support of "most Latin mss." and "all or nearly all Greek". But he acknowledges *We who serve God by the Spirit (spiritu deo),* found in some Latin mss. (the reading of Didymus). However, he darkly adds, those who accept that are in error, refusing to yield to what he calls *weightier authority* (meaning Greek mss.). This is the closest he comes to speaking about any deviant form of text; here he is more interested in a general principle (Greek mss. are more important than Latin), less so in the dogmatic issue.

About seventeen years later, in 416, this verse was part of the text of a lengthy homily (*Serm.* 169 [*PL* 38.915-26]). Augustine begins with a discussion of the variants. In §§1 and 3-4 he still reads, *We who serve the Spirit of God,* repeating that it is supported by most of the Greek mss. that he could find, but now *We who serve God by the Spirit* is coming up fast on the rails, spurred on by most mss. (by which he must mean Latin mss.). So now Augustine is ready to compromise and retain both readings; if the latter is reinterpreted, no suspicion need hang over it. After all, he says, both are meaningful and congruous with the rule of truth. So he 'anthropologises' *We who serve God by the Spirit* and then conflates: *We both serve the Spirit of God and we serve God not in flesh but in spirit.* Honesty may explain the preacher's treatment of the reliability of his text, but I am not sure what Augustine's congregation made of it!

In 420-21 Augustine came full circle. The reading he disapproved of in 399 *(spiritu deo)* and would conflate only after reinterpretation in 416, five years later is now his first choice, though he recognizes two others, the old *spiritui dei* and, a new permutation, *spiritui deo* (*C. du. ep. Pelag.* 3.22 [*PL* 44.604[C] = CSEL 60.512]). Gone are the arguments from "most Latin mss." and the "weightier authority" of "all or nearly all Greek", and the reason is to hand. In the early fifth century the revision of the Old Latin Bible connected with the name of Jerome[25] was gaining ground, and its reading here was *We who serve God by the Spirit.* After following Didymus(?) and Ambrose (πνεύματι θεοῦ// *spiritui dei*), Augustine had overcome his scruples and was not afraid to return to Didymus and the soiled text of Didymus(?)'s opponents (*spiritu domino*// πνεύματι θεῷ) and to a pneumatological exegesis. Its endorsement by his friend Jerome made all the difference.

It is not clear whether Augustine realised that his Latin allowed him to construe *spiritui deo* or *spiritu deo* as datives or ablatives *in apposition* and that he had in *We who serve (by)* ***the Spirit who is God*** an anti-Arian-Pneumatomachian proof text. It seems that Sedulius Scottus in loc. did realise this; commenting on the lemma *qui spiritu*, after *id est, mente, non littera deo servimus*, he proceeds, *In Graeco, melius, spiritui, id est sancto, qui est deus* (*PL* 103.215C).

Is the absence of θεοῦ or θεῷ from P[46] (ca. 200) original? If it were, interpolation might mean that a double effect was achieved. There are (a) a clearer trinitarian effect (at the cost of obscuring an example of the familiar Pauline πνεύματι/σαρκί antithesis, πνεύματι now being less anthropological and more pneumatological),[26] and (b) a greater rhetorical effect (with all three participles now being more evenly qualified). These 'improvements' suggest that P[46] is original.[27]

1 John 4:3a καὶ πᾶν πνεῦμα ὃ μὴ ὁμολογεῖ [*v.l.* **λύει**] τὸν Ἰησοῦν ἐκ τοῦ θεοῦ οὐκ ἔστιν
et omnis spiritus qui solvit Iesum ex deo non est

According to Bede, *solvit* (= λύει), the well-known Latin variant for μὴ ὁμολογεῖ, is part of a larger variation unit. Without naming names he refers to those who *Have erased this clause* [*all* the Latin in bold] *from this epistle, lest their* [christological] *errors be exposed (convincerentur) on the authority of the blessed John* (in loc., *PL* 93.106C = CC 121.311).[28] It was left to two of those who directly or indirectly borrowed from Bede to characterise these men as Arians,

25. Modern Vulgate scholarship is uncertain about Jerome's role in Old Latin New Testament revision outside the Gospels.

26. Even *with* 'God' (whether θεῷ [*PG* 62.257[B]] or θεοῦ [Field 5.113]), by paraphrasing πνεύματι with πνευματικῶς Chrysostom (in loc.) shows that the anthropology could survive, as in Augustine's 416 reinterpretation and Sedulius's second choice, *mente.*

27. E. Fascher, *Textgeschichte als hermeneutisches Problem* (Halle: Niemeyer, 1953), pp. 91-92, concurs.

28. Bede may have misunderstood comments about λύει extant first in Socrates (*HE* 7.32, *PG* 67.809C-12A = GCS, N.F., 1.381) but mediated to him through Cassiodorus's Latin translation (*Historia Tripartita* 12.4.27-8, *PL* 69.1206BC = CSEL 71.668).

to Fulbert(?) certainly (*PL* 141.197BC), Hincmar very probably (*PL* 125.527A; 126.351D).[29] Though for all its use of πνεῦμα this clause concerns Christology rather than Spirit, the formal dependence of even the pejorative πᾶν πνεῦμα (v. 3a; cf. v. 6c and 2 Cor. 11:4b) on τὸ πνεῦμα τοῦ θεοῦ (v. 2a) justifies its inclusion in this list, since, at least for Fulbert(?), the erroneous Christology of the Arian prophet was exposed only by the Spirit of God.

Envoi: it is noteworthy that statements about the Spirit, who, the Truth promised (John 16:13), would be the guide in (or, into) all truth, were themselves not shielded from adaptation. A disciple of Grotius will conclude that truth becomes visible, is even transformed, only through debate.

29. The references to the erasure of this clause in two other borrowers, the *Glossa Ordinaria* and Martin of León, make no mention of heretics; cf. *PL* 114.701AB; 209.279B.

XXVII Translational Tendenz: English Versions and Πνεῦμα in Paul

Gordon D. Fee

Anyone who has tried to write commentaries and has also served on a translation committee knows the perils of the latter undertaking. Besides the ordinary task of trying to offer a minimalist interpretation — over against a maximalist one available in a commentary — there is the difficulty of staying within the boundaries of one's translational theory, whether formal or functional equivalency. These two translational pitfalls have been especially troublesome for English translators (as interpreters) when it comes to rendering certain instances of Paul's use of πνεῦμα, where it is not always clear whether he intends the divine Spirit or the human spirit or simply an attitude. But since capitalization affords the luxury in English of making this distinction, one's understanding of this word is usually self-evident in the translation itself.

The purpose of this paper is to examine the history of translational, and therefore interpretive, tendencies in the history of English translations of πνεῦμα, beginning with the Authorized (King James) Version. I begin with the KJV, rather than its earlier forerunners, since it has so heavily influenced the use of the Bible in English in all Protestant traditions, and since it has had a century-long history of "revision": beginning with the turn-of-the-century (English) Revised Version (ERV, 1885) and American Standard Version (ASV, 1901), through the mid-century Revised Standard Version (RSV, 1948/1952) and the New American Standard Bible (NASB, 1963/1971), up to the revisions of the latter two (New Revised Standard Version [NRSV, 1989] and New American Standard Bible Updated [NASU, 1995]). Since the NRSV was also self-consciously gender inclusive, a group of American evangelicals of a more conservative stripe bought the rights to revise the RSV yet again, calling it the English Standard Version (ESV, 2001), which was equally self-consciously gender exclusive.

To round out the picture, I have also included several translations that cross the twentieth century, including both committee translations and a few of those by individuals. Of the former, pride of place goes to the pioneering Twentieth Century New Testament (TCNT, 1904), followed by the New English Bible (NEB, 1961/1970),[1] the New International Version (NIV, 1973/1978), and two Roman Catholic translations, the Jerusalem Bible (JB, 1966) and the New American Bible (NAB, 1970). These latter four were all revised toward the end of the century: the Revised English Bible (1989), Today's New International Version (TNIV, 2002[NT]), the New Jerusalem Bible (NJB, 1985), and the revised NAB (1986).[2] Of the translations by individuals, I have included those by Weymouth (1903), Moffatt (1913/1924), Goodspeed (1923/1931), Bratcher (TEV/GNB, 1971), and the New Living Translation (NLT, 1997; a committee revision of the Living Bible).

My goal in this investigation is to note how (or whether) the more self-conscious work on the Spirit in the New Testament, which gained momentum in the academy during the last third of the twentieth century, has or has not affected the translation of πνεῦμα in the Pauline corpus. I offer this study in honor of a colleague of long standing,[3] whose seminal work on the Spirit in Paul served as the impetus for much of the scholarly activity on the Spirit in Paul over the past several decades,[4] including my own.[5]

1. The first date in this and following instances is for the publication of the New Testament, followed by that for the entire Bible.

2. The New Testament was revised and the whole published in 1986 without changing the name; I have chosen to designate the revision as NAB².

3. Jimmy Dunn and I first met while standing in line at the annual meeting of the SNTS in Los Angeles in the summer of 1972, just after my review of his *Baptism in the Holy Spirit* (see next note) appeared in the *JBL* (1972, pp. 128-29). That bit of banter led to many years of exchange, which, even though often expressed in friendly disagreement, has never gotten in the way of friendship. I am glad to honor him with this piece that I hope will be useful to many.

4. See his *Baptism in the Holy Spirit: A Re-examination of the New Testament Teaching on the Gift of the Spirit in Relation to Pentecostalism Today* (SBT 2nd ser. 15; London: SCM, 1970).

5. See *God's Empowering Presence: The Holy Spirit in the Letters of Paul* (Peabody, Mass.: Hendrickson, 1994). Since the first 700 pages of this book offer a full exegesis of all these texts, I also need to note that I do not pretend that in the present analysis I am a neutral observer of the data. Indeed, that work turned me into a maximalist when it comes to language of the Spirit in Paul — perhaps overmuch, but always on the basis of careful exegesis of all the texts. My interest in the present subject was piqued while writing that book, especially with how the NIV and others handled 1 Cor. 14:2-16; 2 Cor. 12:18; and Phil. 1:27.

I. On Naming the Spirit

The KJV, which set patterns for many modern revisions/translations, had its own idiosyncrasies in translating πνεῦμα; but, as one might well expect, they were consistently maintained throughout the Pauline corpus. This is especially true when it came to naming the Spirit. Thus, the compound πνεῦμα ἅγιον (or τὸ πνεῦμα τὸ ἅγιον) is always translated "Holy Ghost."[6] However, when this compound appears with a genitive qualifier, the "holy" is lower case and πνεῦμα becomes "Spirit" — "his holy Spirit" (1 Thess. 4:8); "the holy Spirit of God" (Eph. 4:30). This latter phenomenon was most likely influenced by their consistent translation of τὸ πνεῦμα τοῦ θεοῦ as "the Spirit of God," which seems to have been titular for the translators,[7] thus suggesting that in these two cases "holy" was seen as an adjectival qualifier rather than part of the divine name. They also regularly translated the articular τὸ πνεύμα as "the Spirit,"[8] as well as when "the Spirit" has an adjective qualifier ("one," "same").[9]

Except for a couple of idiosyncratic moments,[10] the subsequent translations also regularly render the combination πνεῦμα θεοῦ as "the Spirit of God." But some differences occur with the compound πνεῦμα ἅγιον. The only translation that kept the KJV's "Holy Ghost" was the ERV, an apparent accommodation to "sacred usage" in the church. But in changing to "Spirit" in this combination, not all translators were ready to understand the ἅγιον as part of a compound name, but rather (apparently) as an adjectival qualifier. Thus three translations (Moffatt, Goodspeed, NAB^2) regularly render this compound as "the holy Spirit."

In the case of Moffatt and Goodspeed one suspects that this move was motivated in part by a lack of comfort with the idea of the Spirit as "person." Three things make one think so. First, both of them consistently translate other titular phrases with capital letters (e.g., "Kingdom of God"). Thus in Rom. 14:17 Goodspeed has "the Kingdom of God . . . is a matter of . . . happiness through

6. See 1 Thess. 1:5, 6; 1 Cor. 2:13 (TR); 6:19; 12:3; 2 Cor. 6:6; 13:14(13 Gk.); Rom. 5:5; 9:1; 14:17; 15:13; 2 Tim. 1:14; 3:5.

7. See 1 Cor. 2:11, 14; 3:16; 6:11; 7:40; 12:3; Rom. 8:9. But cf. "the Spirit of the living God" (2 Cor. 3:3), the three instances where Christ is the genitive qualifier (Rom. 8:9; Gal. 4:6; Phil. 1:19), and the two instances of "Spirit of the Lord" (2 Cor. 3:17, 18).

8. See 1 Cor. 2:10 (second occurrence; the first occurrence has the secondary αὐτοῦ, which is translated "his Spirit"); 12:7, 8a; 2 Cor. 1:22; 5:5; Gal. 3:2, 5, 14; 5:17, 17, 22; 6:8, 8; Rom. 8:1 (TR), 2, 10, 11, 16, 23, 26, 26, 27; 15:30; Eph. 4:3; 5:9 (TR); 6:17.

9. For the two exceptions (2 Cor. 12:18; Phil. 1:27) see Section III below.

10. Whereas Goodspeed ordinarily translated πνεῦμα θεοῦ either as "the Spirit of God" or "God's Spirit," in 1 Cor. 7:40 he renders it "God's spirit"; and in Phil. 3:3, the NAB/NAB^2 render the phrase "the spirit of God," which otherwise they translate as "the Spirit of God." Weymouth renders τῆς συνειδήσεώς μου ἐν πνεύματι ἁγίῳ as "my inspired conscience."

the possession of the holy Spirit." Second, they do *not* do the same with the similar use of κύριος with Ἰησοῦς in the Pauline corpus. That is, they consistently render ὁ κύριος as "the Lord," and do the same with the compound "the Lord Jesus"; whereas the latter could just as easily, as with the "holy" Spirit, be understood as an adjectival qualifier. Third, they both eliminate personhood with the two intensive αὐτό's in Rom. 8:16 and 26 — Goodspeed by keeping the KJV's "itself," Moffatt by eliminating the intensive altogether.

What lies behind this same phenomenon in the revised NAB is especially puzzling.[11] On the one hand, the revisers consistently alter the original NAB's "Holy Spirit" to "holy Spirit"; on the other hand, while they often keep the NAB's rendering of τὸ πνεῦμα as "the spirit,"[12] they also at times change it to "the Spirit."[13] It does catch the eye to read Eph. 4:3-4 as "striving to preserve the unity of the spirit through the bond of peace: one hope and one Spirit."

Considerable variation among the translations in rendering πνεῦμα ἅγιον occurs only in 2 Cor. 6:6, which is an exegetical matter, pure and simple. At issue is the unusual appearance of "the Holy Spirit" in a Pauline list that otherwise seems more existential or attitudinal. But the translations that here abandon the ordinary sense of ἐν πνεύματι ἁγίῳ in Paul end up with strange — and lexically unsupportable — locutions like "holiness of spirit" (TCNT, Goodspeed, NRSV) or "spirit of holiness" (JB). Far better, it would seem, to go with Paul's ordinary usage, especially when a good case can be made for its appearance right at this point in the list.[14]

Finally, we should note that the KJV also consistently translates unmodified τὸ πνεῦμα as "the Spirit," whether nominative or accusative.[15] Subsequent

11. They regularly render the combination πνεῦμα θεοῦ and πνεῦμα κυρίου as "the Spirit of God/the Lord," including Phil. 3:3, where the NAB had (the idiosyncratic) "spirit of God." Yet in the three cases of the Spirit in association with Christ, they have "the Spirit of Christ" (Rom. 8:9) and "the Spirit of Jesus Christ" (Phil. 1:19), but "the spirit of his Son" (Gal. 4:6). They regularly capitalize "the one/same Spirit" (1 Cor. 12:4, 8, 9, 11, 13; Eph. 2:18, and 4:4). Otherwise they have "the spirit" in Rom. 2:29; 7:6; 8:2, 4, 5, 6, 9(first occurrence), 13, 15; 1 Cor. 2:4; 14:2, 16; Gal. 3:3; 4:29; 6:8; 4:3; and "the Spirit" in Rom. 8:11(2x), 13, 16, 23, 26, 27; 15:30; 1 Cor. 2:10, 12; 2 Cor. 1:22; 3:6; 5:5; Gal. 3:2, 5, 14; 5:5, 15, 17, 18, 22, 25(2x); Eph. 2:22; 3:5, 16; 5:18; 6:17, 18; Phil. 2:1; Col. 1:8; 1 Thess. 5:19; 2 Thess. 2:13; 1 Tim. 3:16. In a large number of the latter instances, the revisers reversed the original NAB; but in some cases (1 Cor. 4:2; 14:1) they went the other direction.

12. See Rom. 2:29; 7:6; 8:2, 4, 5, 6, 9(first occurrence), 13, 15; 1 Cor. 2:4; 14:2, 16; Gal. 3:3; 4:29; 6:8; Eph. 4:3. In three cases (1 Cor. 2:4; 14:2; Eph. 4:3) they reverse the original NAB, which they also do in 2 Tim 1:7.

13. See Rom. 8:13 (but not earlier in the chapter!); Gal. 5:5, 16, 17(2x), 18, 22, 25(2x) (but not 3:3 and 6:8); Eph. 6:17; and Phil. 2:1.

14. See Fee, *Presence,* pp. 333-35.

15. As subject: Rom. 8:10, 11, 26; 1 Cor. 2:10; as object: Gal. 3:2, 3; 1 Thess. 5:19.

translations generally do the same.[16] The difficulties emerge with the intensive αὐτό in Rom. 8:16 and 26, including how to render the unexpressed subject of ἐντυγχάνει in v. 27. Here especially emerge the tensions between τὸ πνεῦμα as neuter and the Spirit as "person." True to its "literalism," the KJV rendered the phrase "the Spirit itself" in both instances, yet translated v. 27b as "he maketh intercession." The majority of later translations change the intensive to "himself"; others in 8:16 (only) have "the very Spirit" (NRSV), "the Spirit of God" (NEB/REB; GNB, "God's Spirit), and "the Holy Spirit" (NLT),[17] while the NJB has "personally" in 8:26. The NAB², which keeps the "itself" for the intensive, also (with consistency) has "it intercedes" in v. 27!

II. Anarthrous Πνεῦμα in the Oblique Cases

For the most part the KJV, again rather consistently, renders both arthrous and anarthrous πνεῦμα in the genitive and anarthrous dative as "the Spirit,"[18] when the Holy Spirit is the clear referent in context.[19] The later translators tend to follow suit in the genitive when the article is present.[20] But the proclivities of translators emerge in some of the anarthrous constructions. Thus, the NAB has "of spirit" in two instances where apparently they intended the human spirit (Phil. 2:1; 2 Thess. 2:13 [cf. Moffatt]); others have "spiritual" in a few cases,[21] and the NEB has "by inspiration" in Eph. 3:5.

The same tendencies generally hold true for the anarthrous dative (either πνεύματι or ἐν πνεύματι). The problematic instances, where the KJV translated

16. All have "the Spirit": Rom. 8:11, 16, 26; 1 Cor. 2:10, 13 (where the KJV has "Holy Ghost"); and Gal. 3:2 and 5. The NEB/REB has "do not stifle inspiration" in 1 Thess. 5:19. For Rom. 8:10 see Section IV below.

17. For the sake of its contemporary readership, the NLT frequently renders "the Spirit" as "the Holy Spirit" (Rom. 8:5, 6, 13, 16, 23, 26[2x]; 15:30; 1 Cor. 12:4, 11; 2 Cor. 1:22; 3:6[second occurrence]; 5:5; Gal. 3:2, 5, 14; 4:29; 5:16, 17, 18, 22, 25[2x]; Eph. 2:18, 22; 3:5, 16; 4:3; 5:18; 6:18; Col. 1:8.

18. The only occurrence of an articular dative occurs in Rom. 12:11 (τῷ πνεύματι ζέοντες), where only Goodspeed and the RSV translate "the Spirit."

19. Arthrous genitive: Rom. 8:23, 27; 15:30; 1 Cor. 12:7; 2 Cor. 1:22; 5:5; Gal. 3:14; 5:22; Eph. 3:16 (with αὐτοῦ); 4:3; 6:17; anarthrous genitive: 1 Cor. 2:4; Phil. 2:1; 2 Thess. 2:13; anarthrous dative: Rom. 8:13; Gal. 3:3; 5:5, 16, 18, 25(2x); Eph. 2:22; 3:5; 5:18; 6:18; Col. 1:8; 1 Tim. 3:2. Where the KJV went with "the spirit" or "spirit" was in the "spirit/letter" contrasts.

20. Except for the NAB in Gal. 5:23, which inexplicably renders πνεῦμα from 5:5 through 6:8 as "the spirit." This might be related to the "flesh/Spirit" contrast in vv. 16-25, but they have "the Spirit" in 3:3!

21. Gal. 3:3, "begun with what is spiritual" (Weymouth, TCNT, NEB/REB); Eph. 2:22, "a spiritual dwelling" (NEB; cf. NRSV, "built together spiritually").

with lower case "spirit," occur in the three cases where there is a contrast between the "spirit" and the "letter" (Rom. 2:29; 7:6; 2 Cor. 3:6) and in 1 Cor. 14:2 ("howbeit in the spirit, he speaketh mysteries"), which is then picked up in vv. 15b and 16 ("pray/bless with the spirit").

With regard to the "spirit/letter" contrast, the KJV stands near the beginning of a long interpretive tradition in English that understood this phrase as having to do with the "letter" or "spirit" of the law. Thus they have "in the spirit, and not in the letter" in Rom. 2:19, "in newness of spirit, and not in the oldness of the letter" in 7:6, and "not of the letter, but of the spirit" in 2 Cor. 3:6, which they follow with "but the spirit giveth life." One might have thought that both context and consistency in translating nominative τὸ πνεῦμα as "the Spirit" would have caused a double take when they came to the latter passage, but not so.

Of even greater interest is the inconsistency of the subsequent English tradition, where the majority continue with "spirit/letter" in Rom. 2:29,[22] but not in 7:6[23] and 2 Cor. 3:6.[24] One would think that the earlier appearance of this contrast in 2 Corinthians would have determined how they understood Paul's use of it in Romans, especially so since the use of πνεῦμα to express the idea of "inner" in contrast to "outward" is otherwise foreign to Paul, and probably so to the entire Greek world.[25]

The rendering of πνεύματι as "in the spirit" in 1 Cor. 14:2 is equally problematic. In this the KJV was followed by the ERV, ASV, TCNT, JB, NASB/U, NIV, and NAB² (NEB, "no doubt inspired"). The reasons for this are easy to trace. Despite the generally consistent rendering of this dative elsewhere in the corpus as "by/in the Spirit" and the fact that the context here clearly picks up from ch. 12 (that speaking in tongues is "by the one Spirit"), translators appear to have let their understanding (or at least rendering?) of the "Spirit/mind" contrast in vv. 14-15 influence how they would render this occurrence as well.[26]

At issue, therefore, is how one should handle the contrast in vv. 14-15.

22. So ERV, ASV, JB/NJB, NAB/NAB², who follow the KJV, and Weymouth, Moffatt, Goodspeed, RSV/NRSV, REB, who render it with some variation of "spiritual, not literal." The NASB/U, NIV/TNIV, NEB, ESV, GNB, and NLT have some form of "by the Spirit" for πνεύματι.

23. Here only the ERV, ASV, Weymouth, NEB/REB, JB/NJB, NAB/NAB² follow the KJV.

24. Here only the ERV and ASV follow the KJV. All others translate the following nominative as "the Spirit," and only Moffatt, Goodspeed, NRSV, NAB/NAB² (not surprisingly) have "the spirit" for ἀλλὰ πνεύματος.

25. For the full argument as to why this contrast refers to the Spirit and the law, see *Presence*, pp. 489-93.

26. One questions whether this was not also abetted by a rationalistic mind-set that was glad not to attribute to the Spirit the speaking in tongues that involved "speaking to God in mystery."

What seems clear is that in conceding this (basically) private use of praying in tongues, Paul is setting up a contrast between praying and singing with or without one's understanding (hence "with my/the mind" in contrast to speaking in tongues). His following "my spirit/mind" in v. 14 with the articular "spirit" and "mind" in v. 15 and "blessing God in/with the Spirit" in v. 16 should make it clear that this is his intent. But instead the English tradition has let the troublesome "*my* spirit" in v. 14 control their rendering of πνεῦμα in the whole passage. The NEB resolved this exegetical/translational issue rather nicely by rendering "the Spirit in me prays," since the context seems to demand that that is precisely what Paul means.

III. Πνεῦμα with Adjectival Qualifiers

In the opening argument for the need for diversity of Spirit manifestations in 1 Cor. 12:4-11, Paul begins and ends the section by emphasizing "the same Spirit." So also when he lists the variety of manifestations in vv. 8-10, he begins with the thrice-repeated "by the same Spirit" (vv. 8-9a) and "by the one Spirit" (v. 9b) before simply listing five more such Spirit giftings. The KJV and the subsequent English versions all consistently translate this as "by the same/one Spirit." They also all do the same with "one Spirit" in Eph. 2:18 and 4:4.

However, when these identical locutions occur in 2 Cor. 12:18 (τῷ αὐτῷ πνεύματι) and Phil. 1:27 (τὸ ἑνὶ πνεύματι), they were translated in the KJV as "in the same spirit" and "in one spirit." In this they have been followed by the majority of interpreters and translators.[27] But in so doing, while understandable, translators seem also to disregard Paul's own clear usage and opt for a meaning for πνεῦμα that fits the range of meanings for the word "spirit" in English, but for which there is very little, if any, evidence in the Greek world.

This is particularly true when "one spirit" in English means something like *esprit de corps*, for which the Greek equivalent was always μιὰ ψυχή. It is possible, of course, that Paul created this new meaning for τὸ ἑνὶ πνεύματι in Phil. 1:27, for the sake of an emphatic parallel with μιᾷ ψυχῇ. But the pickup of these two words in what immediately follows, where in 2:1 he picks up "the Spirit" and in v. 2 being "like-souled" (σύμψυχοι), suggests that the TNIV has it right in this case.

27. 2 Cor. 12:18 is rendered "same Spirit" by Weymouth, TCNT, NEB/REB, NJB, NLT, and TNIV; only the TNIV has "in the one Spirit" in Phil. 1:27.

VI. On Translating "the Spirit/a spirit of . . ."

Probably related to the usage in 2 Cor. 12:18 noted above is the way translators have handled Paul's recurring use of the semitism πνεῦμα followed by a genitive qualifier that refers to some quality or attitude.[28] The only one of these that the KJV rendered as "the Spirit" is in Rom. 8:2 ("the law of the Spirit of life"). In this it was followed by all others except NAB/NAB[2]. On the other hand, recognizing πνεῦμα ἁγιωσύνης in Rom. 1:4 for the semitism that it is, the majority of subsequent translations — for contextual reasons — render it either as "the Spirit of holiness" or "the Holy Spirit."[29] Likewise, Goodspeed, the NIV/TNIV, and GNB render the echo of Isa. 11:1 in Eph. 1:17 as "the Spirit of wisdom and revelation." The only other instance where such a thing occurs is in 2 Cor. 4:13, which is further complicated by the appearance of "the same." Here Weymouth has "the Spirit of faith" (cf. TNIV[mg], "the same Spirit-given faith").

The one other place where one might have expected some to see a reference to the Spirit with ἐν πνεύματι πραΰτητος is in Gal. 6:1, where it closely follows the appearance of πραΰς as a fruit of the Spirit in 5:23. Very likely at this point the Spirit blends with the semitism, so that Paul's intent is something like "with the Spirit's 'fruit' of gentleness." But both the awkwardness of such a locution in English and the earlier appearance of this phrase in 1 Cor. 4:21 seem to have prohibited such a venture.

V. Πνεῦμα in Various Contrasts

Besides the "Spirit/letter" contrast noted above, the Spirit appears in two other kinds of contrasts in the Pauline corpus, one of which involves a rare instance of (apparent) inconsistency in the KJV. In four places in the corpus where Paul speaks of believers' "receiving" the Spirit, he sets such reception in contrast with a "spirit" they did *not* receive with the coming of the Spirit (Rom. 8:15, "fear leading to slavery"; 1 Cor. 2:12, "this present world"; 2 Cor 11:4, "that of the renegade teachers"; 2 Tim. 1:7, "fear"). Interestingly, only in Rom. 8:15 does the KJV have "the Spirit of adoption." In this instance the majority of later translations, mostly because they choose to render a formal equivalent, have "a spirit of adoption" — whatever that might possibly mean in English! Those who

28. Rom. 1:4; 8:2, 15(2x); 11:8(LXX); 1 Cor. 2:12; 4:21; 2 Cor. 4:13; Gal. 6:1; Eph. 1:17; 4:23; 2 Tim. 1:7.

29. Weymouth, Moffatt, RSV/NRSV, NASB/U, ESV, NIV/TNIV have "Spirit of holiness" (NJB "of the Spirit and of holiness"); NEB/REB, NLT have "Holy Spirit."

choose, more correctly in terms of meaning, to go with "Spirit" do so with a functional equivalent ("the Spirit you received," NEB/REB, TNIV; "the Spirit God gave," GNB).

In the other instances where the KJV has "spirit of," the ERV and ASV alone keep this rendering in 1 Cor. 2:12. In the other two instances one finds a mixed bag: something like "a Spirit different from" in 2 Cor. 11:4[30] and "the Spirit God has given" in 2 Tim. 1:7.[31] In all four of these cases a rendering that puts emphasis on the Spirit seems the better choice.

It is also of interest to watch translators struggle with Paul's contrast between the Spirit and the flesh. For the most part they follow the KJV in rendering πνεῦμα as a referent to the Spirit, although in Rom. 8:6 the KJV already had put "spiritually minded" for τὸ φρόνημα τοῦ πνεύματος. Thus in Rom. 8:4-9 and Gal. 4:29 one sometimes finds either "the spirit" or "spiritual" where it is not always clear what is intended by the translators.[32]

A final passage (2 Thess. 2:2) needs to be noted here, although technically it does not come under the heading "contrast." Of all the occurrences of πνεῦμα in the corpus, this one understandably has received the greatest variety of renderings — no fewer than fourteen among the twenty-two translations! The reasons for this are obvious. Not only is the passage inherently difficult, but even those who recognize that it is almost certainly an oblique reference to the Spirit also recognize that, in light of 1 Thess. 5:19, it points to a prophetic utterance of some kind. Thus while two of our translations (Goodspeed, NJB) offer a direct referent to "the Spirit," the majority offer some form of "prophecy" or "revelation." Thus it is a bit suprising to find that both the NASB/U and ESV opt for "a spirit," where given their proclivities elsewhere, they seem to intend this to refer to a false prophecy and thus to a "foreign spirit."

VI. On Translating Πνευματικός

Understandably, the 1611 translators consistently rendered the adjective πνευματικός as "spiritual," making no distinction between this word as a referent to the Spirit or to something simply immaterial. Very likely the English word "spiritual" often served for them as a referent to the Spirit, especially in

30. Weymouth, Moffatt, TCNT, NEB, NJB, GNB, NLT, TNIV.

31. Goodspeed, TCNT, JB/NJB, NAB, REB, GNB, TNIV.

32. In Rom. 8:4-9, Weymouth and Goodspeed have "spiritual" throughout; this is picked up in vv. 5-9 by TCNT, NEB, and JB, and in vv. 5-6 only by NEB/REB and JB/NJB. In Gal. 4:29 NEB/REB have "spiritual son," while NAB has "in the realm of spirit," which the NAB^2 changed to "child of the spirit."

contexts where the Spirit is prominent (e.g., 1 Cor. 2:10-16). It is less certain whether the Spirit would have been the referent in a passage like Col. 1:9, or indeed what this slippery word might have meant to them.

In any case, the KJV translates the plural πνευματικοί as "he/they that are spiritual" in 1 Cor. 2:15 and Gal. 6:1, where some subsequent translations (rightly, it would seem, in light of the contexts) turn these into "the person with the Spirit" (1 Corinthians) and "those who have the Spirit" (Galatians).[33] It should also be noted that in Col. 1:9 both the GNB and TNIV have taken the clue from the companion, but clearer, passage in Ephesians 1:17, and have thus rendered it "wisdom and understanding the Spirit gives."

VII. Conclusions

In conclusion we may make the following observations:

1. For the most part, the later English tradition of translation tended to follow the lead of the KJV where they had "the Spirit" as the rendering of τὸ πνεῦμα.
2. There is also a tendency to move beyond the KJV on the part of many translations in places where the KJV translators rendered as "spirit" what appear to be certain references to the Holy Spirit. The GNB and TNIV are most consistent in this regard.
3. On the other hand, some earlier translations (TCNT, Goodspeed, Weymouth) have the opposite tendency, namely, at times to render certain references to the Holy Spirit in a more oblique manner.
4. The most notoriously inconsistent with this translational phenomenon is the NAB/NAB², whose waffling with the word would seem to leave the perceptive reader in some degree of confusion.

In the end, however, and in fairness, we should note that besides the (legitimate) differences created by exegetical disagreements, the more notable differences among our English translations can be attributed to two factors: translational theory and ecclesiastical usage. That is, those translations that

33. 1 Cor. 2:15, NIV/TNIV, GNB, NLT; the NIV/TNIV and GNB also (correctly, it would seem) translate the preceding ὁ ψυχικός as "the person without the Spirit" (which others have rendered "unspiritual man/person"; Weymouth, Moffatt, NEB/REB, JB, RSV/NRSV). It should also be noted that the preceding, quite ambiguous dative πνευματικοῖς is rendered "to those who possess the Spirit" (RSV, [NEB/REB], GNB), "to those who are spiritual" (NRSV, ESV, TNIV^mg), and "with Spirit-taught words" (TNIV, NLT).

were designed to update or replace the KJV, especially for the public reading of Scripture as an act of worship, tended also to adhere to formal equivalency as well. Those that were purposely moving away from the KJV tradition, and were interested in serving ecclesiastical purposes as well as the private reading of Scripture, tended toward functional equivalency. This often allowed them greater freedom to express what was perceived to be Paul's meaning put in language that would express that meaning more clearly in contemporary English, which explains the tendencies in the GNB and TNIV.

List of Publications by James D. G. Dunn

1970

Baptism in the Holy Spirit (SBT, second series 15; London: SCM; Philadelphia: Westminster, 1977, viii + 248 pp.

= *El Bautismo del Espiritu Santo* (Buenos Aires: La Aurora, 1977).

'A Note on *dōrea*', *ExpTim* 81 (1969-70): 349-51.

'The Messianic Secret in Mark', *TynB* 21 (1970): 92-117.

= 'Le secret messianique chez Marc', *Hokhma: Revue de réflexion théologique* 18 (1981): 34-56.

= (abbreviated) 'The Messianic Secret in Mark', in *The Messianic Secret* (ed. C. Tuckett; London: SPCK; Philadelphia: Fortress, 1983), pp. 116-31.

'II Corinthians 3.17 — "The Lord is the Spirit"', *JTS* 21 (1970): 309-20.

'The Washing of the Disciples' Feet in John 13.1-20', *ZNW* 61 (1970): 247-52.

'Spirit-baptism and Pentecostalism', *Scottish Journal of Theology* 23 (1970): 397-407.

'Spirit and Kingdom', *ExpTim* 82 (1970-71): 36-40.

1971

'John 6 — A Eucharistic Discourse?', *NTS* 17 (1970-71): 328-38.

'Spirit and Kingdom', *Theology Digest* 19 (1971): 247-50.

1972

'Spirit-and-Fire Baptism', *NovT* 14 (1972): 81-92.

'Rediscovering the Spirit', *ExpTim* 84 (1972-73): 7-12, 40-44.

'Le Baptême de l'Esprit dans l'Experience du Salut', postscript to K. et D. Ranaghan, *Le Retour de l'Esprit* (Paris: du Cerf), pp. 236-45.

1973

'Jesus — Flesh and Spirit: An Exposition of Romans 1.3-4', *JTS* 24 (1973): 40-68.

'I Corinthians 15.45 — Last Adam, Life-giving Spirit', in *Christ and Spirit in the New Testament: Studies in Honour of C. F. D. Moule* (ed. B. Lindars and S. S. Smalley; Cambridge: Cambridge University Press), pp. 127-41.

'New Wine in Old Wineskins: VI. Prophet', *ExpTim* 85 (1973-74): 4-8.

1974

'Paul's Understanding of the Death of Jesus', in *Reconciliation and Hope: New Testament Essays on Atonement and Eschatology. Presented to L. L. Morris* (ed. R. J. Banks; Exeter: Paternoster), pp. 125-41.

1975

Jesus and the Spirit: A Study of the Religious and Charismatic Experience of Jesus and the First Christians as Reflected in the New Testament (New Testament Library, London: SCM; Philadelphia: Westminster), xii + 515 pp.
= *Jesus y el Espiritu* (Salamanca: Secretariado Trinitario, 1981).

'Rom. 7.14-25 in the Theology of Paul', *Theologische Zeitschrift* 31 (1975): 257-73.
= (rev.) 'Romans 7.14-25 in the Theology of Paul', in *Essays on Apostolic Themes: Studies in Honor of H. M. Ervin* (ed. P. Elbert; Peabody, Mass.: Hendrickson), pp. 49-70.

1976

Various articles in *The New International Dictionary of New Testament* (3 vols.; Exeter: Paternoster).

'Rom. 7.14-25 in the Theology of Paul', *Theology Digest* 24 (1976): 230-36.

1977

Unity and Diversity in the New Testament: An Inquiry into the Character of Earliest Christianity (London: SCM; Philadelphia: Westminster), xvii + 470 pp.

'Demythologizing — The Problem of Myth in the New Testament', in *New Testament Interpretation: Essays in Principles and Methods* (ed. I. H. Marshall; Exeter: Paternoster), pp. 285-307.

'According to the Spirit of Jesus', *Theological Renewal* 5 (1977): 16-22.

'Conversion-initiation dans le livre des Actes', *Hokhma: Revue de réflexion théologique* 5 (1977): 21-35.

'The Pentecostals', in *The History of Christianity: A Lion Handbook* (ed. T. Dowley; Herts, Eng.: Lion), pp. 618-22.

1978

'Prophetic "I"-Sayings and the Jesus Tradition: The Importance of Testing Prophetic Utterances within Early Christianity', *NTS* 24 (1977-78): 175-98.

'The Birth of a Metaphor — Baptized in Spirit', *ExpTim* 89 (1977-78): 134-38, 173-75.

1979

'Discernment of Spirits — A Neglected Gift', in *Witness to the Spirit* (ed. W. Harrington; Dublin/Manchester: Irish Biblical Association/Koinonia), pp. 79-96.

'*God as Spirit:* G. W. H. Lampe's 1976 Bampton Lectures', *Theological Renewal* 12 (1979): 29-34.

'"They believed Philip preaching" (Acts 8.12): A Reply', *Irish Biblical Studies* 1 (1979): 177-83.

1980

Christology in the Making: An Inquiry into the Origins of the Doctrine of the Incarnation (London: SCM; Philadelphia: Westminster), xvii + 443 pp.

with D. English et al., *Living with Tension: Proceedings of the Conference of Methodist Chaplains in Higher Education* (Methodist Church Division of Education and Youth).

with G. H. Twelftree, 'Demon-Possession and Exorcism in the New Testament', *Churchman* 94 (1980): 210-25.

= 'La possession demoniaque et l'exorcisme dans le Nouveau Testament', *Hokhma: Revue de réflexion théologique* 51 (1992): 34-52.

Various articles in *The Illustrated Bible Dictionary* (Leicester, Eng.: Inter-Varsity).

1981

'Models of Christian Community in the New Testament', in *The Church Is Charismatic: The World Council and the Charismatic Renewal* (ed. A. Bittlinger; Geneva: World Council of Churches), pp. 99-116.

= 'Models of Christian Community in the New Testament', in *Strange Gifts? A Guide to Charismatic Renewal* (ed. D. Martin and P. Mullen, Oxford: Blackwell, 1984), pp. 1-18.

'Demythologizing the Ascension — A Reply to Professor Gooding', *Irish Biblical Studies* 3 (1981): 15-27.

'Jesus the Prophet', *The Furrow* 32 (1981): 487-95.

= (slightly revised) 'Jesus the Prophet', in *The Burden of Prophecy* (ed. N. McIlwraith, SCM), pp. 27-38.

1982

'The Relationship between Paul and Jerusalem according to Galatians 1 and 2', *NTS* 28 (1982): 461-78.

'Was Christianity a Monotheistic Faith from the Beginning?' *Scottish Journal of Theology* 35 (1982): 303-36.

'Rediscovering the Spirit (2)', *ExpTim* 94 (1982-83): 9-18.

'Levels of Canonical Authority', *Horizons in Biblical Theology* 4 (1982): 13-60.

'The Authority of Scripture according to Scripture', *Churchman* 96 (1982): 104-22, 201-25.

'Debate with Maurice Wiles on Christology', *Theology* 85 (1982): 92-98, 326-30, 360-61.

'Salvation Proclaimed: VI. Romans 6.1-11', *ExpTim* 93 (1981-82): 259-64.

'Algunas reflexiones teólogicas sobre la experiencia religiosa en el Nuevo Testamento', *Estudios Trinitarios* (Salamanca) 16 (1982): 409-25.

1983

'Jesus and the Constraint of Law', *JSNT* 17 (1983): 10-18.

'The Incident at Antioch (Gal. 2.11-18)', *JSNT* 18 (1983): 3-57.

'The New Perspective on Paul', *Bulletin of the John Rylands Library* 65 (1983): 95-122.

'Let John Be John — A Gospel for Its Time', in *Das Evangelium und die Evangelien* (hrsg. P. Stuhlmacher; Tübingen: J. C. B. Mohr), pp. 309-39.

= 'Let John Be John: A Gospel for Its Time', in *The Gospel and the Gospels* (ed. P. Stuhlmacher; Grand Rapids: Eerdmans, 1991), pp. 293-322.

'The Responsible Congregation (1 Cor 14.26-40)', in *Charisma und Agape (1 Ko 12–14)* (hrsg. L. De Lorenzi; Rome: Abtei von St Paul), pp. 201-36, discussion pp. 236-69.

'A Call to Reassess Once More Our Doctrine of Ordination', *Epworth Review* 10.1 (1983): 44-49.

Various articles in *A Dictionary of Christian Spirituality* (ed. G. S. Wakefield; London: SCM).

1984

'Testing the Foundations: Current Trends in New Testament Study' (Inaugural Lecture, University of Durham), 27 pp.; abbreviated in *Times Higher Education Supplement* (7.9.84), 13 pp.

'Mark 2.1–3.6: A Bridge between Jesus and Paul on the Question of the Law', in *NTS* 30 (1984): 395-415.

'In Defence of a Methodology', *ExpTim* 95 (1983-84): 295-99.

Response to R. Nicole, *Churchman* 98 (1984): 208-15.

1985

The Evidence for Jesus: The Impact of Scholarship on Our Understanding of How Christianity Began (London: SCM; Philadelphia: Westminster), xiv + 113 pp.

= *Hoe het Christendom begon* (Ten Have/Baarn, 1987).

'Works of the Law and the Curse of the Law (Gal. 3.10-14)', *NTS* 31 (1985): 523-42.

'Jesus and Ritual Purity: A Study of the Tradition History of Mark 7.15', in *À Cause de L'Évangile* (J. Dupont Festschrift; Cerf: Lectio Divina), pp. 251-76.

'Once More — Gal. 1.18: *historēsai Kēphan:* In Reply to Otfried Hofius', *ZNW* 76 (1985): 138-39.

'Some Clarifications on Issues of Method: A Reply to Holladay and Segal', in *Christology and Exegesis: New Approaches* (ed. R. Jewett), *Semeia* 30 (1985): 97-104.

'Some Ecumenical Reflections on Romans 4', *Aksum-Thyateira: Essays in Honour of Archbishop Methodios* (ed. G. D. Dragas; London and Athens: Thyateira House), pp. 423-26 (double-column pages).

1986

Shinakugaku no Altarashii Shiten (New Perspectives in New Testament Study) (Sugu Shoboh, Japan).

Editor, *The Kingdom of God and North-East England* (with J. I. McDonald, P. Sedgewick, and A. M. Suggate; London: SCM), xi + 81 pp.

'Romans 13.1-7 — A Charter for Political Quietism', *Ex Auditu* 2 (1986): 55-68.

1987

The Living Word (London: SPCK; Philadelphia: Fortress), ix + 196 pp.

with J. P. Mackey, *New Testament Theology in Dialogue* (London: SPCK; Philadelphia: Westminster), viii + 156 pp.

'Enthusiasm', in *The Encyclopedia of Religion*, vol. 5 (ed. M. Eliade; New York: Macmillan), pp. 118-24 (double-column pages).

'Ministry and the Ministry: The Charismatic Renewal's Challenge to Traditional Ecclesiology', in *Charismatic Experiences in History* (ed. C. M. Robeck; Peabody, Mass.: Hendrickson), pp. 81-101.

'"A Light to the Gentiles": The Significance of the Damascus Road Christophany for Paul', in *The Glory of Christ in the New Testament: Studies in Christology in Memory of G. B. Caird* (ed. L. D. Hurst and N. T. Wright; Oxford: Clarendon), pp. 251-66.

'Paul's Epistle to the Romans: An Analysis of Structure and Argument', in *Aufstieg und Niedergang der Römischen Welt*, II.25.4 (Berlin: de Gruyter), pp. 2842-90.

'"Righteousness from the Law" and "Righteousness from Faith": Paul's Interpretation of Scripture in Rom. 10.1-10', in *Tradition and Interpretation in the New Testament: Essays in Honor of E. E. Ellis* (ed. G. F. Hawthorne and O. Betz; Grand Rapids: Eerdmans/Tübingen: J. C. B. Mohr), pp. 216-28.

'Crisis in the Universities', *Methodist Recorder* (Thursday, May 14): 13.

1988

Word Biblical Commentary, Vol. 38 — Romans (2 vols.; Dallas: Word), lxii + 976 pp.

'The Theology of Galatians', in *Society of Biblical Literature 1988 Seminar Papers* (ed. D. J. Lull; Atlanta: Scholars), pp. 1-16.

'Pharisees, Sinners, and Jesus', in *The Social World of Formative Christianity and Judaism: Essays in Tribute to H. C. Kee* (ed. J. Neusner et al.; Philadelphia: Fortress), pp. 264-89.

'Matthew 12.28/Luke 11.20 — A Word of Jesus?', in *Eschatology and the New Testament:*

Essays in Honor of G. R. Beasley-Murray (ed. W. H. Gloer, Peabody, Mass.: Hendrickson), pp. 29-49.

'The New Testament as History', in *Different Gospels: Christian Orthodoxy and Modern Theologies* (ed. A. Walker; London: Hodder & Stoughton), pp. 142-54.

'A Theology of Freedom at Other People's Expense', 'Face to Faith' column, *The Guardian* (May 30): 23.

1989

Christology in the Making: An Inquiry into the Origins of the Doctrine of the Incarnation (2nd ed., with new Foreword; London: SCM, 1989/Grand Rapids: Eerdmans, 1996), xlvi + 443 pp.

'The Spirit of Jesus' and 'The Spirit and the Body of Christ', in *The Holy Spirit: Renewing and Empowering Presence* (ed. G. Vandervelde; Winfield, B.C.: Wood Lake Books), pp. 11-26, 27-43.

'Die Instrumente kirchlicher Gemeinschaft in der frühen Kirche', *Una Sancta* 44.1 (1989): 2-13.

= 'Gli strumenti della Koinonia nella chiesa primitiva', *Studi Ecumenici* 8 (1989): 113-35.

= 'Instruments of Koinonia in the Early Church', *One in Christ* 25 (1989): 204-16.

= 'Los instrumentos de la koinonia en la Iglesia primitiva', *Dialogo Ecumenico* 25 (1989): 351-68.

'Introduction: The Challenge of New Testament Study for Evangelicals Today', in *Introducing New Testament Interpretation* (ed. S. McKnight; Grand Rapids: Baker), pp. 15-19.

'They Set Us in New Paths: VI. New Testament: The Great Untranslated', *ExpTim* 100 (1988-89): 203-7.

Foreword to A. Primavesi and J. Henderson, *Our God Has No Favourites: A Liberation Theology of the Eucharist* (Tunbridge Wells: Burns & Oates, 1989), pp. vii-ix.

'Paul's Knowledge of the Jesus Tradition: The Evidence of Romans', in *Christus Bezeugen: Festschrift für W. Trilling* (hrsg. K. Kertelge et al.; Leipzig: St. Benno), pp. 193-207.

1990

Jesus, Paul and the Law: Studies in Mark and Galatians (London: SPCK), x + 277 pp.

Unity and Diversity in the New Testament: An Inquiry into the Character of Earliest Christianity (London: SCM/Valley Forge, Pa.: Trinity Press International, 2nd, rev. ed. 1990), xxxvii + 482 pp.

= *Edinstvo i mnogoobrazie v Novom Zevete* (Russian ed.; Mockba: BBN, 1997).

'Unity and Diversity in the Church: A New Testament Perspective', *Gregorianum* 71 (1990): 629-56.

'The Holy Spirit', Unit 10 in *Faith and Worship: Local Preachers' Training Course* (ed.

J. S. Lampard; Peterborough: Methodist Publishing House, 1990), 32 (large pages).

'Baptism in the Holy Spirit: Twenty Years On', *Mission and Ministry* 7.4 (1990): 9-12 (three-column pages).

'Recent Trends in the Study of Paul', *Catalyst* 16.3 (1990): 2-3 (three-column pages).

'Christology, New Testament', 'Diversity', 'Judaizers', in *A Dictionary of Biblical Interpretation* (ed. R. J. Coggins and J. L. Houlden; London: SCM), pp. 115-19, 178-79, 369-71 (double-column pages).

1991

The Partings of the Ways between Christianity and Judaism and Their Significance for the Character of Christianity (London: SCM/Philadelphia: Trinity Press International), xvi + 368 pp.

'Paul's Understanding of the Death of Jesus as Sacrifice', in *Sacrifice and Redemption: Durham Essays in Theology* (ed. S. W. Sykes; Cambridge: Cambridge University Press), pp. 35-56.

'The Theology of Galatians: The Issue of Covenantal Nomism', in *Pauline Theology, Vol. 1: Thessalonians, Philippians, Galatians, Philemon* (ed. J. M. Bassler; Minneapolis: Fortress), pp. 125-46 (revised version of 1988 paper).

'What Was the Issue between Paul and "Those of the Circumcision"?' in *Paulus und das antike Judentum* (hrsg. M. Hengel & U. Heckel; 1988 Tübingen-Durham Research Symposium; Tübingen: J. C. B. Mohr), pp. 295-312, with postscript and record of discussion pp. 313-17.

'Fundamental Consensus in the New Testament', in *In Search of Christian Unity: Basic Consensus/Basic Differences* (ed. J. A. Burgess; Minneapolis: Fortress), pp. 200-221.

'John and the Oral Gospel Tradition', in *Jesus and the Oral Gospel Tradition* (ed. H. Wansbrough; JSNTSup 64; Sheffield: Sheffield Academic Press), pp. 351-79.

'Once More, *PISTIS CHRISTOU*', in *Society of Biblical Literature 1991 Seminar Papers* (ed. E. H. Lovering; Atlanta: Scholars Press), pp. 730-44.

'The Formal and Theological Coherence of Romans' and 'The New Perspective on Paul: Paul and the Law', in *The Romans Debate: Revised and Expanded Edition* (ed. K. Donfried; Peabody, Mass.: Hendrickson), pp. 245-50, 299-308.

1992

Jesus' Call to Discipleship (Cambridge: Cambridge University Press), ix + 141 pp.; Japanese ed. (Tokyo: Shinn Shoji, 1996); Spanish ed. — *La llamada de Jesus al seguimiento* (Santander: Sal Terrae, 2001).

Editor, *Jews and Christians: The Parting of the Ways AD 70 to 135* (The Second Durham-Tübingen Research Symposium, September 1989; Tübingen: J. C. B. Mohr, 1992/Grand Rapids: Eerdmans, 1999), including Preface (four pp.) and Concluding Summary (six pp.) of x + 408 pp.

Editor, 'The Lightfoot Centenary Lectures. To Commemorate the Life and Work of

Bishop J. B. Lightfoot (1828-89),' *Durham University Journal* (special issue 1992): 94 pp.

'The Question of Anti-Semitism in the New Testament Writings of the Period', in *Jews and Christians* (as above), pp. 177-211.

'Lightfoot in Retrospect', 'The Lightfoot Centenary Lectures' (as above), pp. 71-94.

'The Justice of God: A Renewed Perspective on Justification by Faith' (The Henton Davies Lecture, Oxford, 1991), *JTS* 43 (1992): 1-22.

'A Word in Time: Understanding the Bible Today' (The Peake Memorial Lecture, 1991), *Epworth Review* 19 (1992): 27-42.

'Yet Once More — "The Works of the Law": A Response', *JSNT* 46 (1992): 99-117.

'Matthew's Awareness of Markan Redaction', in *The Four Gospels: Festschrift for Frans Neirynck* (ed. F. Van Segbroeck; Leuven: Leuven University Press), pp. 1349-59.

'Messianic Ideas and Their Influence on the Jesus of History', in *The Messiah: Developments in Earliest Judaism and Christianity* (ed. J. H. Charlesworth; Minneapolis: Fortress), pp. 365-81.

'"The Body of Christ" in Paul', in *Worship, Theology and Ministry in the Early Church: Essays in Honour of R. P. Martin* (JSNTSup 87; Sheffield: Sheffield Academic Press), pp. 146-62.

'Jesus, Table-Fellowship, and Qumran', in *Jesus and the Dead Sea Scrolls* (ed. J. H. Charlesworth; New York: Doubleday), pp. 254-72.

'Whatever Happened to the Lord's Supper?' *Epworth Review* 19.1 (1992): 35-48 (with responses and reply, pp. 48-55).

Articles on 'Myth' and 'Prayer', in *Dictionary of Jesus and the Gospels* (ed. J. B. Green, S. McKnight, and I. H. Marshall (Downers Grove, Ill.: InterVarsity and Leicester: Inter-Varsity), pp. 566a-69b, 617a-25a (two-column pages).

Articles on 'Christology (NT)' and 'Incarnation', in *The Anchor Bible Dictionary* (ed. D. N. Freedman et al.; 6 vols.; New York: Doubleday), 1:979-91, 3:397-404 (double-column pages).

1993

A Commentary on the Epistle to the Galatians (BNTC; London: A. & C. Black), xxiv + 359 pp.

The Theology of Paul's Letter to the Galatians (Cambridge: Cambridge University Press), xvii + 161 pp.

= Japanese edition (Tokyo: Shinkyo Shuppansha, 1998).

Christian Liberty: A New Testament Perspective (The Didsbury Lectures 1991; Carlisle: Paternoster, 1993/Grand Rapids: Eerdmans, 1994), xi + 115 pp.

Paul for Today (The Ethel M. Wood Lecture, 1993; London: University of London) 29 pp.

(with A. M. Suggate), *The Justice of God: A Fresh Look at the Old Doctrine of Justification by Faith* (Carlisle: Paternoster, 1993/Grand Rapids: Eerdmans, 1994), 87 pp.

'Christology as an Aspect of Theology', in *The Future of Christology: Essays in Honor of*

Leander E. Keck (ed. A. J. Malherbe and W. A. Meeks; Minneapolis: Fortress), pp. 202-12.

'How Controversial Was Paul's Christology?' in *From Jesus to Paul: Essays on Jesus and New Testament Christology in Honour of Marinus de Jonge* (ed. M. de Boer; Sheffield: Sheffield Academic Press), pp. 148-67.

'Pauline Christology: Shaping the Fundamental Structures', in *Christology in Dialogue* (ed. R. F. Berkey and S. A. Edwards; Cleveland: Pilgrim), pp. 96-107.

'Anti-Semitism in the Deutero-Pauline Literature', in *Anti-Semitism and Early Christianity: Issues of Polemic and Faith* (ed. C. A. Evans and D. A. Hagner; Minneapolis: Fortress), pp. 151-65.

'Echoes of Intra-Jewish Polemic in Paul's Letter to the Galatians', *JBL* 112 (1993): 459-77.

'Baptism in the Spirit: A Response to Pentecostal Scholarship on Luke-Acts', *JPT* 3 (1993): 2-27.

'Romans, Letter to the', in *Dictionary of Paul and His Letters* (ed. G. F. Hawthorne, R. P. Martin, and D. G. Reid; Downers Grove, Ill.: InterVarsity), pp. 838-50 (double-column pages).

'Should Paul Once Again Oppose Peter to His Face?' *The Heythrop Journal* 34 (1993): 58-65.

'Lightfoot — The Critic', in *A Christian Heritage* (ed. C. Yeats; Bangor: Headstart History), pp. 58-65.

1994

'The Making of Christology — Evolution or Unfolding?' in *Jesus of Nazareth: Lord and Christ*, I. H. Marshall Festschrift (ed. J. B. Green and M. Turner; Grand Rapids: Eerdmans), pp. 437-52.

'Prolegomena to a Theology of Paul', *NTS* 40 (1994): 407-32.

'Jesus Tradition in Paul', in *Studying the Historical Jesus: Evaluations of the State of Current Research* (ed. B. Chilton and C. A. Evans; Leiden: Brill), pp. 155-78.

'The "Body" in Colossians', in *To Tell the Mystery: Essays on New Testament Eschatology in Honor of Robert H. Gundry* (ed. T. E. Schmidt and M. Silva; JSNTSup 100; Sheffield: JSOT), pp. 163-81.

'Why "Incarnation"? A Review of Recent New Testament Scholarship', in *Crossing the Boundaries: Essays in Biblical Interpretation in Honour of Michael D. Goulder* (ed. S. E. Porter et al.; Leiden: Brill), pp. 235-56.

'John the Baptist's Use of Scripture', in *The Gospels and the Scriptures of Israel* (ed. C. A. Evans and W. R. Stegner; JSNTSup 104; Sheffield: JSOT), pp. 42-54.

'How New Was Paul's Gospel? The Problem of Continuity and Discontinuity', in *Gospel in Paul: Studies on Corinthians, Galatians and Romans for Richard N. Longenecker* (ed. L. A. Jervis and P. Richardson; JSNTSup 108; Sheffield: JSOT), pp. 367-88.

'Training for Ministry', *Methodist Recorder*, May 12, 1994, p. 11.

1995

1 Corinthians (New Testament Guides; Sheffield: Sheffield Academic Press) 118 pp.

'Judaism in the Land of Israel in the First Century', in *Judaism in Late Antiquity: Part 2: Historical Syntheses* (ed. J. Neusner; Handbuch der Orientalisk; Leiden: Brill), pp. 229-61.

'Was Paul Against the Law? The Law in Galatians and Romans: A Test-Case of Text in Context', in *Texts and Contexts: Biblical Texts in Their Textual and Situational Contexts: Essays in Honor of Lars Hartman* (ed. T. Fornberg and D. Hellholm; Oslo: Scandinavian University Press), pp. 455-75.

'Historical Text as Historical Text: Some Basic Hermeneutical Reflections in Relation to the New Testament', in *Words Remembered, Texts Renewed: Essays in Honour of John F. A. Sawyer* (ed. J. Davies, G. Harvey, and W. G. E. Watson; JSOTSup 195; Sheffield: Sheffield Academic Press), pp. 340-59.

'The Colossian Philosophy: A Confident Jewish Apologia', *Biblica* 76 (1995): 153-81.

'In Quest of Paul's Theology: Retrospect and Prospect', in *Society of Biblical Literature Seminar Papers 1995* (Atlanta: Scholars), pp. 704-21.

'Das Problem "Biblische Theologie"', in *Eine Bibel — zwei Testamente* (hrsg. C. Dolmen and T. Söding; Paderborn: Ferdinand Schöningh), pp. 179-93.

'The Historicity of the Synoptic Gospels', in *Crisis in Christology: Essays in Quest of Resolution* (ed. W. R. Farmer; Livonia, Mich.: Dove), pp. 199-216.

'Jesus for Today', *Theology Today* 52 (1995): 66-74.

'In Search of Wisdom', *Epworth Review* 22.3 (September 1995): 48-53.

1996

The Epistles to the Colossians and to Philemon (NIGTC; Grand Rapids: Eerdmans and Carlisle: Paternoster), xvii + 388 pp.

The Acts of the Apostles (Epworth Commentaries; Peterborough: Epworth/Narrative Commentaries; Valley Forge, Pa.: Trinity Press International), xxvi + 357 pp.

Editor, *Paul and the Mosaic Law: The Third Durham-Tübingen Research Symposium on Earliest Christianity and Judaism* (WUNT 89; Tübingen: J. C. B. Mohr, 1996; Grand Rapids: Eerdmans, 2001), xi +368 pp., including Introduction and Bibliography (pp. 1-5 and 335-41).

'In Search of Common Ground', in *Paul and the Mosaic Law*, pp. 309-34.

'The Bible in the Church', in *Essentials of Christian Community: Essays for Dan Hardy* (ed. D. F. Ford and D. L. Stamps; Edinburgh: T&T Clark), pp. 117-30.

'John and the Synoptics as a Theological Question', in *Exploring the Gospel of John: In Honor of D. Moody Smith* (ed. R. A. Culpepper and C. C. Black; Louisville: Westminster John Knox), pp. 301-13.

'Deutero-Pauline Letters', in *Early Christian Thought in Its Jewish Context*, M. D. Hooker Festschrift (ed. J. Barclay and J. Sweet; Cambridge: Cambridge University Press), pp. 130-44.

'The Significance of Matthew's Eschatology for Biblical Theology', in *Society of Biblical Literature Seminar Papers 1996* (Atlanta: Scholars), pp. 150-62.

'The Household Rules in the New Testament', in *The Family in Theological Perspective* (ed. S. C. Barton; Edinburgh: T&T Clark), pp. 43-63.

'"The Law of Faith", "The Law of the Spirit" and "The Law of Christ"', in *Theology and Ethics in Paul and His Interpreters: Essays in Honor of Victor Paul Furnish* (ed. E. H. Lovering and J. L. Sumney; Nashville: Abingdon), pp. 62-82.

'Two Covenants or One? The Interdependence of Jewish and Christian Identity', in *Geschichte — Tradition — Reflexion: Festschrift für Martin Hengel* (ed. H. Cancik et al.; Tübingen: J. C. B. Mohr), pp. 97-122.

= 'Zwei Bünde oder Einer? Die wechselseitige Abhängigkeit der jüdischen und christlichen Identität', in *Studien zu einer neutestamentlichen Hermeneutik nach Auschwitz* (hsrg. P. Fiedler and G. Dautzenberg; Stuttgarter biblische Aufsatzbände 27; Stuttgart: Katholische Bibelwerk, 1999), pp. 115-54.

'A Protestant Response', in *Born Again: Baptism and the Spirit, Concilium* 265 (1996), pp. 109-16; also published in German, French, Dutch, and Spanish.

Articles on 'Baptism' (wholly revised), 'Spirit, Holy Spirit' (revised), and 'Sign', in *New Bible Dictionary* (ed. D. R. Wood; Leicester: Inter-Varsity), pp. 120-22, 1100, 1125-29 (double-column pages).

'Fundamentalism: The Price of Certainty', *Durham First* 3 (Spring 1996): 7-9.

1997

'4QMMT and Galatians', *NTS* 43 (1997): 147-53.

'He Will Come Again', *Interpretation* 51 (1997): 42-56.

= 'El Senor volverá', *Selecciones de Teologia* 36 (1997): 247-54.

= repr. in *Called to One Hope: Perspectives on Life to Come* (ed. J. Colwell; Drew Lectures on Immortality; Carlisle: Paternoster, 2000), pp. 52-66.

'Paul's Conversion — A Light to Twentieth Century Disputes', in *Evangelium Schriftauslegung Kirche: Festschrift für Peter Stuhlmacher* (ed. J. Ådna et al.; Göttingen: Vandenhoeck & Ruprecht), pp. 77-93.

'Paul and Justification by Faith', in *The Road from Damascus: The Impact of Paul's Conversion on His Life, Thought, and Ministry* (ed. R. N. Longenecker; Grand Rapids: Eerdmans), pp. 85-101.

'Jesus and Factionalism in Early Judaism', in *Hillel and Jesus: Comparisons of Two Major Religious Leaders* (ed. J. H. Charlesworth and L. L. Johns; Minneapolis: Fortress), pp. 156-75.

'*KYRIOS* in Acts', in *Jesus Christus als die Mitte der Schrift: Studien zur Hermeneutik des Evangeliums,* O. Hofius Festschrift (ed. C. Landmesser et al.; BZNW 86; Berlin: de Gruyter), pp. 363-78.

'Biblical Concepts of Divine Revelation', in *Divine Revelation* (ed. P. Avis; London: Darton, Longman & Todd/Grand Rapids: Eerdmans), pp. 1-22.

'"Neither Circumcision Nor Uncircumcision, but . . ." (Gal. 5.2-12; 6.12-16; cf. 1 Cor. 7.17-20)', in *La Foi Agissant par l'Amour (Galates 4.12–6.16)* (ed. A. Vanhoye; Rome: Abbaye de S. Paul), pp. 79-110 (discussion on pp. 110-22).

'Once More, *PISTIS CHRISTOU*', in *Pauline Theology, Vol. IV: Looking Back, Pressing*

On (ed. E. E. Johnson and D. M. Hay; Atlanta: Scholars), pp. 61-81 (revised version of 1991 paper).

'In Quest of Paul's Theology: Retrospect and Prospect', in *Pauline Theology, Vol. IV: Looking Back, Pressing On* (ed. E. E. Johnson and D. M. Hay; Atlanta: Scholars), pp. 95-115 (revised version of 1995 paper).

'"Son of God" as "Son of Man" in the Dead Sea Scrolls? A Response to John Collins on 4Q246', in *The Scrolls and the Scriptures: Qumran Fifty Years After* (ed. S. E. Porter and C. A. Evans; Sheffield: Sheffield Academic Press), pp. 198-210.

'Pauline Legacy and School', 'Pseudepigraphy', in *Dictionary of the Later New Testament and Its Developments* (ed. R. P. Martin and P. H. Davids; Downers Grove, Ill./Leicester: InterVarsity Press), pp. 887-93, 977-84.

1998

The Theology of Paul the Apostle (Grand Rapids: Eerdmans/Edinburgh: T&T Clark), xxxvi + 808 pp.

= *La teologia dell'apostolo Paolo* (Introduzione allo studio della Bibbia, Supplementi 5; Brescia: Paideia, 1999).

The Christ and the Spirit: Collected Essays of James D. G. Dunn (Grand Rapids: Eerdmans/Edinburgh: T&T Clark): *Vol. 1, Christology*, xix + 462 pp.; *Vol. 2, Pneumatology*, xvi + 382 pp.

'Whatever Happened to "Works of the Law"?' in *Epitoayto*, P. Pokorný Festschrift (ed. J. Kerkovsky et al.; Praha: Mlyn), pp. 107-20.

'Baptism and the Unity of the Church in the New Testament', in *Baptism and the Unity of the Church* (ed. M. Root and R. Saarinen; Grand Rapids: Eerdmans/Geneva: WCC), pp. 78-103.

'The Pauline Letters', in *The Cambridge Companion to Biblical Interpretation* (ed. J. Barton; Cambridge: Cambridge University Press), pp. 276-89.

'Christ, Adam and Preexistence', in *Where Christology Began: Essays on Philippians 2* (ed. R. P. Martin and B. J. Dodd; Louisville: Westminster), pp. 74-83.

'Paul: Apostate or Apostle of Israel?', *ZNW* 89 (1998): 256-71.

Consultant Editor, *The Complete Bible Handbook: An Illustrated Companion* (ed. J. Bowker; London: Dorling Kindersley); author of 'The Gospels' (300-301), 'Jesus the Messiah' (346-47), 'Acts of the Apostles' (380-81), 'The Mission of Peter' (386-87), 'Hebrews and Hellenists' (388-89), 'The Account of Paul's Missions' (396-97), 'The Letter to the Galatians' (424-25), 'House Churches' (434-35), 'Slavery' (440-41), and 'Pseudepigrapha in the Early Christian Period' (462-63).

'Επιστημονική μηθοδοι στην ἑρμηνεία τῶν 'Ευαγγελίων, Δελτιο Βιβλικων Μελετων 17 (1998): 47-68.

'J. B. Lightfoot', in *Historical Handbook of Major Biblical Interpreters* (ed. D. K. McKim; Downers Grove, Ill.: InterVarsity), pp. 336-40.

'Whatever Happened to Exegesis? In Response to the Reviews by R. B. Matlock and D. A. Campbell', *JSNT* 72 (1998): 113-20.

'Baptism in the Holy Spirit — Yet Once More', *The Journal of the European Pentecostal Theological Association* 18 (1998): 3-25.

'Paul and the Dead Sea Scrolls', in *Caves of Enlightenment: Proceedings of the American Schools of Oriental Research Dead Sea Scrolls Jubilee Symposium (1947-1997)* (ed. J. H. Charlesworth; North Richland Hills, Tex.: Bibal), pp. 105-27.

1999

'Can the Third Quest Hope to Succeed?' in *Authenticating the Activities of Jesus* (ed. B. Chilton and C. A. Evans; New Testament Tools and Studies 28.2; Leiden: Brill), pp. 31-48.

'Jesus: Teacher of Wisdom or Wisdom Incarnate?' in *Where Shall Wisdom Be Found? Wisdom in the Bible, the Church and the Contemporary World* (ed. S. C. Barton; Edinburgh: T&T Clark), pp. 75-92.

'Pauline Theology', in *The New Testament Today* (ed. M. A. Powell; Louisville: Westminster John Knox), pp. 100-109.

'Who Did Paul Think He Was? A Study of Jewish Christian Identity', *NTS* 45 (1999): 174-93.

'Spirit Speech: Reflections on Romans 8:12-27', in *Romans and the People of God*, G. D. Fee Festschrift (ed. S. K. Soderlund and N. T. Wright; Grand Rapids: Eerdmans), pp. 82-91.

'Was Judaism Particularist or Universalist?' in *Judaism in Late Antiquity*, Part III: *Where We Stand: Issues and Debates in Ancient Judaism* (ed. J. Neusner and A. J. Avery-Peck; Handbuch der Orientalisk; Leiden: Brill), 2:57-73.

'"Baptized" as Metaphor', in *Baptism, the New Testament and the Church*, R. E. O. White Festschrift (ed. S. E. Porter & A. R. Cross; JSNTSup 171; Sheffield: Sheffield Academic Press), pp. 294-310.

2000

Editor (with H. Klein, U. Luz, and V. Mihoc), *Auslegung der Bibel in orthodoxer und westlicher Perspektive* (WUNT 130; Tübingen: Mohr Siebeck), xii + 231 pp.

'Scholarly Methods in the Interpretation of the Gospels', in *Auslegung der Bibel*, pp. 105-21.

'Jesus in Paul's Letters', in *Guidelines* September-December 2000 (Oxford: Bible Reading Fellowship), pp. 61-75.

'On the Relation of Text and Artifact: Some Cautionary Tales', in *Text and Artifact in the Religions of Mediterranean Antiquity*, Peter Richardson Festschrift (ed. S. G. Wilson and M. Desjardins; Studies in Christianity and Judaism 9; Waterloo, Ont.: Wilfrid Laurier University), pp. 192-206.

'The Jew Paul and His Meaning for Israel', in *Paulinische Christologie: Exegetische Beiträge*, H. Hübner Festschrift (ed. U. Schnelle and T. Söding; Göttingen: Vandenhoeck & Ruprecht), pp. 32-46.

'The First and Second Letters to Timothy and the Letter to Titus', in *The New Inter-*

preter's Bible, Volume XI (Nashville: Abingdon), pp. 773-880 (double-column pages).

'Christology as an Issue in Inter-Faith Dialogue' (summary), in *Who Is Jesus Christ in a World of Many Faiths?* (Report of the Swanwick Christology Conference, September 1999; London: Churches' Commission on Inter-Faith Relations), pp. 37-39.

'New Testament', in *The Oxford Companion to Christian Thought* (ed. A. Hastings, A. Mason, and H. Pyper; Oxford: Oxford University Press), pp. 473a-77a.

'Jesus in Oral Memory: The Initial Stages of the Jesus Tradition', *SBL Seminar Papers* 136, pp. 287-326.

'Rejoicing in Dialogue: A Response to Lee Keck', *Scottish Journal of Theology* 53 (2000): 390-93 (response to L. E. Keck's review of Dunn's *Theology of Paul the Apostle*, *Scottish Journal of Theology* 53 [2000]: 380-89).

'"Are You the Messiah?": Is the Crux of Mark 14.61-62 Resolvable?' in *Christology, Controversy and Community: New Testament Essays in Honour of D. R. Catchpole* (ed. D. G. Horrell and C. M. Tuckett; Novum Testamentum Supplements 99; Leiden: Brill), pp. 1-22.

2001

Romans: The People's Bible Commentary (Oxford: Bible Reading Fellowship), 189 pp.

'The Bible and Time', in *Time* (ed. B. Beamond; 'Christ and the Cosmos' series 14; Christ and the Cosmos Initiative), pp. 28-42.

'Jesus the Judge: Further Thoughts on Paul's Christology and Soteriology', in *The Convergence of Theology*, G. O'Collins Festschrift (ed. D. Kendall and S. T. Davis; New York: Paulist), pp. 34-54.

'He Will Come Again', in *Called to One Hope: Perspectives on Life to Come* (ed. J. Colwell; Drew Lectures on Immortality; Carlisle: Paternoster), pp. 52-66.

'The Embarrassment of History: Reflections on the Problem of "Anti-Judaism" in the Fourth Gospel', in *Anti-Judaism and the Fourth Gospel: Papers of the Leuven Colloquium*, 2000 (ed. R. Bieringer et al. Assen: Van Gorcum), pp. 47-67.

'Jesus in Oral Memory: The Initial Stages of the Jesus Tradition', in *Jesus: A Colloquium in the Holy Land* (ed. D. Donnelly; New York: Continuum), pp. 84-145.

'*Ex Akoēs Pisteōs*', *Ex Auditu* 16 (2000): 35-46 (D. Moessner, 'Response to Dunn', pp. 47-53).

'The Ascension of Jesus: A Test Case for Hermeneutics', in *Auferstehung Resurrection* (ed. F. Avemarie and H. Lichtenberger; The Fourth Durham-Tübingen Research Symposium in Old Testament, Ancient Judaism, and Early Christianity, Tübingen, 1999; WUNT 135; Tübingen: Mohr Siebeck, 2001), pp. 301-22.

'A Response to Peter Stuhlmacher', in *Auferstehung*, pp. 363-68.

'The Danielic Son of Man in the New Testament', in *The Book of Daniel: Composition and Reception* (ed. J. J. Collins and P. W. Flint; Supplements to Vetus Testamentum 83.2; Leiden: Brill), pp. 528-49.

'Ephesians', in *The Oxford Bible Commentary* (ed. J. Barton and J. Muddiman; Oxford: Oxford University Press), pp. 1165-79 (double-column.pages).

'Diversity in Paul', in *Religious Diversity in the Graeco-Roman World: A Survey of Recent Scholarship* (ed. D. Cohn-Sherbok and J. M. Court; Sheffield: Sheffield Academic Press), pp. 107-23.

'Judaism and Christianity: One Covenant or Two?', in *Covenant Theology: Contemporary Approaches* (ed. M. J. Cartledge and D. Mills; Carlisle: Paternoster), pp. 33-55.

2002

'Noch einmal "Works of the Law": The Dialogue Continues', in *Fair Play: Diversity and Conflicts in Early Christianity*, H. Räisänen Festschrift (ed. I. Dunderberg and C. Tuckett; Leiden: Brill), pp. 273-90.

'The Bible and Scholarship: On Bridging the Gap between the Academy and the Church', *Anvil* 19 (2002): 109-18.

'Beyond the Historical Impasse? In Dialogue with A. J. M. Wedderburn', in *Paul, Luke and the Graeco-Roman World*, A. J. M. Wedderburn Festschrift (ed. A. Christophersen et al.; JSNTSup 217; Sheffield: Sheffield Academic Press), pp. 250-64.

'"How Are the Dead Raised? With What Body Do They Come?": Reflections on 1 Corinthians 15', *Southwestern Journal of Theology* 45 (2002-3): 4-18.

'The Jew Paul and His Meaning for Israel', in *A Shadow of Glory: Reading the New Testament after the Holocaust* (ed. T. Linafelt; New York: Routledge), pp. 201-15.

'"All that glisters is not gold": In Quest of the Right Key to Unlock the Way to the Historical Jesus', in *Der historische Jesus: Tendenzen und Perspektiven der gegenwärtigen Forschung* (ed. J. Schröter and R. Brucker; BZNW 114; Berlin: de Gruyter), pp. 131-61.

'Jesus and Purity: An Ongoing Debate', *NTS* 48 (2002): 449-67.

'The Narrative Approach to Paul: Whose Story?', in *Narrative Dynamics in Paul: A Critical Assessment* (ed. B. W. Longenecker; Louisville: Westminster John Knox), pp. 217-30.

'Has the Canon a Continuing Function?' in *The Canon Debate* (ed. L. M. McDonald and J. A. Sanders; Peabody, Mass.: Hendrickson), pp. 558-79.

'The Incident at Antioch (Gal 2:11-18)', in *The Galatians Debate* (ed. M. D. Nanos; Peabody, Mass.: Hendrickson), pp. 199-234 (repr. of *JSNT* 18 [1983]: 3-57).

2003

'Jesus and the Kingdom: How Would His Message Have Been Heard?' in *Neotestamentica et Philonica*, P. Borgen Festschrift (ed. D. E. Aune et al.; Leiden: Brill), pp. 3-36.

'What Makes a Good Exposition?' (*The Expository Times* Lecture, June 2002), *ExpTim* 114 (2002-3): 147-57.

'Jesus and Holiness: The Challenge of Purity', in *Holiness Past and Present* (ed. S. C. Barton; London: T&T Clark), pp. 168-92.

Jesus Remembered (Christianity in the Making, vol. 1; Grand Rapids/Cambridge: Eerdmans), xvii + 1019 pp.

Editor (with J. W. Rogerson), *The Eerdmans Commentary on the Bible* (Grand Rapids/Cambridge: Eerdmans), 1556 pp.; 'The History of the Tradition: New Testament', pp. 950-71.

Editor, *The Cambridge Companion to Paul* (Cambridge: Cambridge University Press), xx + 301 pp.; Introduction, pp. 1-15.

Index of Names

www.ingramcontent.com/pod-product-compliance
Lightning Source LLC
LaVergne TN
LVHW050951080826
845145LV00005B/1472

* 9 7 8 0 8 0 2 8 7 9 2 5 7 *